NTC's Dictionary of the

UNITED KINGDOM

The Most Practical Guide to British Language and Culture

EWART JAMES

Illustrated by
DUNCAN J. MCKINNON

NTC Publishing Group
NTC/Contemporary Publishing Company

Library of Congress Cataloging-in-Publication Data

James, Ewart, 1942–
    NTC's dictionary of the United Kingdom / Ewart James; illustrated
by Duncan J. McKinnon.
        p.   cm.
    Includes bibliographical references and index.
    ISBN 0-8442-5855-5 (cloth)
    ISBN 0-8442-5856-3 (paper)
    1. English language—Great Britain—Dictionaries.   2. English
language—Northern Ireland—Dictionaries.   3. Northern Ireland—
Civilization—Dictionaries.   4. Great Britain—Civilization—Dictionaries.
I. McKinnon, Duncan J.   II. NTC Publishing Group.   III. Title.
PE1704.J36   1995
941'.003—dc20   95-15517
                                                 CIP

Cover photographs: left, © by J. Moss/H. Armstrong Roberts;
center, © by R. Kord/H. Armstrong Roberts; right, © by Victor Pcholkin/
FPG International

This edition published 1998 by NTC Publishing Group
An imprint of NTC/Contemporary Publishing Company
4255 West Touhy Avenue, Lincolnwood (Chicago), Illinois 60646-1975 U.S.A.
Copyright © 1996 by NTC/Contemporary Publishing Company
Printed in the United States of America
International Standard Book Number: 0-8442-5855-5 (cloth)
                                     0-8442-5856-3 (paper)
18   17   16   15   14   13   12   11   10   9   8   7   6   5   4   3   2   1

Contents

Acknowledgements

Of the many people who have helped make this book happen—mostly without knowing that they had done such a thing—two must be singled out for special thanks:

Louise for her unflagging support, and especially for being my fiercest critic just when that was exactly what I needed to keep to the straight and narrow.

Richard Spears at NTC, for his ever-ready help and advice.

Ewart James
1995

Preface

NTC's Dictionary of the United Kingdom is an illustrated reference work of more than 13,500 entries and almost 17,000 definitions. Inside this dictionary, many thousands of fascinating facts about British language, life, geography and history are waiting to be discovered, and hundreds of explanatory comments and examples are provided. In addition, a bountiful supply of slang, colloquial, regional, archaic, and historical words and expressions are listed and explained upon these pages. An abundance of information about British places, organizations and customs can also be found here. Line drawings enliven and illustrate, maps illuminate, and hundreds of extensive background notes and examples educate the user. Both casual browser and serious student of British culture will be equally well rewarded here.

Although the earliest examples of American innovations with the English language can be traced back to about 100 years before the American Revolution, George Washington and George III both spoke an essentially identical form of the language. Yet well before another fifty years had passed, American and British English had drifted far enough apart for this to be a topic of regular comment and debate, and it has now been long recognized that differences between the various divergent strains of English can lead to serious linguistic and cultural misunderstandings and pitfalls. During World War II, the United States Army issued a little booklet full of helpful advice to every GI heading for England. In a section called "English versus American Language" we find these words:

> Almost before you meet the people you may not understand what they are talking about and they may not understand what you say. The accent will be different from what you are used to and many of the words will be strange or apparently wrong as well ... British slang is something you will have to pick up for yourself.

Such impediments to understanding British English remain today. However, *NTC's Dictionary of the United Kingdom* is a practical and useful tool for decoding those special words and expressions that are uniquely British, and rendering them understandable to the rest of the English-speaking world.

This dictionary provides a real help for visitors to Britain, anyone who enjoys British television and movies, Anglophiles, and those who read British English, whether it is the classics, contemporary novels, or academic, scientific, legal or business papers, or any other kind of document.

Here is a comprehensive, accessible, and readable guide to this fascinating topic, yet is much more than a merely linguistic lexicon. It is a serious, encyclopedic reference presenting and explaining words, concepts, and expressions that reveal the idiom of English as it is spoken in the United Kingdom, and at the same time something of the idiom of British life itself.

Particular attention is given to the differences between contemporary British and American English. This primary dichotomy of the language is used to bring the essential Britishness of British English into a brighter light and a sharper focus. Anyone who is interested in the vast, rich heritage of the English language and British culture will surely find it hard to resist this treasury of often surprising and arcane knowledge.

Scope

NTC's Dictionary of the United Kingdom highlights, catalogs, and explains in American English those parts of the English Language that are specifically British. Words and expressions that are used in different ways in the United States and Britain or that are unique to British English are the substance of this dictionary.

GEOGRAPHIC SCOPE

To focus properly upon this task, geographical criteria for the entries have been clearly drawn. The words and expressions found here reflect the geographical and cultural extent and diversity of the United Kingdom, coming from England, Scotland, Wales and—so far as this is possible—Northern Ireland rather than all of that island. However, words from the Republic of Ireland that have crept into more general British use are included. So have a number of specifically Irish terms that crop up with reasonable frequency in British media reporting of Irish matters.

There is no shortage of varieties of English in the United Kingdom. England alone is home to numerous forms of the language; Cockney to Scouse, West Country to Geordie. Together with Wales, Scotland and Ireland, there are surely more English dialects in the British Isles than the rest of the world together.

The largest living reservoir of the ancient Celtic language in the world today is in Wales. However, in truth the vast majority of the Welsh people conduct their daily business in a sing-song English that betrays their linguistic ancestry but is otherwise largely independent of it. In Northern Ireland people speak in a way that owes more to Scots than the rather more familiar accents of southern Ireland.

In Scotland we find the only variety of the English language that has ever had any real claim to linguistic independence. Compared to the English of the rest of the world, it has a number of unique grammatical features, thousands of unique words, a unique orthography, and a revered body of literature that uses those unique elements—yet it is not a separate language. Because of the unique character of Scots English, there are more regional words and phrases from Scotland listed here than from any other corner of Britain. For all that, what is found here is little more than a sampling of the most common of the many thousands of words and expressions that distinguish Scots from the rest of the language.

LINGUISTIC SCOPE

Classes of Words and Expressions Included

- Those that are unique to British English.
- Those with a British meaning that differs from their usual American meaning.
- Those with a British meaning that is additional to their usual American meaning.
- Those that are archaic in America but remain current in British English.
- Those that are rare or unfamiliar in America but common in British English.
- Those that differ only in spelling.

Words or expressions that have entirely identical meanings and spelling in both Britain and America are not included in this dictionary.

In general, the dictionary offers no information or guidance on pronunciation. For this reason, words such as "leisure", "herb" or "buoy," typically pronounced in markedly different ways on opposite shores of the Atlantic, but otherwise identical in meaning and spelling, are not to be found here*.

A NOTE ON NATIONALITY

Because England is home to about 83% of the British population, the reader should assume an English or British origin unless stated otherwise. Entries with a Scottish, Welsh or Irish origin are labeled thus, but an English one only where there is a particular reason to do so.

Using this Dictionary

1. Headwords are presented in the form in which they normally occur in spoken or written English, and appear in bold type.

2. Except in the case of proper names and abbreviations, headwords do not have a capitalized first letter or terminating period. Those that are abbreviations may be entirely capitalized, have their first letter capitalized or be entirely in lower case as appropriate or normal for that particular headword.

3. Headwords *and thus entries* are listed in absolute alphabetical order, wherein spaces and punctuation, including hyphens, are disregarded.

4. Certain words, particularly definite and indefinite articles placed in front of the headword, and general or non-specific pronouns such as "someone" or "one" placed within a phrasal headword to clarify meaning or use, do not affect alphabetization.

5. Classifications follow each headword and appear in italic type. When there is more than one classification item, these are separated by commas. Classifications include such things as parts of speech, region of origin or primary use, foreign language origin, and slang or colloquial status as appropriate. When there is more than one classification item, these are separated by commas. Most are listed in abbreviated form; for more information on this, see the section Terms, Symbols, and Abbreviations below.

6. Background information is presented in smaller roman type than definitions. Often, these notes take the form of one or several paragraphs expanding extensively upon the primary definition.

7. When an entry incorporates multiple definitions, additional conventions apply.

   If the classification is identical for all definitions, they are numbered and listed sequentially as follows:

   headword *classification* (1) definition; (2) another definition

---

* To satisfy the curious, the British pronounce "leisure" with its "-ei-" sounding not like the "-ea-" in "treason" but the "-ea-" in "treasure," the "h-" in "herb" is never silent and "buoy" sounds exactly like "boy."

For example:

> **master** *noun, out.* (1) a male head of household; (2) an employer, especially of a servant; (3) a male teacher; (4) the principal of certain university colleges; (5) an official of the ➡Supreme Court of Judicature; (6) earlier, a formal prefix title attached to the given name of a boy not old enough to be called "Mr."

If classifications are not identical, then each definition or group of definitions with identical classification is listed in separate paragraphs with paragraph-sequencing letters contained in square brackets, as follows:

> **headword** [A] *classification* (1) definition; (2) another definition
> [B] *another classification* yet another definition

For example:

> **cop** [A] *noun, North* a mound; the crest of a hill
> [B] *verb, sl.* to arrest or capture

9. Curly brackets, "{" and "}" and chevrons, "»," are used to indicate words or phrases belonging in sequence, are interchangable, or otherwise associated together. In the case of multiple gender-related words or phrases, such as {his » her} or {king » queen}, the most common or typical usage is placed first within the brackets, taking precedence over alphabetical order. This is done to simplify searching.

10. Cross-references that refer to another headword from within a definition are highlighted by the symbol "➡" before the word or expression being cross-referred. When this word or expression is plural, quite probably the referred-to headword appears in singular form. Not every possible cross-reference has been implemented, as this would be tedious for frequently used and generally well-known words.

Sources

This dictionary was born out of a growing reservoir of words and expressions accumulated over years of listening, reading and observing the multitude of ways in which English is used and abused in Britain, North America and elsewhere. Taking this large body of disordered information and organizing, cataloging, editing and cross-checking it depended crucially upon a large number of reference and other books and sources. The most significant are listed in the Bibliography.

Although every effort has been made to identify and indicate trademarks or proprietary trade names within the text, this dictionary is not authoritative on trademark identification or use, and the presense or absence of such indication in no way affects the validity of any such name.

Terms, Symbols and Abbreviations Used

abbr.	abbreviation
adj.	adjective
Arab.	Arabic
arch.	archaic; not used in current British English
Aus.	Australian English
C.	century
coll.	colloquial or informal
comp. noun	compound noun
conj.	conjunction
def. art.	definite article
derog.	derogatory
Du.	Dutch
East.	Eastern England or Eastern English
exclam.	exclamation
Fr.	French
Gae.	Gaelic; either Scottish or Irish, depending on the context.
Ger.	German
Gr.	Ancient Greek
Hindi	Hindi
hist.	historical; historic events, people or places.
idiom	idiomatic word or expression
idiom. phr. verb	idiomatic phrasal verb
imper.	imperative
inter.	interrogate
Ir.	Ireland or Irish
It.	Italian
Lat.	Latin
Mid.	English Midlands
North.	Northern England
noun	noun
num.	numerical
out.	out of date; dated; rare in current British English
past tense	past tense
phr. verb	phrasal verb
Port.	Portugese
pos. pronoun	possesive pronoun
prefix	prefix
pref.	preferred; the most common or preferred choice in British English

prep.	preposition
pronoun	pronoun
pr. name	proper name
rh. sl.	rhyming slang; as when "friend" evolves into "china" in the following manner: "mate," already a slang word for "friend," rhymes with "plate," which expands to "china plate," which is then in turn abbreviated to "china." Thus, "china" is rhyming slang for "friend."
Sc.	Scotland or Scottish
sl.	slang
South.	Southern England or Southern English
Span.	Spanish
spell.	spelling
Swedish	Swedish
taboo	taboo; of words or expressions normally considered obscene, offensive or repugnant.
TM	trade mark
Urdu	Urdu
verb	verb
verb. aux	verbal auxiliary
Wal.	Wales or Welsh
West.	Western England or Western English
Yid.	Yiddish
➠	Cross reference symbol
»	Association symbol (linking two or more words or phrases enclosed within curly brackets)
>	Linking symbol, showing the route of a derivation

NTC's Dictionary of the

UNITED KINGDOM

Be not afeard; the isle is full of noises,
Sounds and sweet airs,
that give delight and hurt not.

—William Shakespeare, *The Tempest*

A- *noun* the prefix to a highway number, designating it to be a ➡trunk road

SEE ALSO: ➡M-, ➡B-

A *noun, arch.* a former movie classification indicating suitability for viewing by an adult audience, or children when accompanied by adults

Now replaced by "PG" classification.

A1 *noun, abbr.* (1)➡A1 at Lloyd's; (2) in general, the very best possible quality of anything

(2) is derived from (1).

A1 at Lloyd's *idiom* the best possible classification of the condition of a ship's hull

In the view of ➡Lloyd's Register of Shipping.

A4 *noun* a standard metric page size

Which is 297 x 210 millimeters, or approximately 11¹/₂ x 8¹/₄ inches. This is the normal page size used for most business correspondence in Britain.

AA [A] *noun, arch.* a former movie classification indicating suitability for viewing only by people aged 14 years or older

Now replaced by "PG" classification.

[B] *pr. name, abbr.* the Automobile Association

Similar to the American Automobile Association.

AAA *pr. name, abbr.* the Amateur Athletic Association

The body governing amateur athletics in the United Kingdom, it was founded in 1880.

Abbey National plc *pr. name (TM)* a large national retail bank

Formerly a ➡building society, it became a bank in 1989.

Abbotsford House *pr. name, hist.* a large house some 30 miles south of ➡Edinburgh

Sir Walter Scott built this romantic Gothic pile upon the banks of the ➡Tweed River between 1817 and 1822. It was his home; now it's a museum displaying his large collection of antiquarian relics, and his 9,000-volume library.

abdication *noun, hist.* the formal legal act of resignation of a sovereign from his or her throne

The last British abdication occured in 1936 when ➡Edward VIII was obliged to give up the throne in order to be free to marry Mrs. Wallis Simpson.

Mrs. Simpson was twice divorced and in 1936 this was not considered acceptable for the wife of a British king.

Aberdeen *pr. name, hist.* a city that is the administrative center of the ➡Grampian Region in north eastern Scotland

Aberdeen was originally two cities. Old Aberdeen was incorporated as a city in 1179. The newer city, which is the commercial center of the modern city, developed around the harbor. This is why there were two universities—until they merged in 1860—and three cathedrals. One of these, St Andrew's Anglican Cathedral, is the mother church of the Episcopal Church of the United States, which after independence found itself without a bishop and unable to obtain consecration of new priests from the English Church. This was overcome when an American, Samuel Seabury, was consecrated bishop in a secret ceremony in Aberdeen. Today the city's population, including suburbs, is 215,000 (1988 estimate).

Aberdeen Angus *pr. name* a breed of hornless black cattle bred for beef

➡Aberdeen and ➡Angus are the two former counties in north eastern Scotland where they originated.

Aberdeenshire *pr. name, hist.* a former Scottish county

Now part of the ➡Grampian Region.

Aberdeen Terrier *pr. name* an alternative name for the ➡Scottish Terrier

Aberdeen University *pr. name* the fifth-oldest university in the English-speaking world and the third-oldest in Scotland

It was founded in 1495. A second university was founded in ➡Aberdeen in 1593 and the two only merged into the present single institution in 1860 so that for more almost 240 years, until Durham University was founded in 1832, this small Scottish city could boast as many universities as the whole of England.

Aberdonian *pr. name* a native, inhabitant or citizen of ➡Aberdeen or ➡Aberdeenshire

ablow *adv., prep., Sc.* below

about turn *imper.* a military order to about face

above *prep., coll.* more than

above oneself *idiom, sl.* conceited or overbearing

above stairs *comp. noun, coll., out.* upstairs

abridgement *spell.* abridgment

abroad *adv., arch.* (1) out and about; (2) outdoors

abseil *verb, Ger* to rappel

From the German *abseilen* = "to descend upon a rope".

1

absolute monarchy *comp. noun* a monarchy where the monarch's power is unlimited or unrestricted by constitutional or other laws

SEE ALSO: ➡limited monarchy, ➡constitutional monarchy.

ABTA *pr. name (TM), abbr.* the Association of British Travel Agents

abutter *noun* the owner of adjacent property

{**AC » ACW**} *noun, abbr.* ➡{aircaftsman » aircraftswoman}

academy *noun, Sc.* a high school

ACAS *pr. name, abbr.* the Advisory, Conciliation and Arbitration Service

A government organization set up to mediate between labor unions, employers and other parties to industrial disputes, and to improve industrial relations in general. It replaced the former ➡Trade Board in 1975.

Access *pr. name (TM)* a credit card

Equivalent to and associated with MasterCard (TM).

access broadcasting *comp. noun* TV or radio time set aside for programming by minority or special-interest groups

accident department *comp. noun* a hospital emergency room

accommodation *noun* accommodations

As in a hotel, for example.

accommodation address *comp. noun* a temporary address used by someone who does not have or will not provide a permanent one

accommodation road *comp. noun* an access road

accompanyist *noun* an accompanist

account *noun* a bill

Presented by a hotel, for example.

accountant *noun, Sc.* the chief clerk and assistant manager of a branch office of a bank

{**accoutre » accoutrement**} *spell.* {accouter » accouterment}

accumulator [A] *noun* a system of sequential betting upon horse-races

It automatically turns any winnings from a bet on the first race into the stake for a bet on a second, and so on.

[B] *noun, arch.* a rechargeable wet cell battery

Once commonly used to power radios in the days before transistors or public electricity supplies.

accursed *adj., out.* highly undesirable or despicable

ach *exclam., Sc.* an expression of surprise, regret, irritation, etc.

Achilles' tendon *spell.* Achilles tendon

acid drop *noun* a sour ball

acidie *noun* acedia, apathy or ennui

ack-ack *noun, abbr., hist.* anti-aircraft fire

From "anti-aircraft," abbreviated to "A.A." and then pronounced over military radio, etc., in this way for clarity.

acker *noun, Arab., sl.* cash or low value bank notes

Originally this was military slang, which was in turn a corruption of the Arabic word *fakka* = "coin".

ackle *verb, arch.* to make work

acknowledgement *spell.* acknowledgment

ACORN *pr. name, abbr.* A Classification of Residential Neighbourhoods

A directory of neighborhoods throughout Britain, used by companies to market appropriate products to appropriate areas.

act a part *idiom. phr. verb* to pretend or play a part

acting sub-lieutenant *comp. noun* the lowest rank of commissioned officer in the ➡Royal Navy

Equivalent in rank to an ensign in the U.S. Navy.

action replay *comp. noun* an instant replay on TV

active service *comp. noun* active duty

act of grace *idiom, out.* a pardon or privilege

One which is or has been granted as an act of benevolence and thus cannot be presumed to be a right or entitlement.

Act of Parliament *pr. name* a bill approved by both Houses of ➡Parliament and given the ➡Royal Assent, thus enacted into law

the **Act of Settlement** *pr. name, hist.* the ➡Act of Parliament of 1701, which established that only a Protestant might succeed to the British ➡Throne

This Act still imposes certain limitations upon the behavior of the British ➡Royal Family, in particular what religion they may embrace and whom they may marry.

the **Act of Supremacy** *pr. name, hist.* the ➡Act of Parliament of 1534, which established the supremacy of the monarch over the ➡Church of England and denied any authority to the Pope

the **Act of Union** *pr. name, hist.* (1) the ➡Act of Parliament of 1536, which incorporated ➡Wales into England; (2) the Act of Parliament of 1707, which declared that ➡England and ➡Scotland would "➡for ever after be united into One Kingdom by the Name of ➡Great Britain" and merged the English and Scottish Parliaments into one single ➡Parliament of Great Britain that would meet at ➡Westminster; (3) the Act of Parliament of 1800, which united the Parliaments of Great Britain and ➡Ireland into the United Kingdom Parliament meeting at Westminster

England and Scotland had shared the same monarch since 1603, 104 years before (2), and Ireland had been ruled — in the most part, after a fashion—by England for many hundreds of years before 1800.

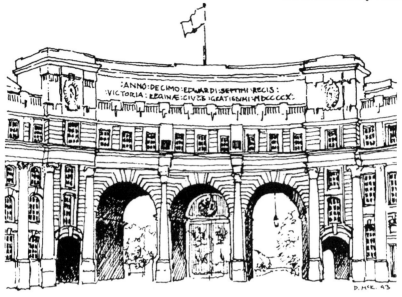

Admiralty Arch

the **Acts of Uniformity** *pr. name, hist.* the ⟶Acts of Parliament, in 1559 and 1662, which established a uniform form of public worship in England

The 1559 Act imposed the ⟶Book of Common Prayer across England, and the 1662 Act required it to be used in all churches; 2,000 ministers who refused to comply were thrown out of their livings.

ACTT *pr. name, abbr.* the Association of Cinematograph, Television and Allied Technicians

A labor union for TV and movie technicians.

Adam *pr. name, hist.* a style of neoclassical architecture that was popular in the 18th C.

Credited to the ⟶Edinburgh architect William Adam and his three sons Robert, James and John.

Adam's {ale » wine} *comp. noun, coll.* water

the **Adam Smith Institute** *pr. name* a right-wing think tank established in 1977

Named for Adam Smith, the Scottish philosopher who published *The Wealth of Nations*, his ground-breaking work that established the intellectual basis of free enterprise economics, in 1776.

ADC *noun, abbr.* an ⟶aide-de-camp

adjournment debate *comp. noun* a short parliamentary debate upon a topic raised by a ⟶private member

When allowed by the ⟶Speaker, these debates are limited to about half an hour at the end of the business day in the ⟶House of Commons.

adjustable spanner *comp. noun* a monkey wrench

admass *noun, coll.* that portion of the population who are supposedly influenced by advertising

admin [A] *adj., abbr., coll.* administrative

[B] *noun, abbr., coll.* administration

admin block *comp. noun, abbr., coll.* an administration building

adminicle *noun, Sc.* collateral evidence concerning what is written in a document that cannot itself be produced in court

admiral *noun* the commander of a fishing fleet

Admiral of the Fleet *pr. name* the highest rank of officer in the ⟶Royal Navy

Equivalent in rank to a Fleet Admiral in the U.S. Navy.

the **Admiral's Cup** *pr. name* the trophy presented by the Royal Ocean Racing Club to the winner of a yacht race held every other year

the **Admiralty** *pr. name, hist.* the former government department that administered the ⟶Royal Navy

Now replaced by the ⟶Admiralty Board.

Admiralty Arch *pr. name* the triumphal arch linking ⟶Trafalgar Square to the ⟶Mall in London

Although built as a memorial to ⟶Victoria, it was for some unknown reason named for the Admiralty Building that it stands beside. As a result, the structure's original function has become somewhat hidden from view over the years.

the **Admiralty Board** *pr. name* the ⟶Ministry of Defence committee administering the ⟶Royal Navy

It replaced the former ⟶Admiralty.

3

the **Admiralty Mile** *pr. name, out.* a nautical mile, equal to 6,080 feet or 1,853.2 meters

The Admiralty Mile and the U.S. Nautical Mile (which is equal to 6,080.20 feet or 1,853.248 meters) have now both been supplanted by the International Nautical Mile, which is equal to 6076.115 feet or 1,852 meters.

ado *noun, out.* (1) business; (2) bustle, trouble or fuss

adopt *verb* to nominate a politician to run for office

adopt as holograph *phr. verb, Sc.* to accept formally that a legal document should be considered to be holograph for legal purposes, even when it is not in fact handwritten

The words "adopted as holograph" must be written out in longhand above the signature of the acceptor, on each and every page of any document that is to be so accepted.

adopted road *comp. noun* a formerly private road that has been reclassified as a public road, requiring publicly-financed maintenance

SEE ALSO: ➡unadopted road

adrenaline *noun* epinephrine

adrenocorticotrophic *spell.* adrenocorticotropic

Stimulating to the adrenal cortex.

Adrian IV *pr. name, hist.* the Pope, from 1154 to 1159

Born in ➡St Albans as Nicholas Breakspear, Adrian IV is the only native of the British Isles ever to become Pope. It is said that he gave ➡Henry II a bull granting absolute ownership of Ireland to the English ➡Crown in perpetuity.

adust *adj., arch.* very thirsty

advance [A] *noun* money that has been lent

[B] *verb* to pay wages before they are due

Advanced Level examination *comp. noun* an examination taken by school students who wish to attend a university

In Scotland, ➡Higher Level examinations fulfill this role.

Advanced Supplementary Level examination *comp. noun* a ➡GCE examination sat by students about to graduate from high school

It is set at a higher academic level than that normally expected from university entrants

adventure playground *comp. noun* a children's outdoors play area equipped with facilities for climbing upon and hiding in; it is generally suitable for adventurous and imaginative play

advert *noun, abbr., coll.* advertisement

advocate *noun, Sc.* a ➡barrister

advowson *noun* a legal right to propose or select the priest to fill a vacant ecclesiastical office which provides its holder with an income

SEE ALSO: ➡patronage.

adze *spell.* adz

A woodcutting tool

Aedh *pr. name, hist.* King of ➡Alba

He reigned for one year from 877 until murdered by the king of ➡Strathclyde in 878.

AEEU *pr. name, abbr.* the Amalgamated Engineering and Electrical Union

A labor union for engineering workers. This is Britain's second largest union, formed by the merging of the ➡AEU and the ➡EETPU in 1992.

aegrotat *noun, Lat., out.* (1) a medical certificate confirming that a university student is medically unfit to attend an examination; (2) a pass certificate awarded to a student who has produced such a medical certificate

It is Latin, meaning "is sick."

aerial *noun* an antenna

aerodrome *noun, out.* an airfield

Particularly a military air base.

aerofoil *noun* an airfoil

aeroplane *noun* an airplane

Aethelstan *pr. name, hist.* King of England

The grandson of ➡Alfred the Great, he was first to establish rule over all of England, in 927. A member of the ➡Royal House of ➡Cedric, he reigned until his death in 939.

AEU *pr. name, abbr., hist.* the Amalgamated Engineering Union

A labor union in the engineering industry, which merged with the ➡EETPU in 1992 to form ➡AEEU.

AEU(TASS) *pr. name, abbr., hist.* the Amalgamated Engineering Union (Technical, Administrative, and Supervisory Section)

A section of the former AEU union, now part of the ➡AEEU.

AFBD *pr. name, abbr.* the Association of Futures Brokers and Dealers

An organization set up under the 1986 Financial Services Act for the purpose of enforcing the codes of conduct established under the auspices of ➡LIFFE.

AFC *noun, abbr.* (1) an ➡Association Football Club; (2) the Air Force Cross

AFDCS *pr. name, abbr.* the Association of First Division Civil Servants

A labor union for the highest-ranking civil servants.

aff *prep., adv., Sc.* (1) of; (2) off

affiliation officer *comp. noun* a court official responsible for enforcing an ➡affiliation order

affiliation order *comp. noun* a legal order placed on a father requiring him to pay for the cost of supporting his child

AFM *noun, abbr.* the Air Force Medal

afoot *adv., out.* (1) in progress; (2) on one's own feet

afore *conj., adv., Ir., prep., Sc.* before

AFRC *pr. name, abbr.* the ➡Agriculture and Food Research Council

African lager *comp. noun, sl.* ➡stout beer
This kind of beer has a very dark color..

afternoon tea *comp. noun* a light afternoon meal served with sandwiches, cakes and tea

afters *noun, coll.* the last course of a meal

afterthought *noun, coll.* the youngest child of a large family
Especially if much younger than all the rest.

afterwards *adv.* afterward

Aga *pr. name (TM)* a large stove, usually located in the kitchen
It is used for heating and cooking, and both coal and oil burning versions are made.

agate *adj., East* active

Age Concern *pr. name* a charity that advocates for and directly aids elderly people
It was founded in 1940.

agee *adj., Sc.* ➡agley

ageing *spell.* aging

agent *noun, Sc.* a lawyer

agent-general *comp. noun* the representative of the government of either (1) a Canadian province or an Australian state in London; (2) the United Kingdom in a Canadian province or an Australian state

aggro *noun, sl.* (1) aggression; (2) deliberate violence or the threat of it, usually by groups of youths; (3) a problem or difficulty

agin *prep., Sc.* against

the battle of **Agincourt** *pr. name, hist.* a major English victory over the French in 1415, during the ➡Hundred Years War
The English army was under the command of Henry V. Agincourt is in France.

agley *adj., adv., Sc.* (1) lopsided or askew; (2) wrong or awry; (3) ajar (of a door)

AGM *noun, abbr.* an ➡annual general meeting

agony aunt *comp. noun, coll.* a journalistic sob sister

agony column *comp. noun, coll.* a column in a newspaper or magazine written as a joint enterprise between an ➡agony aunt and her readers

agricultural *adj., coll.* used to describe clumsy, poor quality or inelegant play in cricket
Such as the play to be expected from a small rural team.

agricultural worker *comp. noun* a farmhand

the **Agriculture and Food Research Council** *pr. name* a government-funded research council established by ➡Royal Charter

It is responsible for conducting research into agricultural, fishing, food and related matters.

ahint *adv., Sc.* (1) behind or remaining; (2) following or formerly; (3) too late
SEE ALSO: ➡hint.

aide-de-camp *comp. noun, Fr.* a military officer who is the confidential assistant of a senior officer
This is French for "camp assistant."

ain *adj., Sc.* own

Aintree *pr. name* a racecourse near Liverpool
The annual ➡Grand National is raced here.

air {bed » cushion} *comp. noun* an air mattress

air chief marshal *comp. noun* the second-highest rank of commissioned officer in the ➡RAF
Equivalent in rank to a four-star general in the USAF.

air commodore *comp. noun* the fifth-highest rank of commissioned officer in the ➡RAF
Equivalent in rank to a one-star general in the USAF.

{aircraftsman » aircraftswoman} *noun* the lowest {male » female} rank in the ➡RAF

air dancing *idiom, sl.* death by hanging

Airedale Terrier *pr. name* a breed of large terrier
Named after the valley of the Aire River in ➡Yorkshire, where they originated.

airer *noun* a rack used to air or dry clothes upon

airf *noun, East* half

the **Air Force List** *pr. name* an official list of all commissioned officers in the ➡Royal Air Force

air hostess *comp. noun* a female flight attendant

airing cupboard *comp. noun* a heated and ventilated closet where sheets, cloths, etc. are stored

air letter *comp. noun, arch.* a letter written upon special lightweight paper, to reduce the cost of sending mail by air

air marshal *comp. noun* the third-highest rank of commissioned officer in the ➡RAF
Equivalent in rank to a three-star general in the USAF.

the **Air Ministry** *pr. name, hist.* the former government department responsible for the ➡RAF
Now absorbed within the ➡Ministry of Defence.

air officer *comp. noun* any officer in the ➡RAF with a rank higher than ➡Group Captain

airs and graces [A] *comp. noun, rh. sl.* suspenders
Derivation: suspenders > ➡braces > graces > airs and graces.
[B] *idiom* artificial or pretentious behavior

airscrew *noun* an aircraft propeller

airt [A] *noun, Sc.* (1) an art or ability; (2) a quarter of the compass, a direction; (3) a manner or style
[B] *verb, Sc.* to guide or direct

*Albert
Memorial*

D. MCK. 9?

air vice-marshal *comp. noun* the fourth-highest rank of commissioned officer in the ➡RAF
Equivalent in rank to a two-star general in the USAF.

airy-fairy *adj., coll.* (1) fairy-like or insubstantial; (2) vague or impractical; (3) trivial or without purpose

ait *noun, arch.* a small island
Typically in the center of a river.

Akela *noun* an adult leading a troop of ➡Cub Scouts
This is the name of the wolf-pack leader in Rudyard Kipling's *Jungle Book*.

à la mode *adj. phr., Fr.* braised in wine
Of beef, not ice cream. It is French for "in the fashion".

alarmist *noun* a fear-monger; someone who raises alarms for trivial reasons

Alba *pr. name, hist.* an ancient kingdom in what is now western and northern Scotland
It formed when ➡Caledonia was annexed by ➡Dalriada in 843 under the rule of ➡Kenneth MacAlpin The usual seat of the kings of Caledonia was ➡Scone, near the modern city of ➡Perth in ➡Tayside. Scone had been the principal residence of the kings of Caledonia and was to remain the place where Scottish kings were crowned until after the ➡Union of the Crowns in 1603.

albatross *noun* a hole played three strokes under par in a game of golf

albert *noun, arch.* a watch chain with a crossbar to enable attachment to a buttonhole
Named after Prince ➡Albert, who popularized the device.

Prince **Albert** *pr. name, hist.* ➡Victoria's husband
German by birth, Albert was the second son of the Count of Saxe Coburg und Gotha. He married ➡Victoria in 1840 and was undoubtedly a major influence upon her and indeed upon British society in general.
Albert was chiefly responsible for inspiring and driving forward—against considerable opposition, it must be said—the concept of the ➡Great Exhibition of 1851. Its success greatly enhanced Albert's reputation.
The strict morality or more accurately, prudery, associated with Victoria is now thought to owe more to Albert's attitude and influence on public behavior than that of the queen herself. Victoria never fully recovered from the shock of his sudden death from typhoid in 1861 and spent the remaining four decades of her reign in semi-mourning.

the **Albert Hall** *pr. name, abbr., hist.* the ➡Royal Albert Hall

the **Albert Memorial** *pr. name* a large monument close by the ➡Royal Albert Hall in west London
It was built in 1876 as the nation's memorial to ➡Albert.

the **Albert Memorial Chapel** *pr. name, hist.* a chapel located to the east of ➡St George's Chapel, within the precincts of ➡Windsor Castle
It was built upon the site of an earlier chapel that had been founded by ➡Henry III in 1340 but had since fallen into ruins. These ruins were almost entirely rebuilt by ➡Victoria to become her personal memorial to the memory of her dead ➡Prince Consort.

Albion *pr. name, hist., Lat.* an ancient name for Britain
Possibly from the Latin, *albus* = "white," which could be a reference to the white cliffs near the modern port of Dover, that face towards France across the English Channel.

the **Aldeburgh Festival** *pr. name* a festival of classical music held annually in ➡Suffolk

{**alderman » alderwoman**} *noun, arch.* a {male » female} member of a local council elected to a position of seniority by other council members
Next in rank to mayor, the rank was abolished in 1974 except in the ➡City of London.

Aldermaston *pr. name* the location of the ➡AWRE
In Berkshire, some 10 miles south of ➡Reading.

Aldershot *pr. name* a town in ➡Hampshire
The location of a military camp since 1855, Aldershot is closely connected with the army. The city's population, including suburbs is 230,000 (1988 estimate).

Aldis lamp *pr. name* a hand-held lamp used to transmit messages in Morse code
Named for A.C.W. Aldis, who invented it.

ale *noun* beer

aleberry *noun, arch.* a drink made from hot ale, spice, sugar and crumbs of toasted bread

ale-dagger *comp. noun, arch.* one used for self-defense in ➡alehouse brawls

alehouse *noun, out.* a ➡pub

A-level *noun, abbr.* an ➡Advanced Level examination

alewife *noun, arch.* the landlady of an ➡alehouse

Alexander I *pr. name, hist.* ➡King of Scots

He fought alongside ➡Henry I of England against the Welsh and married Henry's daughter Sibylla. The son of ➡Malcolm III, he reigned for 17 years from 1107 until 1124 and was known as "The Fierce."

Alexander II *pr. name, hist.* ➡King of Scots

Although married to Joan, sister of ➡Henry II of England, the two monarchs quarreled for years over the exact location of their mutual border, finally settling the issue at the Peace of York of 1237. The son of ➡William I, he reigned for 35 years from 1214 until 1249.

Alexander III *pr. name, hist.* ➡King of Scots

The son of ➡Alexander II, he inherited the Scottish throne at the age of seven and reigned for 37 years from 1249 until 1286. Alexander extended the power of the Scottish crown over the ➡Western Isles and strengthened the authority of the central government. He died after falling from his horse and was succeeded by his granddaughter ➡Margaret, the ill-fated ➡Maid of Norway.

Alexandra Palace *pr. name, hist.* a large Victorian glass palace, similar to the earlier ➡Crystal Palace

It was originally erected in 1862 in Kensington to be the venue of a second exhibition following on the success of the ➡Great Exhibition of 1851. Later, it was moved to its present location in north London in 1873, but had to be rebuilt in 1875 after a fire. It was a military barracks during World War I, and from 1936 became the location of the world's first permanent television channel, operated by the ➡BBC. In 1980 it suffered a second serious fire and although it has since been rebuilt again, it is now little used.

Alfred *pr. name, hist.* King of Wessex

Ruling from 871 until 899, the business of his reign was to prevent the ➡Danes from conquering all of England. He was victorious on land and at sea, and was recognized as leader of all England outside of the ➡Danelaw.

Alfred the Great *pr. name, hist.* King ➡Alfred

The only English monarch ever to have been called "Great".

alight *adj.* (1) on fire; (2) illuminated

the **All-England Club** *pr. name, abbr.* the All-England Lawn Tennis and Croquet Club

Located at ➡Wimbledon, in south London.

Alleynian *pr. name* a member of ➡Dulwich College, either past or present

From the name of the founder, E. Alleyn. The college, in South London, was founded in 1619.

all found *adj. phr., coll.* everything provided

Accommodation and food supplied free by an employer.

all gas and gaiters *idiom, out.* pompous verbosity

the **Alliance** *pr. name, hist.* an electoral pact between the ➡Social Democratic and ➡Liberal Parties that lasted from 1981 and 1988

all-in *adj.* (1) all inclusive; (2) exhausted

allotment *noun* a small area of urban land rented out for the purpose of cultivation

Usually, plots are allotted to apartment-dwellers with no land of their own. The provision of land where poor people could grow their own vegetables began in the latter years of the 19th C. However it was during World Wars I and II that allotments, offering a way to supplement meager food rations, became very popular. Since then, as living standards have risen, their popularity has shown significant decline.

all over bar the shouting *idiom, coll.* all over except for trivial details

all over the {place » shop} *idiom, coll.* (1) everywhere; (2) all over the lot; (3) chaotic

Alloway *pr. name, hist.* a small hamlet two miles from ➡Ayr where Robert Burns was born in 1759

The cottage where he was born is still there, now a museum that is kept as it was in his days.

all-rounder *comp. noun, coll.* a person able to perform several activities well, especially in sports

all serene *adj. phr., coll., out.* all right

allsorts *noun* a mixture of candies

Especially licorice ones.

All Souls College *pr. name* a college of ➡Oxford University, founded in 1438

the **All Souls Parish Magazine** *pr. name, arch., hist.* a former nickname for the ➡*Times* newspaper

Between the two world wars, the editor, G.G. Dawson, Fellow of ➡All Souls College, employed a number of other alumni from the same college, who frequently gathered at their alma mater to discuss policy.

Alfred the Great

all the hours God gives us *idiom, coll.* all the time that is available

all-up *adj., coll.* finished or ruined

Ally Pally *pr. name, abbr.* a popular nickname for ➟Alexandra Palace

almoner *noun, arch.* a hospital-based social worker who aids former patients

almsbox *noun* a box where charitable donations may be deposited, usually in a church

almshouse *noun, arch.* a house supported by charity for the purpose of caring for the poor

Alnwick Castle *pr. name, hist.* originally a Norman keep erected at this ➟Northumberland location to guard against invading Scots.

However the present castle, which has been the home of the same family (the Percys) since it was erected, dates from the 14th C.

Alsatian *pr. name* a German Shepherd dog

althaea *spell.* althea

Better known as the Rose of Sharon.

aluminium *noun* aluminum

amah *noun, hist., Port.* a Chinese or Indian wetnurse

Particularly one looking after a British child during the period of British rule in India. The word derives from the Portuguese word *ama* = "nurse."

the **amber nectar** *idiom, Aus., sl.* beer

Especially ➟lager.

Ambridge *pr. name* a fictitious village that is the location of the BBC's ➟*Archers* radio soap opera

amenity bed *comp. noun* a bed in a private room within a public hospital

amenorrhoea *spell.* amenorrhea

A pathological lack of menses.

the **American Civil War** *pr. name, hist.* the Civil War

American cloth *comp. noun* an enameled or oiled waterproof cotton cloth

Americaneese *noun, derog., sl.* the variety of English spoken in the United States

the **American Museum** *pr. name, hist.* a museum housed in ➟Claverton Manor near ➟Bath

It opened in 1968, with each room styled in the manner of a historic period or geographic region of the United States.

American sock *comp. noun, sl.* a condom

SEE ALSO: ➟French letter.

the **American War of Independence** *pr. name, hist.* the American Revolution

amethyst *noun* in heraldry, (1) ➟purpure; (2) a representation of the planet Mercury

ammonium sulphate *spell.* ammonium sulfate

Amnesty International *pr. name* an organization which campaigns for the release of political prisoners around the world

Founded in London in 1961.

amongst *prep., out.* among

amphitheatre *spell.* amphitheater

Amstrad *pr. name (TM)* a company which manufactures and sells electronic equipment, including personal computers

amusement arcade *comp. noun* an arcade containing slot machines

amusements *noun, coll.* the rides and sideshows at a carnival or fair

Anacreon in Heaven *pr. name, hist.* a drinking song popular in the taverns of early 19th C. London

The tune was borrowed by Francis Scott Key, who attached it to the words of the "Star-Spangled Banner" in 1814.

{**anaemia** » **anaemic**} *spell.* {anemia » anemic}

A hemoglobin deficiency.

{**anaesthesia** » **anaesthesiology**} *spell.* {anesthesia » anesthesiology}

{**anaesthetic** » **anaesthetisation**} *spell.* {anesthetic » anesthetization}

anaesthetics *noun* anesthesiology

The science of anesthetics

anaesthetist *noun* anesthesiologist

analogue *spell.* analog

But in computing and electronics, "analog" is used.

{**analyse** » **analyser**} *spell.* {analyze » analyzer}

{**anapaest** » **anapaestic**} *spell.* {anapest » anapestic}

A term used in prosody.

Ancient Briton *pr. name, hist.* an inhabitant of the pre-Roman British Isles

ancient monument *comp. noun* an old building or other construction considered to be of significant historical interest and accorded legal protection from modification or destruction

the **Ancient Universities** *pr. name, hist.* these are:

(1) the University of Oxford, founded 1096.
(2) the University of Cambridge, founded 1209.
(3) the University of St Andrews, founded 1411.
(4) the University of Glasgow, founded 1451.
(5) the University of Aberdeen, founded 1495.
(6) the University of Edinburgh, founded 1583.
(7) Trinity College, Dublin, founded 1591.

It is because there was a gap of almost two and a half centuries from 1591 until the founding of the first modern university in Britain at ➟Durham in 1832, that these are considered to be "ancient".

By comparison, Harvard University, the oldest in North America, was founded in 1636.

and *conj., pref.* a link used when expressing numbers
For example, 234 is expressed, "two hundred and thirty four" rather than "two hundred thirty four".

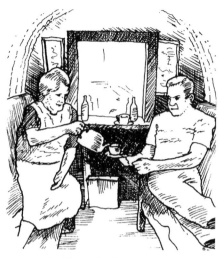

inside an Anderson shelter

Anderson shelter *comp. noun, hist.* an air-raid shelter used to protect civilians during World War II
They were named after Sir John Anderson, ➡Home Secretary at the time, who ordered their distribution in 1938. They were made of curved corrugated iron sheets and were about 6" high, 7" long and 4" wide. Householders were advised to place them in a pit in their yard some 4" deep and then cover with earth.

Andrew *pr. name, sl.* the ➡Royal Navy
Reputedly derived from Andrew Miller, the leader of an early 19th C. ➡press gang.

Andy Capp *pr. name* the hero of a cartoon appearing daily in the *Daily Mirror* newspaper since 1958
A comprehensively lazy individual who never appears without wearing a ➡cloth cap, and rarely without a cigarette in his mouth and pint of beer in his hand.

ane *noun, Sc.* one

anent *prep., out., Sc.* (1) with regard to, concerning; (2) in the presence or view of someone

angel cake *noun* angel food cake

angels on horseback *idiom* oysters wrapped in bacon slices

Angers *pr. name, hist.* an alternate name for the ➡Royal House of ➡Anjou

Angevin *pr. name, hist.* a member of the ➡Royal House of ➡Angers or ➡Anjou

Anglepoise *pr. name (TM)* an adjustable desk lamp

Anglesey *pr. name, hist.* (1) a former Welsh county; (2) an island separated from the Welsh mainland by the Menai Strait
(1) is now part of ➡Gwynedd; (2) is linked to the mainland by both road and rail bridges over the Menai Strait. It is also linked to ➡Holyhead on ➡Holy Island by further bridges

Anglia *pr. name (TM)* a railroad company operating within East Anglia and from there to London
It is part of ➡British Rail.

Anglia TV *pr. name (TM)* a local commercial TV company which is headquartered in ➡Norwich, and is part of the ➡ITV network

Anglican *noun* an Episcopalian
Especially a member of the ➡Church of England.

Anglicism *noun* (1) a fondness for that which is English; (2) a practice which is considered to be characteristically English; (3) a way of speaking or a mannerism which is considered to be characteristically English

Anglo-Catholic *pr. name* an ➡Anglican who favors union between the ➡Church of England and the Roman Catholic Church

Anglo-French *pr. name, hist.* the variety of the French language which developed in England following the ➡Conquest

Anglo-Indian [A] *adj.* concerning or affecting both England and India
[B] *noun* (1) a British person or a person of British descent who has lived in India for a long time; (2) a person of mixed Indian and British descent

Anglo-Irish *pr. name* those Irish citizens who are descended from the English who settled there in the centuries before Irish independence
Included in their numbers are a number of well-known writers such as Swift, Sheridan, Wilde and Shaw.

the **Anglo-Irish Agreement** *pr. name, hist.* a 1985 agreement between the British and Irish governments
It enables the Irish Government to participate in a form of partial co-government of the ➡Six Counties of ➡Northern Ireland, which remains within the United Kingdom.

the **Anglo-Irish Treaty** *pr. name, hist., Ir.* the treaty of 1921 that ended the ➡Anglo-Irish War
26 of ➡Ireland's 32 counties became independent within the ➡British Empire as the ➡Irish Free State.

the **Anglo-Irish War** *pr. name, hist., Ir.* the official British name for the ➡Irish War of Independence
Lasting from 1919 until 1921, this was a brutal terrorist war between the ➡IRA and the ➡Black and Tans. It ended with the ➡Anglo-Irish Treaty.

Anglo-Latin *pr. name, hist.* the variety of Latin developed in England during the Middle Ages

Anglomania

Anglomania *noun* an obsessive interest in England or English things or people

Anglo-Norman *pr. name, hist.* (1) a ➡Norman living in England following the ➡Conquest; (2) the ➡Anglo-French spoken by ➡Normans living in England following the ➡Conquest

{anglophile » anglophobe} *noun* a person with ➡{anglophilia » anglophobia}

{anglophilia » anglophobia} *noun* an obsessive {love » fear} of England or English things or English people

Anglo-Saxon *pr. name, hist.* (1) two of the Germanic tribes who, together with the Jutes, invaded from across the North Sea to occupy most of Britain following the departure of the Romans in the 5th C., and to rule it until the ➡Norman Conquest of 1066; (2) the low German language of these tribes

And that language grew, over many centuries and with much help from Danish, French, Latin, Greek and just about any other language you care to mention, into modern English.

the **Angry Brigade** *pr. name, hist.* a radical anarchist group that made bombing attacks in Britain in the late 1960s and early 1970s

the **Angry Young Men** *pr. name, hist.* a group of young dramatists in the 1950s who were considered politically and morally radical then, although rather moderate by current standards

Their best known member was John Osborne, author of *Look Back in Anger*.

Angus *pr. name, hist.* a former Scottish county

Now part of the ➡Tayside region.

Anjou *pr. name, hist., Lat.* the ➡Royal House of England from 1154 until 1461

The houses of ➡Plantagenet, ➡Lancaster and ➡York are usually thought of as Royal Houses in their own right, but to be strictly accurate all three are subsidiaries within Anjou. "Plantagenet" is said to have been the nickname of Henry II, from the Latin *planta genista* = "sprig of broom," which he supposedly wore at all times. However, it was first used as a Royal House name some 300 years after him. "Lancaster" and "York" derived from the two sides of the ➡Wars of the Roses, who were the parties of the Duke of Lancaster and the Duke of York—both princes of the House of Anjou.

Altogether there were 14 Anjou monarchs. Only three escape one of these other house names; Henry II, Richard I and John. For convenience, the other 11 are listed under ➡Plantagenet, ➡Lancaster and ➡York as appropriate.

annat *noun, hist.* (1) in England, the revenue from the first year of an ecclesiastical benefice; (2) in Scotland, half the annual stipend of a ➡Church of Scotland parish minister, which after his death was required to be paid to his widow until her death

Until 1535 all annat revenue from both countries was paid to the Pope. In England from that year until 1926 when it

was abolished, it was paid to the ➡Crown. The Scottish procedure was established by a law of 1672 and abolished in 1925.

Anne *pr. name, hist.* Queen of Great Britain

She succeeded her brother-in-law, ➡William III, to the throne in 1702. Anne styled herself, "Queen of England, Scotland, France and Ireland, Defender of the Faith, etc., etc." until the ➡Union of the Scottish and English Parliaments in 1707 when she became, "Queen of Great Britain, France and Ireland, Defender of the Faith, etc., etc." She reigned for 12 years until 1714, and was the last member of the ➡Royal House of ➡Stuart to reign. Despite fifteen pregnancies, she died without surviving issue and was succeeded by a distant cousin, ➡George I.

Anne Boleyn *pr. name, hist.* ➡Henry VIII's second wife and the mother of ➡Elizabeth I

It was because Henry had to divorce ➡Catherine of Aragon—his first wife—before he could marry Anne, and because the Pope would not grant this dispensation, that he broke with the Church in Rome, so bringing into being the ➡Church of England and precipitating into England the Reformation already under way elsewhere.

However the new marriage lasted little more than three years, ending with Anne's execution for her alleged adultery with several lovers. It now considered unlikely that any of these charges were true and that her fatal error was to fail in her duty to be delivered of a healthy male heir.

Anne Hathaway's Cottage *pr. name, hist.* the family home of Shakespeare's wife

This sturdy ➡half-timbered and thatched 15th C. structure, which is really more of a farmhouse than a cottage, is about one mile from the center of ➡Stratford-upon-Avon.

Anne of Cleves *pr. name, hist.* the fourth wife of ➡Henry VIII

The daughter of a German duke, she was chosen as Henry's bride for the purpose of cementing a German alliance against France and Spain. However Henry took an immediate dislike to her and the marriage was never consummated. Within six months the political circumstances had changed so that the marriage was no longer necessary and was therefore annulled. Anne lived on in England in comfort for several years after the death of Henry.

annexe *noun, spell.* annex

annual general meeting *comp. noun* a yearly meeting of all members, such as shareholders, of a company or other organization

At this meeting existing officeholders report to members and new officeholders are elected for the following year.

anorak [A] *noun* a windbreaker jacket or parka

A Greenland Eskimo word.

[B] *noun, derog., sl.* a student considered to be dull, conventional and unfashionably dressed

anorectic *spell.* anorexic

Lacking appetite.

another *noun* an unnamed party in a legal action

A N Other *pr. name* in sport, a player who has yet to be named or selected

Gisors (France) Dept LEURE

Haute Normandie

Richard I.

Dieu et mon droit !

British Royal Motto

Co

54016-1444

USA
54016-1444

If you need to make any amendments to your address please complete the
coupon and return this sheet to the address below. Alternatively, please contact
IPC Media on:

Tel: +44 (0) 1444 475675
Fax: +44 (0) 1444 445599

New Address:-
Account No: . . . .
Name: . . . .
Street: . . . .
Town/City: . . . .
               . . . .
Post Code: . . . .
Country: . . . .

FOR ALL SU
EMAIL ipsu

IPC Media Ltd and or IPC E
if you would prefer not to rec

Another Place *pr. name* the ➡House of Lords as referred to within the ➡Chamber of the ➡House of Commons, and *vice versa*

anoxaemia *spell.* anoxemia
A deficiency of arterial oxygen

antheap *noun, out.* anthill

ante-communion *comp. noun* the portion of a service in the ➡Church of England that takes place prior to the act of communion

antenatal *adj.* prenatal

antidisestablishmentarianism *noun, arch.* opposition to ➡disestablishmentarianism

anticlockwise *adj., adv.* counter-clockwise

the **Antipodes** *pr. name, coll.* Australasia
The British tend to consider that Australasia—in particular Australia and New Zealand, although the term is also inclusive of the other islands of the southwestern Pacific—is diametrically opposite the British Isles on the surface of the globe. This is not so, but the Antipodes Islands, 650 miles south-west of Wellington, New Zealand, are very nearly directly opposite London.

antipost *adj.* a bet made before the number of runners in a horse race are known

Antonine's Wall *pr. name, hist.* an ancient 36-mile long earthwork rampart that crosses central Scotland from the ➡Forth to ➡Clyde rivers
It was built between 140 and 142 under the authority of the Roman Emperor Antoninus Pius as a bulwark against the unconquered northern tribes, but was abandoned within 50 years. Although traces of this wall remain, the stone-built ➡Hadrian's Wall is far more intact today.

Antrim *pr. name* (1) a former Northern Irish County (County Antrim) in the ancient province of ➡Ulster; (2) a district in ➡Northern Ireland
The current population of (2) is 50,000 (1990 estimate).

any road *idiom* anyhow or anyway

any work going? *inter., coll.* is there any work available?

Anzac *pr. name, abbr., hist.* (1) the Australia and New Zealand Army Corp.; (2) a soldier from Australia or New Zealand during either World War

apartment *noun* a single room within a building containing other rooms

apartment block *comp. noun* a building containing several ➡apartments

apartments *noun, abbr.* ➡furnished apartments

apence *noun, South* money

APEX *pr. name, abbr., hist.* the Association of Professional, Executive, Clerical and Computer Staff
A labor union for white-collar workers. APEX merged with ➡GMBATU to form ➡GMB in 1989.

apnaea *spell.* apnea
A short period without breathing.

apophthegm *noun* an apothegm or aphorism

apothecaries' measure *comp. noun, arch.* a pharmacists' measure of liquid capacity

apothecaries' weight *comp. noun, arch.* a pharmacists' measure of weight

appal *spell.* appall

{**apparelled** » **apparelling**} *spell.* {appareled » appareling}

appeal *verb* to request a ➡cricketing ➡umpire to decide whether a ➡batsman is ➡out or not
SEE ALSO: ➡howzat.

appeal to the country *idiom. phr. verb* to call a ➡general election

'appen *adv., North* perhaps

appendicectomy *noun* appendectomy

appetising *spell.* appetizing

Appleby *pr. name, hist.* an old town in ➡Cumbria
Although it possesses a Norman castle, the town is now best known for the large horse fair held there every June since the middle of the 18th C.

apple crumble *comp. noun* apple baked into a pie with a crust of ➡crumble

apple fritter *idiom, rh. sl.* ➡bitter beer

apple-pie bed *idiom, coll.* a short-sheeted bed
Made up so that it cannot be used as one, as a practical joke.

apple-pie order *idiom, coll.* perfect condition

apples and pears *idiom, rh. sl.* stairs

apples and rice *idiom, rh. sl.* nice

appointments *noun* furnishings or equipment

approachable *adj.* friendly

approach road *comp. noun* a ➡motorway on-ramp

approved school *comp. noun, arch.* a special residential school for juvenile delinquents

apropos *adj., adv., Fr.* to the point, relevant
From the French, *à propos* = "to the purpose".

APRS *pr. name, abbr.* the Association for the Protection of Rural Scotland
A body set up in 1926 to protect the Scottish countryside.

APT *pr. name, abbr., hist.* Advanced Passenger Train
A high-speed train intended to be introduced on British railroads during the 1980s. However, because of severe technical difficulties principally associated with the tilting mechanism that was supposed to make it possible for the train to travel along curved tracks at very high speed the project was abandoned. The trouble was that in practice the tilting system tended to make passengers violently ill rather than more comfortable as intended.

Aquascutum

Aquascutum *pr. name (TM)* a brand of waterproof raincoat

ARA *noun, abbr.* an Associate of the ➡Royal Academy of Arts

the **Aran Islands** *pr. name* a group of three small and rocky islands off the western coast of Ireland
In descending order of size, the islands are Inishmore, Inishmaan and Inisheer. *SEE ALSO:* ➡Arran.

arbour *spell.* arbor

Arbroath smokie *comp. noun, Sc.* a smoked haddock that has not been split open
Arbroath is a fishing port on the eastern coast of Scotland.

ARC *pr. name, abbr.* the Agricultural Research Council

arcade *noun* a shopping mall

{**archaeological** » **archaeologically**} *spell.* {archeological » archeologically}

{**archaeologist** » **archaeology**} *spell.* {archeologist » archeology}

the **Archbishop of Armagh** *pr. name* ➡Primate of All Ireland and ecclesiastical head of (1) the Roman Catholic Church in all of Ireland; (2) the ➡Anglican Church in all of Ireland

the **Archbishop of Canterbury** *pr. name* ➡Primate of All England and ecclesiastical head of the worldwide ➡Anglican Church

the **Archbishop of Glasgow** *pr. name* ➡Primate of All Scotland and ecclesiastical head of the Roman Catholic Church in Scotland

the **Archbishop of Westminster** *pr. name* ➡Primate of All England and ecclesiastical head of the Roman Catholic Church in England and Wales

the **Archbishop of York** *pr. name* ➡Primate of England and deputy head of the ➡Church of England

the **Archers** *pr. name* a radio soap opera broadcast daily by the ➡BBC since 1951
It was originally created to transmit agricultural information to farmers in an easily-digested manner, but this is now largely forgotten. *SEE ALSO:* ➡Ambridge.

ardour *spell.* ardor

Ards *pr. name* a district in ➡Northern Ireland, in what used to be County ➡Down
The current population is 65,000 (1990 estimate).

area of outstanding natural beauty *comp. noun* an officially designated area of specially protected countryside
Similar to a ➡national park but of lower status.

argent *noun* the heraldic name for the color silver

Argie *pr. name, abbr., sl.* an Argentinean

argie *verb, Sc.* to argue furiously or loudly

argy-bargy *comp. noun* an agitated disputation; a loud and lively discussion

Argyle Street *pr. name* one of the principal shopping streets in ➡Glasgow

Argyll *pr. name, hist.* a former Scottish county
Now part of the ➡Strathclyde region.

Ariel *pr. name, hist.* a series of six British scientific satellites launched between 1962 and 1979

arise out of *phr. verb* to result from

Aristotle *noun, rh. sl.* bottle

Armagh *pr. name* (1) the former Irish County Armagh in the ancient province of ➡Ulster; (2) a district in ➡Northern Ireland; (3) a cathedral city in Northern Ireland which is the seat of the two ➡Archbishops of Armagh
The current population of (2) is 50,000 (1990 estimate).

an **arm and a leg** *idiom* a large amount of money
Especially if the speaker is the one expected to provide it.

the **Armed Forces of the Crown** *pr. name* the collective name for the British army, navy and air force

armiger *noun* a person entitled to heraldic arms

Armistice Day *comp. noun, arch.* a former name for ➡Remembrance Day, November 11
That day in 1918 was the date of the armistice which ended fighting in World War I.

armorial achievement *comp. noun* an heraldic representation of a ➡coat of ➡arms

armory *noun, arch.* ➡heraldry

{**armour** » **armoured**} *spell.* {armor » armored}

{**armourer** » **armoury**} *spell.* {armorer » armory}

arms *noun* an heraldic device

army and navy *idiom, rh. sl.* gravy

the **Army List** *pr. name* the official list of all commissioned officers in the British Army

army rocks *idiom, rh. sl.* socks

arn *pronoun, South* any

around about *adj. phr.* approximately

Arran *pr. name* an island in the ➡Firth of Clyde on the west coast of Scotland
SEE ALSO: ➡Aran Islands.

arras *noun, Fr., hist.* an elaborate tapestry, such as a screen hanging on the wall or walls of a room
Named for the town of Arras in northeastern France, where this form of decoration first developed.

ARRC *noun, abbr.* Associate of the Royal Red Cross

arrestment *noun, Sc.* the legal seizure of possessions or income to enforce debt payment

12

arrow *noun, sl.* a throwing dart in that game

arse *noun, taboo* the ass or buttocks

arse about face *idiom, sl., taboo* facing in the wrong direction

arse around *verb, sl., taboo* to fool around

arse-bandit *comp. noun, derog., sl., taboo* a male homosexual or sodomite

arse-end *comp. noun, derog., sl., taboo* (1) the rear; (2) the final portion

arsehole *noun, sl., taboo* (1) the anus; (2) a contemptible person

arse-licker *comp. noun, derog., sl., taboo* an exceptionally obsequious or toadying person

arse over elbow *idiom, sl., taboo* head over heels

artefact *spell.* artifact

arter *prep., South* after

arterial road *comp. noun, out.* a principle highway

Artful Dodger *idiom, out., rh. sl.* a lodger
An allusion to this character in Dickens's novel *Oliver Twist.*

Arthur *pr. name, hist.* a semi-legendary British king who may or may not have existed
(See box below)

Arthurian *adj.* pertaining to ➡Arthur or the legends associated with him

Arthur Rank *idiom, rh. sl.* a bank
Derived from J. Arthur Rank, who was a former British movie-maker.

Arthur's Seat *pr. name* a volcanic plug rising to 820 feet behind ➡Holyroodhouse in ➡Edinburgh
Vying with ➡Castle Rock to be the most prominent feature of the Scottish capital, the summit offers a magnificent panorama over the city to the ➡Firth of Forth and beyond.

artic *noun, abbr., coll.* an ➡articulated lorry

article *noun, derog., sl.* a contemptible person

articled clerk *comp. noun* one contracted to work for a lawyer for a fixed period of years in return for being taught the skills of that profession
Literally, an apprentice lawyer.

articulated lorry *comp. noun* a trailer truck or rig

artiste *noun* a theatrical entertainer, especially a singer or dancer

the **Arts Council** *pr. name* an independent but government-financed organization charged with supporting and encouraging the arts, especially drama and the other performing arts.

arty-{crafty » farty} *adj., derog., sl.* artsy-craftsy, pretentiously artistic

Arundel Castle *pr. name, hist.* an 11th C. Norman castle in ➡West Sussex
It was built by ➡William the Conqueror to help secure the southern coast against invasion.

ASA *pr. name, abbr.* (1) the Advertising Standards Authority; (2) the Amateur Swimming Association

asafoetida *spell.* asafetida
A fetid resin extracted from certain Asian plants.

ascend the throne *phr. verb* to become monarch

Ascot *pr. name* a racecourse near ➡Windsor, best known for the ➡Royal Ascot race meet.

The Legend of Arthur

It is possible that there may well have been such a king, general or tribal leader who fought in the wars against the waves of ➡ Anglo, Saxons and other Germanic peoples who began to invade the British Isles from across the ➡ North Sea after the Romanised natives had been left to their own devices after the Roman Army had departed in the chaotic conditions following the 5th C. collapse of the Roman Empire.

Although there is no convincing proof or real evidence that Arthur ever lived, he makes his first appearance on paper—with the Latinized name of *Artorius*—as early as the 7th C., in Nennius's *Historia Britonum*. Here he is called a general or duke rather than a king, and leader of the Britons in 12 victorious battles against the Germanic invaders.

The legends about Arthur's court first appeared in Geoffrey of Monmouth's *Historia Regum Britanniæ*, a history of Britain written in 1136, which claims to be a translation from the Celtic of an earlier history of Britain which has never been found. What is certain is that this "translation" first saw the light of day long after the events described in it are all supposed to have happened.

Arthur and his court have been the subject of many fanciful medieval romantic embellishments since then, such as his wonderful redoubt of ➡ Camelot, the tales of his ➡ Knights of the Round Table, and the magician ➡ Merlin.

ASDIC *pr. name, abbr., hist.* a primitive kind of Sonar developed and used by the ➡Royal Navy during World War I

In a fit of immodesty or possibly of a total imaginative failure, the committee responsible for overseeing this innovation, the Admiralty Submarine Detection Investigation Committee, bequeathed to it its own (abbreviated) name.

as ever was *idiom, coll.* unchanged

ASH *pr. name, abbr.* Action on Smoking and Health

A group campaigning against smoking.

ashbin *noun* a trash can able to contain hot ashes

the **Ashes** *pr. name* a mythical trophy supposedly awarded to the victorious side of an annual series of ➡cricket ➡test matches between the English and Australian national teams

The name originated in a spoof epitaph for English cricket, which appeared in a sporting newspaper, following England's defeat at the hands of Australia in the 1882 series of ➡test matches, which concluded by announcing that "the body will be cremated and the ashes taken to Australia."

ashet *noun, Sc.* a large oval plate

the **Ashmolean Museum** *pr. name* the museum of ➡Oxford University

Britain's oldest public museum and originally the collection of Elias Ashmole, who presented it to the university in 1677.

ashpan *noun* a tray placed under a fire-grate so that ashes can be collected and removed more easily

ash-plant *comp. noun* a walking stick made with a sapling taken from an ash tree

ASLEF *pr. name, abbr.* the Amalgamated Society of Locomotive Engineers and Firemen

A labor union for railroad workers.

as queer as a {nine bob » three pound} note *idiom, arch., sl.* obviously worthless, absurd, dishonest or all three

There never was any such thing as a nine ➡bob ➡note or a three ➡pound note.

as safe as houses *idiom* as safe as can be

the **Assaye Regiment** *pr. name, hist.* a nickname for the Royal Highland Fusiliers

A unit of the British Army whose name recalls a distinguished performance at the Battle of Assaye, India, in 1803.

assembly rooms *comp. noun* a public building containing one or more meeting rooms

assentor *noun, out.* one who nominates a candidate for a parliamentary election

Other than the proposer or seconder.

ASSET *pr. name, abbr.* the Association of Supervisory Staffs, Executives and Technicians

A labor union for office workers, engineering technicians, etc.

assisted area *comp. noun* an area designated by the government as qualifying for special aid

Chosen because the area suffers from high unemployment; the purpose is to encourage employers to bring work there.

assist the police with their enquiries *idiom. phr. verb* to be questioned by the police

A common euphemism employed in official statements to the media and public concerning the progress of their investigations into a crime.

assize *noun, arch.* a periodic court

Formerly held at various centers throughout England and Wales, the ➡Crown Court system replaced it in 1972.

Association Football *pr. name* the formally correct name for (1) soccer when played under the rules originally established by the ➡Football Association; (2) the large spherical inflated ball used in the game

assurance *noun* life insurance

as sure as eggs is eggs *idiom, coll.* without doubt

as thick as {a short plank » two short planks} *idiom, coll.* exceptionally dimwitted; highly obtuse

ASTMS *pr. name, abbr.* the Association of Scientific, Technical and Managerial Staff

A labor union for white-collar workers.

the **Astronomer Royal** *pr. name* an honorary title granted to a distinguished British astronomer

*Ashmolean
Museum*

Formerly, the title went automatically to the director of the ➡Royal Greenwich Observatory, but this title is now separated from that office and entirely honorific.

the **Astronomer Royal for Scotland** *pr. name* the director of the ➡Royal Observatory at Edinburgh

Unlike the ➡Astronomer Royal, the holder of this title is expected to work for his or her living.

at a good bat *idiom, coll.* at a high speed

at a loose end *idiom, coll.* at loose ends

at a pinch *idiom, coll.* in a pinch

ATC [A] *noun, abbr.* air traffic control

[B] *pr. name, abbr.* the Air Training Corp.

A part-time training organization for college and school students interested in aviation in general and air force careers in particular. It operates under the control of the ➡RAF.

atheling *noun, hist.* a senior member of the aristocracy of pre- ➡Conquest England

the **Athenaeum** *pr. name* a private club in ➡Pall Mall, London, founded in 1824

the **Athens of the North** *pr. name, coll.* a pretentious nickname for ➡Edinburgh

SEE ALSO: ➡Modern Athens.

athirt *prep., adv., South* across

athletics *noun* track and field sports

Athole brose *comp. noun, Sc.* a concoction of oatmeal, honey and Scotch, sometimes taken together with cream.

the **Atholl Highlanders** *pr. name, hist.* Britain's only private army

It is maintained under a unique ➡royal warrant granted to the Duke of Atholl, at Blair Castle in Scotland. In 1844, during a visit to the Castle, ➡Victoria granted her host the special privilege of the right to his own private army.

Atilla the Hen *pr. name, coll., hist.* a nickname for former ➡Prime Minister Margaret Thatcher

the Battle of the **Atlantic** *pr. name, hist.* the battle between the German navy—mostly using U-boats—and Allied navies which lasted for almost the entire duration of World War II

The German U-boat campaign to destroy Allied shipping bringing supplies from North America and elsewhere to Britain during World War II came very close to succeeding.

the **Atomic Weapons Research Establishment** *pr. name* the military research center located at ➡Aldermaston, where Britain's nuclear weapons were developed in the 1950s

ATS *pr. name, abbr., hist.* Auxiliary Transport Service

A non-combatant unit of women who played a similar role in World War II to that of the ➡WAAC in World War I.

at school *idiom* in or attending school

at table *idiom, coll.* at the table

In Scotland the American form is usual.

attendance allowance *comp. noun* a pension paid by the ➡Department of Social Security to help people who require regular care and help at home due to illness

attendance centre *comp. noun* a place that a court may require a juvenile delinquent to attend

Increasingly it is used as an alternate to prison.

attested {cattle » milk} *comp. noun* {cattle » milk} certified to be free of disease

at the {crease » wicket} *idiom* batting, in ➡cricket

at the double *idiom, coll.* on the double

at the minute *idiom, Ir.* right now, at this instant

the **Attorney General** *pr. name* the senior law officer of England and principal legal adviser to the British government

attract *verb, sl.* to steal

at university *idiom, coll.* at a university

In Scotland the American form is usual.

aubergine *noun* eggplant

auctioneer *noun, Ir.* a real estate broker

Audley End *pr. name, hist.* a very large early 17th C. mansion 15 miles to the south of ➡Cambridge

It is built upon the remains of an earlier abbey granted to Sir Thomas Audley by ➡Henry VIII in 1538.

AUEW *pr. name, abbr.* the Amalgamated Union of Engineering Workers

A labor union for workers in the engineering industry.

August Bank Holiday *pr. name* a public holiday

This is a late August holiday in England and Wales, but is held in early August in Scotland.

auld *adj., Sc.* old

the **Auld Alliance** *pr. name, hist., Sc.* the long-standing military and political alliance of Scotland and France against England

Formally, the alliance lasted from 1295 to 1560, and of course was finally consigned to history in 1603 when Scotland's ➡James IV became James I of England also.

Less formally, this alliance was both deep and close; Joan of Arc's bodyguards were all Scots; Scots fought alongside the French *against* the English at the Battle of Agincourt; the Scots legal system is closely modeled upon the (medieval) French example and not the English; and even 200 years after the ➡Union of the Crowns of England and Scotland in 1603, one of Napoleon's marshals was a Scotsman called MacDonald.

Indeed, traces of the ancient special relationship between Scotland and France are there to be found right up to the present time. *SEE ALSO:* the ➡Auld Enemy.

Auld Clootie *pr. name, Sc.* the Devil

the **Auld Enemy** *pr. name, hist., Sc.* England

SEE ALSO: the ➡Auld Alliance.

auld-farrant *adj., Sc.* old-fashioned

auld lang syne *idiom, coll., Sc.* (1) long ago; (2) old memories and old friendships
Literally, "old long since".

Auld Nick *pr. name, Sc.* the Devil

Auld Reekie *pr. name, coll., Sc.* ➡Edinburgh
Literally, "Old Smokey"

aumbry *noun, arch.* a small cupboard

Aunt Nelly *idiom, rh. sl.* belly

aunt sally *comp. noun, coll.* (1) a game in which sticks or balls are thrown at a wooden target that has been painted to look like the head of an old woman; (2) someone who is subject to unreasonable or persistent attack

Aunty Beeb *pr. name* a nickname for the ➡BBC

au pair *comp. noun, Fr.* a young foreign person, usually a girl, who helps with housework, and especially the care of young children
This is done in return for room, board, a small allowance and an opportunity to learn English. The expression is French, meaning "on equal terms."

Aussie *pr. name, abbr.* an Australian

Austin *pr. name (TM), hist.* a mass production automobile manufacturer founded in 1905 at Longbridge, near ➡Birmingham, and now owned by BMW.
SEE ALSO: ➡Austin 7, ➡baby Austin.

Austin 7 *pr. name (TM), hist.* a small 7 horsepower car, first sold in 1921
The vehicle was greatly influenced by the earlier success of the Model-T Ford in America, and indeed this car was the British equivalent. *SEE ALSO:* ➡Austin, ➡baby Austin.

the War of the **Austrian Succession** *pr. name, hist.* a European war fought from 1740 to 1748, principally between Prussia and France, over the ownership of Silesia
The struggle eventually drew in practically every European power, including Britain, before it was resolved.
As usual, Britain's interest was to prevent the European continent from domination by one power, so that it fought on Prussia's side against the strongest power of the day, France. One principal significance of this war to Britain was that it led the French to connive in and surreptitiously support the ➡Forty-Five Rebellion in an attempt to install a friendly government in London or, at least, divert British interest and resources away from events in Europe. In the end, at the Treaty of Aachen in 1748, the French recognzed the ➡Hanoverian right to the British ➡Throne.
Silesia is in what is now southern Poland.

AUT *pr. name, abbr.* Association of University Teachers
A labor union for professors and other university teachers.

the **Authorised Version** *pr. name, hist.* the Authorized Version of the Bible, which is a translation authorized by ➡James I of England and VI of Scotland and published in 1611
It is also known as the King James Version.

autocar *noun, arch.* an automobile

Autocue *pr. name (TM)* a teleprompter

autocycle *noun, out.* a pedal bicycle with a small two-cycle auxiliary engine added

autolyse *spell.* autolyze
To break down cell tissue.

autumn *noun, pref.* fall (the season)

the **Autumn Double** *pr. name* two horse races that occur around the same time each fall
They are the Cesarewitch and the Cambridgeshire.

auxiliary nurse *comp. noun* a practical nurse

Avalon *pr. name, hist.* the island where ➡Arthur's body is said to have been carried to after his death

Avebury *pr. name, hist.* a village in ➡Wiltshire, which is the location of one of the oldest and largest archeological sites in Europe
The site, believed to be a pre-➡Celtic temple, dates from around 2000 B.C. It consists of a series of circular chalk banks and ditches containing a huge ring of some 100 very large megaliths, which encircle all of the modern village of Avebury. This is a far larger site than the much more famous ➡Stonehenge, and much remains to be explored, discovered and understood. ➡Silbury Hill is close by.

avenue *noun* (1) a line of trees; (2) a tree-lined private access road to a house situated within its own grounds

Aviemore *pr. name* an all-year-round sports resort in the Scottish highlands

avizandum *noun, Lat., Sc.* time taken out by a judge or jury for the consideration of their verdict
From the medieval Latin *avizare* = "advise"

avocado pear *comp. noun* avocado

Avon *pr. name* a county in western England bordering on the ➡Bristol Channel
Avon was formed out of parts of ➡Gloucestershire and ➡Somerset in 1974. The county seat is ➡Bristol and the current population is 920,000 (1991 Census).

avowson *noun* a legal right of presentation

awa *adv., Sc.* away

Awayday *noun* a low-cost, same-day round trip ticket sold by ➡British Rail

away fixture *noun, coll.* an away game or match

away team *comp. noun, coll.* a visiting sports team

awkward customer *comp. noun, coll.* a difficult person to deal with

awkward squad *comp. noun, coll.* (1) originally, a group of raw military recruits; (2) any group not prepared to go along with accepted ways

AWRE *pr. name, abbr.* the ➡Atomic Weapons Research Establishment

Axminster *pr. name* a ➡Devonshire town best known as a kind of carpet

Hand-made carpets were made there for 80 years from the middle of the 18th C. The process had become mechanized early in the 19th C. using techniques and machinery developed by James Templeton of ➡Glasgow and although it retained the name of Axminster, the carpet-making business was moved to ➡Wilton.

aye [A] *adv., Sc.* (1) always; (2) a cautious greeting; (3) an expression of doubt or disbelief

[B] *noun, North, Sc.* yes

aye, aye *adv. phr., Sc.* so that's the way it is

Aylesbury *pr. name* (1) a town that is the administrative center of ➡Buckinghamshire; (2) a breed of white duck

The current population of (1) is 52,000 (1991 estimate); (2) is considered very tasty.

Ayr *pr. name, hist.* a town upon the coast of the Firth of ➡Clyde in Scotland

A seaport and resort, it is best known for its long association with Robert Burns, who was born in nearby ➡Alloway. The current population is 50,000 (1991 estimate).

Ayrshire *pr. name, hist.* (1) a former Scottish county, now part of ➡Strathclyde region; (2) a breed of white or brown dairy cow

azure *noun* the heraldic name for the color blue

B

B- *noun* the prefix to a highway number, designating it to be a minor or local road

SEE ALSO: ➥M-, ➥A-.

BA *pr. name, abbr.* (1) the ➥British Academy; (2) ➥British Airways plc; (3) the ➥British Association

BAA *pr. name, abbr., hist.* the British Airports Authority

A government agency formerly responsible for many of Britain's major airports, including ➥Heathrow, ➥Gatwick and ➥Stanstead serving London, and Glasgow, Edinburgh and Aberdeen in Scotland, until privatized as ➥BAA plc in 1987.

BAA plc *pr. name, abbr.* the company that owns and operates many of Britain's major airports

BAA plc airports are those previously operated by ➥BAA; which the company was formed out of in 1987.

BAAS *pr. name, abbr.* the ➥British Association for the Advancement of Science

babu *noun, arch., derog., Hindi* a native Indian clerk able to write in English

From the Hindi *babu* = "father".

baby Austin *comp. noun, coll., hist.* a nickname for the ➥Austin 7 automobile

baby-{bouncer » jumper} *comp. noun* a framework supporting an elasticated harness for an infant, in order to exercise and develop the child's arms and legs

Baby Buggy *pr. name* an infant's collapsible stroller

babyminder *noun* one who looks after babies or infants in return for a fee

Usually in {his » her} own home, while the child's parent or parents go off to work.

baby's dummy *comp. noun* a baby's pacifier

baby's head *idiom, sl.* ➥steak and kidney pudding

From its appearance.

baccy *noun, abbr., coll.* tobacco

Bach's remedies *pr. name* an alternate medical therapy similar to homeopathy, named for Dr. Edward Bach who developed the technique

back *noun, sl.* a toilet

backbencher *noun, coll.* an ordinary ➥MP

One not entitled to sit on the ➥front bench.

backbenches *noun* the Parliamentary benches where ordinary ➥MPs sit

back boiler *comp. noun, out.* a water-heating tank built into the rear of a domestic stove or coal fire

the **Backbone of England** *pr. name* a nickname for the ➥Pennines

backchat *noun, coll.* back talk

backcloth *noun* a theatrical backdrop

backdoor [A] *adj.* clandestine, improper or secret

Of a way of doing business, for example.

[B] *verb, arch., sl.* to commit adultery

backdraught *spell.* backdraft

back end *comp. noun* (1) late Fall; (2) the rear; (3) the final part

Originally, (1) was the end of the harvest season.

backer-legged *adj., out.* knock-kneed

back garden *comp. noun* a backyard

backhanded compliment *comp. noun, coll., pref.* a left-handed compliment

backhander *noun, sl.* a clandestine, improper or secret payment such as a bribe or informal gratuity

backmarker *noun* the participant with the worst handicap or thought least likely to win a race, etc.

the **back of beyond** *idiom* the middle of nowhere

back passage *noun* the rectum

{backpedalled » backpedalling} *spell.* {backpedaled » backpedaling}

backroom boy *comp. noun, out., sl.* a scientist or other researcher working out of public view

This expression began life as ➥RAF World War II slang.

the **Backs** *pr. name* the gardens and lawns that lie between certain colleges of Cambridge University and the Cam river as it flows through ➥Cambridge

back-shift *comp. noun, coll.* a swing shift

backslang *noun, sl.* a form of ➥cant [b] where a word's letter-order is reversed, supposedly to make it hard for strangers to understand what is being said

For example, 'boy' becomes ➥yob.

19

backstairs

backstairs *noun, out.* a staircase for servants
In a large residence or hotel, for example.

back-to-back housing *idiom* houses joined together by a rear-facing party wall

backward about coming forward *idiom* shy

backwardation *noun* a percentage fee paid for the right to deliver stock late
SEE ALSO: ➡contango.

backward {point » short leg} *comp. noun* fielding players' positions behind ➡cricket ➡stumps

backward thought *comp. noun, coll.* reconsideration; a second thought

backwoodsman *noun, coll.* a member of the ➡House of Lords who rarely attends

backyarder *noun, coll., out.* one who rears chicken in a small way

Baconian *noun, hist.* one who believes that Sir Francis Bacon was the true author of Shakespeare's plays
Bacon was an English philosopher, politician and writer who lived from 1561 to 1626.

bacteraemia *spell.* bacteremia
The transient presence of bacteria in the blood.

bad cess to you *idiom, Ir.* here's wishing you bad luck

baddish *adj.* mildly bad

baddy *noun, coll.* a criminal or villain

bad fist *idiom, coll.* a bad job

bad form *idiom* improper or impolite behavior

bad job *idiom* a bad state of affairs or outcome

badminton *noun* a long drink consisting of claret, club soda and sugar, normally consumed on hot summer days and thus rare in Britain

bad patch *verb, coll.* a difficult period

bad penny *comp. noun, coll.* something or someone that keeps reappearing or cannot be gotten rid of

bad scran *comp. noun, Ir.* bad luck

bad show *comp. noun, coll.* (1) a misfortune; (2) something done badly

BAe *pr. name (TM), abbr.* British Aerospace plc
One of Britain's largest industrial companies.

BAFTA *pr. name, abbr.* the British Association of Film and Television Arts

the Bafta Awards *pr. name, abbr.* awards made each year by ➡BAFTA to outstanding performers in the TV and movie industry

bag [A] *noun* the quantity of game killed during a day's hunting or shooting
[B] *verb, sl.* (1) to claim ownership; (2) to claim the right to be first

bagman *noun, out.* a traveling salesman

the bagpipes *noun* a musical wind instrument
Although most usually associated with Scotland, in fact the bagpipe is an ancient instrument that has been and in many cases still is used to play native music throughout Europe and much of Africa and Asia as well. The traditional Scottish pipe consists of a windbag and reed ➡chanter, together with up to five drone-pipes. Wind is supplied through a valved mouth-tube. In ➡Northumberland, the traditional pipes there are supplied by air pumped in by the movement of the arms upon a bellow.

bags *noun, coll., out.* (1) a large quantity; (2) men's pants
For (2), *SEE ALSO:* ➡Oxford bags.

bagwash *noun* an incomplete laundry; one which has been dried without smothing or ironing

bail *noun* (1) the outer fortifications or walls of a castle; (2) one of the two wooden crosspieces that sit upon ➡cricket ➡stumps

Bailey bridge *pr. name., hist.* a prefabricated steel bridge intended for rapid assembly, developed for the British Army by Sir Donald Bailey and extensively used during World War II

bailie *noun, Sc.* a ➡councilor who is also a magistrate

bailiff *noun, hist.* (1) one who manages a farm or other property on behalf of its landlord; (2) an official who serves writs and carries out arrests on behalf of a ➡sheriff; (3) formerly, the monarch's representative in a region of his or her realm

the Bailiff *pr. name* (1) the senior civilian official of the government of ➡Guernsey; (2) the senior civilian official of the government of ➡Jersey

bailiwick *noun* the territorial domain of a ➡bailiff

bairn *noun, North, Sc.* a young child

bait [A] *noun, arch.* a refreshment break or short halt for a rest while upon a journey
[B] *noun, Mid.* a worker's midday snack
[C] *noun, sl.* bad temper or anger

Baker day *comp. noun, coll.* an in-service training day for teachers
Named after the Secretary of State for Education who instituted the system in 1987. Apparently these days are disliked by many teachers, possibly because for once it is they who are expected to do the learning.

the Bakerloo Line *pr. name* one part of London's rapid-transit subway system
It extends from Harrow & Wealdstone in the northwest to Elephant & Castle in the south. Its name was created by merging the first syllables of ➡Baker Street and the last of ➡Waterloo, two of the principal stations on this route.

Baker Street *pr. name* a central London street
The home—at Number 221b, which does not exist—of Conan Doyle's fictional detective, ➡Sherlock Holmes.

Balmoral Castle

D. MHK. 93

the **Baker Street Irregulars** *pr. name, coll., hist.* (1) the street urchins that ➡Sherlock Holmes supposedly used to spy on the London criminal underworld; (2) a nickname for the ➡SOE
The SOE acquired this name because they were, like ➡Sherlock Holmes, headquartered in ➡Baker Street.

Bakewell tart *comp. noun* a baked pastry cup containing jam and covered by sponge-cake material containing almond
The name is derived from the town of Bakewell in Derbyshire, where they were first devised.

baking tray *comp. noun* a cooking sheet

Balaclava helmet *comp. noun* a warm woolen garment covering the entire head except for eyes, nostrils and mouth
First worn by soldiers at the battle of Balaclava during the ➡Crimean War in 1854.

baldric *noun, arch.* a sword-belt hung over one shoulder to the opposite waist

the **Balfour Declaration** *pr. name, hist.* a promise made in 1917 by the British government, to establish a Jewish national state in Palestine
➡Foreign Secretary Arthur Balfour made this promise on behalf of the government. It was published in the form of a letter to the leading Zionist, Baron Rothschild, and was conditional upon the rights of the existing population there being respected. Later the wording of the declaration was incorporated into the League of Nations Mandate granted Britain to administer Palestine after World War I.

balladmonger *noun, derog., out.* an inferior seller, singer or player of music

ball and bat *idiom, rh. sl.* a hat

Balliol College *pr. name* a college of ➡Oxford University, founded in 1263

ballocks *noun, sl., taboo* the testicles

{**ballocks » bollocks**} *exclam., sl., taboo* a declaration that something is nonsense or untrue

ball of chalk *idiom, rh. sl.* a walk

balloon [A] *noun, derog., Sc., sl.* a braggart, blowhard or pretentious person
[B] *verb* to send a ball high up into the air by kicking, throwing or hitting it

balloon car *idiom, rh. sl.* a ➡saloon bar

balls-up *comp. noun, sl.* a mess, confusion or foul-up

bally *exclam., sl.* a euphemism for ➡bloody

Ballymena *pr. name* a district in ➡Northern Ireland, in what used to be County ➡Antrim
The current population is 55,000 (1990 estimate).

Ballymoney *pr. name* a district in ➡Northern Ireland, in what used to be County ➡Antrim
The current population is 25,000 (1990 estimate).

Balmoral *noun, Sc.* (1) a flat round cap worn by some Scottish soldiers; (2) a heavy-duty front-laced leather boot
From ➡Balmoral Castle.

Balmoral Castle *pr. name, hist.* one of the private homes of the ➡Royal Family
A large house in the ➡Scottish Baronial style, built in northeastern Scotland during the 1850s. It is located some 50 miles west of ➡Aberdeen, where it provided a sanctuary for ➡Victoria and ➡Albert, who could hide away from the world and revel in a sort of romantic Scottishness. After Albert's early death, Victoria spent more and more of her time shut away in this her Scottish hideaway.

balmy *adj., coll.* ➡barmy

BALPA *pr. name, abbr.* the British Air Line Pilots' Association

the **Baltic Exchange** *pr. name* the worldwide market based in London, used for the chartering of vessels and the arranging of marine insurance

bampot *noun, derog., Sc.* a fool or idiot

banana *noun, derog., sl.* a fool

Banbridge *pr. name* a district in ➡Northern Ireland, in what used to be County ➡Down
The current population is 30,000 (1990 estimate).

the Bank of England

Banbury cake *comp. noun* a ➡mincemeat-filled cake
First made in Banbury, ➡Oxfordshire.

the **Band of Hope** *pr. name, hist.* a Victorian temperance society that devoted much effort to saving children from the perils of the demon drink, presumably on the grounds that it's best to catch'em young

Banffshire *pr. name, hist.* a former Scottish county, now part of the ➡Grampian region.

banger *noun, coll.* (1) a noisy old car; (2) a sausage; (3) a firecracker or other noisy firework

bangers and mash *idiom, coll.* a dish of sausages and mashed potatoes

bang off *idiom, sl.* without delay, right now

bang on [A] *idiom, sl.* exactly correct; right on target
[B] *phr. verb, coll.* to remonstrate at length

Bangor *pr. name* a city in ➡Gwynedd, Wales
Its current population is 15,000 (1988 estimate).

bang up *verb, sl.* to lock away, especially in jail

banjax *verb, Gae., Ir.* (1) to confuse; (2) to destroy, defeat, ruin or batter

banjoed *adj., sl.* completely drunk or stoned

the **Bank** *pr. name, abbr., coll.* the ➡Bank of England

bank bill *comp. noun* a check or draft that is drawn by one bank upon another

bank cashier *noun* a bank teller

banker's order *comp. noun* a formal written and signed direction from a customer to his or her

bank to pay money to a third party, usually at regular intervals, such as monthly.

banker's ramp *comp. noun* a real or imaginary conspiracy to manipulate a nation's currency for the benefit of international bankers

bank guaranteed cheque *comp. noun* certified check

bank holiday *comp. noun* a legal public holiday
All official British public holidays are called this. Nominally, these are days when banks alone are required to be closed but they have become accepted as general public holidays. Among others, Christmas Day, New Year Day, Good Friday and the Monday following Easter are bank holidays.

banknote *noun* a piece of paper money
Strictly, a promissory note issued by a bank, which has the legal standing, or serves the purpose, of paper money.

the **Bank of England** *pr. name* Britain's central bank
Founded in 1694 by a Scotsman, to raise funds needed by ➡William III. It is headquartered on ➡Threadneedle Street in the ➡City of London, hence its sometimes nickname of the ➡Old Lady of Threadneedle Street. It is the only authorized source of legal-tender paper money in England, although there are others in Scotland.

the **Bank of Scotland** *pr. name* the first Scottish bank
It was founded in 1695, one year after the ➡Bank of England, and its head office occupies a prominent position on the ➡Mound, in ➡Edinburgh.
Unlike English banks other than the ➡Bank of England, it is authorized to issue its own bank currency, which together with that of the other two principal Scottish banks is legal tender there, and is usually accepted as such in England, too.

the **Bank Rate** *pr. name, hist.* the former name for the British discount rate
The minimum interest rate permitted by the ➡Bank of England, now called the ➡Base Rate.

Bankside *pr. name* part of the southern bank of the ➡Thames River flowing through central London
The location of the ➡Elizabethen theater district where Shakespeare's plays were first performed.

bannock *noun, North, Sc.* (1) a small, unleavened oatmeal loaf; (2) cornbread baked on a griddle

the Battle of **Bannockburn** *pr. name, hist.* a battle between the English under ➡Edward II and the Scots under ➡Robert the Bruce in 1314
A great Scottish victory over a much larger English army, which had arrived there for the purpose of relieving the besieged English garrison of ➡Stirling Castle, which towers over the Field of Bannockburn. This was the decisive battle that ensured Scottish national independence.

the **Banqueting House** *pr. name, hist.* the only surviving part of ➡Whitehall Palace, London, which was largely destroyed by fire in 1698
The first building in Britain to be built in the ➡Palladian Style, in 1622. It was from here that ➡Charles I stepped out upon a gallows platform to be publicly executed in 1649. Today, the building is used for official gatherings and state occasions of various sorts—although the execution of monarchs is now considered to be in bad taste.

banshee *noun, Gae.* a wailing spirit that is said to warn of impending deaths

The word is native to both Scottish and Irish Gaelic. In Irish Gaelic it is *bean sidhe*; in Scots Gaelic *bean sith*. In both it means "woman from fairyland".

bant *noun, out.* to slim by avoiding the consumption of fats, sugar and starch

BAOR *pr. name, abbr.* British Army of the Rhine

The British Army's garrison in Germany, which has been there since the end of World War II and remained there as a contribution to NATO.

bap *noun, Sc.* a large soft bun, somewhat similar to a hamburger bun

bar [A] *noun* (1) the place in a criminal court where those accused stand; (2) a strip placed below the clasp of a military medal, indicating a second awarding of that particular medal

[B] *noun, arch., sl.* one ➠Pound Sterling

[C] *prep.* except, apart from

the **Bar** *pr. name* (1) the imaginary line in a court of law that only officers of the court, such as judges and ➠barristers, may go beyond; (2) the collective name for barristers

In former times, there was a real physical barrier in courts.

bara brith *comp. noun, Wal* raisin bread

BARB *pr. name, abbr.* the Broadcasters Audience Research Board, which measures the audience ratings of television programs

the **Barber Institute of Fine Arts** *pr. name* an art history institute and art gallery, established in ➠Birmingham in 1932.

the **Barbican Centre** *pr. name* a large arts, conference and exhibition complex in central London

This is also the home of the ➠Royal Shakespeare Company and the ➠London Symphony Orchestra.

bar billiards *comp. noun* a variation of the game of billiards which has the pockets located at the center of the table

Barbour jacket *pr. name* a green, waxed cotton waterproof jacket

Popular with ➠Sloane rangers, yuppies and other upper-class city-dwellers when visiting the countryside.

Barchester *pr. name, hist.* an imaginary English town invented by the 19th C. author Anthony Trollope as a setting for his novels

Barclaycard *noun* a Visa (TM) credit card issued by ➠Barclays Bank

Barclays Bank *pr. name* one of the ➠Big Four English retail banks

Formed by the merging of some 20 smaller banks in 1896. The bank's name can be traced back to Robert Barclay, a goldsmith who moved into the banking business on ➠Lombard Street, London, during the 1740s.

bard *noun, Gae., Ir., Wal.* (1) a Welsh or Irish minstrel or poet; (2) the winner of a prize at an ➠Eisteddfod

the **Bard of Avon** *pr. name* William Shakespeare

bargee *noun* a bargeman

bargepole *noun* a long pole used to propel a barge, by pushing against the bottom or sides of a river or canal

Barking and Dagenham *pr. name* a borough within ➠Greater London

Its current population, which is also included within the ➠London urban area total, is 140,000 (1991 Census).

barking mad *idiom, sl.* completely crazy

barleymow *noun* a stack of barley

barm *noun, arch.* the yeasty froth or head upon the top of fermenting beer

barm bread *comp. noun, arch.* bread made with ➠barm

barmy [A] *adj., arch.* full of ➠barm

[B] *adj., sl.* crazy

SEE ALSO: ➠balmy.

Barnardo's *pr. name* a charity which cares for orphaned, destitute and disadvantaged children

Established in 1870 by Dr. Barnardo, a Protestant missionary.

Barnby Rudge *idiom, out., rh. sl.* a judge

A somewhat surprising literary allusion to ➠Dickens's character in the novel of the same name.

Barnet *pr. name* a ➠Greater London borough

Its current population, which is also included within the ➠London urban area total, is 285,000 (1991 Census).

barney *noun, coll.* a loud argument

the **Bar of the House** *pr. name* the rail in the ➠House beyond which only those who are ➠MPs (in the ➠Commons) or a member of the ➠Peerage (in the ➠Lords) may proceed

There is such a physical bar in both the ➠House of Commons and the ➠House of Lords. There are no exceptions to the rule that only members may go beyond the Bar, which is why any non-member, no matter how distinguished, must stand there if he or she wishes to address either House.

baronet *noun* one who is a member of the lowest British order of nobility

barony [A] *noun, Ir.* a subdivision of a ➠county

[B] *noun, Sc.* a large rural estate

Formerly the lands of a baron.

{**barque » barquentine**} *spell.* {bark » barkentine}

A kind of sailing boat.

Barra *pr. name* the southernmost of the principal islands forming the ➠Outer Hebrides chain

barrack *verb* to scoff, jeer or shout in a loud and derisive manner

barrackroom lawyer *comp. noun* a self-importantly disputatious person

{**barrelled** » **barrelling**} *spell.* {barreled » barreling}

barrier cream *comp. noun* a protective skin cream

barrister [A] *noun* a lawyer who has been ➡called to the ➡bar and so may plead in the higher courts
SEE ALSO: ➡solicitor.
[B] *noun, abbr.* a ➡barrister-at-law

barrister-at-law *comp. noun, arch.* a counselor-at-law

barrow *noun* (1) a handcart with two wheels, used by a ➡costermonger or ➡barrow-boy; (2) an ancient burial mound

a barrister

barrow-boy *comp. noun* a man or youth selling from a ➡barrow in a street market

bars *noun* an heraldic representation of multiple horizontal bars across the middle of a shield

bart. *noun, abbr.* a ➡baronet

Bartholomew pig *comp. noun, arch., coll., derog.* a very fat person
The main attraction at Bartholomew Fair, last held on St Bartholomew's Day, 1855, was a whole-roasted pig.

Bart's *pr. name, abbr., coll.* St Bartholomew's Hospital
One of the two oldest hospitals in London and the principal one in the ➡City, it was founded in 1123, and has been a teaching hospital since the 17th C.

barytes *noun* barite
The mineral form of barium sulfate, $BaSO_4$.

Base Rate, the *pr. name* the discount rate
This is the minimum interest rate permitted by the ➡Bank of England, and was formerly called the ➡Bank Rate.

bash *noun, sl.* an attempt

basher *noun, sl.* a person regularly engaged in carrying out uninteresting or boring duties
➡RAF slang.

basin *noun* a bowl

basket *noun, derog., rh. sl.* a euphemism for or variation of "bastard"

Bass *pr. name* Britain's largest brewer and owner of the Holiday Inn (TM) hotel chain
Their trademark, a red triangle, was the first ever to be registered, in 1875. It also has the distinction of appearing on Manet's painting, *A Bar at the Folies-Bergère*, of 1882.

bassalony *noun, coll.* a hazelnut
The word is a corruption of "Barcelona," in Spain, from whence they were first imported

the **Bass Rock** *pr. name* a spectacular volcanic plug thrusting 350 feet up out of the ➡Firth of Forth some twenty miles to the east of ➡Edinburgh
In its time, it has been the location of a group of cells used by hermits, a castle and a prison.

bat *noun, sl.* step, pace or speed

bat and wicket *idiom, rh. sl.* a ticket

bate *noun, sl.* anger, fury or bad temper

Bath *pr. name* a city and spa in ➡Avon, England
Founded as *Aquae Sulis* in the 1st C. by the Romans, who built extensive bathing facilities around the natural hot springs the city is named for. By the 18th C., Bath was highly fashionable once more, which is why it now possesses a considerable quantity of fine Georgian architecture. Incorporated as a city in 1590, the current population is 85,000 (1991 estimate).

bath *verb* (1) to wash oneself in a bath; (2) to wash another in a bath

Bath bun *comp. noun* a round spiced bun covered with currants and icing
From ➡Bath, where they were devised.

Bath chair *comp. noun* a kind of wheelchair

bath cube *comp. noun* a block of bath salts

bathe *verb* (1) to swim in the sea, etc.; (2) to bath

bath ensuite *comp. noun, Fr.* a room with private bath
Hotel terminology from the French *en suite* = "included".

the **Bath Festival** *pr. name* an annual festival of music held at ➡Bath

bathgown *noun* a bathrobe

Bath Oliver *comp. noun* a cheese cracker
From ➡Bath, where they were devised.

bathroom *noun* a room containing a bath, shower or other washing facilities, but normally no toilet
But in Scotland the American meaning is usual.

baths *noun* a publicly owned swimming pool

{**batman** » **batwoman**} *noun* the {male » female} orderly serving as the personal servant of a {male » female} commissioned officer in the British Army or the ➡RAF

batsman *noun* a batter in ➡cricket

battels *noun* an account or invoice presented by an Oxford college for the cost of accommodation or other items supplied

batten *noun* a strip of long thin timber used to hold in place plaster or other wall coverings, etc.

batter *noun, Sc., sl.* a drinking session

battered fish *comp. noun, coll.* a fish fried in batter

batting average *comp. noun* in ➡cricket, a ➡batsman's average runs per inning

Battle Abbey *pr. name, hist.* an ➡️abbey founded by ➡️William the Conqueror upon the site of his victory at the Battle of ➡️Hastings of 1066
Most of the building has now disappeared.

battle cruiser *idiom, rh. sl.* a ➡️pub
Derivation: pub > ➡️boozer > cruiser > battle cruiser.

bauchle *noun, derog., Sc.* (1) an old shoe; (2) an old, useless or worn-out person or thing; (3) a clumsy or slovenly person

baulk *spell.* balk

bawbee *noun, hist., Sc.* (1) a Scots coin worth three ➡️bodles; (2) any coin of small value
By 1707 when it ceased to be legal tender, one bawbee was worth half of one English ➡️penny. For more about Scots currency, SEE ALSO: ➡️pound Scots.

bawdy house *comp. noun, out.* a brothel

bawheid *noun, derog., Sc.* an unpleasant person
Literally, this means "ball-head" in standard English.

bay *noun* a railroad sidetrack used as the terminus point for a branch line, within a station that also possesses tracks that continue on through it

a portion of the Bayeux Tapestry

the **Bayeux Tapestry** *pr. name, hist.* a pictorial depiction of England's conquest by ➡️William in 1066, in particular the Battle of Hastings
This is in truth not a tapestry at all but a linen embroidery. It is about 222 feet long and some 20 inches high and is believed to have been made in England prior to 1082.
It is named for the town of Bayeux in Normandy, western France, because it is now kept in the cathedral there. Its remarkable survival for over nine centuries is believed to be due to the complete absence of gold or silver threads, or jewels, which have caused so many other works of this kind to be looted or destroyed.

the **BBC** *pr. name, abbr.* the ➡️British Broadcasting Corporation

BBC1 *pr. name* a national TV network of the ➡️BBC

BBC2 *pr. name* a national TV network of the ➡️BBC

BBC English *comp. noun, coll.* the form of spoken English that was once commonly heard from announcers on BBC radio and television
In fact it is now quite rarely heard there. SEE ALSO: ➡️received pronunciation, ➡️received standard English, ➡️Oxford English and ➡️King's English.

BC *pr. name, abbr.* (1) the ➡️British Coal Corporation; (2) the ➡️British Council

BEA [A] *pr. name, abbr.* the British Epilepsy Association
[B] *pr. name, abbr., hist.* British European Airways
An airline formed by the government in 1945 for the purpose of serving domestic and European routes and which survived until the present-day ➡️British Airways was created by merging ➡️BOAC and BEA in 1971.

beacon *noun* a hill or other high point considered a suitable location for a warning light or bonfire

be a devil *idiom. phr. verb* to take a chance

beadle [A] *noun, out.* a ceremonial official of a university, church, etc.
[B] *noun, Sc.* an officer assisting a minister of the ➡️Church of Scotland

beak *noun, out., sl.* (1) a judge or magistrate; (2) a school principal

beamer *noun* a ➡️cricket ball that is bowled towards the head of the ➡️batsman
This kind of bowl is usually counted as a no ball. It is also dangerous for the batsman.

beanfeast *noun, sl.* a celebration, party or jolly time
Originally, a celebratory meal consisting of beans and bacon.

beano *noun, abbr., sl.* a ➡️beanfeast

beardie *noun, coll.* a man with a beard

bearskin *noun* a very tall headgear covered with fur, worn by members of the ➡️Guards Regiments when parading on ceremonial occasions

beastie *noun, Sc.* any small animal

beating the bounds *idiom, out.* the ancient custom of marking out parish boundaries by striking certain places along it with special ceremonial sticks
Once a necessity, the event, which is now very rare, is occasionally used as the spurious justification for an annual local festival. SEE ALSO: ➡️common riding.

the **Beatles** *pr. name, hist.* the leading British pop group of the 1960s and 70s
Originating from ➡️Liverpool, the four members of the group became the most popular pop group in history, and an icon of what was called the Swinging Sixties.

beat to quarters *phr. verb, arch.* to call a warship's crew to battle stations

Originally the call was transmitted by the beating of a drum.

Beaumaris Castle *pr. name, hist.* a castle located on the isle of ➡Anglesey in northwestern Wales

It was erected by ➡Edward I during the final years of the 13th C. as an instrument of the English occupation and subjugation of Wales.

beck [A] *noun, North* a brook or small stream

[B] *noun, Sc.* a small bow or nod of recognition

bedder *noun, abbr.* a ➡bedmaker

bedellus *noun, Lat., Sc.* the ➡macers and chief ➡porters at ➡St Andrews, ➡Glasgow and ➡Edinburgh Universities

{**bedevilled » bedevilling**} *spell.* {bedeviled » bedeviling}

Bedford *pr. name* a town in southern England which is the county seat of ➡Bedfordshire

Probably founded by the Romans and certainly established by Anglo-Saxon times, it is best-known for the imprisonment of John Bunyan in the town jail in 1661 for 11 years on the charge of preaching without a license, which is where and when he wrote *Pilgrim's Progress*. The current population is 75,000 (1991 Census).

Bedfordshire *pr. name* a county in southern England, a short distance north of London

The county seat is ➡Bedford and the current population is 515,000 (1991 Census).

bedframe *noun* a bedstead

bedhead *noun* the headboard of a bed

Bedlam *pr. name, hist.* a former London hospital for lunatics which has given its name to any scene or situation of chaos and disorder

It was originally founded as Bethlehem Royal Hospital at the Priory of St Mary Bethlehem in Bishopgate, in the ➡City of London in 1247. "Bedlam" is a corruption or abbreviation of this original name. In 1676 it was moved to Moorfields and soon became one of the famous sights and great disgraces of 17th C. London, when for two pennies, anyone could visit there to look upon the poor inmates and shout insults at them. Eventually, in 1815 it was moved to ➡Lambeth, at the site of what is now the ➡Imperial War Museum, and in 1931 was finally closed down.

Bedlington Terrier *pr. name* a small lightly built terrier with a small head

From Bedlington in ➡Northumberland

bedmaker *noun* a servant who keeps rooms in good order at a college residence, hotel, etc.

Beds. *pr. name, abbr.* ➡Bedfordshire

bedside locker *comp. noun* a nightstand

bedside table *comp. noun* a night table

{**bedsit » bedsitter**} *noun, abbr.* a ➡bed-sitting-room

bed-sitting room *comp. noun* a single-room apartment within a private house

It combines the functions of bedroom and sitting room, usually together with cooking and washing facilities, to provide rental accommodations for a single individual.

the **Beeb** *pr. name, coll.* a nickname for the ➡BBC

SEE ALSO: ➡Aunty Beeb.

bee-baw-babbety *comp. noun, Sc.* a children's kissing game or dance

beefeater *noun, coll.* (1) a ➡Yeoman of the Guard; (2) a warder at the ➡Tower of London

The archaic meaning of the word is "well-fed servant." Strictly, (2) is an incorrect use of the name, but has become attached to the warders at the Tower because their uniforms are superficially so similar to those of the ➡Yeomen of the Guard, who are the only "real" beefeaters.

beef olives *comp. noun* a savory baked dish consisting of thin beef slices wrapped around vegetables or stuffing

a beefeater

beer engine *comp. noun* a pump used to draw beer up from where it is stored in, for example, a beer cellar in order that it can be served from the bar of a ➡pub or hotel

beer from the wood *comp. noun, coll.* draft beer drawn from a wooden cask

beerhouse *noun, out.* a pub licensed to sell beer but not distilled liquor such as whiskey or gin

beer-off *comp. noun, arch., sl.* a packaged liquor store

beer-up *idiom, arch., sl.* a drinking session

bees and honey *idiom, rh. sl.* money

beetle *noun* a game of dice where players attempt to assemble or sketch the component parts of a beetle as they roll the appropriate numbers for the parts with dice

beetle about *verb, sl.* to scurry around

beetle-crusher *comp. noun, coll.* a large shoe or boot

beetle drive *comp. noun* a ➡drive where the participants play the game of ➡beetle

beetle off *verb, sl.* to scurry away

beetroot *noun* the edible root of the common beet

Its formal name is *beta vulgaris*.

beezer *noun, out., sl.* a cheerful person

BEF *noun, abbr., hist.* a ➡British Expeditionary Force

beggar my neighbour *idiom, rh. sl.* unemployed
Derivation: unemployed > ➡on the labour > labour > neighbour > beggar my neighbour.

begorra *exclam., Ir.* a euphemism for or variation of the expression "by God."

{**behaviour** » **behavioural** » **behaviourism**} *spell.* {behavior » behavioral » behaviorism}

{**behaviourist** » **behaviouristic**} *spell.* {behaviorist » behavioristic}

behove *spell.* behoove

{**bejabers** » **bejasus** » **bejebers**} *exclam., Ir.* a euphemism for or variation of "by Jesus"

bejan *noun, Fr., Sc.* a freshman at ➡St Andrews or ➡Aberdeen Universities
From the French, *béjaune* ="young bird."

{**bejewelled** » **bejewelling**} *spell.* {bejeweled » bejeweling}

belabour *spell.* belabor

Belfast *pr. name, hist.* (1) the capital city of ➡Northern Ireland; (2) a district in ➡Northern Ireland, in what used to be partly County ➡Antrim and partly County ➡Down
Belfast grew up around a 13th C. ➡Norman castle, long since destroyed, on the shores of Belfast ➡Lough and was incorporated as a city in 1613. In the 19th C., the city's two main industries were the manufacture of linen and shipbuilding; this is where the ill-fated *Titanic* was built and launched in 1912. The current population, including suburbs, of (1) is 450,000 (1988 estimate). The current population of (2) is 295,000 (1990 estimate).

the *Belfast Gazette pr. name* an official government-published newspaper
It is used only for the purpose of publishing notices of official appointments, bankruptcies, court judgments etc., relating to ➡Northern Ireland.

the *Belfast News Letter pr. name, hist.* Britain's oldest surviving newspaper
Founded in 1737, it scooped the story of the American Declaration of Independence in 1776 when a ship carrying the news called first at Belfast while on its way to London.

the **Belfast Regiment** *pr. name* a nickname for the 3rd Battalion, The Queen's Regiment
A unit of the British Army first formed in ➡Belfast in 1701.

Belgravia *pr. name* a largely residential fashionable area in west-central London close to ➡Hyde Park

Belisha beacon *comp. noun, coll., out.* a flashing yellow light placed at the side of a road to indicate the presence of a pedestrian crossing place
Named after Leslie Hore-Belisha, the ➡Minister of Transport who introduced them in 1934.

bell *noun, sl.* a telephone call

Belleek *pr. name, hist.* a kind of fine translucent porcelain, made in Ireland since the 19th C.
Belleek is a small town in County ➡Fermanagh, ➡Northern Ireland, where this porcelain was first manufactured.

Bell Vue *pr. name* a public gardens and entertainment center in ➡Manchester

the **Belly** *pr. name, sl.* ➡Portobello Road, London

below stairs *idiom, coll., out.* the servants' working areas, such as kitchens in a large house
These were traditionally located in the basement.. *SEE ALSO:* ➡above stairs.

below the gangway *idiom, coll.* the area within the ➡Chamber of the ➡House of Commons where ➡backbench MPs are permitted to sit

belt [A] *verb, arch., Sc.* to punish a school student with a ➡tawse
[B] *verb, sl.* (1) to travel rapidly; (2) to rush about

Beltane *pr. name, Gae.* the traditional Celtic celebration of May Day

belt up *verb, sl.* to shut up

Belvoir Castle *pr. name, Fr., hist.* a 19th C. Gothic-revival mansion some 20 miles from ➡Nottingham
It is situated upon the site of a ➡Norman castle which dated from the 11th C. The mansion's name, which is pronounced "beever," is derived from the ➡Norman French and means "beautiful view."

BEM *noun, abbr.* the British Empire Medal

ben [A] *adv., prep., Sc.* within
[B] *noun, Sc.* the inner room of a ➡but and ben
[C] *noun, Gae., Sc.* a tall mountain

bench *noun* the seats that ➡MPs sit upon in the ➡Chamber of the ➡House of Commons

Bench *pr. name* a division of the ➡High Court

the **Bench and Bar** *pr. name* judges and ➡barristers taken together as a group

bencher *noun* (1) a person who sits in the ➡House of Commons, which is to say, an ➡MP; (2) a senior lawyer practicing in the ➡Inns of Court

bend [A] *noun* an heraldic representation of a diagonal bar across a shield
[B] *verb, sl.* (1) to divert from an honest path; (2) to pervert; (3) to distort for dishonest purposes

bender [A] *noun, derog., sl.* a male homosexual
[B] *noun, sl.* a rough tent-like shelter
Made of saplings bent into a semi-circular form and then covered in waterproof material of some sort.

bend sinister *comp. noun* an heraldic representation of a bar crossing a shield from top left to bottom right
The sign of illegitimacy.

benedick

benedick *noun, arch.* a newly married man who was formerly a confirmed bachelor
From the character of this name in Shakespeare's play *Much Ado about Nothing.*

benefit of clergy *idiom, hist.* (1) the former right of the clergy of the ➡Church of England to be exempt from the jurisdiction of the civil courts in England for certain classes of legal matters; (2) the former right of tonsured clergy such as monks and nuns to be exempt from the jurisdiction of the civil courts in England

the Benefits Agency *pr. name* a government agency, located in ➡Leeds, that issues payments nationally on behalf of local ➡Social Security offices

benefit society *comp. noun* a mutual aid society

Benenden School *pr. name* a leading English ➡public school for girls.
Founded in 1923, it is located in Kent. Benenden's best known student was Princess Anne, the Princess Royal.

the Bengal Tigers *pr. name* a nickname for the 4th Battalion, Royal Anglian Regiment
A unit of the British Army. The name honors their service in India from 1804 to 1823.

Bennery *pr. name, sl.* far left-wing policies
Named after Anthony Wedgwood Benn, a ➡Labour ➡MP. During the 1980s, he introduced a series of extreme-left concepts into Labour Party politics that gave every sign of being on the one hand impossible to implement and on the other guaranteed to ensure defeat at the hands of the voters.

Ben Nevis *pr. name* the highest mountain in Britain
Located in the Scottish ➡Highlands, its height is 4,406 ft.

Bennite *pr. name, sl.* a believer in ➡Bennery

bent *adj., sl.* dishonest, criminal or corrupt

ben the hoose *idiom, Sc.* at the center of a house

Bentley *pr. name, hist.* once a great British automobile marques, bought by ➡Rolls-Royce in 1931.
Originally best known for its great racing successes, it is now associated with luxury rather than extreme speed.

bent shot *comp. noun, derog., Sc., sl.* a male homosexual

{berk » burk} *noun, derog., rh. sl.* a fool or idiot
Derivation: fool > cunt > Berkshire Hunt > berk. "Burk" is an alternative of this which has come into use mainly due to confusion with ➡burke.

Berkeley Castle *pr. name, hist.* a smallish 12th C. fortress about 20 miles to the south of ➡Gloucester
Best known as the scene of the probable murder of ➡Edward II in 1327 after he had been deposed in favor of his son.

Berks. *pr. name, abbr.* ➡Berkshire

Berkshire *pr. name* a county in southern England that is a short way southwest of London
The county seat is ➡Reading and the current population is 715,000 (1991 Census).

Bernicia *pr. name, hist.* a principality in ➡Northumbria
In effect an independent state from 558 until 654 when it was absorbed into ➡Northumbria. The usual seat of the kings of Bernicia was Yeavering, south of ➡Berwick-upon-Tweed in modern ➡Northumberland.

Bertie *pr. name, coll., hist.* a nickname of ➡Edward VII

Berwick *pr. name, hist.* a former Scottish county
Now part of the ➡Borders region.

Berwick-upon-Tweed *pr. name* a town in ➡Northumberland, straddling the ➡Tweed River
Due to its frontier position at the mouth of the ➡Tweed river, Berwick changed nationality many times before settling down to being in England in 1482, although to the present day it is said that many if not most of its citizens feel themselves to be more Scottish than English. The current population is 14,000 (1988 estimate).

BES *pr. name, abbr., hist.* Business Expansion Scheme
A former tax measure introduced to encourage investment in small businesses.

beside the mark *idiom, coll.* beside the point

besom *noun, North., derog., Sc.* (1) a brush or broom; (2) a prostitute or disreputable woman

bespoke tailoring *comp. noun* custom-tailoring

best end of lamb *comp. noun* rib end of neck of lamb

best mince *comp. noun* ground steak

best of British luck *idiom, coll.* lots of good luck

betting shop *comp. noun* a shop where bets are placed, typically on horses or dogs

betty *noun, sl.* a picklock tool used by a burglar

betweenmaid *noun, arch.* a female servant who is an assistant to more than one other servant

bevelling *spell.* beveling

the Beveridge Report *pr. name, abbr., hist.* a report that was used as the basis of Britain's comprehensive social and medical insurance system established after World War II
In full, the title was *A Report on Social Insurance and Allied Services,* written by a committee set up by the government under the chairmanship of William Beveridge in 1942.

the Bevin Boys *pr. name, coll., hist.* a nickname for the young men conscripted to work in coal mines rather than serve in the military during World War II
Named after Ernest Bevin, Minister of Labour at the time, who introduced the policy. At one time, one man in ten was diverted from the armed forces to go down into the coal mines. It's not clear which group got the better deal.

bevvy *verb, Sc., sl.* to drink heavily

Bexley *pr. name* a ➡Greater London borough
Its current population, which is also included within the ➡London urban area total, is 210,000 (1991 Census).

beyond it *idiom, coll.* unable to continue

bind

beyond the pale *idiom* outside or beyond the bounds of acceptable behavior

This was originally the ➡English Pale around ➡Dublin, beyond which Ireland was considered uncivilized territory.

BF *noun, abbr., derog., sl.* a bloody fool

BGM *noun, abbr.* the Burma Gallantry Medal

BhS *pr. name (TM), abbr.* British Home Stores

A national chain of large department stores.

bicky *noun, sl.* the diminutive of ➡biscuit

bicolour *spell.* bicolor

bicycle clip *comp. noun* a metal pants clip

A metal clip worn around the ankle of a bike rider to prevent [his» her} pants from fouling the mechanism of the bicycle.

biffin *noun* a red-colored cooking apple

the **Big Bang** *pr. name, coll., hist.* a number of drastic changes made to the ➡London Stock Exchange, introduced all at once in October 1986

Big Ben, within St. Stephen's Tower

Big Ben [A] *idiom, rh. sl.* ten ➡ p o u n d s sterling

[B] *r. name* the bell of the clock in the tower of the ➡Houses of Parliament

This is the name of the bell only and not the whole structure, which is called St Stephen's Tower. The bell, which was first rung there in 1859, is named after Benjamin Hall, superviser of its casting in 1856.

big dipper *comp. noun* a carnival roller coaster

big end *comp. noun* the larger end of an automobile's connecting rod, which is connected to the crankpin.

the **Big Four** *idiom, coll.* the four largest English retail banks, which are ➡Barclays, ➡Lloyds, ➡Midland and ➡National Westminster Banks

biggen *verb, East* to enlarge

the **Big Smoke** *idiom, coll.* a nickname for ➡London

big wean *comp. noun, derog., Sc., sl.* a childish adult

SEE ALSO: ➡wean.

big wheel *noun* a Ferris wheel

bilberry *noun* a small berry similar to the blueberry

Its formal name is *vaccinium myrtillus.*

bill *noun* a check in a restaurant, etc.

the **Bill** *noun, abbr., sl.* the ➡Old Bill

billiards *noun* a game with a superficial resemblance to pool but played on a much larger table with just three balls in play at a time

Billingsgate Market *pr. name* London's fish market

1,000 years old and formerly located in the ➡City of London, it is now located upon the Isle of ➡Dogs in east London.

Billingsgate pheasant *idiom, arch., sl.* a red herring

Billingsgate talk *idiom, coll.* foul language

billion *noun, num., out.* a trillion, or 10^{12}

Historically, the British billion equals 1,000 American billions, as reported here. However, the American billion is increasingly becoming the standard meaning of the word in Britain.

bill of quantities *comp. noun* a list of the materials required to construct a building

the **Bill of Rights** *pr. name, hist.* a constitutional enactment settling the fundamental form of government and the liberties of the people

Specifically, an ➡Act of Parliament of 1689, called in full, *An Act Declaring the Rights and Liberties of the Subject,* enacted to pass into law the result of the ➡Glorious Revolution, which had established that ultimate sovereignty was Parliament's rather the king's. It also established many civil rights, for example, the prohibition of arbitrary acts by the monarch such as taxation without representation. It guarantees free elections and many other constitutional measures, making it in many ways the nearest thing there is to a written British constitution. However, in truth its creators were not really so much concerned with individual liberty as the establishment of a constitutional monarchy as such.

Bill Stickers Will Be Prosecuted *idiom* a notice equivalent to "Post no Bills"

… and which led to the campaign organized some years ago, complete with marches through London when protesters carrying banners that displayed the slogans, "Free Bill Stickers" and "William Stickers is Innocent".

Billy *pr. name, Ir., Sc.* a Protestant

From ➡King Billy, or ➡William III.

billycock *noun, abbr., arch., sl.* a ➡bowler hat

BIM *pr. name, abbr.* the British Institute of Management

bin *noun* a bucket, basket or other container used for bread or bottled wine

{**bin? » bis?**} *inter, Mid.* are you?

SEE ALSO: ➡bist.

bind *noun, sl.* a complication or nuisance

29

bind over

bind over *verb* to be ordered by a court of law to follow a particular course of action or to behave in a particular manner

bin end *comp. noun, coll.* the last bottle in a wine ➡bin
Usually sold at a discount.

bing *noun* (1) a pile; (2) a slag heap, especially one consisting of the residue of coal mining

Bingham's Dandies *pr. name* a nickname for the 17th/21st Lancers
A unit of the British Army. The name derives from their smart appearance when under the command of Lord Bingham in the early 19th C.

bin liner *comp. noun* a trash bag

bint *noun, coll., derog.* a girl or woman
From the Arabic for "daughter".

biocoenosis *spell.* bioconosis
A community of various organisms living together.

birch [A] *noun* a bundle of birch wood twigs bound together to make a switch used for flogging
[B] *verb* to flog with a ➡birch
For some considerable time now, this form of punishment has confined to the Isle of ➡Man.

bird *noun, sl.* (1) jail; (2) a pretty girl

Birdcage Walk *pr. name* a London avenue named after the aviary once kept there by ➡Charles II

the Bird Catchers *pr. name* nicknames for: (1) the 2nd Dragoons, the Greys; (2) the Royal (1st) Dragoons; (3) the Royal Irish Fusiliers
All are units of the British Army. (1) and (2) both earned this name when they captured French Eagle Standards at the Battle of Waterloo in 1815. Later, the Royal Dragoons merged with the Royal Horse Guards, known as the ➡Blues, to form the ➡Blues and Royals; (3) earned this name when they captured a French Eagle Standard at the Battle of Barossa in 1811. *SEE ALSO:* ➡Blayney's Bloodhounds.

Birkbeck College *pr. name* one of the schools of ➡London University
Founded in 1823 by George Birkbeck.

Birkenhead *pr. name* a town in ➡Merseyside
Today the city's population, including suburbs, is 280,000 (1988 estimate).

birl *verb, Sc.* (1) to whirl, spin or turn quickly; (2) to pour out or serve wine

Birmingham *pr. name* the principal city of the ➡West Midlands ➡Metropolitan County
Britain's largest urban area after London. It was a small town during the Middle Ages, but had already begun to specialize in metalwork by the 16th C. Birmingham started to expand rapidly during the 18th C., exploiting its natural resources of coal and iron, which together with the canals of the 18th C. and railways of the 19th C. made its strategic position at the center of England an exploitable asset rather than a handicap for the first time. Birmingham was incorporated as a city in 1889. The current city population, including suburbs, is 2,350,000 (1988 estimate).

the Birmingham Royal Ballet *pr. name, hist.* a professional ballet company based in Birmingham
Formerly known as ➡Sadler's Wells Royal Ballet, the company acquired its present name when it moved to Birmingham in 1990.

Biro *pr. name (TM)* a ballpoint pen
From the name of its Hungarian inventor.

birr *noun, Sc.* (1) an energetic rush of activity; (2) enthusiasm; (3) a whirring or vibrating sound

birse *noun, Sc.* (1) a bristle or brush; (2) anger

the Birthday Honours *pr. name* the ➡honours list which is announced annually on the date of the sovereign's ➡Official Birthday

biscuit *noun* a cracker or cookie

biscuit tin *comp. noun* a cracker barrel

bish *noun, sl.* a mistake or error

Bishop Barnaby *comp. noun, East* a ladybug

bist? *inter, South* are you?
It is instructive to compare this with *bist du?* which is the familiar form in modern German of "are you?" or more exactly but archaically in English, "art thou?"
SEE ALSO: ➡{bin? » bis?}

bistre *spell.* bister
A brown pigment or color.

{bisulphate » bisulphide » bisulphite} *spell.* {bisulfate » bisulfide » bisulfite}

bit *noun, derog., sl.* a woman

bit of a lad *idiom, coll.* (1) a spirited young man; (2) a man continually making up to women

bit of all right *idiom, sl.* a satisfactory condition

a bit of {all right » crackling » crumpet » fluff » skirt » stuff} *idiom, sl.* a sexually attractive or cooperative woman, as described by a man

a bit off *idiom, coll.* somewhat unfair or unreasonable

a bit on the side *idiom, sl.* an illicit sexual relationship

bits and bobs *idiom, sl.* bits and pieces

bitter *noun* the most common variety of draft beer served in English pubs
It is a bitter-tasting beer strongly flavored with hops and, to the surprise of many visitors, served at room temperature.

a bit thick *idiom* (1) unacceptable; (2) unreasonable

bittock *noun, Sc.* (1) a small portion; (2) a short walk

BL *pr. name, abbr.* the ➡British Library

black *verb, coll.* to boycott, especially a business, especially by a labor union

black-affronted *adj., Sc.* (1) insulted or offended; (2) mortified or embarrassed

the Black and Tans *pr. name, hist., Ir.* the paramilitary police force that operated in Ireland in the years immediately after World War I

Recruited by the British Government to support the ➡Royal Irish Constabulary in their fight with the ➡IRA during the ➡Anglo-Irish War which lasted from 1919 until independence in 1921. Originally the name of a well-known pack of foxhounds in County ➡Limerick, it became attached to this new force from their habit of wearing an outlandish mixture of police and army uniforms depending, it would seem, on what was available at the time. They acquired a reputation for brutality, were deeply resented, and almost certainly did more harm than good to the British cause.

black and white *idiom, rh. sl.* night

black bun *comp. noun, Sc.* a very rich fruit cake

Highly spiced and with a thick crust, it is traditionally eaten at ➡Hogmanay.

Blackburn *pr. name* a town in ➡Lancaster that is an important center of the weaving trade

The current population is 90,000 (1991 estimate).

Black Cap *comp. noun, hist.* the headgear formerly worn by a judge passing a death sentence

It consisted of a small rectangle of black cloth, placed upon the top of the judge's wig. Capital punishment was finally abolished in Britain in 1965.

black-coat worker *comp. noun, arch.* an office worker

black coffee *comp. noun* coffee without cream

the **Black Country** *pr. name* a grimy industrial district near ➡Birmingham in central England

The name was earned in the 18th C. when rapid coal-powered industrialization led to heavy pollution in the area.

blackcurrant *noun* the fruit of the ribes plant

Its formal name is *ribes nigrum*, and although it bears a superficial similarity to the blackberry, is not related.

the **Black Death** *pr. name, hist.* a deadly disease which reached England in 1348

It is believed to have originated in China. The plague of 1348 killed at least one quarter of the population of the British Isles, and there were later visitations in 1361 and 1379. *SEE ALSO:* the ➡Great Plague of 1665.

This was devastation on a scale that we can scarcely imagine today; perhaps the Nazi Holocaust or a nuclear war provide appropriate parallels. Yet within a few decades humanity had recovered; indeed, numerous observers reported that life was better than before.

Callous though it may sound, this was probably because the pressure of overpopulation had been relieved.

Blackfriars *pr. name* an area of central London with this name because Dominican Friars once had a monastery there

the **Black Friars** *pr. name, hist.* the Dominican Order of friars

They acquired this name because of their black mantle.

Blackheath *pr. name* an open area southeast of London once famous for highwaymen and so forth

the **Black Hole of Calcutta** *noun, coll., hist.* any very confined or stuffy place

In 1756, following the capture of the ➡East India Company's Fort William in Calcutta by the Nawab of Bengal, 146 British prisoners were confined in its small (18 ft by 15 ft) and windowless prison. Only 23 survived the suffocating conditions, and ever since, any very confined or stuffy place has been compared with this original Black Hole of Calcutta.

the **Black Horses** *pr. name* a nickname for the 4th/7th Dragoons Guards

A unit of the British Army. Its name was derived from the black color of their facings.

the **Black Isle** *pr. name* a peninsula to the northeast of ➡Inverness, lying between the ➡Cromarty and ➡Moray Firths

As it is neither black nor an island, the origin of this name is not glaringly obvious.

blackleg *noun, sl.* a scab, fink or strikebreaker; a betrayer of fellow workers, etc.

blackmail *noun, hist., North, Sc.* protection money

This is the *original* meaning of the word. It was paid by landowners and others to ➡moss troopers or ➡reivers in the ➡Border country between Scotland and England from the early Middle Ages until the practice was suppressed in the 17th C. following the ➡Union of the Crowns. Although the vast majority of blackmailers were Scots and their victims were English, there were some English blackmailers and Scots victims too. Literally, the word means "hidden rent."

black or white? *inter, coll.* do you want coffee with or without cream?

Blackpool *pr. name* a resort city on the western coast of ➡Lancashire

The resort's most famous landmark is its tower, which is 520 ft. tall and resembles the Eifel Tower in Paris. Today, the city's population, including suburbs, is 265,000 (1988 estimate).

the **Black Prince** *pr. name, hist.* the nickname for Edward ➡Prince of Wales, the son of ➡Edward II

The name is thought to refer to the color of his armor. Edward died a year before his father, who was thus succeeded by his grandson, who became ➡Richard II.

black pudding *comp. noun* a kind of blood sausage

Blackpool Tower

31

Black Rod *pr. name, abbr.* the official responsible for maintaining order in the ➡House of Lords and for summoning ➡MPs to the ➡Lords when the ➡Royal Assent is given to Bills, etc.

In full, "Gentleman Usher of the Black Rod.".The name derives from his staff of office, which is a black rod surmounted with a gold lion.

the **Black Rood of Scotland** *pr. name, hist.* a portion of the "true cross," or rood, left to the Scottish nation in 1093 by St Margaret, wife of ➡Malcolm Canmore

It fell into English hands in 1346 and then became lost during the Reformation.

the **Blackshirts** *pr. name, coll., hist.* a nickname for the ➡British Union of Fascists of the 1930s

The name comes from the color of their uniforms. Led by Sir Oswald Mosley between the World Wars, they modeled themselves on Mussolini's cohorts, also known as Blackshirts for the same reason.

black spot *comp. noun* a length of highway where accidents happen frequently

Blackstone's *pr. name, abbr.* formally and in full, the *Commentaries on the Laws of England*

The definitive treatise on English Common Law first published by the jurist William Blackstone between 1765 and 1770.

the **Black Watch** *pr. name, abbr.* the popular name for this regiment, in use for well over 250 years

Its full name is the Black Watch (Royal Highland Regiment). This is a unit of the British Army raised in 1725 as the 42nd Regiment of Foot, and is perhaps the most famous of all the Scottish Highland regiments. The tartan of their kilts is dark, and this, combined with their original role — to keep watch on rebellious highland clans - earned them this name.

blae *adj., Sc.* (1) blue, blue-gray or dark blue; (2) livid or furiously angry; (3) blue from cold

blaeberry *noun, North, Sc.* a ➡bilberry

blag *verb, sl.* (1) to rob in a violent way; (2) to steal or to scrounge

blagger *noun, derog., sl.* (1) a violent thief or mugger; (2) a scrounger

Blair Castle *pr. name, hist.* a 13th C. castle some 30 miles northwest of ➡Perth in Scotland.

The home of the Dukes of Atholl and the last British castle to withstand a siege, when troops under the command of General Lord Murray resisted an attack by the army of ➡Bonny Prince Charlie in 1746. It was massively rebuilt in the ➡Scottish baronial style during the 19th C. In 1844, during a visit, ➡Victoria granted the Duke of Atholl the unique privilege and right to maintain his own private army, the ➡Atholl Highlanders, which exists to the present day.

blameable *spell.* blamable

blank *verb, coll.* to ignore

{blank » blankety » blankety-blank » blanky} *adj.* a substitute word for an oath or curse not uttered

blastie *noun, derog., Sc.* (1) a shriveled dwarf; (2) an ugly, bad-tempered, or evil child or animal

blast it *exclam., pref., sl.* a euphemism for "damn it"

blate *adj., Sc.* (1) shy or timid; (2) dumb or stupid

Blayney's Bloodhounds *pr. name* a nickname for the Royal Irish Fusiliers

A unit of the British Army that became known by this name after capturing Irish rebels in 1798 while under the command of Lord Blayney. The regiment was disbanded in 1969. *SEE ALSO:* the ➡Bird Catchers.

blazer *noun* a lightweight colored or striped jacket

Often a club, team or school badge is displayed on the top right pocket, and it is worn by sportsmen, schoolboys, etc.

bleat *spell.* blat

bleeder *noun, derog., sl.* an unattractive or disreputable person

{bleeding » blessed} *exclam., sl.* a euphemism for or variation of ➡bloody

the ***Blenheim*** *pr. name, hist.* a bomber flown by the ➡RAF during World War II

Once the fastest bomber in the world with a top speed of 295 mph, it was used mostly in the first part of that war

the Battle of **Blenheim** *pr. name, hist.* a great victory by British and Austrian armies under the command of the Duke of Marlborough, over the French in 1704 during the War of the ➡Spanish Succession

Blenheim is in Germany, about 25 miles to the north of Augburg in Bavaria. *SEE ALSO:* ➡Blenheim Palace.

Blenheim orange *comp. noun* a large round, golden-colored eating apple

A name which reminds us that it was first grown at ➡Blenheim Palace during the 19th C.

Blenheim Palace *pr. name, hist.* a vast 18th C. house some 10 miles to the north west of ➡Oxford

It was built by a grateful nation and presented to the Duke of Marlborough following his victorious generalship during the War of the ➡Spanish Succession. It is named after his most famous victory, the Battle of ➡Blenheim of 1704.

the **Blessed Margaret** *pr. name, coll.* a nickname for ➡Prime Minister Margaret Thatcher

Coined by one of her ministers, Norman St John Stevens.

bletheration *noun, Sc.* blather or foolish gossip

Blicking Hall *pr. name, hist.* a large mansion house built between 1619 and 1629, set in magnificent gardens about 15 miles to the north of ➡Norwich

The first ➡stately home to be given to the ➡National Trust.

blighter *noun, coll., out.* an insignificant man

Blighty *noun, Hindi, sl.* England

From the Hindi *bilayati* = "foreign".

blimey *exclam., sl.* a euphemistic variety of "blind me"

Originally, and in full, this was "God blind me," which was an oath or call for a curse upon oneself.

blowcock

blimp *noun, arch* (1) a World War II barrage balloon; (2) a pompous and reactionary individual
From the title character of a World War II film, *Colonel Blimp*.

blin *adj., Sc.* (1) blind; (2) thick or dense

blind [A] *noun* an awning over a shop window
[B] *verb, sl.* to drive heedlessly and very rapidly, especially without looking ahead

blinder *comp. noun, coll.* an extensive drinking session

the **Blind Half-Hundred** *pr. name* a nickname for the 50th Regiment of ➡Foot
A unit of the British Army that became known by this name because many men suffered from a particularly virulent form of ophthalmia during the Egyptian Campaign of 1801.

blind hedge *comp. noun, coll.* a ditch

{**blinding » blinking » blooming**} *exclam., sl.* a euphemism for or variation of ➡bloody

blindingly stupid *idiom, coll.* very stupid indeed

blind man's holiday *idiom, arch., coll.* a dark night

blin drift *comp. noun, Sc.* drifting snow

blinkers *noun* a horse's blinders

blister *noun, derog., sl.* an irritating person

the **Blitz** *pr. name, abbr., coll., Ger., hist.* a series of German air raids on British cities, especially London, during the winter of 1940 to 41.
An abbreviation of the German *Blitzkrieg* = "lighting war"

bloater *noun* a herring cured by salting and smoking
Often associated with the port of Great Yarmouth in ➡Norfolk.

bloater paste *comp. noun* a kind of fish spread which is sometimes used in sandwiches

blob *noun, sl.* (1) a female breast; (2) a male testicle; (3) an ulcer; (4) a police term for the remains of a victim of a fatal highway accident; (5) a score of zero ➡runs when ➡batting in a game of ➡cricket

blobwagon *noun, sl.* an ambulance attending a road traffic accident
Used mostly by police and paramedics. *SEE ALSO:* ➡blob(4).

block *noun* in ➡cricket, (1) the position before the ➡wicket where a ➡batsman places his bat while waiting to play a ball; (2) defensive play by blocking the ball with a ➡dead bat

block of flats *comp. noun* a large apartment building

block vote *comp. noun* a voting system whereby each delegate's vote is multiplied by the number of individuals she or he supposedly represents
Traditional in the ➡Labour Party and the labor unions, where it is a common substitute or alternative to democracy.

Blois *pr. name, hist.* a ➡Royal House of England
Some authorities consider ➡Stephen, king from 1135 to 1154, to have been a member. However, others consider him a member of ➡Normandy, and the house spurious.

bloke *noun, coll.* a man
As distinct from a woman. Reputedly derived from a secret word used by gypsies.

the **Blood Royal** *pr. name, coll.* the ➡Royal Family

blood sausage *comp. noun* a kind of very dark sausage containing a large amount of dried blood

bloodsports *noun* hunting animals for sport

bloody *exclam., taboo* (1) damned; (2) unpleasant; (3) a general intensifier

the **Bloody Eleventh** *pr. name* a nickname for the 11th Regiment of ➡Foot
A unit of the British Army. Following the Battle of Salamanca in 1812, only 71 men out of the 400 that had been on the roles of the regiment remained fit for duty; so earning the regiment this nickname.

Bloody Mary *pr. name, hist.* a nickname for ➡Mary I
From her habit of dispatching to the afterlife those that she did not see eye-to-eye with on religious matters.

bloody-minded *idiom, taboo* deliberately awkward, perverse or unhelpful

bloody pudding *comp. noun* a kind of ➡blood sausage

Bloody Sunday *pr. name, hist.* (1) an incident in 1887 when two people in a socialist demonstration in ➡Trafalgar Square, London, died after the crowd was fired upon by troops called out to control the event; (2) an incident in 1972 when 13 participants or observers of a banned ➡Irish Republican demonstration in ➡Londonderry, Northern Ireland, died after the crowd were fired upon by troops called out to control the event
In 1972, the British Army maintain that ➡IRA agents in the crowd had fired at troops first although others dispute this … but then they would, wouldn't they?

the **Bloody Tower** *pr. name, hist.* a 14th C. tower at the center of the ➡Tower of London complex
Reputedly where the ➡Princes in the Tower were murdered.

bloom *verb* to coat a photographic lens in order to reduce surface reflection

bloomer *noun* a kind of long crusty loaf with diagonal slashes upon its rounded top

the **Bloomsbury Group** *pr. name, hist.* a group of intellectuals who lived in the Bloomsbury area of London from about 1900 until World War II
The group is best-remembered for their rejection of ➡Victorian morality and a belief in the over-riding importance of art. Membership included Virginia Woolf, Maynard Keynes, Lytton Strachey, E. M. Forster and David Garnett.

blootered *adj., Sc., sl.* very drunk

blot one's copybook *idiom. phr. verb* to damage one's own reputation

blowcock *noun* an emergency release valve upon a boiler or piping

blower

blower *noun, coll.* a telephone

blowlamp *noun* a blowtorch

blow the gaff *idiom. phr. verb* to expose or tell a secret by accident

blue [A] *adj., coll.* pertaining or relating to the ➠Conservative Party

[B] *noun* a sporting representative of ➠Oxford or ➠Cambridge universities

The colors are those used on the team ➠caps. Oxford representatives are dark blue, Cambridge are light blue.

[C] *verb, coll.* to squander or waste money

blue bag *comp. noun* the bag in which a junior ➠barrister carries his or her robes

blue blood *comp. noun* the supposed color of blood in the veins of someone who is noble or royal by birth

blue bonnet *comp. noun, out., Sc.* (1) a round flat woolen man's cap, traditionally dyed blue; (2) a nickname for a Highland Scot

Once the usual head apparel of Scottish ➠Highlanders.

Blue Book *comp. noun* a report issued by ➠Parliament or the ➠Privy Council

bluebottle *noun, derog., sl.* a policeman

From the color of his uniform.

SEE ALSO: ➠bottle and stopper.

bluecoat {boy » girl} *comp. noun, hist.* a student at a ➠bluecoat school

From their traditional uniform, which dates from the 16th C.

bluecoat school *comp. noun, out.* a charity school

In particular but not exclusively, ➠Christ's Hospital in London.

blue ensign *comp. noun* (1) formerly, the ensign flag of the ➠RNR; (2) the ensign flag of a government department

blue-eyed boy *comp. noun, coll.* a favorite person

blue funk *comp. noun, coll.* a state of blind panic or abject terror

Bluemantle *pr. name, out.* a ➠pursuivant of the English ➠College of Arms

blue moon *idiom, rh. sl.* a spoon

blue o'clock *idiom, sl.* the wee small hours; the dead of night

blue ribbon *comp. noun* the ribbon worn by members of the ➠Order of the Garter

Blue Rod *pr. name* an officer of the order of St Michael and St George

the **Blues** *pr. name, abbr.* the ➠Oxford Blues

the **Blues and Royals** *pr. name, hist.* one of the ➠Horse Guards Regiments

Formed in 1969 by amalgamation of the ➠Blues (the Royal Horse Guards) and the ➠Royals (the Royal Dragoons).

Blueshirts *pr. name, coll., hist.* a nickname for Irish Fascists in the 1930s, called this because of the color of their uniforms

This now largely forgotten organization was sufficiently numerous to form a brigade that fought on Franco's side during the Spanish Civil War.

Bluff King Hal *pr. name, hist.* a nickname for ➠Henry VIII

BM *pr. name, abbr.* the ➠British Museum

BMA *pr. name, abbr.* the British Medical Association

BMJ *pr. name, abbr.* the British Medical Journal

The Journal of the ➠BMA.

BNC *pr. name, abbr.* ➠Brasenose College

BOAC *pr. name (TM), abbr., hist.* British Overseas Airways Corporation

Formed in 1939 when the government acquired and merged together ➠Imperial Airways and ➠British Airways. After 1945, when the government created ➠BEA, ➠BOAC was responsible for intercontinental air services to and from Britain until ➠British Airways was created by merging BOAC and BEA in 1971.

Boadicea *pr. name, hist.* a 1st. C. British warrior queen who led a major revolt against the Roman conquerors

Queen of the Iceni tribe, she brought the whole of southern Britain into open rebellion against their Roman conquerors in the year 60. After many victories she was finally routed by the Roman general Suetonius Paulinus, and took poison.

Boadicea is the Latinized version of her name and the one by which she is best known. The alternate, supposedly more accurate, spelling is ➠Boudicca.

boak *verb, Sc.* to vomit

board of green cloth *idiom, coll.* a euphemism for (1) a ➠billiards table; (2) a card table

the **Board of Green Cloth** *pr. name* the committee responsible for managing the domestic business of the ➠Royal Household

Until 1782, it was responsible for managing all royal financial matters and was presided over by the ➠Lord Steward. It is now presided over by the ➠Master of the Household.

the **Board of Inland Revenue** *pr. name* the British equivalent of the Internal Revenue Service, and equally loved

the **Board of Trade** *pr. name, hist.* a former government department that was responsible for trade and commerce matters

Originally established in 1696 as a committee of the ➠Privy Council, for many years it was responsible for all matters concerned with Britain's trade.

It was absorbed into the Department for ➠Trade and Industry in 1970.

boater *noun, out.* a flat-topped straw hat with a broad flat brim

boat race *idiom, rh. sl.* a face

the **Boat Race** *pr. name* an annual rowing race upon the ➠Thames River between crews from ➠Oxford and ➠Cambridge Universities

The contest was first held at Henley-on-Thames in 1829 but moved to its present route between Putney and Mortlake in west London in 1836. It takes place every spring.

the Boat Race

bob *noun, arch., coll.* a ➠shilling

Bob-a-Job-Week *pr. name, coll., hist.* a fundraising scheme used by the Boy Scouts organization in the years after World War II

The idea was that for one particular week every year, Boy Scouts performed household tasks for people in their neighborhood for a ➠bob. However, with the effect of inflation and particularly the introduction of decimal currency in 1971, the name became increasingly inappropriate, and was replaced with "Scout Job Week" in 1972.

bobby *noun, coll.* a policeman

A nickname derived from the given name of Sir Robert Peel, who founded the ➠Metropolitan Police in 1829.

bobby-dazzler *idiom, coll., out.* an excellent or unusual person or thing

bobby-off *imper, East* a euphemism for or variation of ➠bugger off

bob-sleigh *spell.* bobsled

Bob's Own *pr. name* a nickname for the ➠Irish Guards Regiment

A unit of the British Army named after Field-Marshal Earl Roberts, known as "Bob," who was their first Colonel.

bob's your uncle *idiom, sl.* everything's just fine

Reputedly this expression refers to Robert Cecil, Lord Salisbury, who was ➠Prime Minister for most of the last 20 years of the 19th C. and had a propensity to appoint family members to his ➠Cabinet.

BOC *pr. name (TM), abbr.* British Oxygen Company

The largest British supplier of numerous chemicals used by modern industrial processes.

bod *noun, abbr., coll.* a person

The word is an abbreviation of "body"

bodd *noun, East* a bird

bodge *verb, sl.* to botch or bungle

Bodiam Castle *pr. name, hist.* an almost entirely intact 14th C. castle situated a few miles north of the the site of the Battle of ➠Hastings

Built to protect against the threat of invasion from France, it is set in a vast moat so wide at to amount almost to a lake.

bodle *noun, hist., Sc.* a coin worth two ➠pennies Scots

By 1707 when it ceased to be legal tender, one bodle was worth one sixth of an English ➠penny. For more about Scots currency, SEE ALSO: ➠pound Scots.

Bodleian Library *pr. name* the principle library of ➠Oxford University

It is named after Sir Thomas Bodley, who restored it in 1598 when it was already some centuries old.

bodyline bowling *comp. noun* in ➠cricket, a controversial form of fast bowling which is aimed at the batsman instead of the wicket

The intent is to force an easily caught hit as the batsman is obliged to defend himself.

the **body of the kirk** *idiom, Sc.* the main group or party, where most people are seated or to be found

body-servant *comp. noun, arch.* a valet

the **Boer War** *pr. name, Du., hist.* a war in South Africa between British and Dutch settlers

It was fought from 1899 until 1902; *boer* is the Dutch word for "farmer." Dutch settlers in the Transvaal and the Orange Free State resented British intrusion into their territory from Cape Colony and also from the region to the north, now called Zimbabwe.

In the end the British won, but at the cost of 22,000 men dead, while the Boers lost just 6,000 men. However, another 20,000 Boer women and children died in the world's first concentration camps, which the British invented for the purpose of holding the Boer families who had lost their homes as a result of a scorched-earth policy.

boffin *noun, sl.* a research scientist

bog *noun, sl.* a toilet

Originally World War II military slang.

bogey *noun* in golf the strokes which the average player should expect for a particular hole

boggin *adj., Sc., sl.* stinking

bogie *noun* an undercarriage with two or more wheels, pivoted at the rear of a vehicle

Bognor Regis *pr. name, hist., Lat.* a resort town in West ➠Sussex upon the ➠English Channel coast

In a stroke of almost unprecedented pretentiousness, the word "regis" (the Latin for "king") was added to the name of the place after ➠George V had spent some time nearby recuperating from an illness in 1929. It is reputed that some years later the dying king's last words were, "Bugger Bognor." The current population is 41,000 (1991 estimate).

bog-trotter *comp. noun, out., sl.* an Irish vagabond

bogy *noun, sl.* a policeman

boiled *adj., sl.* drunk

boiled shirt *comp. noun* (1) a dress shirt which has had its front starched; (2) a stiffly formal person

boiled sweet *comp. noun* a candy made of boiled sugar

boiler *noun, derog., sl.* (1) an unattractive or stupid woman; (2) a large and shapeless older woman

boiler suit *comp. noun* a coverall suit

bollards *noun* short posts set in or beside a roadway to restrict or exclude vehicular traffic

bolshie *adj., coll.* (1) awkward or unhelpful; (2) foul-tempered

bolthole *noun* (1) a means of escape; (2) a secret place, suitable for hiding in

Bolton *pr. name, hist.* an important medieval town in Lancashire which became a major cotton-spinning and wool center in the 19th C.

It is now a metropolitan borough in ➠Greater Manchester. The current population is 150,000 (1991 estimate).

Bolton Abbey *pr. name, hist.* a 12th C. Augustan priory that never was an ➠abbey, it is some 18 miles west of ➠Harrogate in ➠North Yorkshire

It is still used as the local parish church.

bomb [A] *noun, sl.* (1) a great success; (2) a very large sum of money

[B] *verb, sl.* to cover with graffiti

For example, a wall.

SEE ALSO: ➠dive bomb.

bomb aimer *comp. noun* a bombardier in a bomber

bombardier *noun* a non-commissioned officer in an artillery regiment

Bombay duck *comp. noun* a dried tropical fish which is eaten with curry

Bomber Command *pr. name, hist.* a former ➠command of the ➠RAF responsible for conducting bombing missions over enemy territory

Bomber Command's heyday was in World War II when it conducted the brunt of the strategic aerial bombing of Nazi Germany, greatly assisted after 1942 by the USAAF.

bona *exclam., sl., Span.* excellent, well done

From the Spanish *buena* = "good"

bonce *noun, sl.* (1) a large glass marble used for playing various games; (2) the head

Bond Street *pr. name* one of the principal shopping streets in London

It is best known for its jewelry stores and picture galleries.

bone box *comp. noun, sl.* the mouth

bone china *comp. noun, hist.* the traditionally English form of fine porcelain

This was the first successful western attempt to emulate the fine quality of classical Chinese porcelain, and was manufactured for the first time in the 1790s. by ➠Spode, who discovered that he could greatly enhance the product by adding white bone ash to the clay.

bone-idle *adj.* very lazy

Bonfire Night *pr. name, hist.* ➠Guy Fawkes Night

bonk [A] *noun, sl.* a bang or thump

[B] *verb, sl.* to hit

[C] *verb, sl., taboo* to copulate

bonkers *adj., coll.* crazy

bonnet *noun* the hood of an automobile

{**bonnet » bunnet**} *noun, Sc.* a man's brimless cap

bonnet laird *comp. noun, hist., Sc.* a minor landowner who personally farms his own land rather than renting it to tenant farmers

bonnet piece *comp. noun, hist., Sc.* a gold coin from the time of ➠James V of Scotland

So named because it depicts the king wearing a bonnet.

{**bonnie » bonny**} *adj., North, Sc.* (1) attractive or beautiful; (2) good or pleasing

bonnie fechter *comp. noun, Sc.* a good or powerful fighter for a cause or mission

Bonnie Prince Charlie *pr. name, hist.* the ➠Young Pretender, ➠Charles Edward Stuart

boob *noun, sl.* a goof-up or stupid error

boob tube *comp. noun, sl.* a woman's tight strapless dress top

Boodle's Club *pr. name, hist.* a gentleman's club founded in London in 1762

Located, like so many clubs, in ➠St James's, it is situated upon the site originally occupied by ➠White's until 1755.

book *verb* to reserve in advance

A theater seat, hotel room, travel arrangements, etc.

the **Booker Prize** *pr. name* a leading annual prize awarded for an outstanding work of fiction

Founded in 1969, it is open to British, Irish and Commonwealth authors only.

book in *verb* to check in or register at a hotel

booking clerk *comp. noun* a reservation and ticketing clerk

At a railroad terminus, for example.

booking {hall » office} *comp. noun* a reservation and ticketing hall
At a railroad terminus, for example.

the **Book of Common Prayer** *pr. name, hist.* a book containing the ➡Common Prayer
It was first published in 1549.

the **Book of Kells** *pr. name, hist.* a exceptionally fine illustrated book of the Gospels
It was the work of Scottish monks living on the Isle of ➡Iona off the western coast of Scotland in the 8th C., and it is now kept in the Library of ➡Trinity College, Dublin.

bookstall *noun* a newsstand

book token *comp. noun* a voucher exchangeable for books at most bookstores
Often given as a gift.

boot *noun* the luggage area or trunk of an automobile

bootlace *noun* a shoestring or shoelace

bootrake *noun, arch.* a shoe scraper
A small metal device sometimes still found outside older buildings. They were provided for the purpose of scraping dirt from the sole of shoes before going indoors.

boots *noun* a servant who cleans shoes
Usually those belonging to guests in hotels.

Boots *pr. name (TM)* a national chain of druggists

boozer *noun, sl.* (1) a ➡pub; (2) a drunk

bo-peep [A] *comp. noun, coll.* peek-a-boo
A children's game.
[B] *comp. noun, rh. sl.* sleep

bor *noun, East* a boy or young man
Possibly from the Dutch *boer* = "farmer"

Border Collie *pr. name* a breed of working sheepdog with black and white coloring
Originally from the ➡Border area of Scotland.

Borders *pr. name* a local government region in southeastern Scotland
The current population is 100,000 (1991 Census).

the **Borders** *pr. name* (1) a region encompassing both sides of the Scottish-English border; (2) a region encompassing both sides of the Welsh-English border

Border Terrier *pr. name* a small rough-haired terrier

Border TV *pr. name* a local commercial TV company headquartered in ➡Carlisle
It is part of the ➡ITV network.

bordure *comp. noun* an heraldic representation of a colored edge around a shield

bore *noun* the gauge or diameter of a gun barrel

born to the purple *adj. phr., coll.* born into the ➡Royal Family

borough *noun, hist.* (1) a town incorporated by royal charter; (2) originally, any fortified town; (3) formerly, any town in England that was entitled to send its own ➡MP to ➡Westminster
The most common English spelling. However in Scotland and some parts of England it is spelled ➡burgh. (3) had become serious corrupted by the 18th C. and the system was abolished in the ➡Great Reform Act of 1832.

borrow and beg *idiom, rh. sl.* an egg

borstal *noun, arch.* a reform school
The name was derived from the village in ➡Kent where the first was built in 1907. Borstals were abolished in 1983, when they were replaced by ➡Young Offenders Institutions.

Boscobel *pr. name, hist.* the location in Shropshire of the ➡Royal Oak, 20 miles north of ➡Birmingham

boss *noun* a stud or knob at the center of a shield or other ornamental object

boss-eyed *adj., coll.* (1) blind in one eye; (2) cross-eyed; (3) one-sided; (4) misaligned

boss shot *comp. noun, sl.* (1) a missed shot from a gun; (2) a bad guess; (3) a failed attempt; (4) a mess

bossy-boots *comp. noun, sl.* a domineering or bossy woman or child

Boston *pr. name* a town located upon the ➡Wash
Formerly a major port, Boston is now a decidedly inland town, due to the extensive draining of the flat low-lying land around the Wash since the Middle Ages. A significant number of the Pilgrim Fathers set off to ➡Plymouth from here, from where they sailed to Massachusetts to found, among other places, what is now the modern city of Boston. The current population of this original Boston is 26,000 (1981 estimate).

the Battle of **Bosworth Field** *pr. name, hist.* the battle that ended the ➡Wars of the Roses in 1485
This is where ➡Richard III uttered the memorable words,
A horse! a horse! my kingdom for a horse!
(according to Shakespeare, who was not actually there at the time) and Henry ➡Tudor took the crown after disposing of the horseless Richard.

bother *exclam., abbr.* ➡botheration

botheration *exclam.* confound it

bothy *noun, Sc.* a hut where farm workers sleep

bottle [A] *noun, sl.* courage or self-confidence
[B] *verb* to preserve fruit in glass jars
[C] *verb, arch.* to bundle
Straw, for example.

bottle and stopper *idiom, rh. sl.* a policeman
Derivation: policeman > copper > stopper > bottle and stopper.

bottle out *verb, sl.* to loose one's nerve

bottle party *comp. noun, coll.* a party where guests bring drink to add to the common stock

bottom *noun* reliability or strength of character

bottom drawer *comp. noun* a hope chest

bottom gear *comp. noun* an automobile's lowest gear

bottom of the garden *comp. noun, coll.* the point in a backyard that is farthest from the house

bottom storey *comp. noun* a building's first floor

Boudicca *pr. name, hist.* ➡Boadicea
The alternative spelling of her name, supposedly more accurate than the Latinized version.

bougainvillaea *spell.* bougainvillea
A widely cultivated tropical plant.

bounce *noun* self-confidence

bouncer *noun* a ➡cricket ball that hits the ground after pitching, causing it to rise into the air close to the batsman

bouncing bomb *comp. noun, hist.* a skip bomb
A barrel-shaped spinning bomb dropped from very low-flying aircraft, designed to bounce along a level surface (usually water) to reach a target that would be difficult or impossible to reach from directly above. Invented by British aeronautical engineer Barnes Wallis during World War II, and used first by the RAF 617 (➡Dambusters) Squadron on Germany's Möhne and Eder dams in May 1943.

the **Boundaries Commission** *pr. name* an independent agency which defines and reviews the composition and extent of ➡constituencies for both British and European ➡Parliaments
There is one commission each for England, Scotland, Wales and Northern Ireland.

boundary *noun* the edge of a ➡cricket field

bourn *noun, South* a small stream

Bournemouth *pr. name* a coastal resort town in ➡Dorset upon the southern coast of England
The current city population, including suburbs, is 340,000 (1988 estimate).

Bovril *pr. name (TM)* a concentrated beef extract used as the basis of a hot drink

bovver *noun, rh. sl.* bother or trouble

bovver boot *comp. noun, sl.* a heavy boot worn by ➡bovver boys or ➡skinheads
Usually with a metal toe cap.

bovver boy *comp. noun, sl.* a violent troublemaker

Bow Bells *pr. name, coll., hist.* the bells of the church of St Mary-le-Bow, Cheapside, London
It is said that all true ➡Cockneys are born within the sound of Bow Bells. The bells and interior of the church were destroyed by an air raid in 1941.

bower *noun* a boudoir or small inner room

bowl *verb* to pitch a ➡cricket ball

bowler [A] *noun* the pitcher of a ➡cricket ball
[B] *noun, abbr., coll.* a ➡bowler hat

bowler hat *comp. noun* a derby hat
Named for the 19th C. London hatter who designed it.

bowler-hat *verb, sl.* to retire from the army

bowler hat brigade *comp. noun, coll., out.* London businessmen as a group
From their "traditional" headgear, now rarely seen.

bowling average *comp. noun* the average of ➡runs scored against a ➡bowler per ➡wickets taken in a game of ➡cricket

bowling crease *comp. noun* a line from behind which a ball must be ➡bowled to be legal in ➡cricket

bowling green *comp. noun* a lawn made especially level to play the game of ➡lawn bowls upon

bowl out *phr. verb, coll.* in ➡cricket, (1) to ➡dismiss a batsman; (2) to ➡dismiss an entire side

bowser *noun* a wheeled gasoline tank from which vehicles are fueled

Bow Street {Runner » Officer} *pr. name, hist.* a member of London's first full-time police force
Founded in the 1740s by a magistrate at the central London court in Bow Street to help catch thieves and apprehend individuals who declined to appear in court when required. They were replaced by the modern ➡Metropolitan Police in 1829. For the origin of this name, see ➡runner.

bowt *prep., adv., North* without

box *noun, out.* a Christmas gift for a tradesman

the **box** *noun, sl.* television

box clever *verb* to behave in a clever or cunning way

boxed valance *comp. noun* a box-pleated valance

Boxing Day *pr. name* December 26th
The day following Christmas Day, when ➡boxes were traditionally distributed.

box junction *comp. noun* a highway intersection which must not be entered unless the exit is clear
Indicated by a yellow grid painted upon the road surface.

boxroom *noun* a small room, often in the attic of a house, where boxes, suitcases, etc., are stored

box spanner *comp. noun* a lug wrench

boxty *noun, Ir.* a potato

boychap *noun, South* a youth

boy in blue *idiom, rh. sl.* stew

the Battle of the **Boyne** *pr. name, hist.* a battle in 1690 resulting in the victory of ➡William III over the former ➡James II of England and VII of Scotland
The Boyne is a river about 25 miles north of ➡Dublin in Ireland. James's defeat and subsequent flight to France finally ended his attempt to recover his crown following the ➡Glorious Revolution of 1688.
SEE ALSO: ➡King Billy.

boyo [A] *noun, coll., Wal.* a boy or man
A form of informal address or greeting.
[B] *noun, Ir., sl.* an ➡IRA terrorist

the **boys in blue** *idiom, coll.* the police

BP *pr. name, abbr.* (1) British Petroleum plc; (2) the ➡British Pharmacopoeia

BPC *pr. name, abbr.* (1) the British Pharmaceutical Codex; (2) the ➡British Pharmacopoeia Commission

BR *pr. name, abbr.* ➡British Rail

braces *noun, pref.* suspenders

brachan *noun, Sc.* bracken

Bradford *pr. name* a city in ➡West Yorkshire some 9 miles to the west of ➡Leeds
A center of the wool trade since the Middle Ages, Bradford grew rapidly during the industrial revolution following the development of steam-powered milling in the late 18th C.
It was incorporated as a city in 1847. Its current population, also included within the Leeds area tota, is 450,000 (1988 estimate).

bradshaw *verb, arch., coll.* to follow the line of a railroad as a method of aerial navigation
From ➡Bradshaw's; apparently this was a rather popular technique in the earlier days of aviation.

Bradshaw's pr. name, abbr., hist. a publication which listed passenger railroad schedules
In full, *Bradshaw's Monthly Railway Guide.* It was first published in 1839 and had became a monthly publication by 1841, as it continued until ceasing publication in 1961.

brae *noun, Sc.* (1) the sloping bank of a river, lake or sea shore; (2) a hillside; (3) a steeply rising road; (4) the brow of a hill

braes *noun, Sc.* a mountainous district

the **Braemar Gathering** *pr. name* the best-known annual highland gathering
It is held at Braemar in northeastern Scotland and is regularly visited by the ➡Royal Family, whose Scottish summer retreat is at nearby ➡Balmoral.

brag *pr. name* a card game somewhat like poker

the **Braggs** *pr. name* a nickname for the 28th Regiment of ➡Foot
A unit of the British Army named for General Philip Bragg, their commander from 1734 until 1759. Also known as the ➡Slashers and as the ➡Old Braggs.

Brahms and Liszt *idiom, rh. sl.* drunk
Derivation: drunk > ➡pissed > Liszt > Brahms and Liszt.

braid *adj., Sc.* (1) broad or wide; (2) extended or laid out flat

braid bonnet *comp. noun, arch., Sc.* a traditional Scottish ➡bonnet
It was made from wool, without lining or seam.

Braid Scots *comp. noun, Sc.* the ➡Scots language or dialect spoken without any concessions to English-speaking listeners

brainfag *noun, arch., sl.* nervous exhaustion

brains trust *comp. noun* a brain trust

brake light *comp. noun* an automobile stop lamp

brakesman *noun* a brakeman on a train

brake van *comp. noun* a caboose
From which a train's brakes are operated.

Bramley's *noun* a large green cooking apple
Developed by Matthew Bramley in the 19th C.

Brand's Hatch *pr. name* a car-racing circuit in Kent
First used in 1931 as a grass track for motorcycle racing, it is now the regular location of the British Grand Prix.

brandy-ball *comp. noun* a brandy-flavored candy

Brandy Nan *pr. name, hist.* a nickname for ➡Anne
Who, it is reputed, was not averse to the occasional ➡tincture.

brandysnap *noun* a gingerbread wafer

branks *noun, arch., Sc.* (1) a bridle or halter with wooden side-pieces; (2) an iron gag used to restrain scolding women

brantub *noun* a grab bag

Brasenose College *pr. name* a college of ➡Oxford University, founded in 1509
Over the gates are the arms of the college, which has a brass nose as its central feature. However, the name is believed to be a corruption of an old word, probably Dutch in origin, *brasenhuis* ="brew house" or "brewery." It is supposed that the college was built upon the site of one.

brash *noun, arch.* (1) hedge clippings or other similar vegetative debris; (2) broken up rock or stone; (3) crushed ice

brass [A] *noun, rh. sl.* a prostitute
Derivation: prostitute > tail > rail > brass rail > brass.
[B] *noun, sl.* (1) cheekiness; (2) money; (3) a badge, medallion or ornament

brass farthing *idiom, sl.* the least possible money

brass monkey's weather *idiom, sl.* very cold weather
Derived from the picturesque description of such weather as "so cold it would freeze the balls off a brass monkey."

brass neck *comp. noun, sl.* brazen impudence

brat [A] *noun, North, Sc.* a rough apron worn by some workmen
[B] *noun, sl.* a child
Usually, but not necessarily, derogatory.

braw *noun, Sc.* (1) brave, fine or good; (2) handsome, good-looking or well-dressed; (3) excellent or splendid; (4) fine (of weather); (5) much (of money)

brawn *noun* headcheese

A low-grade jellied meat from the head of a pig, which is finely chopped, boiled, seasoned and molded.

BRB *pr. name, abbr.* the British Railways Board

Better known as ➡British Rail.

BRCS *pr. name, abbr.* the British Red Cross Society

bread and butter *idiom, rh. sl.* a gutter

bread and butter pudding *idiom* a popular dessert

Consisting of buttered bread and sultanas, soaked in eggs and milk and baked until the top is crisp and brown.

break *noun* (1) a school recess; (2) the deviation of a pitched ➡cricket ball upon bouncing

breakdown van *comp. noun* a tow truck

break duck *comp. noun* to score the first run of a ➡cricket inning

breaker's yard *comp. noun* a scrap iron dealer's lot

breakup *noun, coll.* the end of a school's summer term and the start of summer vacation

breast *verb* to complete an ascent

Such as reaching the top of a hill, for example.

breast pin *comp. noun* a brooch that is intended to be worn upon the upper torso

breastsummer *noun* a load-bearing lintel placed over a wide opening

Breathalyser *pr. name (TM), spell.* a Breathalyzer

Brecknock *pr. name, hist.* a former Welsh County, now part of ➡Powys

the **Brecon Beacons** *pr. name* a mountainous region in south Wales, made a ➡national park in 1957

breeches *noun* short pants fastened below the knee

Commonly used in horseback riding.

breeks *noun, Sc.* ➡breeches, pants or ➡trousers

breeze *noun, coll.* an outburst of bad temper

breeze block *comp. noun* a cinder building block

brekkers *noun, sl.* breakfast

Brenda *pr. name, coll.* a satirical nickname for ➡Elizabeth II of England and I of Scotland

Bren gun *comp. noun, hist.* a light machine gun that was fired from the shoulder

It originated from the town of Brno in Czechoslovakia and was used extensively by the British Army during World War II. The first part of its name is based on the first part of this Czechoslovakian town's name.

Brent *pr. name* a borough within ➡Greater London

Its current population, which is also included within the ➡London urban area total, is 225,000 (1991 Census).

brent goose *pr. name* a brant goose

A small breed with a black neck.

breve *noun, out.* a musical term for a note as long as two ➡semibreves

brewer's droop *idiom, sl.* temporary impotence induced by excessive consumption of beer

brewster *noun, arch.* a brewer of beer

Brewster Sessions *pr. name* a court session during which licenses to sell liquor may be issued

brew up *verb, coll.* to make tea

Brian *noun, coll.* a name that supposedly typifies a boring, dull or uninteresting person

Similar to "Irving" or "Melvin," perhaps.

brick [A] *noun* a child's building block

[B] *noun, coll., out.* a solid and reliable person

the **Brickdusts** *pr. name* a nickname for the 53rd Regiment of ➡Foot

A unit of the British Army, named this because of the brick-red color of their facings.

brickfield *noun* a brickyard

brickie *noun, abbr., sl.* a bricklayer

bridewell *noun, arch.* a prison

From the former prison at St Bride's Well in London.

bridge roll *comp. noun* a small, soft roll

It is somewhat similar to a hot-dog bun, but much smaller.

bridging loan *comp. noun* a short-term bank loan

Often to finance purchasing one house while another is sold.

bridleway *noun* a bridle path

brief [A] *noun, coll.* (1) legal case-work performed by a ➡barrister; (2) a ➡criminal barrister

[B] *verb* to instruct a lawyer, especially a ➡barrister

brief bag *comp. noun* the bag in which ➡barristers carry ➡briefs [A](1)

brig *noun, North, Sc.* a bridge

the **Brigade of Guards** *pr. name* the five regiments of ➡Foot Guards

These are the ➡Grenadier, ➡Coldstream, ➡Scots, ➡Irish and ➡Welsh Guards. Among other duties, they guard the sovereign and carry out ceremonial duties in London.

brigadier *noun* the fifth-highest rank of commissioned officer in the British Army

Equivalent in rank to a one-star general in the U.S. Army.

Brighton *pr. name* a town that is the administrative center of East ➡Sussex

This town, less than 50 miles south of London, became a fashionable center for the fashionable elite to bathe in the sea following the publication of Dr. Russell's *Dissertation on the Use of Sea Water in Diseases of the Glands* in 1753. When the Prince Regent set up court there and built the ➡Royal Pavilion during the 1810s, Brighton's fashionable future was secured. The arrival of the railroad in the 1840s secured a yet firmer future for the town as a conveniently accessible yet suitably high-class commuter's residence for prosperous Londoners.

Originally, the town was called "Brighthelmstone" and "Brighton" was an abbreviation or nickname. The current population, including suburbs, is 450,000 (1988 estimate).

brimstone and treacle *idiom, coll.* sulfur and molasses

bring-and-buy sale *idiom* a swap-meet organized to raise funds for a charity

bring low *verb, coll.* to humiliate or ruin

bring to book *verb, coll.* to charge with a crime

Particularly by the police.

the **briny** *noun, sl.* a poetic name for the sea

Bristol *pr. name* a city which is the administrative center of ➡Avon county

An important seaport, serving the wool trade of western England since the early Middle Ages. This is where Cabot sailed from in 1497, searching for the elusive Northwest Passage to China. Of course his quest failed, but the discovery of America gave Bristol great prosperity based upon trade in sugar, slaves and tobacco until it began to lose place to ➡Liverpool and ➡Glasgow in the late 18th C.

Incorporated as a city in 1188, the current city population, including suburbs, is 550,000 (1988 estimate).

Bristol board *comp. noun* a kind of fine pasteboard used by artists as a drawing surface

the **Bristol Channel** *pr. name* an arm of the Atlantic Ocean that lies between Wales and the south western portion of England

At its northeastern corner, it merges into the ➡Severn estuary.

Bristol cream *comp. noun* an especially fine sherry

➡Bristol was the principal entry-port of sherry into Britain *SEE ALSO:* ➡Bristol milk.

Bristol fashion *adj. phr., abbr., coll.* ➡shipshape and Bristol fashion

Bristol milk *comp. noun* a fine dry sherry

➡Bristol was the principal entry-port of sherry into Britain *SEE ALSO:* ➡Bristol cream.

Bristol Old Vic School *pr. name* a drama school opened in ➡Bristol in 1946

bristols *noun, rh. sl., taboo* a woman's breasts

Derivation: breasts > titties > cities > Bristol Cities > bristols. "Bristol City" is a soccer club. *SEE ALSO:* ➡two cities.

brit *noun* a young herring

Brit *pr. name, abbr., sl.* a British person

Britain *pr. name, abbr.* (1) the ➡British Isles; (2) the island of ➡Great Britain; (3) the ➡United Kingdom

the Battle of **Britain** *pr. name, hist.* the great air battle between the ➡RAF and the German *Luftwaffe* over southern England in summer 1940

It was this British victory that forced Hitler to abandon his plans for the invasion of England and so made ultimate Allied victory possible in World War II.

SEE ALSO: ➡Hurricane; ➡Spitfire

Battle of **Britain Day** *pr. name, hist.* September 15th

On this date in 1940, more German aircraft were downed by the ➡RAF than on any other day, and the Germans abandoned their invasion plans. Now it is the day set aside for annual commemoration of the battle.

Britannia *pr. name, hist., Lat.* (1) the Roman name for ➡Great Britain; (2) a female figure who is considered to be the personification of Britain

Britannia first appeared on a coin of the Roman Emperor Antoninus Pius during the 2nd. C., but then vanished again for well over one thousand years until she reappeared on the obverse ("tails") side of British copper coinage from 1665 until quite recently. Normally Britannia carries a trident and shield, and is helmeted and seated.

Britannia metal *comp. noun* an alloy of tin, antimony and copper

It is similar to pewter, yet sometimes is confused with silver.

the **Britannia Royal Naval College** *pr. name* a training college for ➡Royal Naval officer cadets

Located at ➡Dartmouth, ➡Devon.

After a initial period here, training continues at the ➡Royal Naval College, ➡Greenwich.

Britannia silver *comp. noun* 96 per cent pure silver

Britannic *adj.* ➡British

As, for example, in the formalism, ➡Her Britannic Majesty.

British *pr. name, hist.* the ➡Celtic language once spoken by the ancient inhabitants of the British Isles

This is the root from which modern ➡Welsh, ➡Cornish, ➡Manx, ➡Irish Gaelic and ➡Scots Gaelic are derived.

the **British** *pr. name* (1) the inhabitants of all parts of the ➡British Isles; (2) the citizens of the ➡United Kingdom; (3) formerly, all citizens of the ➡British Empire

(1) includes everyone in Ireland because that island is part of the geographical unit known as the ➡British Isles.

the **British Academy** *pr. name* a learned society founded in 1901

It is dedicated to promotion of the humanities.

British Airways *pr. name, hist.* an airline formed after World War I, which was merged with ➡Imperial Airways to form ➡BOAC in 1939

British Airways plc *pr. name* an airline formed by the merging of ➡BOAC and ➡BEA in 1971.

Originally government-owned, it was sold into the private sector in 1987 and is now one of the world's largest airlines.

the **British Association** *pr. name, abbr.* the ➡British Association for the Advancement of Science

the **British Association for the Advancement of Science** *pr. name* a society founded in 1831 in order to promotion knowledge and interest in science among the general population

the British Boxing Board of Control

the **British Boxing Board of Control** *pr. name* the organization regulating professional boxing in Britain

the **British Broadcasting Corporation** *pr. name* a public-service broadcasting organization
(See box below.)

the **British Coal Corporation** *pr. name* a government-owned company operating Britain's underground coal mines
Formerly known as the National Coal Board.

the **British Commonwealth of Nations** *pr. name, out.* a loose association of independent nations that formerly made up the ➠British Empire
Now known more simply as the ➠Commonwealth. South Africa, which was obliged to withdraw in 1961 because of its Apartheid policy, has now rejoined following the change to non-racial government.

the **British Constitution** *pr. name, hist.* a collection of customs, habits, conventions, statutes and legal precedents which taken together form the foundation of the British state
Britain is almost unique in having no written constitution. Nevertheless, the accumulated conventions and precedents appear to provide as secure a basis for the liberty of the ➠subject, the legitimacy of the state, and the rule of law as most nations have with words written upon sheets of paper, and better than most.

the **British Council** *pr. name* an organization charged with promoting British culture and the English language around the world
Established by ➠Royal Charter in 1934, it now has offices in just about every country in the world.

the **British disease** *idiom, hist.* an alternate name for the ➠English disease
SEE ALSO: ➠French disease.

the **British Empire** *pr. name, hist.* the United Kingdom together with all its colonies and overseas dominions
Really, there were two British Empires, but the first ended in 1776. The second, the new empire, the British Empire as it is now thought of, reached its maximum extent in the 1920s when it encompassed a quarter of the land surface of the Earth, and a quarter of the entire human race also. As such, it was the vastest political unit ever to have existed, before or since.
It was supplanted in the 1930's by the ➠British Commonwealth of Nations.

British Empire Medal *pr. name* a medal awarded for meritorious military service
Formerly the Medal of the Order of the ➠British Empire.

British English *pr. name* English as it is written and spoken by the people of the ➠United Kingdom
As distinct from the varieties normally used in the United States, Australia and many other places.

British Expeditionary Force *pr. name, hist.* a British army sent overseas on a specific mission
Especially the armies sent to France in 1914 and 1939.

the **British Film Commission** *pr. name* an organization established to encourage and support the British movie industry and the use of British locations, facilities, etc.

the **British Film Institute** *pr. name* an organization established to encourage the development of the art of the movie both in the cinema and on TV
Its library contains the world's largest collection of movie and TV materials.

British Gas plc *pr. name (TM)* Britain's largest natural gas company
Owned by the government from 1948, privatized in 1986.

the BBC

Originally established in 1923 as the British Broadcasting Company, the name changed to British Broadcasting Corporation in 1927, which it has retained ever since. The corporation had a virtual monopoly over British broadcasting until the establishment of ➠ITV in 1954.

The ➠BBC is a public corporation established by the government under a ➠Royal Charter dating back to 1927. It has complete freedom to develop its own policies and devise its own programming. The only political requirement placed upon it is that it should be balanced in the time it gives to different points of view on political topics, especially the views of the main political parties.

Really, World War II was the heyday of the BBC, when it was the only radio station broadcasting to the people of occupied Europe that was reliable, authoritative and truthful.

It does not generate any revenue by broadcast advertising but is financed by a license fee every household containing a television set is required by law to pay. Today, the BBC is responsible for two nationwide terrestrial TV channels plus five nationwide and many local radio stations within Britain It also has part-interests in some satellite TV channels transmitting to Britain and western Europe. Internationally, it operates the ➠World Service radio service and the World Service Television channel.

the **British Isles** *pr. name* an archipelago in the North Atlantic Ocean off the coast of northwestern Europe

It consists of two major islands, Great Britain and Ireland, together with a large number of much smaller ones.

Britishism *noun* a word or expression particularly associated with Britain

the **British Library** *pr. name* the national library

A copyright library, currently located within the ➠British Museum, but being relocated into a custom-made building at St Pancras, London.

the **British Lion** *pr. name* the animalistic representation of the British nation

The approximate British equivalent of the American Eagle.

the **British Lions** *pr. name* the national rugby team of the United Kingdom

the **British Medical Association** *pr. name* the national professional association of physicians

the **British Museum** *pr. name* one of the major museums of the world

Founded in 1753 in central London, its construction was financed from the profits of a lottery. The museum contains a vast collection of antiquities, including the ➠Elgin Marbles.

the **British Museum (Natural History)** *pr. name, hist.* the former name of the ➠Natural History Museum when it was still a department of the ➠British Museum

British Nuclear Fuels plc *pr. name* a large nuclear fuel reprocessing business

Its principal facility, called ➠THORP, is located on the coast of northwestern England, in Cumbria.

the **British Pharmacopoeia** *pr. name* a published listing of all the drugs and other medical products available in the United Kingdom

Prepared for use by physicians when prescribing for their patients. It specifies the standard that each product must attain though its shelf-life, and what that shelf-life is.

British Rail *pr. name (TM), abbr.* the popular name for Britain's national railroad system

An abbreviation of British Railways Board.
The name "BritRail" is unknown in Britain; using it is likely to generate blank stares among the locals.

British Railways Board *pr. name* a publicly owned corporation, responsible for operating ➠British Rail

British Sky Broadcasting plc *pr. name* a large multi-channel broadcasting organization

The principal purveyors of direct broadcast satellite television to the British public.

the **British Standards Institution** *pr. name* the equivalent of the American Standards Association

Established in 1901 to establish universal standards in the engineering industry but since extended to cover almost every field of commercial activity. The present name was adopted in 1931.

British Standard Time *pr. name, hist.* ➠British Summer Time extended through the whole year

This was introduced in 1968 in an attempt to bring British time more closely in line with that in Western Europe, but proved so unpopular that it was withdrawn in 1971.

British Steel plc *pr. name* Britain's largest steel company, which was government-owned from 1967 until privatized in 1988

British Subject *comp. noun, hist.* a citizen of the ➠British Empire

Now replaced by the status of ➠Commonwealth Citizen.

British Summer Time *pr. name* daylight saving time

One hour ahead of ➠GMT, this is the time to set watches to during the summer. ➠BST lasts from March until October.

British Telecom plc *pr. name* Britain's largest national telecommunications corporation

Originally the telephone system was a government monopoly operated by the ➠Post Office until ➠BT was established and shares sold to the public in the early 1980s.

the **British Tourist Authority** *pr. name* an agency responsible for overseeing and coordinating the tourist industry of Britain

the **British Union of Fascists** *pr. name, abbr., hist.* an far right-wing political party formed in the 1930s

It was founded and led by Sir Oswald Mosley in imitation of Mussolini's Fascists in Italy and the Nazis in Germany and is now long-defunct. Its full name was the "British Union of Fascists and National Socialists," and members were colloquially known as ➠Blackshirts.

British warm *idiom, arch., coll.* a short, thick overcoat once issued to troops by the army

Briton *pr. name* a British person

Brixton briefcase *idiom, sl.* a ghetto blaster

Brixton, in south London, has a large population of immigrants from the Caribbean and Africa.

broad *noun, East* a wide expanse of open fresh water

Broads are found in flat country, typically ➠East Anglia, where there are no natural impediments to prevent a river from becoming very wide.

Broad *pr. name, hist.* a nickname for the ➠Unite, a gold coin worth 20 ➠shillings

It became known by this name because of its size when first issued in 1604. The coin was also known as the ➠Jacobus.

broad arrow *comp. noun, arch.* a distinguishing mark traditionally applied to prison clothing and certain other government property

To aid in rapid identification.

broad bean *comp. noun* the horse bean

Its formal name is *vicia faba.*

Broadcasting House *pr. name* the headquarters building of the ➠BBC

Located in central London close to Oxford Circus, it was specially built for the corporation in 1932.

43

broadcloth *comp. noun* a twilled, densely textured worsted or woolen fabric, usually used to make coats and similar garments

Broadlands *pr. name, hist.* a Palladian mansion some eight miles to the north of ➡Southampton

Broadmoor *pr. name* the best known of Britain's ➡special hospitals
Located a few miles southwest of Windsor, in Berkshire.

the **Broads** *pr. name* the ➡Norfolk Broads

the **Broads Authority** *pr. name* a special statuary authority set up for the purpose of conserving and enhancing the ➡Norfolk Broads

broadsheet *noun* (1) a broadside, being a large paper sheet printed upon one side only; (2) a large-page format newspaper

{**broadways » broadwise**} *adv.* laterally or side-on

broch *noun, hist., Sc.* a prehistoric stone tower, found only in northern Scotland
Usually circular in shape, they are about 30 or 40 feet in diameter and some 30 or 40 feet tall when intact.

brock *noun, Gae., Ir.* badger

brogue *noun, Ir.* (1) a thick Irish accent; (2) a stout walking shoe

broken reed *idiom, coll.* an unreliable person

broker *noun* (1) an official appointed by a court to sell or value goods seized for the payment of a debt; (2) until the ➡Big Bang, a ➡broker-dealer

broker-dealer *comp. noun* a member of the stock exchange who buys and sells stock for clients
Since the ➡Big Bang.

brolly *noun, abbr., coll.* an umbrella

Bromley *pr. name* a ➡Greater London borough
Its current population, which is also included within the ➡London urban area total, is 280,000 (1991 Census).

Brooklands *pr. name, hist.* the world's first custom-built auto racing track
It opened in 1907 and is located in Surrey.

Brooks's *pr. name, hist.* a gentleman's club founded in London in 1764
Named after its first manager, its members have a reputation for indulging in heavy gambling. Now located, like so many other clubs, in ➡St James's.

brose *noun, Sc.* a form of porridge

brothel creepers *comp. noun, out., sl.* brothel stompers; thickly-soled suede shoes

brouhaha *noun* an uproar or commotion

the **brown** *noun* a large flock of game birds flying in a close group together

brown ale *comp. noun* a dark beer with a mild flavor

Brown Bess *pr. name, hist.* a nickname for a kind of flint-lock rifle issued to soldiers under the command of Wellington during the ➡Napoleonic Wars

browned off *idiom, sl.* fed up or very bored

brownie guide *pr. name* a junior ➡girl guide, up to the age of about 8 or 9

browning *noun* a kind of brown flour added to gravy to impart a brown coloring to it

brown job *comp. noun, sl.* a soldier
From the color of his uniform.

brown sauce *noun* a spicy sauce containing various fruits, spices, etc.
Sauce like this is often applied to meat dishes. The best-known brand is ➡HP sauce.

BRS *pr. name, abbr., hist.* British Road Services
A government-owned trucking company, broken up and sold in the 1980s.

Bruce *pr. name, hist.* the ➡Royal House of Scotland from 1306 until 1371
➡Robert I and ➡David II were of this house.

The **Bruce** *pr. name, hist.* ➡Robert I

Brum *pr. name, abbr., sl.* ➡Birmingham

brummagem *adj., coll.* cheap, counterfeit or fake
Derived from ➡Brummagen.

Brummagen *pr. name, hist., Mid.* ➡Birmingham

Brummie *pr. name, sl.* a native, citizen or inhabitant of ➡Birmingham

brumous *adj., arch.* foggy

Brycheiniog *pr. name, hist.* an ancient kingdom in south-central Wales
It is known to have been established by 700.

Brylcreem *pr. name (TM)* a hairdressing for men that was at its most popular and fashionable during World War II
It gave a shiny, sleek appearance to the hair.

the **Brylcreem Boys** *pr. name, coll.* a nickname for the fighter pilots of the ➡RAF who fought in the ➡Battle of Britain
Because of their appearance and the glamour of their role.

BSC *pr. name, abbr.* ➡British Steel Corporation plc

BSI *pr. name, abbr.* the ➡British Standards Institution

BSkyB *pr. name (TM), abbr.* ➡British Sky Broadcasting plc

the **B-Specials** *pr. name, hist.* a semi-military auxiliary police force or militia that formerly operated in ➡Northern Ireland
They were viewed as being anti-Catholic and certainly were composed almost entirely of Protestants; it was this perception led to their disbandment in the early 1970s.

BST *noun, abbr.* (1) ➡British Summer Time; (2) formerly, ➡British Standard Time

BT *pr. name (TM), abbr.* ➡British Telecom plc

BTA *pr. name, abbr.* ➡British Tourist Authority

bubble and squeak *idiom, coll.* meat, vegetables and potatoes chopped up and then fried together

bubble car *comp. noun, arch.* a very small automobile which enclosed the occupants within a transparent bubble-like dome
Briefly popular during the 1950s, most were intended for use by the driver alone or at most driver plus one passenger. The best-known brand were made in Germany by Messerschmidt, who a few years earlier had been best known as manufacturers of military aircraft for the *Luftwaffe*, whose pilots sat in similar transparent bubble-like domes.

bucket shop *comp. noun, coll.* (1) a location where informal and speculative share dealing is conducted; (2) an agency selling heavily discounted airline tickets

Buckfast Abbey *pr. name, hist.* a reconstructed ancient ➡abbey in ➡Devon
It was abandoned as a ruin in the 16th C., but rebuilt in the early years of the 20th C. by some Benedictine monks who personally performed the work, including all the hard physical labor.

Buck House *pr. name, abbr., coll.* ➡Buckingham Palace

Buckingham Palace *pr. name* the official London residence of the sovereign since ➡Victoria came to the throne in 1837
Built in 1705 as the London residence of the Duke of Buckingham, in 1762 it was purchased by ➡George III, who lived there for the rest of his life. It was then left to languish until ➡Victoria chose it as her principal London residence.

Buckinghamshire *pr. name* a county in southern England, immediately to the northwest of London
The county seat is ➡Aylesbury and the current population is 620,000 (1991 Census).

Bucks. *pr. name, abbr.* ➡Buckinghamshire

Buck's fizz *comp. noun* a cocktail consisting of orange juice and champagne
It was first concocted and drunk at Buck's Club in London.

buckshee [A] *adj. adv., sl.* extra or free
[B] *noun, sl.* a bribe

Buddy *pr. name, Sc.* a native, citizen or inhabitant of ➡Paisley, near Glasgow in Scotland

budgerigar *noun* a small green Australian parrot
Formally named *melopsittacus undulatus*, it is a common pet.

the **Budget** *pr. name* the government's annual forecast of revenue and expenditure over the coming year, made public in a speech by the ➡Chancellor of the Exchequor to ➡Parliament
Formerly this was a statement of the government's revenue plans only, made in March, but since 1993 has included spending plans as well and is made in November.

budgie *noun, abbr., coll.* a ➡budgerigar

Buellt *pr. name, hist.* an ancient Welsh kingdom
Known to have been established by 700.

buffer [A] *noun* a shock absorber intended to prevent or reduce impact damage to railroad vehicles
Usually it takes the form of a pair of pneumatic or otherwise sprung devices placed at the front and the rear of railroad vehicles and at the end of railroad tracks.
[B] *noun, abbr., derog., sl.* an ➡old buffer

buffet *noun* a convenience restaurant where light meals, snacks and drinks may be purchased
Often found in such places as airports or railroad terminals

buffet car *comp. noun* a railroad car where snacks and drinks may be purchased

the **Buffs** *pr. name* the 3rd Regiment of ➡Foot
A unit of the British Army descended from a regiment raised in 1572 to fight in Holland, who wore a buff uniform.

bug *noun, arch., sl.* a schoolboy

bugg *adj., East* self-satisfied

bugger *noun, sl., taboo* a very serious or difficult problem or predicament

bugger all *comp. noun, sl., taboo* absolutely nothing

bugger off *imper., sl., taboo* go away, get lost

bugger up *verb, sl., taboo* to spoil or ruin

Buckingham Palace

buggin's turn *comp. noun, coll.* selection by rote rather than merit

bugladders *noun, Sc., sl.* side-whiskers or sideburns

bugs bunny *idiom, rh. sl.* money

builder's merchant *comp. noun* a supplier of lumber, bricks and so forth, to builders

building society *comp. noun* a savings and loan bank
The first was established in 1775.

bulb bowl *comp. noun* a flower bulb planting bowl

bulge the onionbag *idiom. verb. phr.* to score a goal during a game of soccer

bulimia nervosa *comp. noun* bulimarexia, or pathological overeating with induced vomiting

bull [A] *noun, abbr., coll.* the bull's-eye of a target
[B] *noun, sl.* otherwise pointless routine tasks imposed upon troops supposedly as a means of imposing military discipline

bull and cow *idiom, rh. sl.* a row; or argument

the **Bulldog Breed** *pr. name, coll.* the British, as seen by the British

bullock *verb, rh. sl.* to pawn
Derivation: pawn > horn > bullock's horn > bullock.

bull's-eye *comp. noun, coll.* a hard, large, spherical, peppermint-flavored candy

Bull Terrier *pr. name, hist.* a powerful crossbred of terrier and bulldog

bull trout *comp. noun* a salmon trout

bully beef *comp. noun* ➡corned beef

bulrush *noun* ➡reed-mace

bum *noun, sl., taboo* the buttocks

bum bag *comp. noun, sl.* a fanny pack
A small bag attached by a belt around the waist.

bum-bailiff *comp. noun, hist.* a court official employed to effect arrests ordered by the court

bumbledom *noun, coll.* pompous or officious rules or regulations, or the application of them
Derived from an officious character called "Bumble," who was a ➡beadle in Dickens's novel *Oliver Twist*.

bum boy *comp. noun, derog., sl.* a male homosexual

{**bumf » bumph**} *noun, sl.* (1) toilet paper; (2) trashy literature

bumfle *verb, Sc.* to scrunch, crease or crumple up

bum-freezer *comp. noun, sl.* a short coat or jacket

bummaree *noun* a porter at ➡Smithfield

bumper *noun* a ➡bouncer, in ➡cricket

bunce *noun, coll.* a windfall or unexpected profit

bun fight *idiom, coll.* a tea party

bung *verb, sl.* (1) to bribe or tip; (2) to fling or throw

bungaloid *adj., coll., derog.* like a bungalow

Bungalow Bill *idiom, derog., sl.* a slow-witted man
Because there is nothing much going on upstairs.

bunk off *verb, sl.* to play hooky from school

Bunter *noun, derog., sl.* any grossly overweight youth
Originally a fictional schoolboy, Billy Bunter, who appeared in a large number of stories by Frank Richards written between 1910 and the outbreak of World War II.

BUPA *pr. name (TM), abbr.* the British United Providence Association
The largest of a number of associations providing private medical health insurance. BUPA also operates its own chain of hospitals across the country.

bureau *noun* a slant-topped writing desk with drawers

burette *spell.* buret

burgage *noun, hist.* land rented from a feudal lord or from a town upon an annual tenure
Rent might be in form of money but was more commonly paid in the form of labor or military service to the landlord. The arrangement was common during the 15th C.

burgess *noun, hist.* (1) a full citizen of a town or city; (2) an ➡MP representing Oxford or Cambridge Universities; (3) the original name for an ➡MP representing an English ➡borough
(2) Until shortly after World War II, ➡MPs were returned by graduates of the ➡Ancient Universities, who were thus uniquely entitled to two votes as they also could, just like everyone else, vote in the election of the local MP for the ➡constituency where they lived.
On (3): In medieval times, the representatives of counties (or ➡shires) in the ➡Commons were called ➡knights, while the representatives of towns were called burgesses.

burgh *noun, Sc.* (1) a town incorporated by royal charter; (2) originally, any fortified town
This is most common spelling in Scotland and some parts of England, but in most of England the spelling is ➡borough.

Burghley House *pr. name, hist.* an ➡Elizabethan mansion about ten miles north of ➡Peterborough

burke *verb, arch., rh. sl.* to suppress or hush up
Possibly derived from Burke and Hare, two Edinburgh murderers who smothered their victims in order to sell their bodies for dissection by medical students.

Burke's *pr. name, abbr.* a directory of the British aristocracy published annually since 1826
The full title is *Burke's Peerage, Baronetage and Knightage*.

Burlington House *pr. name* a large 17th C. central London building rebuilt and extended in the Palladian style during the 18th C.
The building was again greatly extended around 1870 after the government purchased it, and is now the location of the ➡Royal Academy's annual summer exhibition.

burn *noun, Sc.* a small stream or creek

Burnham Scale *pr. name* the salary scale for teachers in publicly owned schools

burnous *spell.* burnoose

A cloak worn by an Arab.

Robert Burns

Burns Supper *pr. name, Sc.* a formal annual dinner of traditional Scottish fare

It is held each January 25th, the birthday of Robert Burns, Scotland's national poet, who lived from 1759 to 1796. The event celebrates his life and poetry and philosophy and Scottishness and in general, his humanity. The principal feature of the meal is a main dish consisting of ➝haggis, ➝neeps and ➝tatties. The haggis is ceremonially brought into the room held high on a platter, preceded by a piper playing the ➝bagpipes. The master of ceremonies recites Burns's poem ➝*Address to a Haggis* before he formally cuts it open and serves portions to the assembled company.

Other high points of the evening are the "Address to the ➝Lassies," a celebration of Burns's chief interest, and the toast—drunk in ➝Scotch whiskey, of course—to the memory of Burns himself, called the ➝Immortal Memory.

burnt *past tense* burned

Of the verb "to burn".

buroo *noun, Sc., sl.* an unemployment office

Derived from "bureau".

burr *noun* a roughly trilling way of pronouncing the letter "r" which is considered characteristic of the Scottish accent

the **Burrell Collection** *pr. name* an extensive and important collection of paintings, sculpture and other objects of great artistic significance

It is housed in a specially constructed museum in Pollok Park, ➝Glasgow. The collection was gathered by Sir William Burrell and presented to the City of Glasgow in 1944.

bursary *noun* a scholarship paid to a student

Bury St Edmonds *pr. name, hist.* an ancient and historic town in ➝Suffolk

It was a ➝Saxon settlement that became the seat of the kings of ➝East Anglia. Today the population is some 30,000 (1991 estimate).

busby *noun* a tall, fur-covered soldier's hat or helmet now worn only on ceremonial occassions

buses *spell.* busses

bushel *noun, rh. sl.* the throat

Derivation: throat > neck > peck > bushel and peck > bushel.

Bush House *pr. name* the central London headquarters of the ➝BBC's ➝World Service

The building is named for Irvin T. Bush, an American who built it in 1935 as a business venture which proved unsuccessful; it was purchased by the BBC in 1940.

busker *noun* a street actor or musician

bus lane *comp. noun* a highway traffic lane reserved for use by buses and taxis only

They should always be clearly marked on the road surface and with roadside notices. It is against the law to drive in these lanes in any but permitted vehicles.

busman *noun* a male bus driver

bus station *comp. noun, pref.* a bus terminal

busy *noun, sl.* a detective

Busy Lizzie *pr. name* a house plant which is somewhat similar to jewelweed

Its formal name is *impatiens wallerianna.*

but [A] *adv., prep., Sc.* outer

[B] *exclam., Ir., Sc., sl.* an emphasizer sometimes added at the end of a statement

[C] *noun, Sc.* the outer room of a ➝but and ben

but and ben *comp. noun, Sc.* a two-roomed cottage

butchers *noun, rh. sl.* a look or glance

Derivation: look > hook > butcher's hook > butchers. Most often used in the phrase, "take a butchers" = "take a look."

butchery *noun, out.* a slaughterhouse

Bute *pr. name, hist.* a former Scottish county

Now part of the ➝Strathclyde region.

the Isle of **Bute** *pr. name* an island in the Firth of ➝Clyde, on the western coast of Scotland

Butlins' *pr. name (TM)* a company operating a chain of mass-market ➝holiday camps

The first opened at Skegness in ➝Lincolnshire in 1936.

butter bean *comp. noun* a lima bean

butterie *noun, Sc.* a sweet breakfast bun somewhat resembling a croissant

Normally found only in the ➝Aberdeen area.

butter muslin *comp. noun* a particularly fine kind of cheesecloth, orginally used to wrap butter

butter Osborne *comp. noun* a rich and sweet but otherwise plain cookie

buttery *noun, out.* a storage room in a college or university where provisions are kept for disbursement to staff and students

button-backed chair *comp. noun* button-tufted chair

buttonhole *noun* a boutonniere or corsage

buttons *noun, coll., out.* a page boy dressed in ➝livery

button-stick *comp. noun, arch.* a device used to protect the other parts of a uniform while its buttons are being polished

button-through dress

button-through dress *comp. noun* a dress that has buttons down its entire front

butty [A] *noun, arch.* (1) a barge which is towed by another; (2) a fellow worker; (3) a middleman between mine owners and miners

[B] *noun, coll., North* a sandwich made using a buttered bread roll rather than two slices of bread

butty-gang *comp. noun, arch.* a group of men working together on a job and sharing the money earned in equal proportions between them

Buxton *pr. name, hist.* an ancient town in the heart of ➡Derbyshire's ➡Peak District ➡National Park
The Romans established a spa here, and it was fashionable as one again int he 18th C. The current population is about 20,000 (1991 estimate).

buzz bomb *comp. noun, sl. hist.* a ➡V-1
World War II slang.

BWI *pr. name, abbr., hist.* the British ➡West Indies
Those parts of the Caribbean which were or remain British.

by a long chalk *idiom, coll.* by a long way

by a short head *idiom* (1) in a horse race, leading by a very small margin; (2) more generally, very slightly ahead or better

(1) refers to the length of a horse's head.

by-blow *comp. noun, coll.* (1) a blow at something which is not the main or intended target; (2) an illegitimate child

bye-election *noun* (1) a special election held in a single ➡constituency to elect an ➡MP to fill a vacancy occurring between ➡general elections; (2) a similar election to fill a local government elective office between regular election dates

bye *noun* a run taken when a pitched ➡cricket ball was not touched by either batsman or bat
SEE ALSO: ➡extra.

by gum *exclam., sl.* a euphemistic variety of "by God"

by jove *exclam., sl.* a euphemism for "by Jupiter"

byke *noun, Sc.* (1) a beehive or wasps' nest; (2) a bees or wasp swarm; (3) a swarming crowd of people

{by » bye}-law *comp. noun* a local or municipal ordinance

byre *noun* a cow barn
SEE ALSO: ➡cowshed.

by return *comp. noun, abbr., coll.* by return mail

byword *noun* someone or something often referred to as a well-known example

C. *pr. name, abbr., hist.* a ➡Command Paper from 1870 to 1899

CA [A] *noun, abbr., Sc.* a ➡Chartered Accountant
[B] *pr. name, abbr.* the Consumer's Association
A private voluntary group promoting the interests of consumers by monitoring the price, quality and reliability of retail products and services.

ca' *verb, abbr., Sc.* (1) to drive cattle or other animals; (2) to make a request
An abbreviation of "call".

CAA *pr. name, abbr.* the Civil Aviation Authority
The British equivalent of the FAA.

CAB *noun, abbr.* the ➡Citizens' Advice Bureau

cabbage *noun, derog., sl.* someone who is inactive, disinterested or apathetic

caber *noun, Sc.* a long tree trunk or similarly dimensioned heavy pole

cabinet *noun* a meeting of the ➡Cabinet

the **Cabinet** *pr. name* the central executive committee of the government that collectively determines national policy
Members are selected by the ➡Prime Minister, who chairs cabinet meetings and has the power to require the resignation of any individual member at any time. Yet the other members of the Cabinet, when acting in sufficient numbers together, may oblige the Prime Minister to be the one who resigns; in other words, the holder of that office is truly *primus inter pares* = "the first among equals," who, unlike the President of the United States, remains dependent for authority upon the goodwill of the Cabinet as a whole and can never govern without their continuing acquiescence.
The word means "small room" in French and originally consisted of a select group of senior ➡privy councilors who met with the monarch in such a room.

cabinet minister *comp. noun* a senior minister who is a member of the ➡Cabinet

the **Cabinet Office** *pr. name* the Civil Service department or office of the ➡Prime Minister
This office handles matters that relate directly to ➡Cabinet business, controls the Prime Minister's Office and supervises the management and recruitment activities of the Civil Service as a whole, as well as various other offices and agencies of the government.

cabinet photograph *comp. noun, arch.* a small photograph

{cabinet » chancellor's} pudding *comp. noun* a steamed dessert containing dried fruit

the **Cabinet War Rooms** *pr. name, hist.* the offices deep under the ➡Admiralty building in ➡Whitehall from which Winston Churchill conducted the government of Britain during the ➡Battle of Britain and the ➡Blitz
They have been preserved exactly in the condition that they were in during 1941, and are open to the public as a museum. Part of the ➡Imperial War Museum.

Cable and Wireless plc *pr. name (TM)* an international telecommunications conglomerate headquartered in London

caboose *noun* a cabin located upon the deck of a ship and used as a kitchen or galley

ca'canny *imper., Sc.* (1) go carefully; (2) be economical

cack-handed *adj., coll.* (1) left-handed; (2) clumsy or incompetent

Cadbury Schweppes plc *pr. name (TM)* a large confectionery and soft drinks manufacturer

cadcraw *noun, East* a carrion crow

caddie *noun, Sc.* (1) an odd-job man; (2) an ill-dressed youth

cadge *verb, sl.* to obtain by begging

cadogan *noun, out.* a styling for men's hair that involves tying it back with a ribbon
The name derives from the 1st Earl of Cadogan. The style was popular in the later years of the 18th C.

{caecal » caecum} *spell.* {cecal » cecum}
The blind pouch where the small and large intestines join.

Caerdydd *pr. name, Wal.* the ➡Welsh language name for ➡Cardiff

Caerlaverock Castle *pr. name, hist.* a 13th C. castle about ten miles to the south of ➡Dumfries, upon the northern shores of the ➡Solway Firth
It has an unusual triangular layout, and is surrounded by a wide moat. Ravaged by fire and abandoned in 1640 soon after it had fallen to the ➡Covenanters following a 13-week siege, it has remained a ruin ever since.

49

Caerleon *pr. name, hist.* traditionally considered to be one of the residences of ➡Arthur

Called *Isca Silurum* by the Romans, it is located about three miles northeast of Newport in south Wales. There is no convincing evidence of any connection with ➡Arthur.

Caernarfon Castle

Caernarfon *pr. name* a northern Welsh town, the administrative center of ➡Gwynedd

Inhabited since the Romans built their fort of *Siegontium* here, its well-known 13th C. castle is the location chosen for the investitures of the ➡Prince of Wales. The current population is 11,000 (1991 estimate).

Caernarvonshire *pr. name, hist.* a former Welsh County, now part of ➡Gwynedd

Caerphilly *pr. name, hist.* (1) a town in southern Wales, the site of a fortress since Roman times; (2) a mild white cheese, originating from (1)

Caerphilly's present castle, which was built in the 13th C., is the largest in Britain after ➡Windsor. The current population of the town is 40,000 (1991 estimate).

caesarean section *spell.* cesarean section

caesium *spell.* cesium

café *noun, pref.* a snack bar or coffee shop

caff *noun, abbr., sl.* a ➡café

caggy *adj., arch.* bad-tempered

caird *noun, Sc.* a gypsy or vagrant

cairngorm *noun, Gae.* a semi-precious stone

First found in the ➡Cairngorm mountains in Scotland.

the **Cairngorms** *pr. name* the largest British mountain range, located in north-central Scotland

A large area of magnificently rugged scenery, popular for climbing, walking and winter sports.

Cairn Terrier *pr. name* a breed of small fawn-colored, shaggy-coated terriers

Originally used for fox hunting in hilly country in Scotland.

Caithness *pr. name, hist.* a former Scottish county

Now part of the ➡Highland region.

Caius College *pr. name, abbr.* the popular abbreviated name for ➡Gonville and Caius College, ➡Cambridge University

cake-hole *comp. noun, sl.* the mouth

Calcutta Cup *pr. name* an annual trophy played for by the national rugby teams of England and Scotland

Calder Hall *pr. name, hist.* the world's first nuclear reactor to have generated electricity that was sold commercially, in 1956

Now part of the ➡Sellafield nuclear complex on the ➡Cumbrian coast in northwestern England, this reactor originally combined power generation with the production of weapons-grade plutonium. *SEE ALSO:* ➡THORP.

cale *noun, Ir.* ➡kail

Caledonia *pr. name, hist.* (1) the Roman name for ➡Scotland; (2) an ancient kingdom in northern and eastern Scotland

(1) is sometimes still employed as a grandiose alternative to "Scotland." (2) was the independent kingdom of the ➡Picts, already well established when the Romans invaded Britain in the 1st C.; it continued its independent existence until annexed by ➡Dalriada to form ➡Alba in 843.

Caledonian *adj., Lat.* ➡Scottish

the **Caledonian Canal** *pr. name* the navigable waterway that connects the western and eastern coasts of northern Scotland

It consists of a series of short stretches of canal linking together navigable lakes, including Loch ➡Ness, that lie along the length of the ➡Great Glen, enabling navigation from the Atlantic Ocean to the ➡North Sea without risking the dangerous passage around the far north of Scotland.

the **Caledonian Market** *pr. name* a Friday morning antiques market held in Bermondsey Street, in the ➡East End of London

calibre *spell.* caliber

calico *noun* plain cotton cloth, usually white

call *verb* (1) to visit briefly; (2) to disallow a pitched ➡cricket ball

{**callan » calland**} *noun, Sc.* a boy or young man

call box *noun* a public telephone booth

caller *adj., Sc.* cool, fresh or healthy

calliper *spell.* caliper

call to the bar *phr. verb, coll.* to become a ➡barrister

call up *noun, coll.* conscription, a military draft

call within the bar *phr. verb, coll.* to become a ➡{King's » Queen's} Council

Calor gas *pr. name (TM)* a liquefied butane gas that is supplied and stored in pressurized containers suitable for use as a domestic supply

Cam and Isis *pr. name, coll.* the Universities of ➡Cambridge and ➡Oxford taken together

A somewhat poetic rendition, constructed from the names of the rivers they stand upon. *SEE ALSO:* ➡Oxbridge, ➡Camford.

Cambria *noun, hist., Lat.* an ancient name for ➡Wales

This is the Latin *Cambria* which in turn is believed to have been derived from the Welsh ➡*Cymru* = "Wales."

Cambrian *adj., Lat.* ➡Welsh

Cambridge *pr. name* a city which is the administrative center of ➡Cambridgeshire

Cambridge began as an ➡Anglo-Saxon settlement on the Cam river, and a ➡Norman castle was built there in 1068. However it is the ancient and highly prestigious ➡Cambridge University which is its defining feature. Cambridge was incorporated as a city in 1207 and the current population is 100,000 (1988 estimate).

Cambridgeshire *pr. name* a county in the ➡East Anglian region of England, to the north of London

The former counties of ➡Huntingdonshire and Peterborough on the one hand, and ➡Cambridgeshire and the Isle of Ely on the other, which were amalgamated to create Cambridgeshire in 1974. The county seat is ➡Cambridge and the current population is 640,000 (1991 Census).

Cambridgeshire and the Isle of Ely *pr. name, hist.* a former English county

Since 1974 part of ➡Cambridgeshire.

Cambridge University *pr. name* the second-oldest and, together with ➡Oxford, one of the two most venerable universities of the English-speaking world

The university itself was founded in 1209, well before ➡Peterhouse, the most ancient of its colleges that have survived to the present day, was founded in 1284.

Cambs. *pr. name, abbr.* ➡Cambridgeshire

Camden *pr. name* a ➡Greater London borough

Its current population, which is also included within the ➡London urban area total, is 170,000 (1991 Census).

Camelot *pr. name, hist.* the fabled spot where ➡Arthur held his court

And, supposedly, where the Knights of the ➡Round Table held their meetings. The location, or even the certain existence, of Camelot has never been established, but it's believed to be somewhere in southwestern England.

Camford *noun, coll.* a alternate combined name to the better-known ➡Oxbridge for ➡Oxford and ➡Cambridge

SEE ALSO: ➡Cam and Isis; ➡Oxbridge.

camiknickers *noun* a woman's combined bodice-and-panty undergarment

the **Campaign for Real Ale** *pr. name* a voluntary organization that aids, encourages and agitates in favor of the brewing of beer in the traditional manner and its sale in traditional pubs.

Founded by four friends in 1971, it now has many thousands of members and is a very effective pressure group for the preservation of traditional ways of producing and serving beer. Members support the proposition that the availability of traditional—or real—ale is under threat from beer in bottles and cans made by modern chemical processes.

camp bed *noun* a lightweight portable cot

camping {ground » pitch} *comp. noun* a campground

Campion Hall *pr. name* a hall of ➡Oxford University founded in 1896

CAMRA *pr. name, abbr.* the ➡Campaign for Real Ale

canacre *noun, Ir.* the practice of subletting small parcels of land for the purpose of cultivation

Canary Wharf *pr. name* a major prestige office development in London's ➡Docklands area to the east of the ➡City

cancer stick *comp. noun, sl.* a cigarette

candelabra *spell.* {candelabrums » candelabras}

The plural of {candelabrum » candelabra}.

candidature *noun* candidacy

{Candlemas » Canlemas} *pr. name* a Scottish ➡term-day or ➡quarter-day

Now Ferbruary 28, formerly February 2

candour *spell.* candor

candyfloss *comp. noun* cotton candy

canna *verb aux., Sc.* cannot

cannon [A] *noun* in the game of billiards, a carom

[B] *verb, coll.* to collide

canny [A] *adj., North, Sc.* (1) kind or gentle; (2) skillful; (3) cheerful or pleasant

[B] *adj., Sc.* (1) steady, cautious or prudent; (2) frugal; (3) comfortable; (4) fortunate

canonical hours *comp. noun* the hours, which last from 8 a.m. to 6 p.m., during which it is legal to get married in England

cant *noun* the specialized language or jargon of a particular group, class or profession.

Originally it was the secret language of 16th C. criimals.

Cantab *noun, abbr., Lat.* ➡Cambridge University

From the Latin *Cantabrigiensis* = "Cambridge".

Cantabrigian *pr. name* (1) a citizen or resident of ➡Cambridge; (2) a student or graduate of ➡Cambridge University

From the Latin *Cantabrigiensis* = "Cambridge".

canteen [A] *noun* a cafeteria for the staff or employees of an institution

Such as colleges, museums, hospitals, offices or factories.

[B] *noun, abbr.* a ➡canteen of cutlery

canteen of cutlery *comp. noun* a case or chest of flatware or silverware

Canterbury *pr. name, hist.* a city in Kent

An ancient walled city, incorporated in 1448. Canterbury is best known for its 11th C. cathedral, which was the scene of the murder of St Thomas à Becket, ➡Archbishop of Canterbury, in 1170. Today the population of the city is some 125,000 (1988 estimate).

canting arms *comp. noun* a ➡coat of arms that makes an allusion or pun upon the bearer's name

cantrail *noun* a wooden joist supporting the roof of a railroad car

cantrip *noun, Sc.* (1) a magic spell or trick; (2) mischievous behavior

can't say boo to a goose *idiom, coll.* timid or shy

can't say fairer *idiom, coll.* as reasonable as possible

Canute *pr. name, hist.* the popular name for ➡Cnut

canvass *verb* to propose a scheme or plan

CAP *pr. name, abbr.* ➡Common Agricultural Policy

cap [A] *noun* a ➡sporting cap

[B] *verb* (1) to set a maximum level for a tax or charge; (2) to award a ➡sporting cap

(1) is sometimes imposed by the national government upon local administrations considered to be overspending.

[C] *verb, Sc.* to confer a university degree

Cape of Good Hope *idiom, rh. sl.* soap

Capital Transfer Tax *pr. name, hist.* a tax on the payment of large gifts, construed as the transfer of capital from one person to another

Introduced in 1975 to replace ➡Death Duty, then itself replaced with ➡Inheritance Tax in 1986.

capon *noun, arch.* a love letter

capsicum *noun* bell pepper

captain general *comp. noun* an honorary officer

Usually of an artillery regiment.

Captain of the Fleet *pr. name* a naval staff officer responsible for the maintenance of the fleet

carat *spell.* karat

caravan *noun* a mobile or trailer home

caravanner *noun* someone living in a ➡caravan

caravan park *comp. noun* a trailer park or camp

car boot sale *comp. noun, coll.* a sale, usually at the weekend or a public holiday, of used or home-made goods, originally from the trunk of a car

car breaker *comp. noun* an auto wrecker

{**carburetted » carburetter**} *spell.* {carbureted » carburetor}

{**carburetting » carburettor**} *spell.* {carbureting » carburetor}

carcase *spell., out.* carcass

Cardiff *pr. name* the capital city of Wales

Located in ➡South Glamorgan, it was incorporated as a city in 1608 and the current population, including suburbs, is 290,000 (1991 estimate).

Cardiff Arms Park *pr. name* a large international rugby stadium in ➡Cardiff

cardigan *noun* a knitted woolen jacket

Supposedly devised for the 7th Earl of Cardigan in the 1860s.

Cardigan *pr. name, hist.* a former Welsh County, now part of ➡Dyfed

cardphone *noun* a public phone that accepts payment by credit card rather than cash

card-punch *comp. noun* a key punch

cards *noun, sl.* an employee's documents which are normally held by the employer

care *noun, abbr.* child care

Usually by a local government agency or charity.

caretaker *noun* a janitor

However, in Scotland the American word is usual.

carfax *noun* a junction of four highways

car hire *comp. noun* car rental

Carisbrooke Castle *pr. name, hist.* a Norman castle built upon the site of a Roman fortress on the Isle of ➡Wight

Here ➡Charles II was imprisoned for almost a year before being taken to London for his trial and eventual execution.

Carlisle *pr. name* the city which is the administrative center of ➡Cumbria

Founded as *Luguvalium* by the Romans in the 1st C. It was incorporated as a city in 1158 and the current population is 100,000 (1988 estimate).

Carlow *pr. name* a county in the ➡Irish Republic

County Carlow in the ancient province of Leinster.

Carlton Club *pr. name, hist.* a leading ➡Conservative club in ➡St James's, London

Founded in 1832 by ➡Tory opponents of the ➡Great Reform Act of the same year. Originally it was located in Carlton House Terrace, hence the name.

Carlton TV *pr. name* a local commercial TV company headquartered in London, it is part of the ➡ITV network

Carmarthen *pr. name, hist.* a former Welsh County, now part of ➡Dyfed

Carnaby Street *pr. name, hist.* a street in west-central London that became an international center for teenage fashions during the 1960s

Carnoustie *pr. name* a golf course near ➠Dundee, on the eastern coast of Scotland

carny *verb, arch.* to coax

Carolean *adj., hist., Lat.* pertaining to the reigns of ➠Charles I and II

car park *comp. noun* a parking lot

carriage *noun* a railroad passenger car

carriage paid *idiom* prepaid transportation costs

carriageway *noun* (1) a highway traffic lane; (2) a highway intended for use by vehicular traffic

Carrickfergus *pr. name* a district in ➠Northern Ireland, in what used to be County ➠Antrim
The current population is 30,000 (1990 estimate).

carrier bag *comp. noun* a grocery or shopping bag

carry-cot *comp. noun* a baby's portable crib

carry-on *comp. noun, sl.* (1) a love affair; (2) dubious behavior; (3) a confused or excited environment

carry one's bat *idiom. phr. verb* to be ➠not out at the end of a ➠cricket inning

carry the can *idiom. phr. verb* to take the blame

carse *noun, Sc.* fertile land on a river's floodplain

cartridge paper *comp. noun* thick and good-quality drawing paper

carver *noun* a dining-chair with arms
It is intended to be used by the person who carves the meat at the table. This chair should not be confused with the different "Carver chair," named after its reputed inventor John Carver, first governor of the Plymouth Colony.

carve up *verb, sl.* (1) to ruin someone's chances; (2) to divide something into portions

cash desk *comp. noun* where the cash register is located in a store and where purchases are paid for

cash {dispenser » point} *comp. noun* an ➠automated teller machine

cash up *verb* to add up and balance cash at the end of a trading period

cast ill upon *phr. verb, Sc.* to bewitch or curse

Castle Coole *pr. name, hist.* a great house built in the 1790s near ➠Enniskillen in ➠Northern Ireland
Not really a castle at all in the normal sense, but a fine example of neoclassical domestic architecture.

Castle Howard *pr. name, hist.* an especially grand 18th C. stately home located about 15 miles from ➠York in North Yorkshire
Not really a castle at all in the normal sense but a fine example of the baroque style of domestic architecture.

Castlereagh *pr. name* a district in ➠Northern Ireland, in what used to be County ➠Down
The current population is 60,000 (1990 estimate).

Castle Rock *pr. name, hist.* the huge and ancient volcanic plug in the center of ➠Edinburgh which ➠Edinburgh Castle has been built upon

castor sugar *comp. noun* finely granulated white sugar

casualty *noun, abbr., coll.* a ➠casualty department

casualty department *comp. noun* a hospital emergency room

casualty ward *comp. noun* an emergency ward

casual work *comp. noun* temporary employment

cat *noun* the peg used in a game of tipcat

CAT *noun, abbr., out.* College of Advanced Technology
A college providing degree-level courses in science and technology. Most have now been re-classified as universities.

the **cat** *noun, abbr., sl.* a ➠cat-o'-nine-tails

{catalogue » catalogued » cataloguing} *spell.* {catalog » cataloged » cataloging}

{catalyse » catalyser} *spell.* {catalyze » catalyzer}

catapult *noun* a slingshot

catch a cold *verb, sl.* to catch gonorrhea
Military slang.

catch and bowl *phr. verb* in ➠cricket, to be ➠caught out by the ➠bowler

catch at the wicket *phr. verb* in ➠cricket, to be ➠caught out by the ➠wicket keeper

catchment area *comp. noun, coll.* the area providing the rainfall flowing into a river or river system

catch out *verb* to remove a ➠cricket ➠batsman from play by catching a ball he has batted before it reaches the ground

catch pit *comp. noun* a catch basin
A pit dug on a drain line to capture grit, preventing blockages.

catch points *comp. noun* a safety mechanism located on railroad uphill grades
They provide emergency braking for runaway cars. Rails are cut in such a way that an unhitched car running back will become harmlessly derailed.

catch the Speaker's eye *idiom. phr. verb* to be called to speak in the ➠House of Commons
To speak in the ➠Chamber, an ➠MP must be invited to do so by the ➠Speaker of the ➠House.

catch with one's trousers down *idiom. phr. verb* to catch with one's pants down

cateran *noun, Sc.* a Highland rogue or marauder

cater-cornered *adj.* {cater » catty » kitty} -cornered; placed or located diagonally

catering pack *comp. noun* large packages of food

As purchased by hotels, hospitals, etc.

caterpillar penstock *comp. noun* a caterpillar gate; a large steel gate controlling the flow of water through a penstock

cathedral school *comp. noun* a school which is attached to a cathedral

Traditionally, its students sing in the cathedral's choir.

Catherine Howard *pr. name, hist.* the fifth wife of ➡Henry VIII

Following the annulment of his unsuccessful marriage to ➡Anne of Cleves, the king married Catherine within weeks. It was not to last. In less than a year he learned that she had had lovers before their marriage and she rapidly found herself headed for the ➡Tower of London and an appointment with the axman.

Catherine of Aragon *pr. name, hist.* the first wife of ➡Henry VIII and the mother of ➡Mary I

The widow of his elder brother Arthur, Henry married her for reasons of state. Nonetheless, the marriage appears to have been quite happy for some considerable time. However, as Henry became increasingly obsessed with the need for the male heir that it seemed Catherine could not provide, he became resolved to end the marriage.

It was because the Pope would not grant a divorce that he broke with Rome, so creating the Anglican ➡Church of England and beginning the Reformation there.

Catherine Parr *pr. name, hist.* the sixth and last wife of ➡Henry VIII

Twice a widow before her marriage to the king, she provided the stable environment that he and his children from three of his previous wives needed in his last few years. After the king's death she married again for her fourth time.

catherine wheel *comp. noun* a pinwheel firework

cat-o'-nine-tails *comp. noun, hist.* a whip made of rope and possessing nine lashes

Each of the nine lashes was knotted to add to the effectiveness of the device. Once used to administer punishment floggings upon both civilian and military wrongdoers, it continued to be used in the British army and Royal Navy until well into the 19th C. Although its use was not formally abolished as a punishment for civilians until just after World War II, it had fallen into disuse very much earlier than that.

Cat's-eyes *pr. name (TM), coll.* reflector studs set in a highway to aid traffic direction, especially at night

cat's mother *idiom, coll.* an insignificant person

cat's {pyjamas » whiskers} *idiom, coll.* someone or something that is ideal or excellent

cattle-cake *comp. noun* cattle fodder which has been processed into small pellets

cattle-grid *comp. noun* a cattle-guard, a metal grill over a shallow pit set into a rural roadway to prevent the passage of cattle, etc., but not vehicles.

caul *adj., Sc.* cold

caul kail het agin *idiom, Sc.* reheated food

Literally, "cold cabbage heated again."

caur *noun, abbr., arch., Sc.* a street car

But an abbreviation of ➡tramcar, not "street car".

caution *noun* (1) a formal admonishment issued by the police or a court of law; (2) someone or something causing amusement or surprise

caution money *comp. noun* money held as security for good behavior

Cavalier *pr. name, Fr., hist., Lat.* a member of the King's party during the ➡English Civil War

Originally the word meant "knight," having been derived via French from the Latin *caballus* = "horse."

a Cavalier

cavalry twill *comp. noun* a strong woolen fabric

Originally material with a ribbed or twilled weave, which was worn by cavalry troops.

Cavan *pr. name* a county in the ➡Irish Republic

County Cavan in the ancient province of ➡Ulster.

cave *imper, arch., Lat., sl.* look out

From the Latin *cave* = "beware"

Cave *pr. name, hist.* a 19th C. dissident political group with a liberal stance

A biblical reference to the Cave of Adullamite, I Sam. 22:1,2.

the Cavendish Laboratory *pr. name* the principle physics laboratory of ➡Cambridge University

Founded in 1874, its director from 1919 until 1937 was Ernest Rutherford, who made the first demonstration of the splitting of the atom there in 1919.

caviare *spell.* caviar

cavie *noun, Sc.* a chicken coop

{cavilled » cavilling} *spell.* {caviled » caviling}

Cawdor Castle *pr. name, hist.* a 14th C. castle built upon the ruins of an older one, about 12 miles to the east of ➡Inverness in northern Scotland

Shakespeare tells us that ➡Macbeth was ➡Thane of Cawdor before taking the Scottish throne from ➡Duncan. However the present castle was built several centuries after Macbeth's time.

CB *pr. name, abbr.* Companion of the Order of the Bath

CBE *noun, abbr.* a Commander of the Order of the ➡British Empire

CBI *pr. name, abbr.* ➡Confederation of British Industry

CBSO *pr. name, abbr.* the ➡City of Birmingham Symphony Orchestra, founded in 1920

CC *noun, abbr.* (1) a ➡City Council; (2) a ➡County Council; (3) a city councilor; (4) a county councilor; (5) a ➡cricket club

CCC *pr. name, abbr.* ➡Corpus Christi College

CCTA *pr. name, abbr.* the Government Centre for Information Systems

Why this should have become known by the initials "CCTA" is not blindingly obvious.

Cd. *pr. name, abbr., hist.* a ➡Command Paper from 1900 to 1918

CE *pr. name, abbr.* the ➡Church of England

cease trading *idiom. phr. verb* to go out of business

Cedric *pr. name, hist.* the ➡Royal House of England from 927 to 1016

The following English monarchs belonged to this house: ➡Aethelstan, ➡Edmund, ➡Edred, ➡Edwy, ➡Edgar, ➡Edward the Martyr and ➡Ethelred the Unready.

Ceefax *pr. name, (TM)* the ➡BBC's teletext service

CEGB *pr. name, abbr., hist.* the ➡Central Electricity Generating Board

ceilidh *noun, Gae., Ir., Sc.* a party-like gathering for music and dance, etc.

In Ireland usually an informal event, but in Scotland it can often be a much more formal occassion.

Cellnet *pr. name (TM)* a cellular telephone network operated by Telecom Securicor Cellular Radio Ltd.

SEE ALSO: ➡Vodafone.

Celt *pr. name, hist.* (1) a pre-➡Anglo-Saxon inhabitant of the ➡British Isles; (2) a modern descendant of these

(2) now mostly reside in ➡Wales, southern and western ➡Ireland, the ➡Highlands, ➡Cornwall, and the Isle of ➡Man.

Celtic *pr. name* the group of languages that are or were spoken by ➡Celts

This is the language group which includes modern ➡Welsh, ➡Cornish, ➡Manx, ➡Irish Gaelic and ➡Scots Gaelic.

the **Celtic Fringe** *pr. name, coll.* the collective name for those parts of the ➡British Isles usually thought to be principally populated by ➡Celts

Usually considered to be Wales, Ireland, Scotland and Cornwall. However in Scotland only the Highlands are populated, and that very sparsely, by Celts; in reality so far as such things are meaningful nowadays, the vast majority of Scots are almost as ➡Anglo-Saxon as the English and have been for well over 1,000 years.

the **Celtic Twilight** *pr. name, hist.* an Irish literary revival that occurred in the years immediately before and after 1900

The leading member was W.B. Yeats. Why a revival should be called a twilight is a very Irish sort of mystery.

C.Eng. *noun, abbr.* a ➡chartered engineer

the **Cenotaph** *pr. name, Gr.* the British national memorial to the dead of World Wars I and II

Located in ➡Whitehall, London, it was dedicated in 1920. The word means "empty tomb" in Greek.

centenary *noun* centennial

centigramme *spell.* centigram

centilitre *spell.* centiliter

centillion *noun, num.* 10^{603}

The American centillion is a mere 10^{303}.

centimetre *spell.* centimeter

Central *pr. name* a region in central Scotland

The current population is 270,000 (1991 Census).

the **Central Criminal Court** *pr. name* the official name for the ➡Old Bailey in London

the **Central Electricity Generating Board** *pr. name, hist.* the government agency that was formerly responsible for all electrical power generation in England and Wales

Abolished when the industry was privatized in the 1980s.

the **Central Line** *pr. name* one part of London's rapid-transit subway system

It extends from West Ruislip and Ealing Broadway in the west to Epping and Hainault in the north-east.

the **Central Meat, Fish, Fruit, Vegetable and Poultry Markets** *pr. name, hist.* the official and full name for ➡Smithfield

Central Office *pr. name, abbr.* ➡Conservative Central Office

the **Central Office of Information** *pr. name* the agency handling all government publicity, advertising and relations with the media

central reservation *comp. noun* the median strip or divider along the center of a highway

Central Station *pr. name* (1) the principal railroad terminus in central ➡Glasgow for trains for southern Scotland, England and Ireland; (2) the principal railroad terminus in central ➡Newcastle

the **Central Statistical Office** *pr. name* the governmental department responsible for gathering and collating social, economic and other statistics

Originally set up by Winston Churchill in 1941 to provide him with better information with which to fight World War II.

Central TV *pr. name* a local commercial TV company headquartered in ➡Birmingham

It is part of the ➡ITV network.

centre *spell.* center

centreboard *spell.* centerboard

centrefire *spell.* centerfire

centrefold

centrefold *spell.* centerfold

centrepiece *spell.* centerpiece

centring *spell.* centering

century *noun* a ➠cricket score of 100 runs made by a single batsman

Ceredigion *pr. name, hist.* an ancient kingdom which was in west-central Wales

It is known to have been established by 700. During the 9th C., Ceredigion united with ➠Ystrad Towy to form ➠Seisyllwg.

the **Ceremony of the Keys** *pr. name, hist.* the ceremonial securing of the ➠Tower of London which is performed nightly

Every night at 10 o'clock the Chief ➠Yeoman Warder and his party come to lock up the gates of the fortress, where they are challenged by the sentry.
The following dialog then ensues:-
Sentry: "Halt, who comes here?"
Chief Warder: "The Keys."
Sentry: "Whose keys?"
Chief Warder: "{King » Queen} X's Keys."
The guard presents arms.
Chief Warder: "God preserve {King » Queen} X."
Sentry: "Amen."
The Keys are then deposited in the ➠Governor's house.

the **Cerne Giant** *pr. name, hist.* a gigantic figure of a man on a hillside in ➠Dorset

About 180ft tall and carved from the chalk the hill is made of, it is thought to date back to the 2nd C. or possibly earlier.

cert *noun, abbr., sl.* a certainty

Cert. Ed. *pr. name, abbr., arch.* Certificate in Education

the **Certificate of Secondary Education** *pr. name, hist.* an examination taken by students of secondary schools in England and Wales

Replaced with the ➠GCSE in 1988.

cess [A] *noun, hist., Ir., Sc.* a former local land tax
[B] *noun, Ir.* luck

CF *pr. name, abbr.* Chaplain to the Forces

CFE *pr. name, abbr.* a College of Further Education

CGM *noun, abbr.* the Conspicuous Gallantry Medal

CGS *pr. name, abbr.* the ➠Chief of the General Staff

CH *noun, abbr.* Companion of Honour

An award presented to persons considered to have performed a service of special value to the nation.

chair [A] *noun* (1) a university professorship; (2) a metal socket holding a railroad track in place on a tie
[B] *verb* to be carried upon the shoulders of others as a sign of acclaim

{**chairman » chairwoman**} *noun* the chief officer of a corporation and presiding member of its board of directors

The equivalent of a corporate president.

chalk *verb, coll.* to score a point in any game, but particulary darts

chalk and cheese *idiom, coll.* diametric opposites

the **Chamber** *pr. name* the debating chamber of the ➠House of Commons

chambers *noun* (1) the business office of a barrister; (2) a room where a judge listens to submissions that require to be heard in private

In particular, (1) is the room where a barrister meets clients.

champers *noun, abbr., coll.* champagne

champion *adj., coll., out.* excellent

the **Champion of England** *pr. name, hist.* originally a knight who defended the honor of the reigning English sovereign

Later, he rode upon a charger through ➠Westminster Hall on ➠Coronation Day, challenging anyone who disputed the right of that day's candidate to the throne. This ceremony was last observed at the coronation of ➠George IV in 1820. Since then, the Champion has limited his activities to carrying the sovereign's sword upon coronation day.

chancellor *noun* (1) the titular head of a university; (2) the chief secretary of a British embassy

Chancellor of the Duchy of Lancaster *pr. name* the cabinet minister nominally responsible for the ➠Duchy and County Palatine of ➠Lancaster, which is ➠crown land

Because this office now carries no specific duties, the holder is free to take on special tasks arising from time to time.

the **Chancellor of the Exchequer** *pr. name* the principal finance minister of the government and a very senior ➠cabinet minister

The name dates from the early Middle Ages when the king met his treasurer seated at a table covered with a checked cloth.

the **Chancellor of the Garter** *pr. name* the officer of state responsible for sealing commissions

Chancery Division *pr. name* a division of the High Court dealing with business law, including such matters as trusts, probate, bankruptcy and patents

One of the three ➠Divisions of the ➠High Court of Justice of England and Wales, and presided over by the ➠Lord Chancellor.

change ringing *comp. noun* a particular way of ringing church bells which is popular in the ➠Church of England

the **Changing of the Guard** *comp. noun* the formal ceremony of changing the royal guard

Carried out each morning in front of ➠Buckingham Palace and also at the ➠Royal Horse Guards, both in London.

changing room *comp. noun* a locker room

the **Channel** *pr. name, abbr.* the ➠English Channel

Channel 4 *pr. name* a nationwide commercial TV company headquartered in London

channel fleet *comp. noun, sl.* a street

the **Channel Islands** *pr. name* a group of small islands near the western coast of Normandy, France

Although the islands have belonged to Britain since 1066, they are not part of the ➡United Kingdom as such but are self-governing dependencies of the British ➡Crown. However, the United Kingdom takes care of all their defense and external affairs. The Channel Islands are all that remains of the extensive lands in what is now France, that once belonged to ➡William the Conqueror, Duke of Normandy. These islands were the only British territory to be occupied by the Germans during World War II.

SEE ALSO: ➡Isle of Man.

channelling *spell.* channeling

the **Channel Tunnel** *pr. name* the railroad tunnel under the ➡English Channel from England to France

There are really three tunnels. One is for trains from England to France, one for trains from France to England, and the third is a service tunnel.

There had been proposals to dig a tunnel under the English Channel between Britain and the European continent ever since a French engineer suggested it to Napoleon as a way of invading England about 200 years ago. Work on the tunnel began in 1986 and headings from the two sides met in 1990. Passenger services began in 1994.

SEE ALSO: ➡Chunnel

Channel TV *pr. name* a local commercial TV company headquartered in the ➡Channel Islands

It is part of the ➡ITV network.

chanter *noun, Sc.* a reed pipe which plays the melody on the ➡bagpipes

It is also used on its own as a training instrument for those learning to play the ➡bagpipes.

chanty [A] *noun, Sc.* a chamber pot

[B] *spell.* chantey

A song sung by sailors. It is also spelled ➡shanty.

chap [A] *noun, abbr., coll.* a man or boy

Derived, as a now-forgotten abbreviation, from ➡chapman.

[B] *verb, Sc.* to strike, hit or tap

chapel *noun* (1) a church used for non-conformist worship; (2) a non-conformist worshipper; (3) the local of a printers' union

On (3), *SEE ALSO:* ➡father of the chapel.

chapel of rest *comp. noun* a mortuary that is owned by an undertaker

chapel royal *comp. noun* a chapel or church attached to a palace or other royal residence

chapeltry *noun* the territory served by an ➡Anglican chapel

chapman *noun, arch.* a peddler

SEE ALSO: ➡chap

chapper-up *comp. noun, Sc.* a ➡knocker-up

chappie *noun, sl.* diminutive of ➡chap

chappit tatties *comp. noun, Sc.* mashed potatoes

chapter *noun* an ➡Act of Parliament considered as part of the proceedings of a parliamentary session

Each act becomes a chapter in the formal written account of the proceeding of the session.

char [A] *noun, abbr., sl.* a ➡charwoman

[B] *noun, sl.* tea

From the Chinese *cha* = "tea"

charabanc *noun, arch., Fr.* a bus

From the French, *char à bancs* = "seated carriage".

chargehand *noun* a foreman

charge nurse *comp. noun* a nurse responsible for a hospital ward

the **Charge of the Light Brigade** *pr. name, hist.* the most famous event of the ➡Crimean War

During the Battle of Balaclava in 1854, the lightly armed cavalry of the British Army, known as the Light Brigade, was ordered to charge the main artilley placement at the center of the Russian Army lines, an obviously suicidal tactic for a force like that. It is not clear whether the British commander, Lord Raglan, wished the 600 men of the Light Brigade to attack the lightly defended Russian flanks, or the Heavy Brigade to attack the center, but it is clear that his order got garbled or misunderstood.

Tennyson's poem, *The Charge of the Light Brigade,* did more to immortalize this event than anything else:

> *Theirs not to reason why,*
> *Theirs but to do and die:*
> *Into the valley of Death*
> > *Rode the six hundred.*
> *"Forward, the Light Brigade!*
> *Charge for the guns!" he said:*
> *Into the valley of Death*
> > *Rode the six hundred...*
>
> *... Cannon to right of them,*
> *Cannon to left of them,*
> *Cannon in front of them*
> > *Volleyed and thunder'd;*
> *Storm'd at with shot and shell,*
> *Boldly they rode and well,*
> *Into the jaws of Death,*
> *Into the mouth of Hell,*
> > *Rode the six hundred.*

Yet still, although three-quarters of their number were killed or injured, the Light Brigade did capture the Russian position.

charge sheet

charge sheet *comp. noun* a document listing indictments made at a police station

Charing Cross *pr. name, hist.* a location adjacent to Trafalgar Square, Whitehall and the Strand in London

The original cross was erected there by ➡Edward I to commemorate the spot, in what was then the village of Charing, where the coffin of his wife, Eleanor of Castile, stopped for the last time when traveling from Harby in ➡Nottinghamshire, where she had died, to burial at ➡Westminster. The present cross outside Charing Cross Station is a replica erected by the ➡Victorians, the original having been destroyed by Puritans in 1647.

There is another Charing Cross in ➡Glasgow.

Charing Cross Station *pr. name* a principal railroad terminus in central London

For trains to south-east England and the continental ferry ports.

the **Charity Commission** *pr. name* an agency set up by ➡Parliament to supervise charitable trusts

charity school *comp. noun, out.* a school originally funded by charitable donations

charlady *noun* a ➡charwoman

Charles Edward Stuart *pr. name, hist.* the ➡Young Pretender

Charles I *pr. name, hist.* King of ➡Great Britain

A member of the Royal House of ➡Stuart, he styled himself, "Charles, by the Grace of God, King of England, Scotland, France and Ireland, Defender of the Faith, etc." Charles was born in Dunfermline, in ➡Fife, Scotland in 1600 when his father James was as yet Scottish king only. Charles reigned for 23 years from 1625.

Friction with ➡Parliament began almost at once, and after that body had refused to support his demands for taxation, he dismissed them and ruled alone for 11 years after 1628. Eventually, he alienating both the English and Scottish peoples by his attempts at direct taxation. Then he compounded his unpopularity by attempting to impose an English form of religious service upon the strongly Presbyterian Scots, which brought that nation to a condition of open revolt.

When the Scots began to march upon England intent upon forcing the king to accede to their demand for religious freedom, Charles was obliged to summon an English Parliament in 1641, as by then he had no other way to raise the taxes he needed to fund an army to stop the Scots. But Parliament declared that taxation without representation was illegal (incidentally, this precedent was quoted to legitimize the actions of the American revolutionaries 135 years later) and Charles responded by attempting to arrest the leading members of the ➡House of Commons.

This led directly, in 1642, to the ➡English Civil War between King and Parliament. Eventually Parliament prevailed and Charles surrendered to the Scots in 1646. In 1647 the Scots handed him over to their English Parliamentary allies and Charles was executed in 1649 on the charge of high treason.

Charles II *pr. name, hist.* King of ➡Great Britain

A member of the Royal House of ➡Stuart, he styled himself, "Charles the second, by the Grace of God, King of

England, Scotland, France and Ireland, Defender of the Faith, etc., etc." and reigned in England for 24 years from the Restoration in 1660 until 1685, although he was crowned in ➡Scone as ➡King of Scots much earlier, in 1651 — the last British monarch to be crowned in Scotland.

After his Scottish coronation, he marched south with his supporters to take back England from the Parliamentary victors of the recent ➡English Civil War, but was defeated by ➡Cromwell at ➡Worcester. In the aftermath of that defeat, he hid in an oak tree—now remembered as the ➡Royal Oak—and eventually escaped to the ➡Continent, where he lived at various times in France, Germany, Flanders, Holland and Spain, until the end of the ➡Protectorate. Then General Monck forced the issue and Parliament accepted that Charles should return, proclaiming him king in 1660.

Most of his reign turned out to be a vast struggle between his determination to turn England back into a Roman Catholic nation and the even more determined Parliamentary and popular opposition to any such thing. Ultimately he found himself, in his last years, ruling without Parliament and dependent upon subsidies from Louis XIV of France. This was a situation that might well have been the precursor of a second civil war, had he not rather conveniently died before things reached that pass.

Charles was also a patron of both science and the arts—the ➡Royal Society was founded under his auspices—and a king with a number of colorful mistresses, by far the best-known being Nell Gwyn. His last reported words before dying were, "Let not poor Nellie starve," and indeed his brother James, who succeeded him, provided her with a pension.

charlie *noun, sl.* (1) a fool; (2) a ➡night watchman

charlies *noun, sl.* a woman's breasts

charming wife *idiom, arch., rh. sl.* a knife

World War I slang.

charter *verb* to certify

Required of a professional person such as an accountant, architect, engineer, etc. It has this name because their certification is provided by professional institutions, which are authorized to do this by ➡Royal Charters.

Charter 88 *pr. name* a pressure group advocating a written constitution, proportional representation and other reforms in the British political system

chartered accountant *comp. noun* a certified public accountant

chartered architect *comp. noun* a certified architect

chartered engineer *comp. noun* a certified engineer

chartered libertine *comp. noun, coll.* a person who does whatever they like

chartered librarian *comp. noun* a certified librarian

chartered surveyor *comp. noun* a certified surveyor

Charterhouse *pr. name* a leading English ➡public school, now relocated from London to ➡Surrey

Founded in 1611 on the site of a former Carthusian monastery, which was also called a charterhouse.

Chartist *pr. name, hist.* someone who supported the ➡People's Charter of 1838

Chartwell Manor *pr. name, hist.* the country residence, in ➡Kent, of Winston Churchill
Chartwell is now a museum open to the public.

chase up *verb, sl.* to chase down

chat show *comp. noun, coll.* a TV talk show

Chatsworth House *pr. name, hist.* one of the grandest of stately homes, some nine miles west of Chesterfield in ➡Derbyshire
This residence of the Dukes of ➡Devonshire was built late in the 17th C. upon the remains of a much earlier structure.

the **chattering classes** *comp. noun, coll., derog.* certain verbose members of the middle classes, usually of a liberal disposition and often of a pretentiously artistic bias
These people appear to see themselves as social and political attitude-formers, largely untrammeled as they are by the inconvenience of any real-life experience of what they pontificate about, and so lose no opportunity to express their views in a self-important manner among themselves before an audience of whichever lesser mortals are foolish enough to stop and listen to them, usually on radio or TV.

chat up *phr. verb, coll.* to ➡chat with ulterior motive
Especially with a member of the opposite sex

chauve *verb, Sc.* to struggle or work mightily but often with little result

Cheddar cheese *comp. noun* a hard white or yellowish cheese
Originally made in Cheddar, near ➡Bristol.

{**cheerio » cheers**} *exclam., coll.* (1) a toast made upon drinking; (2) good wishes upon arriving or departing; (3) an expression of thanks

cheesed off *adj., sl.* bored or fed up

cheesemonger *noun* a dealer in cheese

the **Cheesemongers** *pr. name* a nickname for the 1st ➡Life Guards
A unit of the British Army. When the regiment was reformed in 1788, some officers were the sons of merchants and thus not "gentlemen"; hence this rather strange name.

cheese-paring *adj., coll.* excessively economical

cheese wire *comp. noun* a length of fine wire with handles at each end, used for cutting cheese

Chelmsford *pr. name* the administrative center of ➡Essex, an ancient town was already the location of Essex's law court in the 13th C.
The current population is 63,000 (1988 estimate).

Chelsea *pr. name* an area of west-central London on the northern bank of the ➡Thames River
The location of the ➡Chelsea Royal Hospital and considered to be London's artistic district during most of the 19th C., it is now one of the most desirable, fashionable and expensive areas of the city to live in.

Chelsea bun *comp. noun* a kind of spiraled bun containing currants and cinnamon

the **Chelsea Flower Show** *pr. name* the annual show of the ➡Royal Horticultural Society, held in the grounds of the ➡Chelsea Royal Hospital

Chelsea pensioners

Chelsea pensioner *comp. noun* one of a number of retired soldiers who are accommodated at the ➡Chelsea Royal Hospital
They wear distinctive uniforms that are red during the summer and blue in the winter.

the **Chelsea Royal Hospital** *pr. name* the home, in ➡Chelsea, for some 400 ➡Chelsea pensioners
Founded by ➡Charles II in 1682 as a home for retired soldiers.

Chelseaware *noun, hist.* various kinds of porcelain wear made in Chelsea during the 18th C.

Cheltenham *pr. name* a spa town in ➡Gloucestershire that has retained much of the look and feel of the elegant and fashionable 18th C. resort that it was
The current population is 77,000 (1991 estimate).

Cheltenham College *pr. name* one of the leading English ➡public schools
Founded in 1841 in ➡Cheltenham, Gloucestershire.

the **Cheltenham Festival** *pr. name* an annual festival that emphasizes modern British music

Cheltenham Ladies' College *pr. name* a leading English ➡public school for girls
Founded in 1853 in ➡Cheltenham, Gloucestershire.

Cheltonian *noun* any member of ➡Cheltenham College or ➡Cheltenham Ladies' College
Either a current or former student.

chemist *noun* a druggist

chemist's shop *comp. noun* a pharmacy or drugstore

cheps *noun, East* (1) the face; (2) the jaw and the area around the mouth

Related to "chops," in the sense of "jawbone of an animal."

{**cheque » cheque-book**} *spell.* {check » checkbook}

In the sense of a written direction to a bank to pay money.

cheque-book journalism *comp. noun, coll.* the purchase by newspapers or TV companies of exclusive rights to stories

cheque card *comp. noun* a check guarantee card

chequer *spell.* checker

In the sense of a pattern of squares.

chequer-board *comp. noun, arch.* a chessboard

Chequers *pr. name* the official country residence of the ➡Prime Minister

It fulfills a similar role to that of Camp David for the U.S. President, which is to provide a sanctuary from the immediate clamor of the "front office." It is near Princess Risborough in the ➡Chilterns, some 25 miles northwest of London. Chequers House was presented to the nation for this purpose by Lord Lee in 1917.

cherry-laurel *comp. noun* a small evergreen bush with fruit that look somewhat like cherries

Its formal name is *prunus laurocerasus*.

the **Cherry-Pickers** *pr. name* a nickname for the 11th Hussars Regiment

A unit of the British Army that acquired this name after a detachment was surprised by the French while picking cherries in a Spanish orchard in 1811. *SEE ALSO:* ➡Cherubims.

the **Cherubims** *pr. name* the 11th Hussars Regiment

A unit of the British Army, who began to be called by this name after adopting crimson trousers as their uniform in 1840. *SEE ALSO:* ➡Cherry-Pickers.

Ches. *pr. name, abbr.* ➡Cheshire

Cheshire *pr. name* a county in northwestern England, just to the south of ➡Manchester

The county seat is ➡Chester, and the current population of the county is 935,000 (1991 Census).

Cheshire cat *comp. noun* a mythical cat that wears a broad grin at all times

A creature made popular by Lewis Carroll's *Alice in Wonderland*, which was published in 1865. However he did not invent the expression which had already had currency for some time by then. Nobody now knows what it was that cats found so amusing about ➡Cheshire.

Cheshire cheese *comp. noun* a mild cheese somewhat similar to ➡Cheddar cheese

The earliest British cheese named after a particular district, it originated, unsurprisingly, in ➡Cheshire, where it has been manufactured long enough ago to have rated a mention in the ➡Domesday Book.

Chester *pr. name* a city which is the administrative center of ➡Cheshire

Founded as *Castra Devana* by the Romans in the 1st C. Chester is the only place of any significance in Britain that has retained its entire medieval city wall intact, and within the wall, much of the half-timbered 16th C. city is intact too. Particularly unusual and interesting are the Rows, which is an entire second-story "shopping mall" dating from ➡Elizabethan times. Chester was incorporated as a city in 1506 and the current population is 115,000 (1988 estimate).

chesterfield *noun* a sofa with heavily padded arms and back, all of the same height

chesty *adj., coll.* prone to or presenting the symptoms of any one of a number of chest diseases

Cheviot *pr. name* a breed of large sheep with a short but thick-wooled coat

From the ➡Cheviot Hills, where they were first bred.

Cheviot Hills *pr. name* a range of hills in southern Scotland and northern England

chevron *noun* an heraldic representation of a bent stripe with an upward point

chew the fat *idiom. phr. verb* to revive an old disagreement or argument

Chichester *pr. name* a city that is the administrative center of ➡West Sussex

Founded as *Noviomagus Regnensium* by the Romans in the 1st C. and incorporated as a city in 1154. The current population is 100,000 (1988 estimate).

the **Chichester Festival** *pr. name* an annual drama festival at this city

chicory *noun* endive

chief *noun* the top third of an heraldic shield

chief constable *pr. name* a police chief

chief fire officer *pr. name* a fire chief

chief inspector *comp. noun* a police officer below the rank of ➡superintendent but above ➡inspector

the **Chief of the Air Staff** *pr. name* the most senior officer of the ➡RAF

the **Chief of the Defence Staff** *pr. name* the most senior British Military officer

the **Chief of the General Staff** *pr. name* the most senior officer of the British Army

the **Chief of the Imperial General Staff** *pr. name, hist.* the most senior military officer of the ➡British Empire

the **Chief of the Navy Staff and First Sea Lord** *pr. name* the most senior officer of the ➡Royal Navy

the **Chief Secretary of the Treasury** *pr. name* the ➡cabinet minister who is effectively second in command of the ➡Treasury

An indication of the importance of the ➡Treasury in comparison with other departments, is that it is the only one with two ministers in the Cabinet.

chief superintendent *comp. noun* a police officer below the rank of ➠commander but above the rank of ➠superintendent

chieftain *noun* the leader of a ➠Highland ➠clan

chief whip *comp. noun* a political party's senior ➠whip in the ➠House of Commons

chiefy *noun, sl.* the person in charge of a military unit

chiel *noun, Sc.* a fellow or young man

child benefit *comp. noun* regular payments made by the government to mothers for each child under the age of 16 residing with them

It is also known as ➠family allowance.

childe *noun, arch.* a poetical term for a noble youth

{**childer » childering**} *noun, Sc.* children

ChildLine *pr. name* a charity that operates a special free and confidential phone number children may call for help if they are subject to physical or sexual abuse at home or elsewhere

childminder *noun* someone who baby-sits for a fee while the parent or parents go to work

chilli *spell.* chili

the **Chiltern Hundreds** *pr. name, hist.* the crown manor of Stoke, Desborough and Burnham in ➠Buckinghamshire, where once a Steward was appointed by the King to suppress the frequent robberies that were occurring in the area.

The original purpose for this office has long vanished, but the office remains. This is because as a nominal office of profit under the Crown, any ➠MP who applies to be Steward of the Chiltern Hundreds is disqualified from sitting in the House of Commons, as would happen if they applied for any other office of profit under the Crown. Because an ➠MP cannot resign, applying for the Chiltern Hundreds has become a convenient device used by any Member of Parliament wishing to vacate his or her seat in the House of Commons.

Chiltern Lines *pr. name (TM)* a railroad company operating between the Chilterns and London

It is part of ➠British Rail.

the **Chilterns** *pr. name* a range of low chalk hills between London and ➠Oxford

Designated an area of outstanding natural beauty.

chimney *noun, pref.* a smokestack

chimney breast *comp. noun* an interior wall that projects out to surround a chimney

chimney stack *comp. noun* a group of chimneys formed into a single structure above a roof

china *noun, rh. sl.* a friend

Derivation: friend > ➠mate > plate > china plate > china.

chinaman *noun* in ➠cricket, a ball pitched from the side by a left-handed ➠bowler

chin-chin *exclam., coll.* (1) a drinking toast; (2) good wishes upon arriving or departing

the **Chindits** *pr. name, hist.* a British-led Allied military force operating behind Japanese lines in Burma during World War II

chine *noun, South* a narrow and deep gorge

Chinese take-away *comp. noun* a carry-out restaurant selling Chinese food

chinless wonder *comp. noun, coll.* a foolish upper-class person, usually male

chip *verb, sl.* to indulge in banter

chip butty *comp. noun, coll., North* a buttered bread roll sandwich filled with French fried potatoes

chipolata *noun* a miniature spicy sausage

chip pan *comp. noun* a deep fat pan used for frying French fried potatoes

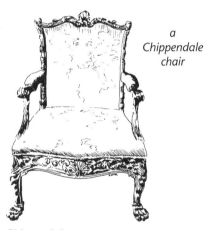

a Chippendale chair

Chippendale *noun, hist.* an 18th C. furniture style

Designed and manufactured by Thomas Chippendale, the leading English cabinetmaker of his day.

chipper *noun, abbr., Sc., sl.* a ➠fish and chip shop

chippings *noun* road gravel

chippy *noun, coll.* (2) a ➠fish and chip shop; (1) a carpenter or ➠joiner

chips *noun* French fried potatoes

chip shop *comp. noun, abbr.* a ➠fish and chip shop

{**chiselled » chiselling**} *spell.* {chiseled » chiseling}

chit *noun, coll.* (1) a memorandum; (2) a note recording money that is owed

chivvy *verb, coll.* to harass

chiz *noun, sl.* a swindle or cheat

choc *noun, abbr., coll.* chocolate

choc-ice

choc-ice *comp. noun, abbr., coll.* a chocolate-covered ice cream bar

chocker *adj., sl.* disgusted, fed-up or near to tears

chock up *verb, coll.* to cram in or make completely full

choir school *comp. noun* a private school attached to a church or cathedral

Especially one where students, in addition to their normal education, are trained to sing with the cathedral or church's choir. *See also:* ➡cathedral school.

choker *noun* a tightly fitting necktie or collar

chokey *noun, sl.* prison

chop [A] *noun, arch., coll., Hindi* a brand or trademark

From the Hindi *chap* = "stamp".

[B] *verb, sl.* to abbreviate, terminate or dispense with

the **chop** *noun, sl.* (1) the act of killing; (2) an employment dismissal

chop and change *verb, coll.* to vacillate

chopper [A] *noun* (1) a short-handled ax with a large blade; (2) a butcher's cleaver

[B] *noun, sl., taboo* the penis

choppers *noun, sl.* teeth

Christ Church College *pr. name* a college of ➡Oxford University founded in 1546

Christian name *comp. noun* a given name

Christie's *pr. name* a firm of fine art auctioneers founded in London in 1766

Christmas box *comp. noun* a gift given to tradesmen and others such as mailmen at Christmas

Originally 26th December, which is still called ➡Boxing Day.

Christmas cake *comp. noun* a rich fruit-filled cake, covered by almond paste and frosting and eaten at Christmas

Christmas Day *pr. name* an English ➡quarter-day

Now December 25, formerly January 6.

Christmas pudding *comp. noun* a rich boiled dessert containing flour, suet, dried fruit and spice, eaten at Christmas

Christ's College *pr. name* a college of ➡Cambridge University founded in 1505

Christ's Hospital *pr. name* one of the leading English ➡public schools

Founded in London by ➡Edward VI in 1552 as a religious home for abandoned infants, it soon became a school. Unusually, fees vary according to parental income.

chronic *adj., coll.* severe or very bad

chronic bronchitis *comp. noun, pref.* bronchiectasis

Although both terms are used in both countries, chronic bronchitis is usual in Britain and bronchiectasis in America.

chucker-out *comp. noun, sl.* a bouncer

Someone employed to eject or refuse admittance to undesirable individuals.

chuckie stain *comp. noun, Sc.* a small pebble

chuck it in *verb, coll.* (1) to quit; (2) to cease trying

chuffed *adj., sl.* satisfied or delighted

chummy *noun, sl.* a police slang term for a prisoner

chump chop *comp. noun* a chop taken from the thick end of a loin of lamb or mutton

the **Chunnel** *pr. name, coll.* a popular name for the ➡Channel Tunnel

{**chunter » chunter on**} *phr. verb, coll.* to grumble or speak inarticulately

the **Church Army** *pr. name* an evangelic movement within the ➡Church of England

Founded in 1882, it was modeled upon the Salvation Army.

the **Church Commissioners** *pr. name* a partly government-appointed organization that oversees the finances of the ➡Church of England

Churchill College *pr. name* a college of ➡Cambridge University founded in 1960

Churchillian *adj., coll.* characteristic of Winston Churchill or other members of his family

the **Church in Wales** *pr. name* the ➡Church of England's sister Episcopalian church in Wales

This was the ➡ established church in Wales under the terms of the ➡Act of Supremacy of 1534, until ➡disestablished in 1920, by which time most Welsh people were Presbyterian.

the **Church of England** *pr. name* the Episcopalian ➡established church in England

It came into being through ➡Henry VIII's dispute with the Pope over the status of his marriage to ➡Catherine of Aragon, and given legal form by the ➡Act of Supremacy of 1534.

The Sovereign is secular head and is Episcopalian while in England. Bishops and archbishops are nominally appointed by the Sovereign upon the advice of the ➡Prime Minister.

the **Church of Ireland** *pr. name* the ➡Church of England's sister church in Ireland

Although it had never attracted the allegience of more than a small minority of the Irish people, this had been the ➡established church in Ireland since the 16th C., until ➡disestablished in 1871.

the **Church of Scotland** *pr. name* the Presbyterian ➡established church in Scotland

The Sovereign is secular head and apparently is magically transformed from an English episcopalian into a presbyterian while in Scotland. All ministers have equal authority and the government of the church is based on egalitarian and democratic principles throughout. Unlike the ➡Church of England, there is no government interference of any kind in its appointments or other matters.

church school *comp. noun* a school operating under the authority of the ➠Church of England

churchwarden *noun* an elected lay representative of a parish of the ➠Church of England, responsible for attending to routine financial matters

churn *noun* a large metal container used for the transportation of milk

CI *pr. name, abbr., hist.* (1) the ➠Channel Islands; (2) the former Imperial Order of the Crown of India

CID *noun, abbr.* a Criminal Investigation Department

A department of the police responsible for detecting those involved in committing crimes.

{**cider » cyder**} *noun* an alcoholic drink made from fermented apple juice

CIE *noun, abbr., hist.* a Companion of the Order of the Indian Empire

cigarette end *comp. noun* a cigarette butt

ciggy *noun, abbr., sl.* a cigarette

CIGS *pr. name, abbr., hist.* the ➠Chief of Imperial General Staff

cinquefoil *noun* an heraldic representation of a formalized five-petaled flower

the **Cinque Ports** *pr. name, hist.* certain seaports on the ➠English Channel coast that were once responsible for maintaining a fleet capable of preventing invasion from Europe

The original five Cinque Ports were Hastings, Sandwich, Dover, Romney and Hythe in the counties of Kent and Sussex. Later, Winchelsea and Rye were added to the list. The naval purpose and requirement, dating back to before the Conquest of 1066, is now long abandoned, but the ceremony associated with it remains.

CIPFA *pr. name, abbr.* the Chartered Institute for Public Finance and Accountancy

the **Circle Line** *pr. name* one part of London's rapid-transit subway system

Spreading out from the original ➠Metropolitan Railway of 1863, the modern Circle Line now takes a large circular route around most of central London, almost all underground.

circs *noun, abbr., coll.* circumstances

circuit *noun* an automobile racing track

circus *noun* an open area where streets come together and traffic circulates

For example, ➠Piccadilly Circus in London.

the **Circus** *pr. name, out., sl.* a nickname for the British secret service

Cirencester *pr. name* a town in ➠Gloucestershire

It was founded as *Corinium* by the Romans, and extensive Roman remains have been discovered in recent years. The current population is 17,000 (1988 estimate).

cispontine *adj., Lat.* upon the northern bank of the ➠Thames River as it passes through London

From the Latin *cis* + *pont* = "nearest or most familiar side + bridge." The original London Bridge was supposedly built by the Romans in 43.

cissy *spell.* sissy

cistern *noun* a dwelling's water storage tank

Usually located in a roof space.

Citizens' Advice Bureau *pr. name* a voluntary organization offering citizens free advice on various matters concerning law, money, etc.

Local offices are found in most towns of any size.

the **Citizen's Charter** *pr. name* a government program to improve the accountability to the public of services provided by government agencies and departments

the **Citizens Theatre** *pr. name* a highly regarded theater that was established in the ➠Gorbals area of ➠Glasgow in 1945

city *noun* (1) any town that contained a cathedral and is or was the seat of a bishop; (2) any town that has been made a city by ➠Royal Charter

the **City** *pr. name* London's principal business district

Geographically roughly coincident with the ➠City of London and similar in function to Wall Street in New York City.

the **City and Guilds** *pr. name, hist.* a body established to improve the education of engineers

Founded in 1878 by the ➠Corporation of the ➠City of London, it established a college of engineering, now part of ➠Imperial College. The City and Guilds continue to set examinations and offer diplomas in scientific and engineering subjects.

city centre *comp. noun* downtown

City Company *pr. name* an ancient corporation or trade guild of the ➠City of London.

city council *comp. noun* the elected body that administers a ➠city

City desk *comp. noun* the business and financial news desk of a newspaper, TV station, etc.

Not the local news desk; the name refers to the ➠City.

City editor *comp. noun* the business and financial news editor of a newspaper, TV station, etc.

Not the local news editor; the name refers to the ➠City.

the **City of Dreaming Spires** *pr. name, coll.* Oxford

From its appearance when viewed by an approaching visitor.

the **City of London** *pr. name* that small part of ➠London that lies within what little remains of the ancient city walls

Approximately one square mile in extent, this is the business heart of Britain.

City page

City {page » pages} *comp. noun* the business and financial news section of a newspaper

the City Remembrancer *pr. name* an official who acts as a sort of ambassador of the ➡City of London Corporation to Parliament

city technology college *comp. noun* a form of ➡state school with an emphasis on technological education, set up in deprived inner-city areas

Their purpose is to provide students with the sort of practical education that is most likely to be useful to them in finding and developing a work career.

civic centre *comp. noun* a central area where city hall and other public buildings are located within a city

the Civic Trust *pr. name* a charity established in 1957 to promote improved town planning and architectural standards

civilisation *spell.* civilization

the Civil List *pr. name* annual payments made by ➡Parliament to the ➡monarch and certain other members of the ➡Royal Family to fund the official business conducted by them

the Civil Service Commission *pr. name* a government agency responsible for the management and organization of the Civil Service

The First Commissioner, who heads this agency, reports directly to the ➡Prime Minister.

the Civil War *pr. name, hist.* the ➡English Civil War; not the *American* Civil War

the Civil War Society *pr. name, hist.* a society whose members come together to re-enact the historic events of the ➡English Civil War

SEE ALSO: the ➡Sealed Knot Society.

civvies *noun, sl.* civilian clothes

World War II military slang.

civvy street *comp. noun, sl.* civilian life

World War II military slang.

clachan *noun, Ir., Sc.* a hamlet

Clackmannanshire *pr. name, hist.* formerly, the smallest Scottish county

It is now divided between the ➡Central and ➡Fife Regions.

claims assessor *comp. noun* insurance claims adjuster

clairvoyante *noun* a female clairvoyant

clamour *spell.* clamor

clan *noun, hist., Sc.* a group of Highland Scots united by a common name and common ancestors

Traditionally, the balance of loyalty is to this group rather than the larger nation or smaller family. A clan is similar in some ways to a Native American tribe.

clanger *noun, coll.* a blunder

clangour *spell.* clangor

clapped out *adj. phr., coll.* tired or worn out

Clare *pr. name* a county in the ➡Irish Republic

County Clare in the ancient province of ➡Munster.

Clare College *pr. name* a college of ➡Cambridge University founded in 1326

Clare Hall *pr. name* a hall of ➡Cambridge University founded in 1966

clarence *noun, arch.* a closed four-wheeled carriage with seats on top

Derived from the Duke of Clarence, later ➡William IV.

Clarence House *pr. name* a royal residence in London, close to ➡St James's Palace

Clarenceux King of Arms *pr. name* the second-ranking ➡Herald of the ➡College of Arms

Named after the Duke of Clarence and responsible for heraldic business in England south of the ➡Trent River.

claret *noun, arch., sl.* blood

clarinettist *spell.* clarinetist

clart *noun, Sc.* (1) mud or dirt generally; (2) an untidy or dirty individual

clarty *adj., Sc.* dirty or sticky

class *noun* (1) a school grade or ➡form; (2) a group of candidates that have performed with equal or similar merit in an examination

Classic FM *pr. name* a commercial radio station, dedicated to classical music, and broadcast nationally

the {Classic Races » Classics} *pr. name* the five principal horse races of England

They are: the 1,000 Guineas, the 2,000 Guineas, the Oaks, the ➡Derby and the ➡St Leger.

classified road *comp. noun* a road significant enough to have been assigned a catagory and identification number which specifies its importance

class-list *comp. noun* a list of candidates and the ➡class (2) that they have been placed in on the basis of their examination performance

clat *noun, East* a trivial or unimportant object

clatty *adj., East, Sc.* messy

Clause 28 *pr. name* a clause in the Local Government Act of 1988 prohibiting local councils from presenting homosexuality as an attractive or acceptable lifestyle in schools and other public places

Clause Four *pr. name* a Communistic-sounding clause in the Constitution of the ➡Labour Party which has been the cause of considerable internal party debate and derisive comments from people outside the party for many years

This clause, which commits the party to a policy of "common ownership of the means of production, distribution and exchange", has for long been the only one of many clauses in the party constitution considered important enough to be printed on the back of the membership cards issued to all party members. It is presently under review.

claver *noun, Sc.* gossip or foolish talk

Claverton Manor *pr. name, hist.* a neoclassical house built in the 1820s close by ➡Bath

Since 1960 it has housed the ➡American Museum.

clawback *noun* the recovery of money already paid out by another means, typically taxation

claymore *noun, Gae., hist., Sc.* a Highlander's traditional large double-edged broadsword

From the Gaelic *claidheamh mór* = "great sword"

clean bowl *phr. verb, coll.* to ➡bowl out or ➡dismiss a ➡cricket ➡batsman by directly hitting the wicket, without first touching the bat or the batter's body

cleansing department *comp. noun* the department of a local council responsible for street cleaning, collection of household garbage, etc.

the **Clearances** *pr. name, abbr., hist., Sc.* the ➡Highland Clearances

clearance sale *comp. noun* a sale held to dispose of surplus stock

clearing bank *comp. noun* a major retail bank that is a member of the ➡LBCH

clearway *noun* a road where stopping is prohibited

clee *noun, East* a claw

cleek *noun, Sc.* (1) a large hook; (2) a door latch

cleg *noun* a horsefly

Cleopatra's Needle *pr. name, hist.* an ancient Egyptian obelisk now found upon London's ➡Thames Embankment

It was brought from Alexandria, Egypt, in 1877 where it, together with an almost identical companion, now in Central Park, New York, had been brought from Upper Egypt by Augustus Caesar in 14 B.C.

Notwithstanding their name, the unromantic truth is that neither Needle has any connection whatsoever with Cleopatra, having been created during the reign of the Pharaoh Thotmes around 1500 B.C., some 1450 years before Cleopatra appeared on the scene. Each obelisk consists of a single block of granite weighing about 205 tons and standing some 60 ft tall.

clerkess *noun, Sc.* a female clerk

clerk in holy orders *comp. noun, out.* a formal name for a clergyman

the **Clerk of the Closet** *pr. name* the senior chaplain to the monarch

the **Clerk of the House** *pr. name* a senior legal official of the ➡House of Commons always present when the ➡House is in session to advise the ➡Speaker on procedural and legal matters

clerk of works *comp. noun* a work supervisor on a construction site

Cleveland *pr. name* a county in northeastern England

Formed from parts of ➡Durham and the ➡North Riding of Yorkshire in 1974. The county seat is ➡Middlesbrough and current population is 540,000 (1991 Census).

clever {clogs » dick} *comp. noun, coll.* a smart aleck

cliché *noun* a kind of metal printing-plate

the **Clickhimin Broch** *pr. name, hist.* a well preserved 5th. C.B.C. ➡broch

It is located on the ➡Shetland Islands

Clifton Suspension Bridge

Clifton Suspension Bridge *pr. name* a road bridge high above the gorge of the ➡Avon River near ➡Bristol in ➡Avon county

It is loosely based upon a design by the great 19th C. engineer, I.K. Brunel, and although work began in 1836 it was not finished until after he had died in 1864.

climber *noun* a climbing plant

Clingfilm *pr. name (TM)* a thin, transparent plastic wrap used for covering food, etc.

clinic *noun* a private or specialized hospital

clinker *noun* something especially good or well done

clip *verb* to cut or tear a ticket to prevent its reuse

Especially on public transport, when entering a theater, etc.

clippie *noun, out., sl.* a ➡bus conductress

From their habit of ➡clipping tickets.

clishmaclaver *noun, Sc.* (1) idle talk or gossip; (2) one who indulges in (1)

C.Lit. *noun, abbr.* a ➠Companion of Literature

the **Cliveden Set** *pr. name, hist.* a group of right-wing politicians and opinion-formers who regularly gathered in the 1930s at Cliveden House

Cliveden is a large country house in ➠Buckinghamshire, which at that time was the residence of Lord and Lady Astor. There is evidence that some members of the Cliveden Set favored making a deal with Hitler.

Cllr. *noun, abbr.* a ➠Councilor

cloakroom *noun, coll.* a euphemism for a rest room

cloaks *noun, abbr., coll.* a ➠cloakroom

clobber [A] *noun, sl.* personal clothes or possessions [B] *verb, sl.* (1) to hit; (2) to beat up; (3) to defeat in a decisive manner

clock [A] *noun, sl.* (1) a person's face; (2) the period of 36 hours following cautioning and arrest of a suspect by the police

(2) is police slang. This is the maximum time a suspect can be held by the police without being charged and brought before a magistrate.

[B] *verb, sl.* (1) to hit someone, especially upon the face; (2) to look at someone in an aggressive and threatening manner; (3) to move back the number of driven miles registered on the odometer of a vehicle so that it appears to have been used less extensively than is actually the case

(3) is reputedly the habitual practice of dishonest used-car dealers. It is, of course, illegal.

clogger *noun, sl.* a soccer player who regularly injures other players

cloot [A] *noun, Sc.* (1) an item of clothing; (2) a household rag or cloth; (3) a diaper; (4) the divisions that make a foot cloven; (5) a whole cloven hoof; (6) an archery target

SEE ALSO: ➠clout

[B] *verb, Sc.* (1) to slap; (2) to patch with cloth; (3) to repair with metal plate

clootie dumpling *comp. noun, Sc.* a dumpling boiled while wrapped in a cloth

close [A] *noun* (1) the precinct of a cathedral; (2) a school playing field; (3) a street which can be entered from one end only

[B] *noun, Sc.* the entryway from a public street to a common tenement stairway or enclosed courtyard

close borough *comp. noun, hist.* a ➠pocket borough

closedown *noun* the cessation of broadcasting for the day by a TV or radio station that does not broadcast through the night

close season *comp. noun* a closed season, when some activity, typically hunting, is illegal

close to the knuckle *idiom, coll.* almost indecent

SEE ALSO: ➠near the knuckle.

closing down sale *comp. noun* a close-out sale

closing time *comp. noun* the time when a ➠pub is required to close under the terms of its license

Usually 11 P.M. or later.

closure *noun* a cloture

First used in the 1880s to break the epic filibusters in the ➠House of Commons, then regularly mounted by Parnell and his Irish obstructionists as a wrecking device in their campaign for Irish independence.

clot *noun, sl.* a fool or blockhead

cloth cap *comp. noun, out.* (1) a flat, cloth-made cap formerly worn by many working-class males; (2) a flat, cloth-made cap worn by some upper-class males, particularly when out on the moors or hills shooting at small inoffensive mammals and birds

SEE ALSO: ➠cloth cap image.

the **cloth cap image** *comp. noun, out.* (1) symbolic of the working class; (2) symbolic of the upper class

Notwithstanding virtually identical cloth caps once being worn by both the working class and upper classes, they have become symbols of both groups. And yet despite this apparent confusion it was not so very difficult to distinguish members of one class from the other, somehow or other. (Hint: the upper class caps were newer and cleaner.) *SEE ALSO:* ➠cloth cap.

cloth-eared *adj. phr., coll., out* (1) partially deaf; (2) not listening or prepared to listen

cloth ears *comp. noun, coll., out* (1) one who is partially deaf; (2) one who does not or will not listen

clothes-peg *noun* a clothespin

clothes rail *comp. noun* a clothes rack

clotted cream *comp. noun* a thick cream made by the process of slowly scalding whole milk

It originated from and continues to be principally made in south-west England. Also known as ➠Cornish cream and ➠Devonshire cream.

clough *noun, North* a steep and narrow valley

clout *noun, North* (1) an item of clothing, household rag or cloth, or a diaper; (2) a piece of leather used for cleaning purposes

SEE ALSO: ➠cloot

Clubland *noun, coll.* an area in West London around ➠Pall Mall, where many clubs are located

cludge *noun, Sc., sl.* a toilet

Clumber Spaniel *pr. name* one of the larger breeds of spaniel, it has a silky white coat and is usually rather slow-moving

It was bred by the Dukes of Newcastle at their home of Clumber Park in ➠Nottinghamshire during the 19th C.

clunch *adj., East* taciturn

Clwyd *pr. name* a Welsh County

The current population is 400,000 (1991 Census).

the **Clyde** *pr. name* a great industrial river, about 100 miles in length

It rises in southwestern Scotland to flow through ➠Glasgow into the ➠Firth of Clyde and then on to the Atlantic Ocean.

the Firth of **Clyde** *pr. name.* the estuary of the ➠Clyde River, on Scotland's western coast

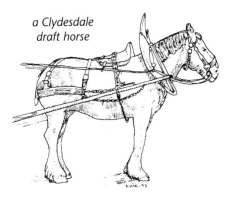

a Clydesdale
draft horse

Clydesdale *pr. name* (1) the valley of the ➠Clyde River; (2) a breed of heavy draft horse

the **Clydesdale Bank** *pr. name* the smallest of Scotland's three principal retail banks

Founded in 1838, its head office is in Glasgow.

Unlike English banks other than the ➠Bank of England, the Clydesdale Bank is authorized to issue its own paper currency, which together with that of the other two principal Scottish banks is legal tender there, and is usually accepted as such in England too.

Clydesdale Terrier *pr. name* a kind of small terrier

clype *noun, Sc.* (1) a tattletale; (2) a slap

Cm. *pr. name, abbr.* a ➠Command Paper since 1986

Cmd. *pr. name, abbr., hist.* a ➠Command Paper from 1918 to 1956

CMG *noun, abbr.* a Commander of the Order of St Michael and St George.

Cmnd. *pr. name, abbr., hist.* a ➠Command Paper from 1956 to 1986

CNAA *pr. name, abbr.* the Council for National Academic Awards

CND *pr. name, abbr, hist.* the Campaign for Nuclear Disarmament

A pressure group founded in 1958 and originally led by Bernard Russell and other prominent people, who were collectively known as the ➠Committee of 100. Its purpose was to campaign for the unilateral nuclear disarmament of Britain Following the end of the Cold War, made possible at least in part by the steadfast refusal of Britain and other Western nuclear powers to unilaterally rid themselves of their nuclear weapons, membership has fallen away somewhat drastically.

Cnut *pr. name, hist.* the Danish king who became King of all England after ➠Edmond II

Better-known as ➠Canute, he reigned in England for 19 years from 1016 until 1035. A member of the Royal House of ➠Denmark, he is best remembered as the king who is said to have stood upon the beach beside the ocean and ordered the tide not to come in; but it did anyway.

coach *noun* a long-distance bus

coach party *comp. noun* a group who are traveling together in a bus

coachwork *noun* the bodywork of a car, etc.

coal *noun* a portion or portions of coal broken into lumps of a size suitable for burning

coal cauldron *comp. noun* a coal scuttle

coalface *noun* (1) the point in a coal mine where a coal seam is actually exposed and available to extract from the ground; (2) a euphemism for wherever it is that the really hard work is being done

coalhole *noun* a small closet used for the storage of household coal

It is, or was, usually or originally located underground.

Coalport *noun* a fine porcelain made in the village of Coalport, ➠Shropshire during the 18th C.

coals to Newcastle *idiom, coll.* goods for sale brought to where there is already a surplus

For many years, ➠Newcastle-upon-Tyne was the center of the British coal-mining industry.

coarse fish *comp. noun* all freshwater fish except trout and salmon.

Coastal Command *pr. name, hist.* a former ➠command of the ➠RAF that was responsible for protecting shipping from attack by enemy warships, especially submarines

Coastal Command played a vital part in the ➠Battle of the Atlantic, finding and destroying U-Boats during World War II.

coastguard *noun* a coastguardsman

coat of arms *comp. noun* the shield, helmet, crest, mantling and supporters formed together into an heraldic design

Strictly, the motto is not part of this.

cob [A] *noun* (1) a rounded heap or lump; (2) a loaf of bread with a rounded top; (3) a corncob

[B] *noun, North* a bread roll

cobblers *noun, rh. sl., taboo* testicles

Derivation: testicles > balls > awls > cobbler's awls > cobblers.

cobbles *noun* (1) coal supplied in lumps about the size of cobblestones; (2) miniature loafs of bread, about the size of a bun

coble *noun, Sc.* a small flat-bottomed rowboat used by salmon fishers

cock *noun, sl.* (1) nonsense; (2) a male friend

cock-a-leekie *comp. noun, Sc.* a soup made from chicken and leek

cock a snook *idiom. phr. verb.* (1) to make a gesture of contempt; (2) to make one's contempt for a person or persons obvious

cocker *noun, sl.* a male companion

As addressed or referred to by another man.

Cocker Spaniel *pr. name* a breed of small spaniel developed in England in the 19th C., to be especially suited for retrieving game birds

It is named after the woodcock, which is particularly effective at recovering things from thickets.

cockle *noun, hist.* a small edible bivalved mollusk

Its formal name is *cardium edule.*

Once they were sold alive on the streets by the pint and the half-pint, but this is now little more than a rapidly fading memory, kept most fresh by the ballad:

In Dublin's fair city where girls are so pretty,
I first set my eyes on sweet Molly Malone,
As she wheeled her wheelbarrow
through streets broad and narrow,
Crying, Cockles and mussels! Alive, alive, oh!

Cockney *pr. name* (1) a native, citizen or inhabitant of London, particularly from the ➽East End; (2) the dialect or accent of London's ➽East End

Traditionally, (1) is a person born within the sound of ➽Bow Bells. The name is believed to have originated from *cokeney* = "cock's egg," an insulting term for a city-dweller in medieval English.

cockneyism *noun* an expression or activity characteristic of a ➽Cockney or of the ➽East End of London

a cock that won't fight *idiom, sl.* a plan or proposal that cannot work

cock-up *comp. noun, sl.* a mess, mistake or muddle

coconut shy *comp. noun* a traditional fairground booth where ➽fairings are awarded to customers who succeed in knocking coconuts over by throwing wooden balls at them

cod *noun, sl.* a trick, hoax or parody

codling *noun* a kind of long, tapered cooking apple

codswallop *noun, sl.* nonsense

{coeliac » coelom » coelomate} *spell.* {celiac » celom » celomate}

Concerning the abdomen.

coenobite *spell.* cenobite

A member of a religious community.

Coeur de Lion *pr. name, Fr., hist.* ➽Richard I

It means "Lion Heart" in French. He is said to have earned this name through his bravery during the Third Crusade.

C of E *pr. name, abbr.* the ➽Church of England

coffee bar *comp. noun* a small café or coffee shop

coffee stall *comp. noun* an outdoor booth that sells coffee and snacks

coffee whitener *comp. noun* coffee creamer

C of S *pr. name, abbr.* the ➽Church of Scotland

{cognisable » cognisance » cognisant} *spell.* {cognizable » cognizance » cognizant}

Concerning identification and legal jurisdiction.

COHSE *pr. name, abbr.* the Confederation of Health Service Employees

A labor union for workers in hospitals, etc., which was absorbed into ➽Unison in 1993.

COI *pr. name, abbr.* the ➽Central Office of Information

coiner *noun* (1) a counterfeiter of coins; (2) an inventor of new words

the Coldstream Guards *pr. name* the 2nd Regiment of ➽Foot Guards

This unit of the British Army began life as General Monck's regiment, which was raised at Coldstream in the Scottish ➽Borders and marched south to overthrow the republican tyranny that the ➽Commonwealth had become, restoring the ➽Monarchy in 1660.

coley *noun* any of a number of edible fish, including pollack, sablefish or coalfish

the Coliseum *pr. name* the largest theater in London's ➽West End theater district

It seats over 2,500 and has been home of the ➽English National Opera since 1968.

collar [A] *noun* (1) a ➽collar of bacon; (2) a neck-chain worn by the holders of certain official offices or knightly orders as a badge of membership or authority

SEE ALSO: ➽Collar of Esses

[B] *noun, rh. sl.* a lie

Derivation: lie > tie > collar and tie > collar.

collar of bacon *comp. noun* the portion of bacon cut nearest to the neck

Collar of Esses *pr. name, hist.* a ➽collar (2) consisting of a series of golden S's linked together

Originally, the symbolic collar worn by members of the House of Lancaster. It is now worn only by the ➽Lord Chief Justice,

➠Lord Mayor of London, ➠King of Arms, the ➠Heralds, the ➠Serjeants-at-Arms, and the Serjeant Trumpeter.

collar-stud *comp. noun, out.* a collar button

collection *noun* an examination that takes place at the end of term at ➠Oxford University

colleen *noun, Gae., Ir.* a girl

college *noun* (1) an independent foundation within a university, with its own master, fellow, students, etc.; (2) an establishment of higher education other than a university; (3) a private high school
(1) is principally associated with ➠Oxford, ➠Cambridge, ➠London and ➠Durham Universities in England, and ➠St Andrews University in Scotland. (3) is unusual, but is the proper name for some such schools.

the **College of Arms** *pr. name* an organization responsible for issuing and recording titles and ➠coats of arms in England, northern Ireland and the Commonwealth
Also known as the ➠Heralds' College.

college of education *comp. noun* a college where schoolteachers are trained

college pudding *comp. noun* an individually-sized steamed pudding consisting of suet and fruit

collie *pr. name* a breed of large, dense-haired sheepdog, originated in Scotland

collieshangie *noun, Sc.* (1) a dog fight; (2) a loud quarrel or brawl

collins *noun, arch., coll.* a bread-and-butter letter, thanking the host upon returning from a visit
From a character in Jane Austin's novel *Pride and Prejudice*.

colliseum *spell.* coliseum

collywobbles *noun, sl.* an apprehensive feeling

the **Colonial Office** *pr. name, hist.* a former government department responsible for administration of ➠Crown Colonies
Now absorbed into the ➠Foreign and Commonwealth Office

colonisation *spell.* colonization

colour *noun* a uniform, badge or ribbon worn in the colors of a club, school, regiment, college, etc.
Used as a badge of membership.

{**colour » colourable**} *spell.* {color » colorable}

{**colourant » colouration**} *spell.* {colorant » coloration}

colourblind *spell.* colorblind

{**colourfast » colourful**} *spell.* {colorfast » colorful}

{**colouring » colourist**} *spell.* {coloring » colorist}

{**colouristic » colourless**} *spell.* {coloristic » colorless}

{**colourman » coloury**} *spell.* {colorman » colory}

colour supplement *comp. noun* a newspaper's Sunday supplement

Colraine *pr. name* a district in ➠Northern Ireland, in what used to be County ➠Londonderry
The current population is 50,000 (1990 estimate).

{**combe » coomb**} *noun, Wal.* a short but deep valley upon a hillside
Derived from the Welsh word ➠cwm.

comber *noun* a member of the perch family of fresh-water fish
Its formal name is *serranus cabrilla*.

combination *noun* (1) a motorcycle which has an attached sidecar; (2) a single undergarment covering both torso and legs

combination-room *comp. noun* a ➠common-room
An expression used at ➠Cambridge University only.

come across *verb, coll.* to meet or find accidentally

come away *phr. verb, coll.* to become detached

come back *phr. verb, coll.* to repeat

come in *phr. verb, abbr.* to ➠come into bat in ➠cricket

come into bat *phr. verb* to commence a session as a ➠batsman in a game of ➠cricket

come off *phr. verb, coll.* to fall off
A horse, for example.

come out *phr. verb, coll.* to go on strike

come over queer *phr. verb, coll.* to feel ill suddenly

come round *phr. verb, sl.* to make an informal visit

the **Comet** *pr. name, hist.* the world's first jet airliner
It first flew in 1949 and entered scheduled service with ➠BOAC in 1952, six years before the first Boeing 707. However the Comet had to be withdrawn from service in 1954 after two crashes, which turned out to be caused by the then little-understood phenomenon of metal fatigue. A modified Comet began to operate the first transatlantic jet service just days before the 707 also did in 1958.

come the innocent *phr. verb, coll.* to pretend innocence

come through *verb, sl.* to survive or succeed

come to no harm *verb, coll.* to be unharmed

come to stay *verb, coll.* (1) to arrive for a long visit; (2) to come to reside permanently

come to the wrong shop *phr. verb, coll.* to ask or seek something in the wrong place

come under the hammer *phr. verb, coll.* to auction

Comfort *pr. name (TM)* a fabric softener

comforter *noun, out.* (1) a baby's pacifier; (2) a woolen scarf

command *noun* a principal division of the ➠RAF

commando *noun, hist.* (1) a member of the ➠Royal Marine Commando; (2) originally, a military group composed of volunteer civilians
(2) was devised by the Boers during the ➠Boer War

Command Paper

Command Paper *pr. name* a paper placed before ➡Parliament on the nominal direction of the ➡Crown
But in reality the government acting in the name of the Crown.

command performance *comp. noun* a movie show or theatrical performance nominally made upon the command of the monarch

the **Commemoration** *pr. name* an annual religious service held in memory of the founders and benefactors of Oxford University

commence [A] *verb* to start to be
[B] *verb, arch.* to take a university degree

commercial traveller *comp. noun* traveling salesman

Commercial Union *pr. name (TM)* a large insurance company

commère *noun, Fr.* a female ➡compère, disk jockey or anchorwoman
From the French for "godmother"

commis chef *comp. noun, Fr.* a junior chef
From the French *commettre* = "entrust"

commissary *noun* an assessor appointed by the court of ➡Cambridge University

commissionaire *noun* a uniformed doorkeeper
Usually found at the entrances to cinemas, theaters, etc.

commissioner *noun, Sc.* a member of the ➡General Assembly of the ➡Church of Scotland
One who has been commissioned by {his = her} parish to attend the Assembly and vote upon its deliberations.

Commissioner for Oaths *comp. noun* a ➡solicitor authorized to perform the duties of a notary public

the **Commissioners of Northern Lighthouses** *pr. name* an agency that controls lighthouses, buoys, lightships and the pilotage of ships around the coasts of ➡Scotland and the ➡Isle of Man
See also: ➡Trinity House.

the **Commission for Racial Equality** *pr. name* an organization set up under race relations legislation for the purpose of working towards the elimination of racial discrimination and the promotion of good relations between different racial groups

commission of the peace *comp. noun* the authority given to a Justice of the Peace

commis waiter *comp. noun, Fr.* a junior waiter
From the French *commettre* = "entrust"

the **Committee** *pr. name, abbr.* the ➡Committee of the House

the **Committee of 100** *pr. name, hist.* the group who founded and originally led ➡CND

the **Committee of the House** *pr. name* a parliamentary committee consisting of the whole of the ➡House of Commons

the **Committee of Ways and Means** *pr. name* a ➡Committee of the House that authorizes the raising of money for public services and approves new or altered taxation

committee stage *comp. noun* the third stage of a parliamentary bill's passage into law
When it is considered in detail, and amendments may be made.

the **Commodore-in-Chief** *pr. name* the supreme commanding officer of the ➡RAF

common *noun, abbr., coll.* (1) common sense; (2) ➡common land

the **Common Agricultural Policy** *pr. name* the farming policy of the ➡EU

the **Common Entrance** *pr. name* an examination taken in preparatory schools, usually at the age of 13, to gain entrance to English ➡public schools
It is called this because it is the common examination used by all English ➡public schools.

commoner *noun* (1) anyone who is not a member of the ➡aristocracy or the ➡Royal Family; (2) a student at ➡Oxford or ➡Cambridge Universities who pays his or her own way

common land *comp. noun* community land that can only be enclosed by special ➡Act of Parliament
Normally this takes the form of open public land, usually in a village or small town.

common law *noun* the unwritten system of English law based on precedent and ancient custom
And also the basis of much U.S. law.

the **Common Market** *pr. name, abbr., hist.* the ➡European Common Market

common or garden *idiom, coll.* garden variety; normsl or usual

common plea *comp. noun* a court action over which the ➡Crown makes no claim of exclusive jurisdiction

the **Common Prayer** *pr. name* the official liturgy of the ➡Church of England
It was first set down in the ➡Book of Common Prayer of 1549 under Archbishop Cramner during the reign of Edward VI, then revised and reissued in 1662, when it was based upon the ➡Authorized Version of the Bible. Here "common" is used in the ecclesiastical sense of a religious service suitable for a particular kind of occasion.

common riding *comp. noun, Sc.* an annual ceremony in many Scottish towns in the ➡Borders, when citizens ride out on horseback to mark the limits of the land belonging to their municipality
Once a necessity, this event which amazingly enough always appears to happen in mid-summer, is now used as the excuse for many an annual local festival. *See also:* ➡beating the bounds.

common room *comp. noun* (1) a shared room used for social and business purposes by certain members of a university of college; (2) those members of a university of college who are entitled to use a ➡️common room, considered as a group

commons *noun* food shared out in common

the **Commons** *pr. name, abbr.* the ➡️House of Commons

Common Serjeant *pr. name* the circuit judge responsible for cases tried in the ➡️City of London

the **Commonwealth** *pr. name, hist.* (1) the short-lived 17th C. republican government of England; (2) a loose association of former members of the ➡️British Empire and ➡️British Commonwealth of Nations

(1) came into being following the execution of ➡️Charles I in 1649 and lasted until the ➡️Restoration of ➡️Charles II in 1660. It was such an unsuccessful, tyrannical and unpopular regime, that republicanism has remained a byword for bad government among many Britons even to the present day. All members of (2) are independent nations who remain members entirely by their own choice.

Commonwealth citizen *comp. noun* a secondary status enjoyed by all citizens of the ➡️United Kingdom, dependent territories and independent countries that are members of the ➡️Commonwealth

It replaces the former status of ➡️British Subject, which was enjoyed by all citizens of the ➡️British Empire. Today the practical significance or value of being a Commonwealth citizen is now almost nil and much less important to the average Briton than being a ➡️European citizen.

Commonwealth Day *pr. name* the original date of the ➡️Sovereign's ➡️Official Birthday

May 24th, which was the natural birthday of ➡️Victoria. The day was known as ➡️Empire Day until 1958.

the **Commonwealth Games** *pr. name* an athletic contest held in a different location every four years and open to national teams from every country of the ➡️Commonwealth

The first, then called the ➡️British Empire Games, was held in Hamilton, Ontario, Canada, in 1930. Unlike the Olympic Games where a single team represents the United Kingdom, England, Scotland, Northern Ireland and Wales send separate national teams to the Commonwealth Games.

the **Commonwealth Institute** *pr. name* a center in London established for the purpose of cultural and educational development and cross-fertilization between ➡️Commonwealth countries

Formerly known as the ➡️Imperial Institute.

Commonwealth Preference *pr. name, hist.* a system of trade preference intended to encourage trade between the members of the ➡️Commonwealth

Introduced at the Imperial Economic Conference held in Ottawa, Canada, in 1932 when it was called ➡️Imperial Preference. It was renamed after World War II; however it

gradually became outdated by the GATT agreement of 1947 and Britain's entry into the ➡️European Economic Community in 1973. It was finally abolished in 1977.

the **Commonwealth War Graves Commission** *pr. name, hist.* an organization maintaining the graves of the nearly one million of the ➡️British Empire and Commonwealth who died in the two World Wars.

communard *adj., Fr.* in the spirit of the ➡️European Community or ➡️European Union

communication cord *comp. noun* an emergency stop request cord or chain in railroad passenger cars

the **Communist Party of Great Britain** *pr. name, hist.* (1) the former name of what is now called the ➡️Democratic Left political party; (2) a tiny, far-left political party

Founded in 1920, the party changed its name in 1991 after the collapse of the Soviet Union. Although the party had two members elected to the ➡️House of Commons in the 1920s and another two in the 1940s, it never came close to being a serious political force in the UK. Coincident with the name change, it admitted for the first time that it has received large subsidies from Moscow during the 1950s, 60s and 70s. When the majority of the 5,000 members of the former ➡️Communist Party of Great Britain voted to adopt the name "Democratic Left" in 1991, a minority determined to stick with the old name, so forming (2), a small splinter group with a few hundred members.

the **Community Charge** *pr. name, hist.* a flat-rate tax levied on every British adult by local councils from 1989 until 1992

Much better known as the ➡️poll tax, this replacement for the former system of personal local property taxation known as the ➡️Rates turned out to be one of the most unpopular impositions on the British people for a long time.

It undoubtedly became one of the most important causes of the departure of Margaret Thatcher from the office of Prime Minister in 1990, as she had been the principal advocate and driving force behind the whole rather ridiculous idea.

Throughout, Rates continued to be levied on business property.

community home *comp. noun* a place where convicted teenagers are housed under supervision

community-service order *comp. noun* a sentence that a court may impose upon an offender as an alternative to jail, fine or conventional probation

Under such an order, the offender must carry out, under supervision, socially useful tasks such as building or repairing facilities for the elderly or helping out at a kindergarten.

companion *noun* a member of the lowest rank of certain merit orders or fraternities, membership of which may only be conferred by the monarch

Companion of Honour *comp. noun* a member of this order, founded in 1917

Companion of Literature *comp. noun* a member of this order, founded in 1961

Company House *pr. name* an executive agency of the ➡Department of Trade and Industry, responsible for collecting and keeping on file information about all private and public companies trading in ➡Great Britain

In fact there are two physical Company Houses: one in ➡Cardiff, responsible for all companies in England and Wales, and another in ➡Edinburgh, responsible for all companies in Scotland.

company sergeant-major *comp. noun* the highest-ranking warrant officer in a British Army company

compassionate allowance *noun* a special payment made to a member of the armed forces when, because of unusual circumstances, normal allowances, pension, etc. are not sufficient

compassionate leave *comp. noun* military leave granted for special reasons such as a family death

compendium *noun* a comprehensive one-volume reference book or textbook

compère *noun, Fr.* a disk jockey or anchorman

From the French for "godfather"

complementary therapy *comp. noun* alternative or fringe medical therapy

compositor *noun* a typesetter

comprehensive school *comp. noun* a state secondary school taking as students all children of the appropriate age that live in a given district, regardless of ability

About 90 percent of all secondary school students in Britain now attend comprehensive schools, which were brought into being for political rather than educational reasons during the 1960s and 70s. The grim and increasingly grimmer products of what is jokingly described as the British education system is the visible and highly unfortunate result.

compulsory purchase *comp. noun* the enforced purchase of land by a local or national government or government agency under the authority of a ➡Compulsory Purchase Order

Compulsory Purchase Order *comp. noun* an order issued by a court enabling the legal enforcement of a ➡compulsory purchase

con *spell.* conn

The steering of a ship.

conceit *verb* to take a fancy to

concentre *spell.* concenter

To bring to the same centerpoint.

concert party *comp. noun* a musical performance presented in a place other than a regular theater

concessionnaire *spell.* concessionaire

conchie *noun, abbr., sl.* a conscientious objector

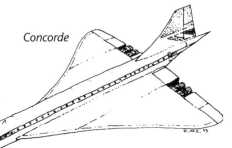

Concorde

the **Concorde** *pr. name* the world's only operational supersonic passenger transport airliner

Designed and built as a joint venture by Britain and France, the Concorde was first flown in 1969 and has been in service with ➡British Airways and Air France since 1976.

conditional discharge *comp. noun* an order made by a court under which a criminal will not be sentenced for one offense unless another is committed within a set period of time

cone off *verb* to deliniate or mark off a road or section of road with traffic cones

the **Confederation of British Industry** *pr. name* the largest and most significant association of industrial companies in Britain

conferment *noun* conferral

confidence trick *comp. noun, coll.* a confidence game

confirmation *noun, Sc.* a grant of probate

conformist *noun* a person who accepts the doctrine and practices of the ➡Church of England

conformity *noun* acceptance of the doctrine and practices of the ➡Church of England

congratters *noun, abbr., coll.* congratulations

Congregation *noun* a general gathering of the senior members of certain universities

Congreve rocket *comp. noun, hist.* the type of artillery rocket used by the British army at the siege of Baltimore during the War of 1812

It is these that are referred to as the "rocket's red glare" in the U.S. National Anthem. The rockets were developed by Sir William Congreve.

Coniston Water *pr. name* a narrow lake, five miles long, located in England's ➡Lake District

conk *noun, sl.* a large or particularly obtrusive nose

conker *noun, coll.* the hard, round nut that is the fruit of the horse-chestnut tree

conkers *noun, coll.* a game played by children

➡Horse-chestnut nuts are threaded with and suspended from strings. They are then swung at each other in turns until one or the other is smashed, the surviving being the victor.

{**Connacht » Connaght**} *pr. name* one of the four ancient provinces of Ireland

It consists of the counties of Galway, Leitrim, Mayo, Roscommon, and Sligo, all within the ➡Irish Republic.

connexion *spell., out.* connection

the **Conqueror** *pr. name, hist.* ➡William I

The Duke of Normandy, victor of the Battle of ➡Hastings in 1066 and the last conqueror of England.

the **Conquest** *pr. name, abbr., hist.* the ➡Norman Conquest of 1066

conservancy *noun* an agency responsible for managing a river, port, or other water resources

conservation area *comp. noun* an area whose environment is legally protected against changes

Conservative *pr. name* a member or supporter of the ➡Conservative Party

Conservative Central Office *pr. name* the headquarters of the ➡Conservative Party

It is in ➡Smith Square, near the Palace of Westminster.

the **Conservative Party** *pr. name* one of the two leading political parties in Britain

The party is disposed towards individual liberty, free enterprise and preservation of the existing order. It is also known as the ➡Tory Party.

Conservative peer *comp. noun* a ➡Conservative member of the ➡House of Lords

Conservativism *pr. name* the philosophies and policies of the ➡Conservative Party

consignment note *comp. noun* a list of goods shipped

consistory court *comp. noun* a ➡Church of England court administering church law within a diocese

It is presided over by the bishop of the diocese.

Consolidated Fund *pr. name* the sum of all government revenues paid into the ➡Exchequer Account at the ➡Bank of England, pledged to meet all government spending and to go towards the reduction of the national debt

consols *noun, abbr.* British Government securities with fixed rates of interest and no redemption date

The name is an abbreviation of "consolidated annuities"

constable [A] *noun* the commandant of a royal castle

For example, the ➡Tower of London or ➡Edinburgh Castle.

[B] *noun, abbr.* a ➡police constable

the **Constable of England** *pr. name, hist.* an ancient office once responsible for the royal stables, now revived for ceremonial purposes at the time of a ➡coronation only

constabulary *noun* a police force

Constantine I *pr. name, hist.* King of ➡Alba

He reigned from 862 until killed in battle by the Danes in 877.

Constantine II *pr. name, hist.* King of ➡Alba

He reigned for 42 years from 900 until he abdicated to become Abbot of the Abbey of ➡St Andrews in 942. He died ten years later in 952.

Constantine III *pr. name, hist.* ➡King of Scots

The son of ➡Culen, he reigned for two years from 995 until killed by his successor in 997.

constant screamer *idiom, rh. sl.* a concertina

The musical instrument.

constituency *noun* the parliamentary district or seat of a ➡MP or ➡MEP

The exact number of constituencies varies according to the rulings of the ➡Boundaries Commissions, but there have been about 650 House of Commons constituencies for some time now, together with 87 larger constituencies electing Members to the ➡European Parliament

constitutional monarchy *noun* the legal form of the British state, where the monarch's power is very severely restricted by the constitution.

Effectively the monarch has just one power left, which is to dismiss any government that attempts to dispense with democracy or the rule of law. Also called a ➡limited monarchy. *SEE ALSO:* ➡absolute monarchy.

consultant *noun* a senior specialist hospital physician or surgeon

the **Consumers' Association** *pr. name* a consumer's pressure group

contango *noun* (1) a delay of one day in the transfer between accounts of securities on the British Stock Exchange; (2) a fee paid by a purchaser in order to effect (1)

SEE ALSO: ➡backwardation.

contango day *comp. noun, out.* the eighth day before the biweekly account settlement day that used to operate on the British Stock Exchange

content *noun* one who votes in favor of a motion being considered by the ➡House of Lords

the **Continent** *pr. name* the European mainland

As distinct from the ➡British Isles. Insularity is not an American monopoly; witness the famous headline in a London newspape, "Fog In Channel, Continent Cut Off."

Continental *adj.* pertaining to the European mainland

As distinct from the ➡British Isles.

continental quilt *comp. noun* a duvet or large quilt

continuation *noun* ➡contango

continuation day *comp. noun* ➡contango day

contract in *verb* to deliberately choose to become involved in or with

contract out *verb* to deliberately choose not to become involved in or with

contraflow

contraflow *noun* the movement of traffic along a highway in the opposite direction to normal

Typically found on a divided highway when both directions of traffic are obliged to share one side of the road temporarily while the other side is being repaired.

contributory *noun* a person legally required to contribute towards paying the debts of a company which has gone out of business

con trick *comp. noun, abbr.* a ➡confidence trick

convenience *noun* a euphemism for a rest room

convention *noun, arch.* a meeting of a ➡Convention Parliament

Convention Parliament *pr. name, hist.* one that has not been summoned by the sovereign

There have been two Convention Parliaments in British history. The first was called by General Monck in 1660 to bring about the ➡Restoration of ➡Charles II.

The second was called in January 1689 to legitimize the ascent of ➡William and Mary to the throne after the removal of ➡James II of England and VII of Scotland in the ➡Glorious Revolution of 1688. It legislated for the ➡Bill of Rights and established the system of constitutional monarchy which has been the basis of government in Britain ever since.

conveyancing *noun, leg.* the legal process of transferring the ownership of property from one party to another

convocation *noun* (1) the governing assembly of a university; (2) a regional assembly or synod of the clergy of the ➡Church of England

coo [A] *exclam., sl.* a euphemistic variation of "God."
SEE ALSO: ➡cor.

[B] *noun, Sc.* a cow
The plural is ➡kye.

cook-chill *verb* to pre-cook and chill food for reheating and consumption later

cooked *adj., sl.* exhausted

cooker *noun* (1) a fruit, especially an apple, intended for cooking rather than eating raw; (2) a stove or cooking range

cookery book *comp. noun* a cookbook

cook-general *comp. noun, out.* a servant responsible for both housework and cooking

cookie *noun, Sc.* (1) a plain and unsweetened bun; (2) a prostitute

Cookstown *pr. name* a district in ➡Northern Ireland, in what used to be County ➡Tyrone
The current population is 30,000 (1990 estimate).

coop *noun* a basket used by fishermen to catch fish

co-op *noun, abbr., coll.* a cooperative store

cooper *noun* a beverage consisting half of ➡stout and half of ➡porter

From the old practice of coopers being given one daily allowance of ➡stout and another of ➡porter, which they habitually mixed and drank together.

co-operate *spell.* cooperate

coorse *adj., Sc.* (1) foul or rough; (2) wicked or evil
(1) is descriptive of weather, (2) of people

cop [A] *noun, North* a mound; the crest of a hill

[B] *verb, sl.* to arrest or capture

cop a packet *idiom. phr. verb* to become badly injured

the Battle of Copenhagen *pr. name, hist.* a naval battle in 1801 during the ➡Napoleonic Wars

The British Fleet, with Nelson second in command, was sent north to disrupt the ships of the Baltic states that had allied themselves with Napoleon. Taking some of his smaller ships in close to Copenhagen, Nelson set about bombarding and destroying the Danish Fleet as it lay at anchor there. It was when his superior signaled his withdrawal in the midst of this action that he put his telescope to his blind eye and thus could truthfully say that he saw no signal. When he eventually did withdraw, the Danish Fleet had been destroyed and subsequently the Danish government made peace with Britain.

coper *noun, arch.* a horse trader

cop it *verb, sl.* (1) to be caught out; (2) to be punished

copper *noun, out.* (1) a bronze coin worth one penny; (2) a large vessel used for boiling, either laundry or cooking

copper-bottomed *adj. phr.* (1) with a bottom covered in copper; (2) undoubtedly genuine, solid or reliable
(1) is usually descriptive of a ship.

cop shop *comp. noun, sl.* a police station

copyhold *noun, arch.* (1) a system of land tenure based on manorial records; (2) land held by (1)

copyholder *noun, arch.* a person holding land under the ➡copyhold system

copyright library *comp. noun* a library entitled to one free copy of every book published in Britain
There are five copyright libraries in ➡Great Britain:
the ➡British Library, London
the ➡Bodleian Library, Oxford
University Library, Cambridge
the ➡National Library of Scotland, Edinburgh
the ➡National Library of Wales, Aberystwyth
There is also one in the ➡Irish Republic, which is ➡Trinity College Library, in Dublin

cor *exclam., sl.* a euphemistic variation of "God."
SEE ALSO: ➡coo.

coracle *noun, hist.* a small boat made from intertwined twigs and clay

They have been made and used since before the arrival of the Romans some 2,000 years ago and are still in occasional use on the inland waters of Ireland and Wales; however, today the clay is usually replaced by canvas or plastic.

corbie *noun, Sc.* a carrion crow, raven or rook

corblimey *exclam., sl.* a euphemism for or variation of "God blind me."
SEE ALSO: ➡gorblimey.

cordial *noun* a fruit-flavored non-alcoholic drink, usually drunk when diluted with water

cordwainer *noun, arch.* a shoemaker

core *noun, Sc.* (1) a group of convivial people; (2) a ➡curling team

co-religionist *spell.* coreligionist

co-respondent *spell.* corespondent

corf *noun* (1) a small wagon used by miners; (2) a basket used to keep caught fish alive under water

Corfe Castle *pr. name, hist.* a spectacularly ruined ➡Norman castle dating from the 12th C., positioned high upon a dominant coastal hilltop on the Purbeck peninsular of the ➡Dorset coast
During the ➡English Civil War, it was subject to a long siege by Parliamentary forces who eventually captured it by underhand means, and then deliberately demolished it.

corgi *noun, abbr., Wal* a ➡Welsh corgi dog

Cork *pr. name* (1) a county in the ➡Irish Republic; (2) a city in the ➡Irish Republic
Both county and city are in the ancient province of ➡Munster.

cork tip *comp. noun, arch.* a cigarette's filter tip

corn [A] *noun* wheat
[B] *noun, Ir., Sc.* oats

Corn. *pr. name, abbr.* ➡Cornwall

cornbrash *noun* a clayey limestone layer belonging to the Upper Jurassic geological period

corn dolly *comp. noun* a figure made of straw
It may be used as decoration or symbol.

corned beef *comp. noun* processed beef, usually sold in cans
Not the same as American-style corned beef, which is called ➡salt beef.

corner shop *comp. noun, coll.* a small local store
Called this because they are often located at street junctions.

cornet [A] *noun* an ice cream cone
[B] *noun, arch.* a cavalry troop's fifth-ranking commissioned officer, who traditionally carried the colors into battle

corn exchange *comp. noun, hist.* a building where corn was traded in the past
Now often used as local venues for exhibitions, concerts, etc.

corn-factor *comp. noun* a dealer in ➡corn

corn flour *comp. noun* cornstarch

Cornish [A] *adj.* pertaining to ➡Cornwall
[B] *pr. name* the version of the ➡Celtic language once spoken in ➡Cornwall
The last native speaker died in the 18th C., and now there are only a handful of people able to speak it as a second language.

Cornish cream *comp. noun* an alternative name for ➡clotted cream

Cornish pasty *comp. noun, coll.* (1) a pastry turnover containing seasoned meats and vegetables; (2) a wide, thickly-soled heavy-duty man's shoe
(2) are called this because they resemble (1) in appearance.

the **Corn Laws** *pr. name, hist.* laws in place since the Middle Ages, which regulated, restricted and taxed grain imports until their repeal in 1846
The original purpose was to protect British farming, but as the population of the British Isles grew and self-sufficiency in food production became increasingly impossible, in actual practical effect these laws just made food more expensive. Following the ➡Napoleonic Wars and a series of bad harvests, the pressure for repeal mounted, particularly through the efforts of the Anti-Corn Law League. However there was great resistance in ➡Parliament where landowning interests had a large influence, and it was not until the ➡Irish Potato Famine of 1845 that repeal was finally forced through.

cornstone *noun* a reddish sandstone layer of the Devonian geological period

Cornwall *pr. name* the county in the most southwestern corner of England
County territory includes the ➡Scilly Isles; the county seat is ➡Truro; the current population is 470,000 (1991 Census).

the **Cornwell Badge** *pr. name* an honor awarded for memorable acts of bravery by Boy Scouts
The name commemorates J. T. Cornwell, a 15-year-old sailor who won the ➡VC for outstanding bravery at the Battle of Jutland during World War I.

coronach *noun, Ir., Sc.* a funeral lament or dirge

coronation *noun* the crowning of a new monarch
Every English coronation since 1066 has taken place at ➡Westminster Abbey in London. Scottish coronations took place at the abbey of ➡Scone; ➡Charles II was the last king crowned there, in 1651.

the **Coronation Chair** *pr. name, hist.* a chair of oak especially made to accommodate the ➡Stone of Destiny, which ➡Edward I removed from Scotland to ➡Westminster Abbey in London in 1296
➡Edward II was crowned upon it in 1308, and so has every English and later every British ➡monarch since that time.

Coronation Chicken *pr. name, arch.* a cold chicken dish specially devised to help people avoid the need to spend time cooking on the day of Elizabeth II of England and I of Scotland's ➡coronation in 1953
It consists of cold chicken with curry sauce, together with a salad containing rice and peas.

Coronation Street *pr. name* the longest-running British TV soap opera

First broadcast in 1960, it tells the story of people living in a street of row houses in an industrial town in northern England.

corporation *noun, out.* a city's municipal government

the **Corporation of the City of London** *pr. name, hist.* the ancient body responsible for the local government of the ➡City of London

the **Corporation of Trinity House** *pr. name* an agency that controls lighthouses, buoys, lightships and the pilotage of ships around the coasts of England, Wales and the ➡Channel Islands

Its origins are unknown, but it was established by the 16th C.

Corpus Christi College *pr. name* (1) a college of ➡Cambridge University founded in 1352; (2) a college of ➡Oxford University founded in 1517

the **Corrective Party** *pr. name* a campaign, masquerading as a serious political party, for the legalization of brothels

Organized and publicized with some style by a prostitute and brothel-keeper with the "trade name" of "Miss Whiplash."

the **corridors of power** *comp. noun, coll.* a euphemism for government ministries and the people who inhabit them

The term was devised by C.P. Snow, physicist and novelist.

corrie *noun, Sc.* a deep, bowl-shaped hollow upon a mountainside; a cirque

corticotrophin *spell.* corticotropin

ACTH, a hormone secreted by the pituitary gland.

cosh [A] *noun, coll.* a bludgeon or blackjack

[B] *verb, coll.* to bludgeon

cosh boy *comp. noun, arch., sl.* a youthful thug equipped with a ➡cosh or bludgeon

co-signatory *spell.* cosignatory

COSLA *pr. name, abbr.* the Convention of Scottish ➡Local Authorities

cos lettuce *comp. noun* a romaine lettuce

From the Greek island of Kos

COSPAR *pr. name, abbr.* Committee on Space Research

A government agency responsible for overseeing the British space program, for what that's worth.

cossy *noun, abbr., Aus., coll.* a costume

Costa del Crime *pr. name, sl., Span.* the southeastern coastal region of Spain

It has become called by this name because of the large number of fugitives from British justice reputed to have gone into hiding there. The name is a play made upon Spain's *Costa del Sol. SEE ALSO:* ➡*Costa Geriatrica.*

Costa Geriatrica *pr. name, sl., Span.* the southern coastal region of England

It has been called by this name because of the large number of retired people living there. The name is a play made upon Spain's *Costa Brava. Geriatrica* is pseudo-Spanish for "old people." *SEE ALSO:* ➡*Costa del Crime.*

cost {a packet » the earth} *phr. verb, coll.* to be very expensive or costly

costard *noun* a variety of large ribbed apple

The root-word of ➡costermonger.

coster *noun, abbr., arch.* a ➡costermonger

costermonger *noun* a barrow-boy selling fruit and vegetables

costumier *noun* a costumer

cosy *spell.* cozy

cot [A] *noun* a crib or small high-sided bed suitable for an infant or young child

[B] *noun, arch.* a kind of small swinging bed once used by officers on board ship

cot case *comp. noun* a patient too ill to get out of bed

cot death *comp. noun* sudden infant death syndrome

the **Cotswolds** *pr. name* an attractive rural area set among hills in ➡Gloucestershire

cottage *noun, sl.* a public rest room habitually used as a place of assignation by homosexuals

cottage hospital *comp. noun* a small local hospital which has no resident medical staff

cottage loaf *comp. noun* bread baked into a round shape with a smaller round piece upon that

cottage pie *comp. noun* a pie rather similar to ➡shepherd's pie

cottar *noun, arch., Sc.* the tenant of a rural cottage without attached land, whose rent is paid in the form of farm labor for the landlord

cottier [A] *noun, arch., Ir.* a peasant farming a ➡smallholding under the ➡cottier tenure system

[B] *noun, coll.* thread

cottier tenure *comp. noun, arch., Ir.* a uniquely Irish system of renting ➡smallholdings

The value of rent was settled by a system of competitive bidding between prospective occupiers.

cotton *noun* thread spun from cotton

cotton reel *comp. noun* a spool of thread

cotton wool *comp. noun* absorbent cotton

cotton wool on top *idiom, coll.* not over-endowed with intelligence

couchant *adj.* lying down

cough sweet *comp. noun* a cough drop or lozenge

could not organize a piss-up in a brewery *idiom, derog., sl., taboo* incapable of organizing anything successfully

couldn't care less *idiom, coll., pref.* could care less, totally disinterested

couldn't half *idiom, coll.* most certainly could

council estate *comp. noun* a development of ➡council houses

the **Council for National Academic Awards** *pr. name* a body awarding degrees to students studying certain approved courses at institutions other than universities
Established by ➡Royal Charter in 1964. It is authorized to award both first degrees and doctorates as appropriate.

council house *comp. noun, coll.* a family dwelling owned by and rented from a ➡local authority

councillor *noun* an elected representative on a ➡county, ➡district, ➡regional, ➡borough, ➡burgh, ➡town or ➡city council

the **Council of Ministers** *pr. name, abbr.* the supreme executive body of the ➡European Union
Located in Brussels, Belgium, together with most of the headquarters staff of the Union.

council tax *comp. noun* a local property tax based upon assessed values of property and land, but in a different and more simplified manner than had previously been the case with ➡Rates
Introduced to replace the unpopular ➡Community Charge or ➡poll tax. It is charged on private property only.

council tax-cap *phr. verb* to impose a maximum value at which the ➡council tax may be assessed
A measure taken by the national government in order to control spending by local authorities.

{**counselled » counselling » counsellor**} *spell.* {counseled » counseling » counselor}

counsellor-at-law *comp. noun, Ir.* a ➡barrister retained in an advisory role only

Counsellor of State *pr. name* a temporary ➡regent appointed when the monarch is briefly absent

counter-passant *adj.* moving the other way
A term used in ➡heraldry.

countess *noun* (1) a woman who is an ➡earl in her own right; (2) the wife or widow of an ➡earl; (3) the wife or widow of a ➡count

count out *phr. verb* to successfully move for the adjournment of the ➡House of Commons on the grounds that a quorum is not present
The quorum for the ➡House of Commons is 40 members.

count palatine *comp. noun, hist.* a lord who possessed sovereign power within his own domain
See also: ➡earl palatine

the **Country Code** *pr. name* a publication of the ➡Countryside Commission recommending an appropriate way to behave while in the countryside

country dance *comp. noun* any one of a number of traditional English or Scottish dances

the **Countryside Commission** *pr. name* a permanent independent agency set up by the government to promote the conservation and improvement of the British countryside

the **Countryside Council for Wales** *pr. name* a permanent independent agency set up by the government to promote the conservation and improvement of Welsh landscape and wildlife

county [A] *noun, hist.* (1) historically, the domain of a count; (2) the principal local administrative unit in Scotland until replaced by ➡regions in 1974; (3) the principal local administrative unit in the ➡Irish Republic; (4) the principal local administrative unit in England and Wales
(1) is the origin of the word. English and Welsh Counties are further sub-divided into ➡Districts.
[B] *noun, coll.* the ➡landed gentry in particular, but also other leading citizens within a ➡county [A]
Or rather, those who think of themselves as such.

county borough *comp. noun, arch.* a large town or city that has the status of a county in its own right

the **County Championship** *pr. name* the principal annual competition between the main regional ➡cricket teams of England, each of which represent a particular county
See also: ➡county cricket

county council *comp. noun* the elected body that administers a ➡county

county court *comp. noun* a local court that considers civil matters only

county cricket *comp. noun* a game of ➡cricket played between teams representing counties
See also: the ➡County Championship.

County Hall *comp. noun* the headquarters building of some county councils

County Palatine *comp. noun, hist.* the territory of an ➡earl palatine or ➡count palatine
In England today, there are still two such territories, ➡Cheshire and ➡Lancaster. These are now no more than curiosities, with little real significance. *See also:* ➡duchy.

county school *comp. noun* a ➡state school operated and financed by the local ➡county council

county town *comp. noun* a county seat

coup [A] *noun, Sc.* a garbage dump
[B] *verb, Sc.* to overturn or overbalance

couped *adj.* in heraldry, the condition of there being nothing below a straight cut
Unlike a ragged break, which is ➡erased.

coupon *noun* an entry form for various sorts of competitions such as ⇒football pools

courgette *noun* a zucchini

course *verb* to hunt with dogs

court [A] *noun* (1) an assembly held by a monarch; (2) a state reception; (3) the residence of a monarch; (4) the retinue or establishment of a monarch [B] *noun, abbr.* a ⇒courtyard

the **Courtauld Institute** *pr. name* a college of art and an art gallery containing the collection of impressionistic paintings gathered by the founder
Associated with ⇒London University, it was founded in 1931 by Samuel Courtland.

court card *comp. noun* a face card

court circular *pr. name* a report published daily listing that day's activities at the royal court, which is published in certain newspapers

court dress *comp. noun* a formal dress suitable to wear at a ⇒court [A] (1)

courtesy light *comp. noun* a car's interior dome light

courtesy title *comp. noun* a title with no legal validity but conferred by social custom upon certain relatives of certain members of the peerage
Thus, the eldest son of a ⇒duke is called a ⇒marquis, the eldest son of a ⇒marquis is called an ⇒earl, the eldest son of an ⇒earl is called a ⇒viscount, etc.

courtier *noun* (1) a servant at a royal ⇒court; (2) a regular visitor to a royal ⇒court

court inspector *comp. noun* an official responsible for keeping order, presenting criminal records, and supervising police officers present within the precincts of a court of law

{**court-martialled » court-martialling**} *spell.* {court-martialed » court-martialing}

the **Court of Appeal** *pr. name* the division of the ⇒Supreme Court of Judicature where both civil and criminal appeals are heard
Presided over by the ⇒Master of the Rolls.

the **Court of Arches** *pr. name* the ⇒Church of England court of appeal presided over by the ⇒Archbishop of Canterbury

the **Court of Common Pleas** *pr. name* the court where ⇒common pleas are heard

the **Court of Protection** *pr. name* a division of the ⇒Supreme Court of Judicature that looks after those who are mentally unfit to care for themselves

the **Court of Saint James** *pr. name* the official name of the ⇒court of the British monarch
The formal address that foreign ambassadors to the United Kindom present themselves to is the Court of St James.

the **Court of Session** *pr. name, Sc.* the supreme civil court of Scotland
Established in 1532 when French influence was particularly strong in Scotland, and modeled on the *Parlement de Paris*.

the **Court of the Lord Lyon** *pr. name, Sc.* the Scottish court of chivalry and heraldry

the **Court of Tynwald** *pr. name* the parliament of the ⇒Isle of Man
The oldest democratic legislative assembly in the world still functioning today. It was established during the time of Viking rule in the 10th C. and consists of a Legislative Council and the ⇒House of Keys, which has 24 members chosen by universal suffrage. No British Act of Parliament applies to the ⇒Isle of Man unless it specifically so states.

court shoe *comp. noun* a woman's light pump shoe

courtyard *noun* the quadrangle of a college of ⇒Cambridge University

Cousin Jack *pr. name, out., sl.* a ⇒Cornishman
Especially one who is a tin miner.

couthie *adj., Sc.* (1) sympathetic, friendly or agreeable; (2) neat, comfortable or pleasant
(1) is descriptive of people, (2) of things and places.

Coutts and Company *pr. name (TM)* a small and highly exclusive London bank
Bankers for the ⇒Royal Family.

covalency *noun* covalence
SEE ALSO: valency.

cove *noun, arch., sl.* a man

the **Covenanters** *pr. name, hist., Sc.* those Scottish Presbyterians who signed one or more of the various national Covenants, but especially the ⇒Solemn League and Covenant of 1638
There were four main Covenants, starting with the one signed by the ⇒Lords of the Congregation in 1557 and ending with the Solemn League and Covenant, which was a formal agreement between the Lords of the Congregation and their English ⇒Parliamentarian allies to preserve Presbyterianism in Scotland and establish it as the state religion in England and Ireland.
However, the name particularly applies to those who remained loyal to the Covenants and their Presbyterian religion after it was declared illegal and practioners persecuted in the years between the Restoration of 1660 and the ⇒Glorious Revolution of 1688.

Covent Garden *pr. name* a theater built on land that was originally the garden and burial ground of ⇒Westminster Abbey
Now the site of the ⇒Royal Opera House; the first theater opened for business here in 1732.

Covent Garden Market *pr. name* London's principal vegetable, fruit and flower market

Originally located in the ➡City of London under the terms of a charter granted in the 17th C. by ➡Charles II, but now moved to Nine Elms, to the east of the ➡City.

Coventry *pr. name* a city in the ➡West Midlands

Incorporated as a city in 1345, the current population, including suburbs, is 350,000 (1988 estimate).

cover *noun* in ➡cricket, (1) a ➡fielder's position behind another on the field; (2) ➡cover point

cover drive *comp. noun* a drive past ➡cover point in a game of ➡cricket

cover in *verb, coll.* to cover or roof over

cover note *comp. noun* temporary insurance certificate issued while full documentation is prepared

cover point *comp. noun* a fielding ➡cricket player's off-side position half-way to the field boundary

cow *noun, derog., sl.* a woman

Especially a particularly fat or coarse one.

coward *noun* an heraldic representation of a tail hanging down between legs

cowboy *noun, sl.* (1) an unqualified, incompetent or reckless business person; (2) an unqualified, incompetent or reckless construction worker

cowboy outfit *comp. noun, sl.* an incompetent or ineffective business, especially in construction

cowd *adj., adv., North* cold

Cowes Week *pr. name* an annual yachting and sailing regatta around the Isle of ➡Wight

Cowes is the principal yachting port on that island.

Cow gum *pr. name (TM)* rubber cement

cowhide *noun, Ir., rh. sl.* shrewd, worldly wise

Derivation: shrewd > wide > hide > cowhide.

cowhorns *noun, sl.* tall curved handles upon a bicycle or motorcycle

cow pat *comp. noun* a cow chip

cowshed *noun* a cow barn

SEE ALSO: ➡barn.

cowslip *noun* the British primula

Its formal name is *primula veris*. Commonly found in cow pastures and such places, it has a fragrant yellow flower sometimes streaked with purple.

Cox's orange pippin *comp. noun* a green-red skinned eating apple

cozzpot *noun, sl.* a policeman

CPM *noun, abbr., arch.* the Colonial Police Medal

CPO *noun, abbr.* a ➡Compulsory Purchase Order

CPRE *pr. name, abbr.* the Council for the Protection of Rural England

A body set up in 1926 to protect the English countryside.

CPRS *pr. name, abbr.* the Central Policy Review Staff

A think tank established in 1971 for the explicit purpose of providing confidential in-depth advice to the ➡Prime Minister of the day on any aspect of government policy.

CPRW *pr. name, abbr.* the Council for the Protection of Rural Wales

A body established in 1928 to protect the Welsh countryside.

CPS *pr. name, abbr.* (1) the Centre for Policy Studies; (2) the ➡Crown Prosecution Service

(1) is a right wing think tank established in 1974 under the aegis of Margaret Thatcher (then in opposition) and others. Many of its policy proposals have since been implemented.

CPSA *pr. name, abbr.* the Civil and Public Servants Association

A white-collar union for civil servants.

crabbit *adj., Sc.* crabbed or sullen

crack *noun, Ir., Sc.* (1) good conversation; (2) pleasant company

cracker *noun, coll.* (1) a sexually attractive person; (2) a dry thin unsweetened biscuit often eaten with cheese

crackers *noun, sl.* crazy

cracking *adj., sl.* exceptionally good

crackling *noun, sl.* an attractive woman considered as a sex object

crag *noun* a steep and rocky hillside or cliff face

craggy *adj.* cragged

cragsman *noun* one who climbs ➡crags

craig *noun, Sc.* (1) a ➡crag; (2) the neck, throat or gullet

Craigavon *pr. name* a district in ➡Northern Ireland, in what used to be County ➡Armagh

The current population is 80,000 (1990 estimate).

Craigievar Castle *pr. name, hist.* a fine example of a Scottish ➡tower house

It is located about 25 miles west of ➡Aberdeen. The building was erected early in the 17th C. and is now the most perfectly preserved of the type.

Craigmillar Castle *pr. name, hist.* an impressively ruined 14th C. castle just outside Edinburgh

➡Mary Queen of Scots was particularly fond of this one of her residences. It was drastically modified and extended during the 16th and 17th Cs., after being burned down in 1544.

Crail's capon *comp. noun, Sc.* a variety of smoked or dried haddock

From the fishing village of Crail, in Fife.

cran *noun, arch., Sc.* a volumetric unit of measure for fresh herrings equal to 37.5 ➡Imperial gallons

crannog *noun, Gae., hist., Ir., Sc.* an prehistoric wooden lake-dwelling, which were huts built upon piles driven into the bed of a lake

79

Cranwell

Cranwell *pr. name* the college where ➡RAF officer cadets are trained

Located in ➡Lincolnshire.

crawl *noun, abbr., sl.* a ➡pub crawl

crawlerboard *noun* a dolly or creeper used by a mechanic working in a car repair shop

crawler lane *comp. noun* a traffic lane reserved for especially slow traffic

Typically where the highway is climbing steeply.

cricket:
the batsman

craw's waddin *idiom, Sc.* a large gathering of crows

Literally, "crow's wedding."

CRE *pr. name, abbr.* the ➡Commission for Racial Equality

creaking gate *comp. noun, coll.* an invalid who neither recovers nor gets worse

cream cracker *comp. noun* a crisp dry ➡cracker, often taken with cheese

creamed potatoes *comp. noun* mashed potatoes with added milk or butter

creamery can *comp. noun, Ir.* a milk ➡churn

cream ice *comp. noun, out.* ice cream

cream tea *comp. noun* an ➡afternoon tea featuring scones with ➡clotted cream

create *verb, sl.* to make a fuss or to complain loudly

the Battle of **Crécy** *pr. name, hist.* an English victory over the French in 1346

credit account *comp. noun, pref.* a charge account

creek *noun* (1) a small inlet or bay upon the ocean shore or the bank of a river; (2) a small coastal harbor

creepie *noun, Ir., Sc.* a footstool

crepe bandage *comp. noun* a gauze bandage

crescent *noun* (1) a curved or crescent-shaped street; (2) those houses or other buildings which are erected along (1).

crew [A] *noun, sl.* a group of aggressive youths

[B] *past tense* crowed

Of the verb "to crow".

crewyard *noun, East* a barnyard

crib [A] *noun* (1) a manger; (2) a model of the Nativity scene, usually associated with Christmas activities; (3) the framework supporting a mine shaft; (4) a cot for a newborn child; (5) an aid to cheating during an examination; (6) a brothel

[B] *verb, coll.* to plagiarize

cricket *noun* an outdoor game of 11 players on each side, who take turns to bat and to bowl

cricket:
the bowler

The heart of the game is an encounter between a ➡batsman, who must defend his ➡wicket—which consists of three ➡stumps with two ➡bails resting loosely upon them—and a ➡bowler, who pitches the ball at the wicket. The bowler succeeds if he can either knock over the bails or cause the batsman to hit the ball in such a way that it is caught by another member of his side before it returns to the ground.

In some ways cricket is the very epitome of England and Englishness, although not Scotland or Ireland, where it has never been popular. The game would appear to have evolved from the medieval game of club-ball, but the earliest references to cricket as such date from the 16th C.

Cricket is usually considered to be a summer game.

cricket bag *comp. noun* a long bag used by a ➡cricketer to carry the equipment used in his sport

cricket ball *comp. noun* a ball used to play ➡cricket

A standard cricket ball has a circumference of just less than 9 inches and weighs between 5½ and 5¾ ounces. It is normally red in color and made from leather with a stitched seam.

cricket bat *comp. noun* a bat used to play cricket

A standard cricket bat, which is traditionally made of willow, has a maximum permitted length of 3 feet and 3 inches, a flat surface below the handle with a maximum width of 4½ inches, and a weight about 2l pounds 10 ounces.

The batsman uses it to protect the ➡stumps from the ball pitched at it by the ➡bowler

the **Cricket Council** *pr. name, hist.* the body that governs the game of ➡cricket worldwide

Until the Cricket Council was formed in 1969, the ➡MCC was the governing body.

cricketer *noun* someone who plays ➡cricket

cricket {pitch » field} *comp. noun* a level and grassed open ground where ➡cricket is played

{crikey » cripes} *exclam., sl.* a euphemism for or variation of "Christ"

the **Crimean War** *pr. name, hist.* a war fought from 1854 until 1856 by Britain, France and Turkey against Russia, nominally over possession of the Crimean Peninsula upon the Black Sea, but the real issue was control of the Black Sea itself

The recently invented telegraph made this in many ways the first modern war, with daily reports from the front making allowing public opinion to influence events in a distant foreign war for the first time in history. The best-known example of this was Florence Nightingale's revolutionary reorganization of the British military hospital at Scutari, which was largely a reaction to newspaper reports of the disgusting conditions there. The Crimean War is also well remembered for the ➡Charge of the Light Brigade.

criminal barrister *comp. noun, sl.* a barrister who specializes in criminal cases

the **Criminal Injuries Compensation Board** *pr. name* an agency set up by the government to administer the disbursement of compensation payments to victims of criminal violence

crimper *noun, sl.* a hairdresser

Crimplene *pr. name (TM)* a synthetic fabric

crinkle-crankle wall *noun* a freestanding wall which meanders around like a snake, so making it resistant to lateral pressure and less likely to fall over

crinkly *noun, sl.* an old person

crisp *noun, abbr.* a ➡potato crisp

crispbread *noun* a thin cracker used by those wishing to loose weight, as an alternative to bread

crivens *exclam., Sc.* a euphemistic for "Christ"

The probable derivation is: Christ defend us » Christ fend us » criffens » crivens.

Crockford's *pr. name* an exclusive gambling club in ➡St James's, London

Crockford's Clerical Directory *pr. name* a reference to the clergy of the ➡Church of England and other Episcopal churches in the British Isles

First published in 1858, with a new edition every other year.

crocodile *noun* a line of children walking in pairs

croft [A] *noun* a small parcel of farmland mostly in Scotland, but occassionly northern England, usually with a small dwelling situated upon it

[B] *verb* to farm a ➡croft

crofter *noun* a person who farms a ➡croft, usually as a tenant

the **Crofters' Commission** *pr. name, Sc.* an agency responsible for developing and regulating ➡crofting in Scotland

cromlech *noun, hist., Wal.* (1) a megalithic stone circle; (2) a prehistoric tomb

crommie *noun, Sc.* a cow with crumpled or misshapen horns

Oliver **Cromwell** *pr. name, hist.* Britain's only republican head of state

A politician, general and leader of the ➡Parliamentary party by the end of the ➡English Civil War. Born in ➡Huntingdon, he entered Parliament in 1629 and was a participant in the events leading up to the civil war, which began in 1642. After proving himself a successful general during that struggle, he was made chairman of the special commission that tried ➡Charles I and condemned him to death in 1649.

Following the king's execution, a republic, known as the ➡Commonwealth, was established in England, and in 1653 Cromwell, like George Washington, was invited to become

Oliver Cromwell, Lord Protector of the Commonwealth

king but also like Washington, declined the offer. Eventually, he took the title of ➡Lord Protector of the Commonwealth, the equivalent of president or dictator of the republic of England, and he retained this office until his death in 1658.

croon *verb, arch., Sc.* (1) to mourn with a loud wailing lament; (2) to roar or bellow

cross *verb* to draw two parallel lines across a check

A crossed check cannot be exchanged for cash but must be paid into the bank account specified upon it. This makes theft more difficult or rather, more pointless. To make the process of crossing fully correct and complete, the words "& Co." should be written between the two lines.

the **Crossbelts** *pr. name* a nickname for the 8th Hussars

A unit of the British Army. During the Battle of Almenara in 1710 they removed the crossbelts from a Spanish regiment they defeated and then wore them over their own shoulders.

crossbencher *noun* a member of either ➡House of ➡Parliament who is independent of any party

Although now very rare in the ➡Commons, they are still unexceptional in the ➡Lords.

the **crossbenches** *noun* the location in the ➡Chamber where ➡crossbenchers sit

Cross Country *pr. name (TM)* a railroad company operating long distance services from Birmingham

It is part of ➡British Rail.

crossing-sweeper *comp. noun, arch.* a person employed to clear horse manure out of the way of pedestrians crossing busy urban streets

The job became redundant in the early years of the 20th C. as filthy and polluting horse-drawn vehicles were replaced with environmentally friendly gasoline-powered automobiles. Or at least that's how it seemed 100 years ago. The more things change, the more they stay the same.

on the **cross** *idiom* on the bias

A direction or manner in which fabric can be cut.

crosstalk *noun* witty discussion or repartee

cross the floor *idiom. phr. verb* to change allegiance from one political party to another

The expression arises from the geometry of the ➡Chamber of the ➡House of Commons. Opposing parties sit facing each other across a central divide known as the Floor of the House.

cross wires *comp. noun* the cross hairs of a gunsight or other optical instrument

crotchet *noun* a quarter note

A musical term.

crouse *adj., Sc.* (1) confident or bold; (2) arrogant or conceited

crowdie *noun, Sc.* a variety of soft cheese from ➡Caithness, Scotland

crown *noun* (1) a ➡monarch's ceremonial headgear; (2) a former British coin with a face value of five ➡shillings, which is one quarter of a ➡Pound, or 25 pence in today's money

Normally made of silver, (2) was often referred to as a "dollar" during the 19th C., as its value was close to that of the U.S. dollar for many years.

the Crown *pr. name* (1) a euphemistic name for the ➡monarch; (2) the emblem of the supreme legal entity, which is the governing authority in the United Kingdom

the Crown Agents *pr. name* an office established under authority of the ➡Crown that acts as purchasing and business agents in Britain for certain foreign governments and former British colonies

Crown Colony *comp. noun* a British colony administered by the ➡Crown

This was the status enjoyed by the thirteen American Colonies until 1776.

Crown Court *comp. noun* a division of the ➡Supreme Court of Judicature

It was established in 1970 to replace the ➡assize court and ➡quarter sessions which were discontinued at that time.

Crown Derby Porcelain *pr. name* high-quality chinaware made in ➡Derby from 1877 until 1890

crowned head *comp. noun* a reigning king or queen

the Crown Estate *pr. name* an agency that collects revenue from land belonging to the ➡monarch

Since 1760, the revenues of these lands have been collected by the government and paid directly into the ➡Exchequer in exchange for the ➡Civil List payments.

the Crown Jewels *pr. name* the state regalia belonging to the ➡monarch

The present-day British regalia dates from after the ➡Restoration as the original English Crown Jewels were destroyed at the time of the ➡Commonwealth. They are kept at the ➡Tower of London, where they are normally available on public display.

The Scottish Crown Jewels, which are much older than the ones in the Tower and are known as the ➡Honours of Scotland, are kept on display in ➡Edinburgh Castle.

On the other hand, the Irish Crown Jewels, which had been kept in Dublin Castle, were stolen from there in 1907 causing a major scandal. They have never been seen since.

crown land *comp. noun* land owned by the ➡sovereign

the Crown Office *pr. name* the department that conducts civil legal business for the government

the Crown Proscecution Service *pr. name* a legal agency of the ➡Crown responsible for the independent review and the conduct of criminal prosecutions in England and Wales

It was established in 1986, when it took over these responsibilities from the police.

Croydon *pr. name* a ➡Greater London borough

Its current population, which is also included within the ➡London urban area total, is 300,000 (1991 Census).

crucial *adj., sl.* excellent or wonderful

cruck *noun, hist.* a curved timber reaching from the ground to the top of the roof of a medieval house

cruet *noun* a small container used to contain salt, pepper, mustard, vinegar, and so forth

cruet-stand *comp. noun* a stand to hold ➡cruets in

Cruft's Dog Show *pr. name* Britain's premier international dog show

It has been held annually in London since 1891; since 1938 it has been organized by the Kennel Club.

cruiserweight *noun* a light heavyweight boxer

cruiseway *noun* a canal reserved for recreational use

crumble *noun* a crust made of flour, sugar and butter, all rolled togther into the consistency of crumbled bread and then cooked

crumblie *noun, sl.* a senile or very old person

crumbs *exclam., sl.* a euphemistic variation of "Christ"

crumpet [A] *noun* a soft, flat cake similar to a muffin, but cooked on one side only

[B] *noun, sl.* a sexually attractive woman

crush barrier *comp. noun* a temporary barrier erected to contain a crowd

crutch *spell.* crotch

The zone between the legs.

cry off *verb* to beg off

cryptaesthesia *spell.* cryptesthesia

Extrasensory perception.

crystal *noun* in heraldry, (1) argent, or silvery white; (2) the representation of ➡Luna

crystallised fruit *comp. noun* candied fruit

the **Crystal Palace** *pr. name, hist.* a vast glass and cast-iron structure designed and built by Joseph Paxton to house the ➡Great Exhibition of 1851

According to statistics published in 1851, it was 1,848 feet long and 408 feet wide. It had a total floor area of 772,824 square feet (almost 18 acres) and consisted of 4,500 tons of iron and 900,000 square feet of glass in 293,655 panels. Paxon's winning design – selected from the 234 other designs in competition with his – was drawn on a sheet of blotting paper and then turned into finished drawings in a remarkably brief nine days. Just as remarkably it was then turned into the finished structure in a mere six months. Originally erected in Hyde Park, after the Great Exhibition was over it was moved to Sydenham in south London in 1854 where it was used as an exhibition and entertainment center until it was destroyed by fire in 1936.

Paxton was formerly a gardener, and there was an obvious similarity in design between the Crystal Palace and a greenhouse.

cry stinking fish *idiom. phr. verb* to belittle or disparage the efforts of oneself, one's family, friends or fellow workers

CS [A] *noun, abbr.* a ➡Chartered Surveyor

[B] *pr. name, abbr., Sc.* the ➡Court of Session

CSA *pr. name, abbr.* the Child Support Agency

An agency set up by the government to collect money due from recalcitrant fathers towards the support of their children by mothers they no longer live with.

CSC *pr. name, abbr.* (1) the ➡Civil Service Commission; (2) the Conspicuous Service Cross

CSE *noun, abbr.* Certificate of Secondary Education

Replaced by the GCSE in 1988.

CSI *noun, abbr.* a Companion of the Star of India

CSM *pr. name, abbr.* a ➡company sergeant-major

CSO *pr. name, abbr.* the ➡Central Statistical Office

CSU *pr. name, abbr.* the Civil Service Union

A white-collar union.

CTC *pr. name, abbr.* (1) a ➡City Technology College; (2) the Cyclists' Touring Club

CU *pr. name, abbr.* ➡Cambridge University

cuckoo-pint *comp. noun* the European arum

Its formal name is *arum maculatum*.

Also known as the ➡wake-robin or ➡lords and ladies.

cuddy *noun, Sc.* (1) a donkey; (2) a horse; (3) a carpenter's trestle; (4) a buffoon

{**cudgelled** » **cudgelling**} *spell.* {cudgeled » cudgeling}

cuittle *verb, Sc.* (1) to whisper; (2) to coax by flattery

culchie *noun, Gae., Ir.* an unsophisticated, rustic person

cul-de-sac *comp. noun, Fr.* a street that can be accessed from one end only

From the French, meaning "bottom of the bag".

Culen *pr. name, hist.* King of ➡Alba

He was the son of ➡Indulf and reigned for five years from 966 until he was murdered in 971.

Cullen skink *comp. noun, Sc.* a soup made with smoked fish

Cullen is a fishing village in ➡Banffshire.

Cullinan Diamond *pr. name* the largest known diamond, presented to Edward VII by the government of South Africa

It was named after the owner of the mine in Johannesburg, South Africa, where it was found in 1905. Uncut, it weighed 3,025 carats. After cutting, the largest stone weighs about 516 carats and now forms part of the British ➡Crown Jewels.

the Battle of **Culloden** *pr. name, hist.* the final, decisive battle between the ➡Jacobites led by ➡Charles Edward Stuart and the army of the British government army under the Duke of Cumberland

This, in 1746, was the last set-piece battle to take place on British soil. It was at this place that the ➡Forty-five Rebellion ended and with it the last hopes of the Jacobites. The battle lasted under an hour and ended with a conclusive and crushing victory for Cumberland and the Hanovarian cause.

The unromantic truth is that despite a popular impression that this was a battle between Scots fighting for their freedom from an English oppressor on the one hand and an English oppressor crushing out their romantic bid for freedom on the other, there were more Scots fighting alongside Cumberland than against him.

Culloden is near ➡Inverness in the north of Scotland.

culpable homicide *comp. noun, leg., Sc.* a criminal charge equivalent to manslaughter

Culzean Castle *pr. name, hist.* a large 18th C. house built to look as if it were a medieval castle, located 13 miles south of ➡Ayr upon the Firth of ➡Clyde

In 1946 an apartment in the castle was presented as a gift from the people of Scotland to General Eisenhower in gratitude for what he had done in World War II.

Cumberland *pr. name, hist.* a former county in the most northwestern corner of England

Now part of ➡Cumbria.

Cumbria *pr. name, hist.* (1) an ancient British kingdom; (2) the county in the most northwestern corner of England

(2) was created out of ➡Cumberland, ➡Westmorland and part of ➡Lancaster in 1974. The county seat is ➡Carlisle and its current population is 485,000 (1991 Census).

Cumbrian

Cumbrian *pr. name* a native, citizen or inhabitant of the county of ➡Cumbria

CUP *pr. name, abbr.* ➡Cambridge University Press

cupboard *noun* a shelved closet

cup final *comp. noun* the final game in a national knock-out ➡soccer competition that has as its prize an ornamental trophy resembling a cup

cuppa *noun, abbr., sl.* a cup of tea

cup tie *comp. noun* a ➡tie game in a national knock-out ➡soccer competition that has as its prize an ornamental trophy resembling a cup

curate *noun* a ➡Church of England ➡vicar or ➡rector's assistant clergyman

curate-in-charge *comp. noun* a clergyman placed in charge of a ➡Church of England parish in the absence of a ➡vicar or ➡rector

curate's egg *idiom, coll.* something not entirely bad
From a cartoon published in ➡Punch in 1895:
Bishop (to a nervous young curate as they have breakfast together): "I see that you have got a bad egg, curate."
Curate: "Oh no, my Lord! Parts are excellent, I assure you!"

curator [A] *noun* a member of the managing board of a university or other institution
[B] *noun, Sc.* the legal guardian of a minor

curl down *phr. verb, coll.* to curl up
For example, with a good book.

curragh *noun, Gae., Ir.* a ➡coracle

current account *comp. noun* a checking account

current bun [A] *noun* a raisin-bread bun
[B] *idiom, rh. sl.* (1) the sun; (2) a son

current form *comp. noun, coll.* present performance
For example, of a sports team.

curriculum vitae *comp. noun, Lat.* a personal résumé
The Latin for "course of life".

the **Curse of Scotland** *pr. name, hist.* the nine of diamonds
Many theories have been put forward to explain the origin of this phrase but none are very convincing. All that is certain is that it has been around for hundreds of years.

curtain up *comp. noun* the commencement of a play or other theatrical entertainment
The phrase refers to the rising of a theatrical curtain.

curtana *noun, hist.* a blunt sword carried before the monarch during the ➡coronation ceremony as a symbol of mercy

customer *noun* what a passenger is now called by ➡British Rail
It is suspected that the name was changed because "passenger" implied travel or movement towards a goal or destination...

cut *adj., sl.* drunk

cut along *phr. verb, sl.* to depart

cut rounds *comp. noun, South* cut scones spread with clotted cream and strawberry jam

cutter *noun* a ➡cricket ball turned sharply on pitching

cut the cackle *imper, sl.* stop talking and get on with what you are supposed to be doing

cutthroat razor *comp. noun* a straight razor

cutting *noun* (1) a channel excavated through a hillside; (2) a clipping from a plant made for gardening reasons
Usually (1) is dug so a railroad, highway, etc. can pass.

cutty *adj., North., Sc.* short or stumpy

cutty sark *comp. noun, Sc.* a short chemise or undershirt

cutty stool *comp. noun, hist., Sc.* (1) a low stool; (2) a ➡Stool of Repentance

cut up rough *phr. verb, coll.* to exhibit resentment, bad temper or anger

CV *noun, abbr., Lat.* a ➡curriculum vitae

CVO *noun, abbr.* a Commander of the Royal Victorian Order

cwm *noun, Wal* a cirque

cwt *noun, abbr.* a ➡hundredweight

cyberphobia *noun* a fear of computers

cycle clip *comp. noun, abbr.* a ➡bicycle clip

cyclopaedia *spell., out.* cyclopedia
An encyclopedia.

cyder *spell., arch.* cider

Cymric *noun, Gae.* Welsh

Cymru *pr. name, Wal.* ➡Wales

cypher *spell.* cipher

d *noun, abbr., Lat.* a ➡penny

The symbol for the old ➡penny, being the first letter of the Latin ➡*denarius* = "penny".

DA *noun, arch., out., sl.* a ➡Duck's Arse

dab hand *comp. noun, coll.* (1) an expert; (2) a skilled amateur

dabs *noun, sl.* fingerprints

Dad's Army *pr. name, coll., hist.* a disparaging nickname for the ➡Home Guard

daft *noun, coll.* stupid, crazy or foolish

daft as a brush *idiom, coll.* completely crazy

daft as a yett on a windy day *idiom, Sc.* completely crazy. SEE ALSO: ➡yett

daftie *noun, Sc.* a thoughtless, foolish or stupid person

Dáil *pr. name, Gae. abbr.* the ➡*Dáil Éireann*

Dáil Éireann *pr. name, Gae.* the lower house of the parliament of the ➡Irish Republic

daily *noun, abbr., coll.* a cleaning woman visiting daily

Daily Mail *idiom, rh. sl.* a story

Derivation: story > tale > mail > Daily Mail. The *Daily Mail* is a newspaper published in London.

daisy-cutter *comp. noun, coll.* (1) a perfect landing by an aircraft; (2) a ➡cricket ball that fails to rise when it is delivered

daisy roots *idiom, rh. sl.* boots

the **Dakota** *pr. name, hist.* the name adopted for the Douglas DC-3 by the ➡RAF during World War II

daks *noun, sl.* a pair of men's pants

Originally the tradename of casual pants sold by Simpsons, a London store, in 1934.

dale *noun, North* a valley

dalesman *noun, North* a man who lives in a ➡dale

Dalriada *pr. name, hist.* an ancient kingdom in western Scotland and northern Ireland

The independent kingdom of the ➡Scots that came into being in the 6th C. It annexed ➡Caledonia to create the new joint kingdom of ➡Alba in 843. Originally Dalriada included land and people in both of what is now Scotland and Ireland, but the Irish territory became detached due to

disruption by Viking invaders in the 8th and early 9th C. The usual seat of the kings of Dalriada was Dunstaffnage, near the modern town of ➡Oban in ➡Argyll.

damager *noun, rh. sl.* a manager

the **Dambusters** *pr. name, hist.* the nickname for 617 Squadron of the ➡RAF

In May 1943, this specially formed ➡Lancaster-equipped squadron destroyed the Möhne and Eder dams that supplied much of the water used by Germany's Ruhr industrial district. Eight of the 19 aircraft that set out failed to return. The ➡bouncing bomb that made the mission possible was invented by aeronautical engineer Barnes Wallis.

dame *noun* (1) the title of a woman who has been awarded a ➡knighthood, an ➡OBE, or certain other awards; (2) a comic character in a ➡pantomime

So far as (1) is concerned, there are various ranks of dame. The title is attached to the primary given name, not the family name, thus it is "Dame Jill Smith" or "Dame Jill," however "Dame Smith" is always incorrect. The husband of a dame carries no special title, so it is "Dame Jill and Mr. Smith." (2) is a man playing the part of an older woman, often the ➡principal boy's mother or aunt.

damehood *noun* the condition of being a ➡dame

dame school *comp. noun, hist.* an elementary school kept and taught by elderly women

damn all *comp. noun, sl., taboo* absolutely nothing

damp {course » proof course} *comp. noun* a waterproof membrane laid across the walls of a building near to but higher than ground level in order to prevent ➡rising damp

dance the Tyburn jig *idiom. phr. verb, arch.* to hang by the neck until dead

SEE ALSO: ➡Tyburn.

dander *noun, Sc.* a ➡dauner

Dandie Dinmont Terrier *pr. name* a small-legged terrier with long body and ears, and possessing a large knot of hair upon the head

Named after a character in Sir Walter Scott's novel *Guy Mannering*, who owned six dogs of this kind.

dandiprat *noun, coll., hist.* (1) a dwarf; (2) a coin issued during the reign of Henry VII

(2) had a face value of three ➡halfpence.

Danegeld *pr. name, hist.* the tribute or tax paid by the ➡Anglo-Saxon kingdoms of England to the ➡Danes, principally between 991 and 1013

An early example of appeasement, as Kipling pointed out when he wrote,

> ... *if once you have paid him Danegeld,*
> *You will never get rid of the Dane.*

the **Danelaw** *pr. name, hist.* that part of England ruled by the Danes from the 9th to 11th Cs.

This territory changed greatly in extent and shape over this period, making exact delineation rather impractical, but at maximum extent it comprised all of northern and most of eastern England; well over half the national territory.

the **Danes** *pr. name, hist.* the name by which those Vikings who invaded England and established the ➡Danelaw in the 9th C. have become known

They came from what is now Norway, as well as the territory of present-day Denmark. Occasional raids along the English coast had developed into long-term occupation and ultimately permanent conquest and settlement of ➡East Anglia and ➡Northumbria; part of ➡Mercia was occupied also.

Only the successful military campaign of ➡Alfred the Great prevented Danish conquest of all of England, and indeed by 10th C., the Danes had accepted the suzerainty of ➡Wessex. However from 980, the Danish attacks resumed, to be bought off for a time by the payment of ➡Danegeld; in 1013 they conquered the entire country and Denmark and England were one kingdom. This ended with the ascent to the English throne of ➡Edward the Confessor in 1042.

danger list *comp. noun* a critical list in a hospital, etc.

danger money *comp. noun* hazardous work pay

darbies *noun, arch., sl.* handcuffs

Darby and Joan *idiom, coll.* a long and happily married elderly couple

Darby and Joan club *comp. noun, coll.* a senior citizens' club

darg *noun, North, Sc.* a day's work

dariole *noun* an individual portion, either sweet or savory, cooked and served in an individual flowerpot-shaped vessel, which has also served as its mold

dark blue *comp. noun, coll.* (1) a present or former student of ➡Harrow School; (2) a present or former student of ➡Oxford University

the **Dark Lady** *pr. name, hist.* the mysterious woman that Shakespeare wrote about in 26 of his sonnets

dart *noun, coll.* a paper airplane

Dartmoor *pr. name, hist.* an extensive area of bleak upland moors in ➡Devon, designated as a ➡national park in 1954

Dartmoor pony *comp. noun* a breed of small pony originating in Dartmoor

Particularly suited for and popular with children.

Dartmoor Prison *pr. name* a remote jail with a particularly forbidding reputation

Located at Princetown in the midst of ➡Dartmoor, it is one of Britain's remotest and bleakest prisons, originally built to house French prisoners of war during the ➡Napoleonic Wars.

Dartmouth *pr. name, abbr.* an informal name for the ➡Britannia Royal Naval College, located at Dartmouth, in Devon

Darwin College *pr. name* a college of ➡Cambridge University founded in 1964

dash [A] *exclam., sl.* a euphemistic variation of "damn" [B] *noun, sl.* money

dash it *exclam., sl.* a euphemistic variation of "damn it"

Datapost *pr. name (TM)* an express package delivery service operated by the ➡Royal Mail

dauner *noun, Sc.* a saunter or casual stroll

Davenport *noun* a writing desk with drawers and a hinged or sloping writing surface

David I *pr. name, hist.* ➡King of Scots

The son of ➡Malcolm III, he grew up in England at the court of ➡Henry I, who was his brother-in-law, and introduced a number of ➡Norman customs into Scotland. He reigned for 29 years from 1124 until 1153.

David II *pr. name, hist.* ➡King of Scots

The son of ➡Robert I, he reigned for a fairly disastrous 42 years from 1329 until 1371. To break the monotony he was deposed for three months in 1332 and then remained out of effective control of most of the land from 1333 until 1356, a period encompassing more than half his reign.

Davis apparatus *comp. noun* a mechanism devised to enable escape from sunken submarines

Davy *pr. name, abbr.* a ➡Davy lamp

Davy lamp *pr. name* a miner's safety lamp

Invented by the English chemist Sir Humphry Davy.

the **day after the fair** *idiom, coll.* when it is too late

day {boy » girl} *comp. noun* a {male » female} student at a boarding school who lives at home

daylight robbery *comp. noun, coll.* highway robbery

In the sense of outrageous overcharging.

day release *comp. noun* a system of part-time training for employees, usually paid for by their employer

Under this arrangement, the employee is permitted one day away from work each week to attend college to be educated in skills that will enhance performance at work.

day return *comp. noun* a discounted same-day round-trip travel ticket

day's a-dawning *idiom, rh. sl.* morning

DBE *pr. name, abbr.* a Dame Commander of the British Empire

DCB *pr. name, abbr.* a Dame Commander of the Order of the ➠Bath

DIC *noun, abbr.* a ➠Detective Chief Inspector

DCM *noun, abbr.* the Distinguished Conduct Medal

DCMG *noun, abbr.* a Dame Commander of the Order of St Michael and St George

DCVO *noun, abbr.* a Dame Commander of the Royal Victorian Order

deacon *noun, Sc.* (1) a master craftsman; (2) the chief official or president of a craft or trade association; (3) a lay person handling the non-spiritual affairs of a ➠Church of Scotland parish church

{**deacon » deaconess**} *noun* the lowest grade of ordained {male » female} minister in the ➠Church of England

dead-and-alive *adj. phr., sl.* monotonous or boring

dead bat *comp. noun* a ➠cricket bat so loosely held that the ball does not bounce away when it hits it

dead cert *comp. noun, abbr., sl.* an absolute certainty

dead chuffed *idiom, sl.* very satisfied or pleased

deadhead *noun* the faded head of a dead flower

dead slow *imper.* travel very slowly

A roadside sign.

deaf aid *comp. noun* a hearing aid

dean *noun* (1) a ➠don in charge of a college chapel at ➠Oxford or ➠Cambridge Universities; (2) a ➠don responsible for undergraduate discipline at a college at ➠Oxford or ➠Cambridge Universities

deanery *noun* a group of parishes under the charge of a ➠rural dean

the **Dean of Faculty** *pr. name, Sc.* (1) the head of a Scottish university faculty; (2) the president of the ➠Faculty of Advocates in Scotland

Dean of Guild *pr. name, Sc.* the president of a ➠Dean of Guild Court

Dean of Guild Court *pr. name, Sc.* a court charged with supervising all building work within a town, to ensure it meets legal requirements

deasil *noun, arch., Sc.* the practice of walking around a person in a clockwise or sunward direction

Doing this is supposed to bring good luck.

Death Duty *pr. name, hist.* a tax levied upon the assets of those who die

It was replaced by ➠Capital Transfer Tax in 1975.

death grant *comp. noun* a payment made by the state to help defray funeral expenses

the **Death or Glory Boys** *pr. name* a nickname for the 17th Hussars

A unit of the British Army whose regimental badge, which was created in memory of General Wolfe, is a Death's Head with the motto "Or Glory."

deave *verb, Sc.* to annoy or to bore

débâcle *spell.* debacle

debag *verb, sl.* to remove a man's pants as a prank

the **Debatable Lands** *pr. name, hist.* a tract of land between the Sark and Esk Rivers, near to the ➠Solway Firth on the western part of the border between England and Scotland

The reason for it being called this is that it was claimed and fought over by both countries for many years.

debenture *noun* a document formally acknowledging a debt

Especially an interest-bearing bond issued by a corporation.

debenture stock *comp. noun* corporate stock consisting of ➠debentures

debit a credit card *phr. verb* to charge a credit card

Debrett's Peerage *pr. name, abbr.* a directory of the members of the British aristocracy

Published annually, its full title is *Debrett's Peerage, Baronetage, Knightage and Companionage.*

deb's delight *idiom, sl.* an upper-class young man who is considered a socially acceptable marriage partner for the daughters of upper-class families

début *spell.* debut

débutante *spell.* debutante

Decca *pr. name (TM)* a long-range navigation system used by ships and aircraft

The system uses phase differences between radio signals from two or more widely-separated transmitters which are integrated by an onboard computer to calculate position.

decent *adj.* generous, kind or helpful

decillion *noun, num.* a novemdecillion, or 10^{60}

The American decillion is 10^{33}.

decimalisation [A] *noun, hist.* the revision of Britain's currency from its former non-decimal system to the decimal system in use today

The decimalization of Britain's currency was first formally proposed to Parliament in 1816, and then again in 1824, 1847, 1853 and 1855, but failed to gain approval on every one of these occasion. There were many more less formal attempts to reform the currency, but the archaic system was not swept away until February 15, 1971. Until then, the basic unit of currency, the Pound—which remained unchanged by decimalization—was divided into 20 shillings. Each shilling, in turn, consist of 12 pennies so that there were 240 pennies per Pound. The decimalization measures of 1971 abolished the shilling and replaced the older penny with a new penny worth 1/100th of a Pound, or 2.4 times as much as an old penny.

[B] *spell.* decimalization

decimetre *spell.* decimeter

declaration

declaration *noun* the cessation of batting by a ➡cricket team before all wickets are down

---

the **Declaration of Arbroath** *pr. name, hist* a declaration, more properly a petiton, made to the Pope by the lords of Scotland in 1320

Composed in Medieval Latin by the Abbot of Arbroath Abbey and Chancellor of Scotland, Bernard de Linton, this remarkable document can lay strong claim to be the first formal written delaration of national independence in history, and perhaps also the first written manifestation of patriotism in the modern sense, as evidenced by this translated extract:

For so long as one hundred of us remain alive we shall never under any circumstances be brought to submit to English rule. It is not for glory, nor riches nor honor that we fight but for freedom alone, which no honest man gives up but with his life ... leave in peace we Scots, who live in this our poor little Scotland ... coveting nothing but that which is our own.

But what is just as remarkable is that for the first time in history we find that the will and the interests of the *people* are placed before those of the king (who was no less a figure than ➡Robert the Bruce at this time; no weakling he) and if the king betrayed the people he was to be removed. This was revolution indeed!

The Declaration was almost exactly contemporaneous with ➡*Magna Carta*; whatever was going on upon this single small island of Great Britain during these years?

---

declutch *verb* to disengage an automobile's transmission clutch

decoke *verb* to remove carbon deposits from an automobile engine

decorate *verb* to paint and wallpaper, etc., a house
Either indoors or externally as appropriate.

Decorated style *comp. noun, hist.* a style of English Gothic architecture using large amounts of geometric tracery and other forms of decoration
It was most popular in the 14th C.

decorator *noun* a tradesman who ➡decorates houses

decree absolute *comp. noun* an order issued by a court making a divorce final, so that either party is free to remarry
See also: ➡decree nisi.

decree nisi *comp. noun, Lat.* a provisional divorce order issued by a court, which will become absolute within a fixed period unless cause is shown why it should not be
From the Latin, *nisi* = "unless." *See also:* ➡decree absolute.

deed box *noun* a strongbox for legal document storage

deed of covenant *comp. noun* a formal written agreement to pay a regular fixed sum over a specified period, usually some years, to a charity, church, etc.
This deed enables the beneficiary to recover from the ➡Inland Revenue the relevant income tax paid by the benefactor.

deed poll *comp. noun* a deed made and executed by a single individual in order to change their name

deedy *adj., arch.* hard-working

{deemster » dempster » doomster} *noun* a judge of the ➡Isle of Man court
Each takes an oath to execute the law, "... as indifferently as the herring backbone doth lie in the middle of the fish."

deep *adj.* of any position near to the boundary of a ➡cricket field

deep {extra cover » fine leg » mid off » mid on » mid wicket » square leg} *comp. noun* fielding players' positions near to the boundary of the cricket field

deep freeze *comp. noun* a freezer

deep-sea diver *idiom, rh. sl.* a five ➡pound note
Derivation: five pound note > fiver > deep-sea diver.

deerstalker *noun* a soft ➡tweed hat peaked at front and rear, with ear flaps that are very often tied together upon the top of the hat
Made famous as the headgear of ➡Sherlock Holmes.

def *adj., sl.* excellent

defaulter *noun* an enlisted {man » woman} found guilty by a court martial—or in the case of the navy, a ship's captain—of a military offense

defence *spell.* defense

Defender of the Faith *pr. name, hist.* a title belonging at first to English monarchs, but since the Union of 1603, to British monarchs

The letters *F.D.* that are on all British coins are an abbreviation of the Latin version of this, *fidei defensor* = "Defender of the Faith," which was granted to ➡Henry VIII by Pope Leo X in 1521 after the king had written against the perceived iniquities of Martin Luther. Then, ironically, Henry too broke with the Pope and established himself as "supreme governor on earth" of the ➡Church of England. But he and his successors have all retained the Pope's titular gift.

---

degree of frost *idiom* degrees below freezing

Deheubarth *pr. name, hist.* an ancient kingdom in what is now southern Wales

Formed by the union in the early years of the 10th C. of the two earlier kingdoms of ➡Dyfed and ➡Siesyllwg. The rest of south Wales consisted of vassal territories of Deheubarth at this time. Deheubarth was gradually eaten away by English encroachment between 1135 and 1201, when at last all of it had fallen under English rule.

Dei Gratia *adv., Lat.* the words on the ➡Great Seal

Latin for "by the grace of God."

deil *noun, Sc.* (1) a devil; (2) a shoemaker's last, or form used for the shaping of shoes

the **Deil haet** *exclam., Sc.* the Devil take it

Deira *pr. name, hist.* a former principality within the ancient kingdom of ➡Northumbria

In effect, an independent state from 558 until 654. The usual seat of the kings of Deira was in what is now the city of ➡York.

dekko *noun, sl.* a glance or quick look

Delhi belly *comp. noun, coll.* another picturesque name for diarrhea, or Montezuma's revenge

Named for New Delhi, the capital city of India and once the scene of many an outbreak of this affliction.

delustre *spell.* deluster

Demerara sugar *comp. noun* brown cane sugar

Named for the Demerara River in Guyana, the former British colony of British Guiana, in South America.

demeanour *spell.* demeanor

demisemiquaver *noun, pref.* a thirty-second note

A musical term.

demister *noun* a car window defroster

demob *noun, abbr., coll.* (1) the demobilization or disbandment of an army, etc.; (2) the discharge of an individual from an army, etc.

the **Democratic Left** *pr. name, hist.* the name adopted by the former ➡Communist Party of Great Britain in 1991

demolition crane *comp. noun* a wrecker boom

demon bowler *comp. noun* a fast ➡cricket ➡bowler

demy *noun* (1) a scholar at ➡Magdalen College, Oxford University: (2) a paper size of 564 x 444 mm , which is approximately 22¼ x 17½ inches

denarius *pr. name, hist., Lat.* a Roman silver coin

From the Latin, *deniases* = "ten ases," because that was its worth—an *as* was a Roman copper coin.

In the Middle Ages *deniases* was used in both France and England as a name for small-value coins generally, whether of silver or copper. Eventually in England the initial "d" was used to delineate a penny until decimalization in 1971.

Denbigh *pr. name* a former Welsh County that is now part of ➡Clwyd

dene *noun* (1) a featureless, sandy area beside the ocean; (2) a narrow wooded valley with a stream

Denmark *pr. name, hist.* the ➡Royal House of England from 1016 until 1066

The following English monarchs belonged to this house: ➡Edmond Ironside, ➡Cnut, ➡Harold Harefoot, ➡Harthacnut, ➡Edward the Confessor and ➡Harold Godwinson.

dentine *spell.* dentin

deoch an doris *comp. noun, Gae., Sc.* a drink offered and taken at the time of parting

This is Gaelic, meaning "drink at the door."

the **Department for Education** *pr. name* the government department responsible for the implementation and supervision of education policies and measures in England and Wales

the **Department of Employment** *pr. name* the government department responsible for the implementation and supervision of policies and measures for the growth of employment, training of the work force and reduction of unemployment

the **Department of Environment** *pr. name* the government department responsible for the implementation and supervision of policies for protection of the environment, planning and land use, government property construction and maintenance, and local government

the **Department of Health** *pr. name* the government department responsible for the implementation and supervision of government health policies and measures in England

Including administration of the ➡National Health Service.

Department of Health and Social Security *pr. name, hist.* a former government department

It was divided up into the ➡Department of Health and the ➡Department of Social Security in 1988.

the **Department of National Heritage** *pr. name* the government department responsible for policies and measures relating to arts, sport, tourism, broadcasting, and the national lottery

Sometimes disparagingly referred to as the ➡Ministry of Fun.

the **Department of Social Security** *pr. name* the government department responsible for policies and measures relating to the workings of the social security system throughout ➡Great Britain

the **Department of Trade and Industry** *pr. name* the government department responsible for policies and measures relating to both internal and international trade and industrial policy

the **Department of Transport** *pr. name* the government department responsible for policies and measures relating to domestic and international transportation matters that concern Britain

dependant *spell.* dependent

depersonalisation *spell.* depersonalization

deposit *noun* a sum of money kept in a bank account

deposit account *comp. noun* a savings account

deputy lieutenant *comp. noun* a deputy or assistant ➡Lord Lieutenant

the **Deputy Prime Minister** *pr. name* a courtesy title given to a senior cabinet minister who acts for the ➡Prime Minister in routine matters while {he » she} is absent

The office has no constitutional significance or implications and certainly does not mean that the holder would automatically become Prime Minister in the event of the death or incapacity of the incumbent.

Derby [A] *pr. name* a city in Derbyshire

Incorporated as a city in 1154, Derby was the nearest to London that Bonny Prince Charlie got to in the course of the ➡Forty-five Rebellion. More recently, it is where Rolls-Royce is headquartered. The current population, including suburbs, is 225,000 (1991 estimate).

[B] *pr. name, abbr.* ➡Derbyshire

[C] *noun* any significant sporting event

the **Derby** *pr. name* an annual horse race at Epsom

It was named after the 12th Earl of Derby, founder of the race. All other "Derbys" (for example, the Kentucky Derby) whether races of horses, other animals, or anything else, are named in emulation of this event and thus this person, even by people who have never heard of the Earl of Derby.

Derby Day *pr. name* the day of the ➡Derby horse race

Treated by many as a sort of informal public holiday.

Derby porcelain *comp. noun, hist.* very fine porcelain figures made between 1750 and 1756

Derbyshire *pr. name* a county in central England

The county seat is ➡Matlock and the current population is 915,000 (1991 Census).

Dere Street *pr. name, hist.* a Roman road that extends Ermine Street northwards from ➡York to ➡Hadrian's Wall and beyond into Scotland, almost as far as present-day Edinburgh

This name is not Roman but one that was given to it by the Saxons centuries later.

derry *noun, abbr., sl.* a derelict building

Derry *pr. name* the Catholic name for the city of ➡Londonderry in ➡Northern Ireland

See also: ➡Londonderry.

derv *noun, abbr.* a kind of diesel fuel used by trucks

The word is an acronym, derived from the initial letters of the following words: **d**iesel-**e**ngined **r**oad **v**ehicles

DES *pr. name, abbr., hist.* the former Department of Education and Science

Now replaced by the ➡Department for Education.

deselect *verb* to decline to re-select or retain a previously elected and currently in office politician as his or her party's candidate for re-election to the same office.

desert rat *comp. noun, coll., hist.* a nickname for a soldier of the 7th Armoured Division

the **Desert Rats** *pr. name, coll., hist.* a nickname for the 7th Armoured Division

A unit of the British Army that fought in the North African campaign during 1941-42. They adopted the jeroba, a small desert rodent of the *dipodidae* family and popularly known as the desert rat, as their divisional sign during their campaign against Rommel in World War II.

The name came to prominence again during the 1990-91 Gulf War, when they fought once more in the desert.

desiccated coconut *comp. noun* coconut which has been shredded and preserved by drying

the **Design Council** *pr. name* an agency charged with the task of improving the standard of British engineering and industrial design

desmond *noun, rh. sl.* a lower second class university degree

Derivation: lower second > 2/2 > two-two > Desmond Tutu (Anglican Archbishop of South Africa) > desmond.

desperadoes *spell.* desperados

des res *comp. noun, abbr., sl.* a desirable residence

Realtor's jargon

dessert *noun* nuts or fresh fruit eaten as the final dish of a meal

dessertspoonful *noun* a unit of measurement used in cookery

The quantity a dessertspoon will hold, about 2.5 fluidrams.

destructor *noun* a trash incinerator

detached house *comp. noun* a house not physically attached to another building

detention centre *comp. noun* a detention home for the short-term incarceration of teenage criminals

Detective Chief Inspector *comp. noun* a police ➡Chief Inspector who is a detective

Detective Inspector *comp. noun* a police ➡Inspector who is a detective

deuce *noun, coll.* bad luck

the **deuce to pay** *idiom, coll.* big trouble

development area *comp. noun* an assisted area where new business is encouraged by relaxed regulatory requirements and tax breaks, all to help counteract high local unemployment

devil *noun, sl.* junior legal counsel

devil's coach-horse *comp. noun* a large beetle

Its formal name is *staphylinus olens*.

the **Devil's Own** *pr. name, hist.* (1) a nickname for the 88th Regiment of ➡Foot; (2) a nickname for the former ➡Inns of Court Rifles

Both are units of the British Army. This name was given to (1) by General Picton to honor their bravery during the ➡Peninsular War; and to (2) by ➡George III, when he learned that the regiment consisted entirely of lawyers.

Devon *pr. name* (1) a county in southwestern England that borders on ➡Somerset to the east and Cornwall on the west, and straddles the peninsula that separates the ➡Bristol Channel from the ➡English Channel; (2) a breed of rust-colored cattle originating from (1)

The county seat of (1) is ➡Exeter and the current population of the county is 1,020,000 (1991 Census).

Devonian *noun* (1) a native of ➡Devon (1); (2) a geological period named for Devon (1)

(2) occurred between the Silurian and Carboniferous periods.

Devonshire *pr. name, hist.* the former name of the English county of ➡Devon

Devonshire cream *comp. noun* ➡clotted cream

dewpond *noun* a shallow pond, usually artificial

These are often found in the villages of the chalky hills of southern England, and have this name because it was once supposed that they filled up from atmospheric condensation.

dexter [A] *noun* the right-hand side of a shield or a ➡coat of arms

[B] *noun, Ir.* a breed of small tough cattle

dextrous *spell.* dexterous

DF *pr. name, abbr.* ➡Defender of the Faith

DFC *noun, abbr.* the Distinguished Flying Cross

DFE *pr. name, abbr.* the ➡Department for Education

DFM *noun, abbr.* the Distinguished Flying Medal

D.G.REX.F.D *idiom, abbr., Lat.* the letters that appear beside the monarch's head on British coins

From the Latin *Dei Gratia Rex Fidei Defensor* = "By the grace of God King, Defender of the Faith." This is one instance where the word *rex*, meaning "king," continues to be used even during the reign of a queen.

DH *pr. name, abbr.* the ➡Department of Health

DHSS *pr. name, abbr., hist.* the ➡Department of Health and Social Security

DI [A] *noun, abbr.* a ➡Detective Inspector

[B] *pr. name, abbr.* Defence Intelligence

diabolical *adj.* seriously incompetent or unacceptable

diaeresis *spell.* dieresis

dial *noun, sl.* the face

{**dialled** » **dialling**} *spell.* {dialed » dialing}

dialling tone *comp. noun* a telephone dial tone

dialogue *spell.* dialog

{**dialyse** » **dialyser**} *spell.* {dialyze » dialyzer}

diamond *noun* in heraldry, (1) ➡sable; (2) a representation of the planet Saturn

diarrhoea *spell.* diarrhea

diary engagement *comp. noun, out.* an appointment

dicey *adj.* risky

dicht *verb, Sc.* to wipe or rub clean in a cursory way

dick [A] *noun, abbr., sl.* a declaration

[B] *noun, coll.* a man

dickens *noun, sl.* a euphemism for the devil

Dickensian *adj.* pertaining to Dickens, his writings or the period when he lived

Charles Dickens was a 19th C. English novelist who wrote primarily of social conditions in Victorian England.

dickory dock *idiom, rh. sl.* a clock

dicky [A] *adj., sl.* unreliable, likely to collapse or to fail

[B] *noun, rh. sl.* (1) a shirt; (2) a word

(1) Derivation: shirt > dirt > dicky dirt > dicky; (2) Derivation: word > bird > dicky bird > dicky.

dicky bow *comp. noun, sl.* a bow tie

dicky seat *comp. noun, coll.* (1) the driver's seat on a horse-drawn carriage; (2) an extra seat at the rear of a vehicle that folds away when not in use

didicoy *noun, sl.* a gypsy

This probably began life as a ➡Romany word.

didna *verb aux., Sc.* did not

the **Die Hards** *pr. name* the 57th Regiment of ➡Foot

A unit of the British Army. At the Battle of Albuera in 1811 with three-quarters of their number dead or wounded, their commander, Colonel Inglis who was himself badly wounded, cried, "Die hard, my men, die hard."

diet *noun, Sc.* (1) a meeting of the governing council of a ➡district or ➡region; (2) a session of a court of law; (3) a church service

diethylstilboestrol *spell.* diethylstilbestrol

$C_{18}H_{20}O_2$, a synthetic colorless crystalline compound, which is also called stilbestrol.

Dieu et mon droit *comp. noun, Fr.* the motto of the British ➡Royal Family

The slogan was first adopted by Richard I before the Battle of Gisors in France in 1198. Its implicit meaning then, and the reason he chose it, was to announce that he was no vassal of France but owed his kingship to God alone. In the battle that followed the French were thrashed.

The literal meaning of the motto, in French, is "God and my right hand."

---

difference *noun* those changes, usually small, which are made to a ➡coat of arms to distinguish between individual members of a family

differencing *noun* the alteration of a ➡coat of arms to distinguish between individual family members

differential *noun* the difference between rates of pay

different to *adj. phr.* different from, different than

digestive biscuit *comp. noun* a semi-sweet whole wheat cookie

diggings *noun, arch.* ➡digs

dig over *verb* to loosen or break up soil in a garden

digs *noun, coll.* furnished lodgings
Such as might be occupied by a student, for example.

dim *adj., coll.* dim-witted

DIN *pr. name, abbr., Ger.* any of a large number of industrial standards established in Germany and now increasingly accepted throughout the ➡EU
From the German, *Deutsche Industrie Norm* = "German Industrial Standard".

dine *noun, Sc.* dinner

dinky *adj., coll.* (1) small; (2) neat; (3) dainty

dinna *verb aux., Sc.* do not

dinna fash yersel *idiom, Sc.* (1) don't trouble yourself; (2) don't get excited, keep calm

dinner jacket *comp. noun* a tuxedo jacket

dinner lady *comp. noun, coll.* a woman who serves lunch at school

dinner pail *comp. noun, coll.* a container for a packed lunch

dioestrus *spell.* diestrus
The condition of having male sexual organs and female ones on separate and individual plants or animals.

dioptre *spell.* diopter
A measure of the refractive power of a lens.

dip [A] *verb* to dim car headlights
[B] *verb, sl.* to become indebted

Dip AD *comp. noun, abbr.* a Diploma in Art & Design

Dip Ed *comp. noun, abbr.* a Diploma in Education

Dip HE *comp. noun, abbr.* Diploma of Higher Education

the **diplomatic service** *comp. noun* all of a nation's diplomats considered as a group

{**dipper » dip-switch**} *noun* a headlight dimmer switch on an automobile

dirdum *noun, Sc.* (1) a heavy blow; (2) a difficulty or complication; (3) a loud argument or scolding; (4) a state of agitated excitement

direct debit *comp. noun* an arrangement whereby a third party may debit a bank account directly under a ➡direct debit mandate

direct debit mandate *comp. noun* a formal written authority from a customer to their bank authorizing a third party to debit their account directly

direct grant *comp. noun* money provided directly by the government to fund certain schools

direct grant school *comp. noun* a school financed by means of a ➡direct grant

direction signal *comp. noun* a vehicle turn signal

Directoire knickers *comp. noun, Fr.* full knee-length womens' underpants
Named after the *Directoire* = "Directory", the governing executive of revolutionary France from 1795 to 1799.
Just why that body should have got involved in designing lady's underwear in the first place is not immediately apparent, but then they *were* French.

director *noun* a member of the managing board of an incorporated business

the **Director of Public Prosecutions** *pr. name* the legal officer who is head of the ➡CPS
Although in exceptional circumstances the Director of Public Prosecutions can be directed by the ➡Attorney General to bring important prosecutions in England and Wales, in the normal course of events the decision whether to prosecute or not rests entirely with this office.

directory enquiries *comp. noun* the telephone information service
For help locating a telephone number in the UK or Irish Republic, call 192. For the rest of the world, call 153.

dirk *noun, Sc.* a long dagger considered to be a traditional item of Highland dress

the **Dirty Half-Hundred** *pr. name* a nickname for the 50th Regiment of ➡Foot
A unit of the British Army. At Vimiera in 1808 they wiped their faces with their sleeves and in the heat, the black dye ran and covered their faces.

the **Dirty Shirts** *pr. name* a nickname for the 101st Regiment of ➡Foot
A unit of the British Army who fought in their shirt-sleeves during the ➡Indian Mutiny of 1857.

disafforest *verb* (1) to remove a forest; (2) to change the legal status of a forest to that of ordinary land

{**discolour » discolourment**} *spell.* {discolor » discolorment}

discount house *comp. noun* a business that discounts bills of exchange

{**disembowelled » disembowelling**} *spell.* {disemboweled » disemboweling}

disenfranchise *verb* disfranchise

disenthral *spell.* disenthrall

disestablishmentarianism *noun, arch.* a belief that the ➡Church of England should cease to be an ➡established church

disfavour *spell.* disfavor

dish [A] *noun, out.* a cup

[B] *verb* to destroy hope or opportunity

{**dishevelled » dishevelling**} *spell.* {disheveled » disheveling}

{**dishonour » dishonourable**} *spell.* {dishonor » dishonorable}

dish out of *verb, sl.* to deprive by cheating

dismiss *verb* in ➡cricket, (1) to put an individual ➡batsman out; (2) to put an entire side out

disna *verb aux., Sc.* does not

disorganisation *spell.* disorganization

dispatch box *comp. noun* (1) a dispatch case, a container for state or military papers; (2) one of the wooden boxes placed upon the central table that lies between the government and ➡opposition ➡front benches in the ➡House of Commons

(1) are used to deliver such documents to or from cabinet ministers, senior military officers and other high state officials. It is while standing beside (2) that senior politicians deliver their speeches to the ➡House.

dispatch office *comp. noun* a shipping department

dispatch rider *comp. noun, hist.* (1) a motorcyclist who carries military documents; (2) formerly, a horseback rider who carried military documents

dispensary *noun* a place where prescriptions are fulfilled and medicines are dispensed

dispensing chemist *noun* a pharmacist qualified to make up and give out drugs prescribed by a physician

displaced person *comp. noun, arch.* a refugee

This rather formal name for a refugee was especially common in the years immediately after World War II.

displayed *noun* an heraldic representation of a bird with wings outspread

dispone *verb, Sc.* to transfer the title of real estate

Dissenter *noun, hist.* an English ➡Nonconformist

the **Dissolution Honours** *pr. name* an extra ➡honours list issued at the ➡Dissolution of Parliament

the **Dissolution of the Monasteries** *comp. noun, hist.* the disbandment and seizing of the buildings and land of the English monasteries and other ecclessiastical establishments such as priories, between 1536 and 1541

(See box below)

the **Dissolution of Parliament** *comp. noun* the ending, nominally by the ➡monarch, of a Parliamentary session, leading to a ➡general election

Parliament dissolves automatically five years after it first meets following a general election, but it is within the right of the ➡prime minister to request the monarch to dissolve parliament sooner than this, which means that he or she can pretty much determine the timing of a general election to suit his or her own party.

dissolve the House *idiom. phr. verb* to call a ➡General Election by ➡Dissolution of Parliament

distance *noun* a unit of length used at horse racetracks

It is 240 yards or 720 feet.

distil *spell.* distill

distressed area *comp. noun* a district or region of the country officially recognized as suffering particularly badly from poverty and unemployment

district *noun* (1) in England and Wales, an administrative unit that is a sub-division of a ➡county; (2) in Scotland, an administrative sub-division of a ➡region; (3) in Northern Ireland, the principle local administrative unit in the province

district heating *comp. noun* a heating system where hot water is supplied to individual homes from a central location

the **District Line** *pr. name* one part of London's rapid-transit subway system

Spreading out from the original Metropolitan Railway of 1863, the modern District Line reaches Ealing Broadway, Richmond and Wimbledon in the west and south, Edgeware Road and ➡Kensington (Olympia) in the ➡West End and Barking and Upminster in eastern London.

district nurse *comp. noun* a visiting nurse

The Dissolution of the Monasteries

Following ➡Henry VIII's break with Rome and his establishment of the independent ➡Church of England under the terms of the ➡Act of Supremecy of 1534, this policy of breaking up and selling off assets in England of the Roman Church was carried out with great ruthlessness by Thomas Cromwell, the king's chief minister at that time. At first the king awarded Cromwell by making him Earl of Essex but then, just four months later, had him executed as a heretic.

Of course, apart from destroying actual or potential centers of residual Papal influence and power in England, the dissolution amounted to a considerable economic windfall for the king, who sold much of the land to raise very considerable sums of money.

district visitor *comp. noun* a ➡Church of England clergyman's assistant who visits the sick

{**disulphate** » **disulphide**} *spell.* {disulfate » disulfide}

div *noun, derog., sl.* a stupid old person
Criminal slang.

dive bomb *verb, sl.* to spray graffiti over a wall, etc.
SEE ALSO: ➡bomb.

dive bomber *comp. noun, sl.* (1) someone who sprays graffiti; (2) someone—such as a vagrant—who collects cigarette butts from the sidewalk with a view to smoking them

dived *past tense* dove
Of the verb "to dive".

diversion *noun* a road detour

diversion sign *comp. noun* a road detour sign

dividend warrant *comp. noun* a written authority to collect a dividend due upon shares in a company

---

the **Divine Right of Kings** *pr. name, hist.* the belief that the authority of kings derives not from the will or wish or consent of their subjects or any other earthly power but directly from God alone

This began life as a medieval theory that kings rule by direct divine direction. It arose in the course of the long struggle between the Pope and the Holy Roman Emperor, but then was used to strengthen monarchy in general when later the institution was threatened by Protestant and Catholic extremists during the Reformation and Counter Reformation. It purported that monarchy by primogeniture was the divine order and thus required unquestioned obedience from a king's subjects.

James I of England and VI of Scotland, and his ➡Stuart successors expounded this belief strongly, which caused vast trouble, not least the ➡English Civil War, and it was not finally demolished as a respectable concept in Britain until the ➡Glorious Revolution of 1688, when the primacy of ➡Parliament was established and thus the "divine right" of ➡MPs to do the ruling themselves.

---

division *noun* (1) a separation of members of the ➡Commons or ➡Lords into two groups who pass through separate lobbies so that their votes can be counted; (2) a parliamentary ➡constituency

division bell *comp. noun* a bell rung in and around the ➡Palace of Westminster to inform ➡MPs to return to the ➡Chamber to vote in a ➡division

divot *noun, Sc.* a small piece of sod or turf

divvy *noun, abbr., coll.* a dividend or share of profits
Particularly those earned by a cooperative venture.

dixie *noun* a large cooking pot used by campers, etc.

Dixons *pr. name (TM)* a large national chain of electronic retail stores

DIY *noun, abbr.* do-it-yourself

DJ *noun, abbr., coll.* a ➡dinner jacket

DMU *noun, abbr.* a diesel multiple unit
A kind of passenger railroad train.

D-Notice *comp. noun, abbr., hist.* a Defence Notice
First introduced in 1912, these were notices issued by the ➡War Office, later the ➡Ministry of Defense, to the press requesting non-publication of particular news items on the grounds that to do so would be damaging to national security. Although never formally abolished, the system has fallen into disrepute and has not been used for a number of years.

do [A] *noun, sl.* (1) a swindle or hoax; (2) a party or celebration; (3) a battle
[B] *verb, sl.* to arrest

do a {**bunk** » **michael** » **mickey** » **runner**} *verb, sl.* to depart rapidly, disappear or escape

do a mischief *verb, coll.* to injure someone

Dobermann pinscher *spell.* Doberman pinscher

do bird *verb, sl.* to serve a jail sentence

dock *noun* the place in a court where the accused sits or stands during a criminal trial

dock asthma *idiom, sl.* theatrically expressed surprise or disbelief displayed by the accused in court
A term used by police and criminals.

docky-bag *noun, East.* a bag that is used to hold a worker's packed lunch
The resemblance to "doggy bag" is clear, but there is no known connection.

docket *noun* (1) a list of goods delivered or received, dues paid, etc.; (2) an order form or voucher

dockland *noun* that part of a city which contains or is adjacent to docks

the **Docklands** *pr. name* the area in eastern London lying along the north bank of the ➡Thames River
The docks are gone and the area is now the focus of extensive redevelopment.

dockyard *noun* a ➡royal dockyard

doctor [A] *noun* a physician
Among medical professionals, only physicians are called "doctor" in Britain. To be strictly correct, surgeons, dentists

and veterinarians should be addressed as "mister," whatever their gender; it derives from "master," being a skilled person.

[B] *verb, coll.* to spay or castrate an animal

doddle *noun, sl.* some action or activity that is easily carried out or trouble-free

dodge *noun* an artful trick or expedient

dodgem car *comp. noun, coll.* a bumper car

dodgy *adj., coll.* (1) tricky or difficult; (2) chancy; (3) evasive; (4) unreliable or unsound

dodgy boiler *comp. noun, derog., sl.* a woman perceived to be the carrier of a sexually transmitted disease

Dod's Parliamentary Companion *pr. name* a publication setting out the procedures and practices of Parliament

It also lists details of sitting ➠MPs. It is regularly revised and kept fully up-to-date. *SEE ALSO:* ➠*Erskine May.*

DoE *pr. name, abbr.* the Department of Employment

do for *idiom. phr. verb* to serve as a housekeeper

dog and bone *idiom, rh. sl.* a telephone

dog end *comp. noun, sl.* a cigarette butt

Dogger Bank *pr. name* a very large underwater sandbank in the middle of the North Sea, some 100 miles off the coast of northern England

The waters of the Dogger Bank are just 10 to 20 fathoms deep, making for a very rich fishing ground. A World War I naval battle between the British and Germany fleets took place there in 1915.

the **dogs** *noun, coll.* greyhound racing

the Isle of **Dogs** *pr. name* a peninsula formed by an undulation of the ➠Thames River as it passes through London's ➠East End

Tradition has it that it was called this because ➠Edward III kept his hunting dogs there.

dogsbody *noun, sl.* (1) a junior naval officer; (2) a drudge; (3) someone of no significance; (4) formerly, a pudding consisting of peas

dog's dinner *idiom, coll.* a dog's breakfast; a mess or shambles

dog's nose *comp. noun, North* a mixture of beer and gin

A popular beverage in northern England.

doings *noun, sl.* the things required

dole *noun, Sc.* in law, the corruption or evil intent that is the essential component of any act which must be present to make it criminal

dolie *noun, derog., sl.* someone who is ➠on the dole

dollar *noun, arch., sl.* twenty-five pence

This use originated in the 19th C., when for many years £1 equaled $4, so that five shillings or one Crown equaled $1. After the currency revisions of 1971, what had been called five shillings became twenty-five pence.

dollop *noun, coll.* an undifferentiated lump, especially of food

doll's house *comp. noun* a dollhouse

dolly *adj., coll.* (1) pretty or attractive; (2) a ➠cricket ball that is easy to hit or catch

dolly bird *comp. noun, coll., out.* a pretty girl

dolly mixture *comp. noun* small candies mixed together in various shapes and colors

dolour *spell.* dolor

Sorrow or distress.

do me good *idiom, rh. sl.* a cigarette

Derivation: cigarette > Woodbine > wood > good > do me good. "Woodbine" was a brand of cigarette especially popular with troops on the Western Front during World War I.

Domesday Book *pr. name, hist.* the records of a detailed survey of England ordered for taxation purposes by ➠William the Conqueror in 1085

It consists of two volumes, written in Latin, which are kept at the ➠Public Records Office in London. It is now of great historical value as it provides a uniquely detailed overview of the entire country as it was more than 900 years ago.

dominie *noun, out., Sc.* a schoolmaster

From the Latin *dominus* = "lord"

Dominion *noun, out.* a self-governing or independent nation within the ➠British Empire, and later the ➠Commonwealth

For example, "Dominion of Canada"

don *noun* a fellow, tutor, scholar or principal of a college at ➠Oxford or ➠Cambridge Universities

Approximately equivalent to an American university professor.

dona *noun, arch., sl.* a woman or girlfriend

From the Spanish *doña* = "wife," "lady" or "mistress"

Donald Bane *pr. name, hist.* ➠King of Scots

The son of ➠Duncan I, he reigned from 1093 until 1094 when he was deposed by ➠Duncan II. Six months later he regained the crown and reigned again until 1097 when he was deposed once again, this time by ➠Edgar, and this time for good.

Donald I *pr. name, hist.* King of Alba

He reigned for four years from 858 until 862.

Donald II *pr. name, hist.* King of Alba

The son of Constantine I, he reigned for 11 years from 889 until deposed in 900.

Doncaster *pr. name, hist.* originally the Roman settlement of *Danum*, now a coal-mining center in South Yorkshire

The current population is 84,000 (1991 estimate).

Donegal *pr. name* a county in the Irish Republic

County Donegal in the ancient province of Ulster.

the **done thing** *idiom, coll.* the acceptable way of doing things

donkey jacket

donkey jacket *comp. noun* a thick weatherproof jacket, somewhat similar to a pea jacket
Popular with construction workers during cold weather.

donkey's years *comp. noun, coll.* a long time ago

donnert *adj., Sc.* dull or stupid

don't care tuppence *idiom, coll.* totally disinterested

don't start *idiom, coll.* do not complain

doodah *noun* a doodad, thingamajig or thingamabob

doodle-bug *comp. noun, hist., sl.* a ➟V-1
World War II slang.

dook *verb, Sc.* (1) to duck; (2) to bathe; (3) to drench

dooker *noun, Sc.* a swimmer

dook for apples *phr. verb, Sc.* to bob for apples
A children's ➟Hallowe'en game.

doolally *adj., sl.* (1) insane; (2) eccentric

Doomsday Book *pr. name, coll., hist.* a common but incorrect spelling of ➟Domesday Book

do one's nut *idiom. phr. verb* to become livid with anger or rage

doonhamer *noun, Sc.* a native or inhabitant of ➟Dumfries

doon the stank *idiom, Sc.* squandered or lost forever

doon the watter *idiom, Sc.* the Firth of ➟Clyde
Which is down the Clyde River from ➟Glasgow.

doorstep *verb, coll.* to indulge in unsolicited door-to-door canvassing or selling

do porridge *verb, sl.* to spend time in jail

Dorchester *pr. name* an ancient town that is the administrative center of Dorset
The current population is 14,000 (1988 estimate).

the **Doric** *pr. name* a rustic accent
Especially a Scottish one. The name is an allusion to the rough way ancient Athenians considered that Greek was spoken by the uneducated inhabitants of the Doric region of Greece. This modern usage was devised by the literati of 18th C. Edinburgh—the ➟Athens of the North, as they liked to call their city—to distinguish what they considered to be their own refined speech from that of the common people.

Dorset *pr. name* a county on the southern coast of England, between ➟Devon and ➟Hampshire
Once the home of a British tribe called the *Dwrtrigs*, a name Latinized by the Romans into *Durotriges*, and then translated by the Saxons into *Dor-saetta*. The county seat is ➟Dorchester and the current population is 645,000 (1991 Census).

dorty *adj., Sc.* bad-tempered or difficult to please

dosh *noun, sl.* money

doss [A] *noun, coll.* a bed
[B] *verb, coll.* to sleep

dossent *verb aux., East* dare not

dosser [A] *noun, abbr., sl.* a ➟doss-house
[B] *noun, sl.* a tramp or other person without proper accommodation

doss-house *comp. noun, coll.* a flophouse or cheap rooming house

dosst *verb, East* to dare

DOT *pr. name, abbr.* the ➟Department of Transport

dot *verb, sl.* to hit or strike

do the Knowledge *idiom. phr. verb* to systematically learn the ➟Knowledge

dotty *noun, sl.* crazy, eccentric or absurd

double-barrelled name *comp. noun, coll.* a hyphenated surname
Such as "Smith-Jones," for example.

double bend *comp. noun* a highway S-curve

double cream *comp. noun* whipping cream

double-decker *comp. noun, coll.* a bus seating passengers upon two decks
Although long considered especially characteristic of London, double-decker buses are ubiquitous throughout Britain The first in London was a horse-drawn bus that had a bench placed on its roof in 1847.

double Dutch *comp. noun, coll.* gibberish

double first *comp. noun, abbr., coll.* (1) a first-class honors degree in two subjects; (2) a person who has been awarded this
(1) is the highest grade of first degree awarded by a British university.

double Gloucester *comp. noun* an orange-red, smooth mellow cheese
Originally made in the Vale of Gloucester. It is called "double" because it is made with ➟double cream.

double saucepan *comp. noun* a double boiler

Double Summer Time *pr. name, hist.* the daylight saving time regime in Britain during World War II
To save fuel and maximize productivity, clocks were moved two hours ahead of ➟GMT all year round from 1941 until 1945. It was briefly reintroduced in 1947, again to save fuel.

doubt [A] *noun, coll.* a cigarette butt
[B] *verb, coll.* to suppose or suspect

douce *adj., Lat., Sc.* (1) sweet or pleasant; (2) respectable; (3) tidy; (4) sober or sedate
From the Latin *dulcis* = "sweet"

doughboy *noun, hist.* a dumpling boiled in seawater, once a staple fare of sailors
It is said that this word became the common nickname of U.S. soldiers in Europe during World War II because the buttons on their uniform resembled these dumplings

doughnut *spell.* donut

douglas *noun, rh. sl.* a third class university degree
Derivation: third class degree > Third > Douglas Hurd, a senior British politician.

Douglas *pr. name* the capital of the ➡Isle of Man, which is also the island's principal seaport and resort
The current population is 22,000 (1988 estimate).

Dounreay *pr. name, hist.* a small settlement near Thurso in the far north of Scotland
It was the location of Britain's first fast breeder nuclear reactor and a center of nuclear research, but is now closed down.

do up *verb, coll.* to zip or button up
For example, a coat.

douse *noun, out.* a blow or hit

dovecot *spell.* dovecote

Dover *pr. name* a seaport in ➡Kent, which is the nearest in England to continental Europe
Here Julius Caesar landed with his army in 55 B.C. The Roman called the port *Dubris;* remains of their lighthouse and castle can still be seen there. It is one of the ➡Cinque Ports. The current population is 35,000 (1988 estimate).

Dover sole *comp. noun* the common European sole
A fish with the formal name of *solea solea.*

do well *verb, coll.* to live well or prosper

{**dowelled » dowelling**} *spell.* {doweled » doweling}

dower house *comp. noun, arch.* a small house located within the grounds of a larger one
Named thus because such houses were often built to be part of the lifetime share of her husband's estate that was retained by a widow.

down [A] *noun* (1) a direction of travel that is away from a capital or major city; (2) high, open rolling land; (3) a trailing or loosing position in a sport, competition or business transaction
(1) usually means away from London; (2) is mostly found in southern England.

[B] *verb, coll.* to swallow a drink

Down *pr. name, hist.* a district in ➡Northern Ireland, in what used to be County Down, a former Northern Irish County
The current population is 60,000 (1990 estimate).

down among the dead men *idiom, coll.* dead drunk

Downing College *pr. name* a college of ➡Cambridge University founded in 1800

Downing Street *pr. name, hist* (1) the street containing the official residence of the British ➡Prime Minister; (2) a euphemism for the British Government
Downing Street is a surprisingly short street off ➡Whitehall in London, with the Prime Minister's residence at ➡No. 10. Additionally, the street contains the official residence of the ➡Chancellor of the Exchequer at No. 11, and the official residence of the government Chief Whip at No. 12.

The street was built in the 1680s by George Downing, an ➡MP. No. 10 was purchased by ➡George II in 1732 and gifted by him to the first ➡Prime Minister, Robert Walpole.

down line *comp. noun* any railroad track used by trains heading away from London

downpipe *noun* a downspout

down the pan *idiom, coll.* down the tubes, wasted, discarded or ruined

down the pub *idiom, coll.* at the ➡pub

down tools *phr. verb, coll.* to cease work

down to the ground *idiom, coll.* completely, utterly or entirely

down train *comp. noun* a train heading away from London

downy *adj., sl.* shrewd or knowing

downy cove *comp. noun, arch.* a quick-witted fellow

dowsing rod *comp. noun* a divining rod

dowt *noun, Sc.* a cigarette butt

D'Oyly Carte Opera Company *pr. name, hist.* a theatrical company founded by and named after Richard D'Oyly Carte
He was impresario and owner of the ➡Savoy Theater in London where all Gilbert and Sullivan operettas had their first performances. Until 1960 the company retained the full copyright on all of Gilbert and Sullivan's work and would not let others perform them without specific permission.

dozy *adj., sl.* lazy or stupid

DP *noun, abbr., arch.* a ➡displaced person

dpc *noun, abbr.* a ➡damp proof course

DPP *pr. name, abbr.* ➡Director of Public Prosecutions

drachm [A] *noun, abbr., arch.* a ➡fluid drachm

[B] *noun, arch.* a unit of weight that was once popular with pharmacists
A drachm is ⅛ th of an ounce.

the Drain *noun, coll.* the ➡Waterloo and City Line

draining board *comp. noun* a drainboard

drainpipes *noun, arch., sl.* very narrow men's pants

Drake's Drum *pr. name, hist.* the legendary drum of Sir Francis Drake
It is said that if struck when invasion threatens, it will call Drake back to save England again as he did when he defeated the Spanish Armada in 1588.

Dralon *pr. name (TM)* a synthetic fabric with a velvety appearance
Often used for upholstery and drapes.

dram *noun, Sc.* a small portion or measure of liquor

Drambuie *pr. name (TM), Gae., hist., Sc.* a Scotch whiskey liqueur
Reputedly the favorite tipple of ➡Bonnie Prince Charlie. It means, in Gaelic, *an dram buidheach* = "the pleasing drink."

dramock *noun, Sc.* raw oatmeal in water

draper *noun* a dry goods merchant

draper's shop *comp. noun* a dry goods store

drapery *noun* (1) dry goods; (2) a ➡draper's shop

{**draught » draughty**} *spell.* {draft » drafty}

draught beer *spell.* draft beer

draughtboard *noun* a checkerboard

{**draughter » draughtsman » draughtsmanship**} *spell.* {drafter » draftsman » draftsmanship}

draught excluder *comp. noun* a weather strip

draught horse *comp. noun* a draft horse

draughts *noun* the game of checkers

draw [A] *noun, out., sl.* a prisoner's term for tobacco [B] *verb, hist.* to drag to execution
Usually inflicted upon a convicted felon. *SEE ALSO:* ➡hanged, drawn and quartered.

drawing pin *comp. noun* a thumbtack or push-pin

draw stumps *verb* to remove ➡cricket ➡stumps from the ground at the end of play for the day

draw the bow *idiom. phr. verb* to make a guess

draw the long bow *idiom. phr. verb* to exaggerate

draw-well *comp. noun* a deep well where water is removed by means of a bucket on a rope

dray *noun, out.* a brewer's horse-drawn cart

the **dreaded lurgi** *idiom, coll., out.* an unspecified, perhaps imaginary, infectious and deadly disease
A popular children's expression of the 1960s.

dreamt *past tense* dreamed
Of the verb "to dream".

dree *verb, Sc.* to suffer or endure

dree ain weird *phr. verb, Sc.* to accept or endure what fate has in store for one

dreich *adj., Sc.* (1) persistent or long-lasting; (2) dismal, dull or dreary; (3) boring or wearisome

dress a bed *verb* to prepare a bed for sleeping in

dress circle *comp. noun* a ➡royal circle

dress coat *comp. noun* a man's tailcoat

dressing gown *comp. noun* a bathrobe

dressing station *comp. noun* a forward military first-aid post

dried milk *comp. noun* dry milk

drier *spell.* dryer

drinking school *comp. noun* a group of people gathered together for the purpose of drinking

drinking up time *comp. noun, coll.* a short period, usually about ten minutes, permitted so that those with drinks bought at the bar of a ➡public house before the compulsory closing time imposed by the law can finish consuming their drinks

drinks cabinet *comp. noun* a liquor cabinet

drinks {cart » trolley} *comp. noun* a portable bar

drinks counter *comp. noun* where a store sells liquor

drinks cupboard *comp. noun* a liquor cabinet

drinks mat *comp. noun* a coaster

drinks party *comp. noun* a cocktail party

drinks table *comp. noun* a table employed as a bar

drive [A] *noun, out.* an organized session of whist, bingo, or various other games
Usually for a large number of people, and often in order to raise money for some charitable cause or other.
[B] *verb* in ➡cricket, to hit the ball hard in a forward direction

{**drivelled » drivelling**} *spell.* {driveled » driveling}

the **Driver and Vehicle Licensing Centre** *pr. name* the ➡Department of Transport office in ➡Swansea, Wales, which holds national vehicle and driver records and issues licenses for both

driving licence *comp. noun* a driver's license

driving mirror *comp. noun* a rear-view mirror

driving seat *comp. noun* a driver's seat

driving test *comp. noun* a driver's test

driving wheel *comp. noun, out.* a steering wheel

'drome *noun, abbr., coll., out.* an ➡aerodrome

drone *noun, arch., sl.* a wealthy but brainless man

drop (someone) in it *idiom. phr. verb* to betray or expose (someone) to danger

drophead *noun, arch., coll.* (1) a convertible automobile; (2) the removable fabric roof of (1)

drop on (one) *verb, coll.* to punish or criticize (one)

drop scone *comp. noun* a pancake

drouk *verb, Sc.* to soak or drench

droukit stour *idiom, Sc.* mud
Literally, "soaking dust."

drove-road *comp. noun* an old track made by the regular passage of cattle over many years

the **Druids** *noun, hist.* an ancient order of priests and magicians who lived in pre-Roman Britain
Little is known about their religious practices or other activities; what little *is* known is based on very brief and always highly cryptic references by Roman authors, who were always scathing, dismissive and basically disinterested in the behavior of people they saw as barbarians.
The modern "Druids," who purport to emulate the activities of their ancient namesakes with ceremonies such as welcoming midsummer dawn at ➡Stonehenge and so forth, are relying upon their own imagination rather than any discernible evidence for the historic validity of what they get up to.
In other words, they've made it all up.

drum [A] *noun, arch.* a tea party held in the afternoon or evening

[B] *noun, sl.* (1) a house; (2) a nightclub; (3) a brothel

drum and fife *idiom, rh. sl.* (1) a knife; (2) a wife
Military slang.

drummer *noun, sl.* a thief

drunk in charge *idiom, abbr.* an abbreviated version of "drunk in charge of a vehicle"
Equivalent to DWI, or "driving while intoxicated".

Drury Lane *pr. name, hist.* a nickname for the ➡Theatre Royal in London
The name of the street which it is upon.

dry *noun, sl.* a Conservative politician favoring right-wing, free-enterprise and individualistic policies
Particularly during the ➡Prime Ministership of Margaret Thatcher, who is reputed to have invented the usage.
SEE ALSO: ➡wet.

dry-arsed *adj., sl., taboo* safe again after danger

dry as dust *adj. phr., coll.* exceptionally dull, boring and uninteresting

dry biscuit *comp. noun* a cracker

Dryburgh Abbey *pr. name, hist.* a ruined 12th C. ➡abbey on the banks of the ➡Tweed river some 40 miles southeast from ➡Edinburgh
Among these ruins are the graves of Sir Walter Scott, author of numerous historical novels, and Field Marshal Douglas Haig, commander of British troops on the Western Front through most of World War I.

dry-cure *verb, out.* to cure meat without pickling

dry goods *comp. noun* all or any non-liquid goods, not just clothing and yard goods

drying {cloth » towel} *comp. noun* a dish towel

drysalt *verb, out.* to ➡dry-cure

drysalter *noun, arch.* a dealer in dry chemicals, drugs, tinned meats, salt, oils, etc.

drystain dyke *comp. noun, Sc.* a ➡drystone wall

drystone wall *comp. noun* a wall built without mortar

DSC *noun, abbr.* the Distinguished Service Cross

DSM *noun, abbr.* the Distinguished Service Medal

DSO *noun, abbr.* the Distinguished Service Order

DSS *pr. name, abbr.* ➡Department of Social Security

DTI *pr. name, abbr.* ➡Department of Trade and Industry

dual *verb, coll.* to convert a two-way highway into a ➡dual carriageway

dual carriageway *comp. noun* a divided highway

dub [A] *noun, Sc.* (1) a muddy or stagnant pool, pond or puddle; (2) a pool visible upon the seashore only at low tide

[B] *verb* (1) to confer a knighthood by touching the recipient's shoulder with a sword; (2) to prepare an artificial fly for use in fishing

dubbie *adj., Sc.* muddy

Dubh *pr. name, hist.* King of ➡Alba
He was the son of ➡Malcolm I and reigned for four years from 962 until murdered in 966.

Dublin *pr. name* (1) the capital city of the ➡Irish Republic; (2) the largest city in Ireland; (3) a county in the ➡Irish Republic; (4) County Dublin in the ancient province of ➡Leinster

dubs *noun, Sc.* mud

dubskelper *noun, Sc.* a person who is continually traveling, whatever the condition of the roads
Literally, "mud-hitter," from the presumed condition of the roads being traveled.

duchess [A] *noun* (1) a woman who is a ➡duke in her own right; (2) the wife or widow of a ➡duke

[B] *noun, sl.* (1) a ➡costermonger's wife; (2) a mother or wife

duchy *noun* the territory of a duke
Similar to a ➡county palatine.

the Duchy and County Palatine of Lancaster *pr. name* crown land nominally administered by the ➡Chancellor of the ➡Duchy of Lancaster on behalf of the government

the Duchy of Cornwall *pr. name* the oldest ➡duchy in England
Instituted by ➡Edward III in 1337 for the purpose of providing an independent income for his son Edward the ➡Black Prince. Ever since, the title and the lands of the duchy have been the property of the ➡Prince of Wales.

the Duchy of Lancaster *pr. name, abbr.* the ➡Duchy and ➡County Palatine of ➡Lancaster

duck *noun* a ➡batsman's score of zero in ➡cricket

duck-hawk *comp. noun* a marsh-harrier
Its formal name is *circus aeruginosus.*

duck's arse *idiom, sl., taboo* hair cut in such a manner that it appears to resemble a duck when viewed from the rear
Amazingly, this was a popular men's style in the 1950s. Hair was swept back and curled in above the neck. *SEE ALSO:* ➡DA

duck's disease *comp. noun, sl.* short legs

{ducks » ducky} *noun, sl.* darling, dear, etc.
A familiar form of address from a woman.

duddie *adj., Sc.* ragged or torn

Dudley *pr. name* a very old industrial town in the western ➡Midlands
Sometimes called the capital of the ➡Black Country, its current population is 192,000 (1991 estimate).

duelled

{duelled » duelling} *spell.* {dueled » dueling}

duff [A] *adj., sl.* counterfeit, broken or worthless

  [B] *noun, North* baking dough
  SEE ALSO: ➧plum duff.
  [C] *verb, sl.* to fail to strike a golf ball

duffle *spell.* duffel

duffle-jacket *comp. noun* a pea jacket

duff up *verb, sl.* to beat up

duke *noun* the highest rank of the peerage

  It has been traditional for the younger sons of the monarch to be made ➧royal dukes.

dukedom *noun* land belonging to a ➧duke

the Duke of Edinburgh *pr. name* a title that has twice been bestowed upon the husband of a reigning British queen when he is not himself the king

  It was bestowed first upon Prince ➧Albert, husband of ➧Victoria, and then more recently upon Prince Philip, husband of ➧Elizabeth II of England and I of Scotland.

Duke of Edinburgh's Award *pr. name* an award given to young people aged between 14 and 25 who have achieved satisfactory results in certain activities designed to test their competence, responsibility and sense of community

  Since the project was introduced in 1962, over two million people have participated. There are five sections: Community Service, Expeditions, Hobbies and Interests, Design for Living and Physical Activities. Badges and certificates are awarded for so-called gold, silver and bronze levels of achievement.

the Duke of Wellington's Bodyguard *pr. name* a nickname for the 5th Regiment of ➧Foot

  A unit of the British Army attached to Wellington's headquarters for a long time during the ➧Peninsular War.

the Duke of York *pr. name* a royal title normally reserved for the second son of the monarch

Dulwich College *pr. name* one of the leading English ➧public schools

  Founded in 1619, it is located in south London.

Dulwich Picture Gallery *pr. name, hist.* the oldest art gallery in England

  It was established in 1814, in the grounds of ➧Dulwich College, south London.

{dumbfound » dumbfounded} *spell.* {dumfound » dumfounded}

Dumfries *pr. name, hist.* a town which is the administrative center of the ➧Dumfries and Galloway region of Scotland

  Where ➧Robert the Bruce murdered the Red Comyn, Robert Burns spent the last five years of his life, Robert Watson-Watt—inventor of radar—was born, and John Paul Jones—founder of the U.S. Navy—was born nearby. The current population is 35,000 (1991 estimate).

Dumfries & Galloway *pr. name* a region in southwestern Scotland

  The current population is 150,000 (1991 Census).

Dumfries-shire *pr. name, hist.* a former Scottish county, now part of the ➧Dumfries & Galloway region

dummy run *comp. noun* a dry run or rehearsal

dummy teat *comp. noun* a baby's pacifier

Dunbartonshire *pr. name, hist.* a former Scottish county

  Now part of the ➧Strathclyde region.

Dunblane *pr. name, hist.* a small town in the ➧Central region of Scotland

  Best known for its parish church, which dates from 1150 and was a cathedral until the Reformation. Its roof was removed in the 16th C., but the whole building was restored in the 19th C.

Duncan I *pr. name, hist.* ➧King of Scots

  The son of ➧Malcolm II's daughter Bethoc, he reigned for six years from 1034 until killed by ➧Macbeth in 1040.
  However, the picture painted of him in Shakespeare's play is not what you could call strictly accurate. Duncan was not a good and wise old king but a reckless and ineffective young one, and possibly Macbeth was the elder of the two. On top of that, Macbeth's claim to the throne was almost certainly better than Duncan's, and he didn't murder him but killed him in battle, which was considered quite normal and acceptable in these days.

Duncan II *pr. name, hist.* ➧King of Scots

  The son of ➧Malcolm III, he deposed ➧Donald Bane and reigned for six months from May until October in 1094 when he was then himself deposed by Donald Bane, who then resumed his interrupted reign.

Dundee *pr. name, hist.* a city that is the administrative center of ➧Tayside, Scotland

  Incorporated as a city in 1179, the current population is 175,000 (1988 estimate).

Dundee cake *comp. noun, Sc.* a rich fruitcake topped with almonds

Dundonian *pr. name, Sc.* a native, citizen or inhabitant of ➧Dundee

Dundrennan Abbey *pr. name, hist.* a ruined 12th C. ➧abbey about 25 miles south west of ➧Dumfries

  Originally built as a Cistercian abbey, this is where ➧Mary Queen of Scots is said to have spent her last night in Scotland before being rowed across the ➧Solway Firth to captivity and eventual execution in England in 1568.

Dunfermline *pr. name, hist.* the ancient ➧royal burgh in ➧Fife that once was the capital of Scotland

  After Malcolm III built a royal palace—little of which survives—here in the 11th C., Dunfermline became the effective capital of Scotland until that honor moved on to Edinburgh in the 13th C. It was also the birthplace of Andrew Carnegie.

Dungannon *pr. name* a district in ➧Northern Ireland, in what used to be County ➧Tyrone

  The current population is 45,000 (1990 estimate)

100

Dunkirk *pr. name, hist.* a French ➡Channel port now forever associated with the massive evacuation of British and Allied troops back to England following the fall of France to the German *Blitzkrieg* in the summer of 1940

Over 350,000 troops were rescued, making the defense of England from Nazi invasion possible. Although really a major defeat that was just prevented, by skill, bravery and luck, from turning into an unmitigated catastrophe, it has nevertheless impressed itself upon the British collective mind as some sort of victory.

Dunlop [A] *noun, rh. sl.* a liar

Derivation: liar > tire > Dunlop tire > Dunlop.

[B] *noun, Sc.* a cheese similar to ➡Cheddar

From Dunlop in ➡Ayrshire, where it originated.

Dunnet Head *pr. name* the most northern point on the British mainland

Not ➡John O'Groats, some 12 miles away, as most suppose

dunnock *noun* a hedge sparrow

dunny *noun, Sc.* (1) an underground passage; (2) a cellar under a tenement building

dunt *noun, Sc.* (1) a heavy knock or blow; (2) an injury caused by a fall or knock; (3) the sound of a heavy fall or knock; (4) a heavy, dull-sounding sound

Dunvegan Castle *pr. name, hist.* a highly picturesque 13th C. fortress located upon the rocky shore of a ➡sea loch in the ➡Isle of Skye

The ancient stronghold of the ➡chieftains of the Clan Macleod for more than 700 years.

duodecillion *noun, num.* 10^{72}

The American duodecillion is 10^{39}.

Dur. *pr. name, abbr.* Durham

Durex *pr. name (TM)* a condom

A trade name for a brand manufactured by the London Rubber Company, but has long been used generically.

Durham *pr. name, hist.* the city that is the administrative center of County ➡Durham

William the Conqueror started building a castle here in 1072 to defend against the Scots. There had been an Anglo-Saxon cathedral at Durham from much earlier times, but this was pulled down in favor of a magnificent new one started in 1093, which remains there to this day.

Durham was incorporated as a city in 1602 and the current population is 85,000 (1988 estimate).

County **Durham** *pr. name* a northeastern English county

The county seat is ➡Durham and the current population is 590,000 (1991 Census).

dust *noun, sl.* money

dustbin *noun* a trashcan

dustcart *noun* a garbage collection truck

duster *noun* a cloth used to dust furniture

dust jacket *comp. noun* a dust wrapper, a removable paper cover around a book

dustman *noun* a garbage collector

dust sheet *comp. noun* a dustcover over furniture

dusty *adj.* unsatisfactory

dusty answer *comp. noun, coll.* an unsatisfactory or brusquely negative reply

dutch *noun, abbr., sl.* wife

An abbreviation of ➡duchess.

dutch barn *comp. noun* a barn that has a roof but no sides, built for the purpose of storing hay, etc.

duvet *noun* a quilt or comforter

dux *noun, Sc.* the academically best student in a class or school

Duxford Airfield *pr. name, hist.* an RAF air base near ➡Cambridge where the ➡Imperial War Museum exhibits its collection of aircraft

Although it is not a military aircraft, there is also a ➡Concorde supersonic passenger aircraft on display here.

DVLC *pr. name, abbr.* the ➡Driver and Vehicle Licensing Centre, in Swansea

dwam *noun, Sc.* (1) a daydream or stupor; (2) a sudden illness or faint

Dyfed *pr. name, hist.* (1) an ancient kingdom in south-western Wales; (2) a Welsh County

(1) is known to have become established by 700. The current population of (2) is 340,000 (1991 Census).

dyke *noun* a natural watercourse

dysmenorrhaea *spell.* dysmenorrhea

Difficult menstruation.

dyspnoea *spell.* dyspnea

Difficulty in breathing.

E

each way bet *comp. noun* a bet that a horse will either win a race or be ➠placed

eagre *noun* a tidal bore, which is a wave that has been produced by a tide channeled into a river estuary or narrow inlet
Characteristically, it becomes larger as the channel narrows.

ealdorman *noun, hist.* the principal government official in a region or district in ➠Anglo-Saxon times

Ealing *pr. name* a ➠Greater London borough
Its current population, which is also included within the ➠London urban area total, is 265,000 (1991 Census).

the **Ealing comedies** *pr. name, hist.* a series of low-budget comedy movies made in the 1940s and 50s at the Ealing Studios in west London
Many are now considered classics of their kind.

ear basher *comp. noun, sl.* an ear bender, someone who is overly loquacious

earl *noun* a British aristocrat with a rank between that of a marquis and a viscount

earldom *noun* the domain of an ➠earl

the **Earl Marshal** *pr. name* (1) the presiding officer of the ➠College of Arms; (2) the master of ceremonies at certain state occasions

the **Earl of Mar's Grey-Breeks** *pr. name* a nickname for the 21st Regiment of ➠Foot
A unit of the British Army whose name reflects the color of the ➠breeks they wore when raised by the Earl of Mar in 1678.

earl palatine *pr. name, hist.* a lord who possessed sovereign power within his own domain
SEE ALSO: ➠count palatine.

Earl's Court *pr. name* an area of west-central London
Now best known for the large exhibition hall there, and for the area's popularity with itinerant Australians. It was named after the medieval court of the Earl of Warwick, who also has a major road in the area named after him.

early closing *comp. noun* the practice of closing all the stores in a town on one afternoon every week

early day motion *comp. noun* a parliamentary procedure that enables an ➠MP to raise a topic for urgent consideration by the ➠House

early days *comp. noun, coll.* too soon for something to have yet happened

Early English *pr. name, hist.* a style of Gothic architectural popular in 13th C. England
The cathedrals of Ely, Salisbury, Wells and Worcester are noted surviving examples.

earnest *noun, out.* a token or pledge of what is to follow
Typically, a deposit paid as a token of serious intent to complete a purchase.

earth *noun* (1) ground; (2) electrical grounding
(1) can be in the sense of background, or in the sense of a location where a hunted animal hides itself.

earth closet *comp. noun* a privy using earth rather than water as the absorbent

earwig *verb, arch, sl.* (1) to eavesdrop; (2) to influence or attempt to influence by secret discussion
(1) is criminal jargon.

ease *verb, sl.* to take time off or to relax
Police jargon.

East Anglia *pr. name, hist.* (1) an ancient kingdom in eastern England; (2) an English region comprising the counties of ➠Norfolk, ➠Suffolk, ➠Cambridgeshire and parts of ➠Essex
This is the lowest-lying, least hilly area of the British Isles. The kingdom of East Anglia was established by 600, but had become a vassal of ➠Mercia by about 740 and remained so until about 835. It became a Danish kingdom between 875 and 917. The usual seat of the kings of East Anglia was Elmham, near the modern city of ➠Norwich.

East Coast *pr. name (TM)* a railroad company operating ➠Intercity services between London and ➠York, ➠Newcastle, ➠Edinburgh, etc.
It is part of ➠British Rail.

the **East End** *pr. name* the area of central London just to the east of the ➠City
Much of the East End is now within the area covered by the ➠London Borough of ➠Tower Hamlets.

Eastender *pr. name* a native, inhabitant or citizen of the ➠East End

Easter Monday *pr. name* a ➠bank holiday which is on the Monday following Easter

the **Easter Rising**

the **Easter Rising** *pr. name, hist., Ir.* the seizure of the General Post Office in Dublin in 1916 by a group of Irish nationalists, who then proclaimed the ➡Irish Republic

Their rebellion lasted a week, by which time all had surrendered to the army and police surrounding them. A number were executed, which turned out to be a serious error by the British government as this only succeeded in generating much renewed sympathy for their cause.

On the other hand, this happened in the darkest days of World War I, when thousands died every week in the trenches of the Western Front in France and life had never been cheaper, so perhaps it was difficult to see that the lives of a dozen or so Irishmen could be that significant in the great scheme of things.

---

the **East India Company** *pr. name, hist.* a company granted a charter by Queen ➡Elizabeth I in 1600 to trade with the East Indies, yet ended up ruling India

By means of treaties, bribery, military alliances and a lot of luck, about 200 years of trading found the East India Company the effective rulers of virtually all of India. This amazing state of affairs, where a vast empire with many millions of inhabitants had effectively become the private property of a company that existed to trade for profit and was owned by people who lived in another country half a world away, is unique in the history of the world. The opportunities for corruption and adventuring became increasingly obvious and unacceptable, and following the ➡Indian Mutiny of 1858, the Company was pushed to one side as the British government took over direct control of India, transforming it into the jewel in the crown of the ➡British Empire.

East Lothian *pr. name, hist.* a former Scottish county, now part of ➡Lothian region

the **East Midlands** *pr. name* the eastern portion of the ➡Midlands area of England

Usually considered to consist of the counties of ➡Derby, ➡Leicester and ➡Nottingham.

the **East Riding** *pr. name, hist.* a major administrative division of the former county of ➡Yorkshire

East Suffolk *pr. name, hist.* a former English County, now part of ➡Suffolk

East Sussex *pr. name* a county on the southern coast of England, between ➡West Sussex and ➡Kent

It was formed out of the eastern part of ➡Sussex in 1974. The county seat is ➡Lewes and the current population is 670,000 (1991 Census). *SEE ALSO:* ➡Sussex.

easy as you know how *idiom, out., sl.* quite easy

This expression began life as ➡RAF World War II slang.

easy-peasy *adj., sl.* very easy

A children's expression.

eatage *noun, arch.* grazing rights

eater *noun, coll.* fruit suitable to be eaten raw, especially apples

E-boat *comp. noun, abbr., coll.* an enemy motorboat

A British naval code name for German motor torpedo boats during World War II.

E-boat alley *comp. noun, abbr., coll.* a route for World War II convoys through the ➡North Sea along the coast of ➡Norfolk and ➡Suffolk

This part of the coastline was subject to regular ➡E-boat attacks in the early years of the war.

EC *pr. name, abbr.* (1) the ➡European Commission; (2) the ➡European Community

Eccles cake *comp. noun* a rather flat round cake filled with currents and covered with pastry

Originally from Eccles, in ➡Greater Manchester.

ECGD *pr. name, abbr.* the ➡Export Credit Guarantee Department

echt *noun, Sc.* eight

ecilop *noun, sl.* the police

Criminals' ➡backslang.

eckies *noun, abbr., sl.* expenses

The kind that are incurred in the course of perfoming one's job. *SEE ALSO:* ➡exes.

the **Economic and Social Research Council** *pr. name* a government-funded research council established by ➡Royal Charter

It is responsible for establishing and maintaining research into economic and social matters and related fields.

economy class *comp. noun, pref.* airline coach class

ecu *noun, abbr.* the ➡European Currency Unit

ED *noun, abbr.* the Efficiency Decoration

Awarded to members of the ➡Commonwealth or Colonial Auxiliary Military Forces from 1930, but now defunct.

Edgar [A] *pr. name, hist.* King of England

He reigned for over 15 years from 959 until 975. A member of the Royal House of ➡Cedric.

[B] *pr. name, hist.* ➡King of Scots

The son of ➡Malcolm III, he reigned for ten years from 1097 until 1107, after deposing ➡Donald Bane.

edge *verb* to strike a ball with the edge of the ➡cricket bat, which is illegal

Edinburgh *pr. name* (1) the capital city of Scotland since the 13th C.; (2) the administrative center of ➡Lothian Region

Founded in the 7th C. by Edwin, King of ➡Northumbria; "Edinburgh" means "Edwin's fortress." Before Edinburgh, ➡Dunfermline was the Scottish capital. The current population, including suburbs, is 450,000 (1988 estimate).

Edinburgh
Castle

Edinburgh Castle *pr. name, hist.* the great fortress that dominates the city of ➟Edinburgh

The first fortifications were erected upon ➟Castle Rock more than 1,200 years ago, but the oldest parts of the present structure date from the 12th C. The castle is high up at the western end of Edinburgh's ➟Royal Mile, looking down over ➟Princes Street in the ➟New Town and the ➟Firth of Forth to the north. The ➟Honours of Scotland are on view here, and the annual Edinburgh Military Tattoo is held on the esplanade in front of the castle during the ➟Edinburgh Festival.

the **Edinburgh Festival** *pr. name* the best-known and most prestigious festival of drama and music in Britain and Europe

It is held in ➟Edinburgh and lasts for three weeks during August and September every year.

the ***Edinburgh Gazette*** *pr. name* an official government-published newspaper

It is used only for the purpose of publishing notices of official appointments, bankruptcies, court judgments and so forth relating to ➟Scotland.

the **Edinburgh Military Tattoo** *pr. name* a military entertainment held upon the esplanade of ➟Edinburgh Castle

It is performed annually at the time of the ➟Edinburgh Festival.

Edinburgh rock *comp. noun* a kind of soft rock-candy bar flavored with peppermint, cinnamon, etc.

It was first made in ➟Edinburgh in 1822 and named after the ➟Castle Rock that ➟Edinburgh Castle stands upon.

Edinburghshire *pr. name, hist.* a former name for the former county of ➟Midlothian

Now part of the ➟Lothian Region of Scotland.

Edinburgh University *pr. name* the sixth-oldest university in the English-speaking world and the fourth-oldest in Scotland, founded in 1583

Edmund *pr. name, hist.* King of England

A member of the ➟Royal House of ➟Cedric, who reigned for over six years from 939 until 946, when he was killed.

Edmund Ironside *pr. name, hist.* King of England

He reigned for 7 months in 1016. "Ironside" is believed to refer to his iron suit of armor, then a rarity. He was a member of the Royal House of ➟Denmark.

Edred *pr. name, hist.* King of England

A member of the ➟Royal House of ➟Cedric, he reigned for nine years from 946 until 955.

educationalist *noun* a student of educational methods and techniques

educationist *noun* a professional teacher

Edward *pr. name, hist.* the son of John ➟Balliot and ➟pretender to the throne of Scotland

After briefly deposing ➟David II in 1332, he acknowledged ➟Edward III of England as his overlord in 1333 and went on to gain effective control over a significant part of the country until 1356, when he surrendered his claim. He died in 1364.

Edward I *pr. name, hist.* King of England

A member of the ➟Royal House of ➟Plantagenet, he styled himself *Rex Angliae, Dominus Hiberniae et Dux Aquitaniae* = "King of England, Lord of Ireland and Duke of Aquitane," and reigned for more than 34 years from 1272 until 1307. Nicknamed ➟Edward Longshanks and also known as the ➟Hammer of the Scots, Edward pursued an aggressive expansionist policy towards both Scotland and Wales.

In Wales he met with considerable success, defeating the local princes and building a series of castles to help keep the territory subject to English rule. However, although he did remove the ➟Stone of Destiny from ➟Scone to ➟Westminster, he had much less conclusive results in Scotland, where he became bogged down in seemingly endless years of indecisive battling against Scottish armies led first by William Wallace and later ➟Robert the Bruce.

In 1290 he confiscated the wealth of all Jews in England and then expelled them from the country. Edward was also responsible for summoning the first Parliament that made some attempt to represent every corner of the land, the "Model Parliament" of 1295.

Edwardian *adj., hist.* pertaining to the period of the reign of any King named Edward, but especially the reign of ➟Edward VII

Edward II *pr. name, hist.* King of England

A member of the ➟Royal House of ➟Plantagenet, he styled himself *Rex Angliae, Dominus Hiberniae et Dux Aquitaniae* = "King of England, Lord of Ireland and Duke of Aquitane," and reigned for over 19 years from 1307.

He was suspected of homosexuality and his barons resented the influence upon him of his favorites, which caused considerable intrigue in his court and trouble across the country, until he was deposed in favor of his son through the machinations of his wife Queen Isabella and her lover in 1327. He was then killed later that same year.

Militarily, his principle "acheivement" was to be humiliatingly defeated by ➟Robert the Bruce, ➟King of Scots, at ➟Bannockburn in 1314, thus driving the English from Scotland and re-establishing Scottish independence.

Edward III *pr. name, hist.* King of England

A member of the ➟Royal House of ➟Plantagenet, he styled himself *Rex Angliae, Dominus Hiberniae et Dux Aquitaniae* = "King of England, Lord of Ireland and Duke of Aquitane" for his first 13 years, thereafter calling himself *Dei Gratia Rex Angliae et Franciae et Dominus Hiberniae* = "By the Grace of God King of England and France and Lord of Ireland" for the remainder of his lengthy reign, which lasted half a century from 1327 until 1377. His claim to the crown of France and his attempts to enforce that claim began the long struggle now known as the ➟Hundred Year's War. All the same, his was the last relatively tranquil reign to be experienced by England for some time.

Edward IV

Edward IV *pr. name, hist.* King of England

He styled himself *Dei Gratia Rex Angliae et Franciae et Dominus Hiberniae* = "By the Grace of God King of England and France and Lord of Ireland" and reigned for 21 years in all, but not continuously.

Firstly, he reigned from 1461 until he was deposed in 1470. Then again, after he was restored in 1471, he reigned until his death in 1483. The first king of the ➡Royal House of ➡York, he came to the throne and held it and lost it and held it again all during the tumult of the ➡Wars of the Roses, a period in history that now seems to resemble nothing more closely than a game of musical thrones.

Edward Longshanks *pr. name, hist.* a nickname for ➡Edward I of England

Edward the Confessor *pr. name, hist.* King of England

A member of the Royal House of ➡Denmark, he reigned for 23 years from 1042 until 1066. He was known for his strong Christian faith and indeed was canonized in 1161. Edward was not called the ➡Confessor because he made a habit of admitting things but because he bore such strong witness to his faith.

It was in order to advance his claim to the English throne in the successional dispute that arose after Edward's death that ➡William invaded England in 1066.

Edward the Martyr *pr. name, hist.* King of England

A member of the ➡Royal House of ➡Cedric, who reigned from 975 until assassinated in 978.

Edward V *pr. name, hist.* King of England

A member of the ➡Royal House of ➡York, he styled himself *Dei Gratia Rex Angliae et Franciae et Dominus Hiberniae* = "By the Grace of God King of England and France and Lord of Ireland" and reigned for two months in 1483 before being deposed on the spurious grounds that his parents' marriage was not valid and thus the throne rightly belonged to his uncle Richard, Duke of York, who did indeed take the crown as ➡Richard III.

Edward, aged 12, was taken with his young brother to the ➡Tower of London and never seen again; most likely Richard had them murdered. *SEE ALSO:* ➡Princes in the Tower.

Edward VI *pr. name, hist.* King of England

He styled himself, "Edward the sixth, by the Grace of God, King of England, France and Ireland, ➡Defender of the Faith and of the ➡Church of England, and also of Ireland, on earth the Supreme Head" and reigned for six years from 1547 until 1553 when he died at the age of 16 having been persuaded to name as successor to his throne his cousin ➡Lady Jane Grey, the very young wife of the son of Edward's guardian, the Duke of Northumberland. He was a member of the ➡Royal House of ➡Tudor and the only son of ➡Henry VIII. His mother, ➡Jane Seymour, never recovered from giving birth to him and was dead 12 days later.

Edward VII *pr. name, hist.* King of the United Kingdom

He styled himself "By the Grace of God, of the United Kingdom of Great Britain and Ireland and the British ➡Dominions beyond the Seas, King, ➡Defender of the Faith, Emperor of India, etc., etc." and reigned for nine years from 1901 until 1910. Edward was the eldest son of ➡Victoria and founder of the ➡Royal House of ➡Saxe-Coburg und Gotha, which was the family name of his father Prince ➡Albert. Because his mother reigned for so long, he did not succeed to the throne until he was almost 60.

Edward VIII *pr. name, hist.* King of the United Kingdom

A member of the Royal House of ➡Windsor who styled himself "By the Grace of God, of Great Britain, Ireland, and of the British ➡Dominions beyond the Seas, King, ➡Defender of the Faith, Emperor of India, etc., etc." Edward reigned for ten months in 1936 before abdicating in favor of his brother the Duke of York—who became ➡George VI—in order to be able to marry Bessie Wallis Warfield, a twice-married American divorcee. It was considered unacceptable for the monarch to be divorced or to be married to a divorced person at that time.

Because of the abdication, he was never crowned and thereafter took the title "Duke of Windsor". After this crisis, they married and went to live abroad until he died in 1972. Mostly they lived in France, but during World War II this was not possible, and Edward was made governor of the Bahamas. The Duchess of Windsor died in 1986.

{Edwig » Edwy} *pr. name, hist.* King of England

The son of ➡Edmond, and so a member of the ➡Royal House of ➡Cedric, he ruled from 955 until his death in 959. There is uncertainty over his exact name.

EEC *pr. name, abbr.* ➡European Economic Community

eedjit *noun, Ir.* idiot

eeh-oop *exclam., North., sl.* an expression of surprise

EETPU *pr. name, abbr.* the Electrical, Electronic, Telecommunication and Plumbing Union

A labor union in the engineering industry, now merged, in 1992, with the ➡AEU into the ➡AEEU.

eff-all *exclam., sl.* a euphemism for "fuck all"

effing and blinding *idiom, sl.* using coarse language

eff off *imper., sl.* a euphemism for "fuck off"

EFTA *pr. name, abbr.* the ➡European Free Trade Association

A free trade area of European countries established in 1960 in response to the then recently established ➡EEC. The original members were Austria, Denmark, Norway, Portugal, Sweden, Switzerland and the UK. Iceland and Finland joined later, but Denmark, Portugal and the UK left in 1973 to join the EEC. Now most of the remaining members are either applying individually to join the ➡EU themselves or are members of the European Economic Area, which is the joint EFTA/EU free trade area and the largest in the world.

egg *noun, arch., coll.* a person or thing

egg-flip *comp. noun* eggnog

eggs and bacon *comp. noun, coll.* any one of a number of possible orange and yellow-colored plants, such as the snapdragon

EGM *noun, abbr.* the ➡Empire Gallantry Medal

Egyptian PT *idiom, arch., sl.* sleeping

This expression originated among the British army based in the Middle East during World War II, founded upon the common preception of that time that all Arabs were lazy at all times without exception.

eiderdown *noun* a quilt or comforter filled with the down of the eider duck or similar soft material

18 *noun* a classification indicating that a movie is considered suitable for viewing only by people age 18 or older

eightsome reel *comp. noun, Sc.* (1) a dance for eight people; (2) the music that accompanys this

EIIR *pr. name, abbr., Lat.* the royal cipher of ➡Elizabeth II of England and I of Scotland, seen on state documents, public buildings, vehicles, etc., except in Scotland
From "Elizabeth II ➡*Regina*". SEE ALSO: ➡ER

Eilean Donan *pr. name, hist.* a modern reconstruction of a 13th C. castle
The original castle was erected in the 1220s, but in 1719 it was a Jacobite stronghold and was bombarded to destruction by ships of the ➡Royal Navy. It is built upon a rocky islet in Loch Duich, connected by a causeway to the Scottish mainland opposite the ➡Isle of Skye.

Eire *pr. name, hist.* the 26 counties of Ireland that became an independent ➡Dominion within the ➡Commonwealth in 1921
This name was adopted in 1937. Previously, the country had been known as the ➡Irish Free State. In 1949 it became a republic, left the ➡Commonwealth, and changed its name again to the ➡Republic of Ireland.

Eisenhower Platz *pr. name, coll., hist.* a nickname for Grosvenor Place, London, during World War II
When every building in the area was occupied by U.S. Military Headquarters Europe.

the **Eisteddfod** *Wal, abbr.* (1) the ➡International Music Eisteddfod; (2) the ➡Royal National Eisteddfod

ejaculatorium *noun, sl.* a room set aside at a sperm bank for the production of sperm
The word is pseudo-Latin.

ekker *noun, abbr., sl.* exercise, particularly at university or school

elasticated fabric *comp. noun* elastic fabric

elastic band *comp. noun* a rubber band

Elastoplast *pr. name (TM)* an adhesive bandage
The equivalent of a Band-Aid.

elbow bender *comp. noun, sl.* a heavy drinker

elder brethern *comp. noun* the ➡elder brothers taken as a group

elder brother *comp. noun* one of the ➡elder brethren of ➡Trinity House

elder of the kirk *comp. noun, Sc.* a lay member elected to a ➡kirk session

eldritch *adj., Sc.* (1) elf-like; (2) strange, ghostly, weird or unearthly

electoral register *comp. noun* a list of the citizens entitled to vote at local and national elections
Compiled annually, copies are kept at town halls, libraries and police stations for perusal by members of the public.

the **Elector of Hanover** *pr. name, hist.* a formal title of those British kings who were also rulers of the German principality or kingdom of ➡Hanover
Certain German kings and princes were known as "electors" (*Kurfürsten* in German; hence *Kurfürstendamm* in Berlin) because traditionally their ancestors had been the people who elected the Holy Roman Emperor. However, by the time ➡George I ascended to the British throne in 1714, the title was meaningless as the Holy Roman Empire itself had become effectively meaningless and the title of Holy Roman Emperor had become no more than a hereditary title of the Emperor of Austria.

electrical point *comp. noun* a ➡power point

electric fire *comp. noun* an electric heater

electric soup *comp. noun, sl.* a particularly powerful alcoholic punch or fortified wine

electric torch *comp. noun* a flashlight

{**electrolysation » electrolyse » electrolyser**} *spell.* {electrolyzation » electrolyze » electrolyzer}

electronic valve *comp. noun* an electron tube or thermionic tube

electroplexy *noun* electroshock or electroconvulsive therapy

electrovalency *noun* electrovalence
A chemical term.

the **Elegant Extracts** *pr. name* a nickname for the 8th Regiment of ➡Foot
A unit of the British Army that acquired this name after a series of courts-martial of officers culminated in 1813 when the regiment's entire body of officers was replaced with others selected or "extracted" from other regiments.

elephant *adj., rh. sl.* drunk
Derivation: drunk > trunk > elephant's trunk > elephant.

the **Elephant and Castle** *pr. name* an area in west-central London just south of the ➡Thames River
The district is named after a ➡pub. So how did this pub acquire such an unusual name? It is an allusion to the habit in classical times of using war elephants to carry structures, called castles, upon their backs for the transportation of archers and other soldiers. Apparently this was once quite a common name for a pub.

eleven-plus *comp. noun, coll., hist.* an examination formerly taken by 11- or 12-year-old children in England and Wales
Its purpose was to determine which kind of secondary school they should go to on the basis of academic ability as measured in this test.

elevenses *noun, coll.* a light refreshment or snack taken mid-morning

Elgin

Elgin *pr. name* a small city in ➡Grampian, Scotland

It boasts a 13th C. cathedral and was incorporated as a city in 1234. The current population is 15,000 (1988 estimate).

Elginism *noun, coll.* the practice of removing culturally valuable items from their natural, native, original or legitimate homes

From the example of Lord Elgin, who brought his Marbles back from Athens to London. (See the next item.)

a portion of the Elgin Marbles

the **Elgin Marbles** *pr. name, hist.* a collection of classical Greek sculptures

This collection includes, in particular, the frieze from the Parthenon, but also other works, including a number by Phidias. Around 1800, the 7th Earl of Elgin, in Athens on diplomatic business, noticed how these works were suffering from neglect and so purchased them and brought them to London at his own expense, where he sold them to the ➡British Museum for much less than their collection and transportation had cost him.

Eliott's Tailors *pr. name* the 15th King's Hussars

A unit of the British Army that was formed when Colonel Eliott enlisted a large group of London tailors into this new cavalry regiment that was supposedly modeled upon the elite Prussian Hussars.

Elizabethan *adj., hist.* pertaining to the time of Elizabeth, but especially that of ➡Elizabeth I of England, in the 16th C.

Elizabeth I *pr. name, hist.* Queen of England
(See box below)

Elizabeth II of England and I of Scotland *pr. name, hist.* Queen of the ➡United Kingdom

She styles herself, "By the Grace of God, of the United Kingdom of Great Britain and Northern Ireland and of Her other Realms and Territories, Queen, Head of the Commonwealth, Defender of the Faith, etc., etc." and has reigned in Britain since 1952. She is a member of the ➡Royal House of Windsor.

ell *noun, arch.* a unit of length of cloth that was equal to about 45 inches

Elsan *pr. name (TM)* a portable chemical toilet

Ely *pr. name* a city in ➡Cambridgeshire, England

Incorporated as a city in 1974, its current population is 10,000 (1988 estimate).

Elizabeth, the Virgin Queen

She styled herself, "Elizabeth, by the Grace of God, Queen of England, France and Ireland, ➡Defender of the Faith and of the ➡Church of England, and also of Ireland, on earth the Supreme Head" and reigned for 44 years from 1558 until 1603. Elizabeth is considered by many to be the greatest monarch ever to have ruled the kingdom of England.

She inherited a realm riven between ➡Puritans and Roman Catholics, yet turned the ➡Church of England into a moderate organization with a moderating influence. She presided over a long period of stability and increasing prosperity, the queen of a united people who would seem by all accounts to have held her in high regard, although perhaps not affection.

The greatest threats came from abroad, principally from the problems and difficulties caused by her cousin ➡Mary Queen of Scots, and the threat from Spain which manifest itself most clearly in the ➡Spanish Armada of 1588.

Elizabeth was the second daughter of ➡Henry VIII and the only daughter of ➡Anne Boleyn, and thus a member of the ➡Royal House of ➡Tudor. She never married, and was succeeded by her nephew and fellow monarch, ➡James VI of Scotland.

the **Emancipation Act** *pr. name, hist.* the ➡Act of Parliament of 1829 that removed virtually all the limitations imposed upon Roman Catholics that had prevented them from holding public office following restrictive laws dating from the anti-Catholic hysteria of the latter years of the 17th C.

the **Embankment** *pr. name, abbr.* the Victoria Embankment in London

It runs along the northern bank of the ➡Thames River.

{**embowelled » embowelling**} *spell.* {emboweled » emboweling}

emerald *noun* in heraldry, (1) a representation of the planet Venus; (2) vert

the **Emerald Isle** *pr. name* a poetic name for Ireland

Emmanuel College *pr. name* a college of ➡Cambridge University founded in 1584

emmet *noun, derog., South* (1) an ant; (2) a tourist

What the natives of ➡Cornwall call the hordes of tourists who invade their region every summer, due to their supposed resemblance to ants.

SEE ALSO: ➡grockle.

{**empanel » empanelled**} *spell.* {impanel » impaneled}

{**empanelling » empanelment**} *spell.* {impaneling » impanelment}

{**Emperor » Empress**} **of India** *pr. name, hist.* an alternate title for the British ➡Monarch devised at the height of the ➡British Empire in the 19th C.

India was of course just one part (albeit the most populous) of the whole British Empire. The title was devised following the proclamation of the king of Prussia as German Emperor (*Kaiser*) in 1871 after Prussia's victory in the Franco-Prussian War, as it would hardly have done for British monarchs in general and ➡Victoria in particular to have been outranked by anyone, especially a junior member of her own family.

SEE ALSO: ➡{King-Emperor » Queen-Empress}.

the **Emperor's Chambermaids** *pr. name* a nickname for the 14th King's Hussars

A unit of the British Army that captured Joseph Bonaparte's silver chamberpot following the Battle of Vittoria in 1813. Joseph was Napoleon's brother and his puppet king of Spain.

Empire Day *pr. name, arch.* the former name for ➡Commonwealth Day, instituted in 1902

the **Empire Free Trade Movement** *pr. name, hist.* a failed campaign to establish free trade throughout the ➡British Empire

Set up in 1929, it collapsed with the onset of the Great Depression a couple of years later.

the **Empire upon which the sun never sets** *idiom, hist.* the ➡British Empire

A bombastic but nevertheless accurate description of Britain's empire during its imperial heyday

employment {**exchange » office**} *comp. noun, arch.* a ➡job centre

the **Employment Service** *pr. name* an executive agency of the Department of ➡Employment set up for the twin purposes of distributing unemployment compensation and helping find work for unemployed persons

EMS *pr. name, abbr.* the ➡European Monetary System

EN *noun, abbr.* an ➡Enrolled Nurse

{**enamelled » enamelling**} *spell.* {enameled » enameling}

enamour *spell.* enamor

ENB *pr. name, abbr.* the ➡English National Ballet

encaenia *noun* a dedication festival

the **Encaenia** *noun* an annual celebration at Oxford University consisting of the recitation of poems and reading of essays in commemoration of the founders and benefactors of the university

encash *verb* to convert checks or other forms of paper money into cash

enclosed order *comp. noun* a cloistered or secluded religious order

enclosure *noun* an area closed off from the general

Especially for the use of a particular group or class of people at, for example, a sporting event.

encyclopaedia *spell.* encyclopedia

the **Encyclopeadia Britannica** *pr. name (TM)* the oldest and largest English-language encyclopedia

It was first published in Scotland in 1768. However, since 1910 the encyclopedia has been American owned and is now distinctly American in outlook, despite its name.

endamoeba *spell.* endameba

An amebic parasite of the gut of insects.

endeavour *spell.* endeavor

endorse *noun* an heraldic representation of a very thin vertical stripe

endorsement *noun* a record of conviction for a traffic violation placed on a driver's license by a court

enew *adj., adv., East.* enough

Enfield *pr. name* a ➡Greater London borough

Its current population, which is also included within the ➡London urban area total, is 250,000 (1991 Census).

enforcement notice *comp. noun* a legal notice requiring that a breach in planning law be remedied

engaged *adj.* busy

Of a telephone.

engaged tone *noun* a telephone busy signal

engine driver *comp. noun* a locomotive engineer

England

England *pr. name* the largest and most populous kingdom within the ➡United Kingdom

➡London is the capital city of both England and the ➡United Kingdom as a whole. Using the word "England" to describe the whole of the United Kingdom, although common, is quite incorrect and deeply offensive to British citizens who are not English, such as those from Wales, Scotland and Northern Ireland. The current population of England is 47,838,000 (1990 estimate).

English *adj.* pertaining to England

Using this word as though it pertains to all of the United Kingdom, although common, is entirely incorrect.

English breakfast *comp. noun* a traditional hot breakfast, washed down by plenty of tea

The meal typically consists of a plate of hot cereal such as porridge, followed by a hot dish such as bacon and eggs, and finishes up with toast and marmalade.

the **English Channel** *pr. name* the arm of the Atlantic Ocean lying between northwestern France and the southern coast of England

It narrows into the ➡Straits of Dover to the northeast.

the **English Civil War** *pr. name, hist.* the 17th C. conflict between King and Parliament

The causes of this bloody war were partly religious and partly political. Underlying everything that was to happen was the long-running struggle between a largely Protestant population on the one hand and a crypto-Catholic monarch on the other, exacerbated by ➡Charles I's belief in the doctrine of the ➡divine right of kings, which led him to believe that he could demand and expect to obtain unquestioning obedience from his subjects.

The particular crisis that brought things to a head, however, was more political than religious. It had long been the practice that Parliament had to approve all taxation measures. This they refused to do in 1642, leading Charles to attempt to arrest the five MPs that he considered to be the leaders of the party that was opposed to him. He failed and when London rallied to Parliament's side, the king went to ➡Nottingham, where he established what was in effect an alternative administration.

Now the country had two alternative governments and the drift to civil war became unstoppable. The first skirmishes were small and local affairs, but by the time of the battle of Marston Moor in 1644, a full-scale war was in progress. Eventually the king, realizing his cause was lost, sought sanctury in Scotland, but eventually the Scots returned him to England to face trial on a charge of treason, and his execution in 1649. After the death of the king, a republican ➡Commonwealth was established in England under the rule of Oliver ➡Cromwell, but eventually this degenerated into a chaotic tyrany and the monarchy was restored in 1660 when Charles II was placed upon the throne.

the **English disease** *idiom, hist.* (1) syphilis; (2) bronchitis; (3) class conflict; (4) economic failure; (5) labor conflicts and strikes; (6) violent and outrageous behavior by ➡soccer fans

What (1) was called by the French in the 16th C. *SEE ALSO:* ➡French disease. What (2) was called by the rest of Europe in the 19th C. What (3) was called by the rest of Europe in the early years of the 20th C. What (4) was called by the rest of Europe from the end of World War II until the mid-1980s. What (5) was called by the rest of Europe from the end of World War II until the mid-1980s. What (6) was called by the rest of Europe in the 1980s.

SEE ALSO: ➡British disease, ➡French disease.

English Heritage *pr. name, abbr.* the historic buildings and monuments commission for England

A government agency established in 1983 with responsibility for the care of such things.

the **English National Ballet** *pr. name, hist.* a ballet company performing classical and modern works

Founded in 1950 and known as the ➡London Festival Ballet until 1989.

the **English National Opera** *pr. name, abbr.* an opera company specializing in performances in English

Founded in 1931 and originally based at ➡Sadler's Wells, it has been based at the ➡Coliseum since 1968.

English Nature *pr. name* an independent agency set up by the government to promote conservation and improvement of English landscape and wildlife

the **English Pale** *pr. name, hist.* the area around ➡Dublin that was colonized by English settlers following its acquisition by ➡Henry II in the 12th C.

Not to be confused with the much later ➡Ulster Settlement in the northern part of the island.

an Engish Setter

English Setter *pr. name* a breed of bird dog with a white, white with black, or brown, long silky coat

the **English Solomon** *pr. name, hist.* a nickname of ➡James I of England and VI of Scotland who was, of course, Scottish

SEE ALSO: the ➡wisest fool in Christendom.

the **English Speaking Union** *pr. name* a society, founded in 1918, that seeks to strengthen ties between the English-speaking nations, especially the United Kingdom and the United States

the **English Stage Company** *pr. name* a theatrical company specializing in the performance of experimental plays and plays by young writers

Established in 1956 at the ➡Royal Court Theatre, London.

English Terrier *pr. name, hist.* a strain of dog, now extinct, cross-bred from the terrier and bulldog to fight other dogs

engrail *verb* to serrate an edge in heraldry

enjoin *verb* to prohibit by legal process

Enniskillen *pr. name, hist.* the county seat of ➡Fermanagh in ➡Northern Ireland
The current population is 11,000 (1991 estimate).

ENO *pr. name, abbr.* ➡English National Opera

enough to be going on with *idiom, coll.* sufficient for the moment

enough to make a cat laugh *idiom, coll.* very funny

{**enquire » enquiry**} *spell.* {inquire » inquiry}

enquiry agent *comp. noun* a private investigator

{**enrol » enrolment**} *spell.* {enroll » enrollment}

enrolled nurse *comp. noun* a nurse better qualified than a practical nurse but not as well qualified as a registered nurse

ENSA *pr. name, abbr., hist.* the Entertainments National Service Association
The World War II British Army entertainment unit.

ensign *noun* a flag incorporating the ➡Union Flag, usually in one corner

entente cordiale *comp. noun, Fr., hist.* a relationship between nations that is less than an alliance but more than a rapprochement
It is French, meaning, "cordial understanding."

the *Entente Cordiale* *pr. name, Fr., hist.* the informal agreement of 1903 between Britain and France
It followed the visit of ➡Edward VII to Paris in 1903 and formed the basis of the future alliance of Britain and France against Imperial Germany during World War I.

enterprise culture *comp. noun* an individualistic society where free enterprise is encouraged

enterprise zone *comp. noun* an economically decayed urban zone, where special government aid and tax holidays are provided to encourage investments into the area from eleswhere and thus, it is hoped, jobs

{**enthral » enthralment**} *spell.* {enthrall » enthrallment}

{**entrammelled » entrammelling**} *spell.* {entrammeled » entrammeling}

entrée *noun* a dish served between the fish and meat courses

entry *noun* a passageway between buildings

entryism *noun* surreptitious infiltration into a political organization or labor union
In order to change or subvert its goals or mission.

entryist *noun* a practitioner of ➡entryism

E-number *comp. noun, abbr.* Europe-number
One of a series of numbers allocated to approved food additives under the Food Labeling Regulations of the ➡EU.

envoy *spell.* envoi
Being the last stanza of a ballad or the concluding remarks of a book, poem, etc.

EOC *pr. name, abbr.* ➡Equal Opportunity Commission

Eochaid *pr. name, hist.* King of ➡Alba
He reigned for 11 years from 878 until deposed in 889.

epaulette *spell.* epaulet

epicentre *spell.* epicenter

epilogue *noun* a short religious message sometimes transmitted at the end of a day's TV broadcasting

the **Episcopal Church of Scotland** *pr. name* the name adopted by the ➡Anglican Church in Scotland

Epsom *pr. name* a racecourse in Surrey
The location of the annual ➡Derby and Oaks races.

EPT *noun, abbr., hist.* Excess Profit Tax
A tax introduced during World War II. Any profit a company made in excess of its pre-war profit was taxed at 100 percent, with 20 percent of this returned upon abolition of the tax after the war. The idea was to prevent unscrupulous businesses profiting from the additional business that came their way as a result of the war. Of course any semi-competent accountant could find numerous ways around this little local difficulty.

{**equalled » equalling**} *spell.* {equaled » equaling}

the **Equal Opportunity Commission** *pr. name* a government commission set up for the purpose of eliminating sexual discrimination and promoting equal employment opportunities between men and women

equerry *noun* an official of the ➡Royal Household who attends upon the needs of an individual member of the ➡Royal Family

Equity *pr. name* a labor union for actors

ER [A] *pr. name, abbr., Lat.* the royal cipher of ➡Elizabeth II of England and I of Scotland, when is Scotland
[B] *pr. name, abbr., arch.* the ➡East Riding
[C] *pr. name, abbr., Lat.* (1) *Elizabetha Regina*; (2) *Edwardus Rex*
(1) = "Queen Elizabeth" and (2) = "King Edward" in Latin.

erased *adj.* in heraldry, the condition of there being nothing below a stem which ends raggedly
Unlike the clean break, when it is ➡couped.

'erbert *noun, arch., sl.* a familiar form of general address made to any man of unknown name
Now rare, it was popular during the late ➡Victorian era when Herbert was a very common given name for a man.

ERD *noun, abbr.* the Emergency Reserve Decoration

eric *noun, out., sl.* a dullard
A childish expression.

Erin

Erin *pr. name, Gae., Ir.* a poetic name for Ireland

As in "Erin's Isle," for example.

erk *noun, sl.* (1) an unpopular person; (2) in the RAF, an ➡aircraftsman; (3) in the RN, a ➡naval rating

ERM *pr. name, abbr.* the Exchange Rate Mechanism

A mechanism employed with varying degrees of success by the ➡EMS to help stabilize the relative values of European currencies one with each other.

ermine *noun* robes worn by judges, members of the ➡House of Lords, etc., on ceremonial occassions

Ermine Street *pr. name, hist.* a Roman road that proceeds from London to ➡York by way of Puckeridge, Godmanchester and ➡Lincoln

This name is not Roman but given to it later by the Saxons.

ERNIE *pr. name, abbr.* Electronic Random Number Indicator Equipment

This is the computer that generates the pseudo-random numbers used to determine winners of ➡Premium Bonds.

Eros *pr. name* the popular but mistaken name for the winged statue at the center of the fountain in ➡Piccadilly Circus, London

In actual fact, the statue is supposed to represent Christian charity. Eros was the Greek god of love, which is not exactly the same thing.

Erse *pr. name, Gae., Ir.* the ➡Celtic or ➡Gaelic language of Ireland

Derived from the early Scots word for "Irish".

SEE ALSO: ➡Gaeilge.

Erskine May *pr. name, abbr.* the main legal reference work concerned with ➡Parliament

In full, its title is *A Treatise upon the Law, Privileges, Proceedings and Usage of Parliament* and the first edition was written by Thomas Erskine May during the 19th C. It is regularly revised and kept fully up-to-date. *SEE ALSO:* ➡*Dod's Parliamentary Companion.*

ESA *pr. name, abbr.* the European Space Agency

The approximate European equivalent of NASA.

Esq. *noun, abbr.* ➡Esquire

Esquire *noun, coll., out.* a title widely used in correspondence in place of "Mister" until quite recently but now becoming less common

In its abbreviated form of "Esq." it replaces "Mr." However, convention requires that "Esq." be placed *after* the surname, not before it, and the first given name is fully expressed. Thus, "Mr. J. Smith" would expressed as "John Smith, Esq." If the person being written to already has some other title such as a knighthood or is a peer, "Esq." is never used.

esquire *noun, hist., Lat.* (1) a servant who carried a knight's shield; (2) a proprietor of land

From the Latin, *scutarius* = "shield-bearer".

ESRC *pr. name, abbr.* the ➡Economic and Social Research Council

essay *noun* an academic report or paper

Essex *pr. name, hist.* (1) an ancient kingdom in southeastern England; (2) a county immediately to the east of London, on the northern banks of the ➡Thames River and estuary, and fronting part of the eastern coast of England

Established by 600, (1) was a vassal of ➡Mercia from about 730 until 825 when it was annexed by ➡Wessex. The usual seat of the kings of Essex was London until the western part of its territory was lost to Mercia about 730, after which the capital moved to ➡Colchester. The county seat of (2) is ➡Chelmsford and the current population is 1,495,000 (1991 Census).

Essex girl *pr. name, coll.* one prosperous but ignorant

A typical product of 1980s ➡Thatcherite economic policies and the worthy partner for ➡Essex man. A superficial and brainless young woman, the butt of many sexist jokes.

Essex man *pr. name, coll.* one prosperous but ignorant

A typical product of 1980s ➡Thatcherite economic policies, who exhibits bad taste and cultural ignorance on a grand scale and reputedly lives in ➡Essex, a somewhat unfashionable county to the northeast of London. *SEE ALSO:* ➡Essex girl.

established church *comp. noun* an official national or state church

The ➡Church of England in England and the ➡Church of Scotland in Scotland are established churches.

established religion *comp. noun* that of the ➡established church

the Establishment *pr. name, coll., hist.* (1) a social group exercising or perceived to be exercising control over the rest of the population; (2) the ➡Church of England when considered as the established church in England

(1) is reputedly resistant to change and considered to comprise such people as senior politicians, civil servants, generals and so forth. (2) is a 19th C. term.

establishmentarianism *noun* a belief that there should be an ➡established church

estate [A] *noun* a large tract of ground surrounding a large house

[B] *noun, abbr.* an ➡estate car

estate agent *comp. noun* a real estate broker

estate car *comp. noun* a station wagon

estate duty *comp. noun, hist.* ➡death duty

the Estates of the Realm *pr. name, hist.* a medieval term for the major classes or orders that constitute society, then considered to be the church, the nobility, and the common people

"Estate" is used here in the sense of status or class. *SEE ALSO:* the ➡Three Estates.

Estuary English *pr. name* a supposedly new British dialect, evolved since the mid-1960s.

An amalgam of traditional ➡Cockney from the ➡East End of London with what is considered to be the somewhat more cultured tones from the western suburbs. The "estuary" in question is that of the ➡Thames River.

Ethelred II *pr. name, hist.* King of England

He reigned for 38 years from 978 until 1016. However, he was temporarily dispossessed of his crown by Swegn Forkbeard, King of Denmark, in 1014. A member of the ➡Royal House of ➡Cedric, he was better known as ➡Ethelred the Unready.

Ethelred the Unready *pr. name, hist.* ➡Ethelred II

Here "unready" does not mean what it sounds like to speakers of modern English but is a corrupted version of the Anglo-Saxon word *unraed*, which means "ill-advised."

Ethelstan *pr. name, hist.* a King of ➡Wessex and ➡Mercia who conquered Northumbria in 927, so delineating for the first time what was to become known as the kingdom of England

He reigned for 12 years from 927 until 939 and founded the ➡Royal House of ➡Cedric.

Eton collar *comp. noun* a large, flat, stiff collar placed outside the coat and traditionally worn with an ➡Eton jacket.

Eton College *pr. name* a leading English ➡public school, and probably the most famous and celebrated of all

Founded by Henry VI in 1440, it is located in Eton, ➡Berkshire, just across the ➡Thames River from ➡Windsor. So far, about 20 future British ➡prime ministers were educated at this school.

Another notable former student was the Duke of Wellington, who is reputed to have said that "the Battle of Waterloo was won on the playing fields of Eton." but this is apocryphal, and was never attributed to him until after his death.

Eton crop *comp. noun, arch.* a short-cut hairstyle common among women in the 1920s.

It was called this as it was supposed to resemble the way boys from ➡Eton College cut their hair.

Eton fives *comp. noun* a variety of the game of ➡fives, played in a court with three walls

Etonian *pr. name* a member of ➡Eton College

Eton jacket *comp. noun* a short jacket, reaching only to the waist, usually worn with an ➡Eton collar

EU *pr. name, abbr.* the ➡European Union

{**eupnoea » eupnoeic**} *spell.* {eupnea » eupneic}

Normal respiration.

Euratom *pr. name, abbr.* the European Atomic Energy Community

eurhythmics *spell.* eurythmics

A method of exercising to the accompaniment of music.

Euro *adj., abbr., coll.* European

Eurobabble *noun, coll.* the specialist jargon used in documents and other writings concerned with or emanating from the ➡EU

eurobin *noun, coll.* a large wheeled trash bin

As specified by ➡EU regulations.

Eurocentric *adj.* Europocentric

eurocheque *noun* a check drawn on any participating bank in the ➡EU

Most European banks participate. The system enables customers in good standing to pay for goods or services or obtain cash from any other participating bank in Europe.

Eurocrat *noun, coll.* a civil servant who works for the ➡European Union

Eurodollar *noun, coll.* U.S. currency held by a European bank

European citizen *comp. noun* a status conferred upon citizens of the ➡United Kingdom under the terms of the ➡Maastricht Treaty of the ➡EU

European citizenship does not replace British citizenship, but automatically confers many of the rights and duties of citizenship of whichever ➡EU member country a European citizen resides in upon that citizen, no matter which EU country the citizen is a native of.

the **European Common Market** *pr. name, hist.* a European free trade area, properly known as the ➡European Economic Community or ➡EEC

It came into being in 1955 and was subsumed, together with certain other trans-national European organizations, into the ➡European Community (➡EC) in 1967. More recently, in 1994, the EC became the ➡European Union (➡EU). Britain and Ireland both joined the EC in 1973.

the **European Community** *pr. name* a former name for what is now called the ➡European Union, from 1967 to 1994

Before 1967 it was known as the ➡European Economic Community.

the **European Currency Unit** *pr. name* a unit of account used for monetary transfer purposes between member states of the ➡European Union

This embryonic international currency, often called the ➡ecu, was established and has been used by the ➡EC and ➡EU since 1978. Under the terms of the ➡Maastricht Treaty, it is intended to eventually become the sole legal currency throughout the ➡EU.

the **European Economic Community** *pr. name, hist.* a former name for the ➡European Union

Formed under the terms of the Treaty of Rome of 1957; its first name change, to ➡European Community, was in 1967.

the **European Monetary System** *pr. name* a system set up to stabilize currency exchange rates between ➡EU member countries and to help towards the eventual establishment of a single common currency for the whole of the ➡EU

the **European Parliament**

the **European Parliament** *pr. name* the parliament of the ➡European Union
All members are elected by universal suffrage for five-year terms. Full sessions of the Parliament meet in Strasbourg, committees meet in Brussels, and the secretariat is based in Luxembourg. There are 71 ➡MEPs elected from England, 8 from Scotland, 5 from Wales and 3 from Northern Ireland.

---

the **European Union** *pr. name* a close economic and political association of western European nations
It includes both the United Kingdom and the Irish Republic. The principal features so far are internal free trade, common external tariffs, common agricultural policies, Europe-wide development projects and close collaboration in defense and foreign affairs. It is seen by many as a proto-superstate or future United States of Europe. Under the terms of the ➡Maastricht Treaty, its name changed from "European Community" to "European Union" in 1994.

Eurotunnel plc *pr. name* the company that owns and operates the ➡Channel Tunnel

Eurovision *noun* a Europe-wide federation of national television networks

the **Eurovision Song Contest** *pr. name* an annual TV competition shown across Europe in which each participating country enters a singer or group with a newly composed pop song, and juries in each European country vote to select a winner
One of the most agonizing examples of Eurotrash that humanity has ever subjected itself to.

Euston Station *pr. name* a principal railroad terminus in central London
The oldest London rail terminal, opened in 1837. However, all traces of the original structures were swept away in 1963 and replaced by an uninspiring modern structure. Euston is used for trains to and from northwest England, western Scotland, north Wales and the ferry ports to Ireland.

evens *noun, sl.* even chances of winning a bet

evensong *noun* evening prayers, as practiced in the ➡Church of England

eventide home *comp. noun* a senior citizens' home
The first of these were set by the Salvation Army.

eventing *noun* an equestrian contest involving ➡showjumping, dressage, and so forth

the **Ever Readies** *pr. name, coll., hist.* a nickname for the ➡TAVR

ever so *adv. phr., coll.* very or extremely

ever so much *idiom, coll.* a vast quantity

the **Eversworded 29th** *pr. name* the 29th Regiment of ➡Foot, also called the Worcester Regiment
When stationed in North America in 1746, they were attacked in their mess by supposedly loyal Indians. Uniquely, to guard against similar surprises in future, officers were permitted to wear swords at mess dinner.

excess *noun* an insurance deductible

excess charge *comp. noun* a penalty payment charged for exceeding the maximum permitted time at a parking meter

exchange contracts *phr. verb* to perform the final legal act that closes a deal, particularly for the sale of property, in England and Wales

exchange controls *comp. noun, hist.* legal restrictions formerly imposed on the movement of currency out of Britain by residents
These measures were introduced at the beginning of World War II and finally abolished in 1979.

the **Exchequer** *pr. name, hist.* (1) the former name for the ➡Treasury; (2) a euphemism for the destination of money paid to the government or the source of money paid by the government; (3) a superior court formerly responsible for revenue matters
The name also survives in the title of the senior minister in charge of the Treasury, who is called the ➡Chancellor of the Exchequer. (3) is now merged with the ➡King's Bench.

the **Excise** *pr. name, hist.* the former government agency responsible for collecting excise duties, but now replaced by ➡HM Customs and Excise

exciseman *noun, arch.* an official employed by the ➡Excise and responsible for collecting taxes and duties on imports, liquor, etc.

exclamation mark *comp. noun, pref.* an exclamation point

exclusion order *comp. noun* an official order issued by the ➡Home Office to prevent a suspected terrorist from entering the country

excuse-me *comp. noun, coll.* a dance where cutting-in is permitted

ex-directory number *comp. noun* an unlisted telephone number

ex-dividend *adj.* excluding the next dividend of stocks and shares

exeat *noun, Lat.* (1) permission granted to a student to be temporarily absent from school or college; (2) permission granted to a priest to move from one diocese to another
Being the Latin for "go out"

exes *noun, abbr., sl.* expenses
The kind that are incurred in the course of performing one's job. SEE ALSO: ➡eckies.

Exeter *pr. name* a city that is the administrative center of ➡Devon

Founded in the 1st C. as *Isca Dumnoniorum* by the Romans and incorporated as a city in 1156, the current population is 105,000 (1991 estimate).

Exeter College *pr. name* a college of ➡Oxford University founded in 1314

exhibition *noun* a grant or scholarship paid by a college or school to maintain a student there

exhibitioner *noun* a student receiving an ➡exhibition

Exmoor *pr. name* a high, exposed and bleak moor in ➡Devon and ➡Somerset, designated a ➡national park in 1954

Exmoor pony *comp. noun* a breed of small pony that originated from ➡Exmoor

Suitable in size and temperament for children to ride.

exon *noun* one of the four commanders of the ➡Yeomen of the Guard

Who are exempt from normal duties, hencef this name.

export *noun, Sc.* a variety of high-quality, strong and dark draft beer served in Scottish pubs

Originally devised for export to various remote regions of the British Empire, hence this name.

the **Export Credit Guarantee Department** *pr. name* a government agency that arranges credit insurance for exporters

express delivery *comp. noun* a special delivery service operated by the ➡Post Office

express package *comp. noun* a letter or package sent by ➡express delivery

{**ex-serviceman » ex-servicewoman**} *noun* a ➡military veteran

extension lead *comp. noun* an electric extension cord

extent *noun, arch.* the value of land or property as assessed for taxation purposes

extra *noun* a run taken when a ➡cricket ball was untouched by either batsman or bat

SEE ALSO: ➡bye.

extra cover *comp. noun* a fielding player's position on the ➡cricket field

extractor fan *comp. noun* a room ventilation fan

extramural class *comp. noun* an extension course

A class taking place away from the premises of the college, etc., that operates it, or a class for those who are not members of the college, etc.

ex-works *idiom* at the factory gate

Used to describe the condition and price of goods as they are when they leave the place where they are made.

eyebath *noun* an eyecup or optic cup used to apply liquid preparations to the eye

eyot *noun, arch.* an ➡ait

eyre *noun, hist.* the circuit followed by a Medieval judge and his court

F

FA *pr. name, abbr.* the ➡Football Association

FAA *pr. name, abbr.* the ➡Fleet Air Arm

the **Fabian Society** *pr. name, hist.* a group of socialists favoring gradual change by democratic means rather than sudden change by revolution
Founded 1884, it was a significant factor in the emergence of the ➡Labour Party in the latter years of the 19th C.
The name derives from the career of Quintus Fabius Maximus, who died in 203 B.C. He was a Roman general known as *Cunctator* = "Delayer", due to his successful delaying tactics against Hannibal in the Third Punic War, between 218 and 202 B.C. By the way, because he adopted similar tactics against the British during the Revolutionary War, George Washington was sometimes known as "the American Fabius."

face-flannel *comp. noun* a facecloth

face like the back end of a bus *idiom, sl.* a spectacularly unattractive visage

facer *noun* a blow in the face

factor *noun, Sc.* an agent managing land or property on behalf of another

Factory Act *pr. name* any one of a series of safety laws concerning the operation of factories
The first Factory Act came into effect in 1802. There have been several since then.

factory ship *comp. noun* a ship that sails with a fishing fleet to provide immediate on-location fish processing facilities

the **Faculty of Advocates** *pr. name, Sc.* the members of the Scottish legal ➡Bar

FA Cup *pr. name, abbr.* the principal annual knock-out soccer competition in England
Organized by the ➡Football Association; the final is played at ➡Wembley.

{**faecal » faeces**} *spell.* {fecal » feces}

faff *noun, coll.* fuss

faff around *verb, coll.* to hesitate, dither or fuss about

fag [A] *noun* a junior student who acts as a servant for an older student
A practice once common at ➡public schools, but now rare.
[B] *noun, sl.* (1) a cigarette; (2) an unwanted or dreary task; drudgery

fag-end *comp. noun, sl.* (1) a cigarette butt; (2) a useless or left-over portion or part

{**faggot » faggoting**} *spell.* {fagot » fagoting}
In the sense of a bundle of sticks.

faggots *noun* a dish consisting of baked balls of seasoned and chopped liver

fag-master *verb* an older school student who employs a ➡fag [A]

fag out *verb, sl.* to exhaust or tire

fain *verb, arch.* to seek a temporary truce
A childish expression.

fair cop *idiom, out., sl.* a clean arrest
Supposedly said by the old-fashioned criminal when apprehended by the old-fashioned policeman: "All right guv, it's a fair cop. I'll come quietly."

fair dos *idiom, coll.* equitable shares

fairing *noun, arch.* (1) a present purchased or won at a fair; (2) fresh fruit eaten at the end of a meal

Fair Isle *pr. name, hist.* a small island midway between the ➡Orkney and ➡Shetland archipelagoes, to the north of the Scottish mainland
Perhaps the most remote inhabited part of the British Isles, it is best known for its unique ➡Fair Isle sweaters.

Fair Isle sweater *comp. noun* a multicolored woolen sweater with a characteristic design
From ➡Fair Isle, where these were first created and are manufactured in the traditionally way.

fair jiggert *idiom, Sc.* very tired

the Office of **Fair Trading** *pr. name* a government department responsible for ensuring that business activities are conducted in a proper manner

fair treat *idiom, coll.* a very pleasurable experience

fairy cake *comp. noun* an iced cupcake

fairy floss *comp. noun* cotton candy

fairy lights *comp. noun* very small colored lights
Commonly used as outdoor decorations or placed upon Christmas trees, etc..

Fairy Liquid *pr. name (TM)* a dish-washing liquid

fairy wool *comp. noun* a fine cloth made from wool

Falkirk

Falkirk *pr. name, hist.* an industrial town in central Scotland, between the ⟶Forth and ⟶Clyde Rivers

Its strategic location helped make it the site of two important battles between Scots and English in 1298 and 1746. The current population is 37,000 (1991 estimate).

Falkland Palace *pr. name, hist.* a former hunting lodge of the Scottish kings, in ⟶Fife some 15 miles to the southeast of ⟶Perth

Built by ⟶James II in the 15th C., but derelict by the early years of the 18th., it was restored in the late 19th C.

Falstaffian *adj.* characteristic of the stout, convivial and jovial knight who is Shakespeare's Falstaff

A fictitious character considered by some to be the essential Englishman. Shakespeare featured him in his plays *Henry IV Parts I and II* and *Merry Wives of Windsor*.

family allowance *comp. noun* ⟶child benefit

family credit *comp. noun* a government payment made to families with a low income in order to supplement their earnings

the **Family Division** *pr. name* the ⟶High Court division handling divorce and child-custody cases

One of the three divisions of the ⟶High Court of Justice .

family income supplement *comp. noun* ⟶family credit

fancy *verb, coll.* to desire or be attracted towards

fancy goods *comp. noun* notions, small ornaments and similar objects

fancy that *exclam., coll.* an expression of surprise

fancy woman *comp. noun, derog., sl.* a mistress

fang *noun, coll.* a tooth

fankle *noun, Sc.* a tangle or muddle

fanny *noun, sl., taboo* the female genitalia

Not the buttocks!

fanny adams [A] *idiom, abbr., sl.* ⟶sweet fanny adams

[B] *comp. noun, arch., sl.* tinned mutton

In 1867 an eight-year-old girl called Fanny Adams was brutally murdered, and there was much publicity over the matter. At about the same time, sailors in the ⟶Royal Navy were issued tinned mutton for the first time, which with gallows humor they dubbed "Sweet Fanny Adams," or just "Fanny Adams."

fantoosh *adj., Sc.* flashy or gaudy

FANY *pr. name, abbr., hist.* the First Aid Nursing Yeomanry

A woman's organization providing non-professional nursing and driving services for the army during World War I. It formed again during World War II.

fardel *noun, Sc.* (1) a three-cornered portion of ⟶scone, ⟶oatcake, bread, etc.; (2) the fourth part or portion of a round of drinks

fare-stage *comp. noun* the length along a public transportation route requiring one unit of payment

farina *noun* a kind of starch

farm *verb* to be the ⟶cricket batsman who is receiving all the balls bowled

Farmer Giles *pr. name* the personification of the supposedly typical British farmer

farmers *noun, rh. sl.* hemorrhoids

Derivation: hemorrhoids > piles > gile > Farmer Giles > farmers.

the **Farne Islands** *pr. name, hist.* a group of small uninhabited islands, little more than rocky outcrops, just off the northeastern coast of England

Best known as the scene of a dramatic rescue by Grace Darling and her father (the lighthouse keeper there) of a group of shipwrecked sailors stranded on one of those exposed rocks one dark and stormy night in 1838.

farragos *spell.* farragoes

The plural of "farrago".

farriage *noun, arch.* a fare charged for travel by ferry

farrier *noun, out.* (1) a blacksmith, especially one who shoes horses; (2) a horse-doctor or veterinarian

farthing *noun, hist.* (1) one quarter of a pre-1971 (old) penny; (2) a coin of the smallest possible value

The farthing ceased to be legal tender in 1961.

fascia *noun* an automobile dashboard

fascia pocket *comp. noun* the glove compartment of an automobile dashboard

See also: ⟶glove pocket

fash *verb, Sc.* (1) to inconvenience, trouble, anger or annoy; (2) to exert oneself, to take pains

Fastnet Rock *pr. name* (1) a dangerous rock located off Cape Clear upon the southwestern coast of Ireland; (2) a lighthouse close by (1)

fast wicket *comp. noun* a game of ⟶cricket that progresses very rapidly

Father Christmas *pr. name* Santa Claus

Someone of this name has been associated with Christmas in England for 400 years at least, but in his modern form he is really the American Santa Claus (originally of Dutch or German origin, of course) who was imported back across the Atlantic Ocean in the 19th C. Certainly "Santa Claus" is known in England but is much less common than "Father Christmas".

However "Santa Claus" *is* his usual name in Scotland, which may be because there is no long tradition of celebrating Christmas there. Indeed the 25th of December was not even a public holiday in Scotland until after World War II, as in the view of Scotland's traditional Presbyterian church, Christmas was a pagan festival with no place in a Christian country. This is also why it was the New Year (⟶Hogmanay) celebrations that formed the central feature of Scotland's traditional mid-winter festival, and it has really only been since the end of World War II that Christmas has come to be celebrated in any significant way in Scotland.

father of the chapel *comp. noun* the leader of the local of a printers' union

the **Father of the House** *pr. name, coll.* the longest-serving ➡MP in the ➡House of Commons
There has yet to be a longest-serving MP who is a woman, but when that happens, no doubt she will be known as the Mother of the House.

fathom *noun* a quantity of wood
6' by 6' in cross-section.

fatstock *noun* fattened livestock ready to go to market

faus *noun, North* a fox

{favour » favourable » favourableness} *spell.* {favor » favorable » favorableness}

{favourably » favourer » favouring} *spell.* {favorably » favorer » favoring}

{favourite » favouritism} *spell.* {favorite » favoritism}

FBA *noun, abbr.* a Fellow of the ➡British Academy

FC *noun, abbr.* a (soccer) Football Club

FCO *pr. name, abbr.* the ➡Foreign and Commonwealth Office

F.D. *pr. name, abbr., Lat.* ➡Defender of the Faith
In Latin, *Fidei Defensor*. This abbreviation is the form found upon British coinage.

FDA *pr. name, abbr.* the First Division (Civil Servants) Association
A labor union for the most senior-ranking civil servants.

feart *adj., Sc., sl.* afraid

fearty *noun, Sc., sl.* a coward

feck *noun, Sc.* (1) an effect; (2) the greater or largest part; (3) the majority
(1) is the root of "feckless."

fed up *adj. phr.* (1) annoyed; (2) bored
Rather than tired or disgusted; a rather subtle distinction, but real nevertheless.

fee *verb, arch., Sc.* to employ or hire for work

feed [A] *noun, coll.* a comedian's straight man
[B] *verb* to supply an actor with cues

feeder *noun* a child's bib

feeding bottle *comp. noun* a baby's nursing bottle

feed store *comp. noun* where cattle food is stored

feein {fair » market} *comp. noun, hist., Sc.* a fair or market where farmers hired workers

feel sick *verb* to feel likely to vomit

feint-ruled paper *comp. noun* paper ruled with very pale or faint lines as an aid to writing

fell *noun, North* (1) a range of mountains or hills; (2) a tract of moorland

fellmonger *noun* a person who removes wool or hair from animal hides before the process of leather-making begins

fellow *noun* a member of a college or a university who participates in its government
Especially at ➡Oxford and ➡Cambridge Universities.

fellow-commoner *comp. noun, arch.* an undergraduate entitled to sit at the fellows' table in a college of Cambridge University

fell-walker *comp. noun, North* one who walks over ➡fells as a pastime or sporting activity

fen [A] *noun, abbr.* ➡fenland
[B] *verb, arch.* to forbid

fencible *noun, arch.* a soldier available or suitable for defense of his local district or town only

fend [A] *verb* (1) to struggle or make an effort; (2) to provide for or support
[B] *verb, Sc.* (1) to rely upon oneself; (2) to scrape a bare subsistence

fenfire *noun* a ➡will-o'-the-wisp

Fenian *pr. name, Gae., Ir.* (1) a member of a 19th C. group of Irish in both Ireland and the U.S. who plotted to remove the British from Ireland; (2) a Catholic Irish person
(1) were also known as the "Irish Republican Brotherhood"; the name "Fenian" derives from the Irish Gaelic word *fianna* = "warrior." (2) is a term of abuse used especially by Protestants in ➡Northern Ireland.

fenland *noun* marshy or flooded low-lying land
Most common in ➡East Anglia.

Fenman *noun* a man who lives in a ➡fen

the **Fens** *noun* a large area of ➡fens in ➡Cambridgshire, ➡Lincolnshire and ➡Norfolk surrounding the ➡Wash
Originally a vast extension of the Wash, this was an area mostly comprising swampy marshland with the occassional island of higher, firmer ground such as the Isle of Ely when in its natural state.
However, since the vast enterprise of draining it was begun with Dutch help in the 17th and 18th Cs., it has been transformed into the richest and most productive farming land in Britain.

fent *noun, East* a portion of cloth

Ferm. *pr. name, abbr.* ➡Fermanagh

Fermanagh *pr. name, hist.* a district in ➡Northern Ireland, in what used to be County ➡Fermanagh, a former County in the ancient province of ➡Ulster
The current population is 50,000 (1990 estimate).

fernytickle *noun, Sc.* a freckle

fervour *spell.* fervor

fesse *noun* an heraldic representation of a wide horizontal stripe across the center of a shield

fesse point *comp. noun* the central point of a shield

the **Festival of Britain** *pr. name, hist.* a series of exhibitions and other events held at various locations throughout the United Kingdom during 1951

The putative reason for holding this festival at that time was to commemorate the centennial of the ➡Great Exhibition of 1851; however, in large part it was really an excuse to celebrate Britain's victory in World War II, which had ended only six years before.

The main center of the festival was the ➡South Bank site in central London; a number of buildings and other temporary but spectacular structures were erected here. Of these structures, only the ➡Royal Festival Hall remains today, although now surrounded by other buildings devoted to various aspects of the arts.

fetch up *verb, coll.* to vomit

Fettes College *pr. name* one of the leading private schools in Scotland

Located in ➡Edinburgh, it was founded in 1870.

fettler *noun, arch.* a railroad repair worker

feu [A] *noun, Sc.* (1) a perpetual lease of land in return for ➡feu duty; (2) a parcel of land so leased

[B] *verb, Sc.* to grant land on a ➡feudal basis

feu charter *comp. noun, Sc.* a legal document granting a ➡feu lease

feudal [A] *adj., hist.* of or characteristic of this system of government

[B] *adj., Sc.* of, or characteristic of, or concerned with, this system of leasing land

feudal superior [A] *comp. noun, hist.* a ➡feudal lord

[B] *comp. noun, Sc.* a landlord who is paid rent in the form of ➡feu duty

the **feudal system** *comp. noun, hist.* a system of government that originated in the chaotic latter days of the Roman Empire

Tenants were indented to their ➡feudal superior with homage, labor, and military service rather than money.

feu duty *comp. noun, Sc.* the rent, fixed in perpetuity, paid for a parcel of ➡feudal land

the **Few** *pr. name, hist.* those ➡RAF pilots who fought in the ➡Battle of Britain of 1940

Never in the field of human conflict was so much owed by so many to so few.

—Winston S. Churchill, speaking in the ➡House of Commons on August 20, 1940.

fey *adj., Sc.* (1) about to die; (2) doomed; (3) elated

Fianna Fáil *pr. name, Gae., Ir.* an Irish political party

From the Irish Gaelic, "Warriors of Ireland." Founded in 1926 by Eamon de Valera as a vehicle for his opposition to the 1921 ➡Anglo-Irish Treaty that brought about the ➡Irish Free State. Its stated goal is a united republic for the whole of the island of Ireland.

{**fibre » fibred**} *spell.* {fiber » fibered}

fibre-board *spell.* fiberboard

fibre-fill *spell.* fiberfill

fibre-glass *spell.* fiberglass

fibre-optic *spell.* fiberoptic

fibre-scope *spell.* fiberscope

Fid. De. *pr. name, abbr., Lat.* ➡Defender of the Faith

In Latin, *Fidei Defensor*.

fiddle *verb, sl.* to swindle, cheat or lie

fiddler *noun, sl.* a swindler, cheater or liar

FIDO *pr. name, abbr., hist.* (1) Fog Intensive Dispersal Operation; (2) the Film Industry Defense Organization

(1) was developed during World War II to help clear fog from the runways at ➡RAF airfields; (2) is an organization established in 1959 to prevent the broadcasting of old movies on British television. It collapsed five years later in disarray, with more old movies than ever appearing on TV.

field *noun* in ➡cricket, (1) the side which is fielding; (2) an individual player who is fielding

field drain *comp. noun* a field tile

field glasses *comp. noun* a pair of binoculars intended for outdoors use

Field Marshal *noun* the highest rank of officer in the British Army

Equivalent in rank to a General of the Army in the U.S. Army.

the **Field of the Cloth of Gold** *pr. name, hist.* the scene of a series of sumptuous meetings held between ➡Henry VIII and Francis I of France in 1529 near Calais on the French ➡Channel coast

Two highly elaborate and ornamental temporary palaces were built, one for each king; there was a stream of huge banquets together with a continuous round of every variety of late medieval entertainment. At this time, Calais was English territory, not French as now.

field of wheat *idiom, rh. sl.* a street

fiery cross *comp. noun, hist., Sc.* a wooden cross burning at one end and dipped in blood at the other

It was taken by runners from place to place to call the men of a ➡Highland ➡clan to arms. It was adopted in modified form as an intimidating symbol by racist whites in Southern states after the Civil War.

fiery pitch *comp. noun* a cricket ➡pitch that causes a ball to rise in a dangerous manner

FIFA *pr. name, abbr., Fr. Fédération Internationale de Football Associations*

Which is French, meaning, "International Federation of ➡Football Associations".

Fife *pr. name* a region in eastern Scotland, on the peninsular which lies between the Firth of ➡Tay and Firth of ➡Forth

The current population is 345,000 (1991 Census).

SEE ALSO: the ➡Kingdom of Fife.

fife and drum *idiom, rh. sl.* a bum

15 *noun* a classification indicating that a movie is suitable for viewing by people aged 15 or older

the **Fifteen** *pr. name, hist.* the failed ➠Jacobite rebellion of 1715

An unsuccessful bid for the British throne, made by the ➠Old Pretender. The whole episode was a fiasco; James was on his way back from Scotland to France and permanent banishment within seven weeks. *SEE ALSO:* the ➠Forty-five.

the **Fifth of November** *pr. name, hist.* ➠Guy Fawkes Night

50 pence piece *comp. noun* a large seven-sided cupro-nickel coin, worth half of one ➠Pound

Fighter Command *pr. name, hist.* a former ➠command of the ➠RAF which was responsible for the air defense of Britain by the interception of encroaching hostile aircraft

Formed in 1936, Fighter Command's heyday was undoubtedly when ➠Air Marshal Hugh Dowding commanded its 50 or so squadrons in the ➠Battle of Britain during World War II.

the **Fighting Fifth** *pr. name* a nickname for the 5th Regiment of ➠Foot

A unit of the British Army which acquired this name from a remark attributed to the Duke of Wellington; "The Ever-Fighting, Never-Failing Fifth".

fig roll *comp. noun* a fig-filled cookie

FIJ *pr. name, abbr.* Fellow of the Institution of Journalists

file *noun* an heraldic representation of a horizontal bar with smaller bars hanging down from it

filibuster *noun, arch., Du.* a pirate

From the Dutch, *vrijbuiter* = "freebooter".

fillebeg *noun, Gae., Sc.* a ➠philabeg

fill {in » up} *verb* to fill out or complete a document, for example

film *noun, pref.* a movie

film-goer *noun* a moviegoer

film star *comp. noun, pref.* a movie star

filter *verb* to operate or use a traffic filter

filter bed *comp. noun* a sewage bacteria bed

filter light *comp. noun* a traffic light separately controlling a vehicle stream turning to the left or right and thus away from the main highway

the **filth** *noun, derog., sl.* the police

FIMBRA *pr. name, abbr.* the Financial Intermediaries, Managers and Brokers Association

An organization set up under the 1986 Financial Services Act for the purpose of enforcing codes of conduct for certain kinds of financial institutions.

Final Reading *comp. noun* a ➠Third Reading

finance house *comp. noun* a finance company

the **Financial Times-Stock Exchange Index** *pr. name* a daily index of the movements of shares on the ➠London Stock Exchange

The British equivalent of the Dow Jones Industrial Average.

the *Financial Times pr. name* the financial and business newspaper that is the British equivalent of the *Wall Street Journal.*

financial year *comp. noun* a year as defined for accounting and tax purposes

The British financial year begins on April 5th.

find *noun* the discovery of a fox while hunting

find one's feet *idiom. phr. verb, coll.* to learn how to perform a new task or cope with a new situation

Fine Gael pr. name, Gae., Ir. an Irish political party

Meaning, in Gaelic, "Tribe of the Gaels." It was founded by William Cosgreave in support of the 1921 ➠Anglo-Irish Treaty that brought about the ➠Irish Free State. It is generally seen as the more conservative Irish party, seeking closer collaboration with Britain.

Fingal's Cave *pr. name, hist.* a large cave on the island of Staffa, in the ➠Inner Hebrides off the west coast of Scotland

Famous for its six-sided rock pillars and the inspirations it has given to Keats, Wordworth, Tennyson and Mendlessohn—to name just four—over the years.

SEE ALSO: the ➠Giant's Causeway, which has been formed in the same geological process of rock crystallization during the cooling phase following an ancient volcanic eruption.

fingers *noun, sl.* (1) a pickpocket; (2) a policeman

finish up *verb, coll.* to end up

Fingal's Cave

fink *verb, sl.* to think

Finnan haddie *comp. noun, Sc.* a haddock cured in the smoke of green wood, turf or peat

Named after Findon—where the food originated—a small fishing village some miles south of ➡Aberdeen. Finnon is the local name for the village.

finnip *noun, sl.* a ➡five pound note

fire {brigade » company} *comp. noun* a fire department

fire lighter *comp. noun* an inflammable material used to start a fire

fire office *comp. noun* an insurance company specializing in fire risks

fireplace suite *comp. noun* a set of fireplace tools

fire practice *comp. noun* a fire drill

fire raiser *comp. noun* an arsonist

fire raising *comp. noun* arson

firkin *noun* a unit of capacity equal to half a ➡kilderkin

firm *noun* a team of hospital doctors and other medical or surgical specialists who work together under the leadership of a ➡consultant

first *noun, abbr., coll.* a ➡first-class degree

first degree *noun, abbr., coll.* a bachelor degree
This should not be confused with a ➡first-class degree.

first-class degree *noun, abbr., coll.* a university ➡first degree awarded with the highest of three possible classes of honor

Each class is further divided into upper and lower grades. The class and grade of a degree is often abbreviated in the form of, for example, 1-1, which is a first-class degree of the upper grade, or 1-2, which is one of the lower grade. See also: ➡second-class degree, ➡third-class degree.

the **First Commissioner** *pr. name* the senior civil servant, with overall responsibility for the entire British Civil Service, and who reports directly to the ➡Prime Minister

first {fitter » footer} *comp. noun, Sc.* the first visitor to enter a house at the start of a new year
Depending upon who or how well equipped that person is, either good luck or bad is signified.
The most lucky arrangement is considered to be a tall dark-haired man carrying something to eat, something to drink, and something to keep the house warm: shortbread, Scotch (what else?) and a lump of coal are the traditional ingredients.

first floor *comp. noun* a second floor
That is, the floor immediately above the ground floor.

the **First Lord of the Admiralty** *pr. name, hist.* the government minister formerly responsible for the Royal Navy

the **First Lord of the Treasury** *pr. name* the official title of the ➡Prime Minister

first post *comp. noun* (1) the first mail collection of the day; (2) the first mail delivery of the day; (3) a military reveille signaled by a bugle call

First Reading *comp. noun* the preliminary presentation of a ➡bill to ➡Parliament in order to obtain permission for it to be introduced

first school *comp. noun* an elementary school for children age 5 to 9 years

the **First Scottish Interregnum** *pr. name, hist.* the two years from the death at sea of the seven-year-old Queen Margaret, ➡Maid of Norway in 1290, until the ascension of ➡John Baliot in 1292

After ➡Margaret of Norway's death, there was no clear line of succession to the Scottish throne and thirteen claimants came forward. Edward I of England was asked to adjudicate, and he awarded the throne to ➡John Baliot. *See also:* ➡Second Scottish Interregnum.

the **First Sea Lord** *pr. name, arch.* the leading naval member of the ➡Board of Admiralty

First Secretary *comp. noun* the title of the chief officer of a government department

the **First War** *pr. name, coll., out.* World War I

firth *noun* a river estuary or ➡sea loch

fiscal *noun, abbr., Sc.* a ➡procurator fiscal

fish and chips *comp. noun* a dish consisting of deep-fried fish and French fries

fish and chip shop *comp. noun* a fast-food, carry-out restaurant selling ➡fish and chips

Fishbourne Palace *pr. name, hist.* the largest Roman building yet discovered in Britain

It is just outside ➡Chichester in ➡West Sussex where it was discovered by accident in 1960, and is now known to extend over an area of 10 acres. It seems to have been built in the 1st C. as the residence of a native British tribal chief who had been rewarded well by the Romans for his cooperation with them. Particularly impressive mosaics have been found.

fish-eaters *comp. noun, coll.* a knife and a fork, especially when used for eating a fish dish

fish finger *comp. noun* a fish stick

fishing *noun, coll.* the art of gathering information while appearing to be doing something else

fishing expedition *comp. noun, hist., sl.* a trip made by single women from good homes to outposts of the ➡British Empire, especially India, in the hope of finding a suitable husband
Most popular in the latter 19th and early 20th Cs.

the **fishing fleet** *comp. noun, hist., sl.* the participants in ➡fishing expeditions, considered as a group

fishmonger *noun* a person dealing in or selling fish

fist *noun, sl.* (1) a hand; (2) handwriting

fitted carpet *comp. noun* a wall-to-wall carpet

fitted cupboard *comp. noun* a built-in closet

fit-up *comp. noun, sl.* a temporary stage

fit up *verb, sl.* to frame someone for a crime

fit-up company *comp. noun, sl.* a traveling theatrical company

Fitzwilliam College *pr. name* a college of ➡Cambridge University founded in 1966

the **Fitzwilliam Museum** *pr. name* the museum of ➡Cambridge University

It was founded when Viscount Fitzwilliam bequeathed his collection and library to the university when he died in 1816.

the **Five Nations Tournament** *pr. name* the annual ➡Rugby Union tournament between England, Scotland, Wales, Ireland and France

fiver *noun, sl.* a ➡five pound note

fives *noun* a kind of handball game particularly associated with ➡Eton College and ➡Rugby School

fivestones *noun* a child's version of the game of jacks, played with five pieces of metal but no ball

five-to-two *idiom, derog., rh. sl.* a Jew

the **Five Towns** *pr. name, hist.* five towns, sitting cheek-by-jowl in ➡Staffordshire that merged to form the city of ➡Stoke-on-Trent in 1910

This, the center of the British ceramics industry, is also known as the ➡Potteries. The five towns were Burslem, Hanley, Longton, ➡Stoke-on-Trent and Tunstall.

fixture *noun, coll.* a scheduled sporting event

fixtures and fittings *idiom* the fixed furnishings of a house or an apartment

It consists of such things as built-in furniture, light fittings, and, possibly, carpets and drapes.

flaff *verb, Sc.* (1) to flutter or fluster; (2) to gust

(2) refers to the behavior of wind.

flaff around *idiom. phr. verb., sl.* to behave in a confused or agitated way

flag *noun, arch.* a lever upon the side of a taxi that was raised to indicate that it was available for hire

Now replaced by an illuminated sign.

flag day *comp. noun* a tag day

When street collectors for charities, etc., exchange small paper flags in return for financial contributions to their cause from passing members of the public.

flageolet *noun* a variety of French kidney bean

flag-list *comp. noun* a list of naval flag officers

flag-officer *comp. noun* (1) an admiral, vice admiral or rear admiral; (2) the commodore of a yacht club

flake out *verb* to collapse or fall asleep with exhaustion

flakers *adj., sl.* exhausted

the **Flamers** *pr. name* the 54th Regiment of ➡Foot

A unit of the British Army named for an event during the American Revolutionary War, when they captured New London, CT, and went on to burn the town and the ships in the harbor.

flaming *adj., coll.* enraged, livid

flaming heck *exclam., sl.* a euphemism for or variation of "fucking hell"

flan *noun* a large, shallow open pastry tart with either sweet or savory filling

Flanders poppy *comp. noun, hist.* a symbol of the many dead of Word War I

From a poem composed in 1915:

In Flanders fields the poppies blow
Between the crosses, row on row,
*   That mark our place; and in the sky*
*   The larks, still bravely singing, fly*
Scarce heard amid the guns below.

We are the Dead. Short days ago
We lived, felt dawn, saw sunset glow,
Loved, and were loved, and now we lie
*   In Flanders fields.*

Take up your quarrel with the foe;
To you from falling hands we throw
*   The torch; be yours to hold it high.*
If ye break faith with us who die
We shall not sleep, though poppies grow
*   In Flanders fields.*

It was written by Lieut.-Col. John McCrae, a Canadian, while serving at ➡Ypres. He died on active service in 1918, after serving four years on the Western Front.
Flanders is in Belgium.

flanker *noun, sl.* a trick, sharp practice, or a swindle

flannel [A] *noun, coll.* (1) nonsense; (2) flattery; (3) a small washcloth

[B] *verb, sl.* to flatter

flannel cake *comp. noun, North* a kind of ➡scone made in ➡Yorkshire

{**flannelled » flannelling**} *spell.* {flanneled » flanneling}

flannelled fools *idiom, coll.* a humorous or derisive term for people who play ➡cricket

flannels *noun* the ➡trousers or pants worn by ➡cricket players

flapjack [A] *noun* a cake made from rolled oats and ➡golden syrup

[B] *noun, arch.* a lady's powder compact

flash *noun* a patch of colored cloth sewn on a military uniform as an emblem indicating unit, rank, etc.

flash cove *comp. noun, arch., sl.* a well-dressed man who is a member of the upper classes

Flash Harry *comp. noun, derog., sl.* a man who dresses in an expensive and flashy manner but lacks taste or elegance

flash of light *idiom, rh. sl.* a gaudily dressed person, particularly a woman

Derivation: gaudy > bright > light > flash of light.

flat *noun* (1) an apartment; (2) a condominium owned by the occupier

the **flat** *noun, abbr.* (1) a flat race, or flat racing; (2) the season for this

(1) is a horse race, or horse racing, taking place on a level course, unlike a steeplechase where hurdles are to be overcome.

flat battery *comp. noun* a discharged or dead battery

flatlet *noun* an efficiency apartment

flatmate *noun, coll.* a roommate or housemate

flat-out *adj., coll.* all-out

flat spin *comp. noun, coll.* (1) an almost horizontal spin by an aircraft; (2) a condition of panic or extreme agitation

flatters *adj., adv., sl.* flat

flautist *spell.* flutist

{**flavour » flavourer » flavourful**} *spell.* {flavor » flavorer » flavorful}

flavouring *noun* a flavor

An ingredient that imparts flavor.

{**flavouring » flavourless » flavoursome**} *spell.* {flavoring » flavorless » flavorsome}

flavour of the month *idiom, coll.* a sarcastic name for the current fashion

flea-pit *comp. noun, sl.* a rundown or dilapidated theater, especially a movie theater

fledgeling *spell.* fledgling

fleech *verb, Sc.* to coax or flatter

fleein *adj., Sc., sl.* very drunk

fleet [A] *adj., adv., arch., Du.* shallow

Probably from the Dutch *vloot* = "shallow," in the sense of water that is not deep.

[B] *noun, South* a creek

the **Fleet** *pr. name* the small stream, now entirely underground, that flows into the ➠Thames River just to the west of the ➠City of London

➠Fleet Street is named after it.

the **Fleet Air Arm** *pr. name* the aviation section of the ➠Royal Navy

It evolved from the ➠Royal Naval Air Service of World War I. In 1918 this was transferred to the then brand-new ➠RAF and renamed the Fleet Air Arm in 1924. It was transferred back to direct naval control in 1939.

fleet chief petty officer *comp. noun* a warrant officer in the ➠Royal Navy

Equivalent in rank to senior chief petty officer in the U.S. Navy.

Fleet Street *pr. name, coll., out.* the collective name for London's newspapers

From this street, which had been the center of London's printing business since about 1500, and where almost all newspapers offices were located until the 1980s.

flesher *noun, Sc.* a butcher

flex *noun* a flexible electrical power cord

flexion *spell.* flection

fley awa *phr. verb, Sc.* to frighten away

flibbertigibbet *noun* a frivolous, gossipy person

flick knife *comp. noun* a switchblade

flies' cemetery *idiom, coll.* a sheet cake of currants sandwiched between shortbread cookie layers

flight lieutenant *comp. noun* a commissioned officer in the ➠RAF

Equivalent in rank to a captain in the USAF.

flight sergeant *comp. noun* a non-commissioned officer in the ➠RAF

Equivalent in rank to a staff sergeant in the USAF.

flim *noun, sl.* any ➠banknote which has a face value of five ➠pounds

flimsy *noun, sl.* (1) thin paper; (2) a copy made on this; (3) women's underwear made from very fine material; (4) a conduct certificate issued to a naval officer by his or her superior at the end of their time spent under that command; (5) a large white five ➠pound ➠banknote once issued by the ➠Bank of England

(5) was in circulation from ➠Victorian times until 1961.

Flint *pr. name, hist.* a former Welsh County, now part of ➠Clwyd

flip *noun, coll.* (1) a short pleasure flight in an aircraft; (2) a brief tour

flipping *exclam, sl.* a euphemistic variation of "fucking"

flit [A] *noun, abbr., coll.* a ➠moonlight flitting

[B] *verb, Ir., North, Sc.* (1) to move house; (2) to permanently leave a district and go live in another

flitter-mouse *comp. noun, arch.* a bat

The mouse-like nocturnal flying mammal, that is.

Compare with the German name *Fledermaus* for this creature.

float *noun* (1) a small cart or electrically powered truck; (2) a sum of money held by a store, etc., so that change can be provided as required

floatage [A] *noun* (1) shipping upon a river; (2) that part of a ship that is above the waterline; (3) the right to gather flotsam

[B] *spell.* flotage

floater *noun, sl.* (1) a government stock certificate considered to be acceptable collateral for a loan; (2) an error; (3) an uncommitted voter

flob *verb, sl.* to spit
An expression mostly used by children.

Flodden Field *pr. name, hist.* a battle in 1513 that ended in a catastrophic defeat for the Scots at the hands of the English
Under the terms of the ➡Auld Alliance, ➡James IV of Scotland marched his army south after ➡Henry VIII of England invaded France. They met the English army sent north to stop them at Flodden, just a few miles south of the ➡Tweed River, which marks the border between Scotland and England. Although James's 30,000 men outnumbered the 20,000 English, the English won, leaving some 10,000 Scots dead on the field, including the king himself. The ➡bagpipe lament *The Flowers o' the Forest* commemorates this great national disaster.

flog [A] *verb, sl.* to sell
[B] *verb, arch.* to resell stolen goods

floorcloth *noun* a cloth used to wash floors

Florence Court *pr. name, hist.* an early 18th C. house eight miles south of ➡Enniskillen, Northern Ireland
It was built by Sir John Cole, who named the house after his wife Florence. It was badly damaged by fire in 1954 but has been completely restored since then.

florin *noun, hist.* (1) a silver coin with a face value of two ➡shillings in ➡old currency; (2) a 14th C. gold coin with a face value of $1/3$ of a ➡pound

flowery *noun, rh. sl.* a prison cell
Derivation: prison cell > cell > dell > flowery dell > flowery.

Flt. Lt. *comp. noun, abbr.* a ➡flight lieutenant

Flt. Off. *comp. noun, abbr.* a ➡flight officer

Flt. Sgt. *comp. noun, abbr.* a ➡flight sergeant

fluff off *imper., sl.* a euphemistic variation of "fuck off"

fluff one's duff *phr. verb, sl., taboo* to masturbate

fluid drachm *comp. noun, arch.* a unit of measurement formerly employed by pharmacists, equal to $1/8$ th of a ➡fluid ounce

fluid ounce *spell.* fluidounce

flummery *noun, coll.* a meaningless or pointless gesture; empty words

flummox *verb, coll.* to bewilder or confuse

flump [A] *noun, coll.* a sudden dull noise
[B] *verb, coll.* to land heavily

flunkey *noun, coll., derog.* (1) a flatterer; (2) a snob

flunkey *spell.* flunky

flunkeys *spell.* flunkies
The plural of flunkey.

flush out *verb* to reveal or expose

flutter *noun* a small bet or speculation

fly [A] *adj., sl.* cunning or knowing
[B] *noun, arch.* a ➡Hackney carriage drawn by a single horse

fly a kite [A] *idiom. phr. verb* (1) to propose a plan that is known to be doubtful; (2) to smuggle things in or out of prison; (3) to write a letter begging for money
[B] *idiom. phr. verb, arch.* (1) to write a check while knowing that it cannot be honored; (2) to discount a bill at a bank while knowing that it cannot be honored by the person upon whom it is drawn

fly at *verb* to attack furiously or rage at

fly-half *comp. noun* a Rugby Football player

flying bomb *comp. noun, hist., sl.* a ➡V-1
World War II slang.

flying officer *comp. noun, abbr.* a commissioned officer in the ➡RAF
Equivalent in rank to a first lieutenant in the USAF.

flying picket *comp. noun* a strike picket who moves rapidly from one location to another in order to support local pickets
The practice was made illegal during the 1980s.

flying squad *comp. noun* a rapid-reaction police unit

flyover *noun* an overpass

flypast *noun* a flyover of aircraft

fly pie *comp. noun, North* a ➡flies' cemetery

fly-swat *comp. noun* a fly swatter

flyte [A] *noun, Sc.* a severe reprimand
[B] *verb, Sc.* (1) to scold or abuse; (2) to quarrel

fly-tipping *comp. noun, coll.* the practice of secretly dumping trash at unapproved locations or without obtaining permission

fly-trap *comp. noun, arch.* a small, open carriage drawn by a single horse

FM *noun, abbr.* a ➡Field Marshal

FO [A] *comp. noun, abbr.* a ➡Flying Officer
[B] *pr. name, abbr.* the ➡Foreign Office

{foetal » foetus} *spell.* {fetal » fetus}

foetid *spell.* fetid

fog [A] *noun* (1) grass that grows after cutting; (2) tall grass that remains after winter; (3) a residue
[B] *verb* to feed cattle with ➡fog [A](1) or (2)

fog bank *comp. noun* a heavy, impenetrable mass of fog, usually at sea

foggage *noun, Sc.* the second crop of grass after hay

foglamp *noun* an automobile's fog light

fold *noun* a hollow or undulation of the land

foldstool *noun* a small table that people at prayer sometimes kneel in front of

folk-ways *comp. noun* traditional customs of a people

folkweave *noun* a loose, roughly woven fabric

follow on *verb* to ➡come into bat for a second time immediately, having scored less ➡runs than the other side in a game of ➡cricket

fontanelle *spell.* fontanel

A membrane-covered space in the skull of an infant, which is located at the interstices between parietal bones which have not yet joined together.

fool [A] *noun* a dessert of stewed fruit and cream, etc., usually made using gooseberry or rhubarb

[B] *noun, hist.* a clown or jester

foolscap *noun, out.* a standard paper size measuring 13¹/₄ by 16¹/₂ inches

It has now been entirely replaced by metric paper sizes. The name comes from an old watermark in the form of a fool's head and cap.

foosty *adj., Sc.* moldy

foot *noun, arch.* infantry

foot-and-mouth disease *comp. noun* hoof-and-mouth disease

football *pr. name, abbr.* (1) the game of ➡Association Football or soccer; (2) the game of ➡Rugby Football

the **Football Association** *pr. name* the body responsible for establishing and regulating the formal rules of the game of ➡soccer throughout the United Kingdom

the **Football League** *pr. name* the body responsible for arranging and controlling ➡soccer competitions between professional teams throughout England and Wales

football {pitch » field} *comp. noun* a playing ground used for games of ➡soccer

football pool *comp. noun* a weekly gambling event

Winning depends upon correctly predicting which of the ➡soccer games organized each week by the ➡Football League result in no-score draws.

footer *noun, abbr., sl.* ➡soccer

A diminutive form of the word ➡football.

Foot Guards *pr. name* the senior infantry regiments of the British Army

The Foot Guards are considered to be the personal bodyguard of the monarch. They consist of the Grenadier, Coldstream, Scots, Irish and Welsh Guards.

footling *adj., coll.* unimportant or trivial

footpad *noun, East* a footpath or sidewalk

footplate *noun* the platform inside a railroad locomotive engineer's cab

Especially on a steam-powered locomotive

Footsie *noun, coll.* originally a humorous rendition of ➡FT-SE Index, now in general use as the colloquial name for this

footslog *noun, coll.* a very lengthy or exhausting march or walk

Especially one across rough or muddy ground.

footway *noun* a pedestrian path or sidewalk

footwell *noun* passenger's legroom in a car

for *prep.* during, or over

For example, as in "for some time" = "over some time".

forby *prep., Sc.* in addition to

force *noun, North* a waterfall

forceput *noun, East* action taken under duress

forces *noun* (1) military personnel; (2) military resources generally

the **Foreign and Commonwealth Office** *pr. name, hist.* the equivalent of the U.S. State Department

foreigner *noun, sl.* illicit work carried out at one's regular workplace for personal benefit

the **Foreign Office** *pr. name, hist.* the former name of the ➡Foreign and Commonwealth Office

Foreign Secretary *pr. name* the British equivalent of the U.S. Secretary of State

forenent *adj., Sc.* (1) opposing or in front of; (2) in exchange or return for

forest *noun, arch., Lat.* uncultivated land that is owned by the monarch

Not necessarily wooded at all, these tracts were traditionally kept as a royal hunting reserve. The word comes from the Latin *foris* = "outside."

forest park *comp. noun* a forest with camping and other facilities for tourists

Similar to a ➡national park.

the **Forestry Commission** *pr. name* the agency administering government-owned forests

foreswear *verb* to renounce something upon oath

foretime *noun, arch.* the distant past

for ever *adv. phr.* for ever more to the end of time

Not to be confused with "forever," meaning "continually."

Forfar bridie *noun, abbr., Sc.* a kind of pie

Forfar is the town in ➡Tayside where these originated. They consist of a circle of pastry that is folded over meat, onions, etc.

for good and all *idiom* finally and for ever more

be **for it** *verb, coll.* to be in immediate danger of punishment or other trouble

the Forth Road Bridge   *the Forth Bridge*

fork lunch *comp. noun* a buffet luncheon

fork supper *comp. noun* a buffet supper

form [A] *adv.* formally or previously

[B] *noun* (1) a school class or grade; (2) formal but possibly empty behavior that accords with tradition or custom; (3) the track record of a race horse; (4) a criminal record

forme *spell.* form

An outdated printing term for a body of text that is secured together for the purpose of being printed as a single unit.

former *noun* a student who is a member of a particular ➡form [B](1) at school

Former Naval Person *pr. name, hist.* a wartime code name for Winston S. Churchill

When communicating with Franklin D. Roosevelt prior to the United States' entry into World War II.

form {master » mistress} *comp. noun* a {male » female} school class teacher

the Forth *pr. name* a 66-mile river flowing through central Scotland

It rises near Aberfoyle in ➡Perthshire and outflows through the Firth of ➡Forth into the ➡North Sea, just to the north of Edinburgh.

the Firth of Forth *pr. name* the estuary of the ➡Forth River, on Scotland's eastern coast

Bounded on the south by ➡Lothian and ➡Edinburgh, and on the north by ➡Fife, this wide river estuary has been bridged just a few miles to the west of Edinburgh, at Queensferry, its narrowest point, by the ➡Forth Bridge and the ➡Fourth Road Bridge.

the Forth Bridge *pr. name* a distinctive three-towered cantilevered bridge carrying a railroad across the ➡Firth of Forth near ➡Edinburgh in central Scotland

It has two equal spans of 1,710 ft., and when completed in 1889 was the world's longest cantilevered bridge, considered to be one of the greatest engineering feats of all time. Because it was built in the years immediately following the

➡Tay Bridge Disaster of 1879, it was designed and constructed with an exceptionally large margin of safety.

Due to the vast area of metal involved, ➡painting the Forth Bridge is a popular euphemism for an endless repetitive task.

the Forth-Clyde Canal *pr. name, hist.* an 18th C. canal across central Scotland

It stretches 38 miles from the ➡Firth of Forth some 20 miles west of ➡Edinburgh to the ➡Clyde west of ➡Glasgow, roughly following the route of the ancient ➡Antonine Wall.

Although this canal is no longer used commercially, it is where Britain's first practical steam-powered boat, William Symington's *Charlotte Dundas*, was first used as a tug in 1802.

for the best *idiom, coll.* with the best intent

the Forth Road Bridge *pr. name* a suspension bridge carrying a highway across the ➡Firth of Forth about a mile west of the older railroad bridge

With its span of 3,300 ft., it was one of the longest suspension bridges in the world when it was completed in 1964.

the Forties *pr. name* the sea area between southern Norway and the northeastern coast of Scotland

Because these waters are reputed to be 40 fathoms deep.

fortnight *noun* two weeks or 14 days

fortnightly *adj., adv.* biweekly

Fortnum and Mason *pr. name* a highly fashionable food store in ➡Piccadilly, London

It is famous for its high quality, high prices and high-class customers, including members of the ➡Royal Family. It was founded in 1707 by a former footman of ➡Anne in partnership with a ➡grocer, and by the 19th C. had developed into a very profitable business supplying Army and Navy officers serving abroad with the sort of high-quality food products that could not normally be found in the remoter corners of the world.

Fort William *pr. name, hist.* a small town and tourist center at the foot of ➡Ben Nevis in the western ➡Highlands of Scotland

Originally a fortress built in the 1690s as part of a campaign to pacify the Highland ➡clans. The 17th C. fort, named in honor of ➡William of Orange, king at the time, was demolished about 200 years later to make way for a railroad.

the **Forty-Five**

the **Forty-Five** *pr. name, hist.* the second ➠Jacobite rebellion, in 1745

(See box on this page.)

forward short leg *comp. noun* a fielding player's position on the ➠cricket field

fosse *noun* a long narrow ditch, canal or trench

the **Fosse Way** *pr. name, hist.* the great Roman road that runs in an almost straight line for some 200 miles from Lyme Bay in ➠Devon in southwest England to ➠Lincoln in east-central England, midway between the ➠Wash and the ➠Humber estuary on the ➠North Sea

It was given this name in ➠Anglo-Saxon times because of the two ➠fosses that run alongside it, one on either side of the actual highway itself. At ➠Lincoln, the Fosse Way joins up with ➠Ermine Street.

foster *verb* to place or allocate a child to a foster home

When done by an official agency, or similar.

fou *adj., Sc.* drunk

founder member *comp. noun* a charter member

fount *spell.* font

A set or style of typeface.

Fountains Abbey and Hall *pr. name, hist.* an abbey and large house near Ripon in ➠North Yorkshire

The abbey was founded in 1132 by Benedictine monks who "defected" to the Cistercian order just three years later, and remains one of the best preserved and most attractive ruins to survive ➠Henry VIII's dissolution of the monasteries. Fountains Hall, built between 1598 and 1611 upon ground once part of the monastic estates and partly using stone from the abbey as building material, is a fine example of a late ➠Elizabethan or early ➠Jacobean mansion. The estate, which encompasses both buildings, has been designated a World Heritage Site.

four-ale *comp. noun, arch.* beer once (long, long ago) on sale at ➠fourpence a quart

four-letter man *comp. noun, sl.* an obnoxious man

the **Four Marys** *pr. name, hist.* the lady companions of ➠Mary Queen of Scots

They were Mary Bethune (or Beaton), Mary Leuson (or Livingstone), Mary Fleming (or Flemyng) and Mary Seaton (or Seyton). Mary Carmichael was not one of them, although she managed to get mentioned in the ballad:

> Yestre'en the queen had four Marys,
> This nicht she'll hae but three.
> There was Mary Beaton and Mary Seaton,
> Mary Carmichael, and me.

fourpence *noun* a sum of four ➠pennies

More common before the currency changes of 1971.

fourpenny *adj.* priced four ➠pennies

More common before the currency changes of 1971.

fourpenny one *comp. noun, arch., sl.* (1) a scolding; (2) a push or shove

the **Four Seas** *pr. name, out.* the seas that surround the ➠British Isles upon all sides

Fourth of July *pr. name* the principal annual celebration at ➠Eton College

Entirely unconnected with the U.S. celebrations held on the same date to commemorate the adoption of the Declaration of Independence in 1776. ➠Eton College was founded in 1440.

fower *noun, Sc.* four

FP *noun, abbr.* a former ➠pupil or student

FPA *pr. name, abbr.* (1) the Family Planning Association; (2) a FormerPupil'sAssociation

(1) is a charity operating a network of birth control clinics throughout Britain and other parts of the world. The first was established by Marie Stopes in London's ➠East End in 1922; (2) is a society for former students of a high school or similar.

FPS *pr. name, abbr.* a Fellow of the Pharmaceutical Society of Great Britain

---

The Forty-Five Rebellion

The name refers to this year of 1745 when Charles Edward Stuart (the ➠Young Pretender, or ➠Bonnie Prince Charlie) attempted to capture the British throne on behalf of his father.

Landing in northern Scotland and joined by a rather small band of clansmen, he marched to ➠Edinburgh where he proclaimed his father to be King ➠James VIII of Scotland. He defeated Sir John Cope at the Battle of Prestonpans near Edinburgh, and moved south into England by way of ➠Carlisle. Meeting little resistance his army continued on to ➠Derby.

By the time he reached that town, there was panic in London where the fall of the ➠Hanovarian regime was momentarily expected. However, the English Jacobites failed to support him as expected and there was confusion among the Scots. Retreating all the way back into northern Scotland, he was decisively defeated by the Duke of Cumberland at the Battle of ➠Culloden near ➠Inverness in the spring of 1746, the last set-piece battle on British soil.

After this Charles escaped, with the aid of Flora Macdonald, to France by way of the Isle of ➠Skye, creating a lasting romantic legend that contemporary accounts would suggest were in no way matched by his rather effete and drink-sodden personality, but there we are.

fracas *spell.* fracases
The plural of fracas.

framboesia *spell.* frambesia
Which is yaws, a highly contagious tropical disease.

France and Spain *idiom, rh. sl.* rain

franking *noun* a marking on a letter or stamp indicating that postage has been paid

franking machine *comp. noun* a postage meter

franklin *noun, hist.* a medieval freeman who owned his own land

fraud squad *comp. noun* a police unit that investigates business frauds

FRCS *pr. name, abbr.* a Fellow of the ➡Royal College of Surgeons

Fred Karno's Army *pr. name, coll., hist.* a nickname for the volunteer British army that was raised at the beginning of World War I
Fred Karno was a well-known music hall comic in the years preceding 1914. The disorganized shambles of the British military effort at the start of the war caused a song with this name to become especially popular with the infantry:

We are Fred Karno's army,
Fred Karno's infantry;
We cannot fight, we cannot shoot,
So what damn good are we?

free church *comp. noun* any Protestant church that is not an ➡established church

the **Free Church of Scotland** *pr. name, hist.* a group who disagreed over doctrine and ceded from the ➡established Presbyterian ➡Church of Scotland in 1843, until 1929 when they resolved their differences and merged together again.

FreeFone *pr. name (TM), arch.* an operator-connected system of toll-free telephone numbers
Now supplanted by ➡0800 and ➡0500 numbers.

free house *comp. noun* a hotel or pub not tied to a particular brewer, thus free to sell any brand of beer
Formerly the vast majority of British pubs were owned by a particular brewer and thus tied to their products, but the proportion is now greatly reduced.

free kick *comp. noun* in ➡soccer, a kick awarded as a minor penalty
It is taken without interference from the opposing team.

freeman *noun, hist.* someone who is not a serf

FreePost *pr. name (TM)* pre-paid postage

free-range *adj.* kept in an unconfined and relatively natural condition
Of chickens, mostly.

free state *comp. noun* an independent nation

Free Stater *pr. name, hist., Ir.* one who supported the terms of the ➡Anglo-Irish Treaty of 1921 and

the ➡Irish Free State which it created, during the ➡Irish Civil War that followed its signing
The more pragmatic advocates of Irish independence, who felt that the terms spelled out within this treaty were the best that they could realistically expect to obtain at the time, and so should be accepted.

freightliner *noun* a freight train that hauls container cars only

French bean *comp. noun* a string bean

French cricket *comp. noun* a simplified form of cricket especially popular with children
Played without stumps, one bat and a soft ball.

the **French disease** *pr. name, hist.* syphilis
As it was called by the English in the 16th C.

French leave *comp. noun, sl.* absent without leave

French letter *comp. noun, sl.* a condom
SEE ALSO: ➡American sock.

French mustard *comp. noun* a mild mustard

French polish *comp. noun* a shellac polish used to apply a high sheen to wooden furniture

the **French Revolutionary Wars** *pr. name, hist.* the wars fought between revolutionary France, attempting to export her form of revolutionary government, and virtually every other European nation, including Britain, between 1792 and 1799
The fighting did not stop in 1799, but Napoleon became First Consul and both the nature and name of the war changed.

fresher *noun, coll.* a freshman

FRIBA *pr. name, abbr.* a Fellow of the ➡Royal Institute of British Architects

FRICS *pr. name, abbr.* a Fellow of the ➡Royal Institute of Chartered Surveyors

fridge *noun, abbr., coll.* a refrigerator

fridge-freezer *comp. noun, abbr., coll.* a unit combining the features of a refrigerator and a freezer

friendly society *comp. noun* a mutual-aid society

Friesian *pr. name* a Holstein cow

frig *noun, abbr.* a refrigerator

fringe *noun* hair bangs

the **Fringe** *pr. name, abbr., coll.* in full, the ➡Edinburgh Fringe Festival
Which is an informal collection of theatrical and other artistic events, exhibitions and so forth, taking place alongside the official ➡Edinburgh Festival, but not part of it.

fringe theatre *comp. noun, coll.* a theatrical performance that exceeds or challenges current mainstream practices
The rough equivalent of "off-off-Broadway."

frisson *noun, Fr.* an emotional thrill
This is the French word for "shiver."

frivolled

{**frivolled » frivolling**} *spell.* {frivoled » frivoling}

Frog *pr. name, derog., sl.* (1) a French person; (2) the French language

frog and toad *idiom, rh. sl.* a road

froggy *adj., derog., sl.* french

frogmarch *verb* to force a person face downwards by holding each of their arms from the rear and make them walk or march forward in this fashion

frogspawn *noun, sl.* a sago or tapioca pudding
An expression mostly used by children.

from a child *idiom, coll.* since infancy or childhood

the **front bench** *comp. noun* (1) those seats in either House of ➡Parliament situated closest to the center of the chamber; (2) ➡frontbenchers as a group

frontbencher *noun, coll.* a government minister or leading member of the ➡Official Opposition
The only members of either of the ➡Houses of Parliament who are entitled to sit upon the ➡front benches.

frontwards *adv.* frontward

froth-blower *comp. noun, sl.* a beer-drinker

frowst *noun* stale or musty warmth
Typically found in a damp, enclosed space, which has not been properly ventilated for some time.

frowsty *adj.* stale or musty

FRS *noun, abbr.* a Fellow of the ➡Royal Society

FRSE *noun, abbr.* a Fellow of the ➡Royal Society of Edinburgh

fruit cup *comp. noun* a fruit-flavored drink

fruiter *noun* a fruit grower or dealer

fruiterer *noun* a ➡fruiter

fruit machine *comp. noun* a slot machine

fruit shortcake *comp. noun* shortcake, served with fruit and whipped cream
See also: ➡shortbread.

fry-up *comp. noun, coll.* (1) an electrocution; (2) the preparation and serving of fried food

fry up *verb, coll.* to electrocute

FSA *noun, abbr.* a Fellow of the ➡Society of Antiquaries

the **FT** *pr. name, abbr.* the *Financial Times*
Unusually, a daily business newspaper printed on pink paper.

FT30 Index *pr. name, abbr.* the ➡FT Index

the **FT Actuaries Indexes** *pr. name, abbr.* the Financial Times Actuaries Shares Index
Which reports the weighted averages for 54 market sectors, covering all the major industrial sectors.

FT Index *pr. name, abbr.* the Financial Times Ordinary Shares Index
This tracks the performance of 30 of the most significant shares quoted on the ➡London Stock Exchange.

the **FT-SE Index** *pr. name, abbr.* the ➡Financial Times - Stock Exchange Index

fubsy *noun, coll.* short and fat (of a person)

fud [B] *noun, Sc.* (1) the buttocks; (2) the tail of a rabbit or hare

[B] *noun, Sc., taboo* the female pudenda

{**fuelled » fuelling**} *spell.* {fueled » fueling}

fug *noun, sl.* stale or smoky air

fuggy *adj., coll.* stale or airless

{**fulfil » fulfilment**} *spell.* {fulfill » fulfillment}

full *adj., sl.* drunk

full age *noun* the legal status of an adult

full marks *comp. noun, coll.* (1) the highest possible examination score; (2) a recognition of excellence

fullock *noun, East* a sudden impulse

full pennyworth *idiom, out.* value for money

full stop *comp. noun* (1) a period marking the end of a sentence; (2) a final and total cessation

full stretch *comp. noun, coll.* (1) full capacity; (2) the maximum extent possible

full toss *comp. noun* a ➡cricket ball pitched directly at the ➡batsman

full whack *comp. noun, sl.* the full price

funbags *noun, sl.* a woman's breasts

funeral parlour *comp. noun* a funeral {parlor » home}

funeral tea *comp. noun* a light meal served to mourners following a funeral

funfair *noun* a carnival or amusement park

fungoid *adj.* of a fungus

funk *verb, sl.* (1) to evade responsibility; (2) to exhibit cowardice or fear

funk hole *comp. noun, sl.* (1) a hiding place used during periods of particular danger; (2) a pretext used to avoid an unpleasant duty or responsibility

funk it *verb, sl.* to ➡shrink or evade a duty, responsibility or challenge

funnel *noun* a smokestack on a ship or locomotive

{**funnelled » funnelling**} *spell.* {funneled » funneling}

fir *noun* the coating that forms on the inside of a pipe, pot, etc., due to the presence of hard water

furnicate *verb, South* to waste time

furnished apartments *comp. noun* a suite of furnished rented rooms

furnisher *noun* a person or store that sells furniture

furore *spell.* furor

Furry Dance *pr. name* a traditional dance performed on the streets of Helston in ➡Cornwall on May 8th every year

further eductaion *comp. noun* adult education that is below university level

furze *noun* gorse

fushion *noun, Sc.* physical, mental or spiritual strength, energy, power or force

fushionless *adj., Sc.* (1) faint-hearted; (2) lacking initiative or ability; (3) weak or without energy

fusilier [A] *noun, hist.* a member of one of several regiments of the British army that were once armed with light flintlock muskets called fusils [B] *spell.* fusileer

fusspot *noun, coll.* a fussbudget

fusty *adj.* moldy, stale or damaged with age

futrat *noun, Sc.* a weasel, stoat or ferret
SEE ALSO: ➡whitrat.

fyrd *noun, hist.* the militia who served the ➡Anglo-Saxon kings of pre-➡Conquest England

G

gaby *adj., North* idiotic or foolish

gadd *verb, East* to run

Gaeilge *pr. name, Gae., Ir.* the ➧Irish Gaelic name for ➧Irish Gaelic

Today, this language is the primary means of communication of some 50,000 people living in those western regions of Ireland known as the ➧Gaeltacht. It is also taught in schools throughout the ➧Irish Republic.

SEE ALSO: ➧Gaelic, the language's very close relative which is spoken in parts of Scotland.

SEE ALSO: ➧Erse.

Gael *pr. name* a Scottish or Irish ➧Celt

Gaelic *pr. name, Gae., Ir., Sc.* the ➧Celtic languages spoken in ➧Scotland and ➧Ireland and formerly, the ➧Isle of Man

All three have the same name and are very closely related, but nonetheless remain separate languages; they are not identical. (By the way; although the Irish pronounce the "ae" in "Gaelic" like the "ai" in "pain," the Scottish pronounciation is like the "a" in "pan.")

Gaelic coffee *comp. noun, Sc.* coffee with cream and ➧Scotch whiskey

Invented as a response to ➧Irish coffee, and usually served in a glass. However, it has never caught on to the same extent as its Irish rival, possibly because it is seen as just too much of a waste of perfectly good ➧Scotch.

the **Gaeltacht** *pr. name, Gae., Ir.* those areas of Ireland where ➧Gaelic is considered the usual daily language

gaff [A] *noun, arch., sl.* (1) a cheap public amusement hall or theater; (2) a building that is someone's home; (3) nonsense

[B] *verb, sl.* to cheat

gaffer *noun* (1) an employer; (2) the foreman of a gang of workmen

gaga *adj., sl.* senile

gala *noun* a festive sporting occasion, particularly one concerned with swimming

gallon *noun, abbr.* an ➧imperial gallon

Galloway *noun* (1) a former county in southwestern Scotland, now part of ➧Dumfries and Galloway Region; (2) a large, hornless breed of cattle with thick black coats, originally from (1)

gallowglass *noun, Gae., hist.* a mercenary or foot soldier from Ireland or the Scottish ➧Western Isles

From the Gaelic *gall* + *oglach* = "stranger + warrior"

Galway *pr. name* a county in the ➧Irish Republic

County Galway is in the ancient province of ➧Connaught.

{**gambolled » gambolling**} *spell.* {gamboled » gamboling}

gambrel roof *comp. noun* a hip roof with gabled ends

games {**master » mistress**} *comp. noun* a {male » female} physical education teacher

the **Gaming Board for Great Britain** *pr. name* a government agency responsible for the supervision of gambling casinos and issuing of gaming licenses

gammon *noun* (1) a ham or a side of bacon; (2) deceptive talk

gammy *adj., sl.* (1) injured; (2) permanently lame

gamp *noun, coll.* a large umbrella

A name derived from Mrs. Sarah Gamp in Dickens's *Martin Chuzzlewit*, who had a large umbrella.

gang *verb, Sc.* to go

gang agley *phr. verb, Sc.* to go wrong

ganger *noun* the foreman of a gang of workmen

gangway *noun* a passageway or aisle between rows of seats

the **Gangway** *pr. name* a cross-aisle in the ➧House of Commons, which separates the area where members of minor parties and dissident members of major parties sit, from the bulk of ➧MPs

gannet *noun, sl.* someone who gobbles down large quantities of food

From the perceived propensity of the sea-bird of this name to consume whole fish in this manner.

Gannex *pr. name (TM)* a distinctive brand of heavy-duty raincoat

ganzie *noun, North* a heavy woolen jersey

{**gaol » gaolbird**} *spell.* {jail » jailbird}

{**gaolbreak » gaoler**} *spell.* {jailbreak » jailer}

gaper *noun* in ➧cricket, a dropped catch

gap site *comp. noun, coll.* a plot of land between buildings that is considered large enough to accommodate another building

garage *noun* (2) a gas station; (1) an automobile repair shop

garda noun, Gae., Ir. an Irish police officer, who is a member of the ➡*Garda Síochána*

the *Garda pr. name, abbr., Gae., Ir.* the ➡*Garda Síochána*

gardant *adj.* in heraldry, full faced

the *Garda Síochána pr. name, Gae., Ir.* the police force of the ➡Irish Republic

This is Irish Gaelic, meaning literally "civil guard."

garden *noun* any enclosed plot of cultivated ground containing a dwelling house; a yard

the **Garden City** *pr. name* (1) a nickname for the city of ➡Norwich; (2) a nickname for the town of Letchworth in ➡Hertfordshire

garden flat *comp. noun* a first-floor apartment incorporating an adjacent garden area as part of the property

the **Garden of England** *pr. name* ➡Kent

the **Garden of Ireland** *pr. name* County ➡Carlow

gardens *noun* a city street or square

For example, "Devonshire Gardens" or "Maybury Gardens"

garden suburb *comp. noun* an attractive and open modern suburban development

garden village *comp. noun* an attractive rural hamlet

gardy loo *exclam., Fr., hist., Sc.* a warning cry once common in the streets of Edinburgh's ➡Old Town as housewives and servants threw slops from their upper windows into the street below

A necessity removed by the installation of main drainage in the 19th C. It is said that the expression derives from the French, *gardez (vous de) l'eau* = "beware of the water".

garibaldi *noun* a shortbread cookie containing currants

garn *exclam., sl.* an expression of disbelief

Possibly a ➡Cockney variation of "go on!"

garnet *adj., arch., sl.* entirely satisfactory

Derived from the name of Sir Garnet Wolseley, commander-in-chief of the British Army in the 1890s, who led several highly successful military expeditions.

Garrick Club *pr. name, hist.* a club that is the traditional preserve of actors, artists and their patrons

Established in 1831, it was named in honor of the leading actor of the 18th C, David Garrick. It is one of the few clubs that as recently as 1992 confirmed in a vote to continue to refuse membership to women.

the Order of the **Garter** *pr. name, abbr., hist.* the highest order of English knighthood

In full, "The Most Noble Order of the Garter."

It was instituted by ➡Edward III in 1348. The name is reputed to originate from an incident in court when the Countess of Salisbury accidentally lost her garter during a court ball. The king was the one who picked it up, and when he noticed the expressions on the faces of the onlookers, bound the blue band round his own knee with the words, ➡*Honi soit que mal y pense.*

Membership of the order is restricted to a maximum of 24 at any one time, and the ➡monarch and the ➡Prince of Wales are always among that number. Selection is at the sole discretion of the monarch. Members of other European royal families may be invited into the ranks as extra-numeries.

the **Garter King of Arms** *pr. name* the principal ➡Herald of the English ➡College of Arms

Called this because he is responsible for attending to the election and installation of Knights of the ➡Garter.

garth *noun, arch.* (1) a paddock; (2) a yard or garden; (3) an open space enclosed within cloisters

gas *verb, coll.* to talk in an idle or boastful fashion

gash *adj., sl.* (1) pointless, broken or useless; (2) additional, extra or not required; (3) unattached

(3) applies to an attractive woman only.

gas mark *comp. noun* a temperature setting on a gas-burning cooking stove

gasometer *noun, out.* a gasholder

A large container used to store ➡town gas under pressure

gasper *noun, sl.* a cigarette

gassed *adj., sl.* drunk

gate [A] *noun, North, Sc.* a street

[B] *verb, out.* to confine within a prescribed area, as punishment for a student at school or college

gateau *noun, Fr.* a very large and creamy layer cake

From the French *gâteau* = "cake"

gatehouse *noun, hist.* a room situated above the gate into a walled city

Once these were commonly used as prisons.

gathman *noun, East* a farmhand responsible for supervising a herd of cattle

Gatwick *pr. name* London's second airport, located about 25 miles south of central London

Operated by ➡BAA plc.

Gatwick Express Railway Company *pr. name (TM)* a railroad company operating services between London and ➡Gatwick Airport

It is part of ➡British Rail.

gaudy *noun, Lat.* an annual college reunion

From the Latin *gaudium* = "joy"

gauger *noun* an official who inspects and evaluates bulk goods in order to assessing duty upon them

gavel *noun, hist.* a form of medieval rent

{**gavelled » gavelling**} *spell.* {gaveled » gaveling}

{**gawker » gawper**} *noun, coll., derog.* someone who ➡{gawks » gawps}

{**gawk » gawp**} *verb, coll., derog.* to stare in a blatant or stupid manner

the **Gay Gordons** *pr. name* a ➡country dance that originated in Scotland

gazette *verb* (1) to announce or publish in a newspaper; (2) to formally announce someone's new official status or appointment

(2) is by means of publication in the ➡*Belfast,* ➡*Edinburgh* or ➡*London Gazette* as appropriate.

gazump *verb, sl.* to raise a selling price, usually of a house or other property, after informally accepting an offer at a lower price

gazump *noun, sl.* a swindler

gazunder *verb, sl.* to lower an offer price, usually of a house, after informally making a higher one

Skillful practitioners of this art wait until the very last moment before contracts making the transaction legally binding are to be signed, so that the seller will hopefully be left with no alternative but to accept the reduced offer. The word has been coined by merging ➡gazump with "under".

GB *pr. name, abbr.* ➡Great Britain

GBE *noun, abbr.* a {Dame » Knight} Grand Cross of the Order of the British Empire

GBH *noun, abbr.* grievous bodily harm

The official police term for intentional serious injury upon a person.

GC *noun, abbr.* the George Cross

GCB *pr. name, abbr.* a {Dame » Knight} Grand Cross of the Order of the ➡Bath

GCE *noun, abbr., arch.* General Certificate of Education

Now replaced by the ➡GCSE.

GCHQ *pr. name, abbr.* the ➡Government Communications Headquarters

GCIE *noun, abbr.* a Knight Grand Commander of the Order of the Indian Empire

GCMG *noun, abbr.* a {Dame » Knight} Grand Cross of the Order of St Michael and St George

GCSE *noun, abbr.* the ➡General Certificate of Secondary Education

GCSI *noun, abbr.* a Knight Grand Commander of the Order of the Star of India

GCVO *noun, abbr.* a {Dame » Knight} Grand Cross of Royal Victorian Order

gear [A] *noun, sl.* (1) clothes; (2) ridiculous talk

[B] *verb* (1) to allocate a portion of a company's dividend to preferred recipients

gearbox *noun* a transmission housing

gearing *noun* (1) leverage, in the business sense; (2) the proportion of a dividend that is allocated to preferred recipients

gear lever *comp. noun* a gear shift

GEC *pr. name (TM), abbr.* General Electric Company

Gee *pr. name, hist.* a radio navigation system used by British bombers over Germany during World War II

Originally called ➡TR1335, Gee employed a triangulation system to fix the aircraft's position. The receiving equipment on the aircraft detected signals from three transmitters and displayed the results on a cathode-ray tube, which the navigator interpreted to determine location.

gee-gee *comp. noun, coll.* a childish name for a horse

geezer *noun* a strange or eccentric man, typically old

gelignite *noun* a form of dynamite that uses a nitrate-based adsorbent

Very popular with miners, construction workers and terrorists.

gelatine *spell* gelatin

gelly *noun, abbr., sl.* ➡gelignite

gen [A] *adj., East* given

[B] *noun, out., sl.* news or information

This expression began life as ➡RAF World War II slang.

Geneagles *pr. name, hist.* a large resort hotel in the ➡Perthshire hills, between Stirling and ➡Perth

The hotel possesses two golf courses; King's Course and Queen's Course were both completed just before the outbreak of World War I in 1914.

general *noun* the second-highest rank of commissioned officer in the British Army

Equivalent in rank to a four-star general in the U.S. Army.

General Accident *pr. name (TM), abbr.* a large insurance company

the **General Assembly of the Church of Scotland** *pr. name* the highest court and supreme governing body of the ➡Church of Scotland

It consists of the ministers and elders of the ➡Kirk presided over by the Moderator, who is also a minister, and is attended by the ➡monarch or, more usually, by his or her deputy, known as the ➡Lord High Commissioner, when it meets in ➡Edinburgh every May.

the **General Certificate of Secondary Education** *pr. name* a standard examination that is expected to be taken by all school students in England and Wales at the age of 15 or 16

the **General Council of the Trades Union Congress** *pr. name* a body elected annually by the ➡Trades Union Congress to manage its affairs over the following 12 months

general degree *comp. noun* an alternate name used by some universities for a ➡pass degree or ➡ordinary degree

General Election *pr. name* the simultaneous universal election of all ➠MPs in the ➠House of Commons

This is how a new government is chosen. In Britain there must be a General Election every five years at most. However, the government of the day is at liberty to call one earlier than this and in actual practice there is usually a General Election every four or four-and-a-half years or so. There may also be a General Election if the government of the day looses a ➠vote of confidence in the ➠House of Commons, and so is obliged to resign.

generalisation *spell.* generalization

the **General Register of Sasines and Land Register of Scotland** *pr. name, Sc.* the executive agency where all registrations of land sales in Scotland must be lodged

general staff *pr. name* the group of officers who together form the high command of an entire army, air force, or navy

the **General Strike** *pr. name, hist.* a strike by all members of all British labor unions

It was called by the ➠TUC in support of already-striking coal miners and lasted from May 4 until May 12, 1926, ending in defeat for the strikers.

the **General Synod** *pr. name* the supreme governing body of the ➠Church of England

General Synod measure *comp. noun, coll.* Any parliamentary statute that is concerned with the ➠Church of England

gentleman *noun, hist.* an amateur player of ➠cricket

As opposed to a ➠player, or professional player.

gentleman-at-arms *comp. noun* a member of the sovereign's bodyguard

gentleman-commoner *comp. noun, arch.* an ➠Oxford University undergraduate entitled to sit at the ➠High Table of their college

Gentleman in Waiting *pr. name* an official of the ➠Royal Household attending upon the personal needs of the king

See also: ➠Groom in Waiting.

gentleman's cloakroom *comp. noun* a euphemism for a men's rest room

gentleman's gentleman *comp. noun, coll.* a gentleman's personal servant, a butler

Gentleman's Relish *pr. name, out.* anchovy paste

Normally consumed after being spread on toast or butter

the **gentlemen's** *noun, abbr.* ➠gentlemen's cloakroom

gentry *noun* those who are just below nobility in social standing

the **gents** *noun, abbr., coll.* a ➠gentleman's cloakroom

gents cloaks *comp. noun, abbr.* a ➠gentleman's cloakroom

genuflexion *spell.* genuflection

gen up *verb, arch., sl.* to gather or to be provided with information

This expression began life as ➠RAF World War II slang.

the **Geological Museum** *pr. name* a leading museum dedicated to geological science

Situated adjacent to the ➠Science Museum in South ➠Kensington, London. It is a department of the ➠Natural History Museum, also located in Kensington.

Geordie *pr. name, coll., North* (1) a native of ➠Tyneside; (2) the dialect of English spoken by a native of ➠Tyneside

George *noun, arch., sl.* an aircraft's automatic pilot

This expression began life as ➠RAF World War II slang.

the **George Cross** *pr. name* a medal awarded for acts of bravery by civilians

Instituted in 1940 by ➠George VI, it is second in rank only to the ➠Victoria Cross. *See also:* the ➠George Medal.

George I *pr. name, hist.* King of ➠Great Britain
(See box opposite.)

George II *pr. name, hist.* King of ➠Great Britain
(See box opposite.)

George III *pr. name, hist.* King of ➠Great Britain, later of the ➠United Kingdom
(See box opposite.)

George IV *pr. name, hist.* King of the ➠United Kingdom
(See box opposite.)

George V *pr. name, hist.* King of the ➠United Kingdom
(See box opposite.)

George VI *pr. name, hist.* King of the ➠United Kingdom
(See box opposite.)

the **George Medal** *pr. name* a medal awarded for acts of civilian bravery considered not quite brave enough to merit the ➠George Cross

Instituted in 1940 by ➠George VI.

Georgian *adj.* pertaining to the time of any of the six British kings named ➠George

gerrof *exclam., sl.* ➠get off it, ➠get out [A]

get across *verb, coll.* to irritate or annoy

get {along » away} with you *imper., coll.* (1) I don't believe you; (2) don't be silly; (3) go away

get a packet *idiom. phr. verb* to become badly injured

get colours *verb* to be selected to join a sporting team

Six Georges

George I styled himself "King of Great Britain, France and Ireland, Duke of Braunschweig-Lüneburg, ➡Defender of the Faith, etc., etc." and reigned in Britain for 12 years from 1714 until 1727. However, George had been ➡Elector of Hanover in Germany since 1692 and so brought the ➡Royal House of ➡Hanover to reign in Britain He was the son of a granddaughter of ➡James I of England and VI of Scotland, which was the basis of his claim (accepted by ➡Parliament in the ➡Act of Settlement) to succeed ➡Anne.

He was never popular, being seen as a foreign interloper to the end of his reign, a perception reinforced by his inability to speak English. It was partly for this reason and partly because of his intense dislike of his son, the ➡Prince of Wales, that he ceased to attend cabinet meetings, which allowed the office of Prime Minister to emerge (in the shape of Robert Walpole) for the first time.

Thus do major steps in the evolution of the British constitution come about.

George II styled himself "King of Great Britain, France and Ireland, Duke of Braunschweig-Lüneburg, Defender of the Faith, etc., etc." and reigned for 33 years from 1727 until 1760. Like his father George I, he was also Elector of Hanover and a member of the Royal House of Hanover. Unlike his father he made some effort to learn English, but was unable ever to rid himself of a strong German accent.

George III styled himself "King of Great Britain, France and Ireland, Duke of Braunschweig-Lüneburg, Defender of the Faith, etc., etc." until the ➡Union of the British and Irish Parliaments in 1801 whereupon his style or title was changed to, "King of the United Kingdom of Great Britain and Ireland, Duke of Braunschweig-Lüneburg, Defender of the Faith, etc., etc."

Altogether, his was a long reign of 59 years from 1760 until 1820. Best known as the king that the American revolutionaries revolted against, but it was really rather unfair to blame George for the behavior of his government, in particular ➡Prime Minister Lord North, who was far more culpable.

During the last nine years of George's reign, from 1811 onwards, the ➡Prince of Wales acted as regent due to the King's insanity.

George was also ➡Elector of Hanover and member of the Royal House of ➡Hanover.

George IV styled himself "King of the United Kingdom of Great Britain and Ireland, Duke of Braunschweig-Lüneburg, ➡Defender of the Faith, etc., etc." and reigned for 10 years from 1820 until 1830, having already been ➡Prince Regent since 1811.

He was also ➡Elector of Hanover and a member of the Royal House of ➡Hanover.

George V styled himself "By the Grace of God, of Great Britain, Ireland, and of the British ➡Dominions beyond the Seas, King, ➡Defender of the Faith, Emperor of India, etc., etc." Altogether, he reigned for 25 years from 1910 until 1936. He founded the ➡Royal House of ➡Windsor when he changed the ➡Royal Family's name from ➡Saxe-Coburg und Gotha because of anti-German sentiment during World War I.

George VI styled himself "By the Grace of God, of Great Britain, Ireland, and of the British ➡Dominions beyond the Seas, King, ➡Defender of the Faith, Emperor of India, etc., etc." until Indian independence in 1947 after which it became, "By the Grace of God, of Great Britain, Ireland, and of the British Dominions beyond the Seas, King, Defender of the Faith, etc., etc." Altogether, he reigned for over 15 years from 1936 until 1952, having inherited the throne unexpectedly when his brother ➡Edward VIII abdicated.

He was a member of the ➡Royal House of ➡Windsor.

get cracking

get cracking *verb, coll.* to get moving or get on with things

{get » git} *noun, derog., sl.* a foolish person
SEE ALSO: ➡git.

get knotted *imper., derog., sl.* go away, get lost

get no change *idiom. phr. verb* to get no help

get off it *exclam., sl.* I don't believe it, don't be absurd
SEE ALSO: ➡gerrof, ➡get out.

get off with (someone) *idiom. phr. verb* to quickly form a romantic or sexual involvement

get one's cards *idiom. phr. verb* to get fired from a job

get one's head down *idiom. phr. verb* (1) to lie down to rest or to go to sleep; (2) to concentrate upon the task in front of one

get one's monkey up *idiom. phr. verb* to become very angry

get one's wind up *idiom. phr. verb, coll.* to become nervous or afraid
SEE ALSO: ➡put someone's wind up.

get on (someone's) wick *idiom. phr. verb* to irritate (someone); to get on (someone's) nerves

get on to (someone) *idiom. phr. verb* to contact (someone) by telephone

get out [A] *exclam., sl.* that's ridiculous
[B] *phr. verb* in ➡cricket, to dismiss a batsman

get-out clause *comp. noun, coll.* an exclusion or loophole in a legal document, such as a contract or insurance policy

get round *verb* to get around, avoid or evade

get shot of *idiom. phr. verb, sl.* to get rid of

get sorted out *idiom. phr. verb* to get organized

get stuffed *imper., sl.* go away, get lost

get the {bullet » chop} *idiom. phr. verb, sl.* (1) to get fired from a job; (2) to be killed

get the frozen mitten *idiom. phr. verb* to be given the brush-off

get the push *idiom. phr. verb* (1) to get fired from a job; (2) to be sent away

get through *idiom. phr. verb* (1) to contact by telephone; (2) to successfully make (someone) listen or understand

getting one's leg over *idiom, sl., taboo* a euphemism for copulation

get up one's nose *idiom. phr. verb* to greatly irritate

get weaving *idiom. phr. verb* (1) to get started; (2) to move along quickly

get yer ➡jotters *idiom. phr. verb, Sc., sl.* to get fired from one's job

get your {finger out » skates on} *imper., coll.* hurry up, get a move on

gey *adj., Sc.* (1) large, considerable; (2) very

geyser *noun* an apparatus that rapidly heats domestic water on demand
As when it is required instantly, for example for a shower.

gey wheen *idiom, Sc.* a large number

GG *noun, abbr.* a ➡Governor-General

ghyll *noun* (1) a deep and wooded ravine; (2) a narrow mountain stream

the Giant's Causeway

the **Giant's Causeway** *pr. name, hist.* a headland upon the northern shore of ➡Northern Ireland
Famous for its thousands of hexagonal rock pillars created by a rock crystallization process during cooling after an ancient volcanic eruption. *SEE ALSO:* ➡Fingal's Cave.

Gib. *pr. name, abbr., coll.* Gibraltar

gie *verb, Sc.* to give

the **Gifford Lectures** *pr. name* a series of lectures on natural theology without reference to sect or creed
Founded by Lord Gifford in 1887 and delivered annually in rotation at the universities of ➡St Andrews, ➡Glasgow, ➡Aberdeen and ➡Edinburgh.

gift of the gab *idiom. phr. verb* the talent of fluent or loquacious speech

gift token *comp. noun* a gift certificate

giggle *noun, sl.* a trivial but amusing person or thing

Gilbertian *adj.* farcical or ridiculous
Derived from the nature of the plots in Gilbert and Sullivan's 19th C. comic operas.

the **Gilded Chamber** *pr. name, coll.* a euphemism for the ➡House of Lords

gill *noun* (1) a quarter of a pint; (2) a ravine or gully
(1) is now most often used in pubs, where Scotch or other liquor is served out in measures such as ¼ or ⅕ th of a gill.

gillie *noun, Gae., hist., Sc.* (1) an attendant or servant of a ➡Highland chieftain; (2) an attendant or servant of a hunter or angler
From the Gaelic *gille* = "youth"

gillie-wetfoot *comp. noun, arch., Sc.* a barefoot ➡Highlander who was employed to carry his master over water while traveling

gillion *noun, num., out.* a billion, or 10^9
Now rare, this word was intended to be used to avoid confusion between the British and American meanings for "billion".
SEE ALSO: ➡milliard.

gilt-edged *adj.* high-quality or reliable
Of a security or other investment.

gin *conj., Sc.* if

gin and It *comp. noun, abbr., coll.* a drink consisting of gin and vermouth
"It" is an abbreviation of "Italian", which is where vermouth came from in the first place, of course.

ginger [A] *noun, arch., derog., rh. sl.* a male homosexual
Derivation: homosexual > queer > beer > ginger beer > ginger.
[B] *noun, Sc.* soda pop of any flavor

gingerade *noun* a kind of soda pop which is flavored with ginger or capsicum

ginger beer [A] *noun* an mildly alcoholic effervescent drink, made from fermented ginger and syrup
[B] *idiom, rh. sl.* a ship's engineer

the **Gingerbread Group** *pr. name* a charity supporting and advocating for single parents

ginger group *comp. noun* an energizing group within a larger group such as, for example, a political party

ginger nut *comp. noun* a gingersnap cookie

ginger pop *noun* ➡gingerade

ginormous *adj., sl.* vast or huge

gin palace *comp. noun, out.* a gaudy, low-class ➡pub

gin-trap *comp. noun* a trap used to capture small animals such as rabbits, etc.

Gippo *noun, derog., sl.* (1) a Gipsy; (2) an Egyptian

Gippy tummy *comp. noun, coll.* another picturesque name for diarrhea, or Montezuma's revenge
Egypt has been the scene of many an outbreak of this.

girdle *noun, North, Sc.* an iron plate, used for baking, with a hooped handle for hanging it over a fire

Girl Guide *comp. noun* a Girl Scout

girn *verb, Sc.* to complain or grumble

giro *noun, It.* a fund transfer system between banks
From the Italian word for "circulation"

the **Giro** *noun, It.* a checking-account system operated through ➡Post Office branches

Girton College *pr. name* a college of ➡Cambridge University founded in 1869

gismo *spell.* gizmo

git *noun, Ir.* a bastard
SEE ALSO: ➡{get » git}.

give (something) a miss *idiom. phr. verb* to stop or to fail to do **(something)**

give (someone) a bell *idiom. phr. verb, sl.* to contact by telephone

give (something) away change *idiom. phr. verb, coll.* to let slip confidential information

give (someone) {his » her} character *idiom. phr. verb, Sc.* to inform (someone) just exactly what you really think of {him » her}.
This is not usually a pleasant experience for the recipient.

give (someone) in charge *idiom. phr. verb* to hand (someone) over to the police

give over *verb, North, sl.* to desist or cease

give (someone) stick *verb, sl.* to subject (someone) to ➡stick

give (someone) the elbow *idiom. phr. verb, sl.* to dismiss or send away (someone)

give the pip *idiom. phr. verb, sl.* to annoy greatly

give way *imper.* yield to other traffic
A road sign.

Gladstone bag *comp. noun* a flexibly sided traveling bag that has two compartments of the same size
Named for William Ewart Gladstone, 19th C. Prime Minister.

glaikit *adj., Sc.* (1) unintelligent; (2) foolish; (3) irresponsible

Glamis Castle *pr. name, hist.* a 14th C. castle in ➡Tayside, much modified and extended during the 19th C., about 12 miles to the north of ➡Dundee
There has been a fortress upon this site since at least as early as the 11th C., although the present structure is younger than that. The oldest part is reputed to be the setting for much of the action depicted in Shakespeare's "Macbeth." Glamis is the family home of Elizabeth, ➡consort of ➡George VI and ➡queen mother of ➡Elizabeth II of England and I of Scotland.

Glamorgan *pr. name, hist.* a former Welsh County
Now broken up into the three counties of ➡West Glamorgan, ➡Mid Gamorgan and ➡South Glamorgan.

glamour *spell.* glamor

glandular fever *comp. noun* infectious mononucleosis

Glasgow

Glasgow *pr. name* the Scottish metropolis and administrative center of ⟶Strathclyde, it is situated upon the ⟶Clyde River

Founded by St Mungo in 543, Glasgow is, perhaps surprisingly to those who think of it as nothing more than a ⟶Victorian industrial town, a much more ancient city than ⟶Edinburgh. Nonetheless, it was when the ⟶Clyde was dredged upon the direction of the municipal council of the city in the 18th C. and Glasgow became accessible as a port for oceangoing ships, that it began to grow dramatically, justifying the saying that, "The Clyde made Glasgow, but Glasgow made the Clyde."

Glasgow became, with ⟶Liverpool and ⟶Bristol, one of the leading transatlantic ports of Britain, building prosperity especially from the tobacco trade. In the 19th C., shipbuilding grew into a major industry to such an extent that by the end of that century, Glasgow was building one quarter of the shipping tonnage of the entire world.

There is a great rivalry with the Scottish capital Edinburgh, less than 50 miles away, but with the current population of the Glasgow urban area at 1,750,000 (1988 estimate), this is by far the largest city in Scotland. The name "Glasgow" is said to mean "dear green place" in ⟶Gaelic.

Glasgow boat *idiom, Ir., rh. sl.* a coat

Glasgow capon *idiom, coll.* salt herring

Glasgow Green *pr. name, hist.* the oldest municipal park in Britain, established as such by 1662

Before that time it had been ⟶Glasgow's common land.

It was on a Sunday morning in 1765 while walking upon a part of Glasgow Green then used as a golf course, that James Watt hit upon the concept of using a separate condenser to greatly improve the efficiency of the steam engine. Thus it might be said that the key idea that made the Industrial Revolution possible was conceived upon Glasgow Green. The ⟶People's Palace is located here.

Glasgow High School *pr. name* one of the leading private schools in Scotland

Located in ⟶Glasgow and founded in 1124.

Glasgow kiss *idiom, sl.* a head butting

the **Glasgow Royal Concert Hall** *pr. name* a large modern concert hall with a seating capacity of 2,500, located in the center of the city

the **Glasgow School of Art** *pr. name* by far the most significant art school in Britain outside London

Founded in 1844, the school occupies a magnificent building designed by Charles Rennie Mackintosh, competed in 1907 and considered to be a masterpiece of *Art Nouveau* architecture.

Glasgow University *pr. name* the fourth-oldest university in the English-speaking world and the second-oldest in Scotland

It was founded in 1451.

glass-cloth *comp. noun* (1) an especially fine cloth used to dry glasses; (2) cloth covered with glass dust so that it can be used as an abrasive

For (2), *SEE ALSO:* ⟶glass-paper.

glasshouse [A] *noun* a greenhouse

[B] *noun, sl.* a military prison

glass-paper *comp. noun* paper covered with glass dust so that it can be used as an abrasive

SEE ALSO: ⟶glass-cloth.

Glastonbury *pr. name* an ancient ⟶Somerset town

Considered by some as a possible location for King ⟶Arthur's fabled Camelot, it is also said to be where Joseph of Arimathea first brought Christianity and the Holy Grail to Britain in 63. There is a Benedictine abbey here which appears to have been founded in Roman times.

Glaswegian *pr. name, Sc.* a native, citizen or inhabitant of ⟶Glasgow

Glaxo *pr. name (TM), abbr.* Britain's largest pharmaceutical company

glaze *verb* to supply or fit glass into a window, door, etc.

glazier *noun* one who ⟶glazes

GLC *pr. name, abbr., hist.* ⟶Greater London Council

gleg *adj., Sc.* (1) quick-witted; (2) intelligent; (3) cheerful

gleg in the uptak *idiom, Sc.* quick on the uptake

glen *noun, Gae., Sc.* a narrow valley, especially one containing a stream

From the Gaelic *gleann* = "valley"

Glenalmond School *pr. name* a leading private school in Scotland

Located in ⟶Tayside, founded in 1841.

glengarry *noun, Sc.* a brimless cap with a central cleft, a pointed front, and ribbons at the rear

the Globe Theatre

The Revolution of 1688

A bloodless *coup* against ➡James II of England and VII of Scotland, with far-reaching constitutional significance.

James's principal offense was his repeated attempts to impose his personal Roman Catholic faith upon a largely Protestant population, which was combined with a contemptuous disregard for the views of ➡Parliament that was grounded in the ➡Stuart kings' foolhardy but persistent belief in the ➡Divine Right of Kings.

When ➡William of Orange, Protestant Dutch prince and husband of James's cousin ➡Mary, landed in England at the head of a large army upon the secret invitation of Parliamentary leaders, the British army and navy abandoned James and declared their support for William. James and his family fled to France and ➡Parliament invited ➡William and Mary, as joint monarchs, to accept the British crown provided they agreed to certain conditions.

It was this that made the Glorious Revolution such a significant event in the history of both Britain and subsequently the United States, because these conditions, which were also binding upon William and Mary's successors, finished the business began during the ➡English Civil War almost half a century earlier. They turned Britain into a ➡constitutional monarchy, where Parliament and not the ➡monarch is the true ➡sovereign and the monarch rules through Parliament as the servant of the people rather than the other way round as the ➡Stuart kings had supposed it should be. The events and the conclusions of the Glorious Revolution taken together with those of the ➡English Civil War before it were considered by many a century later to provide the legal precedents and moral justifications for the actions of the American Colonies against ➡George III in 1776, whose government seemed to have thought these principles did not apply across the Atlantic Ocean.

---

the **Globe Theatre** *pr. name, hist.* the theater where most of Shakespeare's plays were first performed

It was circular in plan with the stage a wooden platform that projected into the open central area where spectators milled around watching the entertainment. Around that and above the stage there were three galleries where those with more money could sit. The galleries and stage were covered by a thatched roof. The theater was built in the Bankside area of London on the south bank of the ➡Thames River in 1599, and demolished to make way for other buildings in 1644 after the ➡Puritans had closed it and all other London theaters the previous year. A replica of this building has recently been constructed at or near the site of the original.

Gloriana *pr. name, hist.* Spencer's adulatory name for ➡Elizabeth I in his work, *The Faerie Queene.*

the **Glorious Revolution** *pr. name, hist.* the bloodless *coup* of 1688 against ➡James II

(See box on opposite page.)

the **Glorious Twelfth** *pr. name, coll.* August 12, which is first day of the grouse-shooting season

Glos. *pr. name, abbr.* ➡Gloucestershire

glossy *noun, coll.* a slick magazine

Often one that has artistic pretensions.

Gloucester *pr. name* a city that is the administrative center of ➡Gloucestershire, it sits upon the ➡Severn River

Founded as *Glevum* by the Romans in the 1st C. Its abbey dates from 681 and the town was incorporated as a city in 1483; the current population is 104,000 (1991 estimate).

Gloucestershire *pr. name* a county in western England which borders upon Wales

The county seat is ➡Gloucester and the current population is 520,000 (1991 Census).

glove box *comp. noun* an automobile glove compartment

SEE ALSO: ➡fascia pocket.

glove money *comp. noun, arch., sl.* a bribe

glycerine *spell.* glycerin

Glyndebourne *pr. name, hist.* the location of an annual opera festival that has been held in the grounds of this large private house in ➡Sussex every summer since 1934

Glywising *pr. name* an ancient Welsh kingdom

Known to have been established by 700.

GM *noun, abbr.* the ➡George Medal

G-man *noun, Ir.* a detective working on political cases

GMB *pr. name, abbr.* the General, Municipal and Boilermaker's Union

A labor union for workers in just about any activity you care to mention. It was formed in 1989 by merging two already large unions, the ➡GMBATU and ➡APEX. The new union had about 800,000 members in 1992.

GMBATU *pr. name, abbr.* the General, Municipal, Boilermaker's and Allied Trade Union

A general labor union for manual workers. It merged with APEX to form GMB in 1989.

GMT *noun, abbr.* ➟Greenwich Mean Time

GM TV *pr. name (TM), abbr.* Good Morning Television

A commercial TV company headquartered in London, this is the part of the ➟ITV network that provides national breakfast programming.

GMWU *pr. name, abbr.* the General and Municipal Workers' Union

A labor union for general blue-collar workers.

gnat's piss *idiom, sl., taboo* a weak or insipid drink

go [A] *noun* an attempt

[B] *verb* to make a sound

Such as to ring a bell or fire a gun.

go about together *idiom, sl.* to go out with each other

goal average *comp. noun* the ratio of goals scored to the number of ➟soccer games played in a series

SEE ALSO: ➟goal difference.

goal difference *comp. noun* the difference between the number of goals scored for and against a ➟soccer team

SEE ALSO: ➟goal average.

goal kick *comp. noun* a ➟free kick allowed to the defenders in a ➟soccer game after the attackers send the ball over the ➟goal line without scoring

goal line *comp. noun* a line that passes through the goal posts and extends to the side-boundary of the play area, forming a ➟soccer field end-boundary

goal mouth *comp. noun* the space between ➟soccer goal posts

gob *noun, sl.* (1) the mouth; (2) a slimy lump

gobbledygook *spell.* gobbledegook

gobdaw *noun, Ir.* a gullible person

{gobsmacked » gobstruck} *adj., sl.* flabbergasted, entirely astonished or dumbstruck

gobstopper *noun, sl.* a jawbreaker candy

go down *verb* to cease to attend a university, implicitly without obtaining a degree

go down {a treat » well} *idiom. phr. verb* to greatly enjoy, especially food or drink

go down with (a disease) *phr. verb, coll.* to become infected with (a disease)

the **gods** *noun, coll.* (1) the top gallery level of a theater; (2) the people sitting on that level; the gallery gods

(1) is usually equivalent to the fourth floor.

God save the {King » Queen} *pr. name* the title and first line of the British national anthem

God slot *idiom. phr. verb* a time set aside for religious programming on television

go extinct *verb, coll.* to become extinct

go for a burton *idiom. phr. verb, sl.* (1) to be killed, particularly in battle; (2) to become broken or destroyed; (3) to become lost

Probably originated from Burton's Ales, of ➟Burton-on-Trent.

go for one's life *idiom. phr. verb* to run as fast as one possibly can

goggle box *comp. noun, sl.* a television set

Goidel *noun, Gae.* a ➟Celt who speaks one of the ➟Goidelic varieties of the ➟Celtic language group

Goidelic [A] *adj., Gae.* characteristic of or relating to Gaelic things or people

[B] *noun, Gae.* that branch of the ➟Celtic language group that includes ➟Scots Gaelic, ➟Irish Gaelic and the ➟Manx of the Isle of Man

go in *verb* to go to commence batting in ➟cricket

going around the houses *idiom* avoiding or delaying coming to the point

goitre *spell.* goiter

go-kart *spell.* go-cart

golach *noun, Sc.* (1) an insect, particularly an earwig or beetle; (2) a contemptible person

the **Gold Cup Day** *pr. name* the day when the Ascot Gold Cup race is run at Ascot racecourse

golden duck *comp. noun* a ➟cricket ➟batsman ➟run out with a score of zero on the first ball

golden handshake *comp. noun, coll.* a gratuity or bonus paid to a senior employee or executive upon leaving the employment of a company

the *Golden Hind* *pr. name, hist.* the ship aboard which Sir Frances Drake circumnavigated the globe between 1577 and 1580, and where ➟Elizabeth I knighted him upon his return

golden syrup *comp. noun* a syrup made from refined molasses

Used in a similar way to corn syrup.

golden wedding *comp. noun* a golden wedding anniversary

Goldsmith's College *pr. name* a school of ➟London University founded in 1891

the **Gold Stick** *pr. name* the gilt rod carried by the Colonel of the ➟Life Guards on state occasions

golf club *comp. noun* a country club

golf links *comp. noun, Sc.* a golf course situated upon or close to the seashore

go like a bomb *idiom. phr. verb* (1) to be a greatly successful business; (2) to function very well

go like the clappers *idiom. phr. verb, sl.* (1) to travel very rapidly; (2) to work very hard

golliwog *noun, out.* a soft doll with black features

gombeen *noun, Gae., Ir.* usury

gombeen man *comp. noun, Gae., Ir.* a moneylender

go missing *verb* to become lost

{gonadotrophic » gonadotrophin} *spell.* {gonadotropic » gonadotropin}
Stimulating to the gonads; that which stimulates the gonads.

gone by *idiom, sl.* too old (of a person)

gone time *idiom, coll.* past or after an expected time or duration

gong *noun, sl.* a military medal

gonk *noun, arch., sl.* a stupid person

{gonorrhoea » gonorrhoeal » gonorrhoeic} *spell.* {gonorrhea » gonorrheal » gonorrheic}

Gonville and Caius College *pr. name* a college of ⟶Cambridge University
Founded in 1348 by Edmund Gonville as a hall, it was raised to college status by Dr. John Caius of ⟶Norwich—physician to ⟶Edward VI, ⟶Mary Tudor and ⟶Elizabeth I—in 1558. He wrote on many matters, including a treatise asserting that Cambridge University was founded in 394 B.C. by Cantaber.

good bat *idiom, sl.* a high speed

good egg *exclam., arch.* well done

a **good few** *comp. noun, coll.* a large number

good form *comp. noun, coll.* the proper way to behave

good job *comp. noun, coll.* a fortunate circumstance

good kick *comp. noun, sl.* a soccer player who can kick the ball especially well

good morrow *exclam., out.* good morning

good on you *exclam., coll.* good for you

Good Queen Bess *pr. name, hist.* ⟶Elizabeth I

goods *noun* freight or cargo transported over land, but not over water or through the air

good show *exclam., coll.* well done

goods lift *comp. noun* a freight elevator

goods train *comp. noun* a freight train

goods van *comp. noun* a delivery truck

goods wagon *comp. noun* a railroad freight car

good wicket *comp. noun, coll.* (1) a ⟶cricket game that's going well; (2) derived and generalized from (1), a good situation to be in

Goodwood House *pr. name, hist.* a stately house that grew out of a 17th C. hunting lodge
Effectively rebuilt in its present style during the 1760s, it is located just a mile or two from ⟶Goodwood racecourse.

Goodwood racecourse *pr. name* a racecourse near ⟶Chichester in ⟶West Sussex

go off *verb, coll.* to start to dislike or lose interest

go off the boil *idiom. phr. verb* (1) to lose the initiative; (2) to lose interest

googly *noun* a ⟶cricket ball bowled so that it spins in the opposite way to that expected

{goolie » gooly} *noun, sl., taboo* a testicle

goon *noun, hist., sl.* what British prisoners of war called their German guards during World War II

go on *verb, coll.* (1) to nag persistently; (2) in ⟶cricket, to commence bowling

go on a bit *idiom. phr. verb* to talk at somewhat excessive length

go on at (someone) *idiom. phr. verb, sl.* to irritate or nag (someone)

go on fire *phr. verb, Ir., Sc.* to take fire or ignite

gooseberry fool *comp. noun* a dessert consisting of sieved gooseberries, cream, custard and sugar

the **Goose Fair** *pr. name* an annual ⟶fair held every October in ⟶Nottingham
It is called this because once geese were sold there.

goosegog *noun, coll.* a gooseberry

go racing *verb, coll.* to attend a horse race meeting

the **Gorbals** *pr. name* a district of ⟶Glasgow once notorious for the grim conditions of its slums and the people who lived in them
Since the 1960s the area has been transformed, when the old slums were demolished and replaced with modern ones.

gorblimey *exclam., sl.* a euphemism for or variation of "God blind me."
SEE ALSO: ⟶corblimey

gorcock *noun, North, Sc.* a male red grouse

Gordon Bennett *exclam., sl.* an exclamation of surprise or annoyance or both
Reputed to be a euphemism for ⟶corblimey or ⟶gorblimey. James Gordon Bennett was a 19th C. New York newspaper baron born in Scotland in 1795 and now forgotten in both his native and adopted lands, but somehow or other preserved as a sort of ⟶Cockney oath uttered when something particularly irritating or annoying happens without warning.
Apparently the real Gordon Bennett's most famous characteristic was to announce his arrival in a restaurant by yanking away the tablecloths of any tables he passed, which might have something to do with this strange immortality.

the **Gordon Highlanders** *pr. name* a Scottish regiment of the British Army
A regiment of this name was originally raised in 1794 by the 5th Duke of Gordon, but the modern Gordon Highlanders was formed when the 92nd and 75th regiments of ⟶foot were merged in the 19th C.

the **Gordon Riots** *pr. name, hist.* severe disorders and riots in London in June 1780, that left about 300 people dead

They were set off by a march to ➡Parliament, led by Lord George Gordon, protesting measures for Roman Catholic emancipation. In order to end the growing chaos as the situation got more and more out of control, troops had to be brought into the capital and used against the citizens, killing many before order was restored.

Gordon Setter *pr. name* a breed of bird dog that has a long black-and-tan coat

From the Duke of Gordon, 19th C. Scottish sportsman.

Gordonstoun School *pr. name* a private school in Scotland that has been attended by some members of the ➡Royal Family

Founded in 1934 by the German educational theorist Kurt Hahn, it is located near ➡Elgin in north-eastern Scotland.

gorilla *noun, sl.* £1,000 (one thousand pounds)

Because it's bigger than a ➡monkey.

SEE ALSO: ➡pony, ➡score.

gormless *adj., coll.* foolish or witless; none too smart

go round the haystack *idiom, rh. sl.* to visit the toilet

Derivation: toilet > ➡back > stack > haystack.

gorse *noun* a spiky yellow European shrub

Its formal name is *ulex europaeus* and it is especially common in Scotland.

Gorsedd *pr. name, Wal* a gathering of Welsh poets and bards, it is the Welsh word for "throne"

go short *verb, coll.* to do without

go sick *verb* to become ill

go slow *noun* a work slowdown

go spare *verb, coll.* (1) to become extremely angry or upset; (2) to become surplus or no longer required; (3) to go to waste

gossip *noun, arch.* a godparent

gossoon *noun, Fr., Ir.* a boy or youth

Perhaps from the French, *garçon* = "boy"

got *past tense* gotten

"Gotten" is now considered to be grammatically incorrect in England and is not used there, despite having been a perfectly correct English word for much longer than "got" and considered entirely proper and normal by Shakespeare, to name but one.

There is a strange inversion of this got/gotten dichotomy when we look at forgotten/forgot; the division between British and American English is far less complete there, but nonetheless is clearly moving in the opposite direction.

By the way, neither "gotten" not "forgot" have ever fallen out of favor in Scotland.

gotcher *exclam., sl.* a variation of "got you"

goth *noun, abbr., sl.* gothic

A species of rock music aficionado who is particularly disposed to adopting a cadaverous style of dress, make up and general appearance.

go the messages *phr. verb, Ir., Sc.* to go shopping

go to earth *verb, coll.* to hide

As an animal does in its burrow.

go to the country *verb, coll.* to call a ➡general election

Done by sending all ➡MPs back to their ➡constituencies throughout the country to face re-election at the same time.

go to the loo *phr. verb, sl.* to go to the bathroom

go up *verb* to enter a university in order to study there

go up the steps *idiom. phr. verb, sl.* to appear on trial at the ➡Old Bailey

go up to town *verb, coll.* to visit London

the **GovernmentCommunicationsHeadquarters** *pr. name* a highly secret electronic intelligence-gathering center headquartered at ➡Cheltenham

Working in close collaboration with the U.S. National Security Agency, ➡GCHQ employs about 10,000 people at Cheltenham and elsewhere around the world.

governor [A] *noun* (1) the official responsible for ruling a colony; (2) the official in charge of a prison [B] *noun, sl.* (1) one's employer; (2) one's father

Governor-General *comp. noun* a person representing the ➡Crown in a ➡Commonwealth country where the British monarch is head of state.

the **Governor of the Bank of England** *pr. name* the official in charge of the ➡Bank of England

gowan *noun, Sc.* a daisy

the **Gower Peninsular** *pr. name* an area considered to be of outstanding natural beauty

It extends into the ➡Bristol Channel upon the southern coast of Wales, just to the west of ➡Swansea.

gowf *noun, Sc.* the game of golf

gowf stick *comp. noun, Sc.* a golf club

gowk *noun, Sc.* (1) a cuckoo; (2) a fool; (3) a trick or a practical joke

gowp *verb, Sc., sl.* (1) to throb with pain; (2) to ache

Gp. Capt. *comp. noun, abbr.* a ➡group captain

GPMU *pr. name, abbr.* the Graphical, Paper and Media Union

A labor union for print trade workers formed in 1991 by the merging of ➡SOGAT 82 and the ➡NGA.

GPO *pr. name, abbr.* the General ➡Post Office

The ➡Post Office's name before 1969.

GR *pr. name, abbr. Georgius Rex*

The Latin for "King George".

grab a pew *imper., coll.* take a seat, sit down

grace *noun* permission to take a university degree

grace and favour {house » residence} *comp. noun* a house or apartment, owned by the sovereign, granted free of rent as a gift of the sovereign

There are grace and favor residences at ➡Windsor Castle, ➡Kensington Palace and ➡Hampton Court.

gracing *noun, abbr., arch., sl.* greyhound racing

gradely *adj., North* faithful or good

gradient *noun* the grade or degree of slope of a highway or railroad

graduand *noun* someone about to be awarded a degree by a university

graduated pension *comp. noun* a retirement pension plan where the value of contributions made during working years determines the size of pension paid

Graecism *spell.* Grecism

Graeco-Roman *spell.* Greco-Roman

graft *noun, coll.* (1) hard work or effort; (2) shady dealings or corruption, especially bribery

grafter *noun, coll.* a hard worker

gralloch *noun, Gae., Sc.* the entrails of a deer
From the Gaelic *grealach* = "intestines"

grammar *noun, abbr., coll.* a ➡grammar school

grammar school *comp. noun, hist.* (1) a ➡state secondary school that concentrates heavily on academic subjects; (2) originally, a school founded earlier than the 17th C. in order to teach Latin
(2) were usually founded in association with a cathedral or some other religious institution.

gramme *spell.* gram

gramophone *noun, out.* a phonograph

Grampian *pr. name* a region in northeastern Scotland
The current population is 505,000 (1991 Census).

the **Grampians** *pr. name* the largest mountain range in the Scottish Highlands
Incorporating the ➡Cairngorms.

Grampian TV *pr. name* a local commercial TV company headquartered in ➡Aberdeen
It is part of the ➡ITV network

gran *noun, abbr., coll.* a grandmother

Granada TV *pr. name* a local commercial TV company headquartered in Manchester
It is part of the ➡ITV network.

granary loaf *noun* a loaf of stoneground bread

grand *noun, sl.* £1,000

grand jury *comp. noun, hist.* a jury which had to find a bill of indictment valid before a criminal case could proceed to full trial
Grand juries originated at the Assize of Clarendon of 1166. They were abolished in England and Wales for most cases in 1933, and finally abolished for all cases under the terms of the Criminal Justice Act of 1948. Today a preliminary hearing before a magistrate fulfills the same role.
There never were grand juries in the Scottish legal system.

grand larceny *comp. noun, arch.* the theft of goods worth more than 12 ➡old pennies
This offense was abolished in 1827.

Grand Met *pr. name, abbr.* Grand Metropolitan plc
A major food, drinks, and hotel corporation that owns, among many other interests, the Inter-Continental hotel chain and the Pillsbury Company.

the **Grand National** *pr. name* Britain's most important steeplechase race
Held annually at ➡Aintree racecourse near ➡Liverpool on a 4½-mile course with 30 fences. The first Grand National was run in 1838, and the race has been called this since 1847.

the **Grand Old Duke of York** *pr. name, hist.* Frederick Augustus, Duke of York and Albany, second son of ➡George III and commander of the British Army in Flanders from 1794 to 1795.

It was Frederick Augustus's apparently futile performance in Flanders that was preserved for posterity in the nursery rhyme:

The grand old Duke of York,
He had ten thousand men,
He marched them up to the top of the hill,
And marched them down again.

In real life he was not old, there was no hill, and he commanded 30,000 men. He became Commander-in-Chief of the British Army in 1798, and his exploits in Flanders are more gloriously commemorated by the only military music, *Marsch des Yorkschen Corps*, to have been composed by none less than Ludwig van Beethoven.

the **Grand Old Man** *pr. name, hist.* a nickname for William Ewart Gladstone, 19th C. Prime Minister

grand tour *comp. noun, hist.* an extensive European tour often lasting up to three years
This was once considered to be an essential component in the education of members of the British upper classes. The custom died out during the first half of the 19th C.; the arrival of railroads may have had something to do with this.

the **Grand Union Canal** *pr. name* the longest canal in Britain
Although the name was devised as recently as 1929, the canal and its various subsidiaries were all built in the 18th and early 19th C. It links ➡London with ➡Birmingham, and the full network including all its many branches, extends to over 240 miles in length.

the **Granite City** *pr. name, coll.* ➡Aberdeen
Called this because it is almost entirely built with locally hewn granite. Because this is so hard and thus slow to weather, much of Aberdeen looks as if it had just been erected yesterday.
Also, granite is naturally radioactive, so Aberdeen has one of the highest levels of background radioactivity in the world, yet its population is also one of the healthiest and longest living. How can that be?

granny {annexe » flat} *comp. noun, coll.* part of a private residence that is used as a self-contained apartment, usually by an elderly relative

granny bond *comp. noun, coll.* the nickname of a form of government savings certificate made available to pensioners only

grant-aided school *comp. noun* a school receiving financial aid from public funds

grass *noun, sl.* a police informer

grasshopper *noun, rh. sl.* a policeman

Derivation: policeman > copper > hopper > grasshopper.

the **Grassmarket** *pr. name, hist.* the ancient marketplace of ➡Edinburgh

It is overlooked by the glowering might of ➡Castle Rock and the great fortress upon it.

grass-snake *comp. noun* a small, non-poisonous snake, the only one native to Britain

Its formal name is *natrix natrix*. This is the common ringed snake and not the common North America greensnake, *opheodrys vernalis*, and known as the grass-snake there.

gratuity *noun* a bonus paid at the end of a period spent in military service

{gravelled » gravelling} *spell.* {graveled » graveling}

gravy-boat *comp. noun* a boat-shaped dish from which gravy is served

Gray's Inn *pr. name* the newest of the ➡Inns of Court

Formerly the residence of the de Grays, a 13th C. legal family.

greaseproof paper *comp. noun* waxed paper

Great Britain *pr. name* (1) geographically, the largest island of the ➡British Isles; (2) politically, ➡Scotland, ➡England and ➡Wales only

the **Great Charter** *pr. name, hist.* an alternate, English-language name for the ➡*Magna Carta*

Greater London *pr. name* an English ➡Metropolitan County

Formed in 1963 to replace the ➡LCC, the current population is 6,675,000 (1991 Census).

Greater Manchester *pr. name* an English ➡Metropolitan County

The principal city is ➡Manchester, the current population is 2,475,000 (1991 Census).

Great Eastern *pr. name (TM)* a railroad company operating commuter services to and from the suburbs to the east of London

It is part of ➡British Rail.

the **Great Exhibition** *pr. name, hist.* an exhibition in 1851, housed in the ➡Crystal Palace, which was especially erected in ➡Hyde Park, London

The first great international exhibition; really this was the first world fair. There were over 13,000 exhibitors from all over the world in the areas of fine arts, machinery, raw materials and manufactures. The exhibition attracted over

6 million visitors and the whole thing made a huge profit, largely used to finance the ➡Victoria and Albert Museum.

the **Great Fire of London** *pr. name, hist.* this started in Master Farryner's bakery in Pudding Lane on September 2, 1666

By the time it was put out five days later by blowing up houses to create a fire break at Pie Corner, 90 churches — including St Paul's Cathedral — and 13,500 houses were destroyed; altogether 460 acres were devastated.

the **great game** *comp. noun, coll., hist.* espionage

the **Great Glen** *pr. name* the long rift valley that runs southwest through Scotland from ➡Inverness and ➡Loch Ness at the apex of the ➡Moray Firth on the ➡North Sea to ➡Oban on the Atlantic Ocean

It is also known as Glen More.

the **Great North Road** *pr. name, hist.* an old name for the principal highway from London to Edinburgh

the **Great Plague** *pr. name, hist.* an epidemic of bubonic plague in 1665

The worst outbreak of bubonic plague in Britain since the ➡Black Death of 1348. Some 75,000 died in London alone, or about 15 percent of the city's half million or so inhabitants. While living in the countryside to avoid the plague, Isaac Newton thought out the principle of universal gravitation and the laws of motion that are named after him.

the **Great Rebellion** *pr. name, hist.* an alternate name for the ➡English Civil War

the **Great Reform Act** *pr. name, hist.* the ➡Act of Parliament of 1832 that brought a modern system of representative democracy to Britain

the **Greats** *pr. name* the final examination for the Bachelor of Arts degree in classics and philosophy at ➡Oxford University

the **Great Seal** *pr. name* the chief seal of the ➡Sovereign, which is used to authenticate important documents of state

great toe *noun* the big toe

the **Great Wen** *pr. name, sl.* a nickname for ➡London

Great Western *pr. name (TM)* a railroad company operating ➡InterCity services between South Wales, the west of England and London

It is part of ➡British Rail.

the **Great Western Railway** *pr. name, hist.* a railroad company absorbed into ➡British Rail in 1947

It had a network stretching west from London to ➡Bristol, south ➡Wales and ➡Cornwall.

the **Great West Road** *pr. name, hist.* an old name for the principal highway from London to Bristol

Grecian knot *comp. noun* a way of dressing women's hair in the manner of the ancient Greeks

gree *verb, Sc.* (1) to come to an agreement; (2) to live together as friends in harmony

green belt *comp. noun* an area surrounding an urban area that is protected from urban encroachment

The idea is to prevent urban sprawl extending over the entire island. It was thought up in the 1930s.

the **Green Berets** *pr. name, sl.* the ➠Royal Marines

There is no connection with the U.S. Army Special Forces, who have the same nickname.

green card *comp. noun* an international automobile insurance certificate

From its green color.

the **Green Cloth** *pr. name, abbr.* the ➠Board of Green Cloth

Green College *pr. name* a college of ➠Oxford University founded in 1979

the **Green Cross Code** *pr. name* a set of road safety rules devised for use by children

the **Green Dragoons** *pr. name* the 13th Hussars

A unit of the British Army thus called because they wore green facings. Later, their facings were colored white.

SEE ALSO: ➠Lilywhites.

green fingers *comp. noun, coll.* green thumbs

greenfly *noun* a green peach aphid

greengage *noun* a small green variety of plum

green goddess *comp. noun, sl.* a military fire truck

Called this because of its color.

greengrocer *noun* (1) a dealer in vegetable and fruit; (2) a vegetable and fruit store

greengrocery *noun* (1) vegetable and fruit; (2) the business of a ➠greengrocer

the **Green Howards** *pr. name* a nickname for the 19th Regiment of ➠Foot

A unit of the British Army called this because of the color of their facings plus the name of the Colonel of the Regiment, Sir Charles Howard, from 1738 to 1748.

the **Green Linnets** *pr. name* a nickname for the 39th Regiment of ➠Foot

A unit of the British Army called this in 1741 because of the color of their facings.

green meat *comp. noun* green vegetables or grass considered as food

Green Paper *comp. noun* a proposal or report made by the government, published for public discussion

Green Park *pr. name* a ➠royal park located in west-central London

Traditionally, no flowers are grown in this park.

the **Green Pound** *pr. name* an imaginary currency unit used to calculate agricultural payments made between countries within the ➠EU

Green Ribbon Day *pr. name* St Patrick's Day, which is March 17

greens *noun, abbr.* green vegetables

Greensleeves *pr. name, hist.* a popular ballad of ➠Elizabethan times

Its air was reputedly written by ➠Henry VIII.

green welly *comp. noun, abbr., coll.* a sort of upscale ➠wellington boot

Supposedly particularly popular with ➠Sloane Rangers.

the **green welly brigade** *comp. noun, abbr., coll.* upper-class city-dwellers who weekend in the country

Where they try to look as if they belong, but invariably fail at least partly because of their preference for ➠green wellies, which no real country-dweller would be seen dead in.

Greenwich *pr. name, hist.* a ➠Greater London borough

A historic area, site of a royal palace since the 15th C. and strongly linked in various ways with the ➠Royal Navy. Greenwich's current population, also included within the ➠London urban area total, is 200,000 (1991 Census).

Greenwich {Mean Time » Time} *pr. name* time upon the ➠Greenwich Meridian and the normal time to set watches to in Britain

Royal Observatory, Greenwich

Except that from March until October, when ➠BST is in force and watches should be set one hour ahead of ➠GMT.

Greenwich Meridian *pr. name* the prime meridian

The baseline from which all longitudes and time zones are based throughout the world, because Greenwich is the location of the original ➠Royal Observatory.

greenyard *noun* a pound for stray animals

greet *noun, Sc.* (1) to weep or lament; (2) to grumble

gregory *noun, rh. sl.* a bank check

Derivation: check > peck > Gregory Peck > gregory.

the **Grenadier Guards** *pr. name* the senior regiment of the ➠Guards Division, raised in 1685

Gretna Green *pr. name, hist.* a hamlet in southwestern Scotland eight miles north of ➠Carlisle, and the first place of any significance—and that not much—to be reached after crossing the border from England

It used to be that in Scotland elopers from England could legally marry without the trouble or expense of obtaining license, banns or priest, as a simple declaration before a witness was sufficient to make a marriage legal. Traditionally, this witness in Gretna was the village blacksmith.

In 1856, a residence of 21 days in Scotland became a legal requirement for marriage but Gretna Green continued to be a popular destination for eloping couples because, unlike England where the minimum age to marry without parental consent was 21, in Scotland it was 16.

grey

grey *spell.* gray

grey area *comp. noun, coll.* an area suffering economic deprivation

greyback *spell.* grayback
An animal.

greybeard [A] *noun* a seeding clematis
[B] *spell.* graybeard

Greyfriars Hall *pr. name* a hall of ➡Oxford University founded in 1910

{**greyish » greyness**} *spell.* {grayish » grayness}

the **Greys** *pr. name, abbr.* the ➡Royal Scots Greys

griddle cake *comp. noun* a pancake

grieve *noun, Sc.* a farm manager or overseer

griff *noun, out., sl.* news

griffin *noun, out., sl.* a betting tip

grill *verb* to broil

Grimsby *pr. name, hist.* a fishing port at the mouth of the ➡Humber river on the east coast of England
It is believed it was first settled in the 9th C. by the ➡Danes; the current population is 92,000 (1991 estimate).

Gripe Water *pr. name (TM)* a solution used to relieve colic in infants

gritting lorry *comp. noun* a truck used to spread sand or gravel over icy roads in winter

grizzle [A] *noun, coll.* the fretful cry of a young child
[B] *verb, coll.* to whine or complain

groat *noun, hist.* a silver coin worth four pence, issued in England between 1351 and 1662

grocer *noun* a dealer in food and certain other household consumables

the **Grocer** *pr. name, coll.* a nickname for ➡Prime Minister Edward Heath
His father was a ➡grocer in ➡Kent.

the **Grocer's Daughter** *pr. name, coll.* a nickname for ➡Prime Minister Margaret Thatcher
Her father was a grocer in Grantham, ➡Lincolnshire, but in addition she succeeded the ➡Grocer as leader of the Conservative Party, and in due course as prime minister.

grockle *noun, derog., sl., South* a tourist
A name used by natives of ➡Cornwall for the horde of tourists who invade their region every summer. *SEE ALSO:* ➡emmet.

grog *noun, hist., out.* rum diluted with water
Formerly a daily ration issued to ➡ratings serving on ➡Royal Navy ships. The word is said to have been derived from Admiral Vernon, who was the first to distribute diluted rather than neat rum to his crews, and who was nicknamed Old Grog, from his cloak made of grogram, a coarse material consisting of wool, mohair and silk, stiffened with gum.

grog-shop *comp. noun, sl.* a low-class ➡public house
Originally one frequented by sailors, used to their daily ration of ➡grog while on board ship.

groise *noun, sl.* a hard worker
A term used by ➡public school students.

groom *noun* an official of the ➡Royal Household

Groom in Waiting *pr. name* an official of the ➡Royal Household attending upon the personal needs of the king
SEE ALSO: ➡Gentlemen in Waiting

grot *noun, sl.* junk

grotty *adj., abbr., sl.* (1) grotesque; (2) ugly, dirty or disgusting

ground *noun, coll., out.* the floor of a room

groundage *noun* the fee or duty that has to be paid for a ship while it is tied up in port

ground floor *comp. noun* street level; the first floor

groundhog *noun* an aardvark

groundnut *noun* a peanut
The agricultural name. When you buy then to eat, they're still called "peanuts."

ground rent *comp. noun* rent paid for the use of the land that a building stands upon
As distinct from rent paid for the use of the building itself.

groundsman *noun* one who maintains a sports ground
Particularly a cricket ground.

ground staff *comp. noun* the staff employed by a cricket club to maintain the facilities

group captain *comp. noun, abbr.* a commissioned officer in the ➡RAF
Equivalent in rank to a colonel in the USAF.

{**grovelled » grovelling**} *spell.* {groveled » groveling}

groyne *spell.* groin
In the sense of a framework or low wall, usually of wood, built out from the shore to prevent or check coastal erosion by sand or current.

Grub Street *idiom, coll.* ➡hack writers as a class
From an actual, physical Grub Street—which has since been renamed Milton Street—in London where such people used to congregate.

grue *verb, Sc.* (1) to feel terror or horror; (2) to shrink in fright or horror; (3) to shudder

gruelling *spell.* grueling

guard *noun* (1) the conductor of a passenger train; (2) the brakeman of a freight train

guardant *adj.* in heraldry, shown with the body placed sideways, face to the front

the **Guards Division** *pr. name* the division of the British Army consisting of the ➡Foot Guards

guardsman *noun* a member of the ➡Foot Guards

guard's van *comp. noun* a caboose

gubbins *noun, coll.* (1) a fool; (2) machinery; (3) trash

guddle [A] *noun, Sc.* (1) a muddle or confusion; (2) a messy worker; (3) a crowbar

[B] *verb, Sc.* (1) to catch a fish by groping with one hand under the stones and banks of a small river or stream; (2) to work in a careless or slovenly way; (3) to create a mess
Considerable patience and very quick reactions are necessary for success with (1), virtues not associated with the other two meanings of the word listed here.

gudgeon pin *comp. noun* a wrist pin, holding together the piston rod and connecting rod of an internal combustion engine

guernsey *noun* a thick woolen sweater
Usually navy blue, and originating from ➡Guernsey.

Guernsey *pr. name* (1) one of the principal islands of the ➡Channel Islands; (2) a breed of fawn and cream-colored dairy cow
(2) is heavier than the ➡Jersey cow and produces very creamy milk; they originate from (1).

guest beer *comp. noun, coll.* a beer from one brewery on sale in a ➡public house owned by another

guest house *comp. noun* (1) a small private hotel; (2) a private house offering paid accommodation

guid bit *comp. noun, Sc.* a long time

Guide *noun, abbr.* a ➡Girl Guide

guide dog *comp. noun* a seeing-eye dog

guider *noun* an adult woman who leads or supervises a troop of ➡girl guides

guidwife *noun, Sc.* a housewife

guild *noun, hist.* an association of Medieval merchants or craftsmen

guildhall *noun, hist.* a hall where ➡guilds once met

the **Guildhall** *pr. name, hist.* an early 15th C. hall, originally built to be used by the various guilds of the ➡City of London
Now used by the ➡Corporation of the City of London for state banquets, etc. It also contains a library and picture gallery.

the **Guildhall School of Music and Drama** *pr. name* a drama college founded in London in 1880

guillotine *noun, coll.* a parliamentary procedure for fixing the maximum time available for discussion of a particular topic

guinea *pr. name, hist.* a gold coin that replaced the ➡Unite and was in circulation as legal tender in Britain from 1663 until 1817
It acquired this name because it was originally made with gold from Guinea in West Africa. At first the Guinea was worth 20 ➡shillings, which is to say one ➡pound. However, for some years its value fluctuated with the price of gold, reaching a high of 30 shillings in 1694. In 1717 its value was fixed at 21 shillings and has not changed since then; in modern currency terms that would be £1.05.

Although the Guinea coin was withdrawn in 1817, it remained customary for such considerations as professional fees, prices at auctions for works of art, race horses, and other items considered to be the preserve of the upper classes to be defined in terms of guineas rather than pounds, notwithstanding the fact that no such currency unit or coin was legal tender. Although this practice has not yet entirely died out, it has become much rarer since the introduction of decimal currency in 1971.

guinea-hen *comp. noun, out.* a prostitute

guinea-pig *comp. noun, hist., sl.* a World War II child evacuee from London or other large city considered particularly exposed to the risk of bombing
In the first weeks of the war, millions were separated from their families and quartered with families in rural areas. These rural families received an allowance of one pound and one shilling, equal to one ➡guinea, per child.

Guinevere *pr. name, hist.* the wife of ➡Arthur

Guinness *pr. name (TM)* a popular brand of ➡stout beer, originating from Ireland

guiser *noun, Sc.* a child in disguise, going from door to door offering trick or treat at ➡Hallowe'en
By the way, this word is the root of "geezer."

gules *noun* the heraldic name for the color red

gullieknife *noun, Sc.* a large knife

gully *noun* a fielding player's position on the ➡cricket field

gum *noun* an adhesive or glue

gumboot *noun* a rubber boot

gun *noun, coll.* a member of a hunting or shooting party

gunge *noun, sl.* any messy or sticky substance

gunge up *verb, sl.* to clog up with ➡gunge

gungy *adj., sl.* messy, sticky, spoiled or ruined

the **Gunpowder Plot** *pr. name, hist.* the plot to blow up ➡James I of England and VI of Scotland, and ➡Parliament on November 5, 1605
It was intended to be the prelude to a Catholic *coup d'etat* but was frustrated at the last minute when the 36 barrels of gunpowder, which had been placed in the cellars of the ➡Palace of Westminster by the plotters, was discovered only the night before the king was due to attend the palace to open a new session of Parliament. The reason the plot failed was that one of the conspirators sent a note to a friend advising him not to be present at the ceremony.

All conspirators were either killed while resisting arrest or tried and hanged. The ringleader of the plot was ➡Guy Fawkes, who has been burned in effigy every November 5th since, to the accompaniment by many fireworks.

the **Gunpowder Treason** *pr. name, hist.* the original, contemporary name for the ➡Gunpowder Plot

gunroom *noun* (1) the room where sporting guns are kept in a large private house; (2) the junior officer's quarters on board a ➡Royal Navy warship
(2) was originally the gunners' quarters.

gunsmith *noun* one who sells, makes or repairs guns

guppie *noun, coll.* a green yuppie

From the abbreviation and merging of "green," signifying environmental concern, etc., with "yuppie."

gurk *verb, sl.* to belch

Gurkha *pr. name* a soldier who is a member of those regiments of the British Army that are recruited from among the Gurkha people of Nepal

Nepal is a small mountain kingdom in the Himalayans, north of India. The inhabitants have provided soldiers for the British Army since 1815. Ferocious fighters, they have distinguished themselves in both World Wars. Following Indian independence in 1947, a number of Gurkha regiments remained with the British army while others transferred to the Indian army. There are still some thousands of Gurkhas in the British army.

GUS *pr. name (TM), abbr.* Great Universal Stores

A major chain of department stores.

gutted *adj., sl.* distraught or completely disillusioned

{**guv » guv'nor**} *noun, abbr., sl.* ➡governor

guy [A] *noun* someone who is dressed in a ridiculous or grotesque manner

[B] *noun, abbr., coll.* an effigy of ➡Guy Fawkes

Guy Fawkes *pr. name, hist.* the leader of the ➡Gunpowder Plot of 1605

His real name was Guido Fawkes.

Guy Fawkes Night *pr. name, hist.* November 5th

When ➡Guy Fawkes is burned in effigy upon bonfires all over the country in celebration of his failure to blow up King and ➡Parliament in the ➡Gunpowder Plot of 1605.

This is the principle annual celebration where fireworks play a major part in the United Kingdom.

guzzle-guts *comp. noun, sl.* someone who is particularly greedy, especially for food

Gwent *pr. name, hist.* (1) an ancient kingdom in southeastern Wales; (2) a Welsh County

The kingdom was known to have been established before 700. The current population of (2) is 430,000 (1991 Census).

GWR *pr. name, abbr., hist.* ➡Great Western Railway

Gwynedd *pr. name, hist.* (1) an ancient kingdom in northern Wales; (2) a Welsh County

(1) was established by about 550, but the kings of Gwynedd accepted the overlordship of the English throne by the middle of the 12th C. English rule became complete in 1283. Currently, the population of (2) is 240,000 (1991 Census).

gybe *spell.* jibe

gymkhana *noun* a competitive event involving horseback riding skills

gymslip *noun* a schoolgirl's sleeveless, pleated and belted tunic

gynaecium *spell.* gynecium

The carpels of a flower.

{**gynaecocracy » gynaecocratic**} *spell.* {gynecocracy » gynecocratic}

Concerning rule by women.

gynaecoid *spell.* gynecoid

Typically feminine.

{**gynaecological » gynaecologist » gynaecology**} *spell.* {gynecological » gynecologist » gynecology}

gynaecomastia *spell.* gynecomastia

The enlargement of male breasts.

gyp [A] *noun* a college servant, especially at ➡Cambridge University

Probably derived from "gippo," the name for a style of short tunic once worn by male servants, although it is possible the word is a variant of "gypsy."

[B] *noun, coll.* pain or discomfort

Probably derived from "gee-gee," a command to a horse to speed up, often reinforced with the use of the spur or whip; hence the pain or discomfort.

gyratory circus *comp. noun, arch.* a traffic circle

SEE ALSO: ➡roundabout, ➡traffic circus.

H

H2S *pr. name, hist.* the code-name for a secret navigation system employed by British aircraft searching for German U-boats during the World War II ➡Battle of the Atlantic

haar *noun, North, Sc.* a cold sea fog, especially on the eastern coast of Scotland or northern England

haberdasher *noun* a dealer in notions and fabric

haberdashery *noun* notions and fabric

Habsburg *spell.* Hapsburg
The name of the former Austrian imperial family. The family themselves spell their name the British way.

HAC *noun, abbr.* the ➡Honourable Artillery Company

hack [A] *noun, abbr., arch.* (1) an ordinary horse; (2) a horse let out for hire
From ➡Hackney, a district in north London where horses for hire were once stabled.
[B] *verb* to kick an opponent upon the shin
Especially in ➡soccer.

{hack » hackette} *noun, coll.* an uninspired or uninspiring {male » female} writer, particularly one who is a journalist

Hackney *pr. name* a ➡Greater London borough
Its current population, which is also included within the ➡London urban area total, is 165,000 (1991 Census).

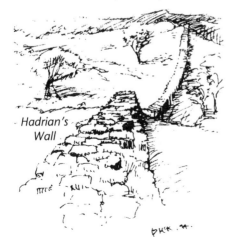

Hadrian's Wall

Hackney carriage *comp. noun, out.* the official name for a London taxi
Originally a carriage drawn by an ordinary (or ➡hack) horse.

Haddo House *pr. name, hist.* an 18th C. Palladian mansion some 25 miles to the north of ➡Aberdeen
It was designed in 1731 by William Adam.

had it *idiom. phr. verb* (1) to be mortally wounded; (2) to be passed one's best

had one's chips *idiom. phr. verb* to be unable to avoid (1) losing a struggle; (2) being punished

Hadrian's Wall *pr. name, hist.* an ancient defensive wall across northern England, somewhat to the south of the Scottish border
It was constructed on the direct orders of the Roman Emperor Hadrian between the years 122 and 127 in order to keep the northern barbarians out of the settled Roman territory in southern half of the island of Great Britain.
The wall, built of stone, was about 16 ft high and at some 9 ft., was wide enough on top for horse-drawn wagons (probably not chariots, as the more romantic among us have supposed) to pass each other. There was a castle every Roman mile (1,000 paces) and turrets between the castles. Also, there were 17 larger forts, each with a substantial garrison, to the south of the wall and on the north there was a *vallum*, or ditch, about 10 ft deep and 30 ft wide running parallel to the wall.
The wall was overrun several times in the 3rd C. and had ceased to be an effective barrier by the end of the 4th C.
Much of the wall remains intact to this day. It runs from Wallsend-on-Tyne in the east to Bowness on the ➡Solway Firth in the west, a distance of about 75 miles across northern England from coast to coast. Today, it is without doubt the most impressive remnant of the Roman Empire left on British soil. SEE ALSO: Antonine's Wall.

hae *verb, Sc.* to have

haem *spell.* heme
$C_{34}H_{32}N_4O_4Fe$, a compound containing iron, which is responsible for the red color of hemoglobin .

haemo *spell., prefix* hema- (which means white-)

haffet *noun, Sc.* (1) the wooden side of a bed or chair; (2) a side-lock of hair

hag *noun, North, Sc.* (1) a raised area of hard ground in a bog; (2) a hollow of soft ground in a moor

haggis

haggis *noun, Sc.* the national dish of Scotland

Consisting of sheep's heart, lungs and liver minced with suet, onions, oatmeal and seasonings. It was traditionally boiled in the animal's stomach but nowadays usually some form of artificial bag is used.

> *Fair fa' your honest, sonsie face,*
> *Great chieftain o' the pudding-race*
> *Aboon them a' ye tak your place,*
> > *Painch, tripe, or thairm:*
> *Weel are ye wordy o' a grace*
> > *As lang's my arm.*
> *...auld Scotland wants nae skinking ware*
> > *That jaups in luggies;*
> *But if ye wish her gratefu' prayer,*
> > *Gie her a haggis!*
> —Robert Burns, *Address to a Haggis*

haggis-basher *idiom, derog., sl.* a ➡Scotsman

ha-ha *noun* a sunken fence

This is a boundary consisting of a trench with retaining wall upon one side, built in this way so that it does not obstruct the view. The origin of the name is a mystery, although unkind people have suggested it is derived from the mirth engendered among spectators as they watch others discovering the existence of the boundary the hard way.

the {hail » hale} { jing-bang » rickmatick} *idiom, Sc.* the whole shebang, enchilada, shooting match ... and so on

Everything {and » or} everybody, in other words.

SEE ALSO: ➡rickmatick.

hairchord *noun* a haircloth upholstery material

hairdresser *noun* a barber

hairgrip *noun* a bobby pin

hairpin bend *comp. noun* a hairpin turn on a highway

hairslide *noun* an ornamental barrette or hair clip

hairwash *noun* shampoo

hairy [A] *noun, out., sl.* a long-haired and probably bearded intellectual

[B] *noun, Sc., sl.* (1) a young woman; (2) a prostitute

hairy grannie *comp. noun, Sc.* a large, hairy caterpillar

haiver *verb, Sc.* (2) to talk nonsense; (2) to vacillate or avoid coming to the point

half [A] *noun, coll.* half a pint

Usually beer, in a pub.

[B] *prep., abbr.* half ➡past

Used to describe time. For example, "half two" = "two thirty".

half a bar *idiom, sl.* ten shillings

In old currency, ten ➡shillings was worth half of one ➡pound.

half-{a-crown » crown} *comp. noun, hist.* a former coin with a face value of 12.5 pence in today's terms

This is 2/6 (two ➡shillings and six ➡pence in old currency) coin, worth half of a ➡crown, also known informally as ➡half-a-dollar and was legal tender until 1970 when it was withdrawn shortly before decimalization in 1971.

half-a-dollar *comp. noun, hist., sl.* ➡half-a-crown

This dates from the 19th C., when £1 = $4 for many years.

half-a-mo *imper., sl.* wait a moment

half-arsed *adj., sl., taboo* half-assed

half-{a-sovereign » sovereign} *comp. noun, hist.* a former gold coin with a face value of 10 shillings

Equivalent to 50 ➡pence in modern terms.

half-blue *comp. noun* someone who has not been formally recognized as a ➡blue, despite representing their college or university in a sport

At ➡Oxford or ➡Cambridge Universities.

half-cut *adj., coll.* partly drunk

half-inch *verb, rh. sl.* to steal

Derivation: steal > pinch > inch > half-inch.

half-{pence » penny} *comp. noun, hist.* a former bronze coin with a face value of half of one ➡penny

Pronounced rather like "hape-knee".

half-timbering

{**halfpennyworth » ha'p'orth**} *noun, arch., coll.* (1) that which could be purchased for one ➡halfpenny; (2) a trivial value

"ha'p'orth" is the more phonetic spelling, but not much more.

half-seas-over *adj., sl.* somewhat drunk

half-term *comp. noun* a time midway through a school term when a short vacation may sometimes be taken

half-timbering *comp. noun, hist.* the most common form of English domestic architecture from the middle of the 15th C. until the late 17th.

A building's timber frame was left exposed, and spaces between the timbers filled with lath and plaster or red bricks.

Halifax [A] *pr. name* the largest ➡building society [B] *pr. name, hist.* a ➡West Yorkshire town that has been a major wool center since the Middle Ages

The current population is 90,000 (1991 estimate).

hall *noun* (1) a large medieval house or mansion; (2) the common dining room of a college; (3) the principal public room of a castle or medieval house

hall of residence *comp. noun* a college dormitory

Hallowe'en *spell., North, Sc.* Halloween

This is an ancient celebration in Scotland and some areas of northern England, but until very recently alien to most of England, where it is only just beginning to be celebrated, mostly by importation from the U. S. *SEE ALSO:* ➡Samhain.

hall porter *comp. noun* a bellhop

hallstand *noun* a hat rack

Hambledon Cricket Club *pr. name, hist.* the most famous of the early cricket clubs, known to be already well-established by the 1760s

It is a village north of ➡Portsmouth, in ➡Hampshire.

hame *noun, Sc.* home

Ham House *pr. name, hist.* a large house in southern London which is one of the best-preserved examples of 17th C. brick-built ➡Restoration domestic architecture

hammer *verb* to declare a member of the ➡Stock Exchange to be in default

The term originated from the practice of making a declaration of default with three taps of a hammer upon the rostrum in the Stock Exchange.

the **Hammer of the Scots** *pr. name, hist.* ➡Edward I

Upon his tomb on ➡Westminster Abbey the inscription reads, *Edwardus Primus Malleus Scotorum hic est* = "Edward the First Hammer of the Scots lies here."

Hammersmith and Fulham *pr. name* a borough within ➡Greater London

Its current population, which is also included within the ➡London urban area total, is 135,000 (1991 Census).

Hampden Park *pr. name* Scotland's national sporting stadium, which is also the home of a small amateur soccer club, Queen's Park

A large stadium in southern ➡Glasgow where many important national and international sporting and other events are held, especially the (soccer) Scottish ➡Cup Final.

the **Hampden roar** *comp. noun, coll.* the distinctive noise of 80,000 voices cheering together when ➡Hampden Park in ➡Glasgow is filled to capacity

Reputedly, the sound can be heard over the entire city.

hamper *noun* a selection of food and drink suitable for a particular occasion

Hampshire *pr. name* a county on the southern coast of England, between ➡Dorset and ➡West Sussex

The county seat is ➡Winchester and the current population is 1,510,000 (1991 Census).

Hampstead *pr. name* a fashionable district on high ground to the northwest of central London

Now best known for the somewhat left-leaning, and often personally bizarre, intellectuals who were its leading denizens in the 1920s and 30s. However, in its time it has provided affluent Londoners with an open area with fresh air and clean water high above the city and relatively safe from the Black Death and Great Plague in medieval and restoration times.

Hampsteads *noun, rh. sl.* teeth

Derivation: teeth > heath > ➡Hampstead Heath > ➡Hampsteads.

Hampstead Heath *pr. name* a large public open area in ➡Hampstead

the Great Hall, Hampton Court

Hampton Court *pr. name, hist.* a royal palace on the banks of the ➡Thames river to the west of London

Originally built in the early 16th C. by Cardinal Wolsey, who quite intentionally set out to equip himself with the most magnificent house in the land, outshining in splendor even the residences of the king himself. He succeeded, and so in due course found himself obliged to gift the house to ➡Henry VIII in order to retain the king's favor. It is certainly one of the finest historical buildings in Britain, and the gardens contain a famous maze.

153

handbag

handbag [A] *noun* a woman's small traveling bag, normally used to carry money and other small items [B] *verb, sl.* to be attacked or hit

By a woman, especially by Margaret Thatcher.

handbasin *noun* a washbasin

hands off *imper.* a warning not to touch or interfere with the controls of a machine, for example

hang about *phr. verb* to hang around

---

hang, draw and quarter *idiom, hist.* the punishment once inflicted upon those found guilty of high treason

To be strictly accurate and correct, this phrase should have been "draw, hang and quarter." Whatever way round, it was certainly not pleasant. Here are the actual words said by the judge to the condemned person:

You are to be drawn on hurdles to the place of execution, where you are to be hanged, but not until you are dead; for, while still living, your body is to be taken down, your bowels torn out and burned before your face; your head is then cut off, and your body divided into four quarters.

---

hanger *noun* a small, wooded area on a steep hillside

Hannah *noun, sl.* a ➡Wren serving with the ➡Royal Marines during World War II

The name comes from Hannah Snell, who joined the marines in the 18th C. by posing as a man

Hanover *pr. name, abbr., hist.* the ➡Royal House of Great Britain from 1714 to 1901

The following English monarchs belonged to this house: ➡George I, ➡George II, ➡George III, ➡George IV, ➡William IV and ➡Victoria. "Hanover" was really an abbreviated version of the full royal name, which was "Hanover and Brunswick-Lüneburg."

Hanoverian *adj., hist.* of or concerning the British ➡Royal House of ➡Hanover

Hansard *pr. name* the official record of proceedings in the ➡House of Commons

Named for Luke Hansard, the printer who first compiled such a record in 1774.

{hansel » hanselled » hanselling} *spell.* {handsel » handseled » handseling}

A gift at the New Year or a foretaste of what's to come.

hansom *noun, abbr., hist.* a ➡hansom cab

hansom cab *comp. noun, hist.* a two-wheeled covered light carriage with seats for two inside and with the driver seated upon an elevated external position at the rear

Hants. *pr. name, abbr.* ➡Hampshire

happy as a sandboy *idiom, coll.* as happy as a clam

happy clappy *comp. noun, coll., derog.* a member of certain kinds of evangelical churches

The kind whose congregations regularly participate in services with frequent bursts of applause, which can appear meaningless to the casual observer.

{harbour » harbourage » harbourer} *spell.* {harbor » harborage » harborer}

hard [A] *noun* a road crossing the tidal part of a beach [B] *noun, abbr., sl.* hard labor

hard at it *idiom, sl.* working hard

hard-by *adj.* nearby

hard {cheese » lines} *idiom, sl.* hard luck

hardcore *noun* heavy, rocky material used to form the foundations under roads, buildings, etc.

hard done by *idiom, coll.* mistreated or ill-served

hard shoulder *comp. noun* a strip of hardened ground alongside the outer lane of a ➡motorway for emergency use only

hardstanding *noun* an area of hard surface used for the parking of automobiles

Hardwick Hall *pr. name, hist.* an ➡Elizabethan house 10 miles south of Chesterfield in ➡Derbyshire

The house is best known for its extensive use of glass; because glass was so expensive while it was being built, large windows were a status symbol. The house was built by Elizabeth, Countess of Shrewsbury, best known as Bess of Hardwick. It contains what are the most spectacular interiors of any Elizabethan house left standing in England today.

Harewood House *pr. name, hist.* an 18th C. Palladian mansion about seven miles to the north of ➡Leeds

Its interiors were designed by Robert Adam, the furniture was supplied by Chippendale, and the grounds were landscaped by Capability Brown; three impressive choices.

harf *noun, sl.* half

harglemen *noun, East* an argument

haricot bean *comp. noun* a variety of French bean

Haringey *pr. name* a ➡Greater London borough

Its current population, which is also included within the ➡London urban area total, is 190,000 (1991 Census).

Harlech Castle *pr. name, hist.* the most dramatically located of the Welsh castles built by ➡Edward I in the later years of the 13th C.

It is about 50 miles to the north of Aberystwyth on the west coast of Wales. Perched high upon a rocky crag that jutted up out of the sea when the castle was built, it is now about half a mile inland as the sea has retreated since the 13th C.

Harlech TV *pr. name* a local commercial TV company headquartered in Cardiff

It is part of the ➡ITV network.

Harley Street *pr. name* a street in London with a heavy concentration of doctor's offices
Considered to be the place to find all the best skilled, highly regarded and most expensive medical practitioners.

harling *noun* a pebble-filled mortar coating for walls

Harold Godwineson *pr. name, hist.* a nickname for ➡Harold II, King of England
Called this because his father was Godwin, Earl of Wessex.

Harold Harefoot *pr. name, hist.* a nickname for ➡Harold I, King of England

Harold I *pr. name, hist.* King of England
A member of the Royal House of ➡Denmark, he reigned five years from 1035 until 1040.

Harold II *pr. name, hist.* King of England
He reigned for 10 months in 1066 until killed in the Battle of ➡Hastings, it is said by an arrow which lodged in his eye. Although victory in that battle led to ➡William becoming the conqueror and thus king of England, it should be remembered that just three weeks earlier Harold had defeated another invader who was also a pretender to his throne, Hardraade of Norway, at Stamford Bridge in the north of England, and then had to march his army hurriedly south to meet William.
Harold, nicknamed "Godwineson," was a member of the Royal House of ➡Denmark.

Harp *pr. name* one of the symbols of Ireland
Because an early Irish king named David took the harp of the David mentioned in the Psalms as his badge or symbol.

the *Harrier* *pr. name* the world's first operational vertical take-off and landing fixed-wing military aircraft
Designed and built by British Aerospace plc, it first flew in 1966 and entered service with the ➡RAF in 1969. It is still in service there, and the ➡Royal Navy uses a version called the Sea Harrier. In the United States, a modified version is made under license by McDonnell Douglas and flown by the U.S. Marine Corp as the AV-8B.

Harris tweed *pr. name, Sc.* the best-known ➡tweed
Genuine Harris tweed is woven, using hand looms, only upon the island of Harris in the ➡Outer Hebrides.

Harrods *pr. name (TM)* Britain's best-known departmental store, in Knightsbridge, London
It evolved from a small ➡grocery store purchased by Charles H. Harrod in 1849; the present building was completed in 1912.

Harrogate *pr. name* a fashionable resort and conference center in Yorkshire
Harrogate has been a spa since the 17th C. The current population is 69,000 (1991 estimate).

Harrovian *noun* a past or present member of ➡Harrow School, near London

Harrow *pr. name* a ➡Greater London borough
Its current population, which is also included within the ➡London urban area total, is 194,000 (1991 Census).

Harrow School *pr. name* one of the leading English ➡public schools
Founded in 1571 and located in northwestern London. Without doubt its best-known former student was Winston S. Churchill, considered a rather poor scholar by his teachers there.

harry *exclam., sl.* a euphemistic variation of ➡bloody

hart *noun* a male red deer more than five years old

Harthacnut *pr. name, hist.* King of England
A member of the Royal House of ➡Denmark, he reigned for two years from 1040 until 1042.

Harwell *pr. name* the location of the principal nuclear research laboratory of the ➡UKAEA
It is at Didcot, near ➡Oxford.

the Battle of **Hastings** *pr. name, hist.* where ➡William the Conqueror, Duke of Normandy, defeated King ➡Harold in 1066
This result ensured the last successful invasion of ➡Britain The site of the battle is near the modern town of Hastings on the coast of what is now ➡East Sussex.

hasty puddding *comp. noun* a dish similar to cornmeal porridge but made with oatmeal

{**hatchelled » hatchelling**} *spell.* {hatcheled » hatcheling}
Concerned with the combing of flax.

hatchety *adj., Mid.* cranky

hatchment *noun* an heraldic representation of a diamond-shaped tablet enclosing a deceased person's coat of arms

Hatfield House *pr. name, hist.* a vast, highly impressive Jacobean mansion, built six miles east of ➡St Albans in ➡Hertfordshire in the early 17th C.
An earlier palace, built in Tudor times, was largely demolished to make way for the present house.
However part of that earlier building survives, having spent many years serving as the stables. It is now being restored to some measure of its former glory.

hatter *noun* a hat seller or maker

hat-trick *comp. noun* (1) in ➡cricket, the taking of three batsmen by three successive balls from the same bowler; (2) in soccer, the scoring of three goals by the same player in one game

hauden doon *phr. verb, Sc.* (1) to load down or burden; (2) to oppress

haulier *noun* a hauler or trucker

hauriant *noun* an heraldic representation of a fish standing upon its tail

have *verb, sl.* to swindle or cheat

have (someone's) guts for garters *idiom* to take extreme retribution
Normally used as a threat.

have a go *idiom. phr. verb* (1) to attack; (2) to attempt

have a monkey on one's back

have a monkey on one's back *idiom. phr. verb* to be a drug addict

have an early night *phr. verb, coll.* to go to bed early

have a slate loose *idiom. phr. verb* to be somewhat mentally unstable

have a word *verb* to discuss

have got to *phr. verb, coll.* to have to

have it {away » off} *idiom. phr. verb, taboo* to copulate

have it taped *idiom. phr. verb* to have everything well under control

have on *verb, sl.* to trick or delude

haver *verb* to hesitate

Havering *pr. name* a ➡Greater London borough
Its current population, which is also included within the ➡London urban area total, is 225,000 (1991 Census).

have up *verb, sl.* to bring to justice

have you got? *inter.* do you have?

Hawaii *noun, rh. sl.* £50
Derivation: fifty pounds > fifty > five-oh > Hawaii Five-0 > Hawaii. From the 1970s TV show *Hawaii Five-0*.

hawker *noun* someone who ➡hawks

H-block *pr. name* that section of the ➡Maze Prison in ➡Northern Ireland set aside for ➡IRA prisoners

HBM *pr. name, abbr.* {His » Her} ➡Britannic➡Majesty

HC *pr. name, abbr.* the ➡House of Commons

HCF *pr. name, abbr.* Honorary Chaplain to the Forces

headbanger *noun, derog., sl.* (1) an enthusiastic follower of heavy rock music who shakes {his »her} head violently in time to the music; (2) a blatantly crazy person; (3) an extremist politician
Derived from the Scots➡hiedbanger; (1) was most common in the 1970s. *SEE ALSO:* ➡idiot dancing; (3) whether of a right- or left-wing viewpoint.

head {boy » girl} *comp. noun, out.* a {schoolboy » schoolgirl} either elected by {his » her} fellow-students or appointed by the school principal to be the leading {male » female} student of the school
SEE ALSO: ➡school captain

{headmaster » headmistress} *noun* a {male » female} principal of a secondary school

headwards *spell.* headward

the Health and Safety Executive *pr. name* a government agency responsible for enforcing health and safety legislation

health centre *comp. noun* a medical center, where doctors and other health practitioners have their offices and can share ancillary services

the Health Service Commissioner *pr. name* an official responsible for investigating complaints about the ➡National Health Service

health visitor *comp. noun* a medical worker who visits families at home, especially those where someone young, old or sick is living
Usually employed by the local council.

heaps *noun, coll.* much or plenty

the Heart of Midlothian *pr. name, hist.* a prison once located in ➡Parliament Square, Edinburgh
Also known as the ➡Old Tolbooth, it was demolished in 1817 but made famous by Sir Walter Scott's novel of the same name, which was published just one year later. It is also the full name of Edinburgh's principal soccer team.

hearty *noun, coll.* a sporty or athletic sort of university undergraduate

Heath Robinson *idiom* Rube Goldberg
Well, not exactly of course, but both were illustrators and cartoonists serving the same purpose in their respective countries, which is to have their names become bywords for bizarre, complex, comical and impossible contraptions. By the way, Heath Robinson was around before Rube Goldberg.

Heathrow *pr. name* London's principal airport, located about 15 miles west of central London
Operated by ➡BAA plc. Heathrow is the busiest international airport in the world.

the Heavies *pr. name* the Dragoon Guards
A unit of the British Army. They acquired this name from their propensity to recruiting men of larger build and height than other regiments.

heavy *noun, Sc.* a variety of strong, dark draft beer served in Scottish pubs

Hebridean *pr. name* a native, citizen or inhabitant of the ➡Hebrides

the Hebrides *pr. name* the ➡Inner Hebrides and the ➡Outer Hebrides islands off the western coast of Scotland, taken together

heck *noun, Sc.* a slatted framework or rack
Used to hold fodder in a stable or to form a sort of elementary bridge so that people or cattle can cross a stream.

hecker *noun, Sc.* a glutton

hectolitre *spell.* hectoliter

hectometre *spell.* hectometer

hedgehopper *noun, sl.* a trainee pilot
From their reputed tendency to fly low.

hee-haw *idiom, sl., Sc.* nothing whatsoever, zilch

heeliegoleerie *adv., Sc.* (1) upside down; (2) in a state of disorder or confusion

heidbanger *noun, derog., Sc., sl.* (1) a violently insane person; (2) a very stupid person
SEE ALSO: ➡headbanger.

heid bummer *comp. noun, coll., Sc.* an ironic or sarcastic name for anyone in a position of authority

heidcase *noun, derog., Sc., sl.* an insane person

heid-the-baw *comp. noun, Sc., sl.* an affectionate nickname for someone considered none too smart

hellish *exclam., coll.* very

Help the Aged *pr. name* a charity founded in 1961 to give aid and comfort to older people, especially those suffering from poverty or isolation

helter-skelter *comp. noun, coll.* (1) a slide spiraling down around a tower, typically at a amusement park; (2) a condition of confused and disorganized hurry

hemidemisemiquaver *noun, pref.* a sixty-fourth note in music

Hemitage Castle *pr. name, hist.* a dramatically imposingly 13th C. tower house in the Scottish ➡Borders some 45 miles to the south of Edinburgh

The fortress of Lord Bothwell, third husband of ➡Mary Queen of Scots. It had fallen into ruins by the 18th C. but has now been partially restored.

hen *noun, Sc.* a casual term of affection for a woman

hen-hertit *adj., Sc.* chicken-hearted, scared

Henley Royal Regatta *pr. name* an annual international rowing regatta held every June upon the Thames River between London and Oxford

hen run *comp. noun* a chicken coop

Henry Beauclerk *pr. name, hist.* ➡Henry I's nickname

Henry Curtmantle *pr. name, hist.* ➡Henry II's nickname

Henry I *pr. name, hist.* King of England

The third surviving son of ➡William the Conqueror, who rode to Winchester and seized the throne—so beating his elder brother Robert, Duke of Normandy, to the prize—upon learning of the death in a hunting accident (which he may have arranged) of his oldest brother, ➡William Rufus.

The following year Robert's attempted invasion of England failed. However, a few years later Henry successfully returned the compliment by invading and conquering Normandy and eventually placing brother Robert in prison, where he was to stay for the rest of his days.

William styled himself *Dei Gratis Rex Anglorum* = "By the grace of God, King of Engand," and reigned for 35 years from 1100 until 1135. He became Duke of Normandy in 1106. A member of the ➡Royal House of ➡Normandy, he was nicknamed ➡Henry Beauclerk.

Henry II *pr. name, hist.* King of England

The grandson of ➡Henry I, he invaded England from his dukedom of Normandy in 1153 in order to take the throne back from the usurper ➡Stephen. Stephen soon made a treaty recognizing Henry as his heir and then conveniently died the following year.

During his reign Henry is best remembered for ordering the murder in his cathedral, of St Thomas â Becket, Archbishop of ➡Canterbury, and also for being the first English king to extend his rule into Ireland.

He styled himself *Rex Angliae, Dux Normaniae et Aquitaniae et Comes Andigaviae* = "King of England, Duke of Normandy and Aquitane and Count of Anjou" and reigned for over 34 years from 1154 until 1189, when he was stabbed to death by an insane monk. Founder of the ➡Royal House of ➡Anjou, he was nicknamed ➡Henry Curtmantle.

Henry III *pr. name, hist.* King of England

Inheriting a disorganized and chaotic kingdom at the age of nine, he ended a very long reign best remembered for his poor judgment and expensive tastes.

Henry, who founded the ➡Royal House of ➡Plantagenet, styled himself *Rex Angliae et Dominus Hiberniae et Dux Aquitaniae* = "King of England and France and Lord of Ireland and Duke of Aquitane" and reigned for 56 years from 1216 until 1272.

Henry IV *pr. name, hist.* King of England

He styled himself *Dei Gratia Rex Angliae et Franciae et Dominus Hiberniae* = "By the Grace of God King of England and France and Lord of Ireland" and reigned for more than 13 years from 1399 until 1413.

The son of ➡John of Gaunt, he invaded England after his cousin ➡Richard II seized his possessions in Lancaster and finally took the throne from Richard after winning the Battle of Conway. Henry founded the ➡Royal House of ➡Lancaster, and was the first king to accept the principle that taxes could only be imposed upon the people if they were raised under the authority of the ➡House of Commons.

Henry V *pr. name, hist.* King of England

Son of Henry IV and member of the ➡Royal House of ➡Lancaster, he styled himself *Dei Gratia Rex Angliae et Regens Franciae et Dominus Hiberniae* = "By the Grace of God King of England and Regent of France and Lord of Ireland" for the 17 years of his reign, which lasted from 1413 until 1422. He spent most of his time expanding his territory in France, with ➡Agincourt in 1415 being his best-remembered victory.

Henry VI *pr. name, hist.* King of England

A member of the Royal House of ➡Lancaster, he styled himself *Dei Gratia Rex Angliae et Franciae et Dominus Hiberniae* = "By the Grace of God King of England and France and Lord of Ireland" and although he inherited the thrones of both England and France at the age of one year when his father Henry V died in 1422, he first assumed royal power in 1442. His reign was hardly a great success.

In France the ➡Hundred Years' War went against him and eventually most of that land was lost to his crown. Although he retained power for 20 years, his incompetent rule back in England was partly responsible for the outbreak of the ➡Wars of the Roses, and was behind his being deposed in 1461. Although he briefly reigned again for six months in 1470, and 1471 he was deposed once again, this time for good, to be murdered in the ➡Tower of London a month or two later.

Henry VII *pr. name, hist.* King of England

Henry's claim to the throne was slender but still the best of any supporter of the House of ➡Lancaster, so that when he defeated and killed ➡Richard III at the Battle of ➡Bosworth Field in 1485, he was immediately crowned king.

The following year he married the daughter of the former Yorkshire king, ➡Edward IV, and thus ended the ➡Wars of the Roses by uniting the rival houses.

He styled himself, *Dei Gratia Rex Angliae et Franciae et Dominus Hiberniae* = "By the Grace of God King of England and France and Lord of Ireland" and reigned for 23 years between 1485 and 1509. He was the founder of the ➡Royal House of ➡Tudor.

Henry VIII

Henry VIII *pr. name, hist.* King of England

He styled himself, "Henry the eighth, by the Grace of God, King of England, France and Ireland, ➡Defender of the Faith and of the ➡Church of England, and also of Ireland, on earth the Supreme Head"—the first monarch of England to be formally styled in English— and reigned from 1509 until 1547. He was also the first monarch to be styled with a post nominal number (that is, the "VIII" of "Henry VIII") during his own lifetime.

A member of the ➡Royal House of ➡Tudor, he is perhaps best known for his six wives. It was Henry's dispute with the Pope over the status of his marriage with the first of these ladies, ➡Catherine of Aragon, that led to his break with Rome and the formation of the ➡Church of England with the monarch as its temporal head, given legal form in the ➡Act of Supremacy of 1534.

Hepplewhite *noun, hist.* a furniture style with a distinctive heart-shaped motif

Named for its 18th C. originator, George Hepplewhite.

the **Heptarchy** *pr. name, hist.* the seven ➡Anglo-Saxon kingdoms of 7th and 8th C. England

herald *noun* (1) an officer of the ➡Herald's College ranking above ➡pursuivant but below ➡King of Arms in rank; (2) a official who makes formal state proclamations

In the English Herald's College there are six heralds, called Somerset, Richmond, Lancaster, Windsor, Chester and York. In the Scottish Herald's College there are three, called Albany, Marchmont and Rothesay.

heraldry *noun* the devising and granting of insignia and the tracing and recording of genealogies

Originally the business of a herald, but now more exactly the knowledge and art of constructing armorial bearings, formerly known as "armory."

the **Heralds' College** *pr. name* the ➡College of Arms

herd *noun* a herder or herdsman

Hereford *pr. name* a city in ➡Hereford and Worcester

Originally a 7th C. Anglo-Saxon settlement, the crypt of its 12th C. cathedral contains the *Mappa Mundi*, a circular map of the world as it was thought to be in 1290 with, as was then the practice, Jerusalem at its center.

Incorporated as a city in 1189 and boasting an older ➡Nelson's Column than London, the current population of Hereford is 50,000 (1988 estimate).

Hereford & Worcester *pr. name* a county in central England, adjacent to the ➡Welsh border

The county seat is ➡Worcester. It was formed out of ➡Herefordshire and ➡Worcestershire in 1974, and the current population is 680,000 (1991 Census).

Herefordshire *pr. name, hist.* a former English county, now part of ➡Hereford and Worcester

her indoors *idiom, sl.* a wife or girlfriend

heriot *noun, arch.* a payment or tribute made in the form of a live animal, a duty performed or the return of borrowed equipment to a feudal lord upon a tenant's death

Heritage Coast *pr. name* sections of the coastline considered especially beautiful and worth protecting

They are managed by the ➡Countryside Commission and often are also located within ➡national parks.

her Ladyship *comp. noun* a form of respectful reference to a ➡Lady in the third person

hersel *noun, Sc.* (1) the mistress of a house; (2) a female boss or woman of great importance

SEE ALSO: ➡herself, ➡himself, ➡hissel.

herself *noun, Ir.* (1) the mistress of a house; (2) a female boss or woman of great importance

SEE ALSO: ➡hersel, ➡himself, ➡hissel.

Hertford *pr. name, hist.* a town some 20 miles to the north of London

The administrative center of ➡Hertfordshire, the current population is 24,000 (1991 estimate).

Hertford College *pr. name* a college of ➡Oxford University founded in 1874

Hertfordshire *pr. name* a county in southern England, immediately to the north of London

The county seat is ➡Hertford and the current county population is 950,000 (1991 Census).

Herts. *pr. name, abbr.* Hertfordshire

hertsome *adj., Sc.* (1) cheering; (2) hearty; (3) encouraging

Heveningham Hall *pr. name, hist.* an 18th Palladian house 25 miles northeast from ➡Ipswich in Suffolk

Hever Castle *pr. name, hist.* a 13th C. castle about 10 miles northwest of Tunbridge Wells in ➡Kent

It was here that ➡Henry VIII courted ➡Anne Boleyn. The castle was purchased by William Waldorf Astor in 1903, who restored it from a condition of considerable dilapidation.

hey presto *exclam.* a conjurer's phrase meaning, "here is an impressive trick"

Heythrop College *pr. name* one of the colleges of London University

HG [A] *noun, abbr.* Her Grace

[B] *pr. name, abbr.* the ➡Home Guard

HGV *noun, abbr.* a ➡heavy goods vehicle

Any sort of large truck or other commercial vehicle

HGV licence *comp. noun, abbr.* the license that is required to drive a large truck, etc.

HH *pr. name, abbr.* {His » Her} Highness

Hibernia *pr. name, Lat.* the Latin name for ➡Ireland

Hibernian *pr. name* a native or inhabitant of Ireland

Hibernicism *pr. name* an ➡Irishism

hide *noun* (1) leather; (2) a blind; (3) formerly, enough land to support a family

(2) in the sense of a camouflaged shelter or place of concealment from which animal may be observed or shot at. (3) was usually between 60 and 120 acres, depending on the quality of land in question.

hide your eyes *imper., coll.* don't look

hiding to nothing *idiom, coll.* a situation that can only lead to failure

hielan *adj., Sc.* (1) ➡highland; (2) primitive; (3) stupid

a {Hieland » Hielan} coo

{Hieland » Hielan} {coo » kye} *pr. name, Sc.* ➡Highland {cow » cattle}

{Hielandman » Hielanman} *pr. name, Sc.* a male ➡Highlander

the **{Hielands » Hielans}** *pr. name, Sc.* the ➡Highlands

the **High** *noun, abbr., coll.* a ➡High Street, but particularly that of ➡Oxford

High Church *pr. name* a style of worship practiced by certain members within the ➡Church of England
It stresses ritual, tradition and Catholic elements.
See also: ➡Low Church.

High Commissioner *pr. name* an ambassador from one ➡Commonwealth country to another

High Court *pr. name, abbr.* ➡High Court of Justice

the **High Court of Justice** *pr. name* a division of the ➡Supreme Court of Judicature dealing with civil law in England and Wales
The High Court is itself divided into three Divisions, ➡Chancery, ➡Family, and ➡{Queen's » King's} Bench; each specializes in certain areas of law.

the **High Court of Justiciary** *pr. name, Sc.* the supreme criminal court in Scotland
This is the court of last appeal; there is no further appeal to the ➡House of Lords in criminal cases as in England and Wales. The judges of this court are the same as those of the ➡Court of Session.

higher *noun, abbr. Sc.* a ➡Higher Level examination

Higher Level examination *comp. noun, Sc.* the higher school leaving examination in Scotland
That is, university entrance level.

Higher National Certificate *pr. name* a certificate of vocational education equivalent to a bachelor degree
Awarded after a minimum of two years full-time or three years part-time study.

Higher National Diploma *pr. name* a certificate of vocational education equivalent to an academic qualification that is higher than high school but lower than bachelor degree level
Awarded after a minimum of two years part-time study.

high-flyer *spell.* high-flier

high heid yin *idiom, coll., Sc.* an ironic or sarcastic name for anyone in a position of authority

high jump *comp. noun, sl.* (1) an execution, particularly a hanging; (2) any severe punishment; (3) job dismissal, the sack

highland *adj.* of the Scottish ➡Highlands

Highland *pr. name* the largest Scottish region
By far the largest but far from the most populous one; the current population is 205,000 (1991 Census).

Highland and Islands Enterprise *pr. name, Sc.* a group of local agencies that work together to encourage and assist business and other ventures for the purpose of progressing the development of the Scottish ➡Highlands and Islands

highland bail *comp. noun, arch., Sc.* the practice of removing oneself from the company of an officer of the law by the expedient of knocking the said officer flat and then running away

Highland cattle *pr. name* a breed of hardy, long-haired cattle native to the Scottish ➡Highlands

the **Highland Clearances** *pr. name, hist.* the forcible mass eviction of ➡Highland ➡crofters between 1785 and 1854

It was carried out, often with great brutality, by their landlords—often also their ➡clan chiefs—who had discovered that they could make more revenue from the land by sheep farming than was possible from the ➡crofters. By the 1820s the crofters had resorted to violence and eventually, far too late for most, in 1886 Parliament gave them security of tenure. However by that time most had emigrated — to Glasgow, to Canada, to the United States, to Australia. As a result of all this, the Scottish Highlands are to this day underpopulated, undertreed and oversheeped.

One of the most surprising and least-known facts of this whole sorry episode was that Harriet Beecher Stowe, author of *Uncle Tom's Cabin*, who visited Britain at the height of her fame in the 1850s, wrote in her so-inaptly named *Sunny Memoirs*, an elaborately tendentious defence of the Clearances and those who had carried them out.

highland dress

highland dress *comp. noun* ➡kilt, ➡sporran, etc.
The traditional dress of the male ➡highlander.

highlander *noun* a native of the Scottish Highlands

the **Highland Fling** *pr. name, Sc.* a lively solo dance, traditionally for men only
Originally a dance in celebration of victory, it is now most often performed by girls and women in competitions at ➡highland gatherings.

highland games *comp. noun* what English people who don't know any better call a ➡highland gathering

highland gathering *comp. noun, Sc.* a Scottish outdoor sporting meet and festival, held annually
Comprising traditional Scottish highland sporting and other events, such as ➡tossing the caber, throwing the hammer, the ➡sword dance, the ➡Highland Fling, etc.

the **Highland Line** *pr. name* an approximately straight line across Scotland defining the boundary between the Scottish ➡Lowlands and ➡Highlands
It proceeds from Dumbarton, west of ➡Glasgow on the west coast, to Stonehaven, south of ➡Aberdeen on the east coast.

the **Highlands** *pr. name* the mountainous wilderness that is the northern half of Scotland

the **Highlands and Islands** *pr. name* that region of Scotland consisting of the ➡Highlands, the ➡Inner and ➡Outer Hebrides, and ➡Orkney and ➡Shetland

high old time *idiom, coll.* a very enjoyable experience

high-rise block *comp. noun* a skyscraper

high school *comp. noun* an English ➡grammar school
But in Scotland a secondary school, as in America.

High Sheriff *comp. noun* (1) the senior legal officer responsible to the ➡Crown for the administration of justice in an English or Welsh ➡county; (2) an honorary official elected annually
(1) has a special responsibility to ensure the safety of ➡High Court judges when on their territory.

High Speed Train *comp. noun* the original name for the ➡InterCity 125 train

High Street *comp. noun* the main street of a town
The most common name for this in England, rather than "Main Street." However in Scotland, "Main Street" is traditional, although "High Street" is now more common.

High Table *comp. noun* (1) a table raised upon a platform where the leading persons at a public ceremony sit; (2) a table where the fellows of a college of ➡Oxford or ➡Cambridge Universities sit

high tea *comp. noun* a main cooked meal served in late afternoon at which tea, bread, etc., are also served
Most common in northern England and in Scotland.

high treason *comp. noun* (1) the murder or attempted murder of the ➡sovereign or any member of the ➡Royal Family; (2) an act of adultery with the wife of the king or of his heir

the **Highway Code** *pr. name* a book containing advice to all road-users, but especially drivers
It was first published by the government in 1931 and regularly updated ever since. Knowledge of its contents must be proven before a driver's license can be issued.

Hilary term *pr. name* the university term that begins in January

Hillingdon *pr. name* a ➡Greater London borough
Its current population, which is also included within the ➡London urban area total, is 225,000 (1991 Census).

the **Hill of Tara** *pr. name, hist.* the seat of government of the high kings of Ireland until the 6th C.
Only a few earthworks now remain of what was once a vast complex, located some 20 miles north of ➡Dublin.

Hillsborough Castle *pr. name, hist.* an 18th C. house about 12 miles to the southwest of Belfast
Until 1972 the official residence of the Governor of ➡Northern Ireland. The 1985 ➡Anglo-Irish Agreement was signed here.

himself *noun, Ir.* (1) the master of a house; (2) a male boss or man of great importance
SEE ALSO: ➡herself.

hind [A] *noun, arch.* a farm manager
[B] *noun, derog.* an ignorant, rustic person
[C] *noun, Sc.* a married farmworker, usually a plowman

the **Hindustan Regiment** *pr. name* a nickname for the 76th Regiment of ➡Foot
A unit of the British Army. They earned this name by their distinguished service in India from 1803 to 1805.

hinnie *noun, Sc.* (1) honey; (2) a term of endearment

hint *adj., Sc.* belonging to the rear
SEE ALSO: ➡ahint.

hip bath *comp. noun* a portable bath

hipster *adj.* hanging not from the waist but the hips
Of a garment.

hipsters *noun* pants that hang from the hips

hire *verb* to rent
Applies to such things as a car, but lodgings—be they a house, hotel room, or anything else—are not hired but rented.

hireable *spell.* hirable

hire car *comp. noun* a rental car

hire purchase *comp. noun* the installment plan

hiring fair *comp. noun, arch.* a ➡mop fair

hirsel *noun, Sc.* a flock of sheep

{His » Her} Majesty's Government *pr. name* the British government

{His » Her} Majesty's Loyal Opposition *pr. name* the ➡Official Opposition

{His » Her} Majesty's Stationery Office *pr. name* a government agency, established since 1786, which is responsible for publishing all the official documents of the British Government

His Lordship *pr. name* a title used when referring in the third party to a man with the rank of ➡lord

hissel *noun, Sc.* (1) the master of a house; (2) a male boss or man of great importance

SEE ALSO: ➡hersel.

hit *adj., rh. sl.* drunk

Derivation: drunk > ➡pissed > missed > hit and miss > hit.

hit for six *phr. verb, coll.* (1) to score six runs by hitting a ➡cricket ball over the boundary without it touching the ground within the field after leaving the bat; (2) to demolish an argument; (3) to successfully subject to a sudden shock or attack

In event of (1), it is not necessary for the batters to actually run between the wickets; the runs will be awarded automatically. (2) and (3) are derived from (1).

hit wicket *verb* to go out in ➡cricket by hitting the ➡wicket with the bat

hive off *verb, coll.* to spin off, as happens when part of a company or organization becomes separate

HK *pr. name, abbr.* the ➡House of Keys

HL *pr. name, abbr.* the ➡House of Lords

HM [A] *pos. pronoun, abbr.* {His » Her} Majesty's [B] *pr. name, abbr.* {His » Her} Majesty

HM Customs and Excise *pr. name, abbr.* {His » Her} Majesty's Customs and Excise

The government agency responsible for collecting customs and excise duties and ➡value added tax, and preventing the importation of prohibited substances, such as narcotics.

HMG *pr. name, abbr.* {His » Her} Majesty's Government

In other words, the British Government.

HMI *pr. name, abbr.* {His » Her} Majesty's Inspectorate

A government department that ensured schools and teachers maintain acceptable standards of teaching in England and Wales. It was replaced by ➡OFSTED in 1992.

HM Land Registry *pr. name* an executive agency where all land sale transactions in England and Wales must be registered.

HMS *pr. name, abbr.* {His » Her} Majesty's Ship

A ship which is part of the Royal Navy's fleet.

HMS Belfast *pr. name, hist.* a World War II ➡Royal Naval battleship that has been preserved as a museum open to the public

Anchored in the ➡Thames River, close to ➡Tower Bridge.

{HMSO » HM Stationery Office} *pr. name, abbr.* {His » Her} Majesty's Stationery Office

HNC *abbr.* ➡Higher National Certificate

HND *abbr.* ➡Higher National Diploma

hoarding *noun* a billboard

hoarstone *noun, hist.* an ancient boundary stone

hob *noun* a stove's flat top surface where pans, etc., can be heated

hobson-jobson *comp. noun* the process by which unfamiliar, usually foreign, words or expressions are substituted with familiar ones which sound somewhat similar, but are unrelated in meaning

The term itself is a garbled anglification of the exclamation, "*Ya Hasan, ya Husayn!*" uttered by Islamic troops of the British Indian Army when on parade during the 19th C. Hasan and Husayn were grandsons of Muhammed. Other examples are ➡subcheese and ➡Wypers

Hobson's choice *idiom* a choice that is no choice; take it or leave it

From Thomas Hobson, a ➡Cambridge carrier in the late 16th and early 17th C., who reputedly insisted that customers could either take the horse next to the door or none at all.

hock *noun, abbr., Ger.* Rhine wine

A generic term for this. It is believed the name is an abbreviation of *Hochheimer*, wine from the small town of Hochheim noted for its high quality. It is situated upon the Main River about three miles from its confluence with the Rhine.

hockey *noun* field hockey, usually a girl's game

{hocus-pocussed » hocus-pocussing} *spell.* {hocus-pocused » hocus-pocusing}

{hocussed » hocussing} *spell.* {hocused » hocusing}

hodden grey *idiom, Sc.* (1) a simple, unaffected person; (2) a coarse, rustic garb made of undyed, homespun woolen cloth

Hodge *noun, coll.* a person who is supposed to represent the typical English farm laborer

hogg *noun, North* (1) a young sheep not yet sheared; (2) wool from (1)

hogget *noun* a yearling sheep

Hogmanay *noun, Sc.* (1) New Year's Eve, December 31; (2) a toast offered or drunk at the New Year; (3) a New Year's gift, especially of ➡Scotch

hogskin *noun* a pigskin

hoick *verb, sl.* to spit

hokey-cokey *comp. noun, hist.* a popular communal dance before and during World War II

From a popular tune of this name.

holdall *noun* a small suitcase with soft sides

hold surgery *verb* to devote time to advising or helping patients, clients or constituents

hold up *comp. noun* a delay caused by traffic congestion

holiday camp *comp. noun* a place where vacationers find accommodation, entertainment and everything else they seek all together on one site

The first British holiday camp was opened upon the coast of ➡Norfolk in 1906.

holiday-maker *comp. noun* a vacationer

holiday with pay *comp. noun* a paid vacation

holidays *noun* vacation time

Holker Hall *pr. name, hist.* a 17th C. stately home some 12 miles to the north of ➡Lancaster

The Lakelands Motor Museum is contained within its grounds.

Holkham Hall *pr. name, hist.* the largest and most intact ➡Palladian mansion in Britain

It was built some 35 miles to the north of ➡Norwich in the 18th C. In the grounds there is a facsimile of ➡Nelson's Column, almost as large and built at about the same time as the one in ➡Trafalgar Square, but in this case to commemorate the work of Coke of Norfolk, Earl of Leicester, who was an early exponent of scientific agriculture in the late 18th and early 19th Cs., and owner of Holkham.

Holland *pr. name, hist.* a major administrative division of the county of ➡Lincoln before reorganization in 1974

holm *noun* an area of flat, low-lying coastal or riverside ground, which is subject to flooding

HOLMES *pr. name, abbr.* the Home Office Large Major Enquiry System

A large computer system used by the ➡Home Office and police to investigate important crimes. Obviously, the acronym was contrived to honor the fictitious detective Sherlock Holmes.

hols *noun, abbr., coll.* holidays

the **Holy Boys** *pr. name* the 9th Regiment of ➡Foot

A unit of the British Army known by this name after their regimental badge was mistakenly thought by the Spanish during the ➡Peninsular War to represent the Virgin Mary.

holy friar *idiom, rh. sl.* a liar

Holy Ghost *idiom, rh. sl.* the mail

Derivation: mail > ➡post > ghost > Holy Ghost.

Holyhead *pr. name* (1) an alternate name for the Welsh ➡Holy Island; (2) The port on (1) where ferries arrive from and depart to Ireland

Although an island, it is linked to the mainland by both road and rail bridges over the narrow ➡Menai Strait that separates it from the rest of Wales.

Holy Island *pr. name* (1) the English one, an island also called ➡Lindisfarne, located in the North Sea about nine miles south of the Scottish border, near ➡Berwick-upon-Tweed; (2) the Welsh one, an island also called ➡Holyhead; (3) the Scottish one, an island in Lamlash Bay off the eastern shore of the Isle of ➡Arran in the Firth of ➡Clyde; (4) the Irish one, an island also called Inishcattra, in Lough Derg, County ➡Clare

The English one is called this because it was one of the first centers of Christianity in Britain, founded in the 7th C. At low tide, it is possible to walk to Lindesfarne from the mainland. Similarly, the Welsh one is linked to Anglesey by two road bridges and one rail bridge. The Irish one is called this because the remains of four 7th C. churches can be found there.

the **Holy Loch** *pr. name, hist.* a Scottish ➡sea loch west of ➡Glasgow in the Firth of ➡Clyde

Where U.S. Navy missile submarines were based for 31 years from 1961 to 1992.

the Palace of **Holyroodhouse** *pr. name, hist.* a 17th C. royal palace at the eastern end of the ➡Royal Mile in Edinburgh

The official residence of the ➡Royal Family in Scotland. It is named after the abbey of the "Holy Rood" (meaning "Christ's Cross") the ruins of which are still to be found in the grounds of the house. The abbey dates from 1128. The present house was built on the instructions of Charles II to replace an earlier one that was built by ➡James IV in 1498. Holyroodhouse is where ➡Mary Queen of Scots lived for about six years and where ➡Bonnie Prince Charlie held his court after taking Edinburgh in 1745.

home and dry *idiom* safe after taking a risk

the **Home Civil Service** *pr. name* all members of the civil service working within the ➡United Kingdom

the **Home Counties** *pr. name* the English counties that are nearest to London

Formerly ➡Kent, ➡Surrey, ➡Essex and ➡Middlesex, now thought of as Kent, Surrey, Essex, ➡Buckinghamshire, ➡Berkshire, ➡Hertfordshire and ➡Sussex. Middlesex was absorbed into ➡Greater London in 1965.

home farm *comp. noun* a farm reserved for the direct use of the owners of a much larger ➡landed estate who rent out the rest to be farmed by others

home fixture *comp. noun, coll.* a sporting event at a team's home base

the **Home Guard** *pr. name, hist.* a citizen's home defense army formed during World War II

Created at the height of the German invasion danger of 1940, they were at first called "Local Defense Volunteers" but the name was changed at the personal direction of Winston Churchill. They were finally disbanded in 1957.

home help *comp. noun* someone paid to do housework

Typically provided to an old person by a ➡local authority

homely *adj.* simple, plain, unaffected or natural

In Britain, it is usually considered flattering to be described as "homely." The word does not imply unattractiveness.

the **Home Office** *pr. name* the government department responsible for law and order, immigration, race relations and various other miscellaneous matters in England

the **Home of Lost Causes** *pr. name, coll.* a sardonic nickname for ➡Oxford University

Homerton College *pr. name* a college of ➡Cambridge University founded in 1824

Home Rule *pr. name, hist., Ir.* the name adopted by many late 19th C. Irish for the concept of Irish independence within the ➡British Empire similar to the status of Canada or Australia at that time

The Irish Home Rule movement was a major factor in British political life for about 50 years, from its early days under Butt and Parnell in the 1870s until the signing of the ➡Anglo-Irish Treaty of 1921.

Home Secretary *pr. name* the ➡cabinet minister responsible for the ➡Home Office

the **Home Service** *pr. name, hist.* a ➡BBC radio station that specialized in news, current affairs, plays, discussions and documentaries

It was given this name during World War II when it was one of two national radio stations broadcast by the BBC, one for civilians and one for the armed forces. This was the one for civilians. *SEE ALSO:* ➡Light Programme.

In 1967 it was renamed ➡Radio 4.

home straight *comp. noun* the home stretch

homework *noun* home assignment

{**homoeopath » homoeopathy**} *spell.* {homeopath » homeopathy}

homoeostasis *spell.* homeostasis

A tendency towards stability.

homoeotherm *spell.* homeotherm

A warm-blooded animal.

homologue *spell.* homolog

That which is homologous.

Honi soit que mal y pense *idiom, Fr.* the motto of the ➡Order of the Garter

It is French, meaning "Evil be to him who evil thinks," or more succinctly and colloquially, "Your suspicion shames you."

honk *verb, Sc., sl.* to vomit

honkers *adj., sl.* drunk

Honkers *pr. name, sl.* Hong Kong

A name for the place most commonly employed by military and upper-class people.

honkin *adj., Sc., sl.* (1) stinking; (2) disgusting

honking *adj., sl.* drunk

honorary *adj.* voluntary and unpaid

The title given to someone doing the work of the secretary or treasurer of a club, society, church, etc., without charge.

{**honour » honourable » honourableness**} *spell.* {honor » honorable » honorableness}

the **Honourable Artillery Company** *pr. name* an ancient regiment of the British Army

Now part of the ➡Territorial Army, this unit was founded in 1537 by ➡Henry VIII as a body of citizens trained as archers to defend London.

Honourable Friend *pr. name* an ➡MP

How MPs in the House call another of their own party.

Honourable Member *pr. name* an ➡MP

How MPs in the ➡House call another not of their own party.

{**honourably » honourer » honourless**} *spell.* {honorably » honorer » honorless}

honours list *noun* a list of people receiving new titles and awards, nominally made by the sovereign but actually selected by the government

The lists are announced twice yearly: at the New Year and upon the sovereign's official Birthday. Also, a third list is usually announced following the dissolution of a Parliament.

the **Honours of Scotland** *pr. name, Sc.* the ➡crown jewels of Scotland

Specifically, the Crown, Scepter and Sword of State, which are kept on display in ➡Edinburgh Castle. They are much more ancient than the British Crown Jewels on display in the ➡Tower of London.

hood *noun* (1) the removable or foldable fabric roof of a convertible automobile; (2) the folding waterproof top on a baby's carriage

hook *verb* (1) to hit a ➡cricket ball from the ➡off-side to the ➡on-side with an upward stroke; (2) to secure the ball with the foot and pass it back through a rugby ➡scrum to the rear on the player's own side

hooker [A] *noun* a rugby player who's job is to ➡hook the ball in a ➡scrum

[B] *noun, Ir.* a small one-masted fishing boat

hoolivan *noun, coll.* a police vehicle equipped with TV cameras and so forth in order to survey hooligans

hoop-la *comp. noun* a game where the objective is to throw a ring over a prize in order to win it

Hooray Henry *comp. noun, sl.* a rich, fashionable, loud-mouthed, conventional, dim-witted young man

hoot *noun, sl.* someone or something that is considered to be very amusing

hooter [A] *noun* (1) an automobile horn; (2) a siren or steam-powered whistle

Typically (2) is sounded for the purpose of informing employees that it is time to start or to stop work.

[B] *noun, sl.* a nose, especially a big or protruding one

hoots *exclam., Sc.* an expression of disagreement, impatience, annoyance, etc.

hoover [A] *pr. name (TM)* a vacuum cleaner

A trade name now employed as the generic term for a vacuum cleaner, no matter who made it.

[B] *verb* to clean with a vacuum cleaner

Hopetoun House *pr. name, hist.* a large 18th C. Palladian mansion 12 miles west of ➡Edinburgh

Construction began in 1699, and the house was enlarged between 1721 and 1754 by William and Robert Adam.

hop-garden *comp. noun* a tract of agricultural land set aside for the cultivation of hops

hop it *imper., sl.* go away, get lost

hop off one's twig *phr. verb, sl.* (1) to die; (2) to leave very suddenly

Hornby *pr. name (TM), arch.* a manufacturer of model railroad systems

horror comic *comp. noun* a comic book containing scenes considered to be excessively violent

163

horse

horse *phr. verb, out., rh. sl.* to defecate
Derivation: defecate > crap > cart > horse and cart > horse.

the horse *idiom, out., rh. sl.* gonorrhea
Derivation: gonorrhea > clap > cart > horse and cart > horse.

horsebox *noun* (1) a horse's stall; (2) a trailer used to transport horses

horse-coper *comp. noun* a horse dealer

horse float *comp. noun, out.* a small horse-drawn cart

the Horse Guards *pr. name, hist.* (1) the cavalry brigade of the ➡Household Troops; (2) a large military barracks on ➡Whitehall in central London
(2) was built in the 1750s adjacent to ➡Horse Guards Parade, for the use of (1).

Horse Guards Parade *pr. name* a parade ground between the ➡Horse Guards and ➡St James's Park, adjacent to ➡Horse Guards in central London
Where the annual ➡Trooping of the Colour ceremony marking the monarch's ➡Official Birthday takes place.

the Horse Marines *pr. name* the 17th Lancers
A unit of the British Army who acquired this name after two troops of the regiment served on board *HMS Hermione* in the Caribbean during 1795.

horses for courses *idiom, sl.* capabilities and requirements that are well matched together

hosepipe *noun* a hose, especially one that is used to water a garden

hosier *noun* a dealer in ➡hosiery

hosiery *noun* stockings and underclothing

hospice *noun* a nursing home for the terminally ill

hostelling *spell.* hosteling
Accommodating oneself at youth hostels while traveling

{hostelry » hostel} *noun, out.* an inn

hot bills *comp. noun, coll.* newly issued Treasury bills

hotch [A] *noun, Sc.* (1) a large, especially a fat, woman; (2) a slut; (3) a jolt, bounce, shrug or twitch
[B] *verb, Sc.* (1) to fidget or wriggle; (2) to cause to jerk or shrug; (3) to shuffle along a bench while remaining seated, to make room for another person

hotchin *adj., Sc.* infested or seething

hot cross bun *comp. noun* a spiced bun with a cross marked upon it in memory of the Crucifixion
Traditionally eaten at Easter.

hotel receptionist *comp. noun* a hotel desk clerk

hotspur *noun, out.* a rash person

hotter *verb, Sc.* to jerk or shudder

hotting *noun, sl.* joyriding in a stolen car

hough *noun* a cut of beef taken from the hock

the hounds *noun, coll.* a pack of foxhounds

Hounslow *pr. name* a ➡Greater London borough
Its current population, which is also included within the ➡London urban area total, is 195,000 (1991 Census).

house [A] *noun* a dorm for students attending a boarding school
[B] *noun, abbr., sl.* the game of ➡housey-housey
[C] *noun, Sc.* a single apartment or dwelling located within an apartment block

the House *pr. name, abbr., hist.* (1) the ➡House of Commons; (2) the ➡House of Lords; (3) ➡Christ Church, ➡Oxford; (4) the London Stock Exchange; (5) formerly, a euphemism for a ➡workhouse

house agent *comp. noun* a realtor

housebreaker *noun* one who demolishes houses

housecarl *noun, hist.* the personal bodyguard of an ➡Anglo-Saxon or Danish king

housecraft *noun* household management skill

the Household Cavalry *pr. name* two regiments, the ➡Life Guards and the ➡Blues and Royals
Among other duties, these regiments guard the sovereign and carry out ceremonial duties in London.

household gods *comp. noun, coll.* a figurative name for the essentials of domestic life

the Household Troops *pr. name* the troops traditionally responsible for protecting the monarch
Comprising the ➡Household Cavalry and ➡Brigade of Guards

houseman *noun* a physician or surgeon who works and lives in a hospital

{housemaster » housemistress} *noun* a {male » female} teacher in charge of a boarding school dorm

the House of Commons *pr. name* (1) all ➡MPs taken together; (2) the ➡Chamber within the ➡Palace of Westminster where ➡MPs sit; (3) the ➡Lower House of ➡Parliament

the House of Keys *pr. name* the legislative assembly of the ➡Isle of Man

the House of Lords [A] *pr. name* (1) all the ➡Peers of the Realm taken together; (2) the chamber within the ➡Palace of Westminster where they sit; (3) the ➡Upper House of Parliament
[B] *idiom, sl.* a euphemism for a men's rest room

the Houses of Parliament *pr. name* the building in ➡Westminster where both the ➡House of Commons and the ➡House of Lords are situated
More properly known as the ➡Palace of Westminster, the present ➡Victorian Gothic structure stands on the site of the original Palace of Westminster, which was built by ➡Edward the Confessor in the 11th C., but was almost completely destroyed by fire in 1834. The present structure was completed in 1867. The ➡Chamber of the ➡House of Commons was

destroyed by a German bomb in 1941, but was completely rebuilt very shortly after World War II ended.

house surgeon *comp. noun* a surgeon who works and lives in a hospital while on duty

housetrain *verb* to housebreak

housey-housey *comp. noun, sl.* a version of bingo played by the military

housing benefit *comp. noun* a payment made by the government to a person with low income so that they are able to afford their rent

The actual amount paid depends upon the precise income and precise rent involved in each individual case.

housing estate *comp. noun* a housing development

housing scheme *comp. noun, Sc.* a public-housing project

{**hovelled** » **hovelling**} *spell.* {hoveled » hoveling}

Hovercraft *pr. name (TM)* a ground-effect vehicle, which travels about above a water or land surface suspended on a cushion of air generated by downward-directed fans

hoverport *noun* a terminal for ➠Hovercraft

hovertrain *noun* a ground-effect train that travels above a specially-constructed concrete track

Hovis *pr. name (TM), Lat.* a trade name for a variety of brown bread From the Latin *hominis vis* = "strength of man"

the **Howard League for Penal Reform** *pr. name* an organization founded in 1866 that is dedicated to reforming and improving the conditions of prisoners

howe *noun, Sc.* (1) a hollow or depression in the ground; (2) a mood of depression

howe backit *adj., Sc.* round-shouldered, hollow-backed

howf *noun, Sc.* (1) a popular meeting place such as a ➠pub; (2) a unroofed space enclosed on all sides; (3) a cemetery

howk *verb, Sc.* (1) to dig or excavate; (2) to investigate or root around; (3) to expose or unearth; (4) to hollow out; (5) to mine or quarry

howzat? *inter.* how is that?

A request to a ➠cricket umpire from the fielding side to rule that the current batsman is out.

HP *noun, abbr.* ➠hire purchase

HP Sauce *pr. name (TM)* the leading British brand of ➠brown sauce

Named after the House of Commons, which is pictured on the label, it is a blend containing vinegar, oriental fruit and spices. It has been on sale since the early years of the 20th C.

HRH *pr. name, abbr.* {His » Her} ➠Royal Highness

HSE *pr. name, abbr.* ➠Health and Safety Executive

HST *pr. name, arch.* a ➠High Speed Train

Now more often called the ➠InterCity 125.

HTV *pr. name (TM), abbr.* ➠Harlech Television

huddle *verb* to throw together in a disorganized heap

SEE ALSO: ➠guddle.

the **Hudson's Bay Company** *pr. name, hist.* a company chartered by ➠Charles II in 1670 to trade in what is now Canada

The company is still in business, making it the oldest chartered company that still is. The Hudson's Bay Company established the colony of British Columbia on the northwestern Pacific coast of North America, which became part of Canada in 1871. It is now headquartered in Winnipeg, Manitoba, and trades in northern Canada.

the Houses of Parliament

D. MCK

165

Hughes Hall *pr. name* a hall of ➠Cambridge University founded in 1886

hulk *verb, out.* to move in a slow and awkward manner

Hull *pr. name, abbr.* ➠Kingston-upon-Hull

hullo *spell.* hello

hum [A] *noun, coll.* a bad smell

[B] *verb, coll.* to emit a bad smell

humanity *noun, arch., Sc.* the study at a university of the classics in general and Latin in particular

the **Humber Bridge** *pr. name* a suspension bridge over the estuary of the ➠Humber in ➠Humberside
Its span is 4,626 ft., 366 ft more than the Verrazano Narrows Bridge, New York City, NY. It was completed in 1978, and was the longest suspension bridge in the world at that time.

Humberside *pr. name* a county on the eastern coast of England, lying between ➠Lincolnshire and ➠North Yorkshire
It was formed out of parts of ➠Lincolnshire and ➠Yorkshire in 1974. The county seat is Beverley and the current population is 835,000 (1991 Census).

humbug *noun* a kind of large, hard-boiled sugar candy
Very often peppermint flavored.

hummel *adj., Sc.* (1) naturally hornless (of cattle or deer); (2) without a sail or mast (of a boat)

{**humour » humourful » humourless**} *spell.* {humor » humorful » humorless}

{**humourlessness » humoursome**} *spell.* {humorlessness » humorsome}

hump *verb, coll.* to lift up or to carry upon the back
SEE ALSO: ➠humph.

the **hump** *noun, sl.* a fit of depression or bad temper

humpback bridge *comp. noun* a hump bridge

hundred *pr. name, hist.* an ancient subdivision in certain English counties
Now of no administrative or political significance, with the sole and rather special exception of the ➠Chiltern Hundreds.

hundreds and thousands *idiom* tiny colored candies sometimes sprinkled over food, such as cakes, in order to decorate them

hundredweight *noun* an imperial or long hundredweight, which is actually 112 lbs.

the **Hundred Years War** *pr. name, hist.* it was fought between England and France from 1337 to 1453, which is a total of a 114 years, in fact
An intermittent struggle over the question of which king should rule large territories that amounted to well over half of what is now modern France.
The trouble started in 1328 when the French King Charles IV died without leaving a male heir and in the ensuing chaos his cousin, who became Philip VI, opportunistically grabbed large chunks of southwestern France that belonged to ➠Edward III of England in 1337.
There were numerous victories and defeats on both sides, including such famous English victories as ➠Crécy and ➠Agincourt and the magnificent campaign inspired by Joan of Arc. However, the war might be said to have run out of steam after a few final engagements in 1453, with England retaining only the ➠Channel Islands and the port of ➠Calais out of their formerly vast French domains. But nonetheless, English and then later British monarchs continued to call themselves kings of France until 1801.

hunner *noun, Sc.* hundred

the **Hunterian Museum** *pr. name, hist.* the museum of the ➠Royal College of Surgeons in London
The foundation of this museum are the 13,000 anatomical specimens collected by John Hunter, a Scottish surgeon who left his collection to the Royal College when he died in 1793. The collection suffered serious bomb damage during World War II.
John Hunter's brother, William, also founded a museum, the ➠Hunterian Museum and Art Gallery, in Glasgow.

the **Hunterian Museum and Art Gallery** *pr. name, hist.* the museum of ➠Glasgow University
The oldest museum in Scotland, it began as the collection of William Hunter, an anatomist who bequeathed it to the university in 1783. It contains an notable collection of coins and many fine paintings.
His brother John also founded a museum, the ➠Hunterian Museum, in London.

hunting *comp. noun* the business of chasing and killing animals without weapons, but with packs of dogs
In Britain, hunting with guns is not called that, but ➠shooting. Fox-hunting, which entails hounds following a scent with horse-riders dressed in ➠hunting pink following, is actually a rather recent innovation.

hunting box *comp. noun, arch.* a hunting cabin
A small dwelling, where hunters can find accommodation when away overnight in a remote location.

Huntingdon *pr. name, hist.* a town in ➠Cambridgeshire, birthplace of Oliver ➠Cromwell
The current population is 20,000 (1991 estimate).

Huntingon and Peterborough *pr. name, hist.* a former English ➠County, now part of ➠Cambridgeshire

hunting pink *comp. noun* the red jacket that is traditionally worn by foxhunters

Huntley *noun, rh. sl.* fate
Derivation: fate > karma > palmer > Huntley and Palmer > Huntley. (Huntley and Palmer make crackers and cookies.)

hunt saboteur *comp. noun* an animal rights activist who attempts to sabotage and in general prevent, hunting, particularly fox-hunts

hunt the gowk! *exclam., Sc.* April fool!

the **hurdies** *noun, Sc.* the rump of a human or animal

hurdle *noun, arch.* a sled-like frame formerly used to drag traitors to the gallows

hurl *verb, Sc.* to travel in or upon a wheeled vehicle

hurlie *noun, Sc.* a handcart

hurlie bed *comp. noun, Sc.* a wheeled bed

hurling *pr. name, Ir.* a variety or close relative of the game of field hockey, which is sometimes called shinny in the United States

Hurling is Ireland's national sport. *SEE ALSO:* ➡shinty

the **Hurlingham Club** *pr. name* a very fashionable sporting club in west London

Originally established for polo players only, it now also caters to many other sporting activities, including tennis, squash and croquet.

the **Hurlingham Polo Association** *pr. name* the governing body of polo in Britain

the ***Hurricane*** *pr. name, hist.* one of the two fighter aircraft that helped the ➡RAF win the ➡Battle of Britain in 1940

167

I

IBA *pr. name, abbr., hist.* the Independent Broadcasting Authority

The agency that succeeded the ➡ITA in responsibility for the licensing and supervising of all British TV and radio except those provided by the ➡BBC. It has, in turn, itself now been replaced by the ➡ITC and the ➡Radio Authority.

ICA *pr. name, abbr.* the Institute of Contemporary Arts

ice [A] *noun, abbr.* ice cream

[B] *verb* to frost, as in baking

ICE *pr. name, abbr.* the Institution of Civil Engineers

ice cream *idiom, rh. sl.* a man

Derivation: man > geezer > freezer > ice cream freezer > ice cream.

ice creamer *comp. noun, derog., sl.* an Italian

ice lolly *comp. noun* a Popsicle

Ich Dien *idiom, Ger.* the motto of the Prince of Wales

It is German, meaning, "I serve." This has been the motto of the Prince of Wales since the time of the ➡Black Prince in the 14th C. It is thought that he borrowed the motto from John, King of Bohemia, who died at the Battle of ➡Crécy in 1346.

I.{Che. CHem.}»E. *pr. name, abbr.* The Institute of Chemical Engineers

ICI *pr. name, abbr.* Imperial Chemical Industries plc

A large chemical corporation formed in 1926 by the merging of four smaller companies.

icing bag *comp. noun* a baker's pastry tube

icing nozzle *comp. noun* a baker's decorating tip

icing sugar *comp. noun* confectioners' or powdered sugar, used in baking

Ickworth House *pr. name, hist.* an early 19th C. stately home at ➡Bury St Edmonds

Its central feature is a most impressive oval rotunda.

identification parade *comp. noun* a police line up

Identikit *pr. name* a reconstructed sketch of a person sought by police, based on the evidence of witnesses

idiot dancing *idiom, derog., out., sl.* solo dancing by an enthusiastic follower of rock music

Most common in the late 1960s and early 1970s and called this because so many observers found the practice simultaneously absurd and comical. *SEE ALSO:* ➡headbanger.

IDSM *noun, abbr., arch.* the former Indian Distinguished Service Medal

IEE *pr. name, abbr.* Institution of Electrical Engineers

IFS *pr. name, abbr.* the Institute of Fiscal Studies

if the cap fits *idiom* if the shoe fits

I.Gas E. *pr. name, abbr.* the Institution of Gas Engineers

IL *pr. name, abbr.* the Institute of Linguists

ILEA *pr. name, abbr., hist.* the former Inner London Education Authority

ilk *noun, Sc.* a family, clan, quality or group

SEE ALSO: ➡ of that ilk.

ilka *adj., Sc.* each or every

Ilkley *pr. name, hist.* a town in ➡West Yorkshire

Best known for the song about the moor to the south of it, *On Ilkley Moor Baht'at* = "On Ilkley Moor Without a Hat," the informal anthem of ➡Yorkshire. The current population is 25,000 (1991 estimate).

ill *adj., Sc.* (1) evil, wicked or immoral; (2) profane or bad; (3) unwholesome; (4) harsh or cruel

(1) refers to people, (2) refers to language or behavior.

ill-favoured *spell.* ill-favored

illuminations *noun* an extensive system of outdoor decorations using colored lights

As seen at resort centers and other entertainment centers

ILR *pr. name, abbr.* Independent Local Radio

imaginary invalid *idiom, coll.* a hypochondriac

I.Mar.E. *pr. name, abbr.* Institution of Marine Engineers

I.Mech.E. *pr. name, abbr.* the Institution of Mechanical Engineers

I.Min.E. *pr. name, abbr.* Institution of Mining Engineers

IMM *pr. name, abbr.* Institute of Mining and Metallurgy

immersion heater *comp. noun* electric water heater

the Immortal Memory *pr. name, Sc.* a toast to the memory of Robert Burns, which is the central feature of a ➡Burns Supper

the Immortals *pr. name* the 76th Regiment of ➡Foot

A unit of the British Army, it earned this name during the Mahratta War of 1803 when almost every man was wounded.

imperial

imperial *adj., arch.* concerning or characteristic of the British Empire

Imperial Airways *pr. name (TM), hist.* the principal British airline between the World Wars

Formed in 1924 by the merging of four smaller airlines, it was aided and encouraged by the government to set up an air transport network intended to help bind together the ➡British Empire, especially the links between London, India and Australia, but also between London and South Africa. In 1939 the company was bought out by the government together with another, smaller airline called ➡British Airways, and the two were merged together into the state-run ➡BOAC.

the Imperial College of Science and Technology *pr. name* a school of ➡London University

Founded in 1907 on land bought with funds left over from the ➡Great Exhibition, the college was created by merging the Royal School of Mines, the Royal College of Science, and the City and Guilds College into one institution.

Imperial College is now one of Britain's leading institutes of advanced scientific education and research.

imperial gallon *comp. noun* 1.2 U.S. gallons; 4.546 liters

the Imperial Institute *pr. name, hist.* a former name for the ➡Commonwealth Institute

imperialist *noun, arch.* one who advocated retention, strengthening, or expansion of the ➡British Empire

imperial pint *comp. noun* 1.2 U.S. pints; 0.568 liters

Imperial Preference *pr. name, hist.* a system of trade preference intended to encourage trade between the various parts of the ➡British Empire

It was first agreed upon at the Imperial Economic Conference held in Ottawa, Canada in 1932, and after World War II it was renamed ➡Commonwealth Preference. However, it became outdated by the GATT agreement of 1947 and Britain's entry into the ➡European Community in 1973. It was finally abolished in 1977.

the Imperial System *pr. name* a statute system of non-metric weights and measures

It was employed or formerly employed in the ➡United Kingdom and throughout the ➡British Empire and later, ➡British Commonwealth. Imperial units of weight and capacity are similar to but not always identical to those of the United States. However, Imperial units of length, area and volume are identical to those of the United States.

imperial ton *comp. noun* 1.12 U.S. tons; 2,240 pounds

the Imperial War Museum *pr. name* Britain's leading military museum, which concentrates on the history of this century's two world wars

First established in 1917 in the ➡Crystal Palace for the purpose of exhibiting the history of World War I while it was still being fought, it moved to its present location in the south London building formerly occupied by ➡Bedlam Hospital, in 1936. The museum also administers ➡HMS Belfast, ➡Duxford Airfield in Cambridgeshire and the ➡Cabinet War Rooms in ➡Whitehall.

{**imperilled** » **imperilling**} *spell.* {imperiled » imperiling}

impolder *verb, Du.* to reclaim land from the sea

Literally, "to make a polder," from the Dutch *inpolderen* = "to reclaim land from the sea".

imposition *noun* schoolwork given as a punishment

impression *noun* a somewhat pretentious name for a print run or the printing of a publication

impressment *noun, hist.* the involuntary recruitment of men into the army or more usually the navy by force

The practice originated in the 13th C. and continued to be used to recruit crews for ➡Royal Navy ships until the 1830s. Originally, individual captains sent ➡press gangs ashore at seaports to recruit in this way for their own ship, but eventually the business was organized centrally and carried out by the Impress Service.

Impressment activities were not confined to the land, and it was considered quite normal and proper to impress sailors from merchant ships at sea. Not all of these merchant ships or sailors were British. It was the impressment of American sailors from American ships during the ➡Napoleonic Wars that provided President Madison with the pretext he sought to declare war on Britain in 1812 in order to attempt the American annexation of Canada while Britain was, he mistakenly thought, fully employed dealing with Napoleon.

It is symptomatic of the relative strengths of Britain and America in these days, that despite the central importance of defeating Napoleon to Britain, the United States effectively lost that war, although without being seriously humiliated by the victor, who was more interested in getting back to dealing with their real enemy, Napoleon.

impropriate *verb* (1) to put church income or property into non-church hands; (2) to attach church income to an organization or individual as if it were property

improver *noun* a person working for little or no money in order to learn a skill or trade

IMRO *pr. name, abbr.* the Investment Management Regulatory Organization

An organization set up under the 1986 Financial Services Act for the purpose of enforcing codes of conduct within the investment management business

I'm so *idiom, rh. sl.* whiskey

Derivation: whiskey > friskey > I'm so frisky > I'm so.

I.Mun.E. *pr. name, abbr.* the Institution of Municipal Engineers

in *prep.* (1) alight; (2) on; (3) batting

(1) of a fire; (2) might refer to being situated on a street, for example; (3) refers to this activity during a game of ➡cricket

in and out *idiom, rh. sl.* the nose

Derivation: nose > snout > out > in and out.

inby *adj., Sc.* (1) indoors; (2) further inside; (3) from outdoors to indoors; (4) inland

in care *idiom* residing in an orphanage or similar institution, usually one operated by a ➡local authority

Of a child, usually by order of a court.

in Carey Street *idiom, coll.* bankrupt

Carey Street in London was where the court that adjudicated bankruptcy cases was formerly located.

incept *verb, arch.* to take a master's or doctor's degree

inch *noun, Sc.* a small island

Now found only in place names.

income support *comp. noun* a payment made from government funds to those not in full-time employment, or with income below a certain level

in credit *idiom* having money in an account, typically one held with a bank

indent *noun* (1) an official requisition made in writing; (2) an order for goods from abroad

the **Independent Broadcasting Commission** *pr. name* the agency charged with supervising all radio and TV programming, both terrestrial and satellite, originating in the UK except those of the BBC

independent school *comp. noun* a private school

Either a ➡public school in England, a private school in Scotland, or a ➡preparatory school.

Independent Television Commission *pr. name* the government agency responsible for licensing and regulating all British TV services, except those supplied by the ➡BBC

the **Independent Television Authority** *pr. name, hist.* a former agency that was responsible for licensing and supervising all British TV transmissions, except these from the ➡BBC

Replaced by the ➡IBA.

Independent Television *pr. name (TM)* a national TV network operated by a federation of commercial TV companies located throughout the country

Independent Television News *pr. name (TM)* a news-gathering and broadcasting organization jointly owned by ➡Channel 4 and the commercial TV companies that are part of the ➡ITV network

➡ITN and its subsidiary ➡WTN (Worldwide Television News) also supply many of the international news reports transmitted by CNN.

index-link *verb* to adjust or index to the cost of living

Indian corn *comp. noun, arch., hist.* corn

Indian ink *comp. noun, hist.* (1) India ink; (2) formerly, a dark pigment imported from China that was used as the base of the earliest versions of (1)

the **Indian Empire** *pr. name, hist.* what India was called when it was a British possession

the **Indian Mutiny** *pr. name, hist.* a rebellion against British rule in India during the 19th C.

It began in 1857 when a new cartridge was issued to use with the Enfield rifles that native troops were armed with. The cartridge was supplied in greased paper, which had to be bitten off before it could be used. Hindu ➡sepoys were persuaded that the fat was from cows, a sacred animals to them, while Muslin sepoys were persuaded that it came from pigs, in their view an unclean animal.

This led to the sepoys killing their British officers and the fall of a number of cities, including Delhi, to mutinous troops. British rule was regained and order fully restored the following year after a considerable struggle.

At the time of the mutiny, British India—including the Indian Army—was still ruled by the ➡East India Company rather than the British Government directly. Following these events, the government in London took direct control of India for the first time.

indian take-away *comp. noun* a carry-out restaurant selling Indian food

indiarubber *noun* an eraser

indicator *noun* a vehicle turn {indicator » signal}

in {dock » the dock} *idiom, sl.* (1) in hospital; (2) undergoing repairs; (3) on trial in a court of law

(1) refers to people; (2) refers to machines.

indraught *spell.* indraft

indubitable *adj.* too obvious to doubt or question

Indulf *pr. name, hist.* King of ➡Alba

He was the son of ➡Constantine II and reigned for eight years from 954 until killed by the Vikings in 962.

industrial action *comp. noun* a job action or strike

In other words, industrial *in*action.

industrial council *comp. noun* a council consisting of representatives of employers and employees in a particular industry

It may meet locally or nationally.

industrial dispute *comp. noun* a labor dispute that may lead to ➡industrial action

industrial estate *comp. noun* an area zoned and prepared for factories and other industrial ventures

inertia selling *comp. noun* the unsolicited sending of goods and products to people in the hope that they will pay for them anyway

The more blatant forms of this practice are now illegal.

infant *noun* (1) a school student under seven years of age; (2) in law, any person under 18 years of age

infant school *comp. noun* a kindergarten

infield *noun* (1) the area of the field adjacent to the ➡cricket ➡wicket; (2) a fielding player's position anywhere in (1)

infill [A] *verb* (1) to fill up a hole or cavity; (2) to locate a new building in a ➡gap site

[B] *noun* material used to [A](1) with

infirmary *noun* a location within a school or other residential institution set aside for tending the sick

inflexion *spell.* inflection

in for a penny, in for a pound *idiom, coll.* (1) once started, there's no way out; (2) all or nothing

in for the long jump *idiom, sl.* (1) due to be hanged; (2) in deep trouble

in future *idiom, coll.* in the future
The American word and meaning is usual in Scotland.

inglenook fireplace

inglenook *noun, hist.* a space within a very large fireplace where people sat to keep warm
It usually contained a bench.

inglenook fireplace *comp. noun, hist.* a large fireplace incorporating ➡inglenooks

Inglis *pr. name, hist., Sc.* the earliest name for the language spoken by the Angles, the Germanic tribe who settled the Scottish lowlands
The sole name of the language until 1494, when it was first called ➡Scottis by Adam Loutful. *SEE ALSO:* ➡Lallans.

ingrowing toenail *comp. noun* an ingrown toenail

in hall *adv. phr.* within a college or university
Especially the refectory or dining room.

in hand *adv. phr.* (1) available; (2) being attended to; (3) under control

Inheritance Tax *pr. name* a tax levied upon gifts or inheritances received
Introduced in 1986 to replace ➡Capital Transfer Tax.

in hospital *adj., coll.* hospitalized; in a hospital
The American word and meaning are usual in Scotland.

{**initialled** » **initialling**} *spell.* {initialed » initialing}

Initial Teaching Alphabet *pr. name* a phonetic alphabet designed to help children learn to read
Financed by a bequest from George Bernard Shaw, it has 44 letters rather than the 26 used in everyday English spelling.

INLA *pr. name, abbr.* Irish National Liberation Army
A republican terrorist organization in Ireland, which is a splinter group that broke away from the ➡IRA in the 1970s.

inland *adj.* not foreign, internal to the country

the **Inland Revenue** *pr. name, abbr.* the ➡Board of Inland Revenue

in marching order *idiom, coll.* organized and equipped ready to go
Originally military, now used more generally

in mufti *idiom, Arab., out., sl.* not in uniform
Army slang. *SEE ALSO:* ➡mufti.

Inner Bar *pr. name* the collective name for those members of the ➡bar who are ➡{King's » Queen's} Counsel

the **Inner Hebrides** *pr. name* the collective name of the various islands scattered along the western coast of Scotland, except for the ➡Outer Hebrides
The largest and best known are ➡Skye, Mull, Jura and Islay.

the **Inner London Education Authority** *pr. name, hist.* the residual education authority responsible for the area of the former ➡LCC until it too was abolished in 1990

Inner Temple *pr. name* the oldest ➡Inn of Court

innings *noun* (1) a ➡cricket inning; (2) a metaphor from cricket for the duration of a person's life

the **Inns of Chancery** *pr. name, hist.* the dormitories once provided for law students studying in London

the **Inns of Court** *pr. name* (1) the four law societies or colleges of English ➡barristers; (2) the buildings they are housed in
They are ➡Lincoln's Inn, ➡Inner Temple, ➡Middle Temple and ➡Gray's Inn, and have been in existence since the 14th C.; all are in central London. All English barristers are required to belong to one of these.

innumerate *adj.* mathematically ignorant or numerically challenged

in-off *idiom, coll* in billiards, pocketing one ball by bouncing it off another

in ordinary *idiom* appointed on a permanent basis
Especially to the household of the ➡monarch.

in pop *idiom, sl.* in pawn

in Queer Street *idiom, sl.* in serious trouble, especially financial

inquiry agent *comp. noun* a private detective

inscribe *verb* to register the holder of a security

inscription *noun* a registered or ➡inscribed security

in service *idiom* employed as a servant

INSET *pr. name, abbr.* in-service training for teachers

inside a week *idiom, sl.* (1) in less than a week; (2) in the midst of a week

inside job *comp. noun, sl.* a crime committed by someone working or living at the scene of the crime

inside leg *comp. noun* the inseam of a pair of pants

in so far *spell.* insofar

inspection pit *comp. noun* a garage grease pit

inspector *noun* a police officer below the rank of chief inspector but above sergeant

inspector of taxes *comp. noun* an official responsible for assessing income tax due
The approximate equivalent of an IRS agent.

{**instal** » **instalment**} *spell.* {install » installment}

instil *spell.* instill

Inst. P. *pr. name, abbr.* the Institute of Physics

instruct *verb* (1) to give information to a lawyer; (2) to authorize a lawyer to act on one's behalf

instructions *noun* a client's directions to [his » her} lawyer

instructor *noun* a teacher of a trade or vocational skill, such as plumbing or automobile repairs

insurance policy *comp. noun* an insurance contract

inswinger *noun* a ➡cricket ball bowled so that it swings in towards the ➡batsman

intake [A] *noun* a ventilation airway into a mine

[B] *noun, North* cultivated land reclaimed from a moor or other wilderness territory

InterCity *pr. name* a high-speed railroad network connecting major cities

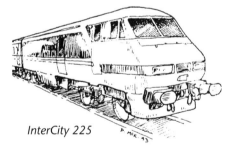

InterCity 225

InterCity 125 *pr. name* a train capable of traveling at 125 miles per hour, operated by ➡British Rail
When introduced in 1976 it was called the ➡High Speed Train.

InterCity 225 *pr. name* a train capable of traveling at 225 kilometers per hour, operated by ➡British Rail
225 kilometers per hour is approximately 140 miles per hour, so it was not really such a giant step forward from the ➡InterCity 125..

interdict *noun, Sc.* a legal injunction

interim interdict *comp. noun, Sc.* a temporary or provisional ➡interdict lasting until the matter under consideration can be settled finally in court

interior sprung mattress *comp. noun* an innerspring mattress

intermediate area *comp. noun* an ➡assisted area in less urgent need of help than a ➡development area

the **International Music Eisteddfod** *pr. name, Wal.* an annual festival of folk dancing and music
Held at Llangollen, in north Wales. Proceedings throughout are held in English.

the **Interregnum** *pr. name, hist.* the period between the termination of the reign of ➡James II of England and VII of Scotland after he fled the country, and the ascension of ➡William III and ➡Mary to the throne of ➡Great Britain
This period, associated with the ➡Glorious Revolution, lasted from December 11 1688 to February 12 1689.

intersterile *adj.* unable to interbreed

interval *noun* an intermission during the performance of a play, etc.

in the air *idiom, coll.* (1) gossip; (2) what is currently fashionable

in the cart *idiom, coll.* in a losing, embarrassing, or difficult situation or predicament

in the club *idiom, abbr., coll.* ➡in the pudding club

in the country *idiom* anywhere upon a ➡cricket field that is a long way from the ➡wickets

in the event *idiom, coll.* (1) as it has happened; (2) as it may happen
(1) refers to the past; (2) refers to the future.

in the picture *idiom, coll.* well-informed

in the pudding club *idiom, sl.* pregnant

in the shop *idiom, coll.* at the store

in the street *idiom, coll.* on the street

intitule *verb* to entitle by an ➡Act of Parliament

in trade *idiom,* owning and operating a shop or other retail business

intrusion *noun, arch., Sc.* the settlement of a ➡Church of Scotland minister upon a congregation without their consent

in two ticks *idiom, coll.* very soon

invalid chair *comp. noun* a wheelchair

invalidity benefit *comp. noun* a government payment to the long-term sick

Inveraray *pr. name, hist.* a small castle and town in the west of Scotland
The town was planned by various members of the Adam family and built as a single entity in the 18th C.

inverness

inverness *noun* a man's sleeveless overcoat with a detachable cape

Named after ➡Inverness, Scotland.

Inverness *pr. name* a northern Scottish town at the eastern apex of the ➡Moray Firth and at the northeastern head of ➡Loch Ness

It is the administrative center of the ➡Highland region and is considered to be the informal capital of the ➡Highlands. The current population is 40,000 (1991 estimate).

Inverness-shire *pr. name, hist.* a former Scottish county

It is now divided between the ➡Highland region and ➡Western Isles Island council.

inverted comma *comp. noun* a quotation mark

This may be either single or double marks, according to taste.

invigilate *verb* to supervise students who are sitting for an examination

invincible ignorance *idiom* ignorance which cannot be removed or overcome because the person who is ignorant declines to recognise that {he » she} indeed are or even may be ignorant, and thus do not see why it is necessary to correct behavious or learn anything new

in work *idiom* employed

IOM *pr. name, abbr.* (1) the Indian ➡Order of Merit; (2) the ➡Isle of Man

Iona *pr. name, hist.* a little island off the south western tip of Mull, in Scotland's ➡Inner Hebrides

A significant place because St Columbus established his monastery here when he arrived from Ireland in 563, and so is now generally considered to be the base from which Christianity spread through post-Roman Britain However, it now appears likely that St Ninian began the process some 150 years earlier from his base on the Isle of ➡Whithorn.

ionisation *spell.* ionization

IOW *pr. name, abbr.* the Isle of ➡Wight

IPCS *pr. name, abbr.* the Institution of Professional Civil Servants

IPEX *pr. name, abbr.* International Petroleum Exchange

Which is located in the ➡City of London.

IPLO *pr. name, abbr.* the Irish People's Liberation Organization

A republican terrorist organization that split away from the ➡INLA in the 1980s.

IPMS *pr. name, abbr.* the Institute of Professionals, Managers and Specialists

A labor union for high-grade civil servants.

Ireland: Isle of Ironies

There has been constant interaction between ➡Ireland and ➡Great Britain from the earliest times. St Columba's missions to introduce Christianity to Scotland sailed from Ireland and the Scots kingdom of ➡Dalriada expanded from northeast Ireland across the North Channel to what is now southwestern Scotland.

But ➡Henry II established English rule around ➡Dublin in 1171 and from that time onwards a regular succession of English and British rulers have attempted to secure their rule over this most difficult of places to govern: ➡Henry VIII, ➡Elizabeth I, ➡Cromwell and ➡William III are remembered particularly, but not with much affection, by most of the Irish people. Part of the problem was that while both England and Scotland had embraced the Reformation and were now largely Protestant states, the Irish had never wavered from Roman Catholicism (which is ironic, because clearly at some time prior to the ➡Synod of Whitby of 664, Ireland had evolved its own form of Christianity, and it was the *English* who were Roman Catholic); this helped foist a spirit of mutual distrust, possibly paranoia.

After the ➡Ulster lords rose against English rule in the last years of Elizabeth's reign and eventually fled to Europe after defeat in 1607, ➡James I of England and VI of Scotland settled Presbyterians, mostly Scots, on the land that had been abandoned in the northern province of ➡Ulster, to form a core of loyal citizens that could be relied upon if there were any more rebellions in the future.

Yet until the disestablishment of the Anglican Church of Ireland and emancipation of Roman Catholics in the early years of the 19th C., Catholics and Presbyterians were *united* against rule from London and *united* in the struggle for Irish independance. Now the ➡Church of Ireland is largely irrelevant and it is a quarrel between Catholics and Protestants—mostly Presbyterians—that is at the root of the present-day problems on this island.

Irony upon ironies: as William Ewart Gladstone, the 19th C. British prime minister said, "Every time we think we have solved the Irish question, the Irish change the question."

Ipswich *pr. name, hist.* a town that is the administrative center of ➡Suffolk, located where the Orwell river flows into the North Sea

Settled by the ➡Danes in the 8th C., it was the birthplace of ➡Henry VIII's ➡Lord Chancellor—and builder of ➡Hampden Court—Cardinal Wolsey. The current population is 121,000 (1991 estimate).

IR *pr. name, abbr.* the ➡Inland Revenue

IRA *pr. name, abbr.* the ➡Irish Republican Army

Ireland *pr. name* the second largest ➡British isle
(See box on opposite page.)

Irish *pr. name* (1) Irish ➡Gaelic; (2) English as spoken by the Irish

Irish bridge *comp. noun* a roughly made open stone drain used to convey water across a roadway
In other words, no bridge at all.

Irish bull *comp. noun* a statement that is ludicrously inconsistent or oxymoronic

the **Irish Civil War** *pr. name, hist., Ir.* a struggle, which lasted from 1922 to 1923, following the signing of the ➡Anglo-Irish Treaty in 1921
It was fought between the ➡Free Staters and the ➡Republicans over the terms of this treaty.

Irish coffee *comp. noun, Ir.* coffee that contains both cream and Irish whiskey
Invented around 1950 as a "traditional" Irish beverage offered to travelers arriving from or leaving for America by flying boat, which at that time refueled in a bay on the west coast of Ireland before continuing the journey.

Irish confetti *comp. noun, sl.* rocks, bricks, and other hard objects thrown in the course of a riot

the **Irish Free State** *pr. name, hist.* the 26 counties of Ireland that became an independent ➡Dominion of the ➡British Empire in 1921
Its name was changed to ➡Eire in 1937. In 1949 it became a republic, left the ➡Commonwealth, and changed its name again to the ➡Republic of Ireland.

Irish Gaelic *pr. name, Gae., Ir.* the Irish version of the ➡Celtic language
SEE ALSO: ➡Gaeilge.

the **Irish Guards** *pr. name* a ➡Guards Division regiment

Irishism *comp. noun* a characteristically Irish word, phrase or action

Irishman's rise *comp. noun, sl.* a reduction in pay

Irish Mile *pr. name, Ir., out.* 2,240 yards or 6,720 feet
Still in occasional use in rural districts of Ireland.

Irish moss *comp. noun* dried seaweed

the **Irish Potato Famine** *pr. name, hist.* catastrophic failures of the Irish potato crops in 1845 and 1846
Because Ireland was then an impoverished and overpopulated country whose people were almost entirely dependent upon the potato for sustenance, the effect of the then-unknown parasitic fungus, *phytophthora infestans*, was devastating. Notwithstanding quite heroic (but now almost entirely depreciated) efforts by the government in London and private charities throughout Britain to feed the people, almost one million died and over a million and a half emigrated to the United States, Canada, Australia, England and Scotland, resulting in the population of Ireland falling from 8.5 million in 1845 to about six million by 1851.

In the years after the famine, it continued to fall for some time and even now the population of the island remains around 5 million. One other major result of this disaster was the repeal of the ➡Corn Laws.

Irish Pound *pr. name* the ➡Irish Punt

Irish Punt *pr. name, Ir.* the principal monetary unit in the ➡Irish Republic

Irish Republic *pr. name, abbr.* the ➡Republic of Ireland

Irish Republican *pr. name, hist., Ir.* an opponent to the terms of the ➡Anglo-Irish Treaty of 1921 and the ➡Irish Free State which was created by it
At that time, Republicans opposed the 1921 treaty principally because of two things:-

First, the ➡Six Counties of ➡Northern Ireland around ➡Belfast remained within the ➡United Kingdom, thus preventing the establishment of an independent state consisting of the whole of ➡Ireland.

Second, although the treaty created an independent Irish state, it remained a ➡dominion within the ➡British Empire, which meant that officeholders were still required to swear an oath of allegiance to the British ➡Monarch, who remained head of state. This was then and remains now the status of other former British dominions, such as Canada or Australia.

the **Irish Republican Army** *pr. name, hist., Ir.* (1) the most significant of several illegal republican paramilitary organizations in Ireland; (2) originally, an underground force raised in 1919 to fight for Irish independence against the ➡Black and Tans and the ➡Royal Irish Constabulary
After the ➡Anglo-Irish Treaty of 1921 granted independence to 26 out of Ireland's 32 counties, the ➡IRA, at first known as the Irregulars, fought against this settlement in the ensuing Civil War. Later, it was kept in existence as a secret organization, by fanatics who would not accept the 1923 settlement that followed.

Although an illegal organization in the Irish Republic since 1931, and proscribed in Britain since 1936, it continued with a low-level campaign of bombings and shootings in ➡Northern Ireland and ➡Great Britain, which eventually trailed off to reach a low point by 1950. Thereafter violent activity slowly began to increase again until by the late 1960s, the situation in Northern Ireland started developing into the terrorist war we have become familiar with in recent years. *SEE ALSO:* ➡Provisional IRA.

the **Irish Sea** *pr. name* the one that lies between the islands of ➡Great Britain and ➡Ireland
It stretches from the ➡North Channel between Ulster and southwestern Scotland to ➡St George's Channel between south eastern Ireland and Wales.

Irish Setter *comp. noun* a bird dog similar to the ⟶English Setter but with a chestnut-colored coat

Irish stew *comp. noun* a stew consisting of mutton, onions and potatoes

Irish Terrier *pr. name* a breed of medium-sized terrier with a rough-haired reddish coat

the **Irish War of Independence** *pr. name, hist., Ir.* the formal Irish name for the ⟶Anglo-Irish War

Irish Water Spaniel *comp. noun* a large breed of spaniel with short tails and curly, heavy topcoats

Irish Wolfhound *pr. name* a breed of tall, heavy-built dogs with rough-haired coats

IRO *pr. name, abbr.* an ⟶Inland Revenue Office

iron *noun, derog., rh. sl.* a male homosexual

Derivation: homosexual > ⟶poof > iron hoof > iron.

Ironbridge *pr. name, hist.* the first bridge ever made from cast iron

It was erected in 1779 over the ⟶Severn River in ⟶Shropshire and consists of about 400 tons of cast iron, which had been slotted and dovetailed together without bolted joints. The bridge spans 100 feet and is now open to pedestrian traffic only.

A village grew up at the site of the bridge, now the location of Britain's foremost museum of industrial archeology.

the **Iron Duke** *pr. name, hist.* a nickname for the Duke of Wellington

the **Iron Lady** *pr. name, coll.* a nickname for ⟶Prime Minister Margaret Thatcher

The name was first bestowed upon her by *Red Star*, the newspaper of the Soviet Ministry of Defense, in 1976.

the **Iron Maiden** *pr. name, coll.* a nickname for ⟶Prime Minister Margaret Thatcher

This was a mistranslation by the British press of the Russian expression ⟶Iron Lady.

ironmonger *noun* a dealer in hardware

ironmonger's shop *comp. noun* a hardware store

ironmongery [A] *noun* (1) hardware; (2) anything made of metal

[B] *noun, sl.* firearms

iron-mould *spell.* iron-mold

A spot on fabric caused by ink or rust

the **Ironsides** *pr. name, hist.* the ⟶Parliamentary army during the ⟶English Civil War

Parliamentary troops became known by this name after Prince ⟶Rupert had bestowed the name ⟶Old Ironsides upon their general, Oliver ⟶Cromwell.

irregular marriage *comp. noun* a marriage performed without publication of banns or otherwise letting the public be informed of the intention to marry

Irvin suit *pr. name, hist.* a flying suit worn by ⟶RAF crews during World War II

From the name of the person who designed it.

I say *exclam., coll., out.* (1) an expression of surprise; (2) something said to draw attention or to commence a discussion

{**ischaemia** » **ischaemic**} *spell.* {ischemia » ischemic}

Localized anemia due to a restricted blood supply.

Isis *pr. name* what the ⟶Thames River is called along its upper reaches

The Roman name for the river was *Thamesis*. Somehow this evolved into "Thames" at London, but as the river flows through ⟶Oxford, it became known as "Isis." There is no connection with the ancient Egyptian goddess of this name.

Island Line *pr. name (TM)* a railroad company operating services on the ⟶Isle of Wight

It is part of ⟶British Rail.

Islington *pr. name* a ⟶Greater London borough

Its current population, which is also included within the ⟶London urban area total, is 155,000 (1991 Census).

ISO *pr. name, abbr.* the Imperial Service Order

I spy strangers *idiom* the words an ⟶MP uses to point out to the ⟶Speaker that there are people in the ⟶Chamber who are not authorized to be there

Because all who are not ⟶MPs are there on sufferance, this is a way to clear out all non-members. *SEE ALSO:* ⟶stranger.

issuant *adj.* in heraldry, rising from top to bottom

ITA *pr. name, abbr.* (1) the ⟶Independent Television Authority; (2) the ⟶Initial Teaching Alphabet

ITC *pr. name, abbr.* ⟶Independent Television Commission

Itma *pr. name, abbr., hist.* the name of a popular World War II radio show

An abbreviation of *It's That Man Again*.

ITN *pr. name, abbr.* ⟶Independent Television News

ITV *pr. name (TM), abbr.* ⟶Independent Television

It won't wash *idiom, coll.* (1) it will not work; (2) nobody will believe it

J

jab *noun, sl.* a medicinal injection

Particularly when a vaccination. *SEE ALSO:* ➧jag.

jack *noun, sl.* (1) a policeman or detective; (2) an odd-job man

Jack and Jill *idiom, rh. sl.* a hill

jack arch *comp. noun* a floor arch

A short brick or concrete arch used to support the deck of a bridge or a heavy floor.

Jack ashore *comp. noun, sl.* a drunk

From the drunken reputation that sailors, or ➧jack tars, have when on shore leave.

jacket potato *comp. noun* a potato baked in its skin

jack-in-office *comp. noun, coll.* a self-important minor civil servant

Jack-in-the-box *idiom, rh. sl.* syphilis

Derivation: syphilis > pox > Jack-in-the-box.

Jack-in-the-Green *pr. name, hist.* a youth concealed in a wooden framework as part of a ➧May Day celebration

jack it in *phr. verb, sl.* to give up or abandon an activity or attempt before it is completed

Jack Jones *idiom, rh. sl.* alone

Jack Russell *pr. name* a breed of small fox terrier with short legs

Developed especially for fox hunting from earlier breeds of terrier by John Russell, the 19th C. ➧vicar it is named after. He wanted a dog small enough to carry in his saddlebag but aggressive enough to tackle a fox, and he got one.

Jack Straw *pr. name, coll.* a worthless man

jack tar *comp. noun, coll.* a sailor

In the days of sail, sailor's hands were regularly covered in tar from the ship's tar-encrusted rigging.

Jack-the-Lad *comp. noun, sl.* (1) a popular rogue; (2) a wanted criminal

Jack the Ripper at work

Jack the Ripper [A] *pr. name, hist.* a name endowed upon himself by the undiscovered murderer of seven prostitutes in the ➧East End of London during 1888 and 1889

All his victims had their throats cut and were otherwise mutilated in a manner which implied that whoever had committed the crimes was knowledgeable about human anatomy. No one was ever arrested for these horrific crimes and although numerous theories have been put forward, there has never been a satisfactory resolution of the mystery of who was Jack the Ripper.

He "signed" his work with little notes such as:

I'm not a butcher,
Nor a Yid,
Nor yet a foreign skipper,
But I'm your own light-hearted friend,
Yours truly,
    Jack the Ripper.

SEE ALSO: the ➧Yorkshire Ripper

Jacobean

Jacobean *adj., hist.* pertaining to the reign of kings named "James" but in particular to that of ➡James I of England and VI of Scotland

This was a period in the earlier years of the 17th C. when English literature flourished as never before or since. The ➡Authorized Version of the Bible and the majority of the works of Shakespeare are to this time's particular credit, rather than the Elizabethan period that preceded it, as many assume in error.

The word comes from the Latin *Jacobus* = "James."

Jacobean architecture *comp. noun, hist.* a 17th C. style emphasizing straight lines and symmetry

Jacobean furniture *comp. noun, hist.* a 17th C. style emphasizing dark oak with rich carvings

the **Jacobites** *pr. name, hist., Lat.* a name adopted by the supporters of ➡James II of England and VII of Scotland, his successors, and the royal ➡Stuart family in general following their eviction from the British throne and flight to France in the ➡Glorious Revolution in 1688

The Jacobites' main strength lay in Scotland, especially in the ➡Highlands, and the north of England. The ➡Forty-Five rebellion marked both a high point of their strength and yet also their swan song as a serious political factor in British politics. The last male ➡Stuart claimant to the British Crown was a cardinal who styled himself Henry IX, yet was in fact paid a pension by ➡George III. He died in 1807.

The word comes from the Latin *Jacobus* = "James."

Jacob's Stone *pr. name, hist.* an alternate name for the ➡Stone of Destiny

Called this because it was believed by some that it was this stone that Jacob rested his head upon when he had his vision of a ladder ascending to Heaven (Genesis xxviii, 11—12)

Jacobus *pr. name, hist.* another name for the ➡Unite, a gold coin worth twenty ➡shillings, issued in 1604

Called this in honor of ➡James I of England and VI of Scotland, who had united the two kingdoms under one crown for the first time. It was also known as the ➡Broad.

Jaffa *pr. name* a large orange with a thick skin

It is imported from the port of Jaffa in Israel.

Jag *noun, abbr., coll.* a ➡Jaguar car

jag *noun, coll., Sc.* a ➡jab, in the sense of an inoculation or injection

Jaguar *pr. name (TM), hist.* a marque of racing and sports automobiles, perhaps best known for its E-Type vehicle of 1961

Although now tending to produce vehicles aimed at the luxury end of the market, the sporting tradition is not quite dead. In 1992 it unveiled the XJ220, reputed to be the fastest production car ever with a top speed of 220 mph and a sticker price well over $500,000. Jaguar was bought by the Ford Motor Company in 1989.

jam [A] *noun* jelly

[B] *noun, coll.* something easy or pleasant

jamboree bags *comp. noun, sl.* a woman's breasts

James I *pr. name, hist.* ➡King of Scots

He reigned for 31 years from 1406 until 1437. Captured by the English while sailing to France just before he inherited the throne, he remained prisoner there until 1424. When he did eventually return to Scotland he turned out to be an effective king, ending the prevailing chaos and founding the ➡Court of Session, which was modeled on the latest French ideas. A member of the Royal House of ➡Stewart, he was assassinated in 1437.

James I of England and VI of Scotland *pr. name, hist.* King of ➡Great Britain

James reigned in Scotland for 58 years from 1567 when his mother ➡Mary Queen of Scots was deposed and he was just one year old. In England he reigned for 22 years from the death of ➡Elizabeth in 1603 until his own death in 1625. Until 1603 he styled himself simply, in the style of all Scots monarchs, as "James, ➡King of Scots".

After 1603 he styled himself much more grandly as "James, by the Grace of God, King of England, Scotland, France and Ireland, ➡Defender of the Faith, etc., etc." It was James's great honor to be the instrument by which the two kingdoms of Great Britain finally came to be united under one crown, ending centuries of warfare.

Further, it was he who authorized the translation of the Bible which is still well known today as the ➡Authorized or ➡King James Version. And it was during his reign (not ➡Elizabeth's, as so many suppose) that Shakespeare wrote the bulk of his plays. James is one of the few British monarchs to have been an author himself, having written at least three books. Two of them set forth the case for the ➡divine right of kings—an obsession of the Stuarts—while the third, *A Counterblast to Tobacco*, adopting a remarkably modern view of the evils of this particular habit.

A member of the Scottish ➡Royal House of ➡Stewart, that spelling became anglified when he moved his court to London. Thus by a change of spelling alone, he founded the British Royal House of ➡Stuart.

James II *pr. name, hist.* ➡King of Scots

He reigned for 23 years from 1437 until killed by the explosion of a cannon while besieging the English in 1460. A member of the Royal House of ➡Stewart.

James II of England and VII of Scotland *pr. name, hist.* King of ➡Great Britain

The second son of ➡Charles I and the younger brother of ➡Charles II, he spent most of his life known as the ➡Duke of York. Indeed, when it was captured from the Dutch, the colony and city of New York were named after him, rather than the city in Yorkshire as most suppose.

When his brother died without an heir in 1685, he succeeded him peacefully enough. However, when it became obvious that he favored his Roman Catholic co-religionists, and particularly when his wife gave birth to a son who could be expected to become a Roman Catholic king in due course, the incipient anti-Papist sentiments of the population in general and ➡Parliament in particular came to the fore. Soon the hostility became too much for him and in the ➡Glorious Revolution of 1688, he was deposed, escaping with his family to France.

He styled himself, "James the second, by the Grace of God, King of England, Scotland, France and Ireland, ➡Defender of the Faith, etc., etc." A member of the ➡Royal House of ➡Stuart, he died in France in 1701.

James III *pr. name, hist.* ➡King of Scots

A member of the Royal House of ➡Stewart, he reigned for 28 years from 1460 until murdered after he lost a battle against rebels near ➡Stirling in 1488.

His Norwegian bride brought ➡Orkney and ➡Shetland to the Scottish crown as her dowry.

James III of England and VIII of Scotland *pr. name, hist.* James Francis Edward Stuart, son of ➡James II of England and VII of Scotland and now best known as the ➡Old Pretender

This was the title adopted by James and his supporters. It made the statement that in their view, he was rightfully King ➡James III of England and VIII of Scotland. He died in 1766.

James IV *pr. name, hist.* ➡King of Scots

He reigned for 25 years from 1488 until killed at the disastrous Battle of ➡Flodden Field in 1513. He was a member of the ➡Royal House of ➡Stewart.

James V *pr. name, hist.* ➡King of Scots

He reigned for 29 years from 1513 when the death of his father at ➡Flodden Field brought him to the throne at the age of one, until 1542 when he suddenly died shortly after losing the Battle of Solway Moss, near ➡Dumfries, to his uncle ➡Henry VIII of England. He was a member of the ➡Royal House of ➡Stewart.

jam *noun* (1) jelly; (2) fruit preserve

jam jar *noun* a glass container for ➡jam

jammy *adj., coll.* (1) easy; (2) lucky; (3) profitable

jam thermometer *comp. noun* a candy thermometer

jam tomorrow *idiom, sl.* a promise of future riches or pleasantness that never arrives

jane *noun, rh. sl.* a prostitute

Derivation: prostitute > whore > Jane Shore > jane. Jane Shore was a mistress of ➡Edward IV.

Jane *pr. name, hist.* an uncrowned queen of England, best known as ➡Lady Jane Grey

Jane Seymour *pr. name, hist.* the third wife of ➡Henry VIII and mother of ➡Edward VI

A ➡lady in waiting to both ➡Catherine of Aragon and ➡Anne Boleyn, Jane spurned Henry's advances unless made honorable by marriage. This may have helped ➡Anne Boleyn on her way to the execution block; certainly it was on the day following Anne's execution that Henry and Jane became betrothed. Jane died 12 days after giving birth to the future ➡Edward VI, having failed to recover from childbirth.

jankers *noun, sl.* military punishment

jar *noun, sl.* a glass of beer

Jarrow *pr. name, hist.* a town on the south bank of the ➡Tyne River in northeastern England

The site of a 7th C. monastery founded by the Venerable Bede. In modern times the name is remembered for the so-

called "Hunger March" of 200 unemployed men from this town who walked the almost 300 miles to London to petition ➡Parliament in 1936. The current population of the town is 25,000 (1991 estimate).

JCB *pr. name (TM)* a vehicle incorporating hydraulically operated excavation equipment, consisting of both a backhoe and a shovel

Ubiquitous on British construction sites, the name is derived from its manufacturers, J.C. Bamford and Co.

JCR *noun, abbr.* a ➡junior common room

Jedburgh Abbey *pr. name, hist.* a 12th C. red sandstone ➡abbey in the Scottish ➡Borders

An Augustinian abbey founded by ➡David I in 1138. Although reduced to a ruin by the English in 1544, what remains today is impressive nonetheless.

jeelie *noun, Sc.* (1) jam or jelly; (2) jello

jeelie piece *comp. noun, Sc.* bread that has been spread with ➡jeelie

jelly [A] *noun* (1) jello; (2) a savory dish consisting of meat set in gelatin

[B] *noun, abbr., sl.* gelignite

[C] *noun, out., sl.* a girlfriend

jelly-baby *comp. noun* a small gelatin-based candy formed into the shape of a baby

jelly bomb *idiom, sl.* a Molotov cocktail

jemmy *noun* a burglar's crowbar or jimmy

jerry *noun, sl.* a chamber pot

Jerry *pr. name, abbr., out., sl.* (1) a German; (2) the German nation

The term was already in use well before World War I and is not usually considered derogatory. The theory that it is derived from a resemblance in shape between the so-called "coal-scuttle" German military helmet and a chamber pot is clearly false as the term pre-dated the introduction of these helmets by about 20 years.

jersey *noun* a long-sleeved knitted sweater

Originally made with wool but now also with various synthetic materials, their design is derived from the sweaters traditionally worn by the fishermen of ➡Jersey.

Jersey *pr. name* (1) one of the principal islands of the ➡Channel Islands; (2) a breed of dairy cow with brown coloring

(2) is lighter than the ➡Guernsey cow and produces unusually rich milk; they originate from (1), of course.

the Jersey Lily *pr. name, coll., hist.* one of the mistresses of Edward ➡Prince of Wales

Emily Charlotte Langtree, who was born on the island of ➡Jersey and lived from 1852 to 1929. She was a famous beauty and also known as Lillie Langtree. Edward, the son of ➡Victoria, later became ➡Edward VII.

Jessie *noun, derog., North, Sc.* an effeminate or cowardly man

Jesus College

Jesus College *pr. name* (1) a college of ➡Cambridge University founded in 1496; (2) a college of ➡Oxford University founded in 1571

the **Jewel in the Crown** *pr. name, coll., hist.* India
When it was the most populous and magnificent possession of the ➡British Empire.

{**jewelled** » **jewellery** » **jewelling**} *spell.* {jeweled » jewelry » jeweling}

Jew's College *pr. name* an institution associated with ➡London University

jiggery-pokery *comp. noun, coll.* trickery or dishonesty

jiggin *noun, Sc., sl.* dancing

jile *noun, Sc.* a jail

jim-jams *comp. noun, sl.* pajamas

jimmy *noun, rh. sl.* one ➡Pound Sterling
Derivation: pound > ➡sovereign > Jimmy Goblin > jimmy.

Jimmy *noun, Sc., sl.* a generic form of familiar greeting especially in ➡Glasgow, applied to any person whose correct name is unknown
Applied without fear or favor to and by men and women alike.
SEE ALSO: ➡John, ➡Kiddo, ➡Moosh, ➡Tosh and ➡Wack.

jimmy riddle *idiom, rh. sl.* an act of urination
Derivation: urinate > piddle > riddle > jimmy riddle.

jings *exclam., Sc.* an expression of surprise

jitty *noun, Mid.* a narrow passageway or alley

jo *noun, Sc.* (1) joy; (2) a boyfriend

jobber *noun, arch.* a wholesale stockbroker, dealing only on the floor of the stock exchange and never directly with the public
With the reorganization of the London Stock Exchange in October 1986, their role was abolished.

Job Centre *comp. noun* a government-run office where job vacancies are displayed

jobsworth *noun, coll., derog.* an official or employee who insists on strict adherence to petty rules
From the phrase, "It's more than my job's worth ..."

Jock [A] *noun, coll.* a Scotsman
[B] *noun, Sc.* (1) a generic term for a man; (2) the Scots version of "John"

the **Jockey Club** *pr. name* the body governing British horse racing
It began in 1750 as a London gentleman's club.

Jockie *noun, Sc.* the diminutive of ➡Jock

Jock Tamson's bairns *idiom, Sc.* the human race

Joe Bloggs *comp. noun, coll.* Joe Blow

joey *noun, arch., sl.* a ➡threepenny bit

John [A] *noun, sl.* (1) a policeman; (2) a familiar form of general address especially in ➡London, applied to any man whose correct name is unknown

For (2) SEE ALSO: ➡Jimmy, ➡Kiddo, ➡Moosh, ➡Tosh and ➡Wack.
[B] *pr. name, hist.* King of England
He styled himself, *Joannes Rex Angliae et Dominus Hiberniae, Dux Normaniae et Aquitaniae et Comes Andigaviae* = "John King of England and Lord of Ireland, Duke of Normandy and Count of Anjou" and reigned for 17 years from 1199 until 1216. A member of the ➡Royal House of ➡Anjou, he was nicknamed ➡John Lackland.
The most unpopular and unsuccessful English king, who is best remembered for being obliged to sign the ➡*Magna Carta* in 1215. What is usually conveniently forgotten is that he persuaded the Pope to cancel it the following year, and so set off a civil war, which lasted until his helpful death soon after this.

John Armstrong *idiom, sl.* a sailor's name for the personification of human effort

John Baliot *pr. name, hist.* ➡King of Scots
The son of Dervorguilla, who was herself the great-great granddaughter of ➡David I, he reigned for four years from 1292 until 1296. He was highly unpopular and, being seen as a puppet of the English king, was known as ➡Toom Tabard. Eventually he abdicated when an English army was sent to remove him. Somewhat surprisingly for these times, he lived for many years after his abdication and died peacefully in 1313.

John Barleycorn *idiom, Sc.* the personification of ➡Scotch whiskey
Perhaps not invented by Robert Burns, but certainly brought into general currency by him in his poem *Tam o'Shanter*:
Inspiring bold John Barleycorn,
What dangers thou canst make us scorn!

John Bull *pr. name* the personification of the English nation and its stalwart people
His name first appeared in a pamphlet, *Law as a Bottomless Pit*, published by a certain Dr. John Arbuthnot in 1712.

John Collins *idiom* a Tom Collins
A tall drink with a gin base.

johndarm *noun, arch., Fr., sl.* a policeman
From the French *gendarme* = "policeman."

John Knox cap *comp. noun, hist., Sc.* an early form of mortarboard, once worn at Scottish universities
Named after the leading proponent of the Presbyterian reformation in 16th C. Scotland.

John Lackland *pr. name, hist.* the nickname of ➡John [B]
Because he kept losing territory, especially in Ireland.

John of Gaunt *pr. name, hist.* Duke of Lancaster, fourth son of ➡Edward III, father of ➡Henry IV, and uncle of ➡Richard II
He lived from 1340 to 1399. Because he was also the great-great grandfather of ➡Henry VII, he was the ancestor of all subsequent English monarchs. He was called "Old Lancaster" by Shakespeare, although just 59 when he died.

John o'Groats *pr. name* a point in ➡Caithness on the northern coast of Scotland that is normally but wrongly presumed to be the most northerly point on the British mainland

In fact Cape Wrath, not far away, is farther north and ➠Dunnet Head, 12 miles to the west, is further north still. *SEE ALSO:* ➠Land's End to John o'Groats.

joiner *noun* a carpenter

joinery *noun* carpentry

joinery shop *comp. noun* a carpenter's shop

joint *noun* a portion of meat suitable for roasting

Joint Committee *pr. name* a committee nominated by and containing members of both the ➠House of Commons and the ➠House of Lords

join up *phr. verb* (1) to connect together; (2) to enlist in the armed forces

{**jollies » jollity**} *noun, abbr.* jollifications
Which is to say, festivities or merrymaking.

jolly *adj.* (1) happy; (2) mildly intoxicated

joskin *noun, East* a simpleton

josser *noun, sl.* a foolish person

jotter *noun* a small notebook or notepad

jotters *noun, Sc., sl.* an employee's documents that are held by his or her employer

jouk *verb, Sc.* to duck or dodge

joy *noun, coll.* success

jubbies *noun, sl.* a woman's breasts

jubbly *noun, sl.* money

the **Jubilee Line** *pr. name* one part of London's rapid-transit subway system
It extends from Stanmore in the north to ➠Charing Cross.

judder [A] *noun* a violent or noisy vibration
Especially by a machine.
[B] *verb* to change volume drastically
Especially of a singer's voice.

judgement *spell.* judgment

judge's marshal *comp. noun* the secretary of a circuit judge

Judges' Rules *pr. name* the rules of evidence employed in English courts

judicial factor *comp. noun, Sc.* an agent appointed by the ➠Court of Session to administer the affairs or property of someone unable to do so themselves

judy *noun, sl.* a woman
Derived from "Punch and Judy".

jug *noun, sl.* a small pitcher
Typically used to serve beer or milk, it is quite unlike the kind that has a cork or rubber stopper.

juggernaut *noun, coll.* a very large or heavy truck

juggins *noun, sl.* an idiot or fool

jug handles *idiom, coll., derog.* protruding ears

jumble *noun* miscellaneous articles, mostly used or discarded, collected for a ➠jumble sale

jumble sale *comp. noun* a rummage sale

jumbo *adj., rh. sl.* drunk
Derivation: drunk > trunk > elephant's trunk > elephant > jumbo.

jumped-up *adj., coll.* presumptuous; self-important

jumper [A] *noun* a knitted pullover or sweater
[B] *noun, sl.* a ticket ➠inspector or conductor on a train or bus

jump-jet *noun, coll.* a jet aircraft that can take off vertically and land in the same manner

junction *noun* road intersection

junior *noun* a ➠barrister who is not a ➠{King's » Queen's} Counsel

junior common room *comp. noun* (1) the common living room within a college used by undergraduates; (2) the members of a university or college who may use the junior common room

junior school *comp. noun* a grade school

junior soph *comp. noun, out.* a sophomore at ➠Cambridge University
Derived from "sophist", not "sophomore" as might be supposed.

junk *noun* a lump or blob

jurat *noun* (1) a elected official in the ➠Cinque Ports similar to an ➠{alderman » alderwoman} elsewhere; (2) an honorary judge in the ➠Channel Islands

just a tick *idiom, coll.* just a moment

justice *noun* a judge of the ➠Supreme Court of Judicature

Justiciar *pr. name, hist.* the principal judicial officer of the king of England until the 13th C.

just so *adv. phr.* exactly as required or expected

just the {**job » ticket**} *idiom, sl.* just right

the Battle of **Jutland** *pr. name, hist.* a 1916 naval battle in the ➠North Sea between the British Grand Fleet and the German High Seas Fleet
The last naval battle of the traditional form where enemy fleets maneuvered close together and came into direct contact with each other. Both sides claimed victory but the truth is that the outcome was indecisive, with the British suffering more damage than the Germans, yet the Germans never again risked sailing out of port to challenge the British Grand Fleet.

K

{K&LTR » Q&LTR} *pr. name, abbr.* the ➡{King » Queen} and Lord Treasurer's Remembrancer

kaffle *verb, East* to sort out

kail *noun, Sc.* (1) a form of curly cabbage; (2) soup, especially cabbage soup

kailyaird *noun, Sc.* a vegetable garden
SEE ALSO: ➡kaleyard.

Kaiser Bill *pr. name, hist.* a nickname for Wilhelm II, German Emperor (or *Kaiser*) in World War I

kaleyard *noun, hist.* a school of 19th C. Scottish romantic fiction dealing with rural life
An anglified version of ➡kailyaird.

kali *noun, North* sherbet
The word is now mostly used by children, but for its most probable origin, see ➡kaliwater.

kalied *adj., North* drunk

kaliwater *noun, Arab., sl.* a sparkling wine, especially champagne
Military slang, from the Arabic *kali* = "alkali," which is the root of *that* English word *also*, by the way.

kangaroo closure *idiom* the enforced closure of a parliamentary committee by means of the chairperson selecting certain amendments for discussion and excluding others

Kangaroo Valley *pr. name, coll.* a nickname for ➡Earl's Court, an area in west London where itinerant Australians tend to congregate

Kate and Sidney *idiom, rh. sl.* ➡steak and kidney pie

Loch **Katrine** *pr. name, hist.* the principal and best-known ➡loch in the ➡Trossachs scenic district some 50 miles to the north of ➡Glasgow

KBE *noun, abbr.* a Knight Commander of the Order of the British Empire

{KB » QB} *noun, abbr.* ➡{King's » Queen's} Bench

KC *pr. name, abbr.* ➡King's College

KCB *pr. name, abbr.* a Knight Commander of the Order of the ➡Bath

KCIE *noun, abbr.* a Knight Commander of the Order of the Indian Empire

KCMG *noun, abbr.* a Knight Commander of the Order of St Michael and St George

{KC » QC} *noun, abbr.* ➡{King's » Queen's} Council

KCSI *noun, abbr.* a Knight Commander of the Order of the Star of India

KCVO *noun, abbr.* a Knight Commander of the Order of the Royal Victorian Order

Keble College *pr. name* a college of ➡Oxford University founded in 1868

kedgeree *noun, Hindi* a dish consisting of cooked or smoked fish, rice, eggs and cream
Originally the Hindi name for an Indian dish that contains rice, onions, pulses, eggs and cream. The name comes from the Hindi *khichri* = "rice and sesame dish."

Kedleston Hall *pr. name, hist.* a large 18th C. house close to the city of ➡Derby, built in a modified Palladian style

keek *verb, Sc.* to peep or glance

keel *noun, abbr., arch., North* (1) a ➡keel-boat; (2) a unit of weight formerly used to measure coal
(2) was equal to 21.2 ➡imperial tons (23.75 U.S. tons) the capacity of a ➡keel-boat.

keel-boat *comp. noun, arch., North* a flat-bottomed boat used to haul coal
Once common on the ➡Tyne River in northeastern England.

keelie *pr. name, Sc.* a ➡Glaswegian term for a working class male ➡Glaswegian

keen *adj.* good or competitive
For example, of a price

keen as mustard *adj. phr., coll.* enthusiastic

keen on *adj. phr., coll.* very attracted to or fond of

keeny *noun, Gae., Ir.* lament or weep

keep [A] *noun, hist.* (1) a fortress; (2) a castle's tower
[B] *verb, coll.* to reside
Particularly at ➡Cambridge University.

keeper *noun* a curator of a museum, art gallery, etc.

keeping one's end up *idiom* (1) in ➡cricket, continuing to bat despite difficulties; (2) doing what is required or expected, but no more

183

keep left *imper.* a direction to keep on left of the road

In Britain, it is the rule of the road to drive on the left, with drivers seated on the right side of their vehicles.

keep wicket *verb* to be ➠wicket keeper in ➠cricket

keep your hair on *imper., coll.* calm down, cool it

keep your head down *imper., sl.* lie low, try not to be noticed

keep your pecker up *idiom, coll.* (1) remain cheerful; (2) don't give up hope

keep yourself to yourself *idiom* remain aloof

Kelper *noun, sl.* a native of the Falkland Islands

Harvesting kelp, a form of seaweed, is a major component of the economy of these British-owned South Atlanic islands.

kelpie *noun, Sc.* a horse-shaped water spirit

Supposedly, these spirits specialize in luring unwary travelers to watery deaths.

kelt *noun, Sc.* a sea trout or salmon that is returning to the sea after spawning

Kelt *pr. name* an alternate spelling of ➠Celt

kelter *spell.* kilter

ken *verb, North, Sc.* (1) to recognize upon sight; (2) to have knowledge or understanding; (3) to be acquainted with someone or somewhere

kenable *adj., Sc.* (1) easy to recognize; (2) obvious

Kendal Green *pr. name* the green cloth traditionally worn by foresters

From Kendal in Cumbria.

Kenilworth Castle *pr. name, hist.* a ruined 12th C. castle about four miles to the south of ➠Coventry

It was once held by ➠John of Gaunt and later presented by ➠Elizabeth I to Robert Dudley, Earl of Leicester, who entertained his monarch at the castle in 1575 with almost three weeks of the most elaborate and spectacular festivities that she was ever to experience.

Reputedly the three weeks cost some £120,000, a phenomenal sum for these days, certainly equivalent to at least several tens of millions of today's dollars.

kenmark *noun, Sc.* (1) a distinguishing mark; (2) a mark or brand of ownership

(1) might be upon an animal, for example.

{**kennelled** » **kennelling**} *spell.* {kenneled » kenneling}

Kenneth II *pr. name, hist.* the first ➠King of Scots

With the acquisition of ➠Lothian from England, Kenneth II took the title ➠King of Scots and his expanded kingdom became known, for the first time, as ➠Scotland. This first Scottish King reigned for 24 years from 971 until 995.

Kenneth III *pr. name, hist.* ➠King of Scots

The son of ➠Dubh, he reigned for eight years from 997 until killed by his successor in 1005.

Kenneth MacAlpin *pr. name, hist.* ➠King of Alba

King of ➠Dalriada from 841, he conquered the ➠Pictish kingdom of ➠Caledonia in 843. The united territory, known as ➠Alba, was ruled by him until 858.

Kensington and Chelsea *pr. name* a Royal Borough within ➠Greater London

Its current population, which is also included within the ➠London urban area total, is 130,000 (1991 Census).

Kensington Gardens *pr. name* a ➠royal park in central London immediately west of ➠Hyde Park

Originally the private grounds of ➠Kensington Palace, its central feature is the ➠Round Pond.

Kensington Palace *pr. name, hist.* a royal palace within ➠Kensington Gardens

Built as the home of the Earl of Nottingham and for this reason originally known as Nottingham House, it was bought by ➠William III in 1689, and until 1760 was the main London residence of the monarch. ➠Victoria was born there in 1819.

kenspeckle *adj., Sc.* conspicuous

Kent *pr. name, hist.* (1) an ancient kingdom in southeastern England; (2) the most southeasterly county in England, situated between London and the ➠Channel Tunnel and the ferry ports to Belgium and northern France

(1) was established by about 450, but became a vassal of ➠Wessex from about 785 until 825 when it was finally absorbed by Wessex. The traditional seat of the kings of ➠Kent was ➠Canterbury. The county seat of (2) is ➠Maidstone and the current population is 1,510,000 (1991 Census).

Kentish *adj.* of ➠Kent

Kentish fire *idiom* long-lasting rounds of voluble approval or disapproval

Kentishman *noun* someone born in ➠Kent, but to the west of the ➠Medway

In contrast to a ➠Man of Kent, who is born east of it.

{**kerb** » **kerbing** » **kerb-stone**} *spell.* {curb » curbing » curbstone}

In the sense of the edge of a street or a sidewalk.

kerb-crawl *verb, coll.* to drive slowly along the side of a street while attempting to persuade pedestrians, usually women, to enter the vehicle

kerb drill *comp. noun* safety precautions taken before crossing a street

In particular, looking both ways for oncoming traffic.

kerfuffle *noun, coll.* a commotion or fuss

Kermit *adj., rh. sl.* a French person

Derivation: French > ➠frog > Kermit the Frog > Kermit.

Kerry *pr. name* a county in the ➠Irish Republic

County Kerry in the ancient province of ➠Munster.

Kerry Blue Terrier *pr. name* a small variety of terrier with a blue-gray silky coat

Kesteven *pr. name, hist.* a major administrative division of ➠Lincoln county before reorganization.

kettle [A] *noun* a tea kettle

[B] *noun, Sc.* a riverside picnic

Especially one upon the ➠Tweed River, when a salmon, newly caught in that river, is cooked and eaten on the spot.

Kew Gardens

Kew Gardens *pr. name* a popular name for the ⟶Royal Botanic Gardens at Kew in west London

There has been a royal garden at Kew since the middle of the 18th C. and scientific work began to be carried out there in the 1840s. Although now primarily a center for scientific research, it is open to the public.

key money *comp. noun, coll.* money paid by a new tenant for a key to [his » her} house or apartment

This is not a deposit, but a form of illegal extortion.

KG *noun, abbr.* a Knight of the ⟶Order of the Garter

the **Khaki Election** *pr. name, hist., sl.* the general election held in 1900

When the ⟶Conservative incumbents set out to profit from the wave of patriotic fervor that followed recent successes in the ⟶Boer War; it worked.

khazi *noun, out., sl.* a communal toilet

Typically found in military barracks and similar places. The word was first heard during the North African campaign of World War II, and it is thought it may possibly be derived from the Italian, *casa* = "house."

khyber *noun, rh. sl.* the buttocks

Derivation: buttocks > ⟶arse > Khyber Pass > khyber. The Khyber Pass is a route through the Himalayas from what is now Pakistan to Afghanistan. In the days of the British ⟶Raj it formed one of the key defensive points on the North West Frontier of Britain's ⟶Indian Empire.

kibble *noun, out.* a kind of iron bucket used in mines to hoist excavated material up to the surface

kick [A] *noun, sl.* a ⟶sixpenny bit

[B] *verb* to cause a ⟶cricket ball to rise high above the ⟶pitch(2)

kick about *verb* to kick around

kick one's heels *verb, coll.* to cool one's heels

Kidderminster *pr. name* a town in ⟶Hereford and Worcester

The current population is 55,000 (1991 estimate).

Kidderminster carpet *pr. name, hist.* a kind of ingrain carpet made at ⟶Kidderminster since 1735

the **Kiddies** *pr. name* the ⟶Scots Guards

A unit of the British Army. When ⟶James II of England and VII of Scotland stationed a large part of his army just to the west of London (close to where the modern ⟶Heathrow Airport now stands) in 1686 in case of riots in London, the ⟶Scots Guards acquired this name because they were the most junior of the three ⟶Guards regiments present.

Kiddo *noun, sl.* a familiar form of address to a man

SEE ALSO: ⟶Jimmy, ⟶John, ⟶Moosh, ⟶Tosh and ⟶Wack.

{**kidnapped » kidnapper » kidnapping**} *spell.* {kidnaped » kidnaper » kidnaping}

Kildare *pr. name* a county in the ⟶Irish Republic

County Kildare in the ancient province of ⟶Leinster.

kilderkin *noun, out.* (1) a unit of liquid measure; (2) a container for liquids with this capacity

(1) is equal to about one-half of a barrel or two ⟶firkins.

Kilkenny *pr. name* a county in the ⟶Irish Republic

County Kilkenny in the ancient province of ⟶Leinster.

Kilkenny cats *comp. noun, Ir.* combatants who fight each other to their mutual destruction

From the story of two cats in the town of ⟶Kilkenny in ⟶Ireland who are supposed to have fought each other until only their tails remained.

killick *noun, sl.* a leading seaman in the ⟶RN

From the symbol of an anchor that appears on his badge, a killick is a kind of small anchor.

kilogramme *spell.* kilogram

kilometre *spell.* kilometer

---

kilt *noun, hist., Sc.* (1) originally, a belted ⟶plaid or a ⟶philabeg; (2) today, a stylized version of (1), commonly but wrongly supposed to be the traditional dress of the male ⟶Highlander

Today the kilt is a kind of knee-length skirt made from tartan and thickly pleated at the rear, but when invented it was no more than a ⟶plaid (2) held together at the waist with a belt.

The true history of the kilt is that it was the invention of Thomas Rawlinson, a Quaker iron-master from ⟶Lancashire, who operated an iron smelting business near ⟶Inverness from 1727 until it failed in 1734. He had found the simple plaids then worn by his highland employees to be dangerous, impractical and indecent, especially on a windy day. This new dress soon became very popular and its use spread rapidly throughout northern Scotland.

Strictly speaking, the kilt is dress for adult males only; women and children may wear kilt-like garments, but these cannot considered true kilts for this reason. And of course, the wearing of the kilt by Irish bagpipe bands on, for example, St Partick's day, is spuriousness compounding spuriousness.

{**kinaesthesia » kinaesthesis » kinaesthetic**} *spell.* {kinesthesia » kinesthesis » kinesthesic} Concerning awareness of bodily movements.

Kincardineshire *pr. name, hist.* a former Scottish county, now part of the ➡Grampian region

kinema *noun, arch.* a movie theater

King Billy *pr. name, coll., hist., Sc.* a nickname for ➡William III in Ulster and Scotland

Perhaps suprisingly, this nickname for a long-dead king is still in daily use among Orangemen and others still reliving ancient religious wars and battles, especially the one upon the ➡Boyne in Ireland in 1690.

King Charles's Spaniel *pr. name, hist.* a small black and tan breed of spaniel with a rounded head

One of various small breeds favored and kept by ➡Charles II.

King Cole *pr. name* a mythical British king

The subject of a nursery rhyme.

kingcup *noun* a marsh marigold

Its formal name is *caltha palustris.*

the **Kingdom of Fife** *pr. name, hist.* a romantic or fanciful name for the region of ➡Fife in Scotland

In the 12th C., Duncan MacDuff, Earl of Fife, ruled this peninsula between the ➡Firths of ➡Forth and ➡Tay as if it were his own private kingdom. In these days, it must be supposed that most of his contemporaries ruled their lands in a similar manner, but for some reason the memory of MacDuff's rule has lingered and to this day the citizens of Fife insist, with more pride and emotion than accuracy, that theirs is the only kingdom within a kingdom within the United Kingdom.

the **Kingdom of the Isles** *pr. name, hist.* an ancient kingdom in what is now part of Scotland

At its maximum extent it consisted of the northwestern coast of the Scottish mainland plus the ➡Inner and ➡Outer Hebrides, ➡Orkney and ➡Shetland.

Originally a Viking territory under the suzerainty of the King of Norway, it reached its greatest extent during the 11th C. By the 15th C., when Christian I of Norway presented Orkney and Shetland to ➡James III as dowry for his daughter ➡Margaret, the rest of what was left of the kingdom was a semi-independent region under the rule of the MacDonalds, whose chief had the hereditary title of ➡Lord of the Isles. This condition of semi-independence lasted until they were defeated in battle by ➡James IV in 1489 and stripped of the title, which was reserved for the Scottish ➡Crown and today belongs to the eldest son of the ➡Monarch.

the **King of Arms** *pr. name* the chief herald of the English ➡College of Arms

the **King of Misrule** *pr. name, hist.* until Tudor times, the director of Christmas festivities in large houses such as manors and castles

Also known as the ➡Lord of Misrule.

the **King over the Water** *pr. name, hist.* a romantic name given by ➡Jacobites to ➡James II of England and VII of Scotland

He acquired this sobriquet after he fled to France following the ➡Glorious Revolution of 1688. In due course this name was inherited by his successor-claimants to the British Throne, being the ➡Old Pretender ("James III"), the ➡Young Pretender ("Charles III") and finally, Henry, Cardinal of York ("Henry IX").

the {**King » Queen**} *pr. name, abbr.* a shortened version of the name of the British national anthem, *God save the* {*King » Queen*}

It is perhaps unique among national anthems, as its title changes with the gender of the incumbent sovereign.

{**King » Queen**}**-Empress** *pr. name, hist.* an alternate title for the British ➡Monarch devised during the height of the ➡British Empire in the 19th C

Technically, the empire in question was the ➡Indian Empire. *SEE ALSO:* ➡{Emperor » Empress} of India.

the {**King » Queen**} **in Council** *pr. name* what the ➡Privy Council is known as when it issues ➡Orders in Council or receives petitions

{**King » Queen**} **of Scots** *pr. name, hist.* the historic title of a reigning Scottish monarch

Who was monarch not of the territory, as was an English monarch, but of the Scottish people themselves, who traditionally had to agree to accept {him » her} as their monarch before {he » she} could reign.

King's Beasts *pr. name, hist.* ten sculptures with an heraldic theme that sit upon either side of the bridge that leads into ➡Hampton Court

Five illustrate the ancestry of ➡Henry VIII and the other five the ancestry of his queen of that particular moment, who was ➡Jane Seymour. The original sculptures were destroyed some time ago and the ones now there are replicas made in 1950. *SEE ALSO:* ➡Queen's Beasts.

the **King's Champion** *pr. name, hist.* see ➡Champion of England

King's College *pr. name* a college of ➡Cambridge University founded in 1441

King's College Chapel *pr. name, hist.* this jewel in the architectural crown of ➡Cambridge is perhaps the finest example of ➡Perpendicular style architecture in the world

Construction began in 1446 upon the direction of ➡Henry VI, founder of the college of which this is the chapel. It was not completed until 1515.

King's College, London *pr. name* one of the schools of ➡London University

It was founded by two archbishops and 30 bishops as an Anglican college in 1828, in direct response to the affront to the ➡established church occasioned by the founding in London of the Nonconformist ➡University College two years earlier. In 1836 the two colleges were brought together to form the ➡University of London. King's College became linked to ➡King's College Hospital in 1839.

King's Cross *pr. name* an area just north of central London, named after a large monument to George IV erected in 1836, that was so unpopular it was demolished less than ten years later

The district is now best-known for its major railroad terminus; it is also probably the largest center of prostitution in London.

King's Cross Station

King's Cross Station *pr. name* a principal railroad terminus in central London

For trains to and from northeast England and eastern Scotland. The present structure, designed by Cubitt and opened in 1852, is considered to be an important and unusual example of 19th C. architecture.

the **King's Evil** *pr. name, hist.* the disease of scrofula, once believed to be curable by a touch from the king

The custom was imported from France before the ➡Conquest by ➡Edward the Confessor. By the time formal touching ceremonies were introduced during the reign of ➡Henry VII, sufferers were given a small gold coin It is reported that ➡Charles II touched almost 100,000 scrofula sufferers during his reign. The last monarch to perform this ceremony was ➡Anne.

King's Lynn *pr. name, hist.* a town in ➡Norfolk which is some three miles from the ➡Wash

This was an important port in the Middle Ages. Better known locally as "Lynn", the "King's" was added when it was granted a charter by ➡Henry VIII in 1537, but the idea has not really become fully accepted by its citizens yet. The current population is 35,000 (1991 estimate).

King's Medal *pr. name, abbr., hist.* in full, either one of (1) the King's Medal for Courage in the Cause of Freedom; (2) the King's Medal for Service in the Cause of Freedom

(1) was instituted in 1945 and awarded to foreigners who helped British forces in enemy-occupied territory during World War II. (2), also instituted in 1945, was awarded to deserving foreigners during World War II not qualified to receive (1).

the **{King's » Queen's} and Lord Treasurer's Remembrancer** *pr. name* the Senior Master of the ➡{King's » Queen's} Bench Division of the ➡High Court of Justice, concerned with the appointment of Sheriffs and with taxation cases

the **{King's » Queen's} Bench** *pr. name* the division of the ➡High Court of Justice dealing with commercial law and claims for damages

One of the three ➡Divisions of the ➡High Court of Justice.

the **{King's » Queen's} Bounty** *pr, name, arch.* a grant of money made by the reigning monarch to the mother of triplets

the **{King's » Queen's} Colours** *pr. name* the identifying flag or flags carried by the regiments of the British Army

the **{King's » Queen's} Council** *pr. name* a senior ➡barrister who is council to the ➡Crown

the **{King's » Queen's} English** *pr. name* correctly written and spoken British English

The expression was used by Shakespeare. *See also:* ➡received pronunciation, ➡received standard English, ➡BBC English, ➡Oxford accent and ➡Oxford English.

{King's » Queen's} evidence *comp. noun* the equivalent of state's evidence

the **{King's » Queen's} Flight** *comp. noun* an alternate name for the ➡Royal Flight

{King's » Queen's} guide *comp. noun* the highest rank of ➡girl guide

the **{King's » Queen's} highway** *comp. noun, out.* the public highway

{King's » Queen's} messenger *comp. noun* a British government diplomatic courier

the **{King's » Queen's} Peace** *pr. name* civil peace and order within the nation

the **{King's » Queen's} Proctor** *pr. name* an official with the right to intervene in divorce or probate cases where collusion or suppression of relevant facts is suspected

the **{King's » Queen's} Regulations** *pr. name* the regulations concerning order and discipline in the British armed forces

the **{King's » Queen's} Remembrancer** *pr. name, hist.* a ➡Treasury official who was responsible for collecting debts due to the ➡Crown

{King's » Queen's} scout *comp. noun* the highest rank of Boy Scout

the **{King's » Queen's} Shilling** *pr. name, hist.* the former custom of giving each army recruit a ➡shilling upon enlistment

Accepting that shilling constituted a legally binding agreement by the recruit that he had indeed joined the army.

the **{King's » Queen's} Speech** *pr. name* a speech made by the sovereign at the ➡State Opening of Parliament, setting out the administration's proposals for the coming session

Although read out by the monarch, the speech is written by the government and the monarch is merely the mouthpiece.

King's Scholar *comp. noun* one holding a scholarship granted by a foundation set up with royal money

King's School *pr. name* (1) a leading English ➡public school, located in Ely, ➡Cambridgeshire; (2) a leading English ➡public school, located in Canterbury, ➡Kent; (3) a leading English ➡public school, located in Rochester, ➡Kent

All three were founded as monastic schools: (1) in 970; (2) in 600; (3) in 604. All three were given new charters by King ➡Henry VIII following his ➡Dissolution of the Monasteries.

187

Kingston-upon-Hull *pr. name* a city in ➡Humberside on the northern bank of the ➡Humber estuary, better known by its abbreviated name of ➡Hull

Chosen as the site of a harbor by ➡Edward I in the 13th C., it was incorporated as a city in 1440. The current population, including suburbs, is 325,000 (1988 estimate).

Kingston-upon-Thames *pr. name* a ➡Royal Borough within ➡Greater London

Its current population, which is also included within the ➡London urban area total, is 130,000 (1991 Census).

Kinross-shire *pr. name, hist.* a former Scottish county, now part of the ➡Tayside region

kinsfolk *noun* kinfolk

kip [A] *noun, sl.* a bed

[B] *verb, sl.* to sleep

kip down *phr. verb, sl.* to go to sleep

kipper [A] *adj., North* energetic

[B] *noun* a dried and smoked herring, often eaten as a breakfast dish

[C] *noun, sl.* an affectionate name for a small child

kip shop *comp. noun, sl.* (1) a cheap boarding-house; (2) a brothel

Kirby Grip *pr. name (TM)* a bobby pin

kirk *noun, Sc.* a church

the **Kirk** *pr. name, Sc.* the ➡Church of Scotland

Kirke's Lambs *pr. name* the 2nd Regiment of ➡Foot

A unit of the British Army. Following their victory in the Battle of Sedgemoor, which ended the Monmouth Rebellion in the West Country in 1685, the regiment, under the command of Colonel Percy Kirke, earned a fearsome reputation for cruelty in the way they hunted out and handled the rebels. It is thought that they became known by this nickname in ironic reference to their behavior at that time, but their emblem already was a Paschal Lamb well before Sedgemoor.

kirk session *comp. noun, Sc.* the lowest court of the ➡Church of Scotland

It consists of the minister and elders of a single parish and is responsible for church government in that parish.

Kirkudbright *pr. name, hist.* a former Scottish county, now part of ➡Dumfries & Galloway region

Kirkwall *pr. name, hist.* a town that is the administrative center of the ➡Orkney Islands

Kirkwall was first settled by Vikings in the 11th C. The current population is 7,000 (1991 estimate).

kirn [A] *noun, Sc.* (1) a confused and churning mixture; (2) a distasteful muddle or jumble

[B] *verb, Sc.* to churn, stir or mix up

kissing gate *comp. noun* a gate hung within a U- or V-shaped enclosure that restricts movement in such a way that only one person can pass through at a time

kissing tackle *idiom, sl.* the mouth

kissing the gunner's daughter *idiom, hist.* corporal punishment onboard a ➡RN ship

Midshipmen due to be flogged were tied to the breech of a cannon, which was known as the "gunner's daughter". ➡Naval ratings were tied to a grating when being flogged. Punishment floggings ceased in the Royal Navy in the second half of the 19th C., although not formally made illegal until after World War II.

the **kiss of life** *idiom* mouth-to-mouth resuscitation

kiss the hand of the Sovereign *phr. verb* to kiss the back of the ➡monarch's fingers

This act signifies acceptance upon being offered an office of state by the ➡Sovereign.

kist *noun, Sc.* (1) a chest; (2) a coffin

(1) both in the sense of part of the body and a storage container.

kit *noun* (1) clothes intended to be worn during a specific activity such as sports, work, military, etc.; (2) gear in the sense of equipment, items or tools, etc.; (3) a wooden tub

kitchen roll *comp. noun* a paper towel

kitchen-sink *adj., coll.* characteristic of an extremely realistic portrayal of some of the more squalid aspects of modern life in a play or movie

kite *noun, out., sl.* an airplane

This expression began life as ➡RAF World War II slang.

Kitemark *pr. name* an official mark, resembling a kite, placed on goods approved by the ➡British Standards Institution

kit-kat portrait *comp. noun, arch.* a portrait of not quite all of the top half of the body, but showing one hand only

Derived from an early 18th C. ➡Whig society called the Kit-Kat Club. Forty-two members had their portraits painted in this style; these are now to be found in the National Portrait Gallery.

kit out *verb, sl.* to provide with all that is required for a particular purpose

Especially clothes.

kittle *verb, Sc.* (1) to please; (2) to tickle; (3) to tease or annoy; (4) to stir a fire

knacker [A] *noun* (1) a buyer of old animals such as horses; (2) a buyer of old buildings, machinery, etc.,

(1) does this for the use or sale of their carcasses. (2) does this in order to reuse or sell their component parts and materials.

[B] *verb, sl.* (1) to exhaust; (2) to kill

knackered *adj., sl.* exhausted

knacker's yard *comp. noun* a place where old animals are disposed of

knackery *noun* a ➡knacker's yard

knag *noun* (1) a dead branch of a tree; (2) a knot in wood; (3) a hat peg

knap *verb* to break up stones with sharp blows from a hammer or similar instrument

knapper [A] *noun* a stone breaker

[B] *verb* to chatter

knave *noun* a jack in a deck of cards

knees-up *noun, sl.* a lively gathering or party

knee-trembler *comp. noun, sl., taboo* an act of copulation performed while standing up

knickers [A] *noun* a woman's or girl's panties

[B] *exclam., sl.* a term of disgust or contempt

knickers in a twist *idiom, coll.* (1) angry; (2) confused; (3) excited

knifeboard *noun, out.* a wooden board that knives are cleaned upon

knight [A] *noun, hist.* (1) a junior medieval nobleman who, after a period of service as a ➠squire, was raised to this rank, which was that of a mounted officer in the service of his ➠feudal superior; (2) a medieval admirer or champion of a noble lady; (3) today, a man honored by the ➠sovereign for merit with a personal non-hereditary nobility that carries with it the title of "Sir"

Today there are various ranks of knight, the highest being baronet. The title is attached to the primary given name, not the surname, thus: "Sir John Smith" or "Sir John"; however, "Sir Smith" is always incorrect. The equivalent female honor to ➠knighthood is to be made a ➠dame, which, when capitalized, is also the title, thus "Dame Jill Smith." The wife of a knight carries the title "Lady," thus "Sir John and Lady Smith."

[B] *verb* to confer a knighthood

knighthood *noun* the condition of being a knight

knightly *adj., adv.* chivalrous

knight marshal *comp. noun* an official of the ➠Royal Household

knight of the road *comp. noun, coll., hist.* (1) a tramp or vagabond; (2) a trucker; (3) a taxi driver; (4) a ➠commercial traveller; (5) formerly, a highwayman

knight of the shire *comp. noun, coll., hist.* (1) the original name for an ➠MP representing a rural area; (2) a depreciative modern term for those ➠MPs representing English rural ➠constituencies.

In Medieval times, two knights were nominated by their peers to represent each county (or shire) in the ➠House of Commons, while towns were represented in a similar manner by ➠burgesses.

Knightsbridge *pr. name* one of the principal shopping streets in London

the **Knights of the Round Table** *pr. name, hist.* the legendary group of knights led by ➠Arthur

Called this because when they reputedly got together at ➠Camelot they all sat down around a large circular table.

knob *noun, sl.* an aristocrat

knock [A] *noun, coll.* a ➠cricket inning

[B] *verb, sl.* (1) to copulate; (2) to astonish

knock back *verb, coll.* (1) to eat or drink very quickly; (2) to disconcert or disparage

knock-down price *idiom, coll.* a low price, a bargain

knocker-up *comp. noun, arch.* a person employed to ➠knock up early workers at their homes to ensure they get to work on time

SEE ALSO: ➠chapper-up.

knock-for-knock agreement *idiom, coll.* a no-fault automobile insurance arrangement under which damage claims are paid out under the vehicle owner's policy, regardless of who might be to blame

knocking copy *idiom, sl.* comparative advertising

knocking-shop *idiom, sl., taboo* a brothel

knock off *phr. verb, sl.* (1) to steal; (2) to seduce

knock on the head *idiom. phr. verb* to stop or prevent a process or plan from proceeding

knock out *verb* to empty a container by tapping

knock up *phr. verb* (1) to be awakened from sleep by knocking on a door or window: (2) to score ➠cricket runs very rapidly

Knole *pr. name, hist.* a very large 15th C. palace some 10 miles near Sevenoaks in ➠Kent

It was built for Thomas Bourchier, ➠Archbishop of Canterbury, confiscated by ➠Henry VIII, and given away by ➠Elizabeth I to the Sackville family, who modified it substantially in the early 17th C.

know-all *comp. noun, coll.* a smart aleck

the **Knowledge** *pr. name, coll.* a highly detailed knowledge of the streets of London that must be accurate enough to pass a very thorough examination set by the ➠Metropolitan Police, before a license to drive a taxi for hire in London can be issued

knuckleduster *noun* a set of brass knuckles

Koh-i-Noor *pr. name, hist.* a large diamond now part of the ➠Crown Jewels in the ➠Tower of London

It originally weighed about 186 carats but has been cut down to about 106 carats. Its origins are lost in the mists of antiquity, but it was known to belong to the Mogul Emperor of India during the 17th C., passed to the Shah of Persia in the 18th C. and then, by way of Afghanistan, to Ranjit Singh of the Punjab. The Punjab was annexed by Britain in 1839, and in 1849 the stone was presented to Sir John Lawrence, British Commissioner in the Punjab. He forgot that he had placed it in his waistcoat pocket for six weeks, but it suffered no harm and still reached London in time to be a major feature at the ➠Great Exhibition in 1851, when it was presented to ➠Victoria. It was at this time that it was cut down to its present size.

There is a tradition that whoever possesses it will suffer bad luck. The name means "Mountain of Light" in Persian.

KP

KP *noun, abbr.* a Knight of the Order of St Patrick

KPFSM *noun, abbr.* the King's Police and Fire Service Medal for Gallantry

KPM *noun, abbr.* the King's Police Medal

{K » Q}FSM *noun, abbr.* {King's » Queen's} Fire Service Medal for Gallantry

{K » Q}GM *noun, abbr.* {King's » Queen's} Gallantry Medal

Instituted in 1974, it is awarded to civilians.

{K » Q}PM *noun, abbr.* the {King's » Queen's} Police Medal

Kronus *spell.* Cronus

According to Greek mythology, one of the Titans, the son of Uranus and father of Zeus. The Romans called him Saturn.

{KS » QS} *noun, abbr.* a {King's » Queen's} Scholar

K.St.J. *noun, abbr.* a Knight of the Order of Saint John

Kt. *noun, abbr.* a Knight

KT *noun, abbr.* a Knight of the ➡Order of the Thistle

kye *noun, Sc.* cattle; the plural of ➡coo

kyle *noun, Sc.* a narrow strait or arm of the sea

kyloe *noun* a breed of small-bodied but long-horned ➡Highland cattle

L

L *noun, abbr.* Liberal

£ *noun, abbr., Lat.* the currency symbol or sign which represents the ➡Pound Sterling

From the first letter of the Latin word *libra* = "pound"

L/Bdr. *pr. name, abbr.* a ➡lance-bombardier

L/Cpl. *pr. name, abbr.* a ➡lance-corporal

label *noun* an heraldic representation of bars that hang down from a ➡file

{**labelled » labelling**} *spell.* {labeled » labeling}

{**labour » laboured » labouredly**} *spell.* {labor » labored » laboredly}

{**labourer » labourism » labourist**} *spell.* {laborer » laborism » laborist}

labour exchange *comp. noun, arch.* a ➡job centre

Labourite *noun* an adherent of the ➡Labour Party

the **Labour Party** *pr. name* one of the two leading political parties in Britain

The Labour Party holds moderately socialist positions on many topics and is closely linked with the labor unions. Originally formed at a meeting of labor unions as the ➡Labour Representative Committee in 1900, it changed to its present name in 1906.

Labour peer *comp. noun* a member of the ➡House of Lords who supports the ➡Labour Party

the **Labour Representative Committee** *pr. name, hist.* the original name of the political grouping established in 1900, which was to became the ➡Labour Party in 1906

LAC *comp. noun, abbr.* a ➡leading aircraftsman

the **Lacedaemonians** *pr. name* a nickname for the 46th Regiment of ➡Foot

A unit of the British Army. In 1777, during the Revolutionary War, their commander reputedly made a long speech while under fire, on the theme of Spartan discipline and the Lacedaemonian military system.

laced mutton *comp. noun, arch., sl.* a prostitute

lace-up *comp. noun* a shoe fastened with a lace

lacking moral fibre *comp. noun, hist.* cowardice

The words on a charge that was frequently brought against troops who broke under the strain of life under fire in the trenches of the Western Front during World War I.

lackland *noun* one who has no land

This was the nickname of ➡John, who managed to lose almost all English land in France.

lacklustre *spell.* lackluster

lacquer *noun* a hair spray

LACW *comp. noun, abbr.* a ➡leading aircraftswoman

ladder *noun* a run in a stocking, etc.

laddish *adj., derog., sl.* of childish or immature behavior in a grown man

the **ladies'** *noun, coll.* a woman's rest room

Ladies' Day *pr. name* the second day of ➡Royal Ascot

On this day, ladies wear their most elegant fashions and, in particular, show off their most outrageous hats.

ladies' fingers *comp. noun* okra

Do not confuse with ➡lady's finger.

the **Ladies' Gallery** *pr. name* a viewing area in the ➡House of Commons reserved for women

lad o' pairts *comp. noun, out., Sc.* a talented and ambitious young man

Lady *noun* the title of a ➡knight's or ➡lord's wife

ladybird *noun* a ladybird beetle; a ladybug

Lady Bountiful *comp. noun, coll.* a benefactress who is condescending to those she helps

Originally a character in *The Beaux' Stratagem*, a play of 1707 by George Farquhar. SEE ALSO: ➡Lady Muck.

Lady Day *pr. name, hist.* the feast of the Annunciation, which is an English ➡quarter-day

Now March 25, but formerly April 6.

Lady Godiva *pr. name, hist.* the patroness of the City of ➡Coventry

In 1040 Leofric, Earl of Mercia and Lord of Coventry, imposed ruinous taxes upon his tenants, which his wife protested. The Earl said he would lift the taxes only if his wife would ride naked through the town. She did so while the entire population kept themselves indoors so as not to see her in this condition, and the Earl kept his promise. The story of Peeping Tom was added much later, in the 18th C.

Lady in Waiting

Lady in Waiting *comp. noun* a ➡Royal Household official attending upon the queen personally
SEE ALSO: ➡Lady of the Bedchamber.

Lady Jane Grey *pr. name, hist.* the name by which England's uncrowned queen ➡Jane is best known

A tragic figure, Lady Jane was a childhood prodigy in Latin and Greek dragged into public life by the machinations of her uncle the Duke of Northumberland, who married her to his son and then persuaded the dying ➡Edward VI, who was his distant cousin, to name her his successor.

Jane reigned for just 14 days in 1553 while she was aged just 15, but when the rightful heir ➡Mary Tudor was proclaimed, all support for her evaporated. She was charged with high treason, thrown into the ➡Tower of London, and executed the following year along with her husband, father and uncle. She was a member of the Royal House of ➡Tudor.

Lady Margaret Hall *pr. name* a college of ➡Oxford University, founded in 1878

Lady Mayoress *comp. noun* (1) a female Lord Mayor; (2) the wife of a ➡Lord Mayor

Lady Muck *comp. noun, coll., derog.* a self-important and pretentious woman
SEE ALSO: ➡Lady Bountiful, ➡Lord Muck.

Lady of the Bedchamber *pr. name* an official of the ➡Royal Household attending upon the personal needs of the queen
SEE ALSO: ➡Lady in Waiting.

the **Lady of the Lake** *pr. name, hist.* Vivien, who was ➡Merlin's girl friend, according to the ➡Arthurian legend

the **Lady of the Lamp** *pr. name, hist.* Florence Nightingale, founder of modern professional nursing
She was called this because of her nightly rounds through the wards at Scutari hospital during the ➡Crimea War.

lady of the town *comp. noun, coll.* a prostitute

Lady Provost *comp. noun, Sc.* (1) a female ➡Lord Provost; (2) the wife of a male ➡Lord Provost

lady's finger *comp. noun* kidney vetch
Its formal name is *anthyllis vulneraria*. It is a herbaceous plant, and should not be confused with ➡ladies' fingers.

{**laevorotary » laevorotation**} *spell.* {levorotary » levorotation}
Concerning the counter-clockwise polarization of light.

{**laevulin » laevulose**} *spell.* {levulin » levulose}

A form of fructose.

lag [A] *noun, arch., sl.* a convict
Now only used in the term ➡old lag.
[B] *verb, arch., sl.* (1) to arrest; (2) to go to prison; (3) to serve a term in prison

lager *noun, Ger., pref.* a light beer, similar to U. S. beer
From the German *Lagerbier* = "storage beer," which is beer specially brewed to make it suitable for long-term storage.

lager lout *comp. noun, coll.* a disruptive, badly behaved, yet affluent youth

laich *adj., Sc.* (1) low; (2) situated in or on the lowest part of a building, such as the basement

lair [A] *noun* a shelter or resting place for cattle
[B] *noun, Sc.* (1) a bed; (2) a muddy place; (3) a family burial plot; (4) lore, knowledge or learning

laird *noun, Sc.* a lord, ➡chief, landlord, estate owner or house owner
The Scottish equivalent of the English ➡Lord of the Manor.

the **Lake District** *pr. name* a picturesque region of mountains and lakes in ➡Cumbria
It was designated a ➡national park in 1954.

Lakeland Terrier *pr. name* a small, rough-coated terrier with a stocky appearance

the **Lake Poets** *pr. name, hist.* a group of 18th and 19th C. poets who lived in the ➡Lake District
Including Wordsworth, Coleridge, De Quincey and Southey.

lakes *adj., rh. sl.* crazy
Derivation: crazy > ➡barmy > Lakes o'Killarney > lakes

the **Lake School** *pr. name, hist.* an alternate collective term for the ➡Lake Poets

Lallans *pr. name, Sc.* (1) the Scottish ➡Lowlands; (2) the traditional ➡Scots language of the Scottish ➡Lowlands; (3) the version of modern literary Scots used by writers in the language
On (2), *SEE ALSO:* ➡Inglis.

Lambeth *pr. name* a ➡Greater London borough
It includes the districts of ➡Vauxhall, ➡Kennington and ➡Brixton; current population, which is also included within the ➡London urban area total, is 220,000 (1991 Census)

the **Lambeth Conference** *pr. name* an assembly of all bishops of the worldwide ➡Anglican church
The first was held in 1876 at the ➡Lambeth Palace under the chairmanship of the ➡Archbishop of Canterbury. The conference is usually called every ten years.

Lambeth degree *comp. noun* an honorary degree awarded by the ➡Archbishop of Canterbury

Lambeth Palace *pr. name* the principal residence of the ➡Archbishop of Canterbury
Not in ➡Canterbury as might be supposed but London, on the southern bank of the ➡Thames River, just across from the ➡Palace of Westminster. The first palace here was erected in the 12th C., but the present structure dates from the 15th C.

the **Lambeth Walk** *comp. noun, hist.* a street dance popular with ➡Cockneys during World War II
Performed with all dancers linked together in a line.

LAMDA *pr. name, abbr.* the London Academy of Music and Dramatic Art
Founded in 1861. Despite the name, LAMDA only trains theatrical professionals; there is no musical training.

Lammas Day *pr. name, Sc.* a Scottish ➡term-day or ➡quarter-day
August 28, formerly August 1

lamppost *noun* a post supporting a street lamp

Lanarkshire *pr. name, hist.* a former Scottish county, now part of ➡Strathclyde region

Lancashire *pr. name* (1) a county in northwestern England; (2) a crumbly white cheese from (1)
(1) is bordered by ➡Greater Manchester and ➡Merseyside to the south, ➡Northumberland to the east and ➡Cumbria to the north. The current population is 1,365,000 (1991 Census).

Lancashire hotpot *comp. noun* mutton stew made with potatoes and onions

Lancaster *pr. name, hist.* (1) a city which is the administrative center of ➡Lancashire; (2) a subsidiary name used for the ➡Royal House of England between 1399 and 1461
(1) was the location of a Roman military camp. Incorporated as a city in 1193, the current population is 125,000 (1988 estimate).
(2) was this because the Royal House before, during, and after, the years referred to was ➡Anjou, with Lancaster a subsidiary name lacking independent existence. Both Lancaster and ➡York derive from the two sides of the ➡Wars of the Roses, which were the parties of the Duke of Lancaster and the Duke of York—both princes of the house of ➡Anjou. The English monarchs belonged to this subsidiary house were: ➡Henry IV, ➡Henry V and ➡Henry VI.

the **Lancaster** *pr. name, hist.* the principal heavy bomber flown by ➡RAF ➡Bomber Command during the second half of World War II
It came into service with the ➡RAF in 1942. With a crew of seven and a maximum bomb load capacity of 22,000 lbs, it was the heaviest bomber used by any power in European operations.

Lancaster House *pr. name* a large house in central London used for international conferences

Lancastrian *pr. name, hist.* (1) a supporter of the ➡Lancastrian claim to the English throne at the time of the ➡Wars of the Roses; (2) today, a native, inhabitant or citizen of ➡Lancaster

lance-bombardier *comp. noun* a lance-corporal in the ➡Royal Artillery

lance-corporal *comp. noun* the lowest rank of NCO in the British Army
Lower than a corporal but higher than a private.

lance-jack *comp. noun, sl.* a ➡lance-corporal

Lancelot of the Lake *pr. name, hist.* one of the Knights of the ➡Round Table

He appears to have spent most of his time either chasing the Holy Grail or Lady Guinevere—who was already married to someone else. That caused all sorts of trouble including disruption of the ➡Round Table and the death of ➡Arthur, but nonetheless, Lancelot somehow always manages to be represented as the model of chivalry, virtue, purity and bravery.

lance-sergeant *comp. noun* a corporal acting with the temporary rank of sergeant

Lancs. *pr. name, abbr.* Lancashire

land agent *comp. noun* (1) a manager of farm land; (2) a real estate agent dealing in farm land

the **landed gentry** *comp. noun* those who are both of superior social class—or think they are—and own significant quantities of the countryside
SEE ALSO: ➡county [B]

land girl *comp. noun, hist.* a woman drafted to work on a farm during World War II
Usually recruited in cities, and so quite unused to farmwork.

landlord *noun* the keeper of a ➡pub or small hotel

the **Landmark Trust** *pr. name* a voluntary organization that saves unusual and historic buildings from demolition

the **land of broad acres** *comp. noun* a poetical metaphor for ➡Yorkshire

Land of Hope and Glory *pr. name* a poetical metaphor for Britain
The phrase is taken from Benson's words of 1902 to Elgar's *First Pomp and Circumstance March* of 1901, which was widely used on occasions of celebration and national pride at the zenith of the ➡British Empire:
Land of Hope and Glory, Mother of the Free,
How shall we extol thee, who are born of thee?
Wider still and wider shall thy bounds be set;
God, who made thee mighty, make thee mightier yet.
It is also the informal anthem of the ➡Conservative Party.

Land of my Fathers *pr.* (1) the informal Welsh national anthem; (2) a poetical name for Wales

landrail *noun* the corncrake bird
A common European rail inhabiting cornfields and grasslands, its formal name is *crex crex*.

Land Rover *pr. name (TM)* an all-terrain, four-wheel-drive vehicle that first went on sale in 1948 and is still very popular
Partially inspired by the Jeep, it now faces increasing competition from Japanese alternatives.

lands *noun, arch., Sc.* a tenement building

Land's End *pr. name* the peninsula on the western coast of ➡Cornwall which, at its tip, is the most westerly point on the British mainland

from **Land's End** to **John O'Groats** *idiom* the whole length of ➡Great Britain
Many wrongly supposed ➡Land's End and ➡John O'Groats to be the points farthest apart on the British mainland.

lang *adj., Sc.* (1) long; (2) tall

language

language *noun, abbr., coll.* a euphemism for bad language or profanity

Lansdowne Road *pr. name* the stadium in ➡Dublin where international rugby matches are held

lantern-slide *comp. noun, arch.* a transparency used in a magic lantern

lanthorn *noun, arch.* a lantern

Laois *pr. name* a county in the ➡Irish Republic
County Laois in the ancient province of ➡Leinster.

larderette *noun* a small pantry

lardy cake *comp. noun* a cake made with lard, dried fruit, bread dough, etc.
It is traditionally served at the end of harvest

lark *noun, coll.* (1) an activity; (2) a trivial escapade

lashings *noun* abundance or plenty

lass *noun, North, Sc.* a girl or young unmarried woman

lassie *noun, coll., Sc.* a diminutive, poetic or affectionate form of ➡lass

last but one *idiom* next to last

last of herrings *comp. noun, out.* a measure of quantity equal to 12 barrels

last of malt *comp. noun, out.* a measure of quantity equal to 10 quarts or 80 bushels

last of wool *comp. noun, out.* a measure of weight equal to 12 sacks or 4,368 lbs

last post *comp. noun* (1) the last mail collection of the day; (2) the last mail delivery of the day; (3) taps, being the final bugle call at night at a military camp, signaling that lights are to be put out; (4) taps, being a call similar to (3) made at military funerals and commemorations

late fee *comp. noun* extra postage charged on a letter mailed after normal collection time

lateral thinking *comp. noun* a way of tackling problems that involves using unusual, or even what at first appear to be irrational, thinking processes

{laurelled » laurelling} *spell.* {laureled » laureling}

LAUTRO *pr. name, abbr.* the Life Assurance and Unit Trust Regulatory Organization
An organization set up under the 1986 Financial Services Act to enforce codes of conduct in the life assurance and ➡unit trust business

lav *noun, abbr., sl.* a ➡lavatory

lavatory *noun* (1) a rest room; (2) a room that usually combines the features of a bathroom and a toilet

lavatory pan *comp. noun* a toilet bowl

lavatory paper *comp. noun* toilet paper

lave *noun, Sc.* the residue or remainder

laver bread *comp. noun* a Welsh dish made from laver, which is a form of seaweed
It is boiled, covered in oatmeal, fried, and then eaten.

lavvy *noun, abbr., sl.* a ➡lavatory

law centre *comp. noun* a legal advice center financed from taxes or public contributions

the Law Commission (England and Wales) *pr. name* a permanent commission set up by ➡Parliament to examine the law and make proposals for modernization and improvement

the Law Courts *pr. name, abbr.* the building housing the ➡Royal Courts of Justice
An imposing structure of 1882, situated upon the ➡Strand and designed to handle all the business of the ➡High Court in London in one place.

Law Lord *pr. name* a member of the ➡House of Lords when that body is sitting as the highest court of appeal, which consists of seven to nine ➡Lords of Appeal in Ordinary and the ➡Lord Chancellor

lawn {bowling » bowls} *comp. noun* a game played on a bowling green with asymmetrically-weighted balls of wood or hard rubber

the Lawnmarket *pr. name* a location upon Edinburgh's ➡High Street that was the former site of public executions

lawn sand *comp. noun* sand mixed with selective weed-killers and fertilizer
Intended to be scattered over a lawn.

Lawrentian *noun* pertaining to (1) T.E. Lawrence, best known as Lawrence of Arabia; (2) D.H. Lawrence, author of *Sons and Lovers*, *Lady Chatterley's Lover*, etc.

the Law Society *pr. name* the professional body that registers ➡solicitors and investigates any complaints about their conduct

lay *verb* to set a table for a meal

layabout *noun* a loafer, one who avoids working

lay about *verb* to hit out in all directions

lay-by *comp. noun* a roadside rest area

lay lord *comp. noun* any member of the House of Lords other than a ➡Law Lord

lay on *verb* (1) to arrange, provide or prepare; (2) formerly, to attack

lay on the table *phr. verb* to put legislation or other proposals on an agenda, especially that of Parliament

layshaft *noun* a countershaft

lay vicar *comp. noun* a cathedral officer who sings portions of the liturgy not reserved for the clergy

LB *noun, abbr.* in ➡cricket, a ➡leg bye

LBC *pr. name, abbr., hist.* London Broadcasting Company
Britain's first commercial radio station, an all-news station that began transmitting in 1974 and went out of business in 1994.

LBCH *pr. name, abbr.* the London Bankers' Clearing House
An organization that meets daily to balance the value of all checks drawn on each member bank against the other so that only the net difference in funds need be transferred from one bank to another. In 1992, there were 13 members.

LBW *adj., abbr.* in ➡cricket, ➡leg before wicket

LCC *pr. name, abbr., hist.* ➡London County Council

LCE *pr. name, abbr.* ➡London Commodity Exchange
Now replaced by the ➡London FOX.

LCJ *pr. name, abbr.* the ➡Lord Chief Justice

Ld *noun, abbr.* Lord

L-driver *comp. noun, coll.* a learning driver
Derived by association with ➡L-Plate.

LDS *noun, abbr.* a Licentiate in Dental Surgery
Which is to say, a fully qualified dental surgeon.

LDV *pr. name, abbr., hist.* Local Defence Volunteers
The original name of the ➡Home Guards.

LEA *noun, abbr.* a Local Education Authority
The agency that is responsible for public schooling within a district or county.

lead [A] *noun* (1) an electric cord; (2) a dog's leash
Meanings derived from the verb "to lead.."
[B] the vertical space between lines of type
These were originally formed using strips of lead.

lead (someone) a {dance » merry dance} *idiom.*
phr. verb to initiate a course of action that causes a lot of trouble and difficulty for someone else

Leadenhall Market *pr. name, hist.* London's meat and poultry market
Originally in the ➡City of London, now partly demolished.

leader *noun* a newspaper editorial

the **Leaderin** *pr. name, sl.* a nickname for former ➡Prime Minister Margaret Thatcher
Reputedly coined by one of her ministers, Norman St John Stevens, it is a pseudo-translation of the feminine version of the German word *Führer* = "Leader," which is *Führerin*.

the **Leader of the House** *pr. name* (1) an ➡MP who is the ➡Cabinet minister responsible for planning and managing the administration's parliamentary business in the ➡House of Commons; (2) in the ➡House of Lords, the chief spokesman for the government
{He » she} is also responsible for arranging the order of business of the ➡House in general, in conjunction with the other parties by way of the ➡usual channels.

the **Leader of the Opposition** *pr. name* the leader of the largest non-governing party in the ➡Commons

Usually the most probable next ➡Prime Minister in the event of a change of government.

leading {aircraftsman » aircraftswoman} *comp. noun, abbr.* the second-lowest ➡RAF rank

leading article *comp. noun* a newspaper editorial

leading counsel *comp. noun* the senior ➡barrister on a particular case

leading note *comp. noun* a leading tone

leading {rating » seaman} *comp. noun* a senior enlisted man in the ➡Royal Navy

leads *noun* (1) frames made of lead, used to hold glass panels within a window frame; (2) strips of lead used to cover a roof; (2) a lead-covered roof
(1) includes the colored panels of stained-glass windows.

lead-swinger *idiom, coll.* a goldbricker

lea farming *comp. noun* a system of crop rotation

the **League Against Cruel Sports** *pr. name* a society that campaigns against blood sports
Founded in 1924 to campaign against ➡hunting in particular.

the **League of Friends** *comp. noun* a local voluntary charitable organization, formed to raise money for schools and hospitals

leal *adj., Sc.* (1) honest; (2) loyal or faithful

leant *past tense* leaned
Of the verb "to lean".

leapt *past tense* leaped
Of the verb "to leap".

Lear *pr. name, hist.* a legendary king of ancient Britain who was the subject of William Shakespeare's play *King Lear*

learnt *past tense* learned
Of the verb "to learn".

lease of life *idiom* lease on life

leat *noun* a flume

leather *noun, derog., sl.* a middle-aged or elderly person who has acquired a lined, leathery skin by spending a great deal of time relaxing in the sun

leather-jacket *comp. noun* a crane-fly grub

leatheroid *noun* a cotton material treated chemically in order to make it resemble leather

leave it out *imper., sl.* desist

leave over *phr. verb, coll.* leave for action or consideration later

LEC *pr. name, abbr., Sc.* a Local Enterprise Company
One of a number of local agencies set up in Scotland by the government for the purpose of enhancing job training and encouraging job-creating employment. In England and Wales, similar agencies are known as ➡TECs.

lecturer

lecturer *noun* (1) one who lectures, particularly at a university or another college of higher education; (2) a university teacher approximately equivalent in grade to an assistant professor in the United States
SEE ALSO: ➡professor, ➡reader and ➡senior lecturer.

Leeds [A] *pr. name* a city in ➡West Yorkshire
A significant center of the woolen trade since the 16th C. In the 19th C. Leeds became the most important clothes manufacturing center in Britain, as it still is. It was incorporated as a city in 1626, and the current population, including suburbs, is 1,450,000 (1988 estimate).
[B] *pr. name (TM)* a large building society

Leeds Castle *pr. name, hist.* a 12th C. turreted castle situated upon two islands in a lake in ➡Kent about 18 miles to the west of ➡Canterbury
Built upon earlier wooden Saxon fortifications, it was presented to Edward I as a gift in 1278 and remained a royal castle until given away to his commander in Ireland by ➡Henry VIII.

leek *noun* the national vegetative emblem of Wales
It is said it came to be emblematic of Wales because ➡St David once arranged for his countrymen to distinguish themselves in battle against the Saxons by wearing leeks in their caps.

leesome *adj., Sc.* pleasant

leet [A] *noun, East, hist.* a subdivision of a ➡hundred
[B] *noun, Sc.* a selected list of candidates for a post

left footer *comp. noun, derog., Sc.* a Roman Catholic

left luggage *comp. noun* baggage checked into a ➡left luggage office for later collection

left luggage office *comp. noun* a baggage check room, where ➡left luggage is deposited
Typically at railroad stations, airports, etc.

leg *noun* that half of the ➡cricket field which, when divided lengthwise through the pitch, contains the striking batsman's feet
The other half is called the ➡off.

legal *noun, sl.* a passenger who pays the exact taxi fare, without any tip

legal aid *comp. noun* legal fees paid from the ➡Legal Aid Fund

the **Legal Aid Fund** *pr. name* the public fund that ➡legal aid is paid from
Supposedly, payments are made only in strictly controlled cases of proven need. This sort of payment is necessary in Britain because contingency fee arrangements between clients and counsel are almost unknown and strongly disapproved of and discouraged. The example of the United States is regularly presented as an awful warning of how badly such fee arrangements can damage and distort a legal system.

leg before wicket *comp. noun* a way to remove a ➡batsman from play in ➡cricket
A batsman is out if he obstructs the ball with any part of his body other than his hand.

leg break *comp. noun* a ➡cricket ball bowled so that it deviates towards the ➡wicket from the ➡leg side following a bounce

leg bye *comp. noun* a ➡cricketing run scored from a ball that strikes off any part of the batsman's ➡leg side except his hand

leg cutter *comp. noun* a fast ➡leg break

legionaire *noun* a member of the ➡Royal British Legion

leg it *verb, sl.* to run away

legless *adj., sl.* unable to stand due to excessive consumption of intoxicating liquor

leg side *comp. noun* that half of a ➡cricket field which is to the right of the ➡bowler

leg slips *comp. noun* a fielding player's position upon the ➡cricket field

leg spin *comp. noun* a kind of spin applied to a ➡cricket ball, causing deviation from the ➡leg side when the ball bounces

leg stump *comp. noun* a ➡cricket ➡stump upon the ➡leg side

leg theory *comp. noun* the ➡cricketing practice of ➡bowling towards the ➡leg side with ➡fielders massed there ready to catch the ball

leg trap *comp. noun* a group of ➡cricketing ➡fielders positioned on the ➡leg side near the ➡wicket

Leicester *pr. name* a city that is the administrative center of ➡Leicestershire
Founded as *Ratae Corieltauvorum* by the Romans in the 1st C., it is where the ➡Fosse Way crossed the Soar River. Incorporated as a city in 1589, the current population, including suburbs, is 410,000 (1988 estimate).

Leicestershire *pr. name* an east-central English county
The county seat is ➡Leicester and the current population is about 860,000 (1991 Census).

Leicester Square *pr. name* a central London square at the heart of the theater district

Leics. *pr. name, abbr.* ➡Leicestershire

Leister *pr. name* one of the ancient provinces of Ireland
It consists of ➡Carlow, ➡Dublin, ➡Kildare, ➡Kilkenny, ➡Laois, ➡Longford, ➡Louth, ➡Meath, ➡Offaly, ➡Westmeath, ➡Wexford, and ➡Wicklow, all in the ➡Irish Republic.

leisure centre *comp. noun* a public facility where sports and other pastimes are catered to

Leithrim *pr. name* a county in the ➡Irish Republic
County Leithrim in the ancient province of ➡Connaught.

lemon *noun, derog., sl.* an unattractive girl

lemonade *noun* (1) lemon-flavored soda drink; (2) formerly, soda pop of any flavor

lemon {cheese » curd} *comp. noun* a lemon-based conserve made with sugar, butter and eggs

lemon squash *comp. noun* a drink made from squeezed or crushed lemons or lemon juice
It is similar to lemonade.

lending library *comp. noun* a library from which books may be borrowed

length *noun* the distance between where the bowler causes the ➡cricket ball to bounce after he has pitched it, and where the ➡batsman stands

lengthman *noun* a railroad track repairman

lengths ahead *idiom* (1) leading a horse race by a considerable margin; (2) superior in general
(1) refers to the length of a horse.

Lent lily *comp. noun* a wild daffodil

Lent term *pr. name* the university term containing the season of Lent

leprechaun *noun, Gae., Ir.* the small mischievous elf of Irish folklore

Lerwick *pr. name, hist.* a town that is the administrative center of the ➡Shetland Islands
First settled by the Vikings, it is the most northerly British town.

lese-majesty *comp. noun, Fr., Lat.* (1) an offense to the dignity of the head of state of a sovereign power; (2) offensive conduct, an affront to dignity; (3) formerly, ➡high treason
From the French, *lèse-majesté*, which is derived in turn from the Latin *laesa majestas* = "injured sovereignty."

let [A] *noun, abbr., coll.* a ➡letting
[B] *verb* (1) to lease property in exchange for a rent; (2) to rent a house, land, car, etc.

letter-book *comp. noun, out.* a book where copies of letters are kept between the pages

letter-box *comp. noun* a mailbox

letter-card *comp. noun* a foldable card that can be sealed closed and then mailed like a letter

letterpress *noun* the written contents as distinct from the illustrations of a book

letters patent *comp. noun* an open written authority from the ➡sovereign granting a specified person or company a particular right, power or exception

letting *noun, coll.* a room, house or apartment that is rented or available to rent

leuco- *spell., prefix* leuko-
It means "white-."

leukaemia *spell.* leukemia

levant *verb* to run away from a debt, especially one incurred by gambling

levanter *noun* someone who ➡levants

levee *noun, arch.* an afternoon assembly at which a king receives only men

level crossing *comp. noun* a railroad grade crossing

{levelled » levelling} *spell.* {leveled » leveling}

the Levellers *pr. name, hist.* an extremely radical republican group that arose in 17th C. England

level pegging *idiom* equal, particularly of a result

Levens Hall *pr. name, hist.* originally a 13th C. ➡peel tower about 15 miles to the north of ➡Lancaster in the northwest of England
It is now a great house with magnificent Elizabethan paneling and patterned ceilings, which are the result of its complete reconstruction in the 16th and 17th C.

Lewes *pr. name, hist.* a town that is the administrative center of East Sussex
Within the town there is a ➡Norman castle dating back to the 11th C. The current population is 16,000 (1991 estimate).

Lewisham *pr. name* a ➡Greater London borough
Its current population, which is also included within the ➡London urban area total, is 215,000 (1991 Census).

libel *noun, Sc.* a formal statement of the basis of a prosecution or lawsuit

{libellant » libelled » libellee} *spell.* {libelant » libeled » libelee}

{libelling » libellous} *spell.* {libeling » libelous}

the Liberal Democratic Party *pr. name, hist.* Britain's third-largest political party
The current name, chosen in 1989, of what had been called the ➡Social and Liberal Democratic Party that had been created by merging the ➡Liberal and the ➡Social Democratic Parties the previous year.

the Liberal Party *pr. name, hist.* the name of the ➡Liberal Democratic Party until 1989

Liberty *pr. name, abbr.* the National Council for Civil Liberties
A pressure group founded in 1934, and known by the abbreviation ➡NCCL until 1989, when "Liberty" adopted.

liberty boat *comp. noun* a boat carrying ➡liberty men

liberty bodice *comp. noun* a tight-fitting ➡under bodice for a woman or girl

liberty man *comp. noun* a sailor granted shore leave

Liberty's *pr. name, hist.* a large department store in the ➡West End of London distinguished by its most unusual mixture of ➡half-timbering with *Art Nouveau* architecture

Lib-Lab *pr. name, abbr., coll., hist.* a member of the ➡Labour Representative Committee elected to parliament under the terms of an agreement made with the ➡Liberal Party, prior to the establishment of the ➡Labour Party in 1906

Lib-Lab Pact

Lib-Lab Pact *pr. name, coll., hist.* a deal by which the ➡Liberal Party helped to sustain in office the minority ➡Labour administration of 1974 to 1979

LIBOR *pr. name, abbr.* the London Interbank Offer Rate, which is the benchmark interest rate for ➡Eurodollar loans being offered on the London market

library ticket *comp. noun* a library card

licence *spell.* license
When a noun. When a verb it is spelled "license".

licensed premises *comp. noun* a public house or ➡licensed restaurant

licensed restaurant *comp. noun* a restaurant permitted to sell liquor with its food

Lifeguard

licensed trade *comp. noun* a euphemism for the business of selling liquor to the public

licensed victualler *comp. noun* an owner of ➡licensed premises

licensee *noun, abbr.* a ➡licensed victualler

licensing hours *comp. noun, coll.* the hours during which ➡licensed premises are permitted to sell liquor under the terms of their license

Lichfield *pr. name* a city in ➡Staffordshire
Incorporated as a city in 1549, the current population is 90,000 (1988 estimate).

licht [A] *adj., Sc.* (1) lightweight; (2) bright
[B] *noun, Sc.* (1) light; (2) enlightenment

lido *noun, out.* a public outdoors swimming pool
From the name of a swimming beach near Venice in Italy.

lie doggo *verb, sl.* lie motionless
In the manner of a dog feigning death in the hope that it will not be noticed.

lie-down *comp. noun* a short rest or snooze

lie in *verb, coll.* to lie in bed after normal rising time

lie of the land *idiom, coll.* the lay of the land

lieutenant *noun* a junior commissioned officer in the British Army

Equivalent in rank to a first lieutenant in the U.S. Army. In the British Army, this word is pronounced, "lef-ten-ant"; in the Royal Navy, it is pronounced, "la-ten-ant," which is closer to but not identical with the U.S. "loo-ten-ant."

lieutenant-general *comp. noun* the third-highest rank of commissioned officer in the British Army
Equivalent in rank to a three-star general in the U.S. Army.

the Lieutenant of the Tower *pr. name* the commander of the Tower of London

the Life Guards *pr. name* the two premier cavalry regiments of the British Army, who form part of the ➡Household Troops

life peer *comp. noun* a member of the ➡House of Lords whose title will die with {him » her}

life-preserver *idiom, arch., sl.* a ➡cosh or bludgeon

LIFFE *pr. name, abbr.* the London International Financial Futures Exchange

lift *noun* an elevator

lift {boy » man} *comp. noun* an elevator operator

lig [A] *noun, East* a lie
[B] *verb, sl.* to freeload or gatecrash

ligger *noun, sl.* a freeloader or gatecrasher

light ale *comp. noun* a light-colored beer

light and dark *idiom, rh. sl.* a park

light blue *comp. noun, coll.* (1) a present or former student of ➡Cambridge University; (2) a present or former student of ➡Eton School

light infantry *comp. noun, arch.* infantry carrying less equipment so that they can move more rapidly

lighting-up time *comp. noun* those hours when it is a legal requirement for vehicles to have the appropriate lights switched on
Defined in law as the period lasting from half-an-hour after local sunset until half-an-hour before local sunrise.

light-minded *adj.* trivial, lacking seriousness

lightning conductor *comp. noun* a lightning rod

the Light Programme *pr. name, hist.* a ➡BBC radio station that specialized in popular entertainment and music
It was called the Forces Programme during World War II when it was one of two BBC national radio stations, one for civilians and this one for the armed forces, renamed Light Programme at the end of the war.
In 1967 it was renamed again as ➡Radio 2.
SEE ALSO: ➡Home Service.

lignocaine *spell.* lidocaine
A local anesthetic.

likeable *spell.* likable

like it or lump it *idiom. phr. verb* like it or not; love it or hate it; willy-nilly

198

Lindsey

Lilliburlero pr. name, hist. now best known as the signature tune of the ➧BBC's ➧World Service, it has a long and interesting history
The very word itself was said to have been one of the watchwords of Irish Catholics when they were busy massacring Irish Protestants in 1641.
It was then adapted as part of a political doggerel with a very catchy tune that was written by Lord Wharton to satirize ➧James II of England and VII of Scotland. This helped build the public mood that led to the ➧Glorious Revolution of 1688. It was reported to have made a huge impression on the entire nation, town and country, army and people, in the King's service and out. Everywhere one went, people were singing it. Later, Wharton boasted that he had "sung a king out of three kingdoms".
A simplified version of it is familiar to most of us as the tune of the nursery rhyme, *{Hush » Rock} -a-bye, Baby.*

Lilli Marlene pr. name, hist. a song popular with both German and British troops in World War II
With words written by a World War II German soldier and sung by Lale Andersen, *Lilli Marlene* became very popular in the German *Wehrmacht* in 1940 and 1941, especially with Rommel's *Afrika Korps,* who were fighting the British 8th Army in North Africa, and it was played nightly to them from Radio Belgrade. This station was picked up by British troops too and soon the song, which tells of the forlorn love of a soldier for a sweetheart he fears he will never see again, became as popular with them as with the Germans.
Soon, a version with English words was prepared and uniquely, *Lilli Marlene* became a simultaneous national hit in both countries at war with each other. Without doubt, if there is one song which epitomizes World War II—at least in Europe—this is it.

Lilo *pr. name (TM)* an inflatable air mattress

the **Lilywhites** *pr. name* the 13th/18th Hussars
A unit of the British Army whose name reflects their adoption of white facings when they changed from being a Dragoon regiment to Hussars, in 1861.
SEE ALSO: ➧Green Dragoons.

Limavady *pr. name* a district in ➧Northern Ireland, in what used to be County ➧Londonderry
The current population is 30,000 (1990 estimate).
Limerick *pr. name* a county in the ➧Irish Republic
County Limerick in the ancient province of ➧Munster.
Lime Street Station *pr. name* the principal railroad terminus in central Liverpool
{limited company » limited liability company} *comp. noun* a company incorporated with limited liability
limited monarchy *comp. noun* a monarchy where the monarch's power is very severely restricted by constitutional and other legal means
SEE ALSO: ➧absolute monarchy, ➧constitutional monarchy.
limmer *noun, derog., Sc.* (1) a prostitute, mistress or whore; (2) a term of contempt for a woman or any female animal
Linacre College *pr. name* a college of ➧Oxford University founded in 1962
Lincoln *pr. name* the city which is the administrative center of Lincolnshire
Founded as *Lindum* by the Romans in 47, it sits astride ➧Ermine Street. The ➧Norman castle dates from 1068 and the huge cathedral beside it from 1072. One of the four surviving original copies of the ➧*Magna Carta* is deposited there. Lincoln was incorporated as a city in 1154, and the current population is 80,000 (1988 estimate).
Lincoln College *pr. name* a college of ➧Oxford University founded in 1427
Lincoln green *comp. noun* a kind of bright green cloth that was originally made in ➧Lincoln
Reputedly worn by ➧Robin Hood and his colleagues.
Lincolnshire *pr. name* a county on the eastern coast of England, lying between the counties of ➧Humberside and ➧Norfolk
The county seat is ➧Lincoln and the current population is 575,000 (1991 Census).
Lincoln's Inn *pr. name* one of the ➧Inns of Court
The name is probably of 14th C. origin and is said to be taken from Thomas de Lincoln, who was king's ➧serjeant and landlord of the original inn.
Lincs. *pr. name, abbr.* ➧Lincolnshire
linctus *noun* a cough syrup
Lindisfarne *pr. name, hist.* ➧Holy Island (1)
Lindsey *pr. name, hist.* (1) an ancient kingdom in eastern England that roughly corresponded with the modern county of ➧Lincolnshire; (2) a major administrative division of the county of ➧Lincolnshire before reorganization in 1974
(1) had become established by the 6th C. It became a vassal state of ➧Mercia from about 715, until finally it was completely absorbed by 800. The usual seat of the kings of Lindsey was what is now the modern city of ➧Lincoln.

199

lineman

lineman *noun* a railroad track walker, who walks along the track to inspect it

linen basket *comp. noun* a laundry basket

linen draper [A] *comp. noun* a dry goods merchant [B] *idiom, rh. sl.* a newspaper

linen drapery *comp. noun, arch.* a dry-goods store

linen-fold *comp. noun* a wooden or stone panelling, ornament or sculpture warped or carved so as to resemble folds of linen cloth

line-of-battle ship *comp. noun, hist.* an 18th C. ➡ship-of-the-line

line of country *idiom, coll.* a field or area of knowledge or expertise

line-out *comp. noun* parallel rows of rugby football players positioned to receive the ball when it is thrown in from the touchline

liner train *comp. noun* a freight train with permanently coupled cars used to transport detachable freight containers

lines *noun, coll* text written out several times as a form of punishment imposed on a school student

linesman *noun* a ➡lineman

link *verb, Sc.* (1) to move along smartly; (2) to skip or dance; (3) to work rapidly

linkman *noun* a TV anchorman

links *noun, Sc.* (1) open rolling grass or gorse-covered ground close to the seashore; (2) a golf course; (3) a chain or string of sausages

The original golf courses were laid out on links (1) such as those at ➡St Andrews.

Linlithgow Palace *pr. name, hist.* a ruined royal palace about 16 miles to the west of Edinburgh

The earliest buildings at this location burned down in 1424; the new one built in its stead was finished later that century, and ➡Mary Queen of Scots was born here in 1542. The new palace was destroyed in an accidental fire during the ➡Jacobite rebellion of 1745 while it was occupied by troops, and it remains a magnificent ruin to this day.

linn *noun, Sc.* (1) a deep, narrow gorge; (2) a waterfall; (3) a pool at the base of a waterfall

lino *noun, abbr.* linoleum

lint *noun, Sc.* flax

lintelled *spell.* linteled

the **Lion and Unicorn** *pr. name* a component part of the British royal ➡coat of arms, representing England and Scotland respectively

the **Lion in the North** *pr. name* Scotland

the **Lion Rampant** *pr. name* the heraldic device of the kings of Scotland

liquid lunch *idiom, sl.* a jocular name for a midday repast consisting of liquor or beer but no solid food

liquid paraffin *comp. noun* a mineral oil laxative

liquorice *spell.* licorice

liquorice allsorts *comp. noun* a confection consisting of various-colored and various-flavored candies containing or wrapped in licorice

Lisburn *pr. name* a district in ➡Northern Ireland, in what used to be County ➡Antrim and County Down

The current population is 100,000 (1990 estimate).

listed building *comp. noun* a building of historical or architectural significance

These are buildings placed on an official list maintained by the ➡Department of National Heritage, which means that they cannot be altered or demolished without special authority. There are three classes of listing:

About 1 percent are Grade I; "buildings of exceptional interest." About 4 percent are Grade II; "particularly important buildings." About 95 percent are Grade III; "warrant every effort to save."

listen in *verb, coll.* to listen to the radio

listing *noun* a cloth's edge or selvage

It may be made of a different material or formed into a different weave than the rest.

the **Litany** *pr. name* what is contained within the ➡Book of Common Prayer

Literae Humaniores *pr. name, Lat.* the ➡Oxford University School of Classics and Philosophy

This is, in Latin, "The more humane studies."

litre *spell.* liter

litter {basket » bin} *comp. noun* a trashcan

litter lout *comp. noun, coll.* a litterbug

little-ease *comp. noun, hist.* a prison cell that was intentionally made too small to permit either standing up or lying down at full length

Little Englander *comp. noun, derog., hist.* (1) someone who does not look beyond England; (2) someone opposed to European union; (3) formerly, someone opposed to imperial expansion

little 'erbert *idiom, arch., sl.* a small boy

SEE ALSO: ➡'erbert.

little finger *comp. noun, pref.* a pinkie

"Pinkie" is unknown in England, but usual in Scotland.

Little Go *idiom, arch., coll.* the traditional name for the initial examination leading to a BA degree at ➡Cambridge University

little Mary *idiom, arch.* the stomach

Little Moreton Hall *pr. name, hist.* perhaps the most impressive ➡half-timbered house in Britain

The oldest parts of this building were erected around about the year 1450. It is located in southern Cheshire some nine miles to the north of ➡Stoke-on-Trent.

the **Liturgy** *pr. name* the ➡Book of Common Prayer

liveable *spell.* livable

live in *phr. verb* to reside where one works
As a domestic employee might, for example.

the **Liver Bird** *pr. name* a mythical bird that is the emblem of the ➡City of Liverpool

live rough *verb, coll.* to ➡sleep rough as a way of life

Liverpool *pr. name* the principal city and major port of ➡Merseyside
Developed first in the 13th C. as a convenient port for travel to and from ➡Ireland, it began to grow vastly in size and importance in the late 18th C., when its hinterland, ➡Lancashire, developed significant manufacturing industries. Liverpool soon became the principal entry port for raw materials, especially cotton from the southern states of the United States, and the main exit port for finished goods from Manchester and Birmingham. More recently, Liverpool has become well-known as hometown of the ➡Beatles. It was incorporated as a city in 1207 and the current population, including suburbs, is 750,000 (1988 estimate)

the **Liverpool and Manchester Railway** *pr. name, hist.* the world's first entirely steam-powered railroad
It opened in 1830 with great ceremony when a train of eight cars carried a large number of celebrities, including the Duke of Wellington, then Prime Minister, the 31 miles from ➡Manchester to ➡Liverpool.
This opening ceremony was also the occasion of the first fatal railroad accident, when an ➡MP from Liverpool, William Huskisson, was hit and fatally injured by the train.

Liverpool Street Station *pr. name* a principal railroad terminus in central London
For trains to and from ➡East Anglia and ferry ports to the continent. It was opened in 1874.

Liverpudlian *pr. name* a native, inhabitant or citizen of ➡Liverpool

liver salts *comp. noun* antacid
Usually sodium bicarbonate.

livery [A] *adj.* strongly cohesive
A characteristic of certain soils.
[B] *noun* (1) special clothing worn by a member of a ➡livery company; (2) the membership of a ➡livery company as a group; (3) distinctive badges or clothes that certain servants may be expected to wear as a sort of uniform

livery company *comp. noun, hist.* one of a number of ancient ➡guilds of the ➡City of London
There are 83 of these guilds, originally medieval trade associates of goldsmiths, butchers, etc., but they are now limited to ceremonial and charity roles.

livery fine *comp. noun, hist.* the fee paid upon joining a ➡livery company

liveryman *noun, hist.* a member of a ➡livery company

living *noun* a religious benefice carrying with it an endowment sufficient for the holder to live on

the **Lizard** *pr. name, hist.* a peninsula on the southern coast of ➡Cornwall, which is the most southerly point on the British mainland
It is from here that Marconi made the first ever transatlantic radio transmission in 1901.

LJ *pr. name, abbr.* the ➡Lord Justice

LL *noun, abbr.* a ➡Lord Lieutenant

Llandudno *pr. name, hist.* a resort town on the coast of ➡Gwynedd, Wales
The current population is 18,000 (1991 estimate).

Llanfair PG *pr. name, abbr., Wal.* ➡Llanfairpwllgwyngyllgogerychwyrndrobwllllantysiliogogogoch
This is the usual abbreviation.
It's hardly surprising that there is one.

Llanfairpwllgwyngyllgogerychwyrndrobwllllantysiliogogogoch *pr. name, Wal.* a village in ➡Anglesey with the longest place name in Britain (and lots of other places too)
The name is usually shortened to ➡Llanfair PG. In full, it means, "The church of St Mary in a hollow of white hazel, near to the rapid whirlpool and St Tysilio's church, near to a red cave", and was almost certainly a 19th C. invention for the purpose of attracting tourists.
The place also has the distinction of being the location of the first-ever branch of the ➡Women's Institute in Britain.

LL B *noun, abbr.* a Bachelor of Law
From the Latin *legum baccalaureus* = "bachelor of law".

LL D *noun, abbr.* a Doctor of Law
From the Latin *legum doctor* = "doctor of law".

LL M *noun, abbr.* a Master of Law
From the Latin *legum magister* = "master of law".

Lloyds Bank *pr. name* one of the ➡Big Four English retail banks
It was founded in 1765 by a Unitarian button maker from ➡Birmingham.

Lloyd's List *pr. name* a newspaper published since 1737, specializing in insurance and shipping news

Lloyd's of London *pr. name* an association of insurance underwriters and investors, called ➡names
Established in 1688 in Edward Lloyd's coffeehouse, it was originally concerned solely with shipping, but is now involved in all areas of insurance business.

Lloyd's Register of Shipping *pr. name* an annual publication classifying the insurance risk status of ships according to the condition of their hulls
The first register was published in 1760 by underwriters at ➡Lloyd's of London, but although still closely connected to that institution, Lloyd's Register is now an entirely separate and distinct entity.

LMBC *pr. name, abbr.* the Lady Margaret Boat Club
Associated with ➡St John's College, ➡Cambridge University.

LME *pr. name, abbr.* the London Metal Exchange

LMF *adj., abbr., hist.* ➡lacking moral fibre

LMH *pr. name, abbr.* ➡Lady Margaret Hall

LMS [A] *noun, abbr.* local management of schools
A system under which school governors and principals are directly responsible for the financial and educational administration of their schools.
[B] *pr. name, abbr.* (1) the London Missionary Society; (2) the London Mathematical Society; (3) formerly, the ➡London, Midland, & Scottish Railway

LNER *pr. name, abbr., hist.* the former ➡London and North Eastern Railway

load of old cobblers *idiom, sl.* utter nonsense
SEE ALSO: ➡cobblers.

loads *noun, coll.* lots, plenty

loaf *noun, rh. sl.* (1) a head; (2) the brains within (1)
Derivation: head > bread > loaf of bread > loaf. *SEE ALSO:* ➡use your loaf.

Loamshire *pr. name* a fictitious English county where various authors have set their tales

loan *noun, out., Sc.* (1) an open area where cows are milked; (2) a track through a field formed by the regular passage of cattle; (3) the part of a farm which surrounds the farm buildings; (4) a street

loaning *noun* (1) a grassy footpath; (2) a pasture

lob [A] *noun, out., sl.* a slow-witted or clumsy person
[B] *verb* to bowl a ➡cricket ball slowly with an ➡underarm pitch

lobby *noun* one of the two corridors adjacent to the ➡Chamber of the ➡House of Commons that ➡MPs file into when they wish to register their votes during a ➡division

lobby correspondent *comp. noun* a journalist reporting upon parliamentary matters

lobscouse *noun, arch.* a sailor's stew consisting of meat, vegetables and sea biscuits
SEE ALSO: ➡Scouse.

local *noun, coll.* a neighborhood ➡pub

local authority *comp. noun* any county, region, district, or other legitimate unit of local government

local train *comp. noun* a train that stops at every depot along its route

loch *noun, Gae., Sc.* (1) a freshwater lake; (2) a ➡sea loch
SEE ALSO: ➡lough.

Lochgelly special *comp. noun, hist., Sc.* a ➡tawse formerly used to punish schoolchildren
From Lochgelly in ➡Fife, where they were manufactured.

Loch Leven Castle *pr. name, hist.* a ruined Medieval castle standing upon an island in the middle of Loch Leven, which is a lake situated beside the town of Kinross in ➡Tayside, some 25 miles to the north of the ➡Firth of Forth

In 1567 ➡Mary Queen of Scots was kept a prisoner here for almost a year until she escaped in a rowboat.

Loch Ness Monster *pr. name* a large, possibly prehistoric, probably fictitious, aquatic animal, reputed to reside in the murky depths of Loch ➡Ness
SEE ALSO: Nessie.

lockage *noun* the height by which a canal lock or system of locks raises or lowers the water level

Lockerbie *pr. name, hist.* a small market town in ➡Dumfries and Galloway, Scotland, about 10 miles to the east of ➡Dumfries
This is where the largest sections of Pan Am Flight 103 fell, after being destroyed by a bomb in mid-air on December 21, 1988. All 259 people on board the aircraft were killed, plus another 11 on the ground in Lockerbie.

lockfast *adj., Sc.* securely locked

lock hospital *comp. noun, arch., coll.* a hospital for patients with sexually transmitted diseases

locksman *noun* a canal lock-keeper

lock-up *comp. noun* premises such as a small shop, workshop, or garage without living quarters, but can be locked up to make secure when left alone

loco *noun, abbr.* a railroad locomotive

locum *noun, abbr., Lat.* a temporary replacement for a doctor or clergyman
From the Latin *locum tenens* = "holding the place"

lodged *adj.* in heraldry, reposed

lodger *noun* roomer

lodgings *noun* a room or rooms not in a hotel but nonetheless rented out for accommodation

logbook *noun, coll.* the informal name for a ➡vehicle registration document

{**logopaedic » logopaedics**} *spell.* {logopedic » logopedics}

logorrhoea *spell.* logorrhea
Verbal diarrhea.

Loiner *noun* a native or inhabitant of ➡Leeds

lollipop [A] *noun, rh. sl.* the police
Derived from ➡slop
[B] *phr. verb, rh. sl.* to inform the police
Derived from both ➡slop and "shop"

lollipop {**lady » man » woman**} *noun, coll.* a school crossing guard
Traffic is halted by holding up a large circular sign on a pole resembling a lollipop, and thus this name.

lollop *verb, sl.* to lounge about

lolly *noun, abbr., sl.* (1) money; (2) candy; (3) a lollipop

Lombard Street *pr. name* (1) a street in the ➡City associated with banking since the 12th C.; (2) a nickname for the London Money Market in general

Lombard Street to a China orange *idiom, coll.* dollars to donuts

Which is to say, very long odds indeed. Lombard Street is the street in the City where the Stock Exchange is.

Loch **Lomond** *pr. name* the largest freshwater lake in ➡Great Britain

About 20 miles northwest of ➡Glasgow.

Londinium pr. name, hist., Lat. the original, Roman name for ➡London

London *pr. name, hist.* (1) the capital city of both ➡England and the ➡United Kingdom; (2) by far the largest British city; (3) the urban area extending beyond the political boundary of ➡Greater London

The earliest reference is to be found in Tacitus's Annals (XIV, ch 33) written in 116 or so and referring to events during the year 61 in ➡*Londinium*. The current population of (3) is 7,700,000 (1991 Census).

London Airport *pr. name* the official name for ➡Heathrow Airport

the **London and North Eastern Railway** *pr. name, abbr., hist.* a former railroad company, absorbed into ➡British Rail in 1947

It had a network stretching north from London up the eastern side of Britain to ➡Edinburgh and beyond.

London Bridge *pr. name* the first bridge built over the ➡Thames River at London

Originally there was a wooden bridge built across the river by the Romans some distance upstream from the present-day ➡Tower of London; it's believed to have been erected in 43. For a long time, this was the only bridge crossing the river in the vicinity of the city.

The first stone bridge, which had houses built upon on both sides from bank to bank, was erected in 1176 and stood until demolished and replaced in 1831. In 1972 another new bridge replaced the 1831 one, which was dismantled and removed to Arizona where it was re-erected as a tourist attraction.

London County Council *pr. name, hist.* a former ➡local authority, which governed London from 1889 until replaced by the ➡GLC in 1963

Londonderry *pr. name, hist.* (1) a district in ➡Northern Ireland, in what used to be County ➡Londonderry; (2) the Protestant name for the city of ➡Derry in ➡Northern Ireland, in what used to be County ➡Londonderry; (3) a former Northern Irish County (County Londonderry) in the ancient province of ➡Ulster

It is said that St Columba founded a monastery here in 564. The 17th C. city wall, built by Protestants to defend themselves from Catholics, is still almost entirely intact. The current population of (1) is 35,000 (1990 estimate). Incorporated as a city in 1604, the current urban population of (2) is 100,000 (1988 estimate).

Londoner *pr. name* someone who is a native, inhabitant or citizen of London

the **London Festival Ballet** *pr. name, hist.* a ballet company performing classical and modern works

Founded in 1950, it has been known as the ➡English National Ballet since 1989.

London fog *idiom, rh. sl.* a dog

London FOX *pr. name, abbr.* the London Futures and Options Exchange

Formed in 1987 as the successor of the ➡LCE.

the ***London Gazette*** *pr. name* an official government-published newspaper

Used only for the purpose of publishing notices of official appointments, bankruptcies, court judgments and so forth, that relate to England and Wales.

the **London, Midland & Scottish Railway** *pr. name, hist.* a former railroad company, absorbed into ➡British Rail in 1947

It had a network stretching north from London up the western side of Britain to Birmingham, Liverpool, Manchester, Glasgow and beyond.

London particular *idiom, hist.* a thick, impenetrable fog once common in ➡London

The almost total elimination of the coal burning to heat homes and power trains, factories and so forth since the end of World War II has effectively banished this phenomenon to the history books: a reminder that environmental problems are neither new nor insoluble!

London Philharmonic Orchestra *pr. name, hist.* an orchestra founded in 1932 by Sir Thomas Beecham

He also founded the ➡Royal Philharmonic Orchestra

London pride *comp. noun* an alternate name for the flower called ➡none-so-pretty

London Regional Transport *pr. name* the organization responsible for public transportation within ➡Greater London

Successor to the London Regional Transport Board set up in 1933 to take over the numerous private bus, streetcar and subway services then operating in the London area and to coordinate them together into a single integrated system.

London School of Economics and Political Science *pr. name* a school of ➡London University

Britain's leading institution devoted to the academic study of politics and economics, founded in 1895.

the **London season** *pr. name, out.* the months of May, June and July, when it is supposedly fashionable to be in London

London Symphony Orchestra *pr. name, hist.* an orchestra founded in 1904

By players fed up with the indignities they were subjected to by the high-handed conductors controlling other orchestras.

London Transport *pr. name, abbr.* ➡London Regional Transport.

the **London Underground**

Underground train

the **London Underground** *pr. name* one of the largest and most comprehensive rapid-transit railroad networks in the world; services extending throughout London and into adjacent suburbs

It is operated by ➠London Regional Transport.

Some of the lines making up the extensive underground sections of the network were excavated as true deep-level tunnels with small diameter bores requiring smaller cross-sectioned cars than is normal on most railroads, and deep station platforms requiring long escalator access from sub-surface ticketing halls.

Other—mostly the older lines— have underground sections that were excavated as trenches and then covered over later with roadways, buildings and so forth, so that is was possible to make the tunnels large enough to accommodate regular railroad car sizes.

London University *pr. name* a large federal university in London

Founded in 1836 by federation of the recently established ➠University and ➠King's Colleges. It now has over 50,000 students and more than 30 independent colleges and institutions throughout London and the surrounding area.

London Weekend TV *pr. name* a local commercial TV company headquartered in London; it is part of the ➠ITV network

longbow *noun, hist.* a hand-drawn wooden bow

The Medieval bow used by the yeomen of England who helped ➠Henry V defeat the French at the Battle of ➠Agincourt in 1415. At some 6 ft 7 in in length, they were a foot or more longer than those in use today.

long clay *comp. noun, arch., out.* a long-stemmed clay churchwarden pipe

long-dated *adj., coll.* not due for early payment

Of an invoice or bill.

long-eared *adj., sl.* stupid

A reference to the ears of an ➠ass.

long field *comp. noun* the area of the ➠cricket playing field behind the ➠bowler

long firm *comp. noun, coll.* corporate swindlers who operate by setting up a dummy company, order goods from trade suppliers, and then vanishing before they have to pay for them

Longford *pr. name* a county in the ➠Irish Republic

County Longford in the ancient province of Leinster.

long jump *comp. noun* a broad jump

Long Kesh *pr. name* the original name for the ➠Maze Prison in ➠Northern Ireland

This name is still used by ➠Republicans.

Longleat House *pr. name, hist.* one of the earliest and grandest of ➠Elizabethan mansions

It was built some 20 miles to the south of Bath in 1580. Britain's first safari park was opened in the extensive grounds of this house in 1966.

long-legged *adj., coll.* very fast

long {leg » off » on} *comp. noun* fielding players' positions on the ➠cricket field

long lie *comp. noun, coll.* time spent lying in bed longer than usual

long-life milk *comp. noun* heat-treated milk

long live the {King » Queen} *exclam.* a declaration of loyalty to the monarch

long odds *idiom* a very considerable improbability

long paper *comp. noun, coll.* a thesis

the **Long Parliament** *pr. name, hist.* the parliament that sat without a ➠general election from 1640, before the ➠English Civil War, until the ➠Restoration of the Monarchy in 1660

long pockets and short arms *idiom, coll.* a psychological inability to spend money

longstop *noun, coll.* (1) the area of a ➠cricket field behind the ➠wicket keeper; (2) a last resort; (3) a final chance or opportunity

(2) and (3) are derived from (1).

long ton *comp. noun* an ➠imperial ton of 2,240 lbs

long toungued *adj. phr., coll.* long-winded, loquacious

long vacation *comp. noun* the summer vacation period of universities and law courts

long wave *comp. noun* radio wavelengths greater than 1,000 meters

longways *adj.* lengthwise

the **Lonsdale Belt** *pr. name, hist.* a trophy belt awarded in 1909 by the Earl of Lonsdale to any boxer, of any weight, who wins a British boxing title

loo *noun, Fr., sl.* a toilet

Probably from the French, *l'eau* = "the water"

look back *verb, coll.* to make a return visit

look in *verb, coll.* to watch television

look like *idiom. phr. verb* to seem probable

lookout *noun* outlook

look out *verb, coll.* to search out or find

look sharpish *imper., coll.* (1) get a move on; (2) keep awake; (3) watch out

look slippy *imper., coll.* get a move on

loon *noun, Sc.* a boy or youth

the **Loony Left** *pr. name, derog., sl.* a deliberately insulting name for those members of the ➠Labour Party intent upon pushing extreme left-wing policies

loose box *comp. noun* a box stall for animals, typically a horse

loose chippings *comp. noun* loose gravel lying upon a highway pavement

A roadside warning sign indicating that gravel has been newly laid upon a road surface but not yet bonded to it.

loose cover *comp. noun* a slipcover for furniture

loose scrum *comp. noun* an informal ➠scrum (1) developed "naturally" in the course of playing Rugbu

lor *exclam., abbr., sl.* a euphemism for or variation of ➠Lord Almighty

lord *noun* (1) an ex-officio title; (2) a title used by a man who may have any one of a number of possible ranks of nobility

Examples of (1) are: ➠Lord Advocate, ➠Sea Lord, ➠Lord Chancellor, etc. (2) may be used by any of the following classes of nobleman: a hereditary peer; a life peer; any son of a duke or marquis; the eldest son of an earl.

the **Lord Advocate** *pr. name, Sc.* the chief law officer of the government in Scotland

Lord Almighty *exclam., sl.* an exclamation of surprise

the **Lord Chamberlain** *pr. name, abbr.* the ➠Lord Chamberlain of the Household

the **Lord Chamberlain of England** *pr. name* a hereditary ceremonial office

the **Lord Chamberlain of the Household** *pr. name* the senior official responsible for managing the ➠Royal Household

Until 1968, he was also responsible for censoring all plays before they were shown in British theaters.

the **Lord Chancellor** *pr. name, abbr.* the ➠Lord High Chancellor of England

the **Lord Chief Justice** *pr. name* the presiding judge of the ➠{King's » Queen's} Bench Division of the ➠High Court

Ex officio a peer, and next in rank to the ➠Lord Chancellor.

the **Lord Clerk Registrar** *pr. name, Sc.* the state archivist of Scotland

Lord Haw-haw *pr. name, hist.* a nickname given by his listeners to William Joyce, who broadcast anti-British propaganda in English from Germany throughout World War II

He was dubbed this because his voice sounded like a caricature of an ➠Oxford accent, although he was in truth a U.S. citizen of Irish descent. After the war he was brought to Britain, tried, found guilty and hanged for treason.

the **Lord High Admiral** *pr. name* the formal naval rank of the monarch

the **Lord High Chancellor of England** *pr. name* the Keeper of the ➠Great Seal and highest ranking judge of England

Ex officio a peer, and presiding officer of both the ➠House of Lords and the ➠Court of Appeal. A member of the ➠Cabinet.

the **Lord High Commissioner** *pr. name, Sc.* the representative of the monarch at the ➠General Assembly of the ➠Church of Scotland

the **Lord High Constable of Scotland** *pr. name, hist.* an ancient office similar to that of the ➠Constable of England

Lord in Waiting *comp. noun* a male officer of the ➠Royal Household who attends upon the personal needs of the king

the **Lord Justice Clerk** *pr. name, Sc.* the vice-president of the ➠Court of Session

Lord Lieutenant *comp. noun* the personal representative of the ➠monarch within a ➠county in England and Wales or a ➠region in Scotland

When the office was created in the 16th C., it carried many responsible executive powers and duties, but is now of ceremonial significance only and considered honorary only.

Lord love a duck *exclam., sl.* a euphemism for or variation of "Lord love me"

the **Lord Lyon King of Arms** *pr. name, Sc.* the chief ➠herald of Scotland

Lord Mayor *pr. name* in certain cities, the ➠Mayor has this ex-officio title

They are the ➠City of London, where the holder is also a ➠Privy Councilor; ➠York, which has had a Lord Mayor since the 14th C.; and more recently the title has been bestowed upon 15 of the largest English provoncial cities

the **Lord Mayor's Banquet** *pr. name, hist.* an event, which has been held every November since the Middle Ages, in London's ➠Guildhall just after the new ➠Lord Mayor takes office

It is provided by the retiring ➠Lord Mayor in honor of his successor and has acquired greater importance over the last 100 years or so, as it has evolved into an occasion when the ➠prime minister of the day is expected to deliver a speech of major significance on the international situation and the place of Britain in the world.

the **Lord Mayor's Show** *pr. name* an annual ceremonial procession celebrating the election of a new ➠Lord Mayor of London

It is held on the second Saturday in November, when the newly elected ➠Lord Mayor is drawn through the streets of the ➠City in a horse-drawn carriage to be presented to the ➠Lord Chief Justice at the ➠Royal Courts of Justice, accompanied by a procession of colorfully decorated vehicles.

Lord Muck *comp. noun, coll., derog.* a self-important and pretentious man
> SEE ALSO: ➡Lady Bountiful, ➡Lady Muck.

Lord of Misrule *pr. name, hist.* the ➡King of Misrule

the Lord of the Isles *pr. name, hist.* the hereditary ruler of the ➡Western Isles of Scotland
> The title was taken over by the Scottish ➡Crown in 1540 and is now one of the titles of the ➡Prince of Wales. SEE ALSO: the ➡Kingdom of the Isles.

lord of the manor *comp. noun, hist.* one endowed with the traditional rights of a lord owning a ➡manor

Lord Ordinary *pr. name, Sc.* a judge of the ➡Outer House of the ➡Court of Session

the Lord President *pr. name, Sc.* the presiding judge at the ➡Court of Session in ➡Edinburgh

the Lord President of the Council *pr. name* the ➡Cabinet minister who presides over meetings of the ➡Privy Council

the Lord Privy Seal *pr. name* a senior member of the ➡Cabinet and the keeper of the ➡Privy Seal

the Lord Protector of the Commonwealth *pr. name, hist.* the head of state and chief executive of the republican Commonwealth in 17th C. England
> Oliver ➡Cromwell carried this title during most of the life of the ➡Commonwealth which had come into being following the execution of ➡Charles I in 1649.

Lord Provost *comp. noun, Sc.* the ➡Provost has this *ex-officio* title in the Scottish cities of ➡Edinburgh, ➡Glasgow, ➡Dundee and ➡Aberdeen

Lord Rector *comp. noun, Sc.* the president of the court at each of the four ancient Scottish universities of ➡St Andrews, ➡Glasgow, ➡Aberdeen and ➡Edinburgh
> The Lord Rector is elected directly by the students.

Lord's *pr. name* the cricket ground that is the headquarters of the ➡Marylebone Cricket Club, in St John's Wood, London

lords and ladies *comp. noun* the European arum
> Its formal name is *arum maculatum* and it is also known as the ➡wake-robin or ➡cuckoo-pint.

the Lord's Day Observance Society *pr. name* a pressure group whose members advocate the strict observance of the Sabbath, including the closing of all stores, etc., on that day

lordship *noun* the condition of being a ➡lord

the Lords of Session *pr. name, Sc.* the judges of the ➡Court of Session as a group

the Lords of the Congregation *pr. name, hist., Sc.* the 16th C. Protestant Scottish lords who deposed ➡Mary Queen of Scots and so helped ensure the triumph of Presbyterianism in Scotland

the Lords Spiritual *pr. name* the collective name for those 26 bishops of the ➡Church of England who are *ex officio* members of the ➡House of Lords

the Lords Temporal *pr. name* the collective name for all those members of the ➡House of Lords who are not ➡Lords Spiritual

the Lord Steward *pr. name, hist.* the senior official of the ➡Royal Household who formerly presided over the ➡Board of the Green Cloth

Loretto School *pr. name* one of Scotland's leading private schools
> Located in Musselburgh on the Firth of ➡Forth some five miles to the east of ➡Edinburgh, it was founded in 1827.

lorry *noun* a truck

lorry driver *comp. noun* a trucker

lose one's rag *idiom. phr. verb* to explode with rage

lost property *comp. noun* missing baggage, etc.

lost property office *comp. noun* a lost and found office
> Typically located at railroad stations, airports, etc.

the lot *noun* everything

Lothian *pr. name* (1) a former Scottish county now part of (2); (2) a region which contains ➡Edinburgh, in east-central Scotland
> The name is supposedly derived from King Lot, brother-in-law of ➡Arthur. The current population is 750,000 (1991 Census).

Lotus *pr. name (TM)* a famous marque of racing and sports automobiles

loud-hailer *comp. noun* a bullhorn

lough *noun, Gae., Ir.* a lake
> SEE ALSO: ➡loch.

Lough Neagh *pr. name* the largest freshwater lake in the ➡British Isles
> About 20 miles west of ➡Belfast, ➡Northern Ireland.

lounge bar *comp. noun* the better-furnished and better-served bar in a ➡public house
> Also called a ➡lounge bar, this is where the drinks are pricier and ladies are encouraged to sit. SEE ALSO: ➡public bar.

lounger *noun, sl.* a goldbricker

Louth *pr. name* a county in the ➡Irish Republic
> County Louth in the ancient province of Leinster.

louvre *spell.* louver

{love » luv » luvvy} *noun, sl.* a casual term of endearment to a stranger, particularly a woman

low [A] *noun, Sc.* a fire or flame
[B] *verb, Sc.* (1) to burn brightly; (2) to blaze with ardor, emotion or excitement

Low Church *pr. name* a party in the ➡Church of England that sees ritual and tradition of little significance and depreciate Catholic elements
> SEE ALSO: ➡High Church.

Lower Chamber *pr. name* the ➠House of Commons

lower deck *comp. noun* (1) a ship's deck that lies directly above the hold; (2) those members of a ship's crew who are petty officers and ratings

Lower House *pr. name* the ➠House of Commons

the **Lower Regions** *pr. name, coll.* Hell

Lowlander *pr. name, Sc.* all Scots except ➠Highlanders
In other words, about 95 percent of Scots.

the **Lowlands** *pr. name* all of Scotland except for the ➠Highlands

low loader *comp. noun* a flatbed truck

lowp *verb, Sc.* (1) to jump or hop; (2) to leap or spring to attention; (3) to walk with long springing steps

lowsin time *comp. noun, Sc.* the end of the day's work, when people go home

Loyalist *noun* an inhabitant of ➠Northern Ireland who resists union with the ➠Irish Republic and professes loyalty to the ➠British Crown

the **Loyal Toast** *pr. name* a toast to the health and long life of the sovereign
It should normally be taken standing up. However, the ➠Royal Navy has the unique privilege of drinking it sitting down, because of the lack of headroom between decks back in the days of wooden warships.

L-plate *comp. noun* a warning sign bearing a large red letter "L" on a white background
One of these signs must be placed on the front and another on the rear of a car that is being driven by someone who is learning how to drive. *SEE ALSO:* ➠L-Driver.

LPO *pr. name, abbr.* ➠London Philharmonic Orchestra

LRT *pr. name, abbr.* ➠London Regional Transport

LSD *noun, abbr., coll., Lat.* (1) pounds, shillings and pence; (2) money in general
This is an abbreviation of the Latin *librae, solidi, denarii*, which loosely translates as "pounds, shillings and pennies", the three currency units of the pre-1971 British monetary system.

LSE *pr. name, abbr.* the ➠London School of Economics

LSO *pr. name, abbr.* the ➠London Symphony Orchestra

LT *pr. name, abbr.* ➠London Transport

LTA *pr. name, abbr.* the Lawn Tennis Association

Ltd. *noun, abbr.* a private incorporated company which has limited liability
A company whose shares are not available for purchase by the public. By law, the words "private limited company" or the abbreviation "Ltd." must be placed after the name.

LTS *pr. name (TM)* a railroad company operating commuter services between London and ➠Southend
It is part of ➠British Rail.

lucky bleeder *exclam.* a lucky person

lucky dip *comp. noun* a grab bag

lucky sod *comp. noun, sl.* a lucky fellow

Lucy Cavendish College *pr. name* a college of ➠Cambridge University founded in 1965
This college admits female students only.

the **Luddites** *pr. name, hist.* groups of early 19th C. textile workers who went around the countryside destroying the newly invented machinery, which they blamed for their own unemployment
Named for Ned Ludd, their almost certainly fictitious leader.

ludo *noun, Lat.* a game similar to Parcheesi, where players move counters over squares by throwing dice
From the Latin for "I play"

luff *noun* the widest part of the bow of a ship
Which is to say, from where the sides begin to curve in.

luggage ticket *comp. noun* a baggage check

luggage van *comp. noun* a baggage car on a train

lughole *comp. noun, sl.* an ear hole
From the originally Scots or dialect *lug*, meaning an ear or ear-like handle or loop.

Lulach *pr. name, hist.* ➠King of Scots
The stepson of ➠Macbeth, he reigned in 1057 for seven months after Macbeth died in battle, until killed himself by ➠Malcolm Canmore in 1058. His nickname was "the Fool".

lum *noun, Sc.* a chimney

lumber *noun* surplus or broken furniture and other articles stored away because they are not required

lumber room *comp. noun* an attic or cellar normally used for the storage of ➠lumber

lumber with *verb, sl.* to encumber with something or someone inconvenient or unwanted

lummy *exclam., abbr., sl.* a euphemism for or variation of "Lord love me"

the **lump** *noun, sl.* the informal employment and payment of casual construction workers, without benefit of income tax and such things

lump sugar *comp. noun* sugar cubes

Luna *noun* an heraldic representation of the moon

Luncheon Voucher *pr. name (TM)* a certificate that may be exchanged for food in restaurants
Supplied by some companies to their employees as a substitute for the direct provision of a subsidized company restaurant or cafeteria.

Lundy *pr. name, hist.* a small rocky islet some 12 miles off the northern coast of ➠Devon
➠Henry III built a castle there in the 13th C. as part of a campaign to prevent piracy. The entire island is now owned by the ➠National Trust.

lunt *noun, Sc.* a puff, cloud or column of steam or smoke

lupin *spell.* lupine
A flower of the genus *Lupinus*, which has long and tapering many-colored spiked flowers.

lurcher *noun* a cross-breed dog midway between a ➠collie and a greyhound

Often used by hunters or poachers.

lurker *noun, sl.* an unauthorized street trader

lustre *noun* a thin fabric with cotton warp and a weft of wool or mohair

Sometimes used to make dresses.

{**lustre » lustreless » lustreware**} *spell.* {luster » lusterless » lusterware}

the **Lutine Bell** *pr. name* a bell hanging at ➠Lloyd's of London, which is rung only when there is news of a ship being lost or of other calamitous events

The bell was salvaged from the *Lutine*, a ship carrying bullion to Holland that sank in the Zuyder Zee in 1799, costing its insurers at Lloyd's a great deal.

It was rung upon news of the assassination of President Kennedy in 1963.

Luton *pr. name* a town in ➠Bedfordshire, England

Currently, the city's population, including suburbs, is 220,000 (1988 estimate).

Luton Hoo *pr. name, hist.* a great house built in the 1770s, about 10 miles north of ➠St Albans in ➠Hertfordshire

It was designed by Robert Adam, greatly modified in the early 19th C., and largely destroyed by fire in 1843. The house was rebuilt in the early 1900s.

LV *noun, abbr.* a ➠Luncheon Voucher

LVO *noun, abbr.* Lieutenant of the Royal Victorian Order

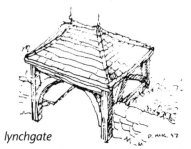

lynchgate

lychgate *noun* a roofed gateway into a churchyard

These were originally provided as a place where a coffin could wait until time for burial.

lyke-wake *comp. noun, arch.* an overnight watch over a corpse

lynchet *noun* a ridge formed on a hillside by plowing

the **Lyon Court** *pr. name, abbr., Sc.* the ➠Court of the Lord Lyon

M

M- *noun, abbr.* the prefix to highway number, designating it to be a ➡motorway

SEE ALSO: ➡A-, ➡B-.

ma'am *noun, abbr.* a form of the word "madam" commonly used when addressing female royalty

the **Maastricht Treaty** *noun* a treaty, signed by all members of the ➡European Community in February 1992, which is intended to accelerate the process of European integration

The principle points agreed were that, the ➡EC should become known as the ➡European Union, there should be a common citizenship, a single currency should be established by 1999, and steps should be taken towards a common European security and foreign policy.

After some considerable difficulties, (not least in Britain) the treaty was ratified by all member states and implemented at the beginning of 1994.

Mac *noun, coll.* a nickname for a Scotsman

macaroni *noun, arch., coll.* a fashionable young man who wears Italian styles and affects Italian manners

An 18th C. term.

Macbeth *pr. name, hist.* ➡King of Scots

The son of ➡Malcolm II's daughter Donada, he reigned for 17 years from 1040 until killed in battle in 1057.

It should be said that the picture of him presented to us in Shakespeare's play of the same name is highly inaccurate. Macbeth had at least as strong a claim to the throne as ➡Duncan, and although murder was a fairly normal and accepted way to succeed in those days, he did not in fact murder his predecessor but killed him in open battle near ➡Elgin, in the north of Scotland.

What's more, the real Macbeth appears to have been a rather good and wise king, popular and confident enough of the stability of his kingdom and loyalty of his subjects to have felt able to go on an extended pilgrimage to Rome in 1050. And although ➡Malcolm Canmore did march against him with help from Siward of ➡Northumbria (not the king of England as Shakespeare tells us) and did defeat and kill Macbeth in battle, the scene of the battle was Lumphanan near ➡Aberdeen, many miles from either Birnam Wood or Dunsinane.

Finally, it was not Malcolm but Macbeth's stepson ➡Lulach who was proclaimed king following the battle, and he reigned for seven months before Malcolm could eventually contrive to take the crown for himself.

the **Mace** *pr. name* (1) the symbol of the authority of the ➡Speaker of the ➡House of Commons; (2) the symbol of the authority of the ➡Lord Chancellor in his capacity as speaker of the ➡House of Lords

macer *noun, Sc.* an official who keeps order and acts as usher in a court of law

machine *verb, coll.* to sew with a sewing machine

machine minder *noun* one who supervises a machine

In a factory, for instance.

mackintosh *noun* a raincoat made with a lightweight, rubberized waterproof material

From Charles Macintosh, 19th C. inventor of this material.

{**mac » mack**} *noun, abbr., coll.* a ➡mackintosh

Maconochie *noun, arch., sl.* (1) tinned stew supplied to soldiers on active duty; (2) the stomach

The name of a supplier of tinned stew to the 19th C. army.

madam *noun, coll.* a conceited young woman

Madame Tussaud's *pr. name, hist.* a waxworks exhibition in ➡Baker Street, London

Anne Marie Grosholtz Tussaud learned her art in late 18th C. Paris where, during the French Revolution, she was required to make death masks of many victims of the Terror.

She moved to London and established her wax exhibition there in 1802. Some of her original death masks from revolutionary Paris are still on display today in the exhibition's Chamber of Horrors.

madding *adj., arch.* frenzied

Now often mistakenly thought to mean "maddening"; Harvey, in *Far From the Madding Crowd*, found the crowd to be frenzied, not maddening.

mad-doctor *idiom, arch.* a doctor who treats the insane

Madeira cake *comp. noun* a particularly rich and very sweet sponge-cake

Named for the mid-Atlantic Portuguese island.

made redundant *verb* to lay off from work

made to measure *comp. noun* made to order; custom-made

made-up road *comp. noun* a paved highway complete with proper drainage and so forth

mad keen *adj. phr., sl.* exceptionally eager or energetic

mad on

mad on *idiom, sl.* very enthusiastic about

MAFF *pr. name, abbr.* the ➡Ministry of Agriculture, Fisheries and Food

maffick *verb, arch., coll.* to celebrate in a particularly wild and noisy manner

Named after Mafeking, a town in South Africa which was relieved after a very long siege in 1900, during the ➡Boer War. This news led to huge and hysterical celebrations in London.

mag *noun, abbr.* a magazine

Magdalen College *pr. name* a college of ➡Oxford University founded in 1458

"Magdalen" is pronounced "mawd-lin".

Magdalene College *pr. name* a college of ➡Cambridge University founded in 1542

"Magdalene" is pronounced "mawd-lin".

Magherafelt *pr. name* a district in ➡Northern Ireland, in what used to be County ➡Londonderry

The current population is 35,000 (1990 estimate).

magic *adj., sl.* wonderful or perfect

Magna Carta *pr. name, hist., Lat.* the ➡Great Charter granted by ➡John to his Barons in 1215

(See box on this page)

maiden *noun, abbr.* in ➡cricket, a ➡maiden over

the **Maiden** *pr. name, hist., Sc.* a nickname for ➡Malcolm IV, ➡King of Scots

maiden assize *comp. noun* an ➡assize that has no cases to try

maiden castle *comp. noun, hist.* a castle that has never been taken

Maiden Castle *pr. name, hist.* the best example of a Iron Age fortification surviving in Britain today

It is located in ➡Dorset, about three miles southwest of Dorchester. The hilltop site is believed to have been occupied for about 4,000 years, although the present fortifications, a series of earth ramparts which have a diameter of about two miles and are terraced up upon the slopes of the hill, are less than 2,500 years old.

maiden over *comp. noun* a ➡cricketing ➡over when no ➡runs are made

the **Maiden Queen** *pr. name, hist.* ➡Elizabeth I

maiden speech *comp. noun* the first speech made in ➡Parliament by a newly elected ➡MP

It is expected that the speech should be non-controversial and in turn, will be listened to without interruption.

Maid Marian *pr. name, hist.* ➡Robin Hood's girlfriend

Originally, a name for the ➡Queen of the May, who featured regularly in medieval ➡Morris dances and May Day celebrations. Only later, in the 17th C., did she become connected with the ➡Robin Hood legend.

maid of honour *comp. noun* (1) an unmarried lady who attends upon a queen or princess; (2) a small custard tart with an almond-flavored filling

(2) are named from Maid of Honour Row, a street in Richmond, ➡Surrey, where they were first made in the 18th C.

the **Maid of Norway** *pr. name, hist.* Margaret, ➡Queen of Scots

Margaret, born in 1282, was the daughter of the King of Norway and became Queen of Scots at the age of four upon the death of her grandfather, ➡Alexander III.

She reigned from 1286 to 1290 and was betrothed to marry Edward, son of King ➡Edward I of England, but perished while on her first voyage from Norway to her Scottish realm at the age of eight.

Maidstone *pr. name, hist.* a town that is the administrative center of ➡Kent

The current population is 76,000 (1991 estimate).

Magna Carta

John fixed his seal on this document in the field of ➡Runnymede beside the ➡Thames River near Windsor, when his only alternative course of action would have been to provoke a rebellion or civil war that he was certain to lose.

Two clauses in the Charter, out of many others that now seem quite irrelevant, have been seen as the fundamental guarantees of personal and political liberties in both Britain and America ever since. One is that no free man may be imprisoned or otherwise punished without due process according to law, and the other is that justice could never be denied, delayed or sold.

As a matter of historical fact, *Magna Carta* was revised and republished several times, and the version which is now most frequently reprinted or quoted dates from 1225, during the reign of ➡Henry III.

There are two original copies of the document kept in the ➡British Museum in London, and one each in ➡Lincoln and ➡Salisbury cathedrals.

The name means ➡Great Charter in Latin.

SEE ALSO: the ➡Declaration of Arbroath.

mail cart *comp. noun, arch.* (1) a cart employed to transport mail by road; (2) a small cart sometimes used to transport children
They were usually horse-drawn.

the **Mail Rail** *pr. name* the world's only underground railroad entirely dedicated to delivering the mail
Operated by the ➡Post Office, it links various mail sorting offices and railroad terminuses in central London on a track that is several miles long and runs through specially constructed tunnels from Whitechapel in the ➡East End to ➡Paddington railroad terminus. The trains are unmanned.

the **Mainland** *pr. name* (1) the island of ➡Great Britain; (2) the main island of the ➡Orkney group; (3) the main island of the ➡Shetland group

mains *noun, Sc.* a ➡home farm

the **mains** *noun* (1) the central distribution network for a power utility such as gas or electricity; (2) household electricity taken from (1) as opposed to electrical power supplied from batteries, etc.

mains razor *comp. noun* an electric razor that uses the public electricity supply rather than a battery

maintained school *comp. noun* a school funded with government money

maintenance *noun* alimony

mair *adj., Sc.* (1) more; (2) physically larger

maisonette *noun* (1) a small house; (2) an apartment or condominium, which has its own entrance and has accommodation on more than one floor

Maister *noun, Sc.* a courtesy title for the eldest son of a Scots ➡viscount or ➡baron who lacks another title

maize flour *comp. noun* cornmeal

maize store *comp. noun* a corncrib

Majesty *noun* a form of title used to address royalty, either directly or indirectly
For example, "Your Majesty," "His Majesty the King" or "Her Majesty's Government."

majesty *noun* a sovereign and impressive stateliness of being

major *adj., out.* a suffix to a surname indicating that its owner is the eldest of that name
Once commonly used among boys attending English ➡pubic schools, where, for example, the eldest of two brothers may be called "Smith-major." *SEE ALSO:* ➡minor.

major-general *comp. noun* the fourth-highest rank of commissioned officer in the British Army
Equivalent in rank to a two-star general in the U.S. Army.

Majorism *noun* the supposed political philosophy favored by ➡Prime Minister John Major and his reputed followers

make a bad fist *idiom. phr. verb, coll.* to do a bad job

make a bomb *idiom. phr. verb, coll.* to make a great deal of money

make a dead set at *idiom. phr. verb, coll.* (1) to attack with vigor and determination; (2) to attempt to attract or interest romantically or sexually

make a good fist *idiom. phr. verb, coll.* to do a good job

make a House *idiom. phr. verb, coll.* to ensure that there are enough ➡MPs present to form a quorum

make a meal of (something) *idiom. phr. verb, coll.* to make a major issue out of (something)

make a {muck » poor fist} of it *idiom. phr. verb, coll.* to bungle, to do a poor job

make a mull of it *idiom. phr. verb, coll.* to perform badly

make at *idiom. phr. verb, coll.* to lunge towards

make noises *idiom. phr. verb, coll.* to talk about or hint

make polite noises *idiom. phr. verb, coll.* to say that which is polite without meaning it

maker *noun, arch.* a poet

make the running *idiom. phr. verb, coll.* (1) to take charge; (2) to establish the pace

Malcolm Canmore *pr. name, hist.* the nickname for ➡Malcolm III, ➡King of Scots
"Canmore" means "Big-Headed".

Malcolm I *pr. name, hist.* King of ➡Alba
He was the son of ➡Donald II and reigned for 12 years from 942 until murdered in 954.

Malcolm II *pr. name, hist.* ➡King of Scots
The son of ➡Dubh, he reigned for 29 years from 1005 until 1034. Malcolm consolidated the territory of Scotland by annexing ➡Strathclyde in 1016.

Malcolm III *pr. name, hist.* ➡King of Scots
The son of ➡Duncan I, he reigned for 35 years from 1058 until 1093 when he died while leading his army through northern England. He gained the throne seven months after killing ➡Macbeth at the battle of Lumphanan, near ➡Aberdeen. Almost his entire reign appears to have been spent at war, usually with the English. He was nicknamed ➡Malcolm Cannier.

Malcolm IV *pr. name, hist.* ➡King of Scots
The son of Henry, Earl of ➡Northumbria, he succeeded to the throne at the age of 11 and reigned for 12 years from 1153 until 1165. He was nicknamed the ➡Maiden.

malkin *noun, coll.* (1) a careless or untidy woman; (1) a cat; (3) a hare

the **Mall** *pr. name, hist.* the principal processional route through London
First built as a broad processional way in the 1660, it stretches from the ➡Admiralty Arch entrance to ➡Trafalgar Square to the ➡Victoria Monument in front of ➡Buckingham Palace.

malmsey *pr. name, hist.* a sweet strong wine

Originally from Greece but now also produced in Spain and other places. It is reputed that the Duke of Clarence, son of Richard ➡Duke of York, was put to death upon the order of his brother, ➡Edward IV, by drowning in a butt of malmsey in 1478. See Shakespeare's *Richard III* for more details, although not necessarily more accuracy.

malthouse *noun* a building built for the processing and storage of malt

malt whisky *comp. noun* ➡Scotch whiskey made with malted barley

Malvern Girls' College *pr. name* one of the leading English ➡public schools

Founded in 1893, it is located in ➡Worcestershire.

mam *noun, abbr., coll.* mother

{**mamilla » mamillary**} *spell.* {mammilla » mammillary}

the Isle of **Man** *pr. name* an island in the ➡Irish Sea midway between ➡Great Britain and ➡Ireland

The island has an area of about 227 square miles and a current population of some 66,000 (1988 estimate)

It is not part of the ➡United Kingdom, but a self-governing dependency of the ➡British Crown. However, the United Kingdom takes care of all its defense and external affairs. *SEE ALSO:* the ➡Channel Islands.

managing director *comp. noun* the chief executive of a commercial business

man and wife *idiom, rh. sl.* knife

Manchester *pr. name* the principal city in ➡Greater Manchester, England

It was founded in 29 as *Mancunium* by the Romans who built a military fort there; this is why the citizens of Manchester are known as ➡Mancunians today.

Flemish weavers began the city's link with the textile industry when they settled there in the 14th C., but Manchester only began to grow from a small local center into a great city in the 18th C. when firstly canals and secondly, in the 19th C., railroads brought cheap coal and raw materials to the city.

Incorporated as a city in 1838, the current population, including suburbs, is 2,350,000 (1988 estimate).

Manchester College *pr. name* a college of ➡Oxford University founded in 1990

Manchester goods *idiom, arch., coll.* cotton textiles

The area around ➡Manchester was where most of Britain's cotton mills were located during the 19th C.

the **Manchester Massacre** *pr. name, hist.* an alternate name for the ➡Peterloo Massacre

the **Manchester Ship Canal** *pr. name, hist.* a canal constructed in the late 19th C. to enable oceangoing ships of up to about 15,000 tons to sail directly into ➡Manchester

About 36 miles long, it is about 30 ft deep and 120 ft wide.

Manchester Terrier *pr. name* a short-haired black-and-tan terrier

Mancunian *pr. name* a native or citizen of Manchester

From the Roman name for the city.

mandrel *noun* a kind of pick used by miners

mangel-wurzel *comp. noun* a large beet normally grown as cattlefood

manky [A] *adj., North, sl.* (1) naughty; (2) spoiled

[B] *adj., sl.* dirty or disgusting

{**manoeuvrability » manoeuvrable » manoeuvre**} *spell.* {maneuverability » maneuverable » maneuver}

Man of Kent *comp. noun* one born in Kent, to the east of the ➡Medway

As distinct from a ➡Kentsman, born *west* of the ➡Medway.

man of straw *comp. noun* (1) someone making a financial or business commitment without the means to fulfill it; (2) a stuffed effigy, traditionally made from straw; (3) a straw hat

the **man on the Clapham omnibus** *idiom, coll., out.* the average person

Clapham is a district in south London.

manor [A] *noun, hist.* (1) a landed estate; (2) the residence of the owner of a landed estate; (3) a medieval territorial unit in England

(3) was an estate under the rule of a lord who had various rights over the inhabitants, especially the right to hold a court.

[B] *noun, sl.* a police precinct

manor house *comp. noun, hist.* the house of a ➡lord of the manor

manse *noun, Lat.* the house of a Presbyterian minister

Particularly in the ➡Church of Scotland. The word comes from the Latin *mansus* = "house."

Mansfield Hall *pr. name* a hall of ➡Oxford University founded in 1886

mansion flat *comp. noun* an apartment within an apartment block

mansion house *comp. noun, hist.* an especially large private residence

Traditionally, the house of a wealthy landed proprietor.

the **Mansion House** *pr. name* the official residence of the ➡Lord Mayor of London, built in the Palladian style in 1753

It incorporates a large room known as the Egyptian Hall, which is used for official banquets and receptions.

mansions *noun* an apartment block

mantua-maker *comp. noun, arch.* a dressmaker

Manx [A] *adj.* pertaining to the ➡Isle of Man

[B] *noun* the native language of the ➡Isle of Man

A variety of ➡Gaelic that is now extinct.

Manx cat *comp. noun* a breed of cat without a tail but with a two-colored coat

Litters of Manx cats usually consist of a mixture of ➡rumpy and ➡stumpy kittens; so in truth the tail has not entirely vanished from the breed.

{**Manxman » Manxwoman**} *comp. noun* a native, citizen or inhabitant of the ➡Isle of Man

the Marble Arch

Marble Arch *pr. name* A triumphal arch originally built as the main entrance arch in front of ➡Buckingham Place, erected there in 1828

However, it proved too narrow for royal carriages, so that in 1851 it was moved to its present position at what was formerly ➡Tyburn Gate and is now called Buckingham Gate. The arch was modeled on Constantine's Arch in Rome.

march *noun, arch.* a border or frontier

the **Marches** *noun, hist.* (1) the ancient frontier between England and Scotland; (2) land on the frontier between England and Scotland that was in dispute for many centuries; (3) the ancient frontier between England and Wales

marching orders *comp. noun, coll.* (1) a military order to march; (2) walking papers, a dismissal

marchioness *noun* (1) the wife or widow of a ➡marquess; (2) a woman who is a ➡marquess in her own right

march past *comp. noun* a military procession past a reviewing point or position

mardie *noun, North, sl.* an effeminate man or one who is ineffectual or weak-willed

mardle *verb, East* to gossip

mardy [A] *adj., North, sl.* (1) bad-tempered; (2) spoiled or over-indulged; (3) marred or ruined

(2) is typically descriptive of a child.

[B] *adj., East* fretful

marg *noun, abbr., coll.* margarine

Margaret *pr. name, hist.* ➡Queen of Scots

The ➡Maid of Norway; also called ➡Margaret of Norway

Margaret of Norway *pr. name, hist.* the ➡Maid of Norway and ➡Queen of Scots

marginal {**constituency » seat**} *comp. noun* a parliamentary district where the sitting ➡MP has a very small majority and thus is in considerable danger of being turned out at the next election

marine *noun* a member of the ➡Royal Marines

the **Maritime Trust** *pr. name* a voluntary organization dedicated to the restoration and maintenance of ships which have played important roles in Britain's history

mark [A] *noun, abbr.* a ➡gas mark

[B] *verb* to follow another closely in order to hinder them in some way

Typically while participating in some sport.

mark (someone's) card *idiom. phr. verb* to warn (someone) off

the **Market** *pr. name, abbr., coll., hist.* the ➡European Common Market

market cross *comp. noun* a cross erected at a crossroads or similar location, where a market is regularly held

market day *comp. noun* the day of the week when an outdoor market is held in a particular town

marketeer [A] *noun, arch.* an advocate or supporter of the ➡European Common Market

[B] *spell.* marketer

market garden *comp. noun* a truck farm

market gardener *comp. noun* a truck farmer

market town *comp. noun* a town that holds an outdoor market each ➡market day

mark out *phr. verb* to set apart

Marks & Spencer *pr. name* a quality departmental store chain with branches all over Britain

Marlborough College *pr. name* one of the leading English ➡public schools

Founded in 1843, it is located in Marlborough, ➡Wiltshire.

Marlborough House *pr. name* a large early 18th C. house in Pall Mall, London

Built for his wife by the Duke of Marlborough, the land it stands upon was leased from the royal family and in 1887 reverted to it. The house is now used primarily for ➡Commonwealth conferences.

marleys *noun, rh. sl.* hemorrhoids

Derivation: hemorrhoids > piles > Marley Tiles > marleys. "Marley Tiles" (TM) is a brand of thermoplastic tiles.

Marmite

Marmite *pr. name (TM)* a yeast spread suitable for toast or bread

marmot *noun* a groundhog

marquess *noun* a peer ranking midway between an ➠earl and a ➠duke

marriage articles *comp. noun, arch.* a prenuptial contract or agreement

marriage guidance *comp. noun* advice given to those with marriage difficulties

marriage lines *comp. noun, coll.* a marriage certificate

marrow [A] *noun* a squash

[B] *noun, North, Sc.* (1) a close friend; (2) a fellow-worker; (3) a spouse; (4) one of a pair

marrowbone jelly *comp. noun* gelatin

marry {above » below} oneself *idiom. phr. verb* to marry someone of {higher » lower} class than oneself

marshall *verb* to merge the ➠coats of arms of different families into one

marshalled *spell.* marshaled

marshalling yard *comp. noun, abbr.* a railroad switching yard

Marshal of the Royal Air Force *comp. noun, abbr.* the highest rank of commissioned officer in the ➠RAF
Equivalent in rank to a General of the Air Force in the USAF.

the Battle of **Marston Moor** *pr. name, hist.* a ➠Parliamentary victory in the ➠English Civil War
Where Oliver ➠Cromwell earned his nickname of ➠Old Ironsides in 1644 by defeating the King's forces, commanded by Prince ➠Rupert. Marston Moor is about seven miles to the west of the city of ➠York.

Martello tower *pr. name, hist.* one of a number of towers built around the British coast during the ➠Napoleonic Wars to defend against French invasion
They are about 40 ft tall, built of stone and circular in form. About 75 were built, and 27 are still almost entirely intact.

Martinmas *pr. name, Sc.* St Martin's Day, which is a Scottish ➠term-day or ➠quarter-day
November 28, formerly November 1

martlet *noun* an heraldic representation of a swallow that has no feet

{marvelled » marvelling » marvellous} *spell.* {marveled » marveling » marvelous}

Mary Ann *comp. noun, derog., sl.* an effeminate male, especially a homosexual

Mary Blane *idiom, rh. sl.* a train

Mary I *pr. name, hist.* ➠Queen of England
(See box on opposite page)

Mary II *pr. name, hist.* ➠Queen of Great Britain
SEE ALSO: ➠William and Mary.

Marylebone *pr. name, Fr.* a London district previously known as ➠Tyburn but now renamed after a church in the area called St Marie-le-bon
From the French, "Mary-the-good"

Marylebone Cricket Club *pr. name, hist.* Britain's leading ➠cricket club
Founded in 1787, it has its grounds at ➠Lord's, in St John's Wood, London. Until the job was taken over by the ➠Cricket Council in 1969, the Marylebone Cricket Club was the body that governed cricket worldwide.

Mary Queen of Scots *pr. name, hist.* the popular name for ➠Mary Stewart
(See box on opposite page)

the **Mary Rose** *pr. name, hist.* the flagship of ➠Henry VIII's navy, which sank off ➠Portsmouth in 1545
It was raised in 1982 and is now displayed at a specially constructed museum in ➠Portsmouth.

Mary Stewart *pr. name, hist.* ➠Mary Queen of Scots
She is sometimes called this, probably to avoid confusion with ➠Mary Tudor, ➠Queen of England.

Mary Tudor *pr. name, hist.* Mary I, ➠Queen of England
She is sometimes called this, probably to avoid confusion with ➠Mary Stewart, best known as ➠Mary Queen of Scots.

mash *noun, abbr., coll.* mashed potatoes

mash tub *comp. noun* where malt is mashed

mason *noun, abbr.* a stonemason, but not a bricklayer

the **Massacre of Glencoe** *pr. name, hist.* the massacre of 38 men, women and children of the Clan MacDonald, in January 1692 as they slept
They were killed in this dark and somber glen in the southwestern Scottish ➠Highlands, upon the orders of the government in London by troops who were members of the Clan Campbell, who had been staying with the MacDonalds as their guests.
To this day there remains bad blood between the MacDonalds and the Campbells. Such things are not quickly or easily forgotten in that part of the world.

masses *adj., coll.* lots, plenty

Mass Observation *pr. name, hist.* a pioneering opinion polling organization that conducted its work during the 1930s and through World War II

massy *adj., coll.* massive, solid or bulky

master *noun, out.* (1) a male head of household; (2) an employer, especially of a servant; (3) a male teacher; (4) the principal of certain university colleges; (5) an official of the ➠Supreme Court of Judicature; (6) earlier, a formal prefix title attached to the given name of a boy not old enough to be called "Mr."
(4) is most common at ➠Cambridge University.

master aircrew *comp. noun, abbr.* a warrant officer in the ➠RAF who is engaged on flying duties

master gunner *comp. noun* a warrant officer of the ➡Royal Artillery or ➡Royal Navy responsible for the gunnery equipment of a battery

Master in Chancery *pr. name* the head clerk of the ➡Chancery Division

master of foxhounds *comp. noun* a person in charge of the hounds used in a hunt

the **Master of the Horse** *pr. name* the senior official of the ➡Royal Household responsible for the personal safety of the sovereign

the **Master of the Household** *pr. name* the senior official of the ➡Royal Household who presides over the ➡Board of the Green Cloth

Two Marys

Mary I *pr. name, hist.* ➡Queen of England, also called ➡Mary Tudor.

A member of the ➡Royal House of ➡Tudor, she styled herself, "Mary, by the Grace of God, Queen of England, France and Ireland, ➡Defender of the Faith" and reigned for five years from 1553 to 1558 following the death of her half-brother, ➡Edward VI.

Her determined Roman Catholicism followed upon her father ➡Henry VIII's break with Rome and his establishment of the separate ➡Church of England, and more recently her young half-brother, Edward VI, had allowed a spirit of intolerant Protestantism to develop in England. As a result she was intensely unpopular, made yet more so by her marriage to the Philip, heir to the crown of Catholic Spain.

In her short reign she allowed draconian persecution of those she considered Protestant heretics. Over 300 were burned at the stake, which proved a propaganda disaster of the first magnitude for the Catholic cause as well as for Mary personally; she ended this particular portion of her career with the nickname of ➡Bloody Mary.

The other major "achievement" of her reign was a short war with France at the instigation of her Spanish husband which brought about the loss of Calais, the last portion of continental soil which had remained part of the territory of the English Crown. It is reported that when she heard the news about the loss of Calais, she said that, "When I am dead and opened, you shall find 'Calais' lying in my heart." She bore no children.

Mary Queen of Scots *pr. name, hist.* the popular name for ➡Mary Stewart or ➡Stuart, ➡Queen of Scots from 1542 until 1567.

A member of the Scottish ➡Royal House of ➡Stewart, she acceded to the Scottish throne at the age of six days in 1542, but was brought up at the French royal court where she spoke French as her first language. There she married the *Dauphin* (the French crown prince) so that when his father died in 1559 she was, at the age of 16, queen of both France and Scotland as well as heir-apparent to the throne of England, because ➡Elizabeth I had no issue and Mary Stewart was her closest living relative.

This was not to be. Her French husband died within a few months of their marriage and two years later, aged 18, she returned to a Scotland that was in the throws of a Calvinist Reformation driven by such as John Knox, who found her Catholic ways anathema. She might have overcome that, but the truth was that she exhibited a lamentable lack of judgment, both personal and political. Both of her marriages in Scotland—first to the Englishman Darnley until his death in a mysterious explosion at his house near Edinburgh, then to the Scotsman Bothwell—were disasters. Her repeated belligerent declarations that Elizabeth was not the legitimate ruler of England made a life-long enemy out of her cousin in London.

However, it was her personal life and especially her blatent Roman Catholicism that made Mary utterly unacceptable as queen to the Scottish Protestant leaders, the ➡Lords of the Congregation. These lords obliged her to abdicated in 1567 in favor of her son, who thus became James VI of Scotland at the age of one year. She was kept a prisoner for most of the rest of her life, firstly in Scotland and then later in England by Elizabeth, who eventually ordered her execution in 1587.

SEE ALSO: ➡Elizabeth I; the ➡Four Marys; ➡James I of England and VI of Scotland.

the **Master of the {King's » Queen's} Musick** *pr. name* the senior official of the ➡Royal Household responsible for organizing the musical requirement of royal and state occasions
Now an honorary title granted to a well-known composer.

the **Master of the Rolls** *pr. name* the senior judge presiding over civil cases in the ➡Court of Appeal
The Master of the Rolls is also responsible for the legal section of the ➡Public Records Office.

mate *noun, coll.* a friend

{matelot » matelote} *noun, arch., Fr.* a sailor
From the French for "sailor."

mater *noun, Lat., out., sl.* mother
This is the Latin for "mother."

materfamilias *noun, Lat., out.* a woman family head
From the Latin, *mater + familia* = "mother" + "family" *SEE ALSO:* "paterfamilias."

maternity allowance *comp. noun* a government payment made to a pregnant woman who does not qualify for ➡maternity pay for whatever reason

maternity pay *comp. noun* a statutory requirement upon an employer to pay a woman employee for 18 weeks after she leaves work to have a baby
To qualify for full maternity pay, a woman has to have worked for the same employer for two years or more.

matey [A] *adj., coll.* friendly, sociable
[B] *noun, coll.* a friend
Often used sarcastically.

maths *noun, abbr., coll.* mathematics
This, never "math," is the common abbreviation.

matinée *spell.* matinee

matinee jacket *comp. noun* a baby's short coat

matiness *noun, coll.* friendliness

Matlock *pr. name, hist.* a town that is the administrative center of ➡Derbyshire
The current population is 21,000 (1991 estimate).

matric *noun, abbr., coll.* matriculation

matron *noun, arch.* a woman in charge of the nursing services of a hospital
Now superseded by ➡senior nursing officer.

mattins *spell.* matins

maucht *noun, Sc.* physical ability, strength or power

maukiflee *adj., Sc.* a bluebottle fly
Its formal name is *calliphora vomitoria.*

maukit *adj., Sc.* (1) filthy or putrid; (2) infested with maggots

maun *verb aux., Sc.* (1) must; (2) must go
(2) is employed without a distinct verb of motion word; for example, "I maun awa" = "I must go away."

maunder *verb* (1) to behave in an idle fashion; (2) to grumble or mumble

the **Maundy Money** *pr. name, hist., Lat.* specially minted coins disbursed personally by the sovereign to selected senior citizens at a ceremony each ➡Maundy Thursday
The number of senior citizens honored in this way each year is equal to the age of the monarch. The coins are made of silver. The name derives from the Latin word *mandatum* for the foot-washing ceremony that Christ performed for his disciples at the time of the Last Supper.

Maundy Thursday *pr. name, hist.* the Thursday before Easter, which is when the monarch disburses the ➡Maundy Money

mauther *noun, East, out.* a young girl

mavourneen *noun, Gae., Ir.* darling or dear
From the Gaelic, *mo mhuirnín* = "my little love"

maxe *verb, coll.* to confuse

in a **maxe** *adj., coll.* confused or bewildered

Mayfair *pr. name* a fashionable district in west-central London
The district acquired this name because of an annual fair formerly held there every May until the middle of the 18th C.

Mayo *pr. name* a county in the ➡Irish Republic
County Mayo in the ancient province of ➡Connaught.

Mayor *pr. name* in England, Wales and Northern Ireland, the principal elected official and chief magistrate of any district council that has the status of a ➡borough (1)
Formerly, the chief magistrate of a city.

Maypole *pr. name* a painted pole decorated with ribbons and garland, danced around on May Day
Traditional English celebrations of May Day included competitions and exhibitions, such as archery and morris dancing, as well as setting up and dancing around the Maypole. All these activities are the vestigial remains of pre-Christian pagan spring festivals. Eventually, the proceedings came to be presided over by ➡Robin Hood and ➡Maid Marion, and for some time during the 16th C. the occasion become known as Robin Hood's Day.

the **mays** *noun* the final degree examinations at ➡Cambridge University
Called this because they happen in the month of May.

May Week *pr. name* a week of celebrations and boat races at ➡Cambridge University during the first week of June, after the ➡mays
No, that was not an error, May Week is indeed in June.

Maze Prison *pr. name* a high-security prison in ➡Northern Ireland
It was especially built in 1971 to contain convicted or suspected terrorist prisoners, from both ➡Republican and Loyalist terrorist groups. Republicans usually referred to the place by its original name, ➡Long Kesh.

MBE *noun, abbr.* a Member of the Order of the ➡British Empire

MC *noun, abbr.* the Military Cross

A decoration established shortly after the start of World War I and awarded to junior officers only.

MCC *pr. name, abbr.* the ➠Marylebone Cricket Club

M.Ch. *pr. name, abbr., Lat.* a Master of Surgery

From the Latin *magister chirurgiae.*

McKenzie friend *comp. noun, coll.* a person who is not a lawyer but appears before a court to help or advise one of the parties to a case

From a case (*McKenzie v. McKenzie,* in 1970) where the precedent of allowing non-professional advisors was set.

McNaughten Rules *pr. name* the legal rules that define the criminal responsibility or otherwise of a purportedly insane person

MCR *noun, abbr.* a ➠middle common room

MD *noun, abbr.* a ➠Managing Director

mead *noun* an alcoholic drink made from fermented honey, malt, yeast and water

meagre *spell.* meager

meal *noun, Sc.* oatmeal

{**meanie » meany**} *noun, coll.* a small-minded or mean individual

measure one's length *verb, coll.* to fall flat upon the ground or floor by accident

Meath *pr. name* a county in the ➠Irish Republic

County Meath in the ancient province of ➠Leinster.

meat safe *comp. noun, arch.* a small cupboard, usually covered in fine wire mesh to keep out flying insects, and used for the storage of meat

meat tea *comp. noun, North, arch.* a ➠high tea where meat is served

Meccano *pr. name (TM)* a mechanical construction toy for children

M.Ed *noun, abbr.* a Master of Education

{**medalled » medalling**} *spell.* {medaled » medaling}

Medicago sativa *noun* alfalfa

A leguminous plant with leaves similar to clover, its formal name is *medicago sativa.*

Medical Officer of Health *pr. name* a local official responsible for public health standards

Always a qualified physician.

the **Medical Research Council** *pr. name* a government research agency

Responsible for establishing and maintaining fundamental research into medical and related fields.

medick *spell.* medic

A leguminous plant like alfalfa, its formal name is *medicago.*

medium pacer *comp. noun* a ➠bowler who pitches ➠cricket balls at a moderately fast speed

medium wave *comp. noun* an AM radio wavelength greater than 100 but less than 1,000 meters

Medway *pr. name* a river which flows north through Kent into the ➠Thames River

A ➠Kentishman lives to the west of the Medway River; but a ➠Man of Kent lives to the east of it.

meetly *adv., out.* suitably, fittingly

meet up with *phr. verb, coll.* (1) to link or connect (roads or rivers) together; (2) to meet with (people)

Meibion Glyndwr *pr. name, Wal.* an illicit group of militant Welsh Nationalists who have make it their business to burn down the homes of English people living in Wales

The name is Welsh, meaning "Sons of Glendower"; Glendower was an ancient Welsh hero.

mêlée *spell.* melee

melton *noun* a heavy woolen cloth with a short nap

The material is named for Melton Mowbray in ➠Leicestershire, where it was first made.

Melton Mowbray *comp. noun* a kind of pork pie

The pie is named for Melton Mowbray in ➠Leicestershire, where it was first made.

Member of Parliament *comp. noun* one elected to represent a constituency in the ➠House of Commons

memorial *noun, Sc.* a document setting out the facts of a legal case and the questions upon which counsel's opinion is sought

memsahib *noun, arch., Urdu* a form of address for a married British woman in India

From "ma'am" plus the Urdu word ➠sahib.

the **Menai Strait** *pr. name, hist.* the narrow channel separating north western Wales from ➠Anglesey

Telford's road bridge over the strait was the largest in the world when it opened in 1826. When Robert Stephenson built his railroad bridge there in 1850 it was one of the first box girder bridges, and is still one of the very few ever to have had the roadway running in a tube through the inside of large box-shaped bridge girders rather than laid on top of them as is more usual.

Stephenson's bridge was badly damaged by fire in 1970 and rebuilt with arches replacing the box girder tubes. A highway was added above the railroad, which was rather a shame.

Mencap *pr. name, abbr.* the Royal Society for Mentally Handicapped Children and Adults

A charity that both directly helps mentally handicapped people and is a pressure group acting on their behalf.

Mendips *pr. name, hist.* a range of hills in ➠Somerset

the **men in grey suits** *idiom, coll.* those ➠Establishment figures who are rarely if ever seen in the light of day but supposedly control events from behind the scenes, like puppeteers pulling upon strings

217

Men of Harlech *pr. name* a patriotic Welsh song
Originally a soldiers' marching song.

mense *noun, Sc.* credit, honor, propriety or dignity

mental *adj., coll.* crazy, uncontrollable or eccentric

Mentmore Towers *pr. name, hist.* an opulent ➡Victorian house in ➡Buckinghamshire some eight miles to the northeast of ➡Aylesbury
Built by the Rothschild family to resemble the most spectacular edifices of the Elizabethan Age; today it is a college of transcendental meditation. *See also:* ➡Wollaton Hall.

me old cock *idiom, out., sl.* my good friend
Term of friendly address to a male acquaintance.

MEP *noun, abbr.* Member of the ➡European Parliament
Elections to this parliament are held every five years.

mepacrine *noun* quinacrine
An anti-malarial drug derived from acridine.

mercat cross *comp. noun, Sc.* a ➡market cross

mercer *noun* a dealer in unusually expensive fabrics, especially silks

merchant *noun* a wholesaler
In Scotland only, the word is also used in the American sense of "storekeeper."

merchant bank *comp. noun* a bank dealing in the underwriting or syndicating of equity or bond issues

the **Merchantile {Marine » Navy}** *pr. name, out.* the Merchant Marine

Mercia *pr. name, hist.* an ancient kingdom that once occupied the greater part of what is now central England, to the Welsh border
Established late in the 6th C., it had accepted the overlordship of ➡Wessex by 829. The usual seat of the kings of Mercia was Tamworth, to the north of the modern city of ➡Birmingham. In 880 it was divided between ➡Wessex and the ➡Danelaw. It was a king of Mercia who built ➡Offa's Dyke.

Mercury *pr. name* a telecommunications company
The principal competitor to ➡BT

Meridian TV *pr. name* a local commercial TV company headquartered in Brighton
It is part of the ➡ITV network

Merionethshire *pr. name, hist.* a former Welsh County, now part of ➡Gwynedd

merk *noun, hist., Sc.* a Scots coin worth 13 ➡shillings Scots and four ➡pennies Scots
By 1707 when it ceased to be legal tender, one merk was worth one ➡shilling and 1½ pennies in English currency. For more about Scots currency, *See also:* ➡pound Scots.

Merlin *pr. name, hist.* ➡Arthur's bard and wizard
He is said to have died in battle about the year 570.
In the later Arthurian romances he has evolved into a wizard, but there is no trace of that particular skill in the earliest stories about him.

merrie England *idiom, hist.* pleasant England
Evocative of a mythical former era when everything was better than now. Here "merrie" does not imply an England full of people who were slightly drunk or participating in mirthful or high-spirited pranks, but rather a pleasing and delightful land, which is the older meaning of the word "merry" or "merrie."

merry *adj., coll.* somewhat drunk; tipsy

the **merry dancers** *comp. noun, coll., out.* the *aurora borealis* or northern lights

the **Merry Monarch** *pr. name, hist.* ➡Charles II

merry thought *comp. noun* a bird's wishbone

the **Mersey** *pr. name* a river in northwest England that outfalls into the ➡Irish Sea at ➡Liverpool
It flows about 70 miles from the ➡Pennines, sweeps to the south of ➡Manchester and then flows past Liverpool, where one railroad and two road tunnels go under the river's estuary.

Merseyrail Electrics *pr. name (TM)* a railroad company operating commuter services in the ➡Merseyside area
It is part of ➡British Rail.

Merseyside *pr. name* an English ➡Metropolitan County
The principal city is ➡Liverpool and the current population is 1,375,000 (1991 Census).

Mersey Sound—the Beatles

the **Mersey Sound** *pr. name, hist.* the particular variety of popular music that originated from ➡Liverpool in the 1960s
Its most famous proponents were the ➡Beatles, of course.

Merton *pr. name* a ➡Greater London borough
Its current population, which is also included within the ➡London urban area total, is 160,000 (1991 Census).

Merton College *pr. name* a college of ➡Oxford University founded in 1264
It was founded in 1264 by Walter de Merton, Bishop of Rochester and ➡Lord High Chancellor. Merton is the earliest college of the university and for this reason its founder is considered to be originator of the Oxbridge collegiate system.

Mespot *pr. name, abbr., arch., sl.* Mesopotamia
The former military slang name for a region of the Middle East approximately equivalent to modern-day Iraq.

mess about *verb* to mess around

messages *noun, Ir., North, Sc.* shopping; that which has been purchased

messan *noun, Sc.* (1) a mongrel dog; (2) a contemptible individual

mess kit *comp. noun* the uniform worn by an army officer while dining at his mess

Messrs *noun, abbr, Fr.* the plural of "Mr.", particularly when applied to a company name
From the French *Messieurs*, which is the plural of *Monsieur* = "Mister" or "sir."

the **Met** *pr. name, abbr.* the ➡Metropolitan Police

metacentre *spell.* metacenter
A term used in physics.

metahaemoglobin *spell.* metahemoglobin

metal *verb* to surface a highway using road metal

{**metalled » metalling**} *spell.* {metaled » metaling}

metalled road *comp. noun* a highway surfaced with road metal

{**metallization » metallize**} *spell.* {metalization » metalize}

metals *noun* the tracks of a railroad

the *Meteor* *pr. name, hist.* the only jet aircraft to enter into operational service with any Allied air force during World War II
The first ➡RAF squadron became operational in 1944. However the first operational German jet, the Me 262, had entered service with the *Luftwaffe* earlier that same year.
Nonetheless, the jet engine that we know today is fundamentally a British invention. All the key patents were British; during World War II, the United States was licensed by Britain to build jet engines for military purposes only, until 1948 when Britain sold the United States a license to use the technology for civilian purposes for about $2.5 million. Quite a bargain.

the **Meteorological Office** *pr. name* the equivalent of the U.S. Weather Bureau, it issues official weather forecasts
Originally established in 1855 as a department of the ➡Board of Trade to provide weather information for shipping, it had become a department of the ➡RAF by World War II. Today it is an executive agency of the ➡Ministry of Defence.

meths *noun, abbr., coll.* ➡methylated spirits

meths drinker *comp. noun, abbr., coll.* someone who drinks ➡methylated spirits
Usually considered to be a tramp or degenerate of some sort.

methylated spirits *comp. noun* alcohol denatured by the addition of methanol

metoestrus *spell.* metestrus

the **Met Office** *pr. name, abbr.* ➡Meteorological Office

metre *spell.* meter

Metroland *pr. name* the outer suburbs to the immediate northwest of London, served by the ➡Metropolitan Railway, later the ➡Metropolitan Line of the ➡London Underground
The name was invented when the network had been newly extended into these leafy parts of ➡Hertfordshire and ➡Buckinghamshire and the railroad company was eager to entice people with the prospect of easy commuting between central London and these attractive semi-rural places.

the **Metropolis** *pr. name, coll.* London

Metropolitan County *noun* a unit of local government in England, resembling a county but comprising a large urban area

the **Metropolitan Line** *pr. name* one part of London's rapid-transit subway system
Spreading out from the original ➡Metropolitan Railway of 1863, the modern Metropolitan Line goes farther out from central London than any other part of the network, reaching Amersham, Chesham, Watford and Uxbridge in the northwest and west, while in the ➡City it goes to Aldgate and in the east it reaches as far as Barking.

metropolitan magistrate *noun* a stipendiary magistrate sitting in the London courts

the **Metropolitan Police** *pr. name* the police force responsible for law and order within London
Founded by Sir Robert Peel in 1829, they replaced the earlier ➡Bow Street Runners and parish constables who had proved quite unable to cope with the crime wave that then seemed in danger of over-running what was already at that date by far the largest city in the world. They were modeled upon the Royal Irish Constabulary, which Peel had established in ➡Dublin some 15 years earlier.

the **Metropolitan Railway** *pr. name, hist.* the first underground mass-transit railroad in the world
It opened for business in 1863, running from ➡Liverpool Street railroad terminus in the ➡City to ➡Paddington railroad terminus in the ➡West End. Passengers enjoyed the luxury of being transported in open cars through dark tunnels full of smoke and fumes belching from the steam-powered trains. It was all considered to be a great triumph of science and industry, the opening being celebrated with a specially-composed *Underground Waltz*.
The route is now part of the modern ➡Metropolitan Line and is also used in part by the ➡Circle Line.

mews *noun* (1) a group of stables, with living quarters above, built around a courtyard; (2) residences that are converted former stables; (3) an alley or narrow back street giving access to (1) or (2).

mezzanine *noun* the space under a theatrical stage

MFH *noun, abbr.* a ➡Master of Foxhounds

MG *pr. name (TM)* a famous marque of sports cars, best known for its MGB series
The name is an abbreviation of "Morris Garages."

MI *noun, abbr.* (1) military intelligence; (2) a myocardial infarction
(2) is another way of saying "heart attack."

MI5 *noun, abbr., hist.* Military Intelligence Department 5, responsible for counterintelligence and security within the ➡UK and now properly known as the ➡Security Service
Whatever happened to Departments 1, 2, 3 and 4?

MI6 *noun, abbr., hist.* Military Intelligence Department 6, responsible for overseas intelligence and espionage and now properly known as the ➡Secret Intelligence Service
Together with ➡MI5, the British equivalent of the CIA

miaow *spell.* meow

MICE *noun, abbr.* a Member of the Institution of Civil Engineers

Michaelmas *pr. name, hist.* the feast of St Michael and an English ➡quarter-day
Now September 29, but formerly October 11.

Michaelmas daisy *comp. noun* the wild aster that blooms in the fall

Michaelmas Term *pr. name* the university term that begins shortly after ➡Michaelmas

M.I.Chem.E. *noun, abbr.* a Member of the Institution of Chemical Engineers

michty me *exclam., Sc.* mighty me
An exclamation of surprise, etc.

mickle *adj., Sc.* an alternate spelling of ➡muckle

{Mick » Mickey » Micky} *noun, derog., sl.* an ➡Irishman

{micropalaeontological » micropalaeontologist » micropalaeontology} *spell.* {micropaleontological » micropaleontologist » micropaleontology}

middle *verb* to strike a ➡cricket ball with the central part of the bat

middle common room *comp. noun* (1) the common living room within a college used by graduates who are not ➡fellows; (2) the members of a university of college who use the middle common room

middle for diddle *imper., sl.* a call to choose who is first to play in a game of darts by throwing one as close as possible to the center of a dartboard

middlemost *adj.* most central

Middlesbrough *pr. name* an industrial town and port that is the administrative center of ➡Cleveland
Currently, the city's population, including suburbs, is 380,000 (1988 estimate).

Middle Scots *pr. name* post-medieval Scots
The form of the language between about 1450 and 1650

Middlesex *pr. name, hist.* a former English county lying immediately to the north of London
Almost all of Middlesex was absorbed into ➡Greater London in 1965 while the remainder was distributed between ➡Surrey and ➡Hertfordshire, so that the county was abolished as a legal entity. The name signifies that it was once the territory of the Middle Saxons.

Middle Temple *pr. name* one of the ➡Inns of Court

midgie [A] *noun, Sc.* (1) a trash can; (2) a trash heap
[B] *noun* a tiny gnat-like fly
A common pest on summer evenings, especially in Scotland before, during and after rain—which is most evenings.

Mid Glamorgan *pr. name* a Welsh County
The current population is 525,000 (1991 Census).

the Midland Bank *pr. name* one of the ➡Big Four English retail banks
Founded in ➡Birmingham in 1836, the Midland bank acquired two London banks and moved its headquarters there in 1898. In 1992 it was itself bought by the Hongkong and Shanghai Banking Corporation.

Midland Main Line *pr. name (TM)* a railroad company operating ➡InterCity services between London and central England
It is part of ➡British Rail.

the Midlands *pr. name* the central area of England
Usually considered to be the counties of ➡Derby, ➡Hereford and Worcester, ➡Leicester, ➡Nottingham, ➡Shropshire, ➡Stafford, ➡Warwick, and ➡West Midlands.

Midlothian *pr. name, hist.* a former Scottish county, now part of ➡Lothian region

mid {off » on » wicket} *comp. noun* fielding players' positions on the ➡cricket field

midshipman *noun* a naval officer of a rank above cadet and below sub-lieutenant

Midsummer Day *pr. name, hist.* the longest day of the year and an English ➡quarter-day
Now June 24, but formerly July 6.

MIEE *noun, abbr.* a Member of the Institution of Electrical Engineers

M.I.Gas.E. *pr. name, abbr.* a Member of the Institution of Gas Engineers

mike [A] *adj., out., sl.* idle or lazy
[B] *noun, out., sl.* a period spent not working
[C] *verb, out., sl.* to avoid work

milch cow *comp. noun, pref.* a cash cow; an easy source of regular income or profit

mild *noun, coll.* a mild-tasting draft beer, commonly served in English pubs
It is lightly flavored with hops and, to the surprise of many visitors, normally served at room temperature.

mild and bitter *comp. noun, coll.* a mixture of ➡mild and ➡bitter beer

Milford Haven *pr. name, hist.* a deep water harbor situated upon the western coast of south Wales
For many centuries the traditional departure point for English kings intent upon invading ➡Ireland, although it did not attract a town around it until the 1790s.
Since 1950, a large oil terminal has developed here, making use of the exceptionally deep water, which enables very large tankers to come very close to shore.

mililitre *spell.* mililiter

milimetre *spell.* milimeter

the **Militant Tendency** *pr. name* an extreme left-wing political organization that regularly attempts to infiltrate the ➡Labour Party
Formed in 1963 as the Revolutionary Socialist League.

milk *noun, pref.* cream
The white liquid often added to coffee. It is usual to be asked if you wish to have *milk* added to coffee, not *cream*.

milk bar *comp. noun, out.* a sort of cross between a coffee shop and an ice cream parlor

*milk
float*

milk float *comp. noun* a lightweight vehicle used for daily house-to-house milk deliveries
Usually battery-powered, and recharged overnight.

milking parlour *comp. noun, arch.* a milking shed

milk pan *comp. noun* a saucepan used to boil milk

milk roundsman *comp. noun* a milkman

milk {round » walk} *comp. noun* a milkman's delivery route

milk stout *comp. noun* a lighter ➡stout than most

millboard *noun* a kind of heavy-duty pasteboard used to bind books

millepede *spell.* millipede

milliard *noun, out.* a billion; 1,000,000,000
SEE ALSO: ➡billion.

Mills bomb *pr. name, hist.* a kind of fragmentation grenade used by the British army in both World Wars

milometer *noun* an odometer

M.I.Mar.E. *pr. name, abbr.* a Member of the Institution of Marine Engineers

M.I.Mech.E. *noun, abbr.* a Member of the Institution of Mechanical Engineers

M.I.Min.E. *noun, abbr.* a Member of the Institution of Mining Engineers

M.I.Mun.E. *noun, abbr.* a Member of the Institution of Municipal Engineers

mince *noun* ground or chopped meat, usually beef

mincemeat *noun* a finely chopped mixture of currants, raisins, apples, spices, suet, and other ingredients
Now mainly used as an ingredient for ➡mincemeat pies. Mincemeat originally consisted mostly of meat with other ingredients added to make it more palatable when eaten in mid-winter, but of the meat only the suet remains now.

mincemeat pie *comp. noun* a small pie filled with ➡mincemeat, now usually only eaten at Christmas

mince pie *idiom, rh. sl.* an eye

mincer *noun* a meat grinder

MIND *pr. name* a mental-health lobbying group
It was formed in 1946 as the National Association for Mental Health; the name was changed in 1970.

the **Minden Boys** *pr. name, coll.* a nickname of the 20th Regiment of ➡Foot
A unit of the British Army, one of the ➡Minden Regiments.

the **Minden Regiments** *pr. name* six regiments that won the most spectacular victory of the ➡Seven Years War, at Minden Heide, Germany, in 1759, against a greatly superior force of French cavalry
The were the 12th Regiment of Foot (the ➡Old Dozen); the 20th Regiment of Foot; 23th Regiment of Foot (the ➡Nanny Goats); the 25th Regiment of Foot; the 37th Regiment of Foot; and the 51th Regiment of Foot.

minder *noun, sl.* a bodyguard, particularly of a criminal

mineral *noun, abbr.* ➡mineral water

mineral water *comp. noun* club soda

mingin *adj., Sc.* (1) stinking; (2) disgusting; (3) dead drunk

mingy *adj.* stingy

minibreak *noun, coll.* a short vacation

minicab *noun* an unlicensed taxi

minim *noun, pref.* a half-note
A musical term.

minister *noun* any politician responsible for a government department

Minister of State *comp. noun* a government minister responsible for a department, but not a member of the ➡Cabinet

Minister of the Crown *comp. noun* a politician responsible for a major department of government and a member of the ➡Cabinet

Minister without Portfolio *pr. name* a ➡Cabinet minister without departmental responsibilities

Ministry *noun* (1) a government department presided over by a ➡minister; (2) the principal building occupied by a government department

the **Ministry of Agriculture, Fisheries and Food** *pr. name* a government department
Responsible for administering agriculture and fishing policy in England only and policies concerned with safety and quality of food throughout the ➡UK.

the **Ministry of Defence** *pr. name* the government department responsible for the administration and support of the ➡Armed Forces of the Crown

the **Ministry of Fun** *pr. name, coll.* a comical name for the ➡Department of National Heritage

the **Ministry of Transport**

the **Ministry of Transport** *pr. name, hist.* the former name for the ➡Department of Transport

minor *adj., out.* a suffix to a surname indicating that the owner is the youngest of that name

This suffix was once commonly used among boys attending English ➡pubic schools, where, for example, the youngest of two brothers may be called "Smith-minor". *SEE ALSO:* ➡major.

mint imperial *comp. noun* a hard-crusted, peppermint-flavored candy

Minton Ware *pr. name, hist.* pottery and porcelain made in the factory founded by Thomas Minton at ➡Stoke-on-Trent in 1793

mint sauce *comp. noun* a sauce of chopped spearmint, sugar and vinegar

One normal accompaniment for roast lamb; an alternate to mint jelly, which is the other.

minute *noun* an official internal government document proposing a course of action

M.I.Prod.E. *noun, abbr.* a Member of the Institution of Production Engineers

MIRAS *noun, abbr.* Mortgage Interest Relief At Source

The disbursement of income tax credits due upon interest paid on mortgages by direct reduction of the monthly payments made by the borrower to the lender, rather than by a refund made later as used to be the case.

misbehaviour *spell.* misbehavior

mischief *noun* a childish irritation

misdemeanour *spell.* misdemeanor

{misdialled » misdialling} *spell.* {misdialed » misdialing}

mise *noun, arch.* settlement by agreement

missive *noun, Sc.* a formal letter setting out a legally binding agreement

miss {off » out} *verb, coll.* to avoid or omit

mistress *noun* (1) a female schoolteacher or tutor; (2) the female principal of a school, college, etc.

Mistress *noun, Sc.* (1) the female heir presumptive of a nobleman; (2) the wife of a ➡master

the **Mistress of the Robes** *pr. name* a woman responsible for a queen's wardrobe

{mitre » mitred » mitring} *spell.* {miter » mitered » mitering}

mixed grill *comp. noun* a dish consisting of a selection of broiled meats, served together with vegetables and so forth

mixen *noun, out.* a dunghill

mix it *phr. verb, coll.* to provoke trouble or start a fight

{mizen » mizen-mast} *spell.* {mizzen » mizzenmast}

mizzle *verb, sl.* to decamp or abscond

MLR *pr. name, abbr., hist.* the Minimum Lending Rate

A former name for the British discount rate, which is the minimum interest rate permitted by the Bank of England and is now called the ➡Base Rate.

m'lud *noun, abbr., coll.* a ➡barrister's term of respectful address to the judge, an abbreviation of "My Lord"

MM *noun, abbr.* the Military Medal

MMC *pr. name, abbr.* the ➡Monopolies and Mergers Commission

MN *pr. name, abbr.* the ➡Merchant Navy

MO *noun, abbr.* a Medical Officer

moaning minnie *comp. noun, hist., sl.* (1) a nickname for a World War II air-raid siren; (2) a nickname for a World War II German mortar; (3) someone who is continually lamenting or complaining

(1) from their repetitive wailing sound; (2) from the shrieking sound made when they were fired.

mobile incident room *comp. noun* a mobile police command post

mobsman *noun, arch.* a well-dressed pickpocket

mocker *noun, sl.* a jinx

mod [A] *noun, arch., coll.* a style of teenage dress popular in the early 1960s

[B] *pr. name, Gae., Sc.* a annual gathering of those who speak ➡Gaelic, centered around musical and literary contests

From the Gaelic word for "assembly" or "council."

MOD *pr. name, abbr.* the ➡Ministry of Defense

mod cons *comp. noun, abbr., coll.* modern conveniences

An expression often used by realtors describing property for sale or rent, which implies that the property being described has all the facilities expected in modern property.

{modelled » modelling} *spell.* {modeled » modeling}

the **Moderations** *pr. name* the first degree examination for the Bachelor of Arts degree in classics and philosophy at ➡Oxford University

the **Moderator** *pr. name, abbr., Sc.* the ➡Moderator of the General Assembly of the Church of Scotland

the **Moderator of the General Assembly of the Church of Scotland** *pr. name, Sc.* a minister of the ➡Church of Scotland chosen to preside for one year over the presbyterian church's ➡General Assembly and to perform certain ceremonial duties on behalf of the whole ➡Kirk

the **Modern Athens** *pr. name, coll.* ➡Edinburgh

SEE ALSO: ➡Athens of the North.

the **Mods** *pr. name, abbr.* the ➡Moderations

mog [A] *noun, abbr., sl.* a ➡moggie

[B] *noun, North* a mouse

moggie *noun, sl.* a cat

MOH *pr. name, abbr.* a ➡Medical Officer of Health

the **Mohocks** *pr. name, hist.* a gang of aristocratic ruffians who infested London's streets during the early years of the 18th C.

They were named in emulation of the Mohawk Indians.

moidare *noun, hist., Port.* a gold coin that was minted in Portugal and circulated in 18th C. England

From the Portuguese *moeda d'ouro* = "money of gold."

moke *noun, sl.* a donkey

moleskin *noun* a heavy-duty cotton fustian material

moley *noun, sl.* a weapon consisting of a potato which has razor blades stuck into it

MOMI *pr. name, abbr.* ➠Museum of the Moving Image

Monaghan *pr. name* a county in the ➠Irish Republic

County Monaghan in the ancient province of ➠Ulster.

monarch *noun* the king, queen, emperor or empress of a kingdom or empire

the **Monday Club** *pr. name* a pressure group of right wing ➠Conservatives

It was founded in 1961. The name originates from their habit of meeting for lunch on Mondays.

money-box *comp. noun* a ➠piggy bank

money for {jam » old rope} *idiom, coll.* a profit for little or no effort or cost

money-grubber *comp. noun* someone interested in amassing money to the exclusion of all else

money-spinner *comp. noun* a money-making person or scheme

monkey *noun, sl.* £500 (five hundred pounds)

See also: ➠gorilla, ➠pony, ➠score.

monkey-engine *comp. noun, coll.* a pile driver

monkey jacket *comp. noun, arch.* a short jacket once popular with sailors

monkey-nut *comp. noun* an unshelled peanut

monkey parade *comp. noun, out., sl.* any place where young people go in search of sexual partners

monkey puzzle *comp. noun* a coniferous tree, a member of the pine family, and native to Chile

It has downward-pointing, intertwined branches with small, close-set leaves. One of the earliest of these trees to be brought to Europe was grown in ➠Cornwall, and when a friend of the owner saw it there for the first time in 1923, he remarked that with these characteristics, it would puzzle a monkey to have to climb such a tree, and promptly named it the "Monkey Puzzle." The name stuck. The tree's formal name is *araucaria araucaria*.

monkey tricks *comp. noun, coll.* shenanigans

monomark *noun* a registered or recognized symbol or identifying mark

Letters and figures serving as an identifying mark for an individual's goods, valuables, letters, etc.

the **Monopolies and Mergers Commission** *pr. name* a government agency that investigates and reports on monopolies or mergers referred to it

Established in 1948 as the Monopolies and Restrictive Practices Commission; the present title was adopted in 1973.

the **Monopolies Commission** *pr. name, abbr.* the ➠Monopolies and Mergers Commission

the Battle of **Mons** *pr. name, hist.* the first great battle of World War I, fought on August 23, 1914, between British and German armies at this Belgium town

By coincidence, Mons is just 25 miles from where the Battle of ➠Waterloo had been fought 99 years before.

Mons Meg *pr. name, hist.* a great 15th C. cannon kept at ➠Edinburgh Castle

Reputedly made at Mons in Belgium, hence the name.

the **Mons Star** *pr. name, hist.* a military service medal issued to all British troops who served in Belgium or France in 1914

The name refers to the Battle of ➠Mons.

the **Montagu Motor Museum** *pr. name, hist.* a museum of old automobiles at Beaulieu, ➠Hampshire

Montgomery *pr. name, hist.* a former Welsh County, now called ➠Powys

the **Monument** *pr. name, hist.* a 202-ft tall column commemorating the ➠Great Fire of London of 1666

This London landmark by Sir Christopher Wren stands at the northern end of ➠London Bridge near the spot where the ➠Great Fire of Londonz began.

mony a mickle maks a muckle *idiom, Sc.* approximately, this means "every little bit helps"

However, because ➠mickle and ➠muckle are just alternate spellings of the same Scots word meaning "large" or "great," the *literal* meaning of the phrase is, "many a large makes a large," which makes little sense.

It is thought that somewhere along the way the wording has changed to its present form from "mony a {little » pickle} maks a muckle." The word ➠pickle means "little," and as both "pickle" and "little" rhyme with "mickle", it's easy to see how such a substitution could have occurred accidentally.

moody [A] *adj., coll.* fake, pretended or counterfeit

[B] *noun, sl.* (1) a period of bad temper; (2) meaningless or nonsense talk

[C] *verb, sl.* to delude with clever words or flattery

moon daisy *comp. noun* a moonflower

moonlight flitting *idiom, coll.* an overnight house move in order to avoid paying rent or other debts

moonraker *noun, arch.* a smuggler

moor *noun* a tract of elevated open rolling scrubland

moorland *noun* a tract of ➠moor

Moosh *noun, North., sl.* a familiar form of general address to any man whose correct name is unknown

See also: ➠Jimmy, ➠John, ➠Kiddo, ➠Tosh and ➠Wack.

moosh [A] *noun, out., sl.* (1) the face; (2) the mouth [B] *verb, out., sl.* (1) to crush or squeeze; (2) to kiss

mop fair *comp. noun, hist.* a fair once held, usually in the fall, for the purpose of hiring farmhands, domestic servants, and so forth

mop up *verb, coll.* to absorb knowledge or news rapidly and enthusiastically

mor *noun, East* a young girl

Moray Firth *pr. name, hist.* an estuary on the eastern coast of northern Scotland that reaches towards ➡Inverness and the ➡Great Glen

Morayshire *pr. name, hist.* a former Scots county, now part of ➡Grampian region

Morgan *pr. name (TM)* a famous marque of hand-built sports automobiles

morning coat *comp. noun* a tailcoat

morning dress *comp. noun* a tailcoat together with striped trousers

morning-room *noun* a parlor or sitting room

Morris *pr. name (TM), hist.* a mass-production automobile manufacturer founded at Oxford in 1912 Now owned by BMW.

morris dance *comp. noun* a traditional English dance

Most common in southern England, it is performed by men in costumes representing various characters such as ➡Robin Hood, Malkin the Fool, Dragon and others, and wearing bells. The dance was originally brought from Spain in the 14th C. where it had been a military dance of the Moors; that is the origin of its name.

Morrison shelter *comp. noun, hist.* an indoor air raid shelter intended to help protect civilians during World War II

They were named after Herbert Morrison, ➡Home Secretary at the time, who officially recommended their use during the ➡Blitz in 1940. They were made from common household possessions such as mattresses and other furniture items, and people were advised to situate them in supposedly secure locations, such as cellars or under stairways.

mort *noun, North* a girl or young woman

Morton's Fork *pr. name, hist.* a logical argument which cannot be won

John Morton, ➡Archbishop of Canterbury and a ➡minister of ➡Henry VII, when charged by the king with extracting additional funds from the rich men of the kingdom, arranged things so that none could avoid paying up:

If the "victim" was obviously prosperous then certainly he could afford to contribute generously.

However if his prosperity was not obvious, then clearly he must have been secreting money away, so he too could afford to contribute just as generously.

mosher *noun, out., sl.* an enthusiastic follower of heavy-metal music, dancing in a very crowded space with whatever small movements are possible

Most common in the 1980s, it was invented in British clubs as a successor to slam dancing. "Most" is probably constructed out of "mash" and "squash."

Mosleyite *pr. name, coll., hist.* a member of the ➡British Union of Fascists

Sir Oswald Mosley was leader of this party, which had its brief moment of glory in the 1930s.

the *Mosquito* *pr. name, hist.* a twin-engined light bomber flown by ➡Bomber Command during World War II

Unusually, it had an all-wooden airframe able to withstand an amazing amount of punishment and, because it carried no defensive armament or extra crew to operate it, the Mosquito was able to avoid interception by flying too fast or too high for the German defenders. As well as a bomber, it was very effective in reconnaissance and night fighter roles. Altogether about 8,000 were built, and it was in service with the RAF from 1941 until 1955.

Moss Bros *pr. name, abbr.* a company that rents out formal clothes for occasions such as weddings

In full, "Moss Brothers."

moss trooper *comp. noun, hist.* a ➡reiver who operated in and around areas of ➡peat moss that formed part of the disputed border between Scotland and England in the 17th C.

Most Honourable *noun* an honorific used as a form of address to a ➡marquess, member of the ➡Privy Council, or member of the Order of the ➡Bath

MOT *pr. name, abbr., hist.* the ➡Ministry of Transport

mother *noun, coll.* any person, of either gender, who takes charge of disbursing tea or coffee within an informal group

Mother Bunch *comp. noun, coll., out.* a fat old woman

Reputedly the name of a famously fat woman who lived during the reign of Elizabeth I.

Mother Hubbard *idiom, rh. sl.* a cupboard

Mothering Sunday *pr. name* the approximate British equivalent of Mother's Day

However, Mothering Sunday and Mother's Day are never the *same* day. Mothering Sunday is the fourth Sunday of Lent, which places it in March or April, while Mother's Day is always the second Sunday in May.

mother of pearl *idiom, rh. sl.* a wife

Derivation: wife > mother > girl > pearl > mother of pearl.

mother's boy *comp. noun, coll.* an effeminate or weak-willed man

mother's help *comp. noun* a household assistant for a mother with children

mother ship *comp. noun* a larger ship that acts as a moveable base for submarines, landingcraft, etc.

mother's meeting *comp. noun, coll.* (1) a gathering of the women of a parish; (2) a discussion of trivial matters considered very important by the participants in the discussion but no one else

mug

Mother's Pride *pr. name* a popular brand of bread
Sometimes used euphemistically as a generic name for bread.

mother's ruin *idiom, sl.* gin

the **Mother's Union** *pr. name* a society for women, devoted to strengthening and supporting traditional family values
Established under the auspices of the ➡Church of England. There is a chapter attached to almost every parish.

mother's wit *comp. noun* mother wit; native or natural intelligence

motor [A] *noun, abbr., coll.* a ➡motor car
[B] *verb* to drive in a car

Motorail *pr. name (TM)* an automobile-ferrying service provided by ➡British Rail
Cars are carried by train over long distances such as between Scotland and London, while drivers and passengers sit in passenger cars attached to the same train

motor car *comp. noun* an automobile

motor firm *comp. noun, out.* a car dealer

motor horn *comp. noun, out.* a car horn

motor mechanic *comp. noun* a car repairman

motor neuron disease *comp. noun* Lou Gehrig's disease

motor racing *comp. noun* car racing

motor spirit *comp. noun, arch.* gasoline

motorway *noun* a superhighway specially built for the sole use of self-propelled vehicles
Typically an expressway or freeway with fully grade-separated access. They are designated by the prefix ➡M-

motorway madness *comp. noun, coll.* dangerous driving upon a ➡motorway in bad weather, especially when fog reduces visibility

MOT Test *comp. noun, abbr., coll.* a compulsory annual roadworthiness test for all automobiles more than three years old
"MOT" is an abbreviation of ➡Ministry of Transport.

{**mould » mouldability » mouldable**} *spell.* {mold » moldability » moldable}

mouldboard *spell.* moldboard

{**moulder » mouldiness**} *spell.* {molder » moldiness}

{**moulding » mouldy**} *spell.* {molding » moldy}

mouldy *noun, arch., sl.* a torpedo

{**moult » moulter**} *spell.* {molt » molter}

the **Mound** *pr. name* an artificial hill built in ➡Edinburgh in the 18th C.
Consisting of some six million tons of material excavated during the construction of the ➡New Town in the late 18th and early 19th Cs. Its purpose was to enable construction of a roadway between a location on the ➡Royal Mile near ➡Edinburgh Castle and the newly built ➡Princes Street.

moustache *spell.* mustache

the **Movie Channel** *pr. name* a pay-TV movie channel
Part of the ➡BSB satellite broadcasting network.

moving staircase *comp. noun, out.* an escalator

Moyle *pr. name* a district in ➡Northern Ireland, in what used to be County ➡Antrim
The current population is 15,000 (1990 estimate).

MP *noun, abbr.* a ➡Member of Parliament

MPS *noun, abbr.* Member of the Pharmaceutical Society

MR *pr. name, abbr.* the ➡Master of the Rolls

MRC *pr. name, abbr.* the Medical Research Council

MRCA *pr. name, abbr.* the Multi-Role Combat Aircraft

{**Mr » Mrs**} **Justice** *comp. noun* an honorific used as a form of address to a ➡High Court judge

Mrs. Duckett *comp. noun, rh. sl.* bucket

Mrs Mop *idiom, sl.* a nickname for a cleaning lady

MSC *noun, abbr.* the Manpower Services Commission

MSFU *pr. name, abbr.* the Manufacturing Science and Finance Union
A large labor union for skilled and professional workers.

MSM *noun, abbr.* the Medal for Meritorious Service

MTB *noun, abbr.* a motor torpedo boat

muck {**about » around**} *verb, coll.* (1) to fool around; (2) to potter around

mucker *noun, sl.* (1) a bad fall; (2) a fellow worker; (3) a friend

muck in *verb* to share equally, especially work

muckle *adj., Sc.* (1) full-grown; (2) large or great; (3) much, lots of; (4) of high rank; (5) self-important

muck sweat *comp. noun, coll.* a heavy sweat

mudguard *noun* the fender or splash guard of a car

the **muesli belt** *comp. noun, coll.* an area where middle-class health food faddists live

muesli belt malnutrition *comp. noun, coll.* undernourishment among ➡muesli belt children

muffin *noun* an English muffin
Which is to say, the *American* "English muffin," not the taller, cup-shaped quick bread made with wheat flour or cornmeal and baked in a pan, which is also called a muffin on both sides of the Atlantic Ocean.

muffin bell *comp. noun, arch.* a bell that was once rung in the street by a muffin man

muffin man *comp. noun, hist.* an 18th C. street seller of hot muffins

mufti *noun, Arab.* civilian clothes worn by someone who is normally dressed in a uniform
Strangely, it's Arabic for an Islamic religious lawyer.

mug [A] *noun, abbr., sl.* a ➡muggins
[B] *verb, sl.* to buy someone a drink

muggins

muggins *noun, coll.* a fool or easy mark

mug's game *idiom, sl.* a foolish or pointless activity

mug up *verb, coll.* to learn by rapid, intensive study
Usually for the purpose of passing a school or college test.

Muhammad *pr. name, spell.* Muhammed
The founder of the Islamic religion.

Muirfield *pr. name, hist.* a golf course near ➡Edinburgh
It belongs to the world's oldest ➡golf club, the Honourable Company of Edinburgh Golfers, founded in 1744.

mull *noun, Sc.* a promontory or headland

mullet *noun* an heraldic representation of a star

mulligatawny soup *comp. noun* a soup, highly seasoned with curry
It originated in India.

multicoloured *spell.* multicolored

multiple smash *comp. noun* a multi-vehicle pile-up on a highway

multiple store *comp. noun* a chain store

multure *noun, arch., Sc.* a fee or duty charged for the grinding of grain
Payable to the proprietor of the mill and consisting of a portion of the grain processed.

{**mum » mummy**} *spell.* {mom » mommy}

mummer *noun, arch.* (1) a masked actor who mimes; (2) a theatrical actor

mummery *noun, arch.* a performance by ➡mummers

mumper *noun, sl.* a beggar

mumping *noun, sl.* the taking of bribes by the police

munch *verb* to eat steadily or continuously

the Munroes *pr. name, Sc.* all 277 Scottish mountains that are over 3,000 ft high
Named for Hugh Munro who published the list in 1891 and died in 1919 having climbed all but one.

Munster *pr. name* one of the ancient Irish provinces
It consists of the counties ➡Clare, ➡Cork, ➡Kerry, ➡Limerick, ➡Tipperary, and ➡Waterford, all in the ➡Irish Republic.

muppet *noun, derog., sl.* (1) a patient in a hospital for the mentally ill; (2) an unpopular teenager

Murryfield *pr. name* a large stadium in ➡Edinburgh where international rugby matches are held

the Museum of London *pr. name* a museum in central London telling the story of the city from prehistory to the present day

the Museum of Mankind *pr. name* a museum in central London containing the ethnological collection of the ➡British Museum
There is an especially comprehensive collection of exhibits illustrating the life and cultures of native peoples from Africa, America and the Pacific.

the Museum of the Moving Image *pr. name* a museum on London's ➡South Bank dedicated to all forms of the moving image
Includes examples from the earliest times through to modern TV, video, lasers, holograms and so forth.

mush *noun, sl.* military prison
Perhaps derived from the association of "mush," a form of thick porridge, with ➡porridge in the sense of time in jail.

mushy peas *comp. noun, North* boiled and mashed peas

musical box *comp. noun* a music box

music centre *comp. noun, coll.* a radio, cassette recorder, CD player, amplifier, speakers, etc. considered as a single entity, or physically built into a single unit

music hall *comp. noun, arch.* (1) a theater used for vaudeville shows; (2) vaudeville shows

in a Victorian music hall

muslin *noun* cheesecloth

mutton [A] *noun, abbr., arch., sl.* ➠laced mutton

[B] *noun, rh. sl.* an eye

Derivation: eye > pie > mutton pie > mutton.

mutton dressed as lamb *idiom, coll.* a middle-aged or older woman who attempts by dress and make-up to make herself look like a young woman

the **Mutton Lancers** *pr. name* a nickname for the 2nd Regiment of ➠Foot

A unit of the British Army. When raised in 1661, the badge of a Paschal Lamb was adopted.

muzzy *adj., coll.* (1) dull, uninspiring or poorly thought out; (2) befuddled due to drink

MVO *noun, abbr.* Member of the Royal Victorian Order

my honourable and learned friend *comp. noun* an honorific used as a form of address by one ➠MP to another of the same party who is also a lawyer

While speaking in the ➠House of Commons.

my honourable friend *comp. noun* an honorific used as a form of address by one ➠MP to another of the same party

While speaking in the ➠House of Commons.

My Lady *comp. noun* an honorific used as a form of address to a woman who carries the title "Lady"

my learned friend *comp. noun* an honorific used as a form of reference by one lawyer when addressing another in court

My Lord *comp. noun* an honorific title used as a form of address to Judges of the ➠Supreme Court of Judicature, Bishops, Noblemen below the rank of ➠Duke, ➠Lord Mayors and ➠Lord Provosts, and the ➠Lord Advocate

my noble friend *comp. noun* an honorific used as a form of address by one peer to another of the same party when speaking in the ➠House of Lords

mystery play *pr. name, hist.* a medieval play with a religious theme

The purpose of these plays, which were typically performed in the street in front of a cathedral or other ecclesiastical edifice, was to impart the Christian message to a largely illiterate population.

{**myxoedema » myxoedemic**} *spell.* {myxedema » myxedemic}

Medical terms related to hypothyroidism.

the {**NAAFI** » **Naafi** » **Naffy**} *noun, abbr.* the Navy, Army, and Air Force Institutes

These are cafeterias, stores and other relaxation and entertainment facilities provided for British military, naval and air force personnel and their families.

Originally set up in the early days of World War II when it was known as the Navy and Army Canteen Board, it was given its current name in 1921.

It is the approximate equivalent of the P.X. which provides similar facilities to members of the U. S. forces.

nab *noun, abbr., arch., sl.* dole; money paid to the unemployed

From ➡NAB.

NAB *pr. name, abbr., hist.* National Assistance Board

Which became the ➡DSS, and then the ➡DHSS.

nabob *noun, hist., Port., Urdu* a person who had become vastly wealthy in India and returned to live in Britain in great style

Originally, a provoncial governor of the Mogal Empire, the word come to English from the Urdu *nawab* via the Portuguese *nababo*.

NACODS *pr. name, abbr.* the National Association of Colliery Overmen, Deputies and Shot-Firers

A labor union for coal-mine supervisors

nae *adj., Sc.* not

{**naevoid** » **naevus**} *spell.* {nevoid » nevus}

Concerning birthmarks.

naff *adj., sl.* (1) unfashionable; (2) useless

naffing *exclam, sl.* a euphemistic variation of "fucking"

naff off *imper, sl.* a euphemistic variation of "fuck off"

Naffy medal *pr. name, hist., sl.* (1) the 1939-45 Star; (2) the Africa Star

(1) was awarded for service in the army during World War II; (2) was awarded for serving in the North African Campaign during World War II. The name is an ironic reference to the ➡{NAFFI » Naafi » Naffy}.

naiant *adj.* in heraldry, swimming

nail *noun, arch.* a unit of length used in tailoring

It is equal to ¹/₁₆ th of a yard or 2¹/₄ inches.

nail pad *comp. noun* a fingernail buffer

nail {**polish** » **varnish**} *comp. noun* fingernail enamel

naipkin *noun, Sc.* (1) a handkerchief; (2) a neckerchief

Nairn *pr. name, hist.* a former Scottish county, now part of ➡Highland region

NALGO *pr. name, abbr.* the National and Local Government Officers Association

A civil servant clerks' union, merged with ➡Unison in 1993.

name [A] *noun* an investor at ➡Lloyd's of London

More specifically, an individual who underwrites insurance risks accepted at Lloyd's, without limit on personal liability.

[B] *verb* to specify a particular ➡MP as being in breach of good order

This action must be carried out by the ➡Speaker or Deputy Speaker before the ➡House of Commons while in session. The member named is then suspended for a period, its length determined by the seriousness of the offense.

nameable *spell.* namable

name after *phr. verb* to name for

name child *comp. noun* one named after someone else

name day *comp. noun* the day before settlement day at the stock exchange, when the names of buyers and sellers are announced

nan *noun, coll.* grandmother

A childish word.

nana *sl., derog.* a foolish person

nancy boy *comp. noun, sl.* a nance, an effeminate man or homosexual

nanny [A] *noun* a nursemaid

[B] *noun, rh. sl.* boat

Derivation: boat > goat > nanny goat > nanny.

the **Nanny Goats** *pr. name* a nickname of the 23rd Regiment of ➡Foot

A unit of the British Army, called this because their regimental mascot is a goat supplied from the Royal herd. *SEE ALSO:* ➡Royal Goats.

nanny state *comp. noun, coll., derog.* a welfare state

nanometre *spell.* nanometer

nap *noun* advice that a horse will win a race

nap hand *idiom* a situation that justifies an expectation of winning

napkin *noun* (1) a ➡nappy; (2) a handkerchief; (3) a head shawl the **Napoleonic Wars** *pr. name, hist.* the great struggle that convulsed all of Europe and much of the rest of the world from 1799 until 1815

A continuation of the ➤French Revolutionary Wars, made grander by the overarching imperialistic vision of Napoleon. In many ways this was the real "World War One", as there was fighting in India, North Africa, the Caribbean and North America—the opportunistic but unsuccessful U.S. attempt to grab Canada which is now known as the War of 1812—as well as Europe.

Britain obtained and retained naval mastery when Nelson defeated the combined French and Spanish fleets at ➤Trafalgar in 1805, but it took another ten years of land fighting in Europe, especially the ➤Peninsular Campaign led by the Duke of Wellington in Portugal and Spain—and Napoleon's own disastrous invasion of Russia—to defeat him. Yet within a year he was back with a renewed Grand Army, to face the combined British and Prussian armies at ➤Waterloo, where it may reasonably be said that the future of the world for the next one hundred years was decided.

napoo *noun, abbr., Fr., sl.* something that either does not exist or is of no use whatsoever

Said to be an abbreviation of the French *il n'y en a plus* = "there is no more of it"

napper *noun, sl.* head

nappy *noun, abbr.* a baby's diaper

An abbreviation of ➤napkin

nappy rash *comp. noun* diaper rash

nark [A] *noun, sl.* (1) a police informer, decoy or stool pigeon; (2) formerly, a policeman

[B] *verb, sl.* to annoy or anger

nark it *imper., sl.* a euphemistic variation of "fuck it"

narky *adj., rh. sl.* sarcastic

Derivation: sarcastic > ➤sarky > narky.

narrow bed *comp. noun, coll.* a euphemism for a grave

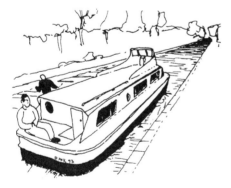

narrow boat *comp. noun* a canal boat

Usually less than 7 ft wide, they are used on the narrow canals found in many parts of England.

narrow circumstances *idiom, coll.* poverty

narrow cloth *comp. noun, out.* cloth that is narrower than 52 inches

the **Narrow Seas** *pr. name, out.* the ➤English Channel and ➤Irish Sea taken together

NAS *pr. name, abbr.* the Noise Abatement Society

nascent *adj.* rising from the center of an ➤ordinary (7)

nasty piece of work *idiom, coll.* an unpleasant person

NAS-UWT *pr. name, abbr.* the National Association of Schoolmasters and Union of Women Teachers

A labor union for teachers.

NATFHE *pr. name, abbr.* the National Association of Teachers in Further and Higher Education

A labor union for university and college teachers.

nation *noun, Sc.* a group of university students who have come from a particular district or region

Particularly at Glasgow and Aberdeen Universities.

the **National Army Museum** *pr. name* a museum of British military history

Located in London, adjacent to the ➤Chelsea Hospital.

the **National Art Collection Fund** *pr. name* the largest British art charity, founded in 1903 to help reduce the number of artistic works going abroad

National Assistance *pr. name, hist.* a former name for ➤Social Security

the **National Covenant** *pr. name, hist., Sc.* an alternative name for the ➤Solemn League and Covenant of 1638

the **National Curriculum** *pr. name* the common curriculum of all state schools in England and Wales

the **National Debt** *pr. name* the total sum of money owed by the British Government to all individuals or institutions it has borrowed money from

the **National Exhibition Centre** *pr. name, hist.* a large exhibition complex comprising 12 halls and other facilities, which opened in 1976

It is adjacent to ➤Birmingham Airport.

the **National Film Theatre** *pr. name* a movie theater operated by the ➤British Film Institute

It is part of the ➤South Bank arts complex in London.

the **National Front** *pr. name* a minor political party with racist and fascist views

the **National Galleries of Scotland** *pr. name* three art galleries in ➤Edinburgh

These are the National Gallery of Scotland, the Scottish National Portrait Gallery and the Scottish National Gallery of Modern Art.

the **National Gallery** *pr. name* perhaps London's best-known art gallery

Founded in 1824, it is located on ➤Trafalgar Square.

National Government *pr. name, hist.* an administration that is formed out of a coalition of the major parties

There have been two National Governments, both in the 20th C. The first was during the economic crisis that followed the Wall Street Crash and subsequent collapse of the ➡Labour government which had been in power at that time.

Another National Government was formed soon after the outbreak of World War II. Normal partisan alignments were suspended during this great national crisis, until the German surrender in May 1945 when a general election was called and normal party politics resumed.

the **National Grid** *pr. name* (1) a network of high-voltage electrical transmission lines connecting power stations, cities, and other locations together into a single system; (2) a system of metric coordinates used on maps of the ➡British Isles published by the ➡Ordnance Survey

the **National Health** *pr. name, abbr.* the ➡National Health Service

National Health Insurance *pr. name, abbr.* a system of compulsory state-run insurance that partially funds the ➡National Health Service

---

the **National Health Service** *pr. name* Britain's national system of universal medical care

It is financed partly by ➡National Health Insurance, partly by fees for certain specific provisions or services, and also from general taxation.

The National Health Service was established in 1948, and provides about nine-tenths of all health-related services in the United Kingdom. People are free to pay for private health care if they wish, but the fact that so few do must be saying something good about the NHS.

---

the **National Hunt Committee** *pr. name, abbr.* the body regulating professional steeplechasing

the **National Insurance Fund** *pr. name, arch.* a former name for the fund financing ➡Social Security

National Insurance stamp *comp. noun, arch.* a stamp, once purchased weekly or monthly at post offices and kept in a payment book

These stamps were proof that an individual had contributed as the law required to the ➡National Insurance Fund during the period covered; they have now been replaced with a computerized record system.

National Liberals *pr. name, hist.* those ➡MPs who left the Liberal Party in 1931 to support the ➡National Governments of 1931 and 1945

In 1948 they formally became the National Liberal Party and in 1966 merged fully with the ➡Conservative Party.

the **National Library of Scotland** *pr. name* a large library in Scotland

A copyright library since 1709. It is located in Edinburgh, where is was founded as the Advocates' Library in 1682.

the **National Library of Wales** *pr. name* the only copyright library in Wales

Established in 1907 and located in Aberystwyth.

the **National Maritime Museum** *pr. name* the leading museum tracing Britain's maritime history

Established in 1937 in the Queen's House, ➡Greenwich.

the **National Monument** *pr. name, hist.* a structure in Edinburgh resembling a ruined Greek temple

Located high up on Calton Hill at the eastern end of ➡Princes Street, it was intended to be a complete, full-size replica of the Parthenon of ancient Athens, built as a memorial to the Scots who died in the ➡Napoleonic Wars. Work was begun in 1822 but soon money ran out and the structure was never finished, with the somewhat bizarre result that can be seen to this day.

the **National Museums of Wales** *pr. name, Wal.* a federation of nine museums situated across Wales

national park *comp. noun* areas designated as places where the country is to be preserved and protected

There are 11 national parks in England and Wales.

They are the ➡Brecon Beacons, ➡Dartmoor, ➡Exmoor, the ➡Lake District, the ➡New Forest, ➡Northumberland, the ➡North York Moors, the ➡Peak District, the Pembrokeshire Coast, Snowdonia and the ➡Yorkshire Dales.

There are no national parks in either ➡Scotland or ➡Northern Ireland, but in Scotland there are forty National Scenic Areas.

the **National Plan** *pr. name, hist.* the grossly overambitious economic plan of the Labour administration of 1964 to 1970

It collapsed ignominiously within a year or so.

the **National Portrait Gallery** *pr. name, hist.* a gallery containing portraits by famous artists or of famous people or both

Founded in 1856, it is located alongside the ➡National Gallery on ➡Trafalgar Square.

the **National Railway Museum** *pr. name* Britain's principal railroad museum, located at ➡York

Opened in 1975, it displays many historic locomotives.

the **National Rivers Authority** *pr. name* a independent body established by Parliament with responsibility for controlling pollution and managing water resources, especially of rivers

the **National Savings Bank** *pr. name* a savings bank operated by the ➡Post Office

231

National Savings Certificate

National Savings Certificate *comp. noun* a savings bond issued by the ➧National Savings Bank, which can be bought from any ➧Post Office
They offer rates of interest that get higher the longer the bonds are held, and are exempt from the income tax that is usually paid on earned interest.

National Scenic Area *comp. noun* approximately, the Scottish equivalent of a ➧national park
There are 40 such areas in Scotland, amounting altogether to more than 13 percent of the total land area of the country.

national service *comp. noun* military conscription

the **National Trust** *pr. name, abbr.* in full, the National Trust for Places of Historic Interest or Natural Beauty

An independent organization set up to preserve and protect buildings and monuments of historic and architectural significance, and areas of countryside of outstanding natural beauty throughout England, Wales and Northern Ireland.

It was established by ➧Act of Parliament in 1907, but all funding comes from its own resources and contributions from the public. There is a separate trust in Scotland.

the **National Trust for Scotland** *pr. name* a similar organization to the ➧National Trust, providing the same services for Scotland

It was established by ➧Act of Parliament in 1931, with the same kind of authority, mandate and resources as the ➧National Trust has in the rest of the United Kingdom.

the **National Westminster Bank** *pr. name* one of the ➧Big Four English retail banks
Formed in 1968 by the merging of two older banks.

the **National Youth Orchestra** *pr. name* an orchestra consisting of the best available amateur teenage musicians in the country
A new 150-strong orchestra is selected by auditions every year.

the **National Youth Theatre** *pr. name* a theatrical company consisting of the best available actors between the ages of 14 and 21 in Britain

the **nation of gentlemen** *pr. name, hist.* Scotland
Called this by ➧George IV on a vist to ➧Edinburgh in 1822.

Nationwide *pr. name* a large ➧building society

NATSOPA *pr. name, abbr.* the National Society of Operative Printers, Graphical and Media Personnel
A labor union that merged with ➧SOGAT 82 in 1981

natter *verb* (1) to talk in an idle way; (2) to grumble

the **Natural Environment Research Council** *pr. name* a government research agency responsible for research into physical and biological science related to environmental matters

the **Natural History Museum** *pr. name* one of the great natural history museums of the world
Located in ➧Kensington, London. The ➧Geological Museum is a department of the Natural History Museum.

the **Nature Conservancy** *pr. name* an agency that manages the natural resources of Britain
It is similar to the U.S. Environmental Protection Agency.

nature reserve *comp. noun* an area of special zoological or botanical interest
There are over 200 nature reserves in Britain.

nature study *comp. noun* the simplified practical natural history as an elementary school subject

NatWest *pr. name, abbr.* ➧National Westminster Bank

naval rating *comp. noun* an enlisted man of the lowest rank in the ➧Royal Navy

navel string *comp. noun, arch.* an umbilical cord

navvy *noun, abbr., verb* an unskilled worker employed in the construction of canals, roads, railroads, etc.
Originally, they were called "navigators."
In the early days of the 18th C. canals, which were the first major civil engineering transportation projects of the modern era, were known as "navigations."

the **Navy List** *pr. name* the official listing of all commissioned officers in the ➧Royal Navy

nay say bad *idiom, Sc.* rather good

NB *noun, abbr., arch.* ➧North Britain

NBA *pr. name, abbr.* the Net Book Agreement
An arrangement that is supposed to protect small independent bookstores by setting a floor on the prices at which books may be sold in the UK; it is becoming increasingly honored more by its breach than observance.

NBG *adj., abbr., sl.* ➧no bloody good

NCB *pr. name, abbr.* the National Coal Board
The former name of ➧British Coal Corporation.

NCCL *pr. name, abbr., hist.* the National Council for Civil Liberties, now known as ➧Liberty

NCU *noun, abbr.* (1) the National Communications Union; (2) the National Cyclist's Union
(1) is a labor union for telecommunications workers.

near as dammit *idiom* (1) very close together; (2) very nearly; almost

nearside *noun* the side of a vehicle next to the curb
Which in Britain is the *left*-hand side.

near the knuckle *idiom, coll.* almost indecent
SEE ALSO: ➧close to the knuckle.

near thing *idiom, coll.* a narrow escape

232

Neasden *pr. name* a suburb in north London that is the regular butt of jokes celebrating the ordinariness of the place and the people who live there

neat *adj.* straight or undiluted
Of a drink.

neb *noun, North, Sc.* (1) a bird's beak; (2) a face; (3) a tip, projection or point; (4) a nose

NEB *pr. name, abbr.* the National Enterprise Board

Nebuchadnezzar *noun* a very large wine bottle, about 20 times as large as normal
From the name of the 6th C. B.C. king of Babylon.

NEC *pr. name, abbr.* (1) the National Executive Committee of the ➡Labour Party; (2) the ➡National Exhibition Centre
(1) is a 26-person group elected annually at the party's conference to administer the day-to-day business of the Labour Party during the following year.

neck *noun, sl.* impudence

neckband *noun* a collar

neckcloth *noun* a cravat

neck-oil *idiom, sl.* beer, especially when available or consumed in large quantities

neckwear *noun, coll.* a collar and tie

NEDC *pr. name, abbr.* the National Economic Development Council
A government-sponsored agency that is there to help plan national economic growth

neddy *noun, coll.* a donkey

Neddy *pr. name, abbr.* a nickname for ➡NEDC

née *spell.* nee

needfire *noun, out.* a fire produced by rubbing two dry sticks together

the **needful** *noun, sl.* money

needle *noun* an outburst of nervousness or bad temper

needle and pin *idiom, rh. sl.* gin

needle and thread *idiom, rh. sl.* bread

needlecraft *noun* needlework

needle {game » match} *idiom* a contest or game where the outcome is important and finely balanced

the **Needles** *pr. name, hist.* three tall rocks made of chalk, which are located just off the western extremity of the Isle of ➡Wight
The outermost one has a lighthouse upon it.

needle time *idiom, out.* the maximum time a radio station may devote to broadcasting recorded music
Once the subject of furious negotiation between radio stations and the Musician's Union, who seemed to imagine fondly that if the time permitted to recorded music was reduced, their members would benefit by being called in to provide live music instead.

needments *noun* things required for a journey

neep *noun, North, Sc.* a turnip

negative capital *idiom* a euphemism for "debt"

négligé *spell.* negligee

negligible quantity *idiom, coll.* a person or thing that does not matter

{**neighbour » neighbourhood » neighbouring**} *spell.* {neighbor » neighborhood » neighboring}

{**neighbourliness » neighbourly**} *spell.* {neighborliness » neighborly}

nelly *noun, rh. sl.* never
Derivation: never > lifetime > breath > puff > Nelly Duff > nelly. *SEE ALSO:* not on your nelly.

Nelson's Column in Trafalgar Square, London

Nelson's Column *pr. name, hist.* a corinithian column in ➡Trafalgar Square, London, erected to commemorate the hero of the great naval victory over the French at ➡Trafalgar in 1805
It is 185 ft tall including the statue of Nelson which stands upon it, and is made of ➡Devonshire granite. The column was completed, with Nelson in place, in 1843, but the four lions that guard its base did not get placed there until 1867, 62 years after the event being commemorated.

the **Nelson touch** *idiom* a brilliantly effective way of resolving problems
After the example of Admiral Lord Nelson

Nemo me impune lacessit *idiom, hist., Lat.* the motto of the ➡Kings of Scots

Meaning in Latin, "No one provokes me with impunity."

NERC *pr. name, abbr.* the National Environmental Research Council

nerk *noun, sl.* a fool

nervy *adj.* anxious, nervous or worried

Loch **Ness** *pr. name* the deepest (at 700 ft.) and longest (at 23 miles) lake in Britain

In the ➡Great Glen and close to ➡Inverness, it is best known as the supposed dwelling-place of ➡Nessie, the ➡Loch Ness Monster.

Nessie *pr. name, coll.* a pet name for the supposed ➡Loch Ness Monster

netball *noun* a kind of basketball

net curtain *comp. noun* a sheer or translucent drape

nett *spell.* net

As opposed to gross.

nettlerash *noun* hives

Network SouthCentral *pr. name (TM)* a railroad company operating commuter services between London and its southern suburbs

It is part of ➡British Rail.

Network SouthEast *pr. name, hist., out.* the former name for all of the extensive rail network in southern and southeastern England that is centered on London and is now operated by a number of separate railroad companies

neuk *noun, Sc.* (1) a nook or recess; (2) an external corner of a building; (3) a corner of a street; (4) a promontory or peninsula

the **never-never** *idiom, sl.* purchase on the installment plan

Newcastle-upon-Tyne *pr. name* the principal city of ➡Tyne and Wear, England

Founded in the 1st C. as *Pons Aelius* by the Romans, who built a bridge over the ➡Tyne River here, at the eastern end of ➡Hadrian's Wall.

A ➡Norman castle, erected in 1080, gave the city its name, and in the 16th C. coal mining began to develop as a significant industry in the surrounding area. Newcastle become the principal port from which coal was shipped down the eastern coast of England to London, by far the most significant market at that time. We are reminded of the way in which Newcastle monopolized this business by the expression ➡coals to Newcastle.

It was the need to transport more and more coal from these inland mines to the city's dockside during the ➡Napoleonic Wars—when labor was in particularly short supply—that did much to make this the place where the first steam-powered public railroads were built, and if the industrial revolution can be said to have a specific geographical place of birth, Newcastle is it.

Incorporated as a city in 1157, the current population of the Newcastle urban area is 800,000 (1988 estimate)

the **New Club** *pr. name, hist.* a leading club in ➡Princes Street, Edinburgh

Founded in 1787 by a group of claret drinkers.

New College *pr. name* a college of ➡Oxford University founded in 1379

the **New English Bible** *pr. name* a completely new translation of the Bible authorized by the principal British protestant churches

The New Testament was published in 1961, and the Old Testament in 1970.

the **New Forest** *pr. name, hist.* an area of more than 90,000 acres in ➡Hampshire made a royal hunting preserve by ➡William the Conqueror in 1079

The name is misleading; it is only partially woodland, the rest being bog and open heath. William the Conqueror's son, ➡William Rufus, was killed in the New Forest while out hunting. The area is especially famous for its ponies, and in 1992 was given the status of a ➡national park.

the **Newgate Calendar** *pr. name, hist.* a record of the escapades of the inmates of ➡Newgate Gaol

First published in 1773 with new editions at regular intervals, just like a modern periodical, until the prison closed in 1880.

Newgate fringe *comp. noun, out., sl.* hair that has grown under the chin

Given this name because the style mimics the appearance of a hangman's rope around the neck.

Newgate Gaol *pr. name, hist.* for many years the local jail for London and ➡Middlesex

This prison was closed in 1880 and the building demolished in 1902. It long had a notorious reputation. Many famous rogues and political prisoners were locked up there, and once executions were commonly conducted in public on the street outside.

New Hall *pr. name* a hall of ➡Cambridge University founded in 1954

This college admits female students only.

Newham *pr. name* a ➡Greater London borough

Its current population, which is also included within the ➡London urban area total, is 200,000 (1991 Census).

Newingtons *noun, rh. sl.* the abdomen

Derivation: abdomen > guts > butt > Newington Butts. Newington Butts is a road in south London.

New Lanark *pr. name, hist.* an idealistic community founded in 1784 by Robert Owen on the upper ➡Clyde 30 miles southeast of ➡Glasgow

This is where Owen founded his proto-socialist experimental community, whose workers were to experience ideal working and living conditions and superior education.

At first his plan appeared to work well, making a profit and ecouraging Owen to build other similar communities—the best-known being New Harmony in Indiana, founded in 1825—but these experiments all did fail in the end of course. However the village built to house these experimental pioneers survives virtually intact to this day at New lanark.

Newmarket [A] *noun* a gambling card game where the object is to play cards matching those on the table
[B] *pr. name* a town in ➡Suffolk, center of the British racehorse breeding and training industry

the **New Model Army** *pr. name, hist.* what the ➡Parliamentary army was known as, following complete reorganization in 1645 during the ➡English Civil War This was the first properly trained and disciplined professional army raised in Britain since the Roman legions left The concept was ➡Cromwell's, it eventually won the war for the Parliament side, and he took the credit.

a soldier of the New Model Army

Newnham College *pr. name* a college of ➡Cambridge University founded in 1871
This college admits female students only.

new penny *noun, coll., hist.* the penny in circulation following ➡decimalisation in 1971, which is worth ¹/₁₀₀ th of a pound
See also: ➡old penny.

Newport *pr. name, hist.* a town in ➡Gwent, Wales, close by the Roman settlement of *Isca*, and an important center since these times
The current population is 110,000 (1991 estimate).

Newry and Mourne *pr. name* a district in ➡Northern Ireland, in what used to be partly County ➡Antrim and partly County ➡Down
The current population is 90,000 (1990 estimate).

newsagent *noun* a newsdealer

New Scotland Yard *pr. name* the headquarters of the ➡Metropolitan Police
It is located just off Victoria Street in west-central London, and should not be confused with ➡Scotland Yard, the former police headquarters near ➡Westminster Bridge.

newsreader *noun* a newscaster on TV or radio

newsroom *noun* a room in a public library, for example, reserved for the purpose of reading newspapers

New Street Station *pr. name* the principal railroad terminus in central ➡Birmingham

newsvendor *noun, pref.* a street newspaper seller

newted *adj., sl.* very drunk
Derived from the expression ➡as pissed as a newt.

Newtonabbey *pr. name* a district in ➡Northern Ireland, in what used to be County ➡Antrim
The current population is 75,000 (1990 estimate).

new town *comp. noun* a town built as a single project after World War II for the purpose of reducing overcrowding in a nearby large city

the **New Town** *pr. name, hist.* a large extension of the city of ➡Edinburgh, built between 1780 and 1830 on open ground to the north of the Royal Mile and the rest of the medieval old town
Considered to be one of the finest examples of Georgian architecture and town planning anywhere, the New Town is now the business heart of Scotland's capital city. ➡Princes Street, the main shopping thoroughfare, offers a truly spectacular urban vista across a valley to the lowering might of ➡Edinburgh Castle.

New Year Honours *pr. name* an ➡honours list announced annually on New Year's Day

next but one *idiom, coll.* following the next, two ahead

next door but one *adj., coll.* two doors along

NF *pr. name, abbr.* the ➡National Front

NFT *pr. name, abbr.* the ➡National Film Theatre

NFU *pr. name, abbr.* the National Farmers Union
An association of farmers. This is not a labor union.

NGA *pr. name, abbr.* the National Graphical Association
A labor union for printers, now merged with the ➡GPMU.

NHI *pr. name, abbr.* ➡National Health Insurance

NHS *pr. name, abbr.* the ➡National Health Service

NHS trust *comp. noun* a self-governing unit of the ➡National Health Service
Although sometimes characterized by their critics as private companies operating for profit, NHS trusts are entirely publicly owned entities that are, however, expected to consider the cost implications of what they are doing. Although coming at the problem from a different direction, NHS trusts appear to bear some significant resemblance to health maintenance organizations.

NI *pr. name, abbr.* (1) ➡National Insurance; (2) ➡Northern Ireland

nib *noun* the point of a pen that makes contact with the writing surface

nice as ninepence *idiom, coll.* very tidy

nice little earner *idiom, sl.* (1) that which makes easy profits; (2) a well-paid job

nick [A] *noun, sl.* (1) the state or condition of something; (2) a police station; (3) a jail
[B] *verb, sl.* (1) to arrest or catch a criminal; (2) to steal

{**nickelled** » **nickelling**} *spell.* {nickeled » nickeling}

nicker

nicker *noun, sl.* a ➡pound
In the sense of money.

nickie-tams *comp. noun, Sc.* straps used by farm workers to tie their pants below the knees in order to keep their upper legs clean

nicotian *noun, sl., out.* a person who smokes

nide *noun* a brood of pheasants

niff *noun, sl.* bad smell

niffy *adj., sl.* smelly

night bell *comp. noun* a bell used to wake up a householder or hotel keeper late at night

night bird *idiom, coll.* someone up and about at night

night boat *comp. noun* a ferry that crosses at night

nightdress *noun* a nightgown

night glass *comp. noun* a telescope especially designed to be used at night

night hag *comp. noun, out.* a nightmare

night hawk *comp. noun* (1) a late-night thief or prowler; (2) the European nightjar
(2) is a nocturnal bird of the *caprimulgus europaeus* family.

nightline *noun* a fishing line left in water overnight

nightpiece *noun* a painting, particularly a landscape, as seen at night

night sister *comp. noun* a senior night nurse

night watchman *comp. noun* (1) one who keeps watch or guard at night; (2) in ➡cricket, a ➡batsman sent on to play near to the end of the day's play in order to be first the following day

nig-nog *comp. noun, derog., sl.* (1) a raw recruit to the army; (2) a fool

the Battle of the Nile *pr. name, hist.* a naval battle during the ➡Napoleonic Wars when the British fleet, commanded by Nelson, destroyed the French fleet at the western mouth of the Nile River in 1798
This had the interesting effect of stranding Napoleon and his army in Egypt for some considerable time, until they could be rescued by another expedition from France.

the Nine Days Queen *pr. name, hist.* ➡Lady Jane Grey, proclaimed queen on July 10 1553
Although ➡Mary Tudor was proclaimed queen in London nine days after Jane, on July 19, Lady Jane Grey reigned on for another five days before formally abdicating.

Nine Men's Morris *pr. name, hist.* a game once popular in the English countryside
It was somewhat similar to checkers.

999 *noun* the telephone number used to call emergency services
It is used in a similar manner to 911, and callers will be connected to police, fire or ambulance services as appropriate. The emergency number used in most of the rest of the ➡EU, which is 112, is being introduced as a parallel emergency number; ultimately, it may replace 999.

ninepence to the shilling *idiom, sl.* lacking intelligence or common sense; simple-minded
There were 12 ➡old pence in a ➡shilling.

the 1922 Committee *pr. name, hist.* a committee comprising all ➡Conservative ➡backbencher ➡MPs
It was formed in 1922 at a meeting in the ➡Carlton Club during a crisis in relations with Turkey which caused the breakup of the Conservative/Liberal coalition government and the resignation of ➡Prime Minister Lloyd George. Since that time the 1922 Committee has remained in existence to ensure that the views of backbenchers cannot be disregarded by leaders of the ➡Conservative Party.

nip out *verb, coll.* to depart or exit briefly

nipper *noun, coll.* (1) a young child, particularly a boy; (2) formerly, a boy assisting an adult workman

nippit *adj., Sc.* (1) bad-tempered; (2) mean

nipple count *idiom, coll.* a measure of the down-market or prurience level of a newspaper
Supposedly measured by the number of unencumbered female breasts visible upon perusal of the publication.

nippy [A] *adj., coll.* snappy or nimble
[B] *noun, arch., sl.* a waitress

NIREX *pr. name, abbr.* the Nuclear Industry Radioactive Waste Executive
The agency handling radioactive waste disposal in Britain.

Nissen hut *comp. noun* a prefabricated hut with a semi-circular cross-sectional roof shape, made from corrugated iron and placed on a concrete base
Similar to a Quonset hut, it is named after its inventor.

nit *noun, abbr., sl.* a nitwit; a stupid person

nitre *spell.* niter

nix [A] *imper., out., sl.* a warning to hide or take care
A childish term
[B] *noun., Ger., sl.* (1) no; (2) nothing
From the German *nichts* = "nothing."

no [A] *adv., Sc.* not
[B] *verb aux., Sc.* cannot

n.o. *idiom, abbr.* in ➡cricket, not out

nob *noun, sl.* a wealthy or high-class person

no ball *comp. noun* an illegally bowled ➡cricket ball

nobble *verb, sl.* (1) to acquire money by dishonest means; (2) to catch or arrest a criminal; (3) to secure support by cheating; (4) to tamper with a racehorse to prevent it from winning

Nobby Clarke *comp. noun, sl.* a nickname acquired by every man with the surname of Clark or Clarke in the British Army, ➡Royal Navy or ➡RAF
A reference to the dress worn by 19th C. government clerks, which was considered to resemble that worn by a ➡nob.

noble *noun, hist.* a gold coin worth one third of a ➡pound, which circulated in 14th C. England

no bloody good *idiom, sl.* useless, a waste of time
Originally military slang. *See also:* ➡NBG.

NOCD *noun, abbr., arch., sl.* not our class, dear
A code word to indicate that the person or thing referred to is not considered to be sufficiently high class for the speaker. *See also:* ➡NTD.

no claims bonus *comp. noun* a reduction in insurance premium applied after a set period—usually a year—when no claim against the policy is made

no cop *adj. phr., sl.* useless

noddy *noun, derog., sl.* a police officer on foot patrol
Named after Noddy, a nursery character who is made of wood and nods his head when speaking.

noddy bike *idiom, derog., hist., sl.* a small, underpowered motorcycle once used by police officers
They had all been withdrawn by 1970. *See also:* ➡noddy.

noddy car *idiom, sl.* a small car
➡Noddy again; he drives a car that is far too small for him.

noddy suit *idiom, sl.* an NCB protection suit sometimes worn by military personnel
It is difficult to don and cumbersome to wear, so movement is difficult and the wearer appears foolish, hence the name.

no distance *adj., adv., coll.* nearby

nod through *phr. verb, coll.* (1) to agree without comment; (2) to count an ➡MP as having voted in the ➡House, although not physically present

nog *noun, North* a strong beer from ➡East Anglia

noggin *noun* a small measure of liquor
Usually the same as a ➡gill.

no-go area *comp. noun, sl.* an area where entry is impossible or prohibited

no-hoper *idiom, sl.* one who makes a habit of failing

no joy *idiom, coll.* a failure

nombril *noun* in heraldry, a position midway between the base of a shield and its ➡fesse point

no names, no pack-drill *idiom, coll.* with discretion, retribution can be avoided

nonce *noun, derog., sl.* (1) a worthless or useless person; (2) a sexual pervert; (3) a prisoner convicted of a sexual offense

Nonconformist *pr. name* an English Protestant who does not accept the doctrine or discipline of the ➡Church of England

non-content *comp. noun* a ➡peer or ➡peeress voting against a motion in the ➡House of Lords

none-so-pretty *comp. noun* a pink flower that grows on sandy or rocky ground
Its formal name is *saxifraga urbium*.

none the less *spell.* nonetheless

none too clever *idiom* sick

non-iron fabric *comp. noun* a permanently pressed fabric, which requires no ironing

nonjuror *noun, hist.* one of the ➡Church of England's clergy who refused to swear allegiance to ➡William and Mary after the ➡Glorious Revolution of 1688

nonplussed *spell.* nonplused

non-profit-making *adj.* non-profit
Of a company or other organization, such as a charity.

nontillion *noun, num.* a septendecillion, or 10^{54}
The American nontillion is 10^{30}.

non-U *adj., arch., coll.* not upper class
See also: ➡U.

noo *adj., adv., conj., pron., Sc.* now

no oil painting *idiom, coll.* not beautiful

no-one *spell.* no one

nor *adj., adv., conj., pron.* neither

Norfolk *pr. name* a county on the eastern coast of England, between ➡Lincolnshire and ➡Suffolk
It is principally famous for being flat. The county seat is ➡Norwich and the current population is 735,000 (1991 Census).

the Norfolk Broads *pr. name* a freshwater recreation area in ➡East Anglia consisting of ➡broads
The area is also important as a nature reserve.

Norfolk jacket *comp. noun* a man's loose-fitting belted jacket

norland *noun, abbr.* the northern part of a territory

Norland *pr. name, abbr. arch.* northern England

normality *noun* normalcy

normal price *comp. noun* a regular price

Norman *pr. name, hist.* one of the mixed Franco-Viking people from ➡William I's domains in western France who came along with him to conquer England in 1066

the Norman Conquest *pr. name, hist.* ➡William I's invasion and conquest of England in 1066

Normandy *pr. name, hist.* the ➡Royal House of England from 1066 until 1135
The following English monarchs belonged to this house: ➡William I, ➡William II and ➡Henry I. ➡Stephen is also usually considered to be a member, although some consider him to be a member of a distinct house called ➡Blois.

Norman English *pr. name* English as influenced by the French-speaking ➡Normans after 1066

Norman French *pr. name, hist.* French as spoken by ➡Normans at the time of the Conquest of 1066
And then by the ruling class of England for another two centuries until it merged with Anglo-Saxon into the creole tongue we now call English. Norman French continued to be used for some time in English courts.

Norn Norse *pr. name* the Norse language formerly spoken in ➡Orkney and ➡Shetland

Norroy and Ulster King of Arms *pr. name* the Third ➡King of Arms of the ➡College of Arms, responsible for heraldic business in England north of the ➡Trent River, plus ➡Ulster in Ireland

Norse *pr. name, hist.* the language of the Vikings

the **Norse** *pr. name, hist.* the Viking people of Scandinavia, especially Norway

Norsman *pr. name, hist.* a Viking

Northampton *pr. name, hist.* a town that is the administrative center of ➡Northamptonshire
A 12th C. ➡Norman castle here was demolished in the 16th C., but many other medieval buildings remain The current population is 165,000 (1991 estimate).

Northamptonshire *pr. name* a county situated in east-central England
The county seat is ➡Northampton and the current population is 570,000 (1991 Census).

north and south *idiom, rh. sl.* mouth

Northants. *pr. name, abbr.* ➡Northamptonshire

North Britain *pr. name, arch.* a once-fashionable name for Scotland devised during the 18th C.

North Briton *pr. name, arch.* a once-fashionable name for a Scot devised during the 18th C.

the **North Channel** *pr. name* the narrow channel at the northern end of the Irish Sea separating the northeastern corner of Ireland from the southwestern corner of Scotland
Where ➡Ireland and ➡Great Britain are closest together. The narrowest part of the channel, between the Mull of Kintyre in Scotland and County Antrim in Ulster, is just 14 miles.

the **North Country** *pr. name, coll.* northern England

North Countryman *pr. name, coll.* a native, citizen or inhabitant of northern England

North Down *pr. name* a district in ➡Northern Ireland, in what used to be County ➡Down
The current population is 75,000 (1990 estimate).

Northern Ireland *pr. name, hist.* that part of the island of ➡Ireland that refused to be separated from the ➡United Kingdom in 1921
Thus remaining within the ➡United Kingdom rather than becoming part of what is now the ➡Irish Republic when Ireland became independent under the terms of the ➡Anglo-Irish Treaty. Northern Ireland consists of six (➡Antrim, ➡Armagh, ➡Down, ➡Fermanagh, ➡Londonderry, and ➡Tyrone) out of the nine counties comprising the ancient Irish province of the ➡Ulster, and so is often mistakenly called by that name. The current population is 1,583,000 (1991 estimate)

the **Northern Ireland Office** *pr. name* the office of state that governs ➡Northern Ireland

the **Northern Line** *pr. name* one part of London's rapid-transit subway system
It extends from Edgware, Mill Hill East and High Barnet in the north to Morden in the south. The Northern Line splits (between Camden Town and Kennington) into two routes through central London, one each for ➡West End and the ➡City.

Northern Sinfonia *pr. name, hist.* the only full-time professional orchestra in northeastern England
It was founded in ➡Newcastle-upon-Tyne in 1958.

North London Railways *pr. name (TM)* a railroad company operating commuter services between London and its northern suburbs
It is part of ➡British Rail.

the **North Riding** *pr. name, hist.* a major administrative division of the former county of ➡Yorkshire

North Sea *pr. name* that body of water north of the ➡Strait of Dover, which separates the ➡British Isles from the rest of the European continent

Northumb. *pr. name, abbr.* ➡Northumberland

Northumberland *pr. name* (1) the most northeasterly county in England; (2) a ➡national park in the northern part of (1)
The county seat is Morpeth and the current population of the county is 300,000 (1991 Census). (1) is bounded on the north by the Scots border and on the south by ➡Hadrian's Wall.

Northumbria *pr. name, hist.* (1) an ancient kingdom located partially in what is now northern England and partially in what is now southeastern Scotland; (2) an alternate name for ➡Northumberland (1)
The kingdom was established by ➡Saxon invaders after the departure of the Romans. Northumbria was divided into the two principalities of ➡Bernicia and ➡Deira from 558 to 654. However, the whole kingdom finally disappeared as a separate entity after invasion and conquest by the Danes in 878. The usual seat of the kings of Northumbria was what is now the modern city of ➡York.

Northumbrian *pr. name* a native, citizen or inhabitant of ➡Northumbria

the **North York Moors** *pr. name, hist.* a ➡national park in ➡Yorkshire consisting of forest and moorland
Most of the park is in Yorkshire, but part is in ➡Cleveland.

North Yorkshire *pr. name* a county in eastern England, between ➡Cleveland and ➡Humberside
Formed out of the East ➡Riding of ➡Yorkshire and portions of the other two ➡Ridings in 1974. The county seat is Northallerton and the current population is 700,000 (1991 Census).

Norwich *pr. name* the largest city in ➡East Anglia and administrative center of ➡Norfolk
Norwich cathedral was founded in 1096 and at 315 ft., its 15th C. spire is the second tallest in England. Norwich Castle was begun at about the same time and Norwich was incorporated as a city in 1194; the current population, including suburbs, is 190,000 (1988 estimate).

Norwich Terrier *pr. name* a small, long-haired breed of terrier with a wiry coat

nosepipe *noun* a section of pipe used as a nozzle

noserag *noun, sl.* a handkerchief

nosering *noun* a ring through the nose of a bull

nose-to-tail *idiom* bumper to bumper

noshery *noun, sl.* a restaurant

no shortage *comp. noun, coll.* plenty

nosh-up *comp. noun, sl.* a big meal

Nostell Priory *pr. name, hist.* a mid-18th C. great house just south of Wakefield in ➧Yorkshire

The building is a mixture of Palladian and neo-classical styles; the interior and parts of the exterior were designed by Robert Adam. It is said that ➧Chippendale was an apprentice here while it was being built.

not a bean *idiom, sl.* without any money

not a {bleeding thing » blind thing » dicky bird » sausage} *idiom, coll.* absolutely nothing

not an earthly *idiom, abbr., sl.* no chance whatever
Derived from an abbreviation of "earthly chance".

not before time *idiom, coll.* late

not cricket *idiom, coll* unreasonable, not fair play

note *noun, abbr.* a ➧banknote

notecase *noun, out.* a wallet or billfold

nothing in it *idiom* nothing to it

nothing loath *adj. phr., coll.* willing

notice board *comp. noun* (1) a bulletin board; (2) a sign board

not long {arrived » here} *idiom, coll.* newly arrived

not much cop *idiom, sl.* of little use

not on *idiom, coll.* unacceptable

not on your nelly *idiom, sl.* emphatically, absolutely not; on no account whatsoever
SEE ALSO: ➧nelly.

not out *comp. noun* in ➧cricket, not bowled, caught or otherwise removed from batting

not proper *idiom* not socially acceptable

---

not proven *adj. phr., Sc.* a third verdict, possible only in a Scottish criminal court
Also known as the ➧Scottish Verdict, it has been paraphrased as, "We know you did it, but can't prove it." Nevertheless, the effect in law of a "not proven" verdict is identical to one of "not guilty".
Originally, Scots law permitted a jury to return just two verdicts, "proven" or "not proven", which were exactly coincident in meaning with the more familiar "guilty" or "not guilty" verdicts of English or American courts.

---

not quite *idiom* almost

not short of a bob or two *idiom, coll.* prosperous
SEE ALSO: ➧bob.

not so dusty *idiom, coll.* just about acceptable

Nottingham *pr. name* a city that is the administrative center of ➧Nottinghamshire

Originally an ➧Anglo-Saxon settlement, it was occupied by the Danes during the 9th C., who turned it into their informal English capital.
There is a ➧Norman castle in the city, which is associated in the public mind with ➧Robin Hood, who supposedly resided in nearby ➧Sherwood Forest and struggled on a regular basis with the Sheriff of Nottingham. Incorporated as a city in 1155, the current population, including suburbs, is 600,000 (1988 estimate).

Nottinghamshire *pr. name* a county located in east-central England

The county seat is ➧Nottingham and the current population is 980,000 (1991 Census).

Notting Hill Carnival *pr. name* an annual ➧West Indian carnival—the largest of its kind in Europe—held in this west London district every August

not to know *idiom, coll.* could not know

Notts. *pr. name, abbr.* Nottingham

not want to know *idiom. phr. verb* to refuse to listen or take notice

noughts and crosses *comp. noun* tick-tack-toe

nous *noun, coll.* common sense, initiative or gumption

novelette *noun, derog.* a light, over-sentimental or romantic short novel

novemdecillion *noun, num.* 10^{114}
The American novemdecillion is 10^{60}.

No Waiting *imper.* no parking
A road sign.

nowt *noun, North* nothing

nozzer *noun, sl.* a new member of a ship's crew

NPA *pr. name, abbr.* Newspaper Publisher's Association

NPL *pr. name, abbr.* the National Physical Laboratory

NR *pr. name, abbr.* the ➧North Riding

NRA *pr. name, abbr.* the ➧National Rivers Authority

NSB *pr. name, abbr.* the ➧National Savings Bank

NSPCC *pr. name, abbr.* the National Society for the Prevention of Cruelty to Children

NTD *noun, abbr., derog., old., sl.* not top drawer
A code used to indicate that the person or thing referred to is not considered to be sufficiently high class for the speaker. *SEE ALSO:* ➧NOCD.

NUBE *pr. name, abbr.* National Union of Bank Employees
A labor union for bank clerks.

nuddy *adj., Aus., sl.* naked

Nuffield College *pr. name* a college of Oxford University founded in 1937

nuffink *noun, sl.* nothing

NUGMW *pr. name, abbr.* the National Union of General and Municipal Workers
A labor union for blue-collar workers

NUJ *pr. name, abbr.* the National Union of Journalists
A labor union for journalists.

NUM *pr. name, abbr.* National Union of Mineworkers
A labor union for miners.

number plate *comp. noun* an automobile license plate

Number Ten *pr. name, abbr.* 10 ➡Downing Street
The official residence of the ➡Prime Minister.

numbles *noun* the entrails of a deer

nun's cloth *comp. noun* a thin woolen material

NUPE *pr. name, abbr.* the National Union of Public Employees
A labor union for public service workers, it merged with ➡Unison in 1993.

nuppence *noun, out., sl.* no money

NUR *pr. name, abbr.* National Union of Railwaymen
A railroad workers' labor union, now merged with the ➡RMT

nurse-child *comp. noun, out.* a foster child

nursery nurse *comp. noun* a nursemaid

nursery slope *comp. noun* a skiing slope suitable for beginners being taught how to ski

nursing chair *comp. noun* a low chair with high back, designed for use by breast-feeding mothers

nursing sister *comp. noun* a senior female nurse

NUS *pr. name, abbr.* (1) the National Union of Seamen; (2) the National Union of Students
(1) is a labor union for sailors. (2) is the national union of university ➡student unions.

NUS *pr. name, abbr.* the National Union of Teachers
A labor union for teachers.

nut-butter *comp. noun* a butter-like food manufactured from nuts

the **Nutcrackers** *pr. name* a nickname for the 3rd Regiment of ➡Foot
A unit of the British Army. This name was earned during their time in Iberia participating in the ➡Peninsular War.

nutmeg *verb, sl.* to kick a ➡soccerball between the legs of a member of the opposing team

nut-oil *comp. noun* an extract of walnuts and hazelnuts

nutter *noun, sl.* a crazy person

nutty slack *comp. noun* small, nut-like lumps of coal

NVQ *pr. name, abbr.* the National Vocational Qualification system
A grading system for technical skills training.

nyaff *noun, Sc.* a self-important yet trivial or insignificant person

nye *spell.* nide
A brood of pheasants.

oak *verb, rh. sl.* to fool around

Derivation: fool around > fool > joke > oak.

Oak-Apple Day *pr. name, hist.* May 29

An annual commemoration of the occasion when after he had lost the Battle of Worcester to Cromwell in 1651, Charles II was obliged to hide in a hollow oak tree at Boscobel for a day and a half to escape capture by Parliamentary troops. He spent the next night hiding in the 16th C. Boscobel House, still there today. The oak tree shown to modern visitors is thought to be a sapling from the original tree.

Confusingly, the battle was fought on September 3; May 29 was Charles' birthday, and a public holiday until the middle of the 19th C.

the **Oaks** *pr. name* an annual horse race at Epsom

OAP *noun, abbr.* an old age pensioner

oast [A] *noun* (1) a small lump or nodule; (2) a conically shaped hop-drying kiln

[B] *noun, abbr.* an oast-house

oast-house *comp. noun, abbr.* a building containing one or more of oast [A](2)

oatcake *noun, Sc.* a thin, unleavened oatmeal cake

Oatmeal Monday *pr. name, hist.* Midterm Monday at Scottish universities

When a poor student's family would bring a sack of oatmeal so that he had food enough to eat during the rest of the term.

OB [A] *noun, abbr.* an outside broadcast

[B] *pr. name, abbr.* the Order of Burma

Oban *pr. name, hist.* a coastal resort and port in the northwestern part of Strathclyde region

The current population is 8,000 (1991 estimate).

OBE *noun, abbr.* the Order of the British Empire

OBI *noun, abbr.* the Order of British India

oblique *noun* an inclined punctuation slash, either "/" or "\"

Oboe *pr. name, hist.* the codename for a secret navigation system employed by British bomber aircraft attacking Germany during World War II

The pilot or navigator listened on headphones to a musical tone that changed pitch when the aircraft veered off course.

obtaining by deception *comp. noun* the legal name for fraud in England and Wales

occupier *noun* a person occupying a house or land

ocean wave *idiom, rh. sl.* a shave

och *exclam., Sc.* an expression of surprise, regret, irritation, etc., mostly uttered by actors pretending to be Scottish

Real Scots tend to say ach instead.

oche *noun* the line behind which darts players must stand when throwing

{**ochre** » **ochreous** » **ochry**} *spell.* {ocher » ocherous » ochery}

ocht *noun, Sc.* ought

octave *noun* a wine cask with ⅛ th the capacity of a pipe or ¼ th the capacity of a hogshead

octillion *noun, num.* a quindecillion, or 10^{48}

The American octillion is 10^{27}.

octodecillion *noun, num.* 10^{108}

The American octodecillion is 10^{57}.

octopuses *spell.* octopudes

OCTU *noun, abbr.* an Officer Cadet Training Unit

These are usually attached to an English public school, and now much less common than they were some years ago.

OD *noun, abbr.* the ordnance datum

odd job *comp. noun* casual work

odd {**jobber** » **job man**} *comp. noun* a casual worker

oddment *noun* a printing term for text other than the main text of a document

odds and sods *idiom, sl.* odds and ends

odds-on *comp. noun, coll.* odds better than even

{**odour** » **odourless**} *spell.* {odor » odorless}

OED *pr. name, abbr.* the Oxford English Dictionary

of account *adj., coll.* significant

off [A] *adv.* spoiled or decayed (of food)

[B] *noun* that half of a cricket field, divided lengthwise through the pitch, which does not contain the striking batsman's feet

The other half is called the leg.

Offaly *pr. name* a county in the Irish Republic

County Offaly in the ancient province of Leinster.

Offa's Dyke *pr. name, hist.* an ancient earthwork that runs from Wye, near Monmouth in the south of Wales, to Prestatyn in the north

It is said to have been built by Offa, King of ➡Mercia, in the 8th C. to defend his ➡Anglo-Saxon people against the native ➡Britons in the wild country further west. Certainly it did for the first time define the boundary between the future England and what was to become Wales.

off by heart *idiom* memorized; know by heart

off colour *idiom, coll.* in poor health

offcut *noun* a remnant; an unsold or unused residual piece of cloth, wood, etc.

offence *spell.* offense

OFFER *pr. name, abbr.* Office of Electricity Regulation

A regulatory agency charged with ensuring that companies who supply electricity do not abuse what are often in effect their supply monopolies.

offer price *comp. noun* a price offered by a potential purchaser to a potential seller

off form *idiom* performing worse than usual

SEE ALSO: ➡on form.

Office *noun* the personnel, buildings and collective persona of a major department of government

Such as, ➡Home Office, ➡Foreign Office, ➡Post Office, etc.

the offices *noun, abbr.* the ➡usual offices

Official IRA *pr. name, abbr., coll.* the Official ➡Irish Republican Army

The original ➡IRA from which the ➡Provisional IRA split in 1969 in order to continue with the campaign of violent terrorism that the Official IRA then wished to discontinue.

the Official Opposition *pr. name* the largest non-governing party in the ➡House of Commons

Usually the most likely to govern if the government changes.

official receiver *comp. noun* an accountant or lawyer appointed by a court to administer the business of an insane or bankrupt person

the Official Referee *pr. name* a person attached to the ➡Supreme Court, to whom disputes may be referred for resolution, provided there is prior agreement of both parties to accept this judgment

the Official Secrets Act *pr. name* Originally, a law of 1911 making it an offense to gather information that would be harmful to the security of the state or to pass such information on to an enemy

There have been several additional acts since then modifying the details, but the principle remains intact.

the Official Unionist Party *pr. name* a Northern Irish political party that strongly supports continuation of the union with the ➡UK

off-licence *comp. noun* a packaged liquor store

off-load *verb, coll.* to get rid of something burdensome by transferring it elsewhere

offside *noun* the side of a vehicle farthest from the curb

Which in Britain is the right-hand side, of course.

offside front seat *comp. noun* the driver's seat in an automobile

off the {chump » head » scone} *idiom, sl.* crazy

off the hooks *idiom, sl.* dead

off the peg *idiom, coll.* off the shelf or off the rack

off you go *imper, sl.* begin now

off your own bat *idiom, coll.* without help

OFGAS *pr. name, abbr.* the Office of Gas Regulation

A regulatory agency charged with ensuring that gas supply companies do not abuse what are often in effect their monopolies.

of great age *adj. phr., coll.* very old

OFSTED *pr. name, abbr.* the Office for Standards in Education

A government Department responsible for ensuring that schools and teachers maintain acceptable standards of teaching in England and Wales. It replaced ➡HMI in 1992.

OFT *pr. name, abbr.* the ➡Office of Fair Trading

OFTEL *pr. name, abbr.* the Office of Telecommunications Regulation

A regulatory agency charged with seeing that telecommunications companies do not abuse what are often in effect their monopolies.

of that ilk *idiom, Sc.* of the same name

A term that is principally used to identify the chief of a ➡Highland clan or the head of an important land-owning family. SEE ALSO: ➡ilk.

OFWAT *pr. name, abbr.* the Office of Water Regulation

A regulatory agency charged with seeing that water supply companies do not abuse what are often in effect their monopolies.

ogham *noun, hist.* an alphabet of 20 characters used by the ancient inhabitants of the British Isles

Characters were formed as patterns made up of parallel lines grouped above or below a horizontal line.

oh *noun* the numeral zero

OHMS *pr. name, abbr.* On {His » Her} Majesty's Service

The letters "OHMS" appear on the front of envelopes mailed by government departments on official business, obviating the need for postage stamps.

oick *noun, derog., sl.* an uncultured, inferior, uneducated or rustic person

From the sound made by a pig, one assumes.

oil can *idiom, hist., sl.* a World War I German trench-mortar, from its appearance

oil the knocker *phr. verb, coll., out.* to bribe or to tip a doorman

oily rag [A] *idiom, rh. sl.* a cigarette

Derivation: cigarette > ➡fag > rag > oily rag.

[B] *idiom, sl.* an incompetent car repairman

the *Oireachtas* *pr. name, Gae.* the legislature of the ➡Irish Republic

Consisting of the President, the ➡*Dáil Éireann*, and the ➡*Seanad Éireann*.

0800- *noun* free-to-caller telephone numbers, similar to U.S. 800 WATS numbers

Operated by ➡British Telecom.

SEE ALSO: ➡0500- phone numbers.

0500- *noun* free-to-caller telephone numbers, similar to U.S. 800 WATS numbers

Operated by ➡Mercury.

SEE ALSO: ➡0800- phone numbers.

old age pension *comp. noun, pref.* a retirement pension

Paid to all women when they reach the age of 60 and to all men when they reach the age of 65.

old age pensioner *comp. noun* a senior citizen, a person receiving the ➡old age pension

the **Old Bailey** *pr. name, coll.* the popular name for the ➡Central Criminal Court, London

From the name of the street it is upon; it stands on the site of the former ➡Newgate Prison, demolished in 1902.

old {bean » boy » chap » fellow » fruit » stick} *comp. noun, coll.* a friendly greeting between men

the **Old Bill** *pr. name, sl.* the police

Especially the ➡Metropolitan Police.

the **Old Bold Fifth** *pr. name* a nickname for the 5th Regiment of ➡Foot

A unit of the British Army.

old boy network *comp. noun, coll.* an informal preferment network for men from similar backgrounds such as school, army, college, etc.

the **Old Braggs** *pr. name* the 28th Regiment of ➡Foot

A unit of the British Army named for General Philip Bragg, their commander from 1734 until 1759. Also known as the ➡Slashers and the ➡Braggs.

old buffer *comp. noun, derog., sl.* a foolish but harmless old man

the **Old {Cavalier » Chevalier}** *pr. name, hist.* alternate names for the ➡Old Pretender

Old Conky *pr. name, hist.* a nickname of the Duke of Wellington, from the shape and extent of his ➡conk.

the **Old Contemptibles** *pr. name, hist.* a nickname for the 160,000 members of the British army ➡Expeditionary Force, commanded by Sir John French, who were sent to France in 1914 upon the outbreak of war with Germany

From an apocryphal direction supposedly issued by the Kaiser to the German Army on August 19, 1914, "It is my royal and imperial command that you exterminate the treacherous English, and walk over General French's contemptible little army."

the **Old Dozen** *pr. name* a nickname for the 12th Regiment of ➡Foot of the British Army

Old English sheepdog

Old English sheepdog *comp. noun* a breed of sheep dog originally from southern England

Now mostly kept as a pet, it has long, gray-white shaggy hair that falls over its eyes.

old fashioned look *idiom* a skeptical or disapproving look

the **Old Firm** *pr. name, Sc., sl.* the two principal ➡Glaswegian soccer teams—Rangers and Celtic—when playing each other

the **Old Fogs** *pr. name, Gae., Ir.* a nickname for the 87th Regiment of ➡Foot

A unit of the British Army. The nickname came from the Gaelic warcry of this Irish regiment at the Battle of Barossa in 1811: *Faugh-a-Ballagh* = "Clear the Way".

Old Ironsides *pr. name, hist.* Oliver ➡Cromwell

A nickname bestowed upon him by Prince ➡Rupert, impressed by the resolution of his ➡Parliamentary opponents during the Battle of Marston Moor in 1644.

the **Old Lady of Threadneedle Street** *pr. name, coll.* a nickname for the ➡Bank of England

From the name of the street it is on.

old lag *comp. noun, sl.* (1) a habitual convict; (2) a former convict

old penny *noun, coll., hist.* the penny that was circulated before ➡decimalisation in 1971, worth $1/240$th of a pound

SEE ALSO: ➡new penny.

Old Pals Act *pr. name, sl.* a mythical law or principle that old friends should help each other

the **Old Pretender** *pr. name, hist.* James Francis Edward ➡Stuart, son of ➡James II of England and VII of Scotland, who was called ➡James III of England and VIII of Scotland by the ➡Jacobites upon the death of his father in 1701

Also known as the ➡Old Cavalier or ➡Old Chevalier. Here, "pretend" is used in the old meaning of to "make a claim to" rather than the modern one, of to "dissemble."

old retainer *comp. noun* old and faithful family servant

Old Sarum *pr. name, hist., Lat.* a notorious ➡pocket borough, abolished in the ➡Great Reform Act

From its Medieval Latin name, *Sarum* = "Salisbury"

243

old school tie

old school tie *idiom, coll.* (1) a necktie carrying a specific pattern or design that only former students of a particular school are entitled to wear; (2) a sentimental code of loyalty to traditional ways and values, sometimes taken to excessive lengths

Old Scratch *pr. name, hist., sl.* the Devil

old sweat *comp. noun, sl.* (1) an old soldier; (2) an experienced individual

the **Old Tolbooth** *pr. name, hist.* an alternative name for the ➡Heart of Midlothian

Old Trafford *pr. name* (1) a major ➡football pitch in ➡Manchester; (2) the principal ➡cricket pitch in ➡Manchester

Not surprisingly, they are adjacent.

old trout *idiom, derog., sl.* an unpleasant old woman

Old Vic *pr. name* a London theater dating from 1818, famous for its Shakespearian productions

Originally opened as the Royal Coburg, it was also known as the Royal Victoria Hall for a while before settling down with its present name, originally an abbreviation of "Victoria".

O-level *comp. noun, abbr., hist.* the ➡Ordinary Level examination once taken by 16- or 17-year-old students

Now replaced by the ➡GCSE.

oliver *noun, rh. sl.* a fist

Derivation: fist > twist > *Oliver Twist* (the novel by Charles Dickens) > oliver.

Olympia *pr. name* a large exhibition hall in London

The first in London, it opened in 1884.

OM *pr. name, abbr.* a member of the ➡Order of Merit

omadhaum *noun, Gae., Ir.* a fool

From the Gaelic *amadán* = "fool"

Omagh *pr. name* a district in ➡Northern Ireland, in what used to be County ➡Tyrone

The current population is 45,000 (1990 estimate).

the **Ombudsman** *noun, coll., Swedish* the ➡Parliamentary Commissioner for Administration

From the Swedish *ombudsman* = "commissioner." Sweden was the first country to appoint this sort of official.

omelette *spell.* omelet

on *noun* the ➡cricketing side which is batting

on a loser *idiom, coll.* in a position or situation from which winning is not possible

on appro *idiom, abbr., coll.* on approval

on behalf of *idiom* in behalf of

ONC *noun, abbr.* the ➡Ordinary National Certificate

on camera *idiom* a stand-up piece, live on TV

once a week *idiom, out., rh. sl.* a judge or magistrate

Derived from ➡beak.

once in a way *idiom, arch.* at least once

oncer [A] *noun, rh. sl.* insolence

Derivation: insolence > cheek > week > once a week > oncer.

[B] *noun, sl.* (1) one ➡Pound ➡Sterling; (2) a unique person, object or event

SEE ALSO: ➡oner.

oncost *noun* an overhead cost

OND *noun, abbr.* the ➡Ordinary National Diploma

one *pronoun, out.* an impersonal version of the personal pronoun "I".

An example would be to say, "one is hungry," instead of, "I am hungry." This usage is now uncommon and usually seems pretentious, but is not extinct.

one and t'other *idiom, rh. sl.* (1) brother; (2) mother

one another *idiom* each other

one day *idiom, coll.* an unspecified future day

the **one o'clock gun** *comp. noun* a cannon fired from a battery on ➡Edinburgh Castle daily at 1 p.m.

one-off *adj.* one-shot; happening only once

one over the eight *idiom, sl.* slightly intoxicated

oner *noun, sl.* a ➡oncer

onfall *verb, arch.* to attack

on form *idiom* performing as expected

SEE ALSO: off form.

ongoings *noun, coll.* goings-on

only here for the beer *idiom* not really interested in what's happening

Originally a popular advertising slogan for Double Diamond (TM) beer in the 1960s.

ono *idiom, abbr.* ➡or near offer

on oath *idiom* under oath, as in a court of law

on-off *adj., abbr.* on-again, off-again

on offer *idiom* for sale at a reduced price

on one's tod *idiom, rh. sl.* alone

Derivation: alone > sloan > Tod Sloan > tod.

on pins *idiom, coll.* nervous or agitated

on points *adj. phr., arch., coll.* rationed

The World War II rationing system was based upon ➡points.

on remand *idiom* held in custody awaiting trial

on song *idiom* performing well

on spec *idiom, abbr., sl.* speculated upon

on suss *idiom, abbr., sl.* on suspicion

on the back boiler *idiom, coll.* on the back burner

on the bash *idiom, sl.* (1) engaging in an extensive drinking session; (2) engaging in prostitution

on the {batter » skite} *idiom, Sc., sl.* (1) on a drinking spree; (2) having a good time

244

on the boil *idiom, coll.* (1) busily active; (2) requiring urgent attention

on the buroo *idiom, Sc., sl.* ➡on the dole

on the cards *idiom, coll.* in the cards; probable

on the credit *idiom, coll.* on credit

on the dole *idiom, sl.* unemployed
Literally, receiving ➡dole money.

on the fiddle *idiom, coll.* working a swindle

on the game *idiom, sl.* (1) engaging in stealing; (2) engaging in prostitution

on the job *idiom, coll.* indulging in sexual intercourse

on the labour *idiom, abbr., arch., sl.* unemployed
Because an unemployed person would have had to have placed his or her name on the register of unemployed people kept at each ➡labour exchange in order to receive ➡dole money.

on the mains *idiom, coll.* connected to the public electricity supply

on the mike *idiom, out., sl.* at loose ends

on the nod *idiom, coll.* agreed without comment

on the parish *idiom, arch., coll.* in receipt of public money for the relief of the poor
Traditionally, such money was paid out by the parish council.

on the phone *idiom, coll.* (1) connected to the telephone system; (2) speaking on the telephone

on the plate *idiom, coll.* requiring to be done

on the razzle *idiom, coll.* having a good time

on the streets *idiom, coll.* (1) homeless; (2) engaging in prostitution as a streetwalker

on the strength *idiom, coll.* (1) on the payroll; (2) a member of the team

on the trot *idiom, coll.* (1) busily occupied; (2) in rapid succession

on the up and up *idiom, coll.* successful and getting more so

on to *spell.* onto

on yer bike *imper., sl.* (1) get on with things; (2) exert yourself; (3) get lost

oof *noun, rh. sl., Ger., Yid.* cash
Derivation: cash > *ooftisch* (in Yiddish which, in its turn, was derived from the German *auf dem tische* = "on the table" in English) > oof

oofy *noun, sl.* rich
Derived from ➡oof

op. *noun, abbr.* (1) a surgical operation; (2) a military operation

open cast mine *comp. noun* a strip mine

open day *comp. noun* a day when the public may visit somewhere they are normally excluded from
For example, a school, prison, army base, or such.

opening time *comp. noun, coll.* the time at which ➡public houses may legally open for business

open Parliament *verb* to ceremonially declare that a ➡Parliamentary ➡session has begun
Traditionally carried out by the ➡Sovereign.

open prison *comp. noun* one whose inmates remain there on the honor system
Rather than because of crude physical devices such as walls, guards, and so on.

the Open University *pr. name* a university lacking a campus in the normal sense, but which teaches mostly by television, radio and correspondence
Founded in 1969, this is now a large enterprise with some 80,000 enrolled students in the early 1990s. Students need no formal entrance qualifications to begin study.

Opera North *pr. name, hist.* an opera company that was originally the northern branch of ➡English National Opera
Independent since 1981, it's based at the Grand Theatre, Leeds.

operating theatre *comp. noun* an operating room
Called a theater because surgical operations were originally conducted before audiences of students, and indeed curious members of the general public too.

ophthalmic optician *comp. noun* an optometrist

---

the **Opium Wars** *pr. name, hist.* the first was an invasion of China between 1839 and 1842; the second was a joint invasion of China by Britain and France between 1856 and 1860

Both wars were fought to protect the illegal importation of opium into China by the ➡East India Company, which was vastly profitable. These disgraceful episodes are difficult to comprehend today. Yet the first resulted in the ceeding to Britain of a small Chinese harbor called Hong Kong. During the second, Peking was captured and the Chinese Emperor's palace was destroyed.

---

oppo *noun, abbr., sl.* an opposite number or counterpart

the **Opposition** *pr. name* the ➡Official Opposition

OPSS *pr. name, abbr.* the ➡Office of Public Service and Science

Optic *pr. name (TM)* a metering device attached to the neck of a bottle
Usually spirits, usually in pubs, to control the quantity poured.

or *noun* the heraldic name for the color gold

Oracle *pr. name (TM)* a teletext service operated by ➡ITV and ➡Channel 4

the **Orange Lilies** *pr. name* a nickname for the 35th Regiment of ➡Foot

A unit of the British Army raised in ➡Belfast in 1701 by the Earl of Donegal. They wore orange facings in honor of ➡William of Orange. Later, white plumes taken from the French Regiment of Royal Roussillion, following Wolfe's victory at Quebec in 1759, provided the lilies.

Orange lodge *pr. name* a local branch of the ➡Orange Order

Orangeman *pr. name* a member of an ➡Orange lodge

Orangeman's Day *pr. name* July 12th

A holiday in ➡Northern Ireland that commemorates the Protestant victory at the Battle of the ➡Boyne in 1690.

the **Orange Order** *pr. name* a society dedicated to the support and strengthening of Protestantism in Ireland.

It was originally a secret society and probably began as a group of Freemasons when it was emerged in 1795.

The name honors ➡William of Orange, who defeated ➡James II of England and VII of Scotland and his Catholic supporters at the Battle of the ➡Boyne in 1690.

orange squash *comp. noun* a drink consisting of the juice of crushed oranges

It is often sold in concentrated form.

orbital *noun, sl.* a party occuring just outside London

From being located just beyond the ➡orbital motorway.

orbital motorway *comp. noun* a beltway

Orcadian *noun* a native or inhabitant of the ➡Orkney Islands

order book *comp. noun* (1) a book where tradesmen, for example, enter the orders that have been placed with them by customers; (2) a euphemistic way of describing the volume of work waiting to be carried out by a business

order form *comp. noun, pref.* an order blank

Order in Council *pr. name* a directive or order by the ➡Sovereign, issued with the advice and consent of the ➡Privy Council

orderly book *comp. noun* a book where regimental orders are recorded

orderly officer *comp. noun* an officer of the day

orderly room *comp. noun* a room in a barracks or military base where the administrative business of a unit is conducted

the **Order of Merit** *pr. name* an award for significant achievement

Founded in 1902, it is divided into military and civilian classes. Only 24 persons may hold the Order at any one time.

the **Order of Saint Michael and Saint George** *pr. name, abbr., hist.* an order of knighthood

In full this is, "The Most Honourable Order of St Michael and St George". Instituted in 1818, its membership is now limited to people serving in the diplomatic and foreign services.

the **Order of the Bath** *pr. name, abbr., hist.* the most senior English order of knighthood

In full, the order is known as The Most Honourable Order of the Bath.

The name derives from the ancient ceremony of bathing upon the inauguration of a knight, formerly observed as a symbol of purity. Founded by ➡Henry IV, the last knights to be created in a ceremony that was complete with the full bathing routine were inducted by ➡Charles II in 1661.

order paper *comp. noun* a document listing the order of business in the ➡House of Commons

ordinary *noun* (1) stock or shares that are not deferred or preferred; (2) a physician with a permanent appointment to the ➡Royal Household; (3) formerly, a meal served to the public at a fixed time for a fixed price; (4) an establishment that provided such meals as described in (3); (5) a judge who has immediate *ex officio* jurisdiction; (6) formerly, a priest attended those about to be hanged; (7) one of the primitive shapes that are used in the design of a ➡coat of arms

(5) is in distinction to one that is a deputy. (7) includes such heraldic shapes as ➡bend, ➡pale, ➡pile, etc.

the **Ordinary** *pr. name, hist.* the correct name for the ➡penny farthing bicycle

ordinary degree *noun, abbr., coll.* a university ➡first degree awarded without any one of three possible classes of honor

The lowest class of degree awarded by British universities. See also: ➡first-class degree, ➡second-class degree, ➡third-class degree.

Ordinary Level examination *comp. noun* the ➡GCE or ➡SCE ordinary (that is, not university entrance level) school leaving examination

the **Ordinary National Diploma** *pr. name* a certificate of vocational education equivalent in level of knowledge to ➡GCE ➡A-Level

ordinary shares *comp. noun* common stock

ordnance datum *comp. noun* mean sea level as defined for the purposes of the ➡Ordnance Survey

The leveling datum from which all heights above sea level are usually measured in Great Britain, as it has been established to be over many years at Newlyn in ➡Cornwall. Previously, sea level at ➡Liverpool was used.

Ordnance Map *pr. name* a map published by the ➡Ordnance Survey the **Ordnance Survey** *pr. name* an executive agency of the government responsible for making accurate maps of Britain

Originally, map making was undertaken by the ordnance department of the army, hence this name.

organdie *spell.* organdy

organisation *spell.* organization

Oriel College *pr. name* a college of ➠Oxford University founded in 1326

Orkney *pr. name* a Scottish ➠Island Council, formerly a Scottish county

The current population is 20,000 (1991 Census).

the **Orkneys** *pr. name* an archipelago of more than 70 islands some 30 miles north of the Scottish mainland

Until transferred, with the ➠Shetlands, to the Scottish ➠Crown in 1468 to compensate for the non-payment of the dowry of the bride of ➠James III, the Orkneys were Norwegian.

orle *noun* an heraldic representation of a narrow emblematic border close to the edge of a shield

or near offer *idiom, abbr.* words found in small advertisements for items on sale by individuals

It means that a price close to but not as large as the one suggested might be acceptable.

orra *adj., Sc.* (1) strange, odd, or unusual (of people); (2) spare or superfluous

orraman *noun, Sc.* a handyman or farmhand

orthocentre *spell.* orthocenter

{**orthopeadic » orthopeadics » orthopaedist**} *spell.* {orthopedic » orthopedics » orthopedist}

OS *pr. name, abbr.* the ➠Ordnance Survey

Osborne biscuit *comp. noun* a plain cookie

Named for ➠Osborne House.

Osborne House *pr. name, hist.* Victoria's residence upon the Isle of ➠Wight

Where she died in 1901, and now preserved as it was then.

Osterley Park *pr. name, hist.* a great house about 12 miles west of London, built before 1576

The house was drastically remodeled by Robert Adam between 1763 and 1780.

ostler *noun, arch.* a man responsible for stabling guests' horses at an inn

OTC *noun, abbr.* the Officers' Training Corp.

Usually attached to universities and English ➠public schools; now becoming much less common.

OTE *noun, abbr., coll.* on-target earnings

A shorthand way of stating in an advertisement offering a job in sales, what earnings would be if the expected level of earned commission is added to basic pay.

the **Other Place** *idiom* a name used in ➠Oxford for ➠Cambridge University, and vice versa

other ranks *comp. noun* all soldiers other than commissioned officers

OTT *adj., abbr., sl.* ➠over the top

OU *pr. name, abbr.* (1) ➠Oxford University; (2) the ➠Open University

ought one? *inter.* (1) should you?; (2) should I?

outby *adv., Sc.* (1) outwards or a short distance off; (3) offshore or out to sea

outcast *noun, Sc.* a quarrel

outdaacious *adj., East* outrageous

{**outdoor relief » out-relief**} *comp. noun, hist.* assistance offered to those poor who are not living in a poorhouse

the **Outer Bar** *pr. name* those members of the ➠bar not ➠{King's » Queen's} Counsel

outer garments *comp. noun* outerwear

the **Outer Hebrides** *pr. name* a 120-mile long archipelago some 30 to 50 miles off the northwestern coast of the Scottish mainland

These are also called the ➠Western Isles.

The largest islands are Lewis, North Uist and South Uist; the principal settlement is ➠Stornoway on ➠Lewis.

the **Outer House** *pr. name, Sc.* the House of the ➠Court of Session where judges sit alone

outfitter *noun* a haberdasher or men's clothing store

out for the count *adj, coll.* down for the count

outgang *noun, Sc.* (1) an exit or means of departure; (2) a result; (3) an expense

{**outgeneralled » outgeneralling**} *spell.* {outgeneraled » outgeneraling}

outgoings *noun* expenditure, expenses or costs

outhouse *noun* an outbuilding other than a privy

outmanoeuvre *spell.* outmaneuver

out of *prep.* out

out of order *idiom, sl.* (1) dishonest; (2) not following the customary rules; (3) stoned or drunk

{**outrivalled » outrivalling**} *spell.* {outrivaled » outrivaling}

outside broadcast *comp. noun* a live TV show not made in a studio, and usually out of doors

outsider *noun* a competitor not expected to win

outsize *adj.* extra-large

Of clothes for the fuller figure.

the **Outward Bound Trust** *pr. name* an organization that helps and encourages young people to participate in various outdoor activities such as canoeing, orienteering, sailing, and so forth

outwith

outwith *prep., Sc.* (1) outside, away from; (2) uncontrolled by

the Oval *pr. name* a cricket ground that is the headquarters of the Surrey Cricket Club in Kennington, south London

It was Australia's win here in 1182 that led to the tradition of the annual competition for the ➡Ashes.

oven cloth *comp. noun* a pot holder

over *noun* in ➡cricket, (1) a series of six balls all bowled from one end of the ➡pitch by the same bowler; (2) a call by the umpire to change to bowling from the other direction

overall *noun* a loose-fitting protective coat-like garment worn over normal clothes

To provide protection from dirty or wet environments

overalls *noun* (1) pants or dungarees worn as protective covering; (2) close-fitting pants worn as part of a military uniform

overarm *adj.* with the arm above shoulder level

A ➡cricketing term for a style of pitching.

overbid *verb* to bid more than previously

overdraft *noun* (1) a line of credit with a bank; (2) a bank account containing a negative sum of money

overhead railway *comp. noun* an elevated railroad

the Overlord Embroidery *pr. name, hist.* A large embroidery depicting the events of D-Day when the Allies landed on the shore of Normandy to begin the liberation of Nazi-occupied Europe in 1944

A deliberate attempt to emulate its ancient predecessor, the ➡Bayeux Tapestry. The Overlord Embroidery is at 271 feet some 49 feet longer than the earlier work. It is on public display at the D-Day Museum in ➡Portsmouth.

overpitch *verb* to bowl a ➡cricket ball that pitches very close to the stumps, making it easy to hit

overrider *noun* an automobile bumper guard

Overseer of the Poor *comp. noun, hist.* a parish official who was responsible for giving assistance to the poor from public funds

overslaugh *verb* to miss one military duty because another takes precedence

overspill *noun* (1) a liquid that overflows or is spilled; (2) surplus population moved from a congested area or one without sufficient resources (such as housing, work, schools, etc.) to another that is more congenial

over the moon *idiom, coll.* very pleased indeed

over the {road » way} *idiom, coll.* upon the other side of the street

over the top *idiom, sl.* exceeding reasonable limits; beyond a joke

Particularly of dress or behavior.

The expression originated during the trench warfare of World War I, when "going over the top" meant climbing up out of a trench and into no-man's-land with a view to charging at the enemy, but quite probably getting shot dead by them in the process. Since then, "going over the top" has become a euphemism for doing anything that is excessive, especially if outragious, stupid or suicidal.

owd *adj., North.* old

ower *prep., Sc.* (1) over; (2) excessive

owner-driver *comp. noun* someone who owns the car they drive

owner-occupier *comp. noun* someone who owns the house they live in

own goal *idiom, sl.* (1) a soccer goal scored in error against one's own side; (2) an accidental action that hurts oneself or one's own side; (3) a suicide; (4) a terrorist blown up by {his » her} own bomb

(3) and (4) are police slang.

owt *pronoun., North* anything

Oxbridge *pr. name* (1) a name for ➡Oxford and ➡Cambridge Universities taken together; (2) what it is that these two universities have in common

SEE ALSO: ➡Cam and Isis; ➡Camford

oxe fence *comp. noun* a strong fence, plus railings, hedge and ditch, built to contain cattle

Oxfam *pr. name, abbr., hist.* the Oxford Committee for Famine Relief

A charity founded in 1942 by people in ➡Oxford who were concerned with the fate of people in occupied Europe who were going hungry because of the then-prevailing conditions. Oxfam is now involved in numerous relief and development projects in Third World countries.

Oxfam shop *comp. noun* a shop run by ➡Oxfam where people donate their cast-off clothes, etc., which are then sold to make money for the charity

There is a network of more than 500 such shops covering almost every corner of the United Kingdom.

Oxford [A] *pr. name* a city upon the ➡Isis River, which is the location of one of the most prestigious universities in world; it is also the administrative center of ➡Oxfordshire

Oxford is known to have been an established settlement as early as the 10th C., and has grown into a major industrial center in the course of the 20th C., but it is the university, founded in 1096 and the oldest in the English-speaking world, which is without doubt the defining feature of this city.

Incorporated in 1154, the city's current population is 110,000 (1988 estimate).

[B] *idiom, arch., rh. sl.* five ➡shillings

Derivation: five shillings > dollar > scholar > Oxford scholar > Oxford.

This originated in the 19th C., when £1 = $4 for a great many years, so that five shillings equaled $1.00

Oxford accent *comp. noun, out.* a way of pronouncing English that is supposedly characteristic of members of ➟Oxford University
SEE ALSO: ➟received pronunciation, ➟received standard English, ➟BBC English, ➟{King's » Queen's} English and ➟Oxford English.

Oxford bags *comp. noun* men's pants with wide legs
Fashionable at ➟Oxford University before World War II.

the **Oxford Blues** *pr. name, hist.* a nickname for the ➟Royal Horse Guards
A unit of the British Army that has this name because of their blue uniforms of 1661, and their commander of 1690, the Earl of Oxford. Now part of the ➟Blues and Royals.

Oxford English *comp. noun* a version of the English language supposedly characteristic of members of ➟Oxford University
SEE ALSO: ➟received pronunciation, ➟received standard English, ➟BBC English, ➟{King's » Queen's} English and ➟Oxford accent.

the *Oxford English Dictionary pr. name, hist.* a massive enterprise, without doubt the definitive lexicographical work on the English language
Although *Webster's* is older, its *Third Edition* defines a "mere" 450,000 words while the *Revised Edition* of the ➟OED of 1989 defines about 615,000.

Oxfordshire *pr. name* a county in central England

The county seat is ➟Oxford and the current population is 555,000 (1991 Census).

Oxford Street *pr. name* one of the principal shopping streets in London

Oxford University *pr. name* the oldest and, in company with ➟Cambridge, one of the two best-known universities in the English-speaking world
Founded in 1096, well before ➟Merton—the most ancient of the colleges surviving today—was established in 1264.

Oxo *pr. name (TM)* a concentrated extract of beef

Oxon. *pr. name, abbr.* ➟Oxfordshire

Oxonian *pr. name* (1) a citizen of ➟Oxford; (2) a member of ➟Oxford University

oxter *noun, Ir., North., Sc.* the armpit

oxyhaemoglobin *spell.* oxyhemoglobin

oxysulphide *spell.* oxysulfide

oyer and terminer *comp. noun, Fr., hist.* the authority given to a circuit judge to hold court
From the Norman-French legal phrase *oyer et terminer* = "hear and determine."

oyster on the shell *comp. noun, coll.* oysters on the half shell

Oz *pr. name, sl.* Australia

Ozzie *pr. name, sl.* an Australian

P

p *noun, abbr.* a ⇒penny

The present-day abbreviation for a penny. Before decimalization in 1971, ⇒d was used.

P&O *pr. name (TM), abbr., hist.* (1) the Peninsular and Orient Steam Navigation Company; (2) the Peninsular and Oriental Shipping Company

(1) was a steamship company founded in 1837. Best known as provider of a regular service between Britain and India by way of the Mediterranean Sea, Suez Canal and Red Sea, during the heyday of the British Empire. The company is still in business, now involved in ferry services across the English Channel and North Sea, luxury cruising and exhibition management. (2) is the present-day name of (1).

p&p *noun, abbr.* ⇒postage and packaging

PA [A] *noun, abbr.* a personal assistant

A highfalutin executive's highfalutin secretary.

[B] *pr. name, abbr.* the ⇒Press Association

PACE *noun, abbr.* Police and Criminal Evidence Act

A law governing police powers and the law of evidence in England and Wales.

paceman *noun* one who bowls a ⇒cricket ball at high speed without spin

pack *noun, abbr.* a ⇒pack of cards

package holiday *comp. noun* a vacation trip with all arrangements, such as travel, accommodation, meals, etc., included in the price

SEE ALSO: ⇒package tour.

package tour *comp. noun* a guided vacation tour with all arrangements, such as travel, accommodation, meals, etc., included in the price

SEE ALSO: ⇒package holiday.

pack-drill *comp. noun* military punishment in the form of a forced march while wearing full marching equipment

packed lunch *comp. noun, coll.* a box lunch

packet [A] *noun, arch.* a ⇒packet-{boat » steamer}

[B] *noun, arch., sl.* a bullet or shell

A World War I expression.

[C] *noun, coll.* a lot of money won or lost

packet-boat *comp. noun* a ship that transports mail and possibly passengers

packet steamer *comp. noun* a steam-powered ⇒packet-boat

pack {in » up} *verb, sl.* (1) to give up (of people); (2) to cease to function (of machines)

packing-case *comp. noun* a box or frame used to protect goods while in transit

packing-sheet *comp. noun* a sheet used to pack goods while in transit

pack it in *verb, sl.* (1) to give up; (2) to die

pack of cards *comp. noun* a deck of cards

pack off *verb, coll.* to send someone away peremptorily

pack out *verb, coll.* to fill completely with people

pad *noun, out.* a path or narrow roadway

Paddington fair *comp. noun, arch., sl.* a public execution

⇒Tyburn was located in the Paddington area of London.

Paddington Station *pr. name* a principal railroad terminus in central London

For trains to and from southwest England and south Wales. The present structure, designed by I. K. Brunel for his ⇒Great Western Railway, was opened in 1854, replacing a temporary wooden building of 1838 that had stood nearby.

paddle steamer *comp. noun* a paddle-wheeler powered by steam

paddy *noun, abbr., sl.* a ⇒paddywack

Paddy *pr. name, sl.* an Irishman

From the name, "Patrick."

paddywack *noun, out., sl.* a burst of anger or excitement

padnag *noun, coll.* an unenthusiastic or slow horse

pad the hoof *phr. verb, sl.* to walk

paean *spell.* pean

paedo- *spell., prefix* pedo-

Concerning a child or children.

page *noun, hist.* (1) a hotel bellboy; (2) formerly, a trainee knight

page three girl *idiom, coll.* a nubile young lady photographed in a state of undress

Traditionally these photographs are found displayed upon page three of the *Sun*, a nationally available daily tabloid publication loosely described as a newspaper.

Paget's Irregular Horse *pr. name* a nickname for the 4th Hussars

A unit of the British Army. When they returned in 1842 from 20 years service in India under the command of Colonel Paget, the regiment had lost almost 900 officers and men. Their replacements were poorly trained and unsurprisingly the standard of drill fell badly, which is how they acquired this name.

painting the Forth Bridge *idiom* an endless task

The ➠Forth Rail Bridge is famous for being so vast that as soon as the bridge has been painted from one end to the other, it's time to start over. In other words, it is an endless task.

paintwork *noun* (1) paint applied to a surface; (2) the activity of painting

pair-oar *comp. noun* an oar pulled by two rowers

pair of steps *comp. noun* a folding household stepladder

a **pair of virginals** *noun, hist.* an alternate name for the ➠virginals

Paisley *pr. name, hist.* a town six miles to the southwest of ➠Glasgow

There has been an abbey there since the 12th C. The current population is 83,000 (1991 estimate) and is included in the ➠Glasgow urban area total.

Paisley pattern *comp. noun* a bright and colorful Persian or Indian-originated pattern that is woven from cashmere or fine wool

From ➠Paisley, where these highly complex patterns were first mass-produced during the 19th C.

Paisley shawl *comp. noun* a shawl of cashmere or fine wool, incorporating a ➠Paisley pattern

Paki *pr. name, abbr., derog., sl.* a ➠Pakistani

A native of Pakistan or descendant of one, living in Britain.

Paki bashing *comp. noun, sl.* the victimization of Pakistanis and other Asian residents in Britain

By white youths, usually for racial motives.

the **Palace** *pr. name, coll.* ➠Buckingham Palace

the **Palace of Westminster** *pr. name* the ➠Houses of Parliament

palaea- *spell., prefix* paleo-

Old-, ancient- or prehistoric-

palais de dance *comp. noun, arch., Fr.* a public dance hall

This is French, meaning "dance palace."

pale *noun* an heraldic representation of a wide vertical stripe down the middle of a shield

the **Pale of Dublin** *pr. name, hist.* an alternate name for the ➠English Pale

palish *adj.* rather pale

pallet *noun* a representation of a narrow vertical stripe, used in heraldry

pall mall *comp. name, hist.* a late medieval game, which combined many of the features of present-day skittles and croquet

Pall Mall *pr. name* a central London avenue

Now the location of many clubs, it was built in the late 17th C. upon the site of a ➠pall mall alley.

Palmerston's Follies *pr. name, hist.* a chain of forts around ➠Portsmouth and ➠Plymouth

Their construction was ordered in 1859 by the Prime Mininster, Lord Palmerston, when invasion from France threatened. The danger never materialized, so the forts were seen as a waste of money.

paltsgrave *noun, Du.* a ➠count palatine

From the Dutch *palts* + *grave* = "palatinate + count."

pan [A] *noun, abbr., coll.* a ➠lavatory pan

[B] *noun, Sc.* the skull or cranium

Pancake Day *pr. name* Shrove Tuesday

Upon this day, it is traditional to eat pancakes in England.

panda car *comp. noun* a police patrol car

From the way some appeared during the 1960s, when a wide black vertical stripe was painted over an otherwise white body.

pan drop *comp. noun, Sc.* a hard peppermint candy

panel [A] *noun, hist.* a list of doctors within a local area who were registered as willing to treat those whose treatment would be paid by the government

Abolished in 1948 when the establishment of the ➠National Health Service made this system unnecessary.

[B] *noun, Sc.* the accused party in a criminal trial

panel-beater *comp. noun* a repairer of damaged vehicle bodywork

{**panelled** » **panelling**} *spell.* {paneled » paneling}

panic {merchant » monger} *comp. noun* someone who spreads panic

pan loaf *comp. noun, Sc.* (1) a hard-crusted bread baked in a pan; (2) an affected and over-refined accent which some people imagine impresses others

Somewhat surprisingly, (1) does not come from the French word for bread, but from the container the loaf is baked in (2) is usually associated with the Kelvinside and Morningside areas of ➠Glasgow and ➠Edinburgh, respectively, where people speaking in this manner appear to congregate.

pannage *noun* entitlement to use a pasture for pigs

Or to money or food provided instead.

pannikin *noun* a small metallic cup or its contents

pantechnicon *noun* a furniture transportation vehicle

The name is derived from the ➠Pantechnicon.

the **Pantechnicon** *pr. name, hist.* a bazaar which sold artistic work in London about 150 years ago

When it became unsuccessful, it was converted into a furniture warehouse. *SEE ALSO:* ➠pantechnicon.

pantihose *spell.* panty hose

panto *noun, abbr., coll.* a ➠pantomime

pantomine *noun* (1) a theatrical entertainment based loosely on a traditional nursery or fairy tale; (2) exaggerated or other absurd behavior

(1)s are particularly popular with children. An unusual feature is that the hero, called the ➟principal boy, is played by a young woman, while the leading older female character, or ➟dame, is played by a man. Performed annually around Christmas time since the 18th C., they incorporate currently popular songs, dancing and topical jokes.

pants *noun* drawers or underpants

papa *noun, coll.* father
A childish name.

paper carrier *comp. noun* a disposable shopping bag

paper chase *comp. noun* a cross-country run where the trail is set by earlier runners leaving scraps of paper behind them as they go

paper handkerchief *comp. noun* a disposable tissue

para *noun, abbr., coll.* a paragraph

the **Parachute Regiment** *pr. name, hist.* founded in 1940 upon the direct instructions of Winston Churchill, this is a unit of the British Army with a particular reputation for toughness

parade of shops *comp. noun* a line of shops along one side of a highway
Sometimes along a frontage road.

{paraesthesia » paraesthetic} *spell.* {paresthesia » paresthetic}
Tingling or creeping sensations on the skin.

paraffin *noun* kerosene

paraffin stove *comp. noun* a kerosene-burning stove

paraffin wax *comp. noun* the solid form of paraffin mineral oil

{paralysation » paralyse} *spell.* {paralyzation » paralyze}

{paralyser » paralysis} *spell.* {paralyzer » paralyses}

paralytic *adj., sl.* extremely drunk

{parcelled » parcelling} *spell.* {parceled » parceling}

parish *noun* the smallest British unit of government

parish council *comp. noun* the body responsible for administering a ➟parish

parish lantern *idiom, arch., coll.* the moon

parish pump *adj. phr., coll.* (1) trivial; (2) very local

parish register *comp. noun* a book recording all christenings, marriages, and deaths in a parish
It is traditionally kept at the parish church.

parkin *noun, coll.* a kind of gingerbread containing oatmeal and molasses

Park Lane *pr. name* a central London avenue
It separates ➟Mayfair from ➟Hyde Park.

park up *verb, coll.* to park vehicles close to each other
Probably derived from "close up"

parkway *noun* a railroad station surrounded by extensive parking lots
Usually located outside a metropolitan area to attract commuters and others from their cars and onto trains, hopefully reducing highway traffic congestion.

parky *adj., coll.* bitterly cold
Particularly of mornings, the air, and so forth.

Parl *noun, abbr.* ➟Parliament

Parliament *pr. name, Fr., hist.* (1) the ➟House of Commons and the ➟House of Lords taken together; (2) that which, together with the ➟Sovereign, forms the supreme legislature of the ➟United Kingdom
The approximate equivalent of the U.S. Congress. The name is derived from the French verb *parler* = "to speak." The first English Parliament so named, was called during the 13th C.

parliamentarian *noun, hist.* (1) a member of either the ➟House of Commons or the ➟House of Lords; (2) a supporter of the ➟Parliamentary side during the ➟English Civil War
(1) is especially applied to members of either ➟House who are experts in the practices and precedents of the institution.

Parliamentary *adj.* established by, related to, or connected with ➟Parliament

parliamentary clerk *comp. noun* a senior legal official of ➟Parliament

the **Parliamentary Commissioner for Administration** *pr. name* an official who investigates complaints about government
Complaints must be made by members of the general public and referred to the commissioner by an ➟MP. This official is also called the ➟Ombudsman

the **Parliamentary Labour Party** *pr. name* those ➟MPs who are members of the ➟Labour Party

parliamentary language *comp. noun* (1) specifically, that which it is permissible to use in ➟Parliament; (2) generally, that which is considered to be polite

parliamentary private secretary *noun* an ➟MP who is assistant to a government minister who is not a ➟secretary of statean

parliamentary privilege *pr. name* the right of ➟MPs to be exempt from the law of slander when speaking in the ➟Chamber of the ➟House

parliamentary under-secretary of state *noun* an ➡MP appointed to act as a deputy for a senior minister who is a ➡secretary of state

Parliament House *pr. name, hist.* a building in ➡Edinburgh erected in the 1630s to house the Scottish Parliament

The Scottish Parliament, which had previously met in Edinburgh Castle, used this new building until it subsumed itself into the United Kingdom Parliament at ➡Westminster under the terms of the ➡Act of Union of 1707.

Parliament House is now the home of the ➡Court of Session and the ➡High Court of Justiciary, making it the supreme law court of Scotland.

Parliament Square *pr. name* (1) a square in ➡London in front of the ➡Houses of Parliament, with ➡Westminster Abbey upon its south side; (2) the square in front of ➡Parliament House, ➡Edinburgh

parlivue *noun, Fr., sl.* an informal discussion or chat

From the French *parlez-vous* = "you speak"

parlour *spell.* parlor

parlour maid *comp. noun, out.* a maid serving at table

parochial church council *comp. noun* a body that administers the secular business of a parish church of the ➡Church of England

parrot-fashion *adj.* repetitive like a parrot

parson and clerk *comp. noun, arch.* a children's game where sparks from burning paper represented people

Parson's Pleasure *pr. name* a naturally formed pool in the ➡Isis River near Oxford, where nude male bathing has been permitted for many years

partan *noun, Sc.* (1) a common crab; (2) an ugly or stupid person

part exchange *comp. noun* a trade-in taken as part payment for a purchase

particoloured *spell.* parti-colored

parting *noun* a part, which is to say an imaginary line upon the head from which hair is combed away

part-work *comp. noun* a book published in regular installments over an extended period of time

party *adj.* the heraldic condition of being divided into differently colored parts

pash [A] *noun, abbr., sl.* a passion or infatuation [B] *noun, out.* the head

pass a comment *verb, coll.* to comment

passant *comp. noun* the heraldic term for a representation of a walking figure with the face in profile, which is emblematic of resolution

passant gardant *comp. noun* an heraldic representation of a walking figure with a full face

Emblematic of resolution and prudence.

passant regardant *comp. noun* an heraldic representation of a rearward-looking walking figure

pass degree *comp. noun* the lowest class of degree conferred by a university

passenger light *comp. noun* a car's interior light

passing bell *comp. noun* a bell rung to announce a death

Typically but not always a church bell.

passing out parade *comp. noun* a military drill celebrating the graduation of officer cadets

passman *noun* someone who obtains a pass degree

pass mark *comp. noun* the minimum performance standard needed to pass an examination

pass out *verb* to graduate as an officer

past *prep., pref.* after

Of time. For example, "ten past two" = "ten after two."

past it *adj., coll.* unable to continue because of age

pasty *noun* a pastry cup made without a dish to mold or form it with

Pat *noun, abbr., sl.* an Irishman

pat-a-cake *noun* patty-cake, a children's game

patch *noun, coll.* the area that a police officer patrols or is responsible for

patches *noun, sl.* pieces sewn onto a prisoner's uniform to enable easy identification by the Police or public in the event of escape

patent agent *comp. noun* a patent attorney

the **Patent Roll** *pr. name* a listing of all the patents issued in the course of a year

pater *noun, Lat., sl.* a father

This is Latin for father.

paterfamilias *noun, Lat.* a male head of a family

From the Latin *pater* + *familia* = "father + family."

SEE ALSO: materfamilias.

pathetic *adj., coll.* contemptibly or pitifully insufficient or inadequate

pathfinder *noun, out.* an aircraft sent ahead to mark out targets for the main force of bombers

patience *noun* solitaire

The card game.

patrial *noun* someone with a ➡patrial right

patrial right *comp. noun* the right to live in the United Kingdom because a parent or grandparent was or is a native there

patrol *noun* a person officially appointed to control traffic for the purpose of making a road crossing safe for children

patron *noun* someone who has right of ➡patronage

patronage *noun* the right of presenting a clerical candidate to a church office which provides its holder with an income
SEE ALSO: ➡advowson.

patter merchant *comp. noun, coll.* a person who gets into or out of situations by fast talking

pattern *verb, coll.* to equal, imitate or copy

pattie *noun, rh. sl.* a ➡first class degree
Derivation: first class > Patty Hearst > pattie.

Paul Jones *pr. name* a partner-changing dance
Named for John Paul Jones, the Scottish naval adventurer who founded the U.S. Navy. Originally this was a barn-dancing set; the ladies form an outward circle and move in the opposite direction to the gentlemen, who form an inward circle.

pavement *noun* a sidewalk

pavement artist *comp. noun* a person who draws on sidewalk flagstones with chalks in the hope of attracting money from passersby

pavilion *noun* a building at a sports ground containing locker rooms, eating facilities and so forth

paviour *noun* a person who paves a street, etc.

Pavlova *noun* a dessert which consists of fresh fruit and cream in or upon a meringue
Named for the Russian ballerina of this name, who is reputed to have had this repast invented for her.

pawky *adj., North, Sc.* dryly humorous

pawnee *noun, coll., Hindi, out.* water
From the Hindi *pani* = "water."

pax *exclam, Lat., sl.* a call for a truce
Usually by children at play. It is the Latin word for peace.

Pax Britannica *pr. name, hist., Lat.* that period in history when Britain was—to use modern terminology—the world's sole military and economic superpower
It could be considered to extend at the very most for 99 years: from the eclipse of France after Wellington's victory over Napoleon at the Battle of ➡Waterloo in 1815, until the rise of Germany and the outbreak of World War I in Europe in 1914.
The expression is Latin, meaning "British Peace." The phrase, first used in the 19th C., derives from the historic example of *Pax Romana*, the long period of peace in the ancient world enforced by the might of Imperial Rome.

---

pay *noun, abbr., sl.* a military paymaster

Pay-As-You-Earn *pr. name* a system of income tax collection by deduction as the money is earned
SEE ALSO: ➡PAYE..

pay bed *comp. noun* a bed in a public hospital for a paying patient

paybob *noun, sl.* a naval paymaster

pay claim *comp. noun* a demand from a labor union for increased wages

pay-day *comp. noun* a day when stock transfers have to be paid for

PAYE *pr. name, abbr.* ➡Pay-As-You-Earn

paying guest *comp. noun* someone who pays for {his » her} board

pay-in slip *comp. noun* a banking deposit slip

the Paymaster General *pr. name, hist.* the minister responsible for the department that makes payments on behalf of the government
Originally, the office was created in the early 19th C. to organize pay to members of the Army and the Navy. Now, the range of payments it is responsible for is much wider.

pay packet *comp. noun* a pay envelope

payphone *noun* a telephone booth

pay round *comp. noun, coll.* a recurring discussion about pay between labor union and employer

pay scot and lot *idiom. phr. verb, out.* (1) to share in a financial burden; (2) to pay local taxes, thus qualifying to vote

the PBI *noun, abbr., arch., sl.* the poor bloody infantry
That is, ordinary foot-slogging troops. This was an expression coined during World War I.

PC *noun, abbr.* (1) a police ➡constable; (2) a ➡Privy Councillor

PCAS *pr. name, abbr., hist.* the Polytechnics Central Admissions System
Merged, in 1992, with the ➡UCAS.

PCC [A] *noun, abbr.* a ➡parochial church council
[B] *pr. name, abbr.* ➡Press Complaints Commission

PDSA *pr. name, abbr.* the ➡People's Dispensary for Sick Animals

the Peak District *pr. name* a picturesque area of moorland and peaks located mainly in north ➡Derbyshire, designated a ➡national park in 1951

peaky *adj.* (1) sickly or unwell; (2) weak; (3) anemic

pean *noun* in heraldry, ➡or-spotted ➡sable

pearl *noun* (1) picoted lace; (2) in heraldry, argent; (3) a heraldic representation of Luna

pearl bulb *comp. noun* a kind of translucent light bulb

pearly *noun* the traditional pearl-button-covered dress of a London ➡costermonger or his wife

pearly king

pearly king
and
pearly queen

pearly {king » queen} *comp. noun* a London ⟶{costermonger » costermonger's wife}, wearing {his » her} traditional ⟶pearly

peas *adj., rh. sl.* hot

Derivation: hot > pot> pod >peas in the pod > peas.

the **Peasant's Revolt** *pr. name, hist.* a rising in 1381 against an unpopular ⟶poll tax

The ⟶Archbishop of Canterbury was beheaded and the rebels, led by Wat Tyler and John Ball, occupied London for a short while. ⟶Richard II, who was then aged just 14, offered them free pardons and attention to their grievances. Most dispersed home, satisfied. However a hard core remained, and after Wat Tyler was killed attempting to attack the boy-king, severe repression followed.

Of course, Richard's promises were not kept.

pease pudding *comp. noun* a savory pudding made of boiled peas and eggs with ham or pork

pea-souper *idiom, arch., out.* a dense, choking fog

Formerly a common event in London, these heavy and dangerous fogs, which once killed thousands of people each winter, are now virtually unknown, following the Clean Air Act of the 1950s and the dramatic fall in coal-burning as road transportation replaced steam-powered rail transportation.

Could it be that not all environmental problems are getting worse, that not all are insoluble, that rail transportation is not necessarily environmentally friendly, and that sometimes automobiles can make the environment—at least for a while—better rather than worse?

peat moss *comp. noun, Sc.* a peat bog, a swamp

peat reek *comp. noun, Sc.* (1) the smoke from a peat fire; (2) the distinctive aroma of ⟶Scotch distilled in the traditional manner over a peat fire

pebble-dash *comp. noun* a pebble-filled mortar coating for an external wall

Pebbles are thrown (or dashed) at a wet mortar layer placed on the surface earlier.

pebble-glass *comp. noun, coll.* an especially thick lens

As may be used in reading glasses, for example.

pec *noun, arch., Lat., sl.* money

From the Latin *pecunia* = "money"

pech *verb, Sc.* to puff, pant or gasp for breath

pecker *noun, coll.* (1) courage; (2) the mouth

Peckham rye *idiom, rh. sl.* a necktie

Peckham is a district in eastern London.

peckish *adj., coll.* somewhat hungry

pedal bin *comp. noun* a garbage can that opens when a pedal is stepped upon

{**pedalled » pedalling**} *spell.* {pedaled » pedaling}

{**pedestalled » pedestalling**} *spell.* {pedestaled » pedestaling}

pedestrian crossing *comp. noun, pref.* a crosswalk

256

pedestrian precinct *comp. noun* an area set aside for use by pedestrians only

pedlar *spell.* peddler

pedlar's French *comp. noun, coll., out.* (1) a thieves' jargon or cant; (2) nonsense

pee *noun, abbr., coll.* a penny
Specifically, a "new" penny, of the kind introduced in 1971. SEE ALSO: ➡p.

Peebleshire *pr. name, hist.* a former Scottish county, now part of ➡Borders region

peeler *noun, hist., sl.* an early policeman
Derived from Sir Robert Peel, who founded London's ➡Metropolitan Police in 1829.

peelie-wally *adj., Sc.* sickly, pale, thin or ill-looking

peel tower *comp. noun, hist.* any one of a number of small square towers built near the Scottish-English border in the 16th C. as defensive redoubts

peenie *noun, Sc.* an apron

peep-toe *comp. noun, coll.* an open-toed shoe

peer *noun* a male member of any one of the five ranks of British nobility
These are: ➡duke, ➡marquess, ➡earl, ➡viscount and ➡baron.

the Peerage *pr. name* the ➡peers as a group or class

peeress *noun* (1) a female ➡peer; (2) a courtesy title for the wife or widow of a ➡peer

peerie [A] *adj., Sc.* tiny or insignificant
[B] *noun, Sc.* a spinning top

peerie-heidit *adj., Sc.* mentally confused
Literally, "tiny-headed," or if you prefer, "spinning-headed."

Peer of the Realm *pr. name* a ➡peer entitled to sit in the ➡House of Lords

peever *noun, Sc.* (1) the game of hopscotch; (2) the flat stone used in (1)

peg [A] *noun, abbr., coll.* a ➡clothes-peg
[B] *verb, coll.* (1) to drink; (2) to pin laundry up on a clothesline

peg down *verb, coll.* to restrict with rules, regulations, laws, etc.

peg out *verb, coll.* to collapse

pelican crossing *comp. noun* a variety of ➡pedestrian crossing incorporating traffic lights that can be controlled by pedestrians wishing to halt traffic so they may cross in safety
The word "Pelican" is a rough acronym of PEdestrian LIght CO(A)Ntrol.

Pelmanism *pr. name (TM)* (1) a system of memory training; (2) a card game based on this.
Devised by the Pelman Institute.

pelmet *noun* a curtain valance

Pembroke College *pr. name* (1) a college of ➡Cambridge University founded in 1347; (2) a college of ➡Oxford University founded in 1624

Pembrokeshire *pr. name, hist.* a former Welsh County, now part of ➡Dyfed

the Pembrokeshire Coast *pr. name* a coastline in southwestern Wales together with some offshore islands, designated a ➡national park in 1952

penal servitude *comp. noun, arch.* imprisonment

{**pencilled** » **pencilling**} *spell.* {penciled » penciling}

pendant *noun* a nautical pennant

pendragon *noun, Wal.* a title of ancient British chiefs
From the Welsh *pen* + *dragon* = "head + standard"

penfriend *noun* a pen pal

penguin *noun, arch., sl.* (1) a non-flying flying machine; (2) an early flight-simulator, for pilot training
This word began life as ➡RAF World War II slang.

the Peninsular War *pr. name, hist.* a long campaign fought in the Iberian Peninsula during the ➡Napoleonic War, between 1808 and 1814
For most of the war, it was the only part of the land campaign in Europe that Britain was able to participate in. Portugal, Britain's only remaining continental ally at that time, was invaded by Napoleon's forces in 1807. The following year, the British army landed there and captured the Portuguese national capital, Lisbon. The first attempt to march into Spain to support a more widespread revolt against the greatly-resented French-imposed government failed, but after a number of great difficulties, the British under the command of Wellington, together with their Spanish allies, won two great victories against the French at Salamanca and Vitoria (where they captured the entire baggage train of Napoleon's brother Joseph, the puppet king of Spain) and went on to drive the French out of the Iberian Peninsula entirely by 1814.

the Pennines *pr. name* the principal mountain range of northern England
It runs from Northumberl to ➡Staffordshire. SEE ALSO: ➡Backbone of England.

the Pennine Way *pr. name* a long distance footpath that extends for some 250 miles along the top of the ➡Pennines

penn'orth *noun, abbr., arch., coll.* an alternate spelling of ➡pennyworth, reflecting more closely the usual pronunciation

penny [A] *noun, hist.* (1) a coin; (2) a monetary unit
Prior to 1971, it was worth $1/240$ th part of a ➡Pound, and its abbreviated symbol was "d." Since 1971, it has been worth $1/100$ th part of a Pound and its abbreviated symbol is "p."
[B] *noun, rh. sl.* a smile
Derivation: smile > mile > penny-a-mile > penny.

penny-a-liner *idiom, arch., sl.* a hack writer
From the going rate of payment when the expression was thought up.

penny black

*a Penny
Black*

penny black *comp. noun, hist.* the world's first adhesive postage stamp

First issued in 1840 with a face value of one ➡penny, to be used with the ➡penny post. These stamps are now sought by collectors and are valuable.

penny {blood » dreadful} *comp. noun, hist., sl.* a cheap, low-quality novel or periodical containing tales of sensational and garish violence and crime

A major source of popular entertainment during the Victorian era, especially among children and less-educated adults.

the **penny drops** *idiom, sl.* at last, it is understood

penny farthing *comp. noun, coll., hist.* an early form of bicycle, properly called the ➡Ordinary, with one large and one small wheel

The name is a reflection of the fact that in terms of relative sizes its wheel arrangement resembled coins with these two names, which were in common use during the 19th C.

a **penny for your thoughts?** *inter, coll.* what you are thinking?

penny-in-the-slot machine *comp. noun, out., sl.* a slot machine

penny post *comp. noun, hist.* the world's first national flat-rate public postal service

It was introduced in 1840. A letter would be delivered anywhere within the ➡British Isles, provided it had a ➡penny black stamp attached to it. An interesting survival from this time when Britain was the only country in the world with this sort of flat-rate postal system is that British postage stamps still do not have the name of the country issuing them written upon them.

penny Scots *comp. noun, hist., Sc.* the lowest denomination of Scots coin

By 1707 when it ceased to be legal tender, one Scots penny was worth one twelfth of an English ➡penny. For more about Scots currency, *SEE ALSO:* ➡pound Scots.

pennyworth *noun, out.* what is worth one penny

Penrhyn Castle *pr. name, hist.* a large 19th C. house about two miles south of ➡Bangor in Wales

It was built in the early 19th C. to look as if it were a ➡Norman castle some six or seven centuries older than it really is. Incorporated within it are the remnants of a medieval farmhouse that had already stood upon this site.

Penshurst Place *pr. name, hist.* a rather strange house five miles north west of Tunbridge Wells in ➡Kent

Its earliest parts date back to the 14th C. but over the centuries it has developed into a most unusual jumble with elements of the architectural styles of many different periods, as each generation has added its unique contribution.

pensioner *noun* a ➡Cambridge University undergraduate receiving no financial support from his or her college

pension scheme *comp. noun* retirement pension plan

the **Pensions Ombudsman** *pr. name* an official who investigates complaints about pensions

pentobarbitone *noun, out.* pentobarbital

$C_{11}H_{18}N_2O_3$, a granular narcotic sedative and hypnotic drug dispensed in the form of a sodium or calcium salt, once commonly used to relieve insomnia.

Not to be confused with ➡phenobarbitone.

Penzance *pr. name, hist.* a ➡Cornwall fishing port and resort, which is the most westerly town in England

The town has an unusually mild climate, thanks to the Gulf Stream. The current population is 21,000 (1991 estimate).

the **People's Charter** *pr. name, hist.* a document formalizing the demands for reform made by a grass-roots movement in 1838

Supporters were known as ➡Chartists. The six principal demands laid down in their charter were:

> A ➡general election every year
> Universal suffrage (only for men, of course)
> Voting districts of approximately equal size
> Voting by secret ballot
> Payment of ➡MPs
> No property qualifications required to become an ➡MP

All except the first have long been met and now seem quite unexceptional, or even dated. At the time they did not just seem, but indeed were, revolutionary. The movement collapsed after its petition to Parliament failed in 1848.

the **People's Dispensary for Sick Animals** *pr. name* a voluntary organization that provides free veterinary treatment for the pets of poor people

the **People's Palace** *pr. name, hist.* a museum upon ➡Glasgow Green, Glasgow

Opened in 1898 as a cultural center for the poor of the city, it is now a magnificent museum of social history.
SEE ALSO: ➡PDSA.

PEP *pr. name, abbr.* a ➡Personal Equity Plan

peppercorn rent *comp. noun* a nominal rent

pepper pot *comp. noun* a pepperbox

perambulator *noun* a baby's carriage or buggy

Per ardua ad astra *idiom, Lat.* motto of the ➡RAF

This is Latin, meaning "By work to the stars."

per cent *spell.* percent

per cents *comp. noun* stock yielding fixed-rate interest

perch *noun, arch.* a unit of length equal to 5.5 yards, 16.5 feet, one ➡pole, or one ➡rod

{**perilled** » **perilling**} *spell.* {periled » periling}

perish *verb* (1) to cause to be ruined; (2) to cause to die; (3) to rot or deteriorate

(3) applies particularly to rubber or objects made of rubber.

perisher *noun, sl.* an irritating person, specially a child

perishing [A] *adj., coll.* (1) extremely cold; (2) confounded

[B] *adv., coll.* confoundedly

perjink *adj., Sc.* (1) neat or tidy; (2) prim or strait-laced; (3) exact or fussy

Permanent Secretary *pr. name* the most senior civil servant advising a ➡secretary of state

Permanent Under-secretary *pr. name* the most senior civil servant advising a ➡minister

permanent way *comp. noun* a railroad roadbed

pernickety *adj., Sc.* (1) persnickety, obsessed with detail; (2) requiring great care

(1) is of people; (2) is of things or deeds.

the Perpetual Peace *pr. name, hist.* a peace treaty concluded between England and Scotland in 1502

It lasted until Scotland invaded England in 1513, a whole 11 years later.

perry *noun* a drink, similar to cider, but made from fermented pear juice

Personal Equity Plan *comp. noun* a government scheme that permits certain limited purchase of shares, under certain specific conditions, to be exempt from income or capital gains tax

Perspex *pr. name (TM)* a tough transparent acrylic thermoplastic

Similar to Plexiglas (TM) and used in similar situations.

Perth *pr. name* a city in ➡Tayside, Scotland

It lies on the ➡Tay River adjacent to ➡Scone, where the Scottish kings were traditionally crowned and so was the effective capital of Scotland for many years. Perth was incorporated as a city in 1210 and the current population is 45,000 (1988 estimate).

Perthshire *pr. name, hist.* a former Scottish county, now divided between ➡Central ➡Tayside regions

petalled *spell.* petaled

peter *noun, sl.* a prison cell

Peterborough *pr. name* a city in ➡Cambridgeshire

First settled in ➡Anglo-Saxon times around a Benedictine abbey founded in 650, it was incorporated as a city in 1874 and the current population is 150,000 (1988 estimate).

Peterhouse College *pr. name* a college of ➡Cambridge University

Founded in 1284 by Hugo de Basham, Bishop of Ely. It is the smallest and earliest college of the university.

the Peterloo Massacre *pr. name, hist.* the killing of 11 people and the injuring of about 500 more at the hands of troops in 1819 in ➡Manchester

In 1819 about 50,000 people gathered at St Peter's Field, Manchester to hear about parliamentary reform. Fearing a riot, the magistrates ordered troops to disperse the crowd, with the disastrous results described above. This caused great indignation throughout the country and probably aided the cause of reform.

Obviously, the name was modeled on ➡Waterloo, the great battle that had happened just four years earlier.

petersham *noun* a ribbon of thickly corded silk, used for trimmings in dressmaking

The name derives from Lord Petersham, a 19th C. army officer.

pethidine *noun* a soluble analgesic sometimes given to children

the Petition of Right *pr. name, hist.* a resolution by both ➡Houses of Parliament of 1628 that declared that only Parliament could authorize taxes and people could only be imprisoned by due process of law

The reluctant acceptance of the Petition by ➡Charles I was considered by many to be the most important advance in the cause of constitutional government and personal liberty since ➡*Magna Carta* four centuries before.

petrol *noun* gasoline

petrol bomb *comp. noun* a Molotov cocktail

petrol gauge *comp. noun* a gasoline gauge

petrol pump *comp. noun* a gasoline pump

petrol station *comp. noun* a gas filling station

Petticoat Lane *pr. name* a street in London's ➡East End where an outdoor market has been held every Sunday morning for over 200 years

petticoat tails *comp. noun, Sc.* triangular ➡shortbread slices

the Petty Bag Office *pr. name, hist., Lat.* a former office of the Court of ➡Chancery that attended to matters of common law

Called this because writs were kept in a little sack: *in parva baga*. When common law business moved to the jurisdiction of the ➡High Court of Justice, the office was abolished.

petty session *noun* a session of a court where lesser charges are considered

petty treason *comp. noun, hist.* (1) the crime of murder of his or her master by a servant; (2) the crime of murder of her husband by a wife

(1) and (2) were both abolished in 1828.

Petworth House *pr. name, hist.* a drastically modified late medieval house about 14 miles to the north east of ➡Chichester, Sussex

It was extensively rebuilt in a baroque style in the late 15th C. and then rebuilt and remodeled again after a major fire in 1714. It was subject to further bouts of significant remodeling in the 1760s, 1770s, and the 1870s.

pew *noun, coll.* a seat

pewage *noun* ➡pew rent

pew rent *comp. noun* a rent paid for exclusive use of a particular pew in a church

PG *noun, abbr.* a ➡paying guest

phagedaena *spell.* phagedena
A virus that infects bacteria.

phenacetin *noun* acetophenetidine, a derivative of phenol used to treat fevers

phenobarbitone *noun* phenobarbital
$C_{12}H_{12}N_2O_3$, a crystalline sedative and hypnotic barbiturate dispensed in the form of a sodium or calcium salt, commonly used to treat epilepsy
Not to be confused with ➡pentobarbitone.

phial *noun* vial

philabeg *noun, Gae., Sc.* a belted ➡plaid, which was the original form of the ->kilt
From the Gaelic *feileadh-beag* = "little fold".

philtre *spell.* philter
A love potion.

{**phiz » phizog**} *noun, abbr., sl.* a face
A jocularly abbreviated version of "physiognomy".

phone box *comp. noun, abbr* a telephone booth

Phonecard *pr. name (TM)* a card containing magnetically stored prepaid units used to pay for phone calls from specially designed telephone booth.
The cards, which are the size of credit cards and can be used for no other purpose, are sold by shops, post offices, railroad stations, etc.

phone through *phr. verb, coll.* to call by telephone

phonograph *noun, arch.* an early kind of gramophone
It could record as well as play, and used cylinders, not disks.

photo *noun, rh. sl.* Guinness (TM)
Derivation: Guinness > finish > photo finish > photo.

Photofit *pr. name (TM)* a system employed by the police to reconstruct the appearance of a suspect's face from the evidence of witnesses
The likenesses are built up from photographs of the component parts such as eyes, chins, mouths, etc.

physical jerks *comp. noun, coll.* physical exercises

pi *adj., abbr., sl.* pious

piastre *spell.* piaster

pibroch *noun, Gae., Sc.* a lament or military music suitable for the Scottish ➡bagpipes
From the Gaelic *piobaireachá* = "art of piping." Originally any music played on the pipes had this name.

Piccadilly *pr. name* a central London shopping street

Piccadilly Circus *pr. name* a major road junction in central London
London's nearest equivalent to New York's Times Square.

the **Piccadilly Line** *pr. name* one part of London's rapid-transit subway system
It extends from ➡Heathrow Airport and Uxbridge in the west to Cockfosters in the north. The line has two stations at Heathrow, one serving Terminals 1, 2 and 3, with the other serving Terminal 4.

Piccadilly Station *pr. name* a principal railroad terminus in central ➡Manchester
For trains to and from the south.

piccaninny *spell., derog., taboo.* pickaninny

pick *noun, out.* something which is thrown

pickerel *noun* a small or young pike

pickle [A] *noun, coll.* a troublesome child
[B] *noun, Sc.* (1) a kernel of grain; (2) a small particle or speck; (3) difficult or awkward work

Pickwickian *adj.* (1) of speech that is either understood or intended to be understood in an unusual sense; (2) stout and convivial
From the hero of Charles Dickens's novel *Pickwick Papers*, who made a habit of talking thus, and was also stout and convivial.

Picts *pr. name, hist., Lat.* the ancient pre-Scots inhabitants of Scotland
Reputedly they went about covered in blue paint and nothing else. It must be said that this seems improbable in view of the highly bracing nature of the Scottish climate; it is not a convincing choice of location for the founding of a nudist movement. The Pict kingdom survived, if somewhat chilled, until ➡Kenneth MacAlpin, first King of Picts and Scots, unified most of what is now Scotland in the 9th C.
From the Latin word *picti* = "painted"

picture-goer *noun* a moviegoer

picture house *comp. noun, arch.* a movie theater

the **pictures** *noun, pref.* the movies
In the sense of movies being viewed, not movies being make.

pie *spell.* pi
Spilled or mixed-up printer's type.

piece *noun, North, Sc.* a snack
Often a sandwich or something similar.

piece of goods *idiom, derog., sl.* a woman

piece rate *comp. noun* the payment rate for piecework

piece tin *comp. noun, North, Sc.* a snack container

pie funnel *comp. noun* a funnel made of pottery
It is used to support the pastry covering of a large pie and also to permit the escape of steam while it is being baked.

pieman *noun, arch.* a street vendor of pies

pig [A] *noun* any kind of swine of any age
[B] *noun, Sc.* crockery, especially earthenware vessels

pigeon-hearted *adj. adv., coll., derog.* cowardly

pigeon pair *comp. noun* (1) a boy and girl that are the sole children of a family; (2) twins that consist of a boy and a girl

pigeon's milk *comp. noun, coll.* an imaginary item children on a fool's errand may be asked to fetch

piggery *noun* (1) a hog farm; (2) a pigpen

piggy *noun* another name for the game of tipcat

In this game, one player tries to keep a short wooden peg airborne by striking it repeatedly with a bat, while other players attempt to catch it.

SEE ALSO: ➠{piggy » pig} in the middle

{piggy » pig}-in-the-middle *comp. noun, coll.* (1) a children's game; (2) someone placed in a difficult situation between two others

(1) is a variant of ➠piggy, where two players throw a ball back and forth while a third person in the middle tries to catch it. (2) is derived from (1).

pig it *verb, coll.* to live in squalor

pig-meat *comp. noun* pork, bacon or ham

pigs *noun, abbr., rh. sl.* ➠pig's ear

pig's ear *comp. noun, rh. sl.* beer

pig sticker *comp. noun, arch., coll.* (1) a very sharp and lengthy knife such as a bayonet; (2) a pork butcher

pigsty *noun, coll., derog.* (1) a pigpen; (2) a house or a room that is in a filthy or slovenly condition

pi jaw *idiom, arch., sl.* a long, boring lecture on morality

From the abbreviation of "pious" to "pi." The term is usually employed by school students describing their teachers.

pike *noun, North* a mountain with a summit that comes to a distinct point

pikelet *noun, North, Wal.* a thin crumpet or pancake

Derived from the Welsh *pyglyd* = "bread."

pile [A] *noun* in heraldry, a narrow triangle

[B] *noun, arch.* the reverse side or tails of a coin

the Pilgrims' Way *pr. name* a footpath that runs from ➠Winchester, ➠Hampshire to ➠Canterbury, ➠Kent

Believed to be the route taken by medieval pilgrims going to the shrine of St Thomas à Becket at ➠Canterbury Cathedral.

pill [A] *noun, abbr., arch.* pillage

[B] *noun, arch., sl.* (1) nonsense; (2) a ball; (3) a cigarette; (4) an army physician

[C] *verb, arch.* to flake away or peel off

[D] *verb, sl.* to fail in an examination at college, etc.

pillar box *comp. noun* a mailbox

The name refers to its pillar-like appearance.

pillar box red *comp. noun* a bright red color

The traditional color of British mail boxes.

pillock [A] *noun, out.* (1) a rabbit dropping; (2) a worthless person

[B] *noun, sl.* a fool or idiot

pillow-biter *comp. noun, derog., sl.* a passive male homosexual partner

pillow-fight *noun* a children's mock fight at bedtime

pills *noun, sl., taboo* the testicles

pilot officer *comp. noun* the lowest rank of commissioned officer in the ➠RAF

Equivalent in rank to a second lieutenant in the USAF.

Piltdown Man *pr. name, hist.* a famous scientific forgery

Supposedly the fossilized skull of a very early primitive man, possibly the long-sought-after "missing link" between *Homo sapiens* and earlier species.

"Discovered" in 1908 near Piltdown Common in ➠Sussex, it was later shown to be a hoax assembled from portions of both human and ape skulls.

pimento *spell.* pimiento

Pimm's *pr. name (TM)* fruit-flavored alcoholic drink

pinafore *noun* (1) an apron with a bib; (2) a sleeveless protective covering worn over the clothes

(2) is normally worn by women to protect their clothes while they are performing housework, etc.

pinafore dress *comp. noun* a woman's sleeveless and collarless dress, worn over a blouse

pindown *noun, coll.* an illegal form of punishment inflicted upon some children being "cared for" by certain social workers

It consisted of confining the children, dressed only in their nightclothes and without any personal possessions, in solitary confinement for long stretches. They were forbidden to talk to anyone and were given pointless and soul-destroying tasks to perform.

Pindown developed during the early 1980s and was stopped by the ➠High Court when a girl attempted suicide after being subjected to this, and others became clinically depressed.

pingle *verb, East* to eat without enthusiasm

pink *noun* (1) a young salmon; (2) a minnow

pinkers *noun, sl.* ➠pink gin

pinking *noun* abnormal or badly timed ignition in an automobile engine; knocking

pink gin *comp. noun* a once-fashionable drink consisting of gin, some water, and a drop of Angostura bitters

Angostura bitters is a red extract of spices originating from Angostura in Venezuela. That's what causes the drink to take on a pink hue.

pink'un *idiom, sl.* a newspaper, such as the ➠*Financial Times*, that is printed upon pink paper

pinny *noun, abbr., coll.* an apron

An abbreviation of ➠pinafore.

pint [A] *noun* a volumetric unit of measurement of quantities of shellfish

It is, believe it or not, the quantity of shellfish that can be put into a container with a volume of one pint.

[B] *noun, abbr.* an ➠imperial pint

[C] *noun, coll.* this quantity of beer

Especially as an order for this in a pub.

pinta *noun, abbr., coll.* a pint of milk

The word may be thought of as a corruption of "pint of"; it was invented for an advertising campaign designed to encourage increased milk consumption during the 1960s.

pin tuck *comp. noun* a very narrow tuck in clothing

pip [A] *noun* (1) a diamond-shaped insignia worn on their shoulders by army officers to denote rank; (2) a short, high-pitched mechanical sound

[B] *verb, coll.* (1) to blackball; (2) to defeat; (3) to hit with a shell from a gun

the **pip** *noun, sl.* a strong feeling of irritation or disgust

pip at the post *idiom. phr. verb* to defeat at the very last moment

pipe-cot *comp. noun, arch.* a ship's hammock

pipe down *verb* to dismiss a sailor from duty

pipe major *comp. noun* an NCO in command of the military ➡bagpipers of a Scottish army unit

pip emma *comp. noun, out., sl.* p.m. or afternoon

From the letter-names formerly used by military signalers to avoid confusion.

pipe one's eyes *phr. verb, sl.* to weep

the **Pipe-Rolls** *pr. name, hist.* the records of the annual accounts of the British ➡Exchequer for the years from 1131 to 1831

These invaluable historic records are kept in the ➡Public Records Office in London; they have this name because they are stored in tightly wound rolls that look like pipes.

pip out *verb, coll.* to die

pip-pip *exclam, arch., sl.* good-bye

the **pips** *noun, coll.* six short high-pitched sounds, produced mechanically or electronically and transmitted by radio as a time signal

piss-artist *comp. noun, derog., sl., taboo* (1) a drunkard; (2) a person who boasts of knowledge or skills that in truth they do not have

pissed *adj., sl., taboo* drunk

Does NOT mean "angry," but "pissed off" does.

pissed as a newt *idiom, sl., taboo* very drunk indeed

See also: ➡newted.

piss off *verb, sl., taboo* to depart rapidly and immediately

piss oneself *verb, sl., taboo* to wet one's pants

piss-taker *comp. noun, sl., taboo* one who mocks

piss-up [A] *comp. noun, sl., taboo* a session of extensive drinking

[B] *verb, sl., taboo* (1) to mess up; (2) to fail

pissy *adj., sl., taboo* (1) tawdry or third-rate; (2) unacceptable

{**pistolled » pistolling**} *spell.* {pistoled » pistoling}

pit [A] *noun* (1) that part of a theater's auditorium that is at or below street level; (2) the people in (1)

[B] *noun, sl.* a bed

pitch *noun* (1) an outdoors location, such as a field where business, sporting or leisure activity takes place; (2) the area at the center of a cricket field that lies between the two bowling ➡creases

(2) extends 5 ft on either side of the ➡wickets.

pitch and toss *comp. noun* a game of chance where players bet on the outcome of tossed coins

pitch up *verb* to bowl a ➡cricket ball so that it bounces near to the ➡batsman

pitch wickets *verb* to place ➡cricket ➡stumps into the ground upon a cricket pitch

Pitlochry *pr. name, hist.* a resort town in the ➡Highlands some 25 miles to the north of ➡Perth

Best known for its summer-long festival of plays and music.

pit pony *comp. noun, hist.* a pony that worked underground hauling coal

PLA *pr. name, abbr.* the ➡Port of London Authority

place *verb* to show in a horse race

That is, to be one of the first three horses to finish the race.

place-bet *comp. noun, coll.* a bet that the horse backed will be ➡placed in the race

place card *comp. noun* one that indicates where a person is to sit at a table

placeman *noun, hist.* a politician appointed to a public office of profit as a favor or reward

The practice was finally abolished in Britain in 1870. Henceforth all civil service appointments have been made strictly on the basis of a candidate's performance in public examinations.

placet *noun, Lat.* an affirmative vote in the assembly or council of a church or university

From the Latin for "it pleases".

plack *noun, hist., Sc.* a Scots coin worth two ➡bodles

By 1707 when it ceased to be legal tender, one plack was worth one third of an English ➡penny. For more about Scots currency, *See also:* ➡pound Scots.

plaid *noun, Gae., hist., Sc.* (1) a length of twilled woolen cloth originally woven in multishaded stripes that generated a russet or brown effect, but was later imbued with a ➡tartan pattern; (2) a (1) which was once worn over the shoulder as the principle or sole component of a Scottish ➡highlander's dress, who also used it as his blanket

The plaid was worn by all classes of highlander until the invention of the ➡kilt in the 18th C., but the better off and nobility among them wore it as an upper garment only, enclosing their lower limbs with ➡trews. Thus, the wearing of the plaid alone was a badge of poverty or undesirability.

Plaid Cymru pr. name, Wal. a political party favoring Welsh independence

The name means, in Welsh, "Party of Wales". The party was founded in 1925.

plain as a pikestaff *idiom, coll.* glaringly obvious

plain sailing *idiom* smooth sailing

plaint *noun* a legal charge or accusation

plait *noun* a pleat or pigtail of hair

planning permission *comp. noun* formal permission obtained from a local council, which is required before any house, office, factory, or other structure of any size or significance may be erected

Plantagenet *pr. name, hist., Lat.* a subsidiary name for the ➠Royal House of England from 1216 to 1399

Formally, the royal house before, during and after these years was ➠Anjou, with "Plantagenet" a subsidiary name without independent existence or validity.

"Plantagenet" is reputed to have been the nickname of Henry II, from the Latin *planta genista* = "sprig of bloom," something he supposedly wore regularly. However, it was first used as a name for the royal house about 300 years after he had lived.

The following English monarchs belonged to this subsidiary house: ➠Henry III, ➠Edward I, ➠Edward II, ➠Edward III and ➠Richard II.

planter *noun, hist.* (1) an English or, more usually, a Scottish Protestant settler in 17th C. ➠Ulster; (2) a person placed in an evicted Irish tenant's house and land during the 19th C.

plasmolyse *spell.* plasmolyze

To experience plasmolysis.

Plas Newydd *pr. name, hist.* a 16th C. great house in the ➠Isle of Anglesey, which looks over the ➠Menai Strait to the ➠Welsh mainland

Extensively remodeled between the 1780s and 1820s, it was then refurbished again in the 1930s and is now a unique mixture of neoclassical and gothic styles.

plaster *noun, abbr.* (1) a medical adhesive tape used to cover or bind wounds; (2) a medical plaster cast

plastic explosive *comp. noun* a putty-like explosive material that can be shaped or molded by hand

Plasticine *pr. name (TM)* children's modeling clay

plate basket *comp. noun* a linen-lined basket used for storing or carrying cutlery

platelayer *noun* a railroad track layer

plate-rack *comp. noun* a rack where plates and other dishes are left to drain after washing

plates of meat *idiom, rh. sl.* feet

platform ticket *comp. noun* a ticket that gives access to a platform in a train station, but not the train

Used by non-travelers accompanying departing passengers to their train, or to meet them as they alight from their train.

play-brick *comp. noun* a child's building block

player *noun, hist.* a professional player of ➠cricket

As opposed to a ➠gentleman, or amateur player.

play gooseberry *verb, coll.* to be a third person present when the other two wish to be alone

playgroup *noun* a group of preschool children who play together under adult supervision

play {hell » merry hell} *idiom. phr. verb* to cause endless difficulties

playschool *noun* a kindergarten

play silly buggers *idiom. phr. verb, taboo* to refuse to be serious when frivolity is not appropriate

play the goat *idiom. phr. verb* to fool around

play the wag *verb, sl.* to play hooky from school

play up *verb* (1) to cause trouble; (2) to irritate or annoy; (3) to flatter; (4) to participate in a sport or game with all possible effort or energy

{PLC » plc} *noun, abbr.* a publicly incorporated corporation with limited liability

These are corporations, often large, with shares that are traded publicly on the stock exchange. By law, the words "public limited company" or the abbreviation 'PLC' or 'plc' must be placed after their name.

pleader *noun, arch., sl.* an attorney

plimsole *spell.* plimsoll

Plimsoll line *comp. noun* the Plimsoll mark or load line of an ocean-going cargo ship

Devised by Samuel Plimsoll, a 19th C. English politician.

plonk *noun, sl.* a cheap, poor-quality wine

plonker *noun, sl.* (1) a big, loud, wet kiss; (2) a stupid mistake; (3) a foolish or unimaginative person

plough *verb, coll.* to fail an academic examination

the Plough *pr. name* the Great Bear or Big Dipper

The constellation of *Ursa Major.*

{plough » ploughboy » plougher} *spell.* {plow » plowboy » plower}

ploughland *noun, arch.* as much land as could be plowed by one team of eight oxen in one year

{ploughman » ploughmanship} *spell.* {plowman » plowmanship}

ploughman's lunch *comp. noun* a popular ➠pub lunch of cheese, pickle and salad with bread

Plough Monday *Pr. name, arch.* the first Monday after Epiphany

When plowmen traditionally returned to work after Christmas.

{ploughshare » ploughstaff} *spell.* {plowshare » plowstaff}

plouk *noun, Sc.* a pimple, boil, or small growth

PLP *pr. name, abbr.* the ➠Parliamentary Labour Party

PLR *noun, abbr.* the ➧Public Lending Right

PLU *noun, abbr., sl.* people like us

A code word indicating that a person is socially acceptable.

pluck *verb, arch.* to reject an examination candidate

plug-hole *comp. noun* the drain in a sink, bathtub, etc.

plumcake *noun* a cake full of currants, raisins, etc.

plum duff *comp. noun* a plain pudding consisting mostly of flour and containing raisins

plum pudding *comp. noun* an alternate name for a ➧Christmas pudding

plunk school *verb, Sc.* to play hooky from school

the **Plutonium Blonde** *pr. name, coll.* a nickname for ➧Prime Minister Margaret Thatcher

plutter *verb, Sc.* (1) to dabble or splash about in water with hands or feet; (2) to work or move about aimlessly or without purpose; to dabble or putter

Plymouth *pr. name* a city and port in ➧Devon

Although it had been established in Anglo-Saxon times, Plymouth first became significant in the 15th C. when it was realized that its harbor would be an ideal base for the English fleet, and indeed it is from here that Drake sailed to defeat the ➧Spanish Armada in 1588. It is also from Plymouth that the Pilgrim Fathers set off for America in 1620.

Incorporated as a city in 1439, the current population, including suburbs, is 260,000 (1988 estimate).

the **Plymouth Brethren** *pr. name* an evangelical Christian sect founded in Ireland in 1828

The name refers to the fact that they first evangelized in England at ➧Plymouth in 1830.

PM *pr. name, abbr.* the ➧Prime Minister

PMG *pr. name, abbr., hist.* (1) the ➧Postmaster General; (2) the ➧Paymaster General

PMRAFNS *pr. name, abbr.* the Princess May's ➧Royal Air Force Nursing Service

PNEU *pr. name, abbr.* the Parents' National Educational Union

PO *noun, abbr.* (1) a ➧postal order; (2) a ➧pilot officer

po *noun, sl., abbr.* a child's name for a chamber pot

poach *verb, coll.* to recruit someone by enticing [him » her} away from {his » her} present employer

pochle *verb, Sc.* to steal, fake, or fiddle a little; to slightly adjust facts to better fit a theory, as it were

pocketbook *noun* a small notebook that will fit within a pocket

pocket borough *comp. noun, hist.* a parliamentary electoral district that was in the corrupt power to give of a private individual or family

Abolished by the ➧Great Reform Act of 1832.

pocket money *comp. noun* an allowance paid to a child, usually by his or her parents

podgy *spell.* pudgy

the **Poet Laureate** *pr. name* a poet appointed to be a member of the ➧Royal Household

In return for this appointment, he or she is expected to produce poems to order in celebration of significant national occasions such as coronations or state funerals. Past Poet Laureates have included among there numbers John Dryden, William Wordsworth, and Alfred, Lord Tennyson.

Poet's Corner *pr. name* an area on the south transept of ➧Westminster Abbey dedicated to the memory of poets

Here are the graves of, or monuments to, many famous poets, from Chaucer onwards.

po-faced *adj.* deadpan or humorless in appearance

poind *verb, Sc.* to impound a debtor's property, upon the authority of a court

point [A] *noun* (1) a railroad switch, where two tracks meet; (2) a fielder's position on the ➧cricket field [B] *noun, abbr.* a ➧power point

point duty *comp. noun* the work of a police officer directing traffic at a junction

points *noun, hist.* a system of allocating quantities of various products under the rationing system used in Britain during World War II

pointsman *noun* (1) a police officer on ➧point duty; (2) a person controlling railroad switches

point taken *idiom, coll.* I see what you mean

poker school *comp. noun* a group of people gathered together to play poker

pole *noun, arch.* a unit of length equal to 5.5 yards, which is 16.5 feet, one ➧rod, or one ➧perch

poleaxe *spell.* poleax

polecat *noun* a small flesh-eating mammal with brownish fur, of the weasel family

The animal has probably acquired this name from it's propensity to prey upon poultry, hence the "pole." Its formal name is *mustela putorius,* and it is unrelated to the North American polecat or skunk..

the **Police Complaints Authority** *pr. name* an independent office that investigates complaints about the police in England and Wales

In Scotland, this work is carried out by the ➧Procurator Fiscal.

police constable *comp. noun* the lowest rank of police officer

police van *comp. noun* a police patrol wagon

policies *noun, Sc.* the grounds belonging to and surrounding a large house

polis *noun, Sc.* the police

political agent *comp. noun* a political campaign manager

the **poll** *noun, Gr., sl.* students who obtain no more than a ➧pass degree from ➧Cambridge University
From the Ancient Greek *hoi polloi* = "the many" or, more colloquially and cruelly, "the common herd."

polling station *comp. noun* a voting place

Pollok House *pr. name, hist.* a mid-18th C. stately house set within Pollock Park about three miles south of central ➧Glasgow
The ➧Burrell Collection is also to be found in a specially constructed building in this same park

poll tax *comp. noun, coll., hist.* (1) in the 1380s, a tax of one ➧shilling per head, which was highly unpopular and partially responsible for inducing the ➧Peasant's Revolt; (2) in the 1980s, the universal name for the short-lived and unlamented ➧Community Charge, which was highly unpopular and partially responsible for inducing the fall from prime ministerial office of Margaret Thatcher

Polo *pr. name (TM)* a mint candy similar to a lifesaver

polo-neck *comp. noun* a turtleneck, but higher

polony *noun* a sausage containing partly cooked pork
A corruption of "bologna," the Italian city.

poly bag *comp. noun* a flexible, often transparent, bag made from polyethylene
Use to carry shopping and so forth.

polycythaemia *spell* polycythemia

Polyfilla *pr. name (TM)* a powder that mixes with water to form a paste that sets hard with the consistency of plaster, and is used to fill cracks and similar flaws in domestic plasterwork

polysulphide *spell.* polysulfide

polytechnic *pr. name, hist.* a college of higher education
These had been entitled to award degrees for some time; in 1992 they were all turned into full universities.

polythene *noun* polyethylene

Pomfret cake *comp. noun, arch.* an older name for a ➧Pontefract cake

{**pommelled » pommelling**} *spell.* {pommeled » pommeling}

the **Pompadours** *pr. name* a nickname for the 35th Regiment of ➧Foot
A unit of the British Army that when it was raised in 1755 had facings of purple, which was also the favorite color of Louis XV's mistress, Madame de Pompadour.

Pompey *pr. name, sl.* a nickname for ➧Portsmouth

ponce *noun, derog., sl.* (1) an effeminate homosexual; (2) a pimp

ponce about *verb, sl.* to act in an affected or effeminate manner

pondage *noun* (1) a store of water; (2) the volume of water in a pond

pong *noun, coll.* a stink or unpleasant smell

pongo *noun, sl.* (1) a soldier; (2) an orangutan; (3) a foreigner

pons asinorum *idiom, Lat.* specifically, this is the proof of Pythagoras's theorem in Euclidian geometry which states that the square on the hypotenuse of a right-angled triangle is equal to the sum of the squares on the other two sides, but more generally it is any proposition that is considered difficult to comprehend and is viewed as a test of intelligence
The expression is Latin for "asses bridge."

Pontefract cake *comp. noun* a small candy consisting mostly of licorice
Made at Pontefract, formerly called Pomfret, in ➧Yorkshire. *SEE ALSO:* ➧Pomfret cake.

Pontius Pilate's Bodyguard *pr. name* a nickname for the 1st Regiment of ➧Foot, better known as the ➧Royal Scots
This is the oldest regiment in the British Army; it was first raised in 1633.
It is said that when a French officer claimed his own regiment was so ancient that it was on duty on the night of the Crucifixion, the commander of the Royal Scots replied to him, "Had we been on duty, we would not have slept at our post."

pontoon *noun, Fr.* blackjack
From the French *vingt-et-un* = "twenty-one"

pony [A] *noun, sl.* £25 (twenty-five pounds)
SEE ALSO: ➧gorilla, ➧monkey, ➧score.
[B] *verb, rh. sl.* to defecate
Derivation: defecate > crap > trap > pony and trap > pony.

pony club *pr. name* a club devoted to encouraging children to take up horseback riding

pony-treck *phr. verb* to travel around the countryside on a pony, in a casual manner as a leasure activity

pooch *noun, Sc.* (1) a pocket in pants, jacket, etc.; (2) a purse

{**poof » poofter**} *noun, Aus., derog., sl.* a male homosexual

pool *noun* a game played on a billiard table
It should not be confused with the U.S. game of the same name. Each player has his or her own ball, and the objective is to pocket those of all the other players in a set sequence, the winner taking all the stakes.

the **Pool of London** *pr. name* a wide stretch of the ➧Thames River lying between ➧London Bridge and the ➧Tower of London

the **pools** *noun, abbr.* the ➧football pools

265

the **Poor Law**

the **Poor Law** *pr. name, hist.* a system established in 1601 to cater for the destitute and others unable to look after themselves

It was financed by a local tax called the ➡Poor Rate. The system evolved over the years, and by the middle of the 19th C. the destitute poor were required to live in workhouses where conditions were deliberately kept unpleasant and the inhabitants were required to work to earn their keep. The last vestiges of the system were finally buried in the 1940s when the modern social security system was established.

poorly *adj.* somewhat unwell

the **Poor Rate** *pr. name, hist.* a former local tax

This money was used for the relief of the poor under the terms of the ➡Poor Law.

poor show *idiom, coll.* not good enough, disappointing

pop *verb, sl.* to pawn

pope's eye *comp. noun, Sc.* a cut of beef

pope's head *comp. noun, arch.* a long-handled broom

pop in *verb, coll.* to visit briefly

popper *noun, coll.* a snap button on clothing

poppet *noun, coll.* (1) a small or dainty person; (2) a term of endearment

poppet-head *comp. noun* a framework at the head of a mineshaft that supports the ropes used for hoisting up men and materials

popping crease *comp. noun* a line marked on the ground of a ➡cricket pitch four feet in front of the ➡wicket, beyond which a ➡batsman must not stray in order to prevent himself from being ➡stumped.

Poppy Day *pr. name* ➡Remembrance Day

Called this because it is customary to wear a poppy in memory of those who died in the poppy-strewn cornfields of Flanders in Belgium during World War I.

SEE ALSO: ➡Flanders poppy.

pop round *verb, coll.* to briefly visit nearby

pop-shop *comp. noun, out., sl.* a pawn shop

popsy *noun, coll.* a term of endearment for an attractive woman or girl

pork pie *comp. noun* a pie containing chopped pork

Normally served cold, it is a common food in pubs.

{**porky » porky pie**} *idiom, rh. sl.* a ➡lie

porridge [A] *noun* oatmeal

[B] *noun, sl.* time spent in jail

port *noun, hist., Sc.* a gate or door through the defensive wall of a town

Portaloo *pr. name (TM)* a transportable toilet

A familiar sight on construction sites and many other temporary locations.

portcullis *noun, hist.* an iron grating hung over the gateway into a castle, walled town, or other fortified place, which could be lowered to prevent entry

porter *noun* (1) a bitter, dark-brown beer made from charred malts; (2) the doorkeeper of a hotel, public building, etc.

porter's knot *comp. noun, arch.* a kind of shoulder pad supported by a loop around the forehead, for the purpose of carrying heavy loads

the Isle of **Portland** *pr. name* not an island but a peninsula on the ➡Dorset coast located just to the west of the coastal resort of Weymouth

Portland stone *comp. noun* a high-quality limestone

Stone from the Isle of ➡Portland, much used in public buildings in London and elsewhere.

Portmeirion *pr. name, hist.* a privately owned village built in 1925, five miles from ➡Harlech in Wales

The village was conceived as a vacation center or sort of proto-theme park for tourists. It was used as the location of the 1967 TV series "The Prisoner."

Portobello Road *pr. name* a street in west London where there is a daily market

Established since the 1870s, now best known for its antiques.

the **Port of London Authority** *pr. name* the public agency that manages the Port of London

Portsmouth *pr. name* a city and port in ➡Hampshire

Portsmouth first became significant during the reign of ➡Henry VII. He established a naval dockyard there in 1496, and it has been the home port of the ➡Royal Navy ever since. Nelson's flagship from the Battle of ➡Trafalgar, HMS ➡Victory, is on view in the harbor.

Incorporated as a city in 1194, the current population, including suburbs, is 425,000 (1988 estimate).

the **Portsmouth defence** *comp. noun, coll.* a legal stratagem by which a man accused of assault pleads guilty but claims in mitigation that he was outraged by the homosexual advances made to him by the man he assaulted

➡Portsmouth is the chief port of the ➡Royal Navy, so such incidents are reputedly commoner there than most places.

Port Sunlight *pr. name, hist.* a model village built in 1888, some five miles south of ➡Liverpool

It was built to provide homes for workers at the Sunlight Soap factory, hence the name.

Portuguese parliament *comp. noun, sl.* an out-of-control discussion where everyone talks at once and no-one listens

Originally a sailor's expression.

posh [A] *adj., abbr., arch.* port out, starboard home

The way first-class ticket holders sailed from England to India and back, as this arrangement minimized exposure to the sun, making their voyage more pleasant.

Despite a popular myth to the contrary, this is most unlikely to be the origin of the word when it is used in the sense of "upper class or elegant," as the word was being used with that meaning for some time before the predilections of colonial administrators had been catered for in the manner mentioned. It is much more probably derived from early 19th C., now archaic, meanings of the word as a noun, which are now given here:

[B] *noun, arch., sl.* (1) a dandy; (2) money

positive vetting *comp. noun* an exhaustive inquiry into the background of a candidate for high-security or sensitive work in the military or the civil service

Conducted by the security services to ensure that a candidate is suitable in this regard.

post [A] *noun, arch.* a naval commission to command a vessel of 20 guns or more

[B] *noun, coll.* (1) mail collection; (2) mail delivery

the **Post** *pr. name* the Mail

postage and packaging *comp. noun* shipping and handling

postal card *comp. noun, arch.* a postcard

postal order *comp. noun* a money order

postbag *noun* a mailbag

postbox *noun* a mailbox

Post Captain *noun, hist.* a ➡Royal Naval rank for an officer awarded a ➡post commission

In use from about 1730 until 1815 .

post code *comp. noun* the equivalent of a zip code

poste restante *idiom, Fr.* (1) general delivery mail; (2) the location within a post office where (1) is kept while awaiting collection

From the French, "letter remaining."

post-free *adj.* postage paid

post-haste *spell.* posthaste

postie *noun, abbr., coll.* a ➡{postman » postwoman}

{postman » postwoman} *noun* a {mailman » mailwoman}

postman's knock *comp. noun* the game of post office

postmaster *noun* a scholar at ➡Merton College, ➡Oxford University

Postmaster General *pr. name, hist.* a government minister in charge of postal services

This office was abolished in 1969.

post-obit *comp. noun, abbr.* a post-obit bond

A bond from borrower to lender securing repayment of a sum due upon the death of a third person from whom the borrower is expected to inherit sufficient funds to repay the debit.

the **Post Office** *pr. name (TM)* the public authority responsible for providing a mail service

A royal monopoly since 1635. With the Penny Post of 1840, it became the world's first flat-rate mail service, and introduced the world's first adhesive mass-produced postage stamps. The Post Office ceased to be a government department in 1969 and since then its monopoly has become significantly restricted.

Post Office Counters *pr. name (TM)* the division of the ➡Post Office that operates retail post offices

post town *comp. noun* any town with a post office

post war credits *comp. noun, hist.* tax credits that were due because of extra taxes paid during World War II

pot [A] *noun* a ➡snooker shot that pockets a ball

[B] *noun, Ir.* the hole which remains in the ground after peat has been excavated

pot and pan *idiom, rh. sl.* a father or husband

Derivation: father > old man > pan > pot and pan.

potato crisp *comp. noun* a potato chip

poteen *noun, Gae., Ir.* illicitly distilled Irish whiskey

pothole *noun* a natural sinkhole formed by water erosion over geological time

They may link together to form extensive systems of caves and underground waterways in limestone regions.

potholer *noun* a spelunker

pot plant *comp. noun* a houseplant

pot-pourri *spell.* potpourri

potted *adj.* summarized in a pedestrian manner

potted heid *comp. noun, Sc.* a dish consisting of the meat from the head of a cow which is boiled, finely chopped, and served cold in jelly made from stock

potter about *verb* to putter

the **Potteries** *pr. name* an area in ➡Staffordshire that is the center of the British china and earthenware product industry

Now almost entirely within the city of ➡Stoke-on-Trent.

potty *adj., sl.* (1) somewhat crazy; (2) trivial

Pound *noun, abbr.* what the ➡Pound Sterling is usually called

poundage *noun* (1) a commission or fee which is paid at a rate of so much per ➡Pound Sterling; (2) the portion of a business's earnings which are paid out as wages

pound and pint *comp. noun, arch.* a sailor's ration

As laid down in 19th C. government regulations.

pound and pinter *comp. noun, arch.* a ship whose crew received the regulation ➡pound and pint ration

pound coin *comp. noun* a coin worth one ➡Pound

pound note *comp. noun* a ➡banknote worth one ➡Pound

Now discontinued, except in Scotland where they are still issued by the ➡Royal Bank of Scotland.

pound Scots *comp. noun, hist., Sc.* the principal monetary unit of Scotland until 1707

Originally Scots and English currency was roughly equal in value, but Scots money began to depreciate against the English in the late 14th C. By the time of the ➡Union of the Parliaments in 1707 when the old Scottish currency was replaced with the English, a pound Scots was worth one English ➡shilling and eight English pennies, which is to say, just $1/12$ th of an English pound.

the **Pound Sterling**

the **Pound Sterling** *pr. name* the principal monetary unit of the United Kingdom

It usually called by its abbreviated form, the ➡Pound. Nowadays it consists of 100 pennies, but formerly consisted of 240 old pennies or 20 shillings. It is said that the name originally derived from the coin being worth one pound (weight) of "sterling" ("pure") silver.

pouring cream *comp. noun* half-and-half cream

powder monkey *comp. noun, hist.* a young boy on a warship who carried gunpowder from the powder magazine to the guns during battle

They scrambled through the bowels of the ship, along narrow passageways too constricted for full-grown men to use.

power-assisted steering *comp. noun* power steering

power cut *comp. noun* an electrical power failure

power {point » socket} *comp. noun* an electrical power outlet

Powis Castle *pr. name, hist.* some 20 miles to the west of ➡Shrewsbury, it was originally a 13th C. frontier fortress close to the English border

Over the years, Powis Castle has been transformed from a fortress into a large house incorporating examples of various kinds of architecture, especially Elizabethan and baroque.

Powys *pr. name, hist.* (1) an ancient kingdom in central Wales; (2) a Welsh County

(1) was ruled by the kings of ➡Gwynedd from about 850, but the princes of Powys became independent rulers after Gwynedd accepted English mastery in the middle of the 12th C. English rule arrived for Powys in 1269. The current population of (2) is 115,000 (1991 Census).

PPE *noun, abbr.* philosophy, politics and economics

An Oxford University degree course particularly popular with those who are thinking of a future career in politics.

PPP *pr. name, abbr.* Private Patients Plan

An association providing private medical health insurance.

PPS *noun, abbr.* (1) a ➡Parliamentary Private Secretary; (2) a second postscript to a letter

(2) is an abbreviation of the Latin *post postscriptum*, where *postscriptum* is the past participle of the verb "to write." Thus PPS is in this sense, the past participle of the past participle of the verb "to write," as it were.

PRA *pr. name, abbr.* the President of the ➡Royal Academy of Arts

practise *spell.* practice

praecocial *spell.* precocial

Of birds that can feed themselves as soon as hatched.

praelector *noun* a ➡fellow at ➡Cambridge University who presents candidates for degrees

praemunire *noun, arch., hist.* the crime of asserting the authority of the Pope in England

Especially that he has any over the ➡Church of England.

praepositura *noun, Sc.* a wife's legal right to incur debts on behalf of her husband in order to obtain food and other household essentials

praepostor *noun* a school ➡prefect or monitor

{praetor » praetorian guard} *spell.* {pretor » pretorian guard}

prairie oyster *comp. noun* an unshelled but otherwise intact raw egg, seasoned and swallowed whole

Reputedly a cure for a hangover.

pram *noun, abbr.* a ➡perambulator

prang *verb, out., sl.* (1) to bomb accurately; (2) to collide with a vehicle; (3) to crash one's own aircraft or car; (4) to shoot down an enemy aircraft

This expression began life as ➡RAF World War II slang.

prat *noun, sl.* a silly person

{precancelled » precancelling} *spell.* {precanceled » precanceling}

precept *noun* a court warrant requiring the party it is served upon to pay local taxation

precognition *noun, Sc.* the initial questioning of a witness to establish whether or not there are grounds for proceeding to trial

pree *verb, Sc.* to taste or sample

preen *noun, Sc.* (1) a pin; (2) a fishhook

prefect *noun* in some schools, a senior student responsible for the discipline of others

preference {shares » stock} *comp. noun* stock with a divident entitlement that takes priority over ordinary stock

preggers *adj., sl.* pregnant

the **preliminaries** *noun* items such as title page, introduction and so forth, at the front of a book

the **Premier** *noun* the ➡Prime Minister

premiss *spell.* premise

A logical proposition from which conclusions may be drawn.

Premium {Bond » Savings Bond} *pr. name* a government security that offers the chance to win cash prizes as an alternative to earning interest

prep *noun, abbr., coll.* (1) ➡preparation; (2) time set aside for (1)

prepacked meal *comp. noun* a packaged meal

preparation *noun* school homework

preparatory school *comp. noun* a private fee-paying school for children age 7 to 13, where they are prepared for entry to an English ➡public school

prep school *comp. noun, abbr.* a ➡preparatory school

the **Pre-Raphaelite Brotherhood** *pr. name, hist.* a group of 19th C. English painters who tried to emulate the paintings of 15th C. Italian painters who had worked in the period prior to Raphael

Members included Rossetti, Millais and Hunt.

presence chamber *comp. noun* a room in which the ➡Sovereign formally receives visitors

presenter *noun* a TV show host

presently *adj.* soon; shortly

the **President of the Board of Trade and Secretary of State for Trade and Industry** *pr. name* the ➡cabinet minister responsible for the ➡Department of Trade and Industry

the **Press Association** *pr. name* the leading news agency for domestic British news
Established in 1868 by a group of newspapers from all parts of Britain except London.

press {button » fastener » stud} *comp. noun* a snap fastener for clothing

the **Press Complaints Commission** *pr. name* an independent press watchdog organization
It replaced the ➡Press Council in 1991.

Press Council *pr. name, hist.* an independent press watchdog, replaced by the ➡Press Complaints Commission in 1991
Replaced by the ➡Press Complaints Commission in 1991.

press cutting *comp. noun* a press or newspaper clipping

press cutting agency *comp. noun* a service which collects newspaper clippings for clients

press gallery *comp. noun* an area in the ➡House of Commons set aside for journalists reporting debates

press gang *comp. noun, hist.* a group of men commanded by an officer empowered to recruit men into the army or, usually, the navy, by ➡impressment

pressman *noun, out.* a journalist

pressmark *noun* a mark on a book that indicates its proper place in a library

press-on towel *comp. noun* an adhesive sanitary napkin

press-up *comp. noun* a push-up

Prestel *pr. name* an interactive viewdata service

Preston *pr. name* a city that is the administrative center of ➡Lancashire
An important port on the estuary of the Ribble River in ➡Lancashire, and a significant center of the wool trade since the Middle Ages. The current population, including suburbs, is 250,000 (1988 estimate).

pretence *spell.* pretense

pretender *noun, arch.* someone who makes a false or unaccepted claim to a throne

the **Prevention of Terrorism Act** *pr. name, hist.* a law giving special powers to police and courts in ➡Northern Ireland in order to fight terrorism
First introduced as a temporary measure in 1984.

the **Preventive Service** *pr. name* a service department of ➡HM Customs which is responsible for preventing smuggling

prezzie *noun, abbr., coll.* a present or gift

price ring *comp. noun* a cartel of traders who fix prices among themselves

prick *verb* to mark off an item in a list by making a small hole on or beside it

priest of the blue bag *idiom* a barrister
From the color of robe-bags once carried by junior counsel

priest's hole *comp. noun, arch.* a secret place where Catholic priests hid during times of persecution

priest-vicar *comp. noun* a minor canon

primary education *comp. noun* elementary education

primary school *comp. noun* an elementary school

the **Primate of All England** *pr. name* the ➡Archbishop of Canterbury

the **Primate of England** *pr. name* the ➡Archbishop of York

the **Prime Meridian** *pr. name* longitude zero
Which is to say the ➡Greenwich Meridian.

Prime Minister *pr. name* the chief executive of the British Government, chair of the ➡Cabinet, ➡First Lord of the Treasury and first minister of the ➡Crown

Not the head of state: that is the ➡Sovereign. The office came about because ➡George I did not speak English, making it difficult to chair meetings of the ➡Cabinet as the monarch had traditionally done, thus he chose Sir Robert Walpole, ➡First Lord of the Treasury, who filled that role for 21 years from 1721, becoming known as the king's "prime," or first, minister. The Prime Minister is always either the leader of the party whose members constitute an absolute majority of the ➡MPs in the ➡House of Commons, or the leader of the largest party in a coalition of parties, which together have a majority in the House of Commons.

Although not absolutely necessary for the Prime Minister to be an MP, it is now considered unrealistic, both politically and practically, for the office to be held by someone who is not an MP. The last Prime Minister who held office while sitting in the ➡House of Lords was Lord Salisbury, whose third and last administration ran from 1895 to 1902. The last Prime Minister to enter the office while not an MP was Sir Alex Douglas-Home, whose administration ran from 1963 to 1964. He had sat in the Lords as Lord Home, but as soon as he became Prime Minister, he resigned his peerage and entered the Commons as MP for a Scottish ➡constituency after winning a ➡bye-election there.

the **Prime Minister's Office** *pr. name* the government office which provides support services for the ⟶Prime Minister and his personal staff

the **Primrose League** *pr. name* an association formed in 1883 for the furtherance of ⟶Conservative political principles

Primus *pr. name (TM)* a portable oil-burning stove

the **Primus** *pr. name* the presiding bishop of the Episcopal church in Scotland

Prince Consort *pr. name* a title that *may* be conferred upon a queen's husband who is not a king because his wife reigns in her own right

It was conferred upon Prince ⟶Albert, husband of ⟶Victoria, but has not been conferred upon Prince Philip, husband of ⟶Elizabeth II of England and I of Scotland.

prince of the blood *idiom* a son or grandson of a British ⟶sovereign

---

Prince of Wales *pr. name* a title normally conferred by the sovereign upon his or her eldest son

A title first used by Dafydd ap Llewelyn in 1214, and recognized by the English kings within a few years. However, when ⟶Edward I had completed the conquest of Wales in 1301, he conferred the title upon his eldest son, Edward. Since then, the title has been reserved by the monarch for this purpose. The motto of the Prince of Wales is *Ich dien* = "I serve" in German, first adopted by the ⟶Black Prince at the Battle of ⟶Crécy in 1346.

{**prince** » **princess**} **regent** *comp. noun* a {prince » princess} who acts as ⟶regent

the **Prince Regent** *pr. name* the future ⟶George IV who, as ⟶Prince of Wales, eldest son, and heir to the throne of ⟶George III, was made ⟶regent in 1811 when it had become apparent that his father's insanity was irreversible

He has a well-deserved reputation as the most licentious of Britain's kings, but is also remembered as responsible for the fabulous ⟶Royal Pavilion in Brighton.

Prince Royal *pr. name* the eldest son of a monarch

the **Princes in the Tower** *pr. name, hist.* the 12-year-old ⟶Edward V and his younger brother Richard, Duke of York

They were lodged in the ⟶Tower of London in 1483 while their uncle Richard, Duke of Gloucester, usurped the throne to become ⟶Richard III.

The princes disappeared at that time, and were generally assumed to have been murdered on the orders of their uncle but there is no conclusive evidence of this. However, bones found under the ⟶White Tower in 1674 were interred in ⟶Westminster Abbey and in 1933 were examined and found to be of two children of appropriate age.

Princess of Wales *pr. name* a title normally conferred upon the wife of the ⟶Prince of Wales

Princess Royal *pr. name* a title that may be conferred upon the eldest daughter of the monarch

Princes Street *pr. name* the principal shopping street of ⟶Edinburgh

Only the north side of this street has buildings along it, allowing spectacular views over a valley to the ⟶Royal Mile and ⟶Edinburgh Castle. It was named after the future ⟶George IV, then ⟶Prince of Wales.

principal *noun* a high-grade civil servant

principal boy *comp. noun* the young male hero of a ⟶pantomime, a role traditionally played by a woman

the **Principality** *pr. name, abbr.* Wales

the **Principality of Wales** *pr. name* the formal name for ⟶Wales

pringle *noun, sl.* an aggressive, young working-class male with pretentions of upper-class mobility

From their supposed disposition to wear Pringle (TM) sweaters.

Prinny *pr. name, hist.* the future ⟶George IV's nickname while still ⟶Prince of Wales

printer's devil *comp. noun, hist.* a printer's boy assistant

printshop *noun* a printing office

prison bird *comp. noun, arch., sl.* a jailbird

prisoner at the bar *comp. noun* a prisoner on trial on a criminal charge

prison house *comp. noun* a prison building

prison officer *comp. noun* a prison guard

prison without bars *comp. noun* an ⟶open prison

private address *comp. noun* a home address

private bill *comp. noun, hist.* a ⟶parliamentary bill concerning an individual person or company alone

From ⟶Henry VIII's break with Rome and establishment of the ⟶Church of England until the passing of the Matrimonial Causes Act of 1857, the only way to obtain a divorce in England and Wales was by means of such a private bill, ruling out divorce for any but the very rich and well-connected. *SEE ALSO:* ⟶private member's bill.

private company *comp. noun* a company with limited membership and whose shares are not quoted on the Stock Exchange

private hire *comp. noun, coll.* a car rented together with a driver

private hotel *comp. noun* one not open to all comers

private means *comp. noun* unearned income

private member *comp. noun* a ➡backbencher ➡MP

private member's bill *comp. noun* a bill introduced into ➡Parliament by an individual MP

As such it is not part of the government's legislative program. *SEE ALSO:* ➡private bill.

private notice question *comp. noun* an urgent written question put to a minister by the ➡Speaker of the House on behalf of a ➡MP

Normally there will be a verbal answer on the same day.

private patient *comp. noun* one treated privately

As opposed to being treated under the auspices of the ➡National Health Service.

private practice *comp. noun* a medical practice that is not conducted under the auspices of the ➡National Health Service

private ship *comp. noun* any ship in the ➡Royal Navy other than a flagship

---

the **Privy Council** *pr. name* the ➡Sovereign's private council of state

All cabinet members and many other eminent people from both Britain and other ➡Commonwealth countries are members. Originally this was the royal executive which ruled the state, but eventually it had become far too large and unwieldy for this and by the 16th C. had been supplanted in this role by a small inner group of ➡Privy Counsellors, known as the ➡Cabinet.

Uniquely, all meetings of the Privy Council take place with those present standing up, which may help explain why they are normal of very short duration.

Privy Counsellor *comp. noun* a member of the ➡Privy Council

privy parts *comp. noun, arch.* the private parts

the **Privy Purse** *pr. name* an allowance made to the monarch that is provided from public funds

the **Privy Seal** *pr. name* a seal attached to documents that are either not important enough for the ➡Great Seal or will receive it later

prize court *comp. noun* a wartime court that decides the disposition of captured ships and cargoes

PRO *abbr. North* the ➡Public Record Office

proceed to *phr. verb* to take a university degree

process *verb* to go in procession

proctor *noun* one of two university officers appointed annually, responsible for disciplining students

procurator fiscal *comp. noun, Sc.* a legal officer appointed by the ➡Lord Advocate, whose duties combine most of the functions of coroner and public prosecutor, with supervision of the legal aspects of police investigation of a crime

producer *noun* the director of a TV or stage play

professor *noun* a university teacher approximately equivalent in grade to a U.S. senior professor.

SEE ALSO: ➡lecturer, ➡reader and ➡senior lecturer.

prog *noun, sl.* a ➡proctor at ➡Oxford or ➡Cambridge Universities

{**programme » programmed » programming**} *spell.* {program » programed » programing}

However, it should be noted that a British computer runs a "program" after it has been "programed," which happens when "programing" is finished.

progress *noun, arch.* an official, formal state journey

prom *noun, abbr.* (1) a promenade or strolling place; (2) a ➡promenade concert

promenade concert *comp. noun* a concert where the audience, who are not provided with anywhere to sit, "promenade" or walk about while the music is being played

Originally such concerts were held in public parks, like Vauxhall Gardens or ➡Hyde Park in early 19th C. London, following the example of similar events that had been popular some years earlier in Paris.

the **Promenade Concerts** *pr. name* a series of annual concerts of classical music organized by Sir Henry Woods from 1895 onwards

In 1927 the BBC took them over, and they are now performed in the ➡Royal Albert Hall and broadcast on radio and TV.

promenader *noun* one attending promenade concerts

the **Proms** *pr. name, abbr.* the ➡Promenade Concerts

prooestrus *spell.* proestrus

The time immediately before estrus.

propeller shaft *comp. noun* a drive shaft

propelling pencil *comp. noun* a mechanical pencil

proper *adv., sl.* (1) total, completely or very; (2) in a correct and polite way of speaking

proper charlie *idiom, sl.* a complete fool

propone *verb, Sc.* (1) to advance a legal defense; (2) to propose an action or resolution to a court

proproctor *noun* a deputy university ➡proctor

propshaft *noun, abbr.* a ➡propeller shaft

prorogation *noun* termination without dissolution of a ➡Parliamentary session by ➡Royal Proclamation

This only happens when a ➡general election is called.

protect *verb* to provide the money needed to meet expenses, costs, and so forth

the **Protectorate**

the **Protectorate** *pr. name, hist.* an alternate name for the short-lived republican ➡Commonwealth of England during the 17th C.
From 1653 to 1659, England was governed by Oliver ➡Cromwell and later his son Richard, as ➡Lord Protectors of the ➡Commonwealth; effectively, they were dictators.

proud *adj.* projected slightly above a level surface

provenance *spell.* provenience

provident society *comp. noun* a mutual-aid society

the **provinces** *noun* the whole of England and Wales, apart from London and the territory immediately surrounding it

provisional driving licence *comp. noun* a special driver's license issued to permit someone to learn to drive while supervised by a fully qualified driver

Provisional IRA *pr. name, abbr., coll.* the Provisional ➡Irish Republican Army
The faction of the ➡IRA that broke away from the original ➡Official IRA in 1969 in order to follow a policy of violent terrorism against the Protestant Irish, the British military and British civilians both in Ireland and Great Britain in the belief that somehow or other this would advance their goal of a single state encompassing all of the island of Ireland. The organization has been proscribed in both ➡Northern Ireland and the ➡Irish Republic.

the {**Provisionals » Provos**} *pr. name, abbr., coll.* the ➡Provisional IRA

the **Provisional** *Sinn Féin* *pr. name, Gae., Ir.* the political wing of the ➡Provisional IRA
From the Irish Gaelic, meaning "We Ourselves"

Provo *pr. name, abbr., coll.* a member of the ➡Provisional IRA

provost [A] *noun* the principal of certain ➡Cambridge and ➡Oxford colleges
[B] *noun, Sc.* the principal elected official and chief magistrate of a Scottish city or burgh
Equivalent in rank to a ➡mayor.

proxime accessit *idiom, Lat.* a person who comes second best in a university examination
The Latin for "came very close"

PRS *pr. name, abbr.* (1) the President of the ➡Royal Society; (2) the Performing Rights Society

pruif *noun, Sc.* (1) the ➡precognition by a judge or commissioner appointed by the court to determine whether the evidence against the ➡panel is sufficient to warrant a trial; (2) a trial held before a judge in the absence of a jury

PSA *pr. name, abbr.* the Property Service Agency
A government executive agency responsible for providing and maintaining government property.

PSBR *noun. abbr.* the ➡Public Sector Borrowing Requirement

The government's fiscal deficit, in other words.

pseud *noun, coll.* a person who purports to be an intellectual but is not

PSV *noun, abbr.* a public service vehicle

psychoanalyse *spell.* psychoanalyze

PTA *pr. name, abbr.* a Passenger Transport Authority

pub *noun, abbr., coll.* a ➡public house or tavern

publican *noun* a saloon-keeper

public bar *comp. noun* the cheaper and less luxurious bar in a ➡public house
SEE ALSO: ➡saloon bar.

public call box *comp. noun* a telephone booth

public company *comp. noun* a company whose shares are quoted on the Stock Exchange and may be bought by any member of the public

public convenience *comp. noun, pref.* a public rest room

public house *comp. noun* a saloon or bar licensed to sell liquor for consumption on the premises

Public Lending Right *pr. name* the right of authors to payment related to the frequency of borrowings of their works from public libraries in Britain
Established by ➡Act of Parliament in 1984 and financed by the government. It applies to British authors only.

publicly-owned corporation *comp. noun* a company owned by the state but in all other respects operates as a commercial business

the **Public Record Office** *pr. name, hist.* where the official government documents of England and Wales are stored
Important historical documents such as the ➡Domesday Book are to be found here.

public school *comp. noun* (1) in England, an independent, private, fee-paying school; (2) in Scotland, a ➡state school run by a ➡local authority

the Office of **Public Service and Science** *pr. name* a government agency directly managed by the ➡Cabinet Office

public transport *comp. noun* transportation available for public use

pud *noun, abbr.* a ➡pudding

pudding *noun* a dessert

pudding basin *comp. noun* a large and deep glazed bowl used to make ➡{steam » steamed} puddings

puddock *noun, Sc.* a frog

puff and dart *verb, rh. sl.* to start or commence

Puffing Billy *pr. name, hist.* the world's first steam-powered locomotive riding on smooth rails
It began operating in 1813 along track laid between a coal mine and the dock where coal from that mine was loaded

272

onboard ships — a distance of some five miles — upon the ➟Tyne River in ➟Northumberland. Puffing Billy can now be seen in the ➟Science Museum in London.

puff-puff *comp. noun* a childish name for a train
Particularly a steam-powered one, of course.

pug *noun* a small locomotive used to shunt railroad cars around a switching yard

puggy *noun, Sc.* (1) a monkey; (2) the bank in a game of cards; (3) a fruit machine

puissance *noun* a ➟showjumping event that involves persuading horses to jump over large objects

pukka *adj., coll., Hindi, out.* (1) authentic; (2) reliable; (3) of full measure
Originally Hindi, meaning "well cooked" or "substantial".

pukka sahib *comp. noun, Hindi, out., Urdu* a gentleman
Originally the Hindi, ➟pukka plus the Urdu *sahib*, which means "lord," "master" or "friend."

pull *verb, coll.* (1) to pick up a potential sexual partner; (2) to hit a ➟cricket ball to the left

pull about *verb, sl.* (1) to treat roughly; (2) to knock from side to side

pull a face *verb, coll.* to grimace

pull a {flanker» stroke} *verb, sl.* to pull a fast one

pull a pint *verb* to draw draft beer from its barrel using a pump operated by a lever on a ➟pub's bar

pull-in *comp. noun* a roadside stopping place

pull the moody *idiom. phr. verb* to sulk

pull the other one *imper., coll.* pull the other leg

pulpit *noun, arch., sl.* the cockpit of an aircraft
This expression began life as ➟RAF World War II slang.

{pummelled » pummelling} *spell.* {pummeled » pummeling}

pumpkin *noun* a kind of large-fruited winter squash

pump room *comp. noun, out.* a room at a spa where waters supposedly possessing health-giving properties are available to bath in, drink, or do with whatever else takes your fancy

pun *verb* to compact earth, etc., by pounding

punce *verb, Sc.* to hit gently or to nudge

Punch *pr. name, hist.* a humorous magazine, first published in London in 1841, discontinued in 1992
The leading British vehicle for cartoonists, its full title was *Punch, or the London Charivari*; the magazine took its name from the "Punch and Judy" puppet show.

punch-bag *comp. noun* a punching bag

punch-up *comp. noun, coll.* a fistfight

puncture *noun* a flat tire

punnet *noun* a small basket for soft fruit
Particularly strawberries, which are often sold by the punnet.

Punt *noun, abbr., Ir.* the ➟Irish Punt

punter *noun, sl.* (1) an ordinary person; (2) a customer; (3) a gambler; (4) a prostitute's client

pup *noun, coll.* an unpleasantly aggressive young man

pupil [A] *noun* (1) a student at elementary or high school; (2) a student under the guidance of a particular instructor or teacher
[B] *noun, Sc.* legally, a boy younger than 14 or a girl younger than 12

pupillage *spell.* pupilage

Purbeck stone *comp. noun* a hard building limestone
From Purbeck, which is in Dorset.

the Purcell Room *pr. name* a musical recital hall in the ➟South Bank complex, London

purchase tax *comp. noun, hist.* a tax on purchases
Somewhat similar sales taxes in the U.S.. It was abolished when ➟value added tax was introduced in 1973.

pure *adj., Sc., sl.* completely, entirely

pure dead brilliant *idiom, Sc.* wonderful, marvellous

Purdy *pr. name (TM)* a very high-quality and expensive shotgun

Puritan *pr. name, hist.* one of a group of English Protestants, largely Calvinist, who regarded the Bible as the sole legitimate source of authority. Considering the 16th and 17th C. ➟Church of England to be insufficiently reformed, they sought the complete "purification" of Christianity. Puritans had a large influence on the ➟Parliamentary party during the ➟English Civil War and comprised about one-third of the Pilgrim Fathers who sailed in the *Mayflower* to Massachusetts in 1620.
Following the ➟Restoration and the Act of Uniformity of 1662, they became known as ➟Dissenters or ➟Nonconformists.

puritan woman

the Puritan Revolution *pr. name, hist., out.* an alternate name, now rare, for the ➟English Civil War

purler *noun, coll.* a blow that causes the victim to fall head first

purlieu

purlieu *noun, arch.* a portion of land at the edge of a forest which was once part of that forest
Usually still subject to the laws governing forests, even if there is not a tree in sight.

purpose-made *adj.* made for a specific purpose

purpure *noun* the heraldic name for the color purple

purse *noun* a woman's change purse

the **Purse Bearer** *pr. name* the official who carries the ➞Great Seal ahead of the ➞Lord Chancellor upon ceremonial occasions
Called this because he carries it in a purse.

pursuivant *noun* an official of the ➞College of Arms below the rank of herald
There are four in England: Rouge Dragon, Blue Mantle, Portcullis and Rouge Croix.
In Scotland there are three Pursuivants Ordinary: Unicorn, Carrick and Dingwall or Kintyre, together with two Pursuivants Extraordinary: Linlithgow and Falkland.

purveyance *noun, arch.* the right of a ➞monarch to purchase provisions at a fixed price

push {bike » bicycle} *comp. noun, sl.* a pedal bike

pushchair *noun* a baby's stroller

push-start *phr. verb, coll.* to start a car by pushing it to turn over the engine and get it firing

push the boat out *idiom. phr. verb, coll.* to celebrate in a big way

put (someone's) gas at a peep *idiom. phr. verb, coll., Sc.* to humiliate or cut (someone) down to size

put about *verb, coll.* to spread a rumor

put a {lid on » sock in} **it** *idiom. phr. verb* (1) to stop it; (2) to be silent

put a spoke in (someone's) wheel *idiom. phr. verb* to prevent or delay (someone's) intended action

put back *phr. verb* to delay

put down *phr. verb* to kill an animal humanely or for humane reasons

put it to (someone) *idiom. phr. verb* to challenge (someone) to deny

put one's wind up *idiom. phr. verb, coll.* to induce terror or fear
SEE ALSO: ➞get one's wind up

put (someone) on the mat *idiom. phr. verb* to call (someone) on the carpet; to reprimand severely

put on the slate *idiom. phr. verb.* to record a debt
Originally, one that was written with chalk upon a slate provided for the purpose in a store, bar, etc.

put out of misery *idiom. phr. verb* (1) to ➞put down an animal; (2) to end a suspenseful situation

put paid to *idiom. phr. verb* to finish off, end or kill

put the black on *idiom. phr. verb* to threaten blackmail

put the boot in *idiom. phr. verb* (1) literally, to attack by kicking; (2) metaphorically, to attack by other means, either physical or verbal

put the lid on *idiom. phr. verb, sl.* to terminate

put the mockers on *idiom. phr. verb, sl.* (1) to curse; (2) to ruin or stop

put to flight *phr. verb* to rout or to cause to run away

putty medal *comp. noun, coll.* a trivial or humorous reward for a small service

PW *noun, abbr.* a policewoman

{**pyaemia** » **pyaemic**} *spell.* {pyemia » pyemic}
Blood poisoning.

pygmy *spell.* pigmy

pyjama *spell.* pajama

{**pyorrhoea** » **pyorrhoeal**} *spell.* {pyorrhea » pyorrheal}
Inflammation of the gums and loosening of the teeth.

Pyrex *pr. name (TM)* heat-resistant glass cookware

pyrolyse *spell.* pyrolyze
Chemical change caused by heat.

pyrosulphate *spell.* pyrosulfate
A chemical.

QARANC *pr. name, abbr.* the Queen Alexandra's Royal Army Nursing Corps

QARNNS *pr. name, abbr.* the Queen Alexandra's Royal Naval Nursing Service

QBI *idiom, abbr., arch., sl.* quite ➡bloody impossible
This expression began life as an ➡RAF World War II description of severe flying conditions.

Q-car *noun, coll., out.* an unmarked police car crewed by officers in civilian clothing

quack *noun, sl.* a medical practitioner

quadrillion *noun, num.* a septillion, or 10^{24}
The American quadrillion is 10^{15}.

the **Quaestor** *pr. name, Lat., Sc.* the chief financial officer at ➡St Andrew's University
From the Latin for "seeker"

quaff *verb, out.* to drink deeply or to gulp

quaggy *adj., coll.* shakily or difficult

quagmire [A] *noun* soft and yielding ground
Such as that found in a bog, marsh or ➡fen.
[B] *noun, coll.* a tricky situation or predicament, which it is difficult to get out of

quahog *spell.* quahaug
An edible clam.

quaich *noun, Sc.* a small two-handled drinking cup
Originally made of wood and practical, it is now usually of pewter or silver, and entirely ornamental.

quango *noun, abbr.* a quasi-autonomous non-governmental organization
A semi-independent organization mainly funded by the government, is concerned with a matter of public interest, and whose senior appointments are made by the government.

quant *noun, East* a pole used to propel a punt with
Used on the ➡Broads of ➡Norfolk. It is equipped with a projection to prevent it from becoming stuck in mud.

quantity surveyor *comp. noun* one who estimates the quantities of materials and costs involved in erecting buildings and other structures, and later, from inspection and measurement of the actual structure, the payment contractors are entitled to receive for their work.

quare *adj, Ir.* strange or unusual

quare impedit *comp. noun, Lat.* a writ issued against an objector when there is a disputed presentation in benefice
Meaning, in Latin, "why does he hinder?"

{**quarrelled » quarrelling**} *spell.* {quarreled » quarreling}

quarter [A] *noun* (1) eight bushels of grain; (2) one quarter of a ➡hundredweight, which is to say 28 pounds or two ➡stones (1)
[B] *verb, hist.* to divide a body into four parts following its death by hanging
For fuller details, see ➡hang, draw and quarter.

quarter-bloke *comp. noun, sl.* a quartermaster

quarter-day *comp. noun, hist.* a day upon which quarterly payments fall due, legal contracts come into force or cease to be enforced, etc.
In England, Wales and Northern Ireland they are:
Lady Day, March 25 *(formerly April 6)*
Midsummer Day, June 24 *(formerly July 6)*
Michaelmas, September 29 *(formerly October)*
Christmas, December 25 *(formerly January 6)*
In Scotland, quarter-days are called ➡term-days, and fall upon different dates.

quarter-light *comp. noun* a side window of a car, other than the main door window

quartermaster sergeant *comp. noun* a non-commissioned officer in the British Army
Equivalent in rank to a technical sergeant in the U.S. Army.

quartern *noun, arch.* a quarter of a pint

quartern loaf *comp. noun, arch.* a 4-lb loaf of bread

quarters *noun* the hindquarters of an animal

quarter sessions *comp. noun, arch.* a civil and criminal court that was formerly held quarterly at various locations around England and Wales
Replaced by the ➡Crown Court system in 1970.

quattuordecillion *noun, num.* 10^{84}
The American quattuordecillion is 10^{45}.

quaver *noun, pref.* an eighth note
A musical term.

Queen-Anne

Queen-Anne *comp. noun* the styles of architecture and furniture of the time of ➡Anne

Queen Anne is dead *idiom, coll.* that's very old news

queen cake *comp. noun* a soft cake containing raisins

Queen Dowager *comp. noun* the widow of a king

Queen Elizabeth Hall *pr. name* a concert hall in London's ➡South Bank Complex

Queen Mary and Westfield College *pr. name* a school of ➡London University founded in 1882

Queen Mary's Dolls House *pr. name, hist.* an exquisitely detailed doll house, down to the last item such as miniature bottles of wine, books, paintings upon the walls, and so forth
A present by the nation to Queen Mary, wife of King ➡George V, in 1924. It is now kept at ➡Windsor Castle.

Queen Mother *comp. noun* a ➡Queen Dowager who is mother of a reigning monarch

Queen of the May *pr. name* a girl chosen to preside over celebrations on May Day in a rural village
She was often called ➡Maid Marion in the 16th and 17th Cs.

the Queen of the South *pr. name* ➡Dumfries

Queen Regnant *comp. noun* a queen reigning in her own right rather than as the wife of a king

the Queen's Award for Export Achievement *pr. name* an award given to British companies making a significant proportion of their sales as exports
Established in 1976 in partial replacement of the former ➡Queen's Award to Industry established since 1965.

the Queen's Award for Technological Achievement *pr. name* an award given to British companies making significant technical advances
Established in 1976 in partial replacement of the former ➡Queen's Award to Industry established since 1965.

the Queen's Award to Industry *pr. name* an award given to British companies making outstanding technical and exporting achievements
Established in 1965, replaced in 1976 by the ➡Queen's Award for Export Achievement and the ➡Queen's Award for Technological Achievement.

the Queen's Bays *pr. name* a nickname for the 2nd Dragoon Guards
A unit of the British Army called this because of the bay-colored horses they rode from 1767 while other cavalry regiments had black ones.

the Queen's Beasts *pr. name, hist.* ten sculptures with an heraldic theme, located in ➡Kew Gardens
They illustrate the ancestry of ➡Elizabeth II of England and I of Scotland, and were first seen in public outside ➡Westminster Abbey in 1953 at the time of her coronation.
SEE ALSO: ➡King's Beasts.

the Queensberry Rules *pr. name* the rules of boxing
Initiated by the Marquis of Queensberry in 1867.

the Queen's Club *pr. name* an exclusive sports club in west London
Founded in 1886, the club provides facilities for playing real tennis, lawn tennis and rackets.

Queen's College *pr. name* (1) a college of ➡Oxford University founded in 1340; (2) a college of ➡Cambridge University founded in 1448

the Queen's Gallery *pr. name* an art gallery inside ➡Buckingham Palace
It contains a selection of paintings and other works from the royal collection, and is open to the public.

the Queen's House *pr. name, hist.* Britain's first Palladian building, designed for Anne, wife of ➡James I of England and VI of Scotland, but finished for Henrietta Maria, wife of ➡Charles I
Now part of the complex of buildings at ➡Greenwich, including the original ➡Royal Observatory and the ➡Royal Naval College, occupying the site of the former royal palace that once stood there.
Today it is the home of the ➡National Maritime Museum.

Queen Street Station *pr. name* a principal railroad terminus in central ➡Glasgow
For trains to and from eastern and northern Scotland.

queer *noun, sl.* (1) drunk; (2) unwell, faint or giddy

queer roll *phr. verb, sl.* to rob a homosexual

queer the pitch *idiom. phr. verb, sl.* to secretly spoil or ruin an opportunity

question master *comp. noun* a quiz game host

question time *pr. name* time set aside in the ➡House of Commons when ➡backbenchers and members of the ➡Shadow Cabinet may question members of the government, including the ➡Prime Minister, about the business of their departments
One hour, from 2:30 to 3:30 p.m., is set aside for questions every Monday, Tuesday, Wednesday, and Thursday while the ➡House is in session.
Questions to the Prime Minister are usually answered every Tuesday and Thursday between 3:15 and 3:30 p.m.
The reality is that the majority of questions are presented beforehand in writing and answered in the same manner, so that what is seen in the ➡Chamber of the ➡House represents just the tip of the iceberg.

queue [A] *noun, pref.* people or vehicles waiting in line [B] *verb, pref.* to wait in line

queue jump *phr. verb, coll.* to move in front of those waiting in line

queue up *verb, pref.* to form a line

quick off the mark *idiom* quick starting or reacting

quickset *noun* a hedge consisting of transplanted plant cuttings, particularly hawthorn

quid *noun, sl.* one ➡Pound Sterling

quids in *idiom, sl.* (1) going well; (2) making a profit

quieten down *verb* to become quiet or quieter

quiff [A] *noun* a tuft of hair across the forehead

[B] *noun, derog., sl.* a male homosexual

[C] *noun, sl.* a clever trick

This is naval slang.

quill driver *comp. noun, out.* (1) a clerk; (2) a hack writer

quin *noun, abbr.* a quintuplet

quine *noun, Sc.* (1) a daughter; (2) a young girl; (3) an unmarried woman; (4) a female servant; (5) a bold woman or hussy; (6) a mistress or concubine

quindecillion *noun, num.* 10^{90}

The American quindecillion is 10^{48} .

quint *noun* a sequence of five cards from the same suit

quintillion *noun, num.* a nontillion, or 10^{30}

The American quintillion is 10^{18}.

quite a lad *idiom, coll.* a spirited young man

quite so *idiom, coll.* (1) it is agreed; (2) that is true

quod *noun, sl.* prison

quorate *adj.* with a quorum attending

Quorn *pr. name (TM)* a kind of textured vegetable protein extracted from edible fungus

Named after the small ➡Leicester village of Quorn. The product is popular with vegetarians.

quote *verb* to state a price or a cost estimate

R *noun, abbr.* (1) ➡Railway; (2) ➡Royal; (3) ➡*Rex*; (4) ➡*Regina*

(3) or (4) are the full versions of the alternate final parts of a shortened form of the royal signature used on state documents, coinage, etc., which is an abbreviation of either ➡*Rex* or ➡*Regina* as appropriate, attached to the royal signature after a Latinized version of the monarch's given name.

For example, Queen ➡Elizabeth would sign herself as *Elizabetha R* on such a document.

R&A *pr. name, abbr.* the ➡Royal and Ancient Golf Club

ra *adj., adv., Sc., sl.* the; the definite article

RA [A] *pr. name, abbr.* (1) the ➡Royal Academy of Arts; (2) the Ramblers' Association; (3) the Royal Artillery
[B] *noun, abbr.* a Royal Academician
Which is to say, a member of [A](1).

rabbit [A] *noun* a novice or poor game player
[B] *noun, rh. sl.* inconsequential chatter
Derivation: chatter > talk > rabbit and pork > rabbit.
[C] *verb, sl.* to borrow but fail to return
Navy slang.

rabbit {away » on} *phr. verb, sl.* to talk or chatter at length without purpose or to come to the point
SEE ALSO: ➡rabbit [B].

RAC *pr. name, abbr.* (1) the Royal Automobile Club; (2) the ➡Royal Armoured Corps

racecard *noun* a schedule of planned races

racecourse *noun* a racetrack

racegoer *noun* someone who goes to races

race meeting *comp. noun* a gathering for the purpose of conducting a series of races

Rachmanism *noun* the exploitation of slum tenants by an unscrupulous landlord
From the name of a notorious landlord in 1960s London.

rack off *verb* to draw off the dregs from a bottle or barrel of wine or beer, etc.

rack rent *comp. noun* the highest possible rent that can be extracted from a property

rackwheel *noun* a cogwheel

racoon *spell.* raccoon

racquets *noun* the game of racquetball

RADA *pr. name, abbr.* Royal Academy of Dramatic Art
Founded in 1904 at His Majesty's Theatre and moved to its own site in London in 1905.

RADC *pr. name, abbr.* the Royal Army Dental Corps

the Radcliffe Library *pr. name* a library in ➡Oxford
Founded with a bequest from Dr. Radcliffe early in the 18th C.

Radical *pr. name, hist.* a label first applied to 19th C. ultra-liberals who in large measure drew their inspiration from the French Revolution

Radio 1 *pr. name* a national ➡BBC radio station
It specializes in pop/rock.

Radio 2 *pr. name* a national ➡BBC radio station
It specializes in golden oldies, easy listening and popular entertainment. Prior to 1967, it was called the ➡Light Programme.

Radio 3 *pr. name* a national ➡BBC radio station
It specializes in intellectual material such as classical and avant-garde music, drama, literature, academic lectures and discussions. Prior to 1967, it was called the ➡Third Programme.

Radio 4 *pr. name* a national ➡BBC radio station
It specializes in news, current affairs, middle-weight plays and discussions. Prior to 1967, it was called the ➡Home Service.

Radio 5 Alive *pr. name* a national ➡BBC radio station
It specializes in continuous sports and news coverage.

the Radio Authority *pr. name* an agency responsible for the licensing and supervising of all British radio transmissions except those of the ➡BBC.
Successor to the ➡ITC.

radiogram *noun, arch.* a radio and record player combined into a single unit

Radley College *pr. name* one of the leading English ➡public schools
Founded in 1847, it is located in ➡Oxfordshire.

Radnorshire *pr. name, hist.* a former Welsh County, now part of ➡Powys

RAF *pr. name, abbr.* the ➡Royal Air Force

RAF Germany *pr. name* those ➡RAF units based in Germany and responsible for tactical air support in the Central Region of NATO

the RAF Museum *pr. name, abbr.* the ➡Royal Air Force Museum

RAFVR *pr. name, abbr.* the ➧Royal Air Force Volunteer Reserve

rag *noun, coll.* a rowdy celebration

rag and bone man *comp. noun* a traveling dealer in old clothes, household goods, etc.

rag day *comp. noun, coll.* the one day each year when students dress up in unusual costumes and perform street entertainments and stunts in order to raise money for charity

ragged school *comp. noun, arch.* a kind of free school once operated as a charity for poor children

Raglan sleeve *comp. noun* a sleeve cut all the way up to the neckline without shoulder seams
A design originated by British Field Marshal Lord Raglan.

rag paper *comp. noun* paper made from rags

Railcard *pr. name (TM)* a card sold by ➧British Rail entitling the owner to reduced-cost rail travel

railman *noun* a ➧railwayman

RailTrack *pr. name (TM)* a company that maintains and operates all railroad tracks owned by British Rail, and upon which all other British railroad companies operate their trains
It is part of ➧British Rail.

railway *noun, pref.* a railroad
An interesting example of apparent transatlantic word transposition—in the earliest references to this new means of transportation, early 19th C. Britons most commonly used the word "railroad" while their American contemporaries apparently preferred "railway."

railway {carriage » coach} *comp. noun* a railroad passenger car

railway halt *comp. noun* a railroad flag stop or way station

railway line *comp. noun* a railroad track

railwayman *noun* a railroad employee

railway marshalling yard *comp. noun* a railroad switching yard

railway station *comp. noun, pref.* a railroad depot or train station

rain off *verb* to rain out

rain stair-rods *idiom. phr. verb* to rain very heavily

raise the wind *idiom. phr. verb, coll.* to raise money required for a particular purpose

raising agent *comp. noun* a leavening agent, such as yeast or baking powder, when used in baking

the **Raj** *pr. name, Hindi, hist.* British rule in India
From the Hindi word *raja* = "king."

rake's progress *comp. noun* a steady decline from prosperity and happiness to poverty, misery and ruin due to excessive indulgence in various vices
From a series of 18th C. engravings by Hogarth, called by this name and illustrating how such a fall can happen.

RAM *pr. name, abbr.* the ➧Royal Academy of Music

RAMC *pr. name, abbr.* the Royal Army Medical Corps

Rameses *pr. name, spell.* Ramses
There were 11 ancient Egyptian Pharaohs with this name.

rammy *noun, Sc.* (1) a free-for-all; (2) a fight

ramp [A] *noun* a speed bump
[B] *verb* to swindle or cheat
Particularly when done by charging extremely high prices.

rampant *adj.* in heraldry, raised up upon hind legs with face in profile, indicative of magnanimity

rampant gardant *adj.* in heraldry, raised up upon hind legs with a full face, indicative of prudence

rampant regardant *adj.* in heraldry, raised up upon hind legs with a rearward-looking face, indicative of circumspection

ram-raid *comp. noun, sl.* a ➧smash-and-grab robbery where access is made into a store by ramming into its front with a vehicle

ramstam *adj., Sc.* headstrong or rash

rancour *spell.* rancor

randan *noun, sl.* a spree

randem *noun, out.* a carriage driven by three horses harnessed in tandem

randie [A] *adj., Sc.* (1) aggressive; (2) boisterous or wild; (3) coarse or obscene
(3) refers especially to language.
[B] *noun, Sc.* (1) a frolic; (2) a loud-mouthed or bad-tempered woman; (3) a slut; (4) an offensive beggar

randy *adj.* (1) lusty or eagerly promiscuous; (2) sexually boastful

range *verb* to justify text
A term used by printers.

ranger *noun* (1) a keeper of a ➧royal, ➧national or ➧forest park; (2) a senior ➧girl guide

rant *noun, Sc.* a boisterous good time

RAOC *pr. name, abbr.* the Royal Army Ordnance Corps

rap *noun, arch., Ir.* a counterfeit Irish ➧halfpenny

RAPC *pr. name, abbr.* the Royal Army Pay Corps

rape *noun, hist.* one of the ancient divisions of ➧Sussex

rapparee *noun, hist., Ir.* a 17th C. freebooter or bandit

{rappelled » rappelling} *spell.* {rappeled » rappeling}

rare tear *idiom, Sc.* a good time

RASC *pr. name, abbr.* the Royal Army Service Corps

rasher *noun* a thin slice of bacon

rat-arsed *adj., sl.* very drunk indeed

rateable *adj.* liable to pay ➧Rates

rateable value *comp. noun* the value of property or land, as assessed to determine what value of ➧Rates are to be paid by its owner

rate-cap *verb* to impose a maximum value at which ➧Rates may be assessed
A measure taken by the central government to control spending by local authorities.

rate of knots *idiom, coll.* a high speed

ratepayer *noun* a person or business that pays ➧Rates

the Rates *noun* a local property tax based on assessed values of property and land
Formerly it was assessed on all property, but now only on business property.

rather *exclam., out.* a strong expression of agreement

rating [A] *noun* the total sum to be collected in the form of ➧Rates each year within the territory of an individual ➧local authority
[B] *noun, abbr.* a ➧naval rating

ratted *adj., sl.* very drunk

RAVC *pr. name, abbr.* the Royal Army Veterinary Corps

rave *noun, abbr., sl.* a ➧rave-up

{ravelled » ravelling} *spell.* {raveled » raveling}

rave-up *comp. noun, sl.* a wild party

Rawlplug *pr. name (TM)* a masonry anchor bolt similar to a Mollybolt

Rayburn *pr. name (TM)* a cooking stove

razor-edge *noun, coll.* (1) a very sharp edge; (2) a critical situation; (3) a mountain ridge which forms a distinct dividing line; (4) a boundary line marking a sharp division

razor-edged *adj, coll.* sharp
Of a disagreement.

razor-slasher *comp. noun, sl.* a criminal who attacks with a straight razor

RCA *pr. name, abbr.* the Royal College of Arts

RCGP *pr. name, abbr.* the Royal College of General Practitioners

RCM *pr. name, abbr.* the ➧Royal College of Music

RCN *pr. name, abbr.* the Royal College of Nursing

RCO *pr. name, abbr.* the Royal College of Organists

RCOG *pr. name, abbr.* the Royal College of Obstetricians and Gynaecologists

RCP *pr. name, abbr.* (1) the Royal College of Pathologists; (2) the Royal College of Physicians; (3) the Royal College of Psychiatrists

RCPSG *pr. name, abbr.* the Royal College of Physicians and Surgeons of Glasgow

RCR *pr. name, abbr.* the Royal College of Radiologists

RCS *pr. name, abbr.* (1) the Royal College of Science; (2) the Royal College of Surgeons; (3) the Royal Corps of Signals

RCST *pr. name, abbr., hist.* the Royal College of Science and Technology
Now the University of Strathclyde, in ➧Glasgow

RCSE *pr. name, abbr.* the Royal College of Surgeons of Edinburgh

RCVS *pr. name, abbr.* the Royal College of Veterinary Surgeons

RD [A] *idiom, abbr.* ➧refer to drawer
[B] *noun, abbr.* the Decoration for Officers of the ➧Royal Naval Reserve

RDC *noun, abbr., arch.* a ➧Rural District Council

RE [A] *noun, abbr.* Religious Education
The teaching of religion as a topic at school. *SEE ALSO:* RI.
[B] *pr. name, abbr.* (1) the ➧Royal Engineers; (2) the Royal Society of Painter-Etchers and Engravers

reach-me-down *idiom, sl.* (1) hand-me-down; (2) ready-made
Typically, of clothes.

read *noun* a period of time spent reading

read and write *phr. verb, rh. sl.* to fight

reader *noun* a university teacher approximately equivalent to a professor in the United States
SEE ALSO: ➧lecturer, ➧professor and ➧senior lecturer.

reader's ticket *comp. noun* a certificate or token signifying right of access to a particular library

the readies *noun, abbr., sl.* cash or ready money

Reading *pr. name* a town that is the administrative center of ➧Berkshire
A great Benedictine abbey, founded there in 1121 but now almost entirely destroyed, was the institution which made Reading a place of significance in medieval times. The current population, including suburbs, is 210,000 (1988 estimate).

reading age *comp. noun* the mental age of an individual expressed in terms of reading ability

reading room *comp. noun* a room in a library or similar, set aside for the purpose of reading

ready money *comp. noun* cash, or money in any form that is available for immediate use

ready-reckoner *comp. noun, arch.* a book containing tables listing the detailed results of frequently required arithmetic calculations, particularly the sort regularly used in business
These books virtually disappeared overnight after the introduction of the pocket calculator.

ready, steady, go *imper., coll.* ready, set, go

reaforestation *noun* reforestation

real ale *comp. noun* a draft beer that has been brewed and served in the traditional manner

really *adv., coll.* real

In, for example, "This is really good" = "This is real good."

real money *comp. noun, coll.* actual physical ➡banknotes or cash

---

real tennis *comp. noun* the original form of the modern game of tennis

Here, "real" means "royal." Believed to have originated in medieval monastaries, it had graduated to become the sport of kings by the 15th C., hence this name. The game is played in a four-walled indoor court with a hard ball, and is still played that way today at, for example, the ➡Queen's Club in London.

---

rear [A] *noun, sl.* institutional latrines

Possibly this refers to their traditional location within or behind a building such as a school or college.

[B] *verb* to care for, nurture and educate a child

rear-commodore *comp. noun* a yacht club official

{rebelled » rebelling} *spell.* {rebeled » rebeling}

recce *noun, abbr., out.* reconnaissance

received pronunciation *comp. noun* the form of spoken English which is most common among educated people in southern England

SEE ALSO: ➡received standard English, ➡BBC English, ➡Oxford English, ➡King's English.

received standard English *comp. noun* the form of written or spoken English common among educated people in southern England

SEE ALSO: ➡received pronunciation, ➡BBC English, ➡Oxford English, ➡King's English.

receiving order *comp. noun* a court direction instructing the appointment of an official receiver

reception *noun* the front desk of an hotel

reception order *comp. noun* a legal authority issued by a court placing a patient in a mental hospital

reception room *comp. noun* a room suitable for receiving visitors or guests

recess [A] *noun* a temporary closure of Parliament

Such as happens every year during the period of the summer vacation, and other times.

[B] *noun, sl.* a prison toilet

{reconnoitre » reconnoitrer} *spell.* {reconnoiter » reconnoiterer}

recorded delivery *comp. noun* certified mail

recorder *noun* (1) the principal magistrate in some English cities; (2) a senior lawyer appointed to act

as part-time judge; (3) a ➡County Court judge in ➡Northern Ireland

recreation ground *comp. noun* public land set aside for sports, games and other outdoor recreations

rector [A] *noun* a clergyman in charge of a ➡Church of England parish and receiving the full attached income

[B] *noun, Sc.* a school principal

rectorial *noun, Sc.* the election of a Scottish university's ➡Lord Rector

rectory *noun* the benefice and residence of a ➡rector of the ➡Church of England

recusancy *noun, hist.* a refusal by a Roman Catholic to attend a ➡Church of England service

Failure to attend church on Sunday was a statutory offense in England from 1570 to 1791.

recusant *noun* someone who refuses to submit to authority or obey regulations

the **Red Arrows** *pr. name* the ➡RAF aerobatics team

Formed in 1965. Unsurprisingly, they fly red aircraft.

red-arse *comp. noun, sl.* a new recruit to the army

red biddy *comp. noun, sl.* a mixture of denatured alcohol and cheap wine

Redbreast *noun, hist., sl.* a ➡Bow Street Runner

From the bright red waistcoat that was the outstanding feature of their uniform.

redbrick *adj., coll.* a mildly pejorative term sometimes applied to any English university founded more recently than ➡Oxford or ➡Cambridge, but especially one founded in the 19th C.

They are called this name because in so many cases their buildings were built in the Gothic revival style popular at that time, but using red bricks. The universities to whom the name could most aptly be applied are ➡Birmingham, ➡Bristol, ➡Leeds, ➡Liverpool, ➡Manchester, ➡Reading and ➡Sheffield. The Universities of ➡London and ➡Durham, also founded in the 19th C., are not considered part of this group.

Redbridge *pr. name* a ➡Greater London borough

Its current population, which is also included within the ➡London urban area total, is 220,000 (1991 Census).

redcap *noun* a military policeman

From the color of their caps.

redcoat [A] *noun, coll.* a steward at one of ➡Butlins' ➡holiday camps

From the distinctive color of his or her uniform clothing.

[B] *noun, arch., hist.* a British soldier

From the scarlet color of many regimental uniforms, which originated with the ➡New Model Army and only began to be phased out in favor of khaki in the final years of the 19th C.

the **Red Devils** *pr. name* nicknames for (1) the army skydiving display team; (2) the ➡Parachute Regiment

From the color of their caps.

red {duster » ensign} *comp. noun* the ensign flag of the ➡Merchant Navy the **Red Feathers** *pr. name* a nickname for the 46th Regiment of ➡Foot

A unit of the British Army who, during the Revolutionary War, participated in the defeat of the Continental Army at Brandywine in 1777. When the Americans promised revenge, the 46th, in an act of bravado, dyed their cap feathers red to make themselves easier to identify.

red fox *comp. noun* a fox native to the British Isles

Its formal name is *vulpes vulpes.*

redgum *noun* a gum rash that infects teething infants

the **Red Hand** *pr. name, abbr.* the ➡Red Hand of Ulster

the **Red Hand of Ulster** *pr. name, hist.* a red right hand held upright with fingers clenched together

The symbol of the O'Neill family and of ➡Ulster.

redhat *noun, sl.* a military staff officer

red horse *comp. noun, arch., sl.* ➡corned beef

Military slang.

{**redialled » redialling**} *spell.* {redialed » redialing}

red lead *comp. noun, arch., sl.* canned tomatoes

Military slang.

red rag *comp. noun, sl.* an object or idea that infuriates

In the way that a red cloth allegedly enrages a bull.

red ribbon *comp. noun* a ribbon worn by a member of the Order of the ➡Bath

red rose *comp. noun, hist.* (1) the emblem of the House of ➡Lancaster; (2) the emblem of the County of ➡Lancashire

red squirrel *comp. noun* a variety of squirrel native to the British Isles

Its formal name is *sciurus vulgaris,* not *sciurus hudsonicus,* which is native to North America.

red 'un *comp. noun, arch., sl.* a ➡sovereign coin

redundancy *noun* (1) dismissal from a job that is no longer required; (2) unemployment

redundancy payment *comp. noun* payment made by an employer to compensate for a job layoff

redundant *adj.* (1) no longer required for work; (2) unemployed

reed *noun* straw which has been prepared from wheat to be used in thatching

reedmace *noun* cattail

Its formal name is *typha latifolia,* and it is a tall water plant used for making matting, etc. *SEE ALSO:* bulrush.

reefer *noun, out.* a midshipman

A reef is one of a number of strips that a ship's sail is or was made up of, and originally a reefer was a member of a ship's crew who took in or shortened its sails.

reefing jacket *comp. noun* a close-fitting, thick-clothed, double-breasted jacket

reef knot *comp. noun* a square knot

reef-point *comp. noun* a short length of rope attached to a sail to secure it when reefed

reek *noun, Sc.* smoke

reel [A] *noun* a bobbin or spool used for thread

[B] *noun, Sc.* (1) a lively ➡Highland dance for two, three or four couples; (2) the music for (1)

reest *verb, Sc.* to balk

reeve *noun, hist.* (1) the local agent of an ➡Anglo-Saxon king; (2) the manorial magistrate responsible for ensuring that ➡villeins discharged their feudal obligations

referee *noun* a person testifying to the ability or character of an applicant, usually for employment

refer to drawer *idiom* a banker's note of refusal to honor a check

reflexion *spell.* reflection

Reform Club *pr. name, hist.* a leading ➡Liberal club in ➡St James's, London

Founded in 1832 by ➡Whig supporters of the ➡Great Reform Act of that year.

reform school *comp. noun* a reformatory

refresher *noun* additional fees paid to a ➡barrister when a case takes longer than originally expected

refreshment room *comp. noun* a restaurant at a rail or bus terminal

{**refuelled » refuelling**} *spell.* {refueled » refueling}

refuse bin *comp. noun* a trashcan

refuse collection vehicle *comp. noun* a garbage truck

refuse collector *comp. noun* a garbage collector

regardant *adj.* in heraldry, looking backwards

Emblematic of circumspection.

the **Regency** *pr. name* the period from 1811 to 1820

When George, ➡Prince of Wales—later ➡George IV—acted as ➡regent during the insanity of his father, ➡George III.

Regency style *comp. noun* styles of architecture and furniture from the time of the ➡Regency

regent *noun* one who acts in the place of a monarch

the **Regent House** *pr. name* the general assembly of senior resident members of ➡Cambridge University

Regent's Park *pr. name* a ➡royal park just to the north of central London

The centerpiece of the ➡Prince Regent's project to develop west-central London in the 1810s, it extends over an area of 488 acres that had been a royal hunting park since the ➡dissolution of the monasteries in the 16th C. It contains the London Zoological Gardens.

Regent's Park Hall *pr. name* a hall of ➡Oxford University founded in 1810

Regent Street *pr. name* a principal London street
Construction began in 1813, during the ➡Regency and upon the ➡Prince Regent's personal initiative. It proceeds north through what is now called the ➡West End of London from the Prince's home at Carlton House, to ➡Regent's Park.

regicide *noun* (1) the crime of murdering a king; (2) someone who commits (1)

the **Regicides** *pr. name, hist.* those responsible for the execution of ➡Charles I in 1649

regimental colours *comp. noun* the ➡{King's » Queen's} Colours

regimental sergeant-major *noun* a warrant officer in the British Army
He normally assists the regimental adjutant and is equivalent in rank to a sergeant-major in the U.S. Army.

regiment of foot *comp. noun, arch.* an infantry regiment

Regina *noun, Lat.* a reigning queen
The Latin for "queen"

{*Regina* v. x … » *Rex* v. x …} *idiom* the form of title of the monarch as it appears in lawsuits when one party is the ➡Crown (and the other is x …)

Region *noun* the largest Scottish local government unit
Similar in scope and powers to an English county.

Regional Railways Cardiff Valleys *pr. name (TM)* a railroad company operating local services centered on ➡Cardiff in south Wales
It is part of ➡British Rail.

Regional Railways Central *pr. name (TM)* a railroad company operating local services in ➡Birmingham and central England
It is part of ➡British Rail.

Regional Railways North East *pr. name (TM)* a railroad company operating local services in northeastern England
It is part of ➡British Rail.

Regional Railways North West *pr. name (TM)* a railroad company operating local services to and from ➡Manchester
It is part of ➡British Rail.

Regional Railways South Wales and West *pr. name (TM)* a railroad company operating local services in southwestern England and south Wales
It is part of ➡British Rail.

Registered General Nurse *comp. noun, arch.* formerly, a ➡State Registered Nurse

registered post *comp. noun* registered mail

register office *comp. noun* a place where an official register of births, marriages and deaths are kept and civil marriages are performed

registrar *noun* (1) an administrative officer of the ➡High Court; (2) a hospital staff doctor authorized to admit new patients

Registrar General *pr. name* the government official who conducts regular population censuses

registrary *comp. noun* the official registrar of ➡Cambridge University

registration number *comp. noun* a vehicle license plate number

registry office *comp. noun* a ➡register office

regius *adj.* royal
Now only found in ➡Regius professor. SEE ALSO: ➡Rex

Regius professor *comp. noun* a professorial chair that was founded and funded by the monarch
Regius professorships are found only at the ancient universities of ➡Oxford and ➡Cambridge in England and ➡St Andrews, ➡Glasgow, ➡Aberdeen and ➡Edinburgh in Scotland

regnal year *comp. noun* a year numbering system that begins counting from zero afresh, every time a new ➡monarch comes to the thronen

regnant *adj.* reigning

reightsharp *adj., East* sane

reign *verb* to exercise royal office
To reign is not to rule. In Britain, the monarch reigns but does not rule. The people, through ➡Parliament, rule.

Reithian *adj.* characteristic of high-minded public service broadcasting in the manner of Lord Reith, first Director General of the ➡BBC

reive *verb, arch., Sc.* to rob or pillage

reiver *noun, arch., Sc.* a raider

{**relabelled** » **relabelling**} *spell.* {re-labeled » re-labeling}

relieving officer *comp. noun, arch.* an official once responsible for looking after poor or insane people who had nowhere else to turn for help

remand {**centre** » **home**} *comp. noun* an institution where people ➡on remand are held upon the authority of the court, while awaiting trial

REME *pr. name, abbr.* the Corps of Royal Electrical and Mechanical Engineers

Remembrance {**Day** » **Sunday**} *pr. name* the Sunday nearest November 11th, when the dead of two World Wars are honored
Similar to Veterans Day.

remembrancer *noun* a reminder or *aide mémoire*

remission *noun* a reduction in the duration of a prison term granted for good behavior

remittance man *comp. noun, hist.* one who has emigrated to a distant colony but remains dependent on money sent from home
The implication was that this was a worthless or idle person who has been bribed to go away.

{**remodelled** » **remodelling**} *spell.* {remodeled » remodeling}

remould [A] *noun* a re-treaded tire

[B] *spell.* remold

removal van *comp. noun* a moving van or truck

remove [A] *noun* a name for some classes or grades at certain schools

[B] *verb* to promote to a higher grade or class at certain schools

remover *noun* a house mover

removing cream *comp. noun* cleansing cream

Renfrewshire *pr. name, hist.* a former Scottish county, now part of ➡Strathclyde region

rent *noun, derog., sl.* (1) money acquired by criminal means; (2) money earned from homosexual prostitution

rent boy *comp. noun, sl.* a young male prostitute

renter [A] *noun* a distributor of movie films

[B] *noun, sl.* a ➡rent boy

rent service *comp. noun* the payment of rent in whole or part by personal service rather than money

repair engineer *comp. noun* a repairman

repertory theatre *spell.* repertory theater

report *verb* to announce to the ➡House of Commons that a committee has completed its deliberations upon a bill before the House

report stage *comp. noun* a debate on a bill before the ➡House of Commons after a committee has ➡reported upon it

{**reprogrammable » reprogramme**} *spell.* {reprogramable » reprogram}

{**reprogrammed » reprogramming**} *spell.* {reprogramed » reprograming}

the **Republic of Ireland** *pr. name* the 26 counties of ➡Ireland that became an independent ➡Dominion within the ➡Commonwealth in 1921

This name was adopted in 1949, when it became a republic and left the ➡Commonwealth. Previously, it had first been known as the ➡Irish Free State, and then from 1937 as ➡Eire.

require *verb* to be or to feel obliged

reservation *noun, abbr.* a ➡central reservation

reserved list *comp. noun* a list of retired naval officers who remain liable to be called back for service in the event of an emergency

reserved occupation *comp. noun, arch.* one that exempts a practitioner from military service

reserve price *comp. noun* a minimum or upset price for property on sale at an auction

reset *verb, Sc.* (1) to receive stolen goods for the purpose of resale; (2) to protect an enemy of the state or a fugitive from justice

Resident *pr. name, hist.* (1) a representative or agent of the British government in a semi-independent state or territory under British protection; (2) a representative or agent of the British Viceroy at the court of an Indian prince

Resident Commissioner *pr. name, hist.* an administrator of a district or region of a British colony or other territory under British protection

the **Resignation Honours** *pr. name* a special ➡honours list published only when a ➡prime minister resigns

resit *verb, coll.* to sit an examination again after failing to pass it previously

resurrection man *comp. noun, arch.* a resurrectionist, a body snatcher

the **rest** *noun* the reserve fund of a bank

the **Rest** *pr. name* the ➡rest of the ➡Bank of England

Restart *pr. name* a government project to get long-term unemployed people back to work

restaurant car *comp. noun* a railroad dining car

restbalk *noun* an unplowed ridge left between the furrows of a plowed field

resting *adj., coll.* what an actor calls unemployment

rest on one's oar *idiom. phr. verb* to lay on one's oar; to relax one's efforts

---

the **Restoration** *pr. name, hist.* the re-establishment of the monarchy under ➡Charles II in 1660

Which came about following the failure and growing unpopularity of the republican government of the ➡Commonwealth under the increasingly dictatorial and chaotic ➡Protectorate of ➡Cromwell's son Richard. Eventually, General Monck forced the issue by marching upon London at the head of an army, and Parliament, accepting that the republic had failed and Charles II should rule, proclaimed him king in 1660. However, constitutional matters were not really resolved until the ➡Glorious Revolution, 28 years later in 1688.

Charles II

restricted area *comp. noun* an area where an especially low or unusual speed limit is imposed on traffic

restrictive practice *comp. noun* a formal or informal arrangement made between the practitioners of a particular trade or profession for the purpose of restricting output or avoiding competition between each other

retail price index *pr. name* the consumer price index

retainer *noun* reduced rent paid on unoccupied property
Paid to preempt it from being rented to others.

retiral *noun, Sc.* retirement from work or elected office

retire *verb* to voluntarily terminate a ➡cricket ➡innings as ➡batsman without being got out

retirement pension *comp. noun* an ➡old age pension

return [A] *noun* (1) the re-election of an ➡MP; (2) the election of an ➡MP for the first time; (3) an official announcement or declaration of (1) or (2); (4) a formal report by a ➡sheriff on the progress of a writ
[B] *noun, abbr.* a ➡return ticket

returning officer *comp. noun* an official responsible for supervising an election and declaring the result

return ticket *comp. noun* a round-trip ticket for a journey by bus, train, plane, etc.

return to office *verb* to elect to a public office

Reuters *pr. name, (TM)* a major news agency
Established in 1851 by Julius Reuter, a German immigrant.

{**revelled » revelling**} *spell.* {reveled » reveling}

revenue officer *comp. noun* an official charged with enforcing the collection of duties and taxes

reverse *verb* to back up a vehicle

reverse charge call *comp. noun* a collect phone call

reverse {**charges » the charges**} *phr. verb, pref.* to call collect by telephone

reversing light *comp. noun* a vehicle back-up light

revise *verb* to review in order to improve understanding or knowledge
Especially in order to perform well at an examination.

the **Revised Version** *pr. name, hist.* a revision of the ➡King James ➡Authorized Version of the Bible published in Britain between 1881 and 1885

revivor *noun* a procedure to revive a legal suit after the death of one of the parties to it

the **Revolution of 1688** *pr. name, hist.* an alternate name for the ➡Glorious Revolution

Rewley House *pr. name* a college of ➡Oxford University founded in 1990

Rex noun, Lat. a reigning king
The Latin for "king." *SEE ALSO:* ➡regius.w

RFA *noun, abbr.* a Royal Fleet Auxiliary
A ship providing support services to the Royal Navy.

RFC [A] *noun, abbr.* a ➡Rugby Football Club
[B] *pr. name, abbr., hist.* the ➡Royal Flying Corps

RGN *noun, abbr., arch.* a ➡Registered General Nurse

RGS *pr. name, abbr.* the ➡Royal Geographical Society

RHA *pr. name, abbr.* the Royal Horse Artillery

Rhenish [A] *adj.* of or relating to the Rhine River and the region surrounding it in Germany
[B] *noun* Rhine wine

RHG *pr. name, abbr.* the Royal Horse Guards

Rhodes scholar *comp. noun* the holder of a ➡Rhodes Scholarship

the **Rhodes Scholarships** *pr. name* scholarships paid annually to a limited number of students from the United States, various Commonwealth countries, and Germany, so that they may study at ➡Oxford University for two or three years
Named after the founder, Cecil Rhodes, an imperialist, business magnate, and politician who was born in Britain but made his career and his fortune largely in southern Africa. He died in 1902. The money for the scholarships was provided under the terms of his will.

the **Rhondda Valley** *pr. name, hist.* an area in ➡Mid Glamorgan, ➡South Wales, which came to symbolize the Welsh coal-mining industry
Coal was first mined in the Rhondda in the early years of the 19th C. and both coal production and population peaked in the early years of the 20th C. The last coal was mined there in 1990.

RHS *pr. name, abbr.* (1) the Royal Historical Society; (2) the ➡Royal Horticultural Society; (3) the Royal Humane Society

rhyne *noun, arch.* a wide and open ditch

RI [A] *noun, abbr., out.* Religious Instruction
The teaching of religion as a school subject. *SEE ALSO:* RE.
[B] *pr. name, abbr.* (1) {*Rex et Imperator » Regina et Imperatrix*} (2) the Royal Institute of Painters in Water Colours; (3) the ➡Royal Institution
(1) is {King and Emperor » Queen and Empress} in Latin.

RIBA *pr. name, abbr.* Royal Institute of British Architects

RIC *pr. name, abbr.* the Royal Institute of Chemistry

Richard *Coeur de Lion* *pr. name, hist.* ➡Richard I

Richard I *pr. name, hist.* King of England
A member of the ➡Royal House of ➡Anjou, Richard grew up in Aquitaine, France, and spent a mere six months in England throughout his entire reign. Thus his link with England was about as little as he could get away with, except for going some considerable way towards ruining its finances in order first, to pay for the Third Crusade, in which he played a starring role, and second, to pay a huge ransom so that he could be released from captivity when he was taken prisoner on his way home from the Holy Land.

Yet somehow he became a hero, which is reflected in his nickname, ➡*Coeur de Lion* (➡Lionheart in French). He styled himself *Rex Angliae, Dux Normaniae et Aquitaniae et Comes Andigaviae* = "King of England, Duke of Normandy and Aquitane and Count of Anjou", and reigned from 1189 until 1199.

Richard II *pr. name, hist.* King of England

A member of the ➡Royal House of ➡Plantagenet, he was the son of the ➡Black Prince and succeeded his grandfather, ➡Edward III, to the throne when he was just 10 years old. He showed considerable courage and skill in facing down the ➡Peasants' Revolt when he was 14, and is considered to have created a cultured and civilized court around him. He foiled a plot against him led by his cousin Bolingbroke in 1387, whom he banished abroad the following year. Such mercy turned out to be a mistake when Bolingbroke returned with an army the year after that.

Richard styled himself *Dei Gratia Rex Angliae et Franciae et Dominus Hiberniae* = "By the Grace of God King of England and France and Lord of Ireland" and reigned for 22 years from 1377 until deposed and taken prisoner by Bolingbroke, who became ➡Henry IV in 1399. Richard died the following year. There is no proof that he was murdered, but is was certainly very convenient for all concerned, except of course for Richard himself.

Richard III *pr. name, hist.* King of England

A member of the ➡Royal House of ➡York, Richard styled himself *Dei Gratia Rex Angliae et Franciae et Dominus Hiberniae* = "By the Grace of God King of England and France and Lord of Ireland" and reigned for two years from 1483 until he was killed at the Battle of ➡Bosworth Field.

His reputation as an evil villain derives largely from the need of later Tudor monarchs to blacken the name of the monarch that the founder of their royal house, ➡Henry VII, had usurped, together with Shakespeare's willingness to play the part of Royal propagandist in his play *Richard III*. However, the real Richard was certainly no angel, and was almost without doubt responsible for the murder of the two young ➡Princes in the Tower.

Richmond *pr. name, hist.* a town in ➡North Yorkshire, best known for the ruined ➡Norman castle lying within it

The current population is 7,000 (1991 estimate).

Richmond Park *pr. name* a large ➡royal park southwest of London, in ➡Surrey

Richmond-upon-Thames *pr. name, hist.* a borough within ➡Greater London

The borough derives its name from the palace built there in 1499 by ➡Henry VII, who had previously been Earl of Richmond in ➡Yorkshire. Current population, also included within the ➡London urban area total, is 155,000 (1991 Census).

{**rick » wrick**} *verb* to sprain

rick in the back *comp. noun* a pain in the back

rickmatick *noun, Sc.* a collection or group of objects or people

The word is a corruption of "arithmetic."

RICS *pr. name, abbr.* the Royal Institute of ➡Chartered Surveyors

ride *noun, out.* a path, especially one through woods, which is suitable for horseback riding

rideable *spell.* ridable

rider *noun* (1) a comment, opinion, or recommendation added to the verdict of a court of law; (2) a supplement to a parliamentary bill added at its ➡third reading in the ➡Commons

Riding *noun, hist.* one of the three historic divisions of the counties of ➡Yorkshire and ➡Lincolnshire

Originally the word was "thriding", which is more obviously related to "third"; it seems the initial "th" got lost over the years. The divisions of Yorkshire were called this because they were each a third part of the county: ➡East Riding, ➡North Riding and ➡West Riding. Once, the three divisions of ➡Lincolnshire were also called "ridings".

Rievaulx Abbey *pr. name, hist.* a 12th C. Cistercian ➡abbey, now a ruin, 20 miles north of ➡York

rig *noun, Sc.* (1) a backbone; (2) a strip down the back of an animal; (3) the ridge of a roof; (4) a long narrow hill; (5) a narrow strip of land, suitable for plowing in one operation

right as ninepence *idiom, coll.* in perfect condition

right charlie *idiom, sl.* a complete fool

right down to the ground *idiom, coll.* complete in every last respect

right 'erbert *comp. noun, arch., sl.* a stupid, cheeky or objectionable person

SEE ALSO: ➡'erbert.

right-ho *exclam., coll., out.* a term of agreement

Right Honourable *pr. name* a courtesy title applied to certain people of high rank

Those who have the ranks of ➡Earl; ➡Viscount; ➡Baron; are ➡Privy Counsellors; ➡Lords Justice of Appeal; ➡Lord Mayors of ➡London, ➡York or ➡Belfast; or the ➡Lord Provosts of ➡Edinburgh or ➡Glasgow may expect this appellation.

right one *idiom, sl.* a foolish person

right shut *adj. phr., coll.* completely shut

For example, a door.

right smart *adj. phr., coll.* very clever

right up one's street *idiom, coll.* particularly attractive or suitable to or for one

Rigmarie *noun, hist., Sc.* a Scots coin of the reign of ➡Mary Queen of Scots

Its name derives from the Latin words *Reg. Marie* = "Queen Mary" that appeared as part of the legend upon it. *Reg.* is an abbreviation of ➡*Regina*; the coin was worth very little.

rigour *spell.* rigor

rigout *noun, sl.* a set of clothes

ring *verb* to call on the telephone

the ring *noun, coll.* bookmakers as a class

Ring-a-Ring-a-Roses

Ring-a-Ring-a-Roses *idiom Ring Around the Rosie*, the children's rhyme and game

The British name is probably somewhat closer to the original, which appears to have been *Ring of Roses*.

When it began, this song and game "celebrated" the dark purplish blotches called buboes from which bubonic plague takes it name. They are formed on the groin and neck due to subcutaneous hemorrhaging caused by the infection and might be said to resemble a ring that is composed of dark rose-like colors and shapes. These spots tended to be very dark by the time the victim had died, which was why this deadly disease, which first reached England in 1348, became known as the ➡Black Death.

Sneezing and crazed dancing (caused by neurological disorders) are other symptoms of the disease that were also worked into this charming little song, as is the result: falling down, which is to say, dropping dead. Which is exactly what about a quarter of Britain's population did in 1348.

ring back *verb, coll.* to return a telephone call

ring off *verb* to terminate a telephone call

ring road *comp. noun* a beltway or bypass road

ring through *verb, coll.* to call on the telephone

ring up *verb, coll.* to call on the telephone

RIO *pr. name, abbr.* the Royal Institute of Oil Painting

the **Riot Act** *pr. name, hist., out.* a law of 1715 under which people rioting were required to disperse within one hour of this Act being read to them by a magistrate, or automatically become guilty of a felony

This law was repealed in 1973.

Ripon *pr. name* a city in ➡North Yorkshire

A monastery was established here around 660, and the town was incorporated as a city in 886. The current population is 15,000 (1988 estimate).

ripping *adj., coll., out.* wonderful, fine or splendid

ripping yarn *idiom, out.* an enjoyable adventure tale

rise *noun* a raise in pay

rising damp *comp. noun* moisture which has been absorbed into a wall from the ground

rissole *noun* a sort of meat patty containing spices and crumbled bread, fried before being eaten

ritualisation *spell.* ritualization

{**rivalled » rivalling**} *spell.* {rivaled » rivaling}

River [A NOTE ON THE USE OF THIS WORD IN BRITISH ENGLISH.]
The word "River" is placed *before* the river name as in "River Thames", not *after* it as in "Hudson River".

River Ouze *idiom, rh. sl.* an alcoholic drink
Derivation: drink > booze > Ouze. The Ouse is a river in eastern England that flows into the ➡Wash.

RL *noun, abbr.* ➡Rugby League

RLPO *pr. name, abbr.* the Royal Liverpool Philharmonic Orchestra

RM *pr. name, abbr.* (1) the ➡Royal Mail; (2) the ➡Royal Marines

RMA *pr. name, abbr.* the ➡Royal Military Academy

RMS *noun, abbr.* (1) ➡Royal Mail Steamer; (2) the Royal Society of Miniature Painters

RMT *pr. name, abbr.* the National Union of Rail, Maritime and Transport Workers
A labor union for transport workers.

RN *pr. name, abbr.* the ➡Royal Navy

RN(V)R *pr. name, abbr.* Royal Naval (Volunteer) Reserve
Now the ➡RNR.

RNAS [A] *comp. noun, abbr.* a Royal Naval Air Station
[B] *pr. name, abbr., hist.* the Royal Naval Air Service

RNIB *pr. name, abbr.* the ➡Royal National Institute for the Blind

RNID *pr. name, abbr.* the ➡Royal National Institute for the Deaf

RNLI *pr. name, abbr.* the ➡Royal National Lifeboat Institution

RNR *pr. name, abbr.* the Royal Naval Reserve
Formerly the ➡RN(V)R

RNRD *pr. name, abbr.* Royal Naval Reserve Decoration

road *noun* an underground passageway in a mine

the **Road Fund** *pr. name, hist.* a fund established by the government from ➡vehicle excise tax revenue, for the purpose of constructing, maintaining and improving bridges, highways, etc.

In truth, this fund is now mythical, as revenue raised by the ➡vehicle excise tax just goes straight into general taxation along with all other revenue or taxation, and the money spent by the government on roads is about one quarter of what is collected in this way.

road fund licence *comp. noun* a certificate of payment of ➡vehicle excise tax, which must be displayed on any vehicle driving on the highway

roadholding *noun* an automobile's aptitude for remaining on the highway while being driven

roadman *noun* a highway repair man

road tax *comp. noun, coll.* the ➡vehicle excise tax

road up *comp. noun* highway under repair
A roadside warning sign.

road works *comp. noun* highway construction

roan *noun, Sc.* a rainwater gutter along a roof's eaves

roanpipe *noun, Sc.* a downspout

roast beef and Yorkshire pudding *comp. noun* an entrée considered the most traditionally English

Despite its name and reputation, this dish is actually French in origin. *SEE ALSO:* ➡Yorkshire pudding.

Robert I *pr. name, hist.* ➡King of Scots

His family name was originally "de Bruge" because they had come to Scotland from the city of Bruge in what is now Belgium. Robert was descended, through marriage, from ➡David I and although just one of 13 claimants to the Scottish throne, was crowned King of Scotland at ➡Scone in 1306 after murdering his chief rival, the Red Comyn, in a church in ➡Dumfries.

For the first eight years of his reign he fought a campaign to rid Scotland of its English occupiers which finally triumphed when ➡Edward II's army was routed at ➡Bannockburn, close by ➡Stirling Castle, in 1314. In all he reigned for 23 years until 1329, founding the ➡Royal House of ➡Bruce.

He is the great Scottish national hero-king, known best as ➡Robert the Bruce or more simply, just The ➡Bruce.

Robert II *pr. name, hist.* ➡King of Scots

The son of Marjorie, who was daughter of ➡Robert the Bruce, and Walter, hereditary holder of the title of Steward of Scotland, and thus founder of the ➡Royal House of ➡Stewart. He reigned for 19 years from 1371 until 1390.

Robert III *pr. name, hist.* ➡King of Scots

A member of the ➡Royal House of ➡Stewart, he reigned for 16 years from 1390 until 1406.

Robert the Bruce *pr. name, hist.* ➡Robert I, ➡King of Scots, as he is better known

robin *noun* the ➡robin redbreast

Robin Hood *pr. name, hist.* the traditional folk-hero outlaw of numerous English ballads and folktales

The earliest surviving mention of Robin Hood is to be found in Langland's *Piers Plowman* of 1377. A collection of Robin Hood ballads was published in 1489; there his adventures were set around Barnsdale in ➡Yorkshire rather than the more familiar ➡Sherwood Forest in ➡Nottinghamshire, which, together with his adversarial relationship with the Sheriff there, appears to be a later invention.

His name is now attached liberally to anyone who acts illegally but with good intent, especially if they steal from the rich and disburse part or (more improbably) all of their ill-gotten gains to the poor. However, there is no evidence that the original Robin Hood ever really existed.

---

robin redbreast *comp. noun* a popular name for the common European ➡robin

Its formal name is *erithacus rubeculs.*

A small brown bird, native to Europe, which is similar in appearance to but not the same as the red-breasted thrush *turdus migratorius*, popularly called a robin in North America.

Robinson College *pr. name* a college of ➡Cambridge University founded in 1977

ROC *pr. name, abbr. hist.* the Royal Observer Corps

A voluntary organization established in 1925 and granted the right to be called "Royal" in 1941. It tracked and identified enemy aircraft flying over Britain. During World War II 32,000 observers provided warnings of approaching enemy aircraft, supplimenting the rudimentary radar system of these times.

Rochester *pr. name* a city on the ➡Medway in ➡Kent

Founded by the Romans in the 1st C. as *Durobrivae*, this is an important river crossing. The ➡Norman castle and cathedral were began in the 11th C. and the town was incorporated as a city in 1189; the current population, including suburbs, is 245,000 (1988 estimate).

the Rock *pr. name, coll.* Gibraltar

The great rock at the southernmost tip of Spain, which has been a British possession since 1704, a status confirmed by the Treaty of Utrecht in 1713. The great strategic significance of Gibraltar is that it dominates and thus controls the narrow Straits of Gibraltar that is the only shipping passage between the Atlantic Ocean and Mediterranean Sea.

rockbed *noun* a hard, rocky bottom

rock cake *comp. noun* a cake containing dried fruit

It has a rugged texture somewhat resembling rock.

rockery *noun* a rock garden

rocket *noun, coll.* a strong reprimand

the Rocket *pr. name, hist.* an early steam-powered railroad locomotive built by Stevenson

Winner of the Rainhill Trials of 1829, set up to determine which was the most reliable and suitable locomotive to use on the soon-to-open ➡Liverpool and Manchester Railway.

rock of ages *idiom, rh. sl.* wages

rock salmon *comp. noun* any of a number of different species of fish, but usually dogfish and catfish

rod *noun, arch.* (1) a unit of length equal to 5.5 yards, 16.5 feet, one ➡pole, or one ➡perch; (2) a unit of area equal to 30.25 square yards, 272.25 square feet, or one ➡square perch

rodent officer *comp. noun* a rat catcher

rodham *noun* a raised footpath or roadway

One built on the dry bed of a river in the ➡East Anglian ➡fens.

rod in pickle *idiom, coll.* trouble in store

The expression is supposed to have arisen from the reputed habit in former times of storing rods in vinegar to make them more supple and thus more painful when applied to a guilty fundament as punishment.

Roedean School *pr. name* a leading English ➡public school for girls
Founded in 1885, it is located in ➡Brighton, East Sussex.

roger *verb, sl., taboo* to copulate

roil *spell.* rile

rolled gold *comp. noun* thin gold film
Made for its application upon other metal by rolling

rolled oats *comp. noun* husked and crushed oats

Roller *noun, abbr., sl.* a ➡Rolls-Royce automobile

rolling in it *idiom, coll.* having plenty of money

rolling press *comp. noun* a printing press with a revolving cylinder
Used by a copperplate printer.

rolling stone *comp. noun, coll.* a person who does not remain long at the same address, job, etc.

rollmop *noun* a rolled-up pickled herring

roll-neck *comp. noun* a turtlenecked garment

roll-on *comp. noun* (1) an elastic corset; (2) a deodorant applied to the skin with a rolling ball in the mouth of its container

roll-on roll-off *comp. noun* a vehicular ferry with large doors at both bow and stern, permitting vehicles to drive directly on board and ashore again at the end of the voyage

Rolls-Royce *pr. name (TM), hist.* bestknown as the manufacturers of automobiles that have a reputation for being the epitome of extravagance and luxury
Founded in 1904, the company has been involved in aviation as well as automobile from the start; indeed the design and manufacture of aircraft engines has always been by far the largest part of its business.

roly-poly pudding *comp. noun, coll.* a dessert consisting of a strip or sheet of suet pastry covered with jam or fruit, then rolled and baked or steamed

roman candle *comp. noun, sl.* the characteristic progress of a parachutist whose parachute fails to open

Romanes Lecture *pr. name* an annual lecture given at ➡Oxford University by an eminent authority upon a literary or scientific topic
Established in 1891 by C.J. Romanes.

Roman road *pr. name, hist.* one of the many roads built in Britain by the Romans when Britain was part of the Roman Empire from the 1st to 4th C.
Substantial traces of several still remain, and some modern roads are built along routes first established by the Romans.

rood *noun, arch.* a unit of square measurement equal to one quarter of an acre

roof light *comp. noun* a car dome light

roost *noun, Sc.* a tidal race experienced among or between the ➡Orkney or ➡Shetland islands

rootle *verb* to turn up ground by rooting around
Especially when done by an animal.

rooty gong *comp. noun, hist., sl.* a medal once awarded to army personnel serving in India

ropey *adj., coll.* (1) low-grade or substandard; (2) somewhat unwell

rope-yarn *comp. noun* the material from which strands of rope are made

roro *noun, abbr.* ➡roll-on roll-off

rorty *adj., sl.* (1) enjoyable; (2) fond of amusement; (3) unsophisticated or crude; (4) down to earth

Roscommon *pr. name* a county in the ➡Irish Republic
County Roscommon in the ancient province of ➡Connaught.

rose *noun* a many-holed nozzle used to sprinkle water over a large area with hose or watering can

Rose *noun* the national vegetative emblem of England

Roseland *pr. name, coll.* southeastern England apart from London
Where it is supposed that life is rosy.

rose-tinted spectacles *comp. noun* rose-colored glasses

rosiner *noun, Gae., Ir.* a stiff drink

RoSPA *pr. name, abbr.* the Royal Society for the Prevention of Accidents

Ross and Cromarty *pr. name, hist.* a former Scottish county, now divided between ➡Highland region and ➡Western Isles Island council

Rosslyn Chapel *pr. name, hist.* a small 15th C. chapel in the village of Roslin, tix miles south of ➡Edinburgh
Best known for its extensive, highly detailed and original stone carvings, in particular the spirally banded Prentice Pillar, traditionally supposed to have been carved by an apprentice without the permission of his master.

the **Ross-Shire Buffs** *pr. name* a nickname for the 78th Regiment of ➡Foot
A unit of the British Army, named after the color of their facings and their recruitment area in northern Scotland.

rot *verb, sl.* (1) to joke; (2) to tease or annoy

rota *noun* a duty roster

Rotavator *pr. name (TM)* a machine for rotary cultivation or tilling
It is similar to a Rototiller.

a Roman road

rotten borough *comp. noun, hist.* a parliamentary electoral district with exceptionally few—indeed in some cases no—electors

Abolished by the ➡Great Reform Act of 1832.

Rotten Row *pr. name* a horseback-riding path through ➡Hyde Park in London

It is conjectured, but without proof, that the name is a corruption of the French *route du roi* = "route of the king".

rotter *noun, out., sl.* an objectionable person

rouble *spell.* ruble

The Russian currency unit.

rouf *noun, sl.* four

Criminal ➡backslang for "four."

rough diamond *comp. noun, coll.* a diamond in the rough

rough grazing *comp. noun* undeveloped pasture

rough justice *comp. noun, coll.* treatment that is approximately fair

rough luck *comp. noun, coll.* bad luck

rough tongue *comp. noun, coll.* rude or harsh language

rough work *comp. noun, coll.* violence

round *noun* a delivery route for a newspaper ➡roundsman, a milkman, or similar

roundabout *noun* (1) a merry-go-round or carousel; (2) a traffic circle

For (2), SEE ALSO: ➡gyratory circus, ➡traffic circus.

roundarm *verb* to ➡bowl a ➡cricket ball with the arm held horizontally at shoulder level

round brackets *comp. noun* parentheses, being a pair of curved marks, thus ( )

roundel *noun* a circular icon painted on ➡RAF aircraft as an identification mark

rounders *noun* a game somewhat similar to softball

the **Roundheads** *pr. name, hist.* ➡Parliamentarians

They were members of the ➡Parliamentary party during the ➡English Civil War. The name derives from their Puritan habit of cropping their hair very short.

the **Round Pond** *pr. name* a large pond in ➡Kensington Gardens, London

It has been there since 1728, and is now principally known as a place where people sail toy boats.

roundsman *noun* a routeman

the **Round Table** *pr. name, hist.* the table that ➡Arthur's ➡Knights of the Round Table are said to have sat around

It was circular so that no one member of the group had precedence over another. The table was located at ➡Camelot.

round the twist *idiom, sl.* round the bend; insane

round the houses *idiom, rh. sl.* men's pants

Derivation: pants > ➡trousers > houses > round the houses.

round towel *comp. noun* an endless towel, upon a roller

roup *noun, North, Sc.* a public auction, especially of the possessions of a bankrupt individual or business

rout *noun, arch.* a fashionable reception or gathering held in the evening

routeing *spell.* routing

route march *comp. noun* a long-distance military training march

rover *noun, arch.* the former name of a ➡venture scout

Rover *pr. name (TM), hist.* a mass-production automobile manufacturer founded in 1900 at ➡Coventry

rowanberry *noun, Sc.* the scarlet-colored berry of the ➡rowan tree

rowan tree *comp. noun, Sc.* a mountain ash tree

Formally named *sorbus aucuparia*, a member of the rose family found in Scotland and northern England; not to be confused with the *sorbus americana* found in North America

{**rowelled** » **rowelling**} *spell.* {roweled » roweling}

rowing boat *comp. noun* a rowboat

rowlock *noun* an oarlock

Rowton house *comp. noun* a kind of lodging house for destitute men

Named after Lord Rowton, a 19th C. social reformer.

Roxburgh *pr. name, hist.* a former Scottish county, now part of ➡Borders region

royal *adj.* (1) from, of, established by, belonging to, under the authority of, in the service of, worthy of, or in the family of, a king or queen; (2) majestic, splendid or stately

the **Royal Academy of Arts** *pr. name, hist.* an institution established to encourage painting, sculpture and architecture

It was founded in 1768 with Sir Joshua Reynolds as first president, and originally shared premises with the National Gallery on ➡Trafalgar Square, but since 1868 has been located in ➡Burlington House in London.

the **Royal Academy of Music** *pr. name* an institution providing musical training

Founded in 1822, it is associated with ➡London University.

the **Royal Aircraft Establishment** *pr. name* the principal government aerospace research center

It is located at Farnborough, ➡Hampshire.

the **Royal Air Force** *pr. name* the British air force

Founded in 1918 by merging of the army's ➡Royal Flying Corp and the navy's ➡Royal Naval Air Service into a single independent third military service alongside the Army and Navy, the first independent air force in the world.

the **Royal Air Force Museum** *pr. name* a museum of the history of flight in general and of the ➡RAF in particular

There are about 65 historic aircraft on display at its Hendon, north London, location

the **Royal Albert Hall**

the Royal Albert Hall

the **Royal Albert Hall** *pr. name, hist.* a large, domed concert hall in London, built in 1871 as a memorial to Victoria's ➠Prince Consort, ➠Albert

Although the building appears to be circular, it is in reality oval. It was partially financed from the profits of the ➠Great Exhibition; however most funding came from selling 999-year leases on a number of the seats in the auditorium.

the **Royal American Regiment** *pr. name, hist.* the original name of the King's Royal Rifle Corp

The unit was first raised at Philadelphia in 1755. It has now been absorbed into the ➠Royal Green Jackets.

the **Royal and Ancient Game** *pr. name, Sc.* an alternative, more grandiose, name for golf

Why this name? Because the game was played by the kings and queens of Scotland as long ago as the 15th C., and perhaps earlier. ➠James IV is the first monarch known to have played, and ➠Mary Queen of Scots was playing golf when she was told of the death of her second husband, Lord Darnley.

the **Royal and Ancient Golf Club** *pr. name, Sc.* the venerable golf club on the ➠links along the seashore at ➠St Andrews in ➠Fife, Scotland.

It was founded in 1754 as the Society of St Andrews Golfers, originally with a course of 22 holes. It was granted the right to call itself "Royal" by permission of ➠William IV in 1834, but of course the title is also a reference to the alternate, earlier name for the game.

Today St Andrews is the world center for the game.

the **Royal Armoured Corps** *pr. name* the collective name for the mechanized units of the British Army

the **Royal Armouries** *pr. name, hist.* Britain's oldest museum, located inside the Tower of London

This museum of armor, located in the ➠White Tower, began in the 16th C. as ➠Henry VIII's personal collection.

the **Royal Arms** *pr. name* the personal arms of the ➠monarch of the ➠United Kingdom of Great Britain and Northern Ireland

(See box below)

the **Royal Artillery** *pr. name* the collective name for the artillery units of the British Army

Royal Ascot *pr. name* a horse race meeting held at ➠Ascot every June

Called this because the ➠Royal Family regularly attends.

The Arms of the British Monarch

In *England* these are correctly emblazoned as follows:-

Quarterly,

first and fourth ➠gules—➠three lions ➠passant ➠gardand in ➠pale ➠or (for England)
second gule—or, a ➠lion rampant with a double ➠tressure flory-counterflory gules (for Scotland)
third gule—➠azure, a ➠harp or, stringed ➠argent (for Ireland).
All this is surrounded by the ➠Garter.
Crest—Upon the royal helm, the imperial crown proper, thereon a lion ➠statant gardant or, imperial crowned proper.

Supporters,

➠Dexter—a lion rampant guardant or, imperially crowned .
Sinister—a unicorn ➠argent, armed, crined, and unguled or, gorged with a coronet composed of crosses patée and fleur de lis, a chain affixed thereto, passing between the forelegs and reflexed over the back.

Motto

➠Dieu et mon Droit in the compartment below the shield, with the ➠Union rose, ➠shamrock and ➠thistle engrafted on the same stem.
➠Honi soit qui mal y pense along the surrounding garter, although not all is visible.

In *Scotland* there are the following changes:

Quarterly,

The Lion of Scotland is placed in the first and fourth gules and the Lions of England are placed in the second gule.

Supporters,

These are transposed, with the unicorn argent on the dexter and the lion rampant on the sinister.

(On both versions, the lion rampant represents England and the unicorn argent represents Scotland.)

royal assent *comp. noun* the final constitutional step leading to the creation of a new law

A parliamentary bill becomes law only when it has received the Royal Assent, now little more than a formality. This is still given in ➡Norman French, beginning with the words *"La Reine remercie ses bons sujets, accepte leur benevolence, etc ..."*

the **Royal Ballet** *pr. name, hist.* Britain's national ballet company

Founded in 1931 as the Vic-Wells Ballet and renamed the ➡Sadler's Well Ballet in 1946, it was given its present name by ➡Royal Charter in 1956. It is now based at the Royal Opera House, ➡Covent Garden, London, a venue it shares with the ➡Royal Opera.

the **Royal Bank of Scotland** *pr. name* Scotland's largest and second-oldest bank, founded in 1727

Its head office is in ➡Edinburgh. Unlike English banks other than the ➡Bank of England, the Royal Bank of Scotland is authorized to issue its own paper currency, which together with that of the other two principal Scottish banks is legal tender there, and is usually accepted as such in England too.

Royal Birkdale *pr. name* a golf course near ➡Liverpool, established in 1897

royal borough *comp. noun* a borough holding a charter from the crown that historically entitled it to special privileges

Royal Botanic Gardens, Edinburgh *pr. name* the oldest botanic gardens in Britain, founded in 1670

Although primarily a center for scientific research, it is open to the public.

Royal Botanic Gardens, Kew *pr. name* the official name for ➡Kew Gardens, founded in 1759

Although primarily a center for scientific research, it is open to the public.

the **Royal British Legion** *pr. name* the approximate equivalent of the American Legion

royal burgh *comp. noun, Sc.* a Scottish burgh holding a charter from the crown that historically entitled it to special privileges

Royal Charter *comp. noun* a written grant of authority issued directly by the ➡monarch

Usually for the purpose of establishing a company, city, borough, burgh, or some other type of organization. The charter sets out the functions and extent of the powers of the organization so established.

royal circle *comp. noun* the first curved balcony or mezzanine level of a theater

It is equivalent to the second floor in a conventional building, and is also known as the ➡dress circle.

the **Royal College of Arts** *pr. name* a central London college founded in 1837, it issues higher degrees in the graphic arts

the **Royal College of Music** *pr. name* an institution in London providing a professional musical training

Founded in 1883, it is associated with ➡London University.

royal commission *comp. noun* a commission of inquiry set up by the government to look into some matter of national concern

Similar to a Presidential Commission.

the **Royal Courts of Justice** *pr. name* the building that houses the ➡Supreme Court of Judicature, which is located on the ➡Strand, London

Royal Court Theatre *pr. name, hist.* the first venue for several plays by George Bernard Shaw in early 20th C. London

the **Royal Crescent** *pr. name, hist.* an 18th C. architectural gem in the city of ➡Bath, Avon

Considered to be the finest ➡crescent in Britain.

Royal Crown Derby Porcelain *pr. name* very high quality chinaware made in ➡Derby after 1890

royal dockyard *comp. noun* a navy yard

Royal Doulton *comp. noun, hist.* (1) a style of brown salt-glazed stoneware; (2) a style of fine art china

(1) was first made by Henry Doulton in Lambeth, London, in 1815 and (2) has also been made by his company, since the 1870s. The company was authorized to add "Royal" to its name by ➡Edward VII in 1901.

royal duke *comp. noun* (1) a duke who is also a prince; (2) the sovereign of a duchy or small state

the **Royal Engineers** *pr. name, hist.* the technical units of the British Army

Including Sappers, Miners, the Royal Corps of Signals and even, until the formation of the independent ➡RAF in 1918, the ➡Royal Flying Corps.

the **Royal Exchange** *pr. name, hist.* the original location of London's embryonic 16th C. stock market

Opened by Queen ➡Elizabeth I in 1568, the building was burned down for the first time in the ➡Great Fire of 1666 and for a second time in 1838; the present structure dates from 1844. In 1928 it was purchased by an insurance company and has been used as their offices since.

the **Royal Family** *pr. name* the family that the monarch belongs to

the **Royal Festival Hall** *pr. name* the concert hall that is the centerpiece of the ➡South Bank complex in London

the **Royal Fine Arts Commission** *pr. name* a government-financed independent organization set up to consider and report on the artistic implications of any major public project, primarily architectural ones, in England and Wales

the **Royal Fine Arts Commission for Scotland**

the **Royal Fine Arts Commission for Scotland** *pr. name* similar to the ➡Royal Fine Arts Commission, but for Scotland

the **Royal Flight** *pr. name* a small fleet of aircraft used to transport members of the ➡Royal Family and senior members of the government

The reigning monarch and the heir to the throne are supposed never to travel together in the same aircraft. The aircraft of the Flight are theoretically part of the ➡RAF fleet.

Also known as the ➡{King's » Queen's} Flight.

the **Royal Flying Corps** *pr. name, hist.* the aviation division of the Army, which provided the principal British air presence over the Western Front during most of World War I

Formed in 1912, it was merged with the ➡Royal Naval Air Service to form the ➡Royal Air Force in 1918.

Royal Geographical Society *pr. name, hist.* an institution founded in London in 1788

Originally calling itself the African Association, it is dedicated to finding out more about the world. In the past it regularly sponsored expeditions to unexplored regions, most famously those by David Livingstone to Africa in the 19th C.

the **Royal Goats** *pr. name* the ➡Nanny-Goats

An alternate nickname.

the **Royal Green Jackets** *pr. name* an army regiment formed in 1866

Royal Highness *comp. noun* a title that may be used by the king, queen, children of the monarch, and any male grandchildren of the monarch

the **Royal Holloway and Bedford New College** *pr. name* a school of ➡London University founded in 1849

the **Royal Horticultural Society** *pr. name, hist.* Britain's leading association of gardeners

Founded at a meeting in a London bookshop in 1804, it is now best known as organizer of the ➡Chelsea Flower Show.

royal house *noun* a dynastic line of monarchs

the **Royal Household** *pr. name* those people who are domestic employees of the ➡Royal Family

the **Royal Institution** *pr. name* a society founded in London in 1799 for the purpose of diffusing and popularizing scientific knowledge

the **Royal International Horse Show** *pr. name* a large international ➡showjumping event held every year at ➡Olympia, London

royalist *noun* one who favors a monarchy

the **Royal Mail** *pr. name* the government department that collects and delivers the mail

Royal Mail Steamer *comp. noun, arch.* a steam packet boat that carried the ➡Royal Mail

the **Royal Marine Commando** *pr. name* a unit of the ➡Royal Marines specially trained as amphibious troops, specialsts in sabotage and inflitration

the **Royal Marines** *pr. name* a corps of soldiers originally assigned to sail aboard men-of-war

Unlike the U.S. Marines, the Royal Marines are not an independent military force, but a unit of the ➡Royal Navy. They were founded in 1664.

the **Royal Maunds** *pr. name* the ➡Maundy Money

the **Royal Mews** *pr. name, hist.* the royal stables

Close by Buckingham Palace, where state coaches are kept.

the **Royal Mile** *pr. name, hist.* the main thoroughfare of Edinburgh's ancient ➡Old Town

It runs for about a mile from ➡Holyrood House in the east, to ➡Edinburgh Castle in the west. Both were once the residences of Scottish kings and queens.

the **Royal Military Academy** *pr. name* the British Army's officer training college

Founded in 1799 as the Royal Military College and located near what was then the village of ➡Sandhurst in ➡Berkshire.

the **Royal Mint** *pr. name* the government organization that manufactures all British coinage

Located until 1810 within the ➡Tower of London and then close by on Tower Hill, in 1968 it was moved to Llantrisant, near Pontyclun in Wales.

the **Royal Museum of Scotland** *pr. name* a museum in Edinburgh formed in 1985 by amalgamating two existing museums in the city

These were the Royal Scottish Museum, founded 1866, and the National Museum of Antiquities of Scotland, founded 1817.

the **Royal National Eisteddfod** *pr. name, Wal.* an annual congress of Welsh bards and the national Welsh festival of music, literature and drama

Held at different locations in Wales each year, with the proceedings conducted entirely in Welsh.

the **Royal National Institute for the Blind** *pr. name* a voluntary organization founded in 1863 to provide help to blind people

the **Royal National Institute for the Deaf** *pr. name* a voluntary organization founded in 1911 to provide help to deaf people

the **Royal National Lifeboat Institution** *pr. name* a voluntary organization founded in 1824 to provide a comprehensive lifeboat rescue service around the coast of Britain

the **Royal National Theatre** *pr. name* an ensemble of three theaters in London's ➡South Bank complex

the **Royal Naval College** *pr. name, hist.* a collection of impressive 17th C. buildings housing the ➡Royal Navy's officer training college besides the ➡Thames River at ➡Greenwich since 1873

the **Royal Navy** *pr. name, hist.* Britain's navy

There has been a fleet in being continuously since it was first formed by ➡Alfred the Great in the 9th C.

the **Royal Northern College of Music** *pr. name* an institution in ➡Manchester that offers a professional musical training

Founded in 1973 by an amalgamation of the Northern School of Music and the Royal Manchester School of Music.

the **Royal Oak** *pr. name, hist.* an oak tree at Boscobel in ➡Shropshire

Which ➡Charles II hid in for a day following the defeat of his forces by ➡Cromwell at the Battle of ➡Worcester on September 3, 1651. *SEE ALSO:* ➡Oak-Apple Day

the **Royal Observatory** *pr. name, hist.* the astronomical observatory established at ➡Greenwich by ➡Charles II in 1675 in order to improve the effectiveness of maritime navigation

For many years an important center of scientific astronomy, the growing atmospheric pollution generated by London made seeing increasingly difficult and in 1948 the institution moved to the 15th C. castle of Herstmonceux in ➡East Sussex. In 1990 it moved once more, this time to ➡Cambridge, while its principal observatory is now located at Las Palmas in the Canary Islands.

the **Royal Opera** *pr. name, hist.* Britain's premier opera company, performing in London since 1732

Based at the ➡Royal Opera House, ➡Covent Garden, London, which it shares with the ➡Royal Ballet.

the **Royal Opera House** *pr. name* the leading theater in London for ballet and opera

The home of both the ➡Royal Ballet and the ➡Royal Opera, it is also known as ➡Covent Garden because of its location. The present theater is third on this site since 1732.

royal park *comp. noun* public parks maintained by the government in the name of the ➡monarch

There are 12 such parks in London alone.

the **Royal Pavilion** *pr. name* one of the most spectacular architectural sights in Britain, located in ➡Brighton

Originally built in the late 18th C. when it was called the Marine Pavilion, and then rebuilt between 1815 and 1820 for the ➡Prince Regent in an extravagant oriental style with onion-shaped domes, minarets, etc., and a partly-Chinese interior, all of which has turned it into what must be Britain's most voluptuously extravagant public building.

the **Royal Philharmonic Orchestra** *pr. name, hist.* an orchestra founded in London by Sir Thomas Beecham in 1946

It has this name due to its collaborative association with the ➡Royal Philharmonic Society. Beecham also founded the ➡London Philharmonic Orchestra.

the **Royal Philharmonic Society** *pr. name, hist.* a society founded in 1813 in London for the purpose of promoting music, particularly by sponsoring composers and holding concerts

The Royal Philharmonic Society is immensely proud of the fact that for some time it sponsored none other than Beethoven and it was they who commissioned his *Ninth (Choral) Symphony*, whose last movement, based on Schiller's poem *An die Freude* and loosely translated as "Ode to Joy," has since become the anthem of the ➡European Union.

Royal Prerogative *pr. name* the personal rights and powers of the monarch, in theory without limit

But in practice they are now almost nonexistent.

royal progress *comp. noun, arch.* a ➡progress made by the ➡monarch or other members of the ➡Royal Family

the **Royal Regiment** *pr. name, arch.* a former name of the ➡Royal Scots

the **Royals** *pr. name, abbr., coll.* (1) the ➡Royal Family; (2) the ➡Royal Marines; (3) the Royal Dragoons cavalry regiment

(3) is a unit of the British Army, amalgamated with the Royal Horse Guards as the ➡Blues and Royals since 1969.

royal salute *comp. noun* a ceremonial salute by cannons fired at the Tower of London on appropriate royal occasions

the **Royal Scots** *pr. name* the 1st Regiment of ➡Foot

Raised in 1633, this is the senior regiment of the British Army, previously known as the ➡Royal Regiment.

the **Royal Scots Greys** *pr. name* one of oldest Scottish regiments in the British Army

Raised in 1678 and named for the color of their horses.

the Royal Pavilion

the **Royal Scottish Academy of Music and Drama** *pr. name* the principal Scottish institution offering dramatic and musical training
Established, as the Glasgow Athenaeum, in 1847.

the **Royal Scottish Academy** *pr. name, hist.* founded in 1826 for the purpose of encouraging painting, sculpture and architecture
It is housed in a building modeled upon a classic temple, erected in front of the ➡National Gallery of Scotland at the foot of the ➡Mound, upon ➡Princes Street in Edinburgh.

the **Royal Scottish Observatory** *pr. name, hist.* an astronomical observatory established upon Calton Hill in ➡Edinburgh in 1818 and granted a ➡royal charter in 1822
Its principal observatory is now located upon Hawaii.

Royal Scottish Orchestra *pr. name, hist.* an orchestra founded in ➡Glasgow in 1891 as the ➡Scottish National Orchestra
It has existed informally since 1844. The orchestra was granted its right to use the royal appellation in 1991.

the **Royal Shakespeare Company** *pr. name* one of the world's major theater companies
It has bases at both the ➡Shakespeare Memorial Theatre in ➡Stratford-upon-Avon and at the ➡Barbican in London. Despite its locations and its name, the ➡RSC performs a very wide range of plays apart from the Shakespearean repertoire that is expected. Its right to use the royal appellation was granted in 1961.

the **Royal Society** *pr. name, hist.* the oldest and most illustrious scientific society in Britain and possibly the world
Although many of the leading members had met regularly on an informal basis since 1645 to discuss scientific matters, it was incorporated under a ➡Royal Charter granted by ➡Charles II in 1662. In many ways it serves in the role of a national academy of science, and fellowship of the Royal Society is the most coveted of honors among scientists.

Royal Society of Arts *pr. name, abbr., hist.* in full, this is the Royal Society for the Encouragement of Arts, Manufactures and Commerce
Established in London in 1754 to improve educational and working standards in such areas as industrial design.

the **Royal Society of Edinburgh** *pr. name, hist.* founded at Edinburgh in 1783 as a scientific society similar to London's older ➡Royal Society, but with additional interests in the arts

the **Royal Standard** *pr. name* the personal flag or banner of the ➡monarch
Which consists of a banner in shape and quarterings, and is flown upon any royal palace when the monarch resides there.

the **Royal Tank Regiment** *pr. name* a unit of the ➡Royal Armoured Corps

the **Royal Tournament** *pr. name* a military display held each July in London
It is usually held in Earl's Court and is open to the public.

Royal Troon *pr. name* a golf course in Strathclyde, 25 miles southwest of Glasgow on ➡links along the shore of the ➡Firth of Clyde
Founded in 1878, it has been permitted to use the word "Royal" in its title since 1978.

royalty *noun* (1) a person or persons of royal rank; (2) royal power, status or right

the **Royal Victoria Chain** *pr. name* a decoration instituted by ➡Edward VII in memory of his mother ➡Victoria and which is bestowed upon foreign monarchs to mark special events

royal warrant *comp. noun* a warrant authorizing a business to supply a specific kind of goods to a particular member of the ➡Royal Family
These are considered to be a considerable honor for a business.

Royal Worcester *pr. name* a style of porcelain that has been in continuous production in ➡Worcester since 1751

the **Royal Yacht** *pr. name* a large yacht used by members of the ➡Royal Family during official visits around the world
Nominally a ship of the ➡Royal Navy, the current royal yacht, *Britannia*, was built on the ➡Clyde in 1953 and is 412 ft long. Reputedly, it can be used as a hospital ship in time of war.

rozzer *noun, sl.* a policeman

RP *noun, abbr.* ➡received pronunciation

RPC *pr. name, abbr.* the Royal Pioneer Corps

RPI *pr. name, abbr.* the ➡retail price index
It is published monthly by the government statistical office and is the principal measure of inflation in the economy.

RPO *pr. name, abbr.* ➡Royal Philharmonic Orchestra

RPS *pr. name, abbr.* the Royal Photographic Society

RRC *noun, abbr.* the Royal Red Cross

RS *pr. name, abbr.* (1) the ➡Royal Society; (2) the Royal Society of Portrait Painters; (3) the ➡Royal Scots

RSA [A] *noun, abbr.* a Royal Scottish Academician
[B] *pr. name, abbr.* (1) the ➡Royal Society of Arts; (2) the ➡Royal Scottish Academy

RSC *pr. name, abbr.* (1) the ➡Royal Shakespeare Company; (2) the Royal Society of Chemistry

RSD *pr. name, abbr.* the Royal Society of Dublin

RSE *pr. name, abbr.* the ➡Royal Society of Edinburgh

R.Sigs. *pr. name, abbr.* the Royal Corps of Signals

RSM *noun, abbr.* a ➡regimental sergeant-major

RSPB *pr. name, abbr.* the Royal Society for the Protection of Birds

A society founded in ➥Manchester in 1889 for the purpose of protecting wild birds. It now has over 750,000 members and manages over 100 nature reserves.

RSPCA *pr. name, abbr.* the Royal Society for the Prevention of Cruelty to Animals

A society founded in 1824, it was granted authority to use the word "Royal" in its title by ➥Victoria in 1840.

Rt. Hon. *pr. name, abbr.* ➥Right Honourable

RU *noun, abbr.* the game of ➥Rugby Union

rub-a-dub-dub *idiom, rh. sl.* a pub

rub along *idiom. phr. verb* to get by or manage without too much difficulty

rubber *noun, abbr.* an ➥indiarubber eraser

rubbish [A] *noun* (1) trash or debris; (2) absurd or nonsensical ideas or proposals

[B] *verb, coll.* (1) to discard as useless; (2) to criticize with exceptional severity

rubbish bin *comp. noun* a trashcan

rubbish tip *comp. noun* a garbage dump

ruby *noun* in heraldry, (1) ➥gules; (2) a representation of the planet Mars

RUC *pr. name, abbr.* the Royal Ulster Constabulary

The Northern Irish police force, descended from the Royal Irish Constabulary set up by Sir Robert Peel in Dublin in 1814, and as such the oldest properly organized modern police force anywhere.

London's ➥Metropolitan Police was established, also by Peel, in 1829.

ruckle *verb* to ruck or crease

ruddy *exclam., sl.* a euphemistic variation of ➥bloody

Rugby *pr. name, hist.* a town in ➥Warwickshire about 11 miles to the east of ➥Coventry

An important railroad junction and engineering center since the early 19th C., however it is probably best known as the venue of ➥Rugby School. The current population is 65,000 (1991 Estimate).

Rugby fives *comp. noun* a variety of the game of ➥fives played in a court with four walls

Rugby Football *comp. noun, hist.* a football game without time-outs, interference or forward passing, but with kicking, dribbling, later passing and tackling

The name derives from ➥Rugby School, England, where it originated in 1823, and is now played in two distinct forms, ➥Rugby League and ➥Rugby Union.

Rugby League *comp. noun* a professional version of ➥Rugby Football with teams of 13 per side

Rugby School *pr. name* one of the leading English ➥public schools

Founded in 1567, it is located in ➥Rugby, ➥Warwickshire. This is where Thomas Hughes' novel *Tom Brown's Schooldays* was set and the game of ➥Rugby Football was invented.

Rugby Union *comp. noun* an amateur version of ➥Rugby Football with teams of 15 per side

rugger *noun, abbr.* ➥Rugby Football

Rule 43 *pr. name* a rule in the ➥Home Office Prison Rules Book under which prisoners considered at special risk from other prisoners are kept isolated in a special section of prison

Typically this is done because of the nature of the offense the prisoner has committed, especially sex crimes.

Rule, Britannia! *pr. name, hist.* a popular patriotic song written at the express command of the ➥Prince of Wales and first heard in 1740

The words of the first verse are:-

When Britain first, at Heaven's command,
Arose from out the azure main,
This was the charter, the charter of the land,
And guardian angels sung this strain:
"Rule, Britannia; Britannia rules the waves;
Britons never, never will be slaves."

---

rum [A] *adj.* strange or odd

[B] *adj., abbr., coll.* ➥rummy

rumble *verb, sl.* to discover something that had been deliberately hidden

rumbustious *adj..* rambunctious

rum cove *comp. noun, out., sl.* a man of doubtful reputation or character

rum customer *comp. noun, sl.* a difficult person, one not to meddle with

rummy *adj., coll.* (1) strange or peculiar; (2) difficult or risky

rumour *spell.* rumor

the **Rump Parliament** *pr. name, hist.* what remained of the ➥Long Parliament between 1648 and 1653

rumpy *noun* any member of a litter of ➥Manx kittens that is born with no tail

SEE ALSO: ➥stumpy.

rumpy-pumpy *comp. noun, sl., taboo* a euphemism for copulation

run *noun* the unit of scoring in ➥cricket

A run is scored when both ➥batsmen exchange ends of the pitch after the ball has been batted and before it can be returned into play. Clearly, this exchange has to be conducted as rapidly as possible, so batsman run between the ➥creases.

run around *phr. verb* to move from place to place without ceasing

runner *noun, arch., sl.* (1) a ➡robin redbreast; (2) a ➡Bow Street Runner; (3) a police officer

(1) comes from the ➡Bow Street Runners' other nickname, ➡redbreast, derived from the color of their uniform. This, in turn, became part of their semi-official name of Bow Street Runner, which neatly brings this path of name-origin pretty much back to where it started. For a while the nickname was inherited by the members of the ➡Metropolitan Police, which replaced them in 1829.

runner bean *comp. noun* a twining vine or scarlet runner

running bowsprit *comp. noun* a bowsprit that can be drawn in when not required to carry sail

---

Runnymede *pr. name, hist.* the field beside the ➡Thames River, near Egham in ➡Surrey, where ➡John put his seal upon ➡*Magna Carta* in 1215

Three memorials have been erected here in the couse of the 20th C.

The first commemorates the British airmen who died in World War II and was dedicated by ➡Elizabeth II of England and I of Scotland in 1953.

The second, commemorating Runnymede's importance in the history of the establishment of civil rights and personal liberty in both Great Britain and the United States, is modeled after a classical temple and donated by the American Bar Association in 1957.

The third is a memorial to President Kennedy which is set in land that was presented by the British people to the American people. It, too, was dedicated by ➡Elizabeth II of England and I of Scotland, in 1965.

---

run on the spot *phr. verb* to run in place

run out *verb* to ➡stump a ➡cricket ➡batsman while he is away from his ➡crease

runrigg *noun, hist., Sc.* an early system of joint strip-farming where ➡rigs were rotated yearly

runt *noun, Sc.* (1) an old or decayed tree stump; (2) the hardened or withered stem of a plant; (3) an old cow fattened for slaughter

run-up *comp. noun* a period of preparation before a significant event

Prince **Rupert** *pr. name, hist.* the son of the eldest daughter of ➡James I of England and VI of Scotland

A German prince who came to England to command an army for his uncle, ➡Charles I, during the ➡English Civil War.

rural dean *comp. noun* a member of the Church of England clergy who is responsible for supervising other clergy within a ➡deanery

rural district *comp. noun, hist.* a small country area governed by a ➡Rural District Council

Replaced by the ➡District in 1974.

Rural District Council *pr. name, hist.* the elected body that governed a ➡rural district

Rural Protection Societies *pr. name, hist.* three societies set up in the 1920s to campaign for the preservation and protection of the British countryside

rush-bearing festival *comp. noun, out.* an annual rustic festival which involves taking rushes and spreading them over the floor of a church

Once an annual necessity in the Middle Ages but now very rare and of ceremonial significance only.

rush one's fences *idiom phr. verb* to attempt to move or work too fast

rusticate *verb* to suspend from school or college, usually as a punishment

rustre *noun* an heraldic representation of a lozenge containing a round hole

Rutland *pr. name* a former English county

Now part of the county of ➡Leicester, Rutland was the smallest of the former English counties.

RV *pr. name, abbr.* the ➡Revised Version of the Bible

RWS *pr. name, abbr.* the Royal Society of Painters in Water Colours

the **Ryder Cup** *pr. name* a professional golf competition between Britain and the United States held every two years

s *noun, abbr., hist.* a ➡shilling

The standard abbreviation for the ➡shilling, which ceased to be legal tender in 1971. *SEE ALSO:* ➡sh.

S4C *pr. name, abbr., Wal* ➡*Sianel Pedwar Cymru*

sab *noun, abbr., coll.* a ➡hunt saboteur

sable *noun* the heraldic name for black

sabre *spell.* saber

sabretache *spell.* sabertache

A satchel worn by cavalry officers. From the German, *Säbeltasche* = "saber-pocket."

Sabrina *pr. name, hist.* the Roman name for the ➡Severn River

the **Sacred Isle** *pr. name* Ireland

From its large number of saints.

{SAC » SACW} *noun, abbr.* a ➡senior {aircraftman » aircraftwoman}

Sadler's Wells Theatre *pr. name* a London theater dating from 1756

A popular venue for opera and ballet.

SAE *noun, abbr.* stamped and addressed envelope

The equivalent of SASE

safe {constituency » seat} *comp. noun* a parliamentary district where the sitting ➡MP has a very large majority and so is in little danger of being turned out at the next election

sag *verb, North, sl.* to play hooky from school

sahib *noun, arch., Urdu* a form of address to a British man in India, usually by a native of inferior status

The word is Urdu, meaning "friend," "master," or "lord".

sailing-boat *comp. noun* a sailboat

sailing master *comp. noun* the navigating officer on board a yacht

the **Sailor King** *pr. name, hist.* ➡William IV, King of the ➡United Kingdom

He joined the navy as a midshipman at the age of 14 and had risen to the rank of ➡Lord High Admiral by the time he was king. Mind you, being heir to the throne does not hurt your promotion prospects.

sailor's blessing *comp. noun, sl.* a curse

sailor's farewell *comp. noun, sl.* a parting curse

sain *verb, arch.* (1) to make the sign of the cross; (2) to bless or consecrate

Sainsbury's *pr. name (TM)* Britain's largest chain of supermarkets

St Albans *pr. name* a city in ➡Hertfordshire, near the remains of the Roman city of *Verulanium*

A Benedictine abbey was founded here in the 8th C. The 11th C. cathedral was originally a church associated with the abbey; the town that grew up around it was incorporated as a city in 1553; the current population is 65,000 (1988 estimate).

St Andrew *pr. name, hist.* the patron saint of Scotland

He first become the patron saint of the ➡Picts during the 8th C. and was later adopted by the ➡Scots. By the way, St Andrew is also the patron saint of Russia.

the **Order of St Andrew** *pr. name, hist.* an alternate name for the Order of the ➡Thistle

St Andrews *pr. name, hist.* a small but ancient coastal city in ➡Fife, Scotland

It is said that a storm drove a ship containing the bones of ➡St Andrew onto the Fife shore here during the 4th C., but there is no evidence to support this. However, his relics apparently did turn up sooner or later and a church was dedicated to him at this spot, which became a center of scholarship and Christianity in the early middle ages.

A bishop was appointed to St Andrews in the 9th C. and an Archbishop from 1472, making this the seat of the primate of Scotland. It is the home of Scotland's oldest and Britain's third-oldest university, founded in 1412. The world center of golf, the ➡Royal and Ancient Club, is also to be found in St Andrews. The current population is 11,000 (1990 estimate).

St Andrew's Cross *pr. name* Scotland's national flag

It consists of two diagonal white stripes on a blue background and is a component of the ➡Union Flag.

St Andrew's Day *pr. name* November 30, Scotland's national day

St Andrews University *pr. name* the third-oldest university in the English-speaking world and the oldest in Scotland, founded in 1412

Red gowns worn by students are a feature of St Andrews.

St Anne's College *pr. name* a college of ➡Oxford University founded in 1952

St Antony's College *pr. name* a college of ➡Oxford University founded in 1950

St Asaph

St Asaph *pr. name, hist.* a village in ➡Clwyd, about 20 miles east of ➡Conway, which is home to the smallest cathedral in Britain

The first church on this site is said to have been established by St Mungo in 560 or so, and the present cathedral, which dates from the 13th C., was considerably restored during the 19th C. *SEE ALSO:* St David's.

St Bartholomew the Great *pr. name, hist.* the oldest surviving church building in London, founded as a priory in 1123

St Benet's Hall *pr. name* a college of ➡Oxford University founded in 1897

St Bride's *pr. name, hist.* the site of a church in London since the 5th C., it is believed

The present structure has the tallest spire of any of Wren's churches, but that spire was all that remained after the rest was destroyed in the ➡Blitz of World War II. It has now been entirely rebuilt to his original design.

St Catherine's College *pr. name* (1) a college of ➡Cambridge University founded in 1473; (2) a college of ➡Oxford University founded in 1962

St Clement Danes *pr. name, hist.* a 17th C. church in the ➡Strand, London, which is now closely associated with the ➡RAF

St Cross College *pr. name* a college of ➡Oxford University founded in 1965

St David *pr. name, hist.* the patron saint of Wales

St David's *pr. name, hist.* a tiny village in ➡Dyfed, about 25 miles northwest of ➡Pembroke on the westermost point of Wales, where it is said St ➡David founded a monastery in the 6th C.

This is Britain's smallest ➡city, as a cathedral was built there in the 12th C. *SEE ALSO:* St Asaph.

St David's Day *pr. name* March 1, the Welsh national day

St Edmund Hall *pr. name* a college of ➡Oxford University founded in 1278

St Edmund's College *pr. name* a college of ➡Cambridge University founded in 1896

St Edward *pr. name, hist.* ➡Edward the Confessor

King of England from 1042 until 1066, canonized in 1161.

St George *pr. name, hist.* the patron saint of England

St George's Channel *pr. name* the channel at the southern end of the ➡Irish Sea separating southeastern ➡Ireland from southwestern ➡Wales

St George's Chapel, Windsor *pr. name* the royal chapel of ➡Windsor Castle

Built in the ➡perpendicular style of the 15th and 16th C., it is the final resting place of many kings and the venue for the ceremony of the Order of the ➡Garter.

St George's Cross *pr. name* the English national flag

It consists of a red cross on a white background and is a component of the ➡Union Flag.

St George's Day *pr. name* April 23, England's national day

St Giles' Cathedral *pr. name* the 15th C. Gothic church in ➡Parliament Square, ➡Edinburgh

This name is really a misnomer. Although often incorrectly called the cathedral church of the city, it is actually the High ➡Kirk in Edinburgh of the Presbyterian ➡Church of Scotland, which has no bishops, and therefore cannot have any cathedrals. Its most distinctive architectural feature is a Gothic openwork crown placed upon a square tower.

St Grouse's Day *pr. name, coll.* August 12th

A facetious name for first day of the grouse shooting season.

St Hilda's College *pr. name* a college of ➡Oxford University founded in 1893

This college admits female students only.

St Hugh's College *pr. name* a college of ➡Oxford University founded in 1886

St James's *pr. name* a street in London's ➡West End

It leads from ➡Piccadilly to ➡St James's Palace, and is at the epicenter of the rash of gentleman's clubs that have grown up in this part of London over many years.

St James's Palace *pr. name* a royal palace in ➡Pall Mall, London

A redbrick palace in the ➡Tudor style built in 1532 by ➡Henry VIH upon the site of the former St James's Leper Hospital. It was the principal London residence of British monarchs from 1697 until 1837, and to this day the formal address that foreign ambassadors to the United Kindom present themselves to remains the ➡Court of St James's, although the ➡Royal Family moved to ➡Buckingham Palace in 1837.

St James's Park *pr. name* a ➡royal park in central London, which the ➡Mall passes through

the **St John Ambulance Brigade** *pr. name* an organization of volunteer first-aid workers who attend public events in England

St John's College *pr. name* (1) a college of ➡Cambridge University founded in 1511; (2) a college of ➡Oxford University founded in 1555

St Katharine's Dock *pr. name, hist.* an open museum of historic ships

A working dock from 1828 until 1978, it is located in London's ➡Docklands.

St Kilda *pr. name, hist.* a small island group about 50 miles to the west of the ➡Outer Hebrides

The most westerly point of the ➡United Kingdom, these islands have been unpopulated since 1930, except by a large number of seabirds and sheep. They were designated a World Heritage Site in 1987.

St Leger *pr. name* an annual horse race for three-year-olds held at ➡Doncaster

St Luke's summer *comp. noun* a period of good weather in late October

St Margaret's Westminster *pr. name, hist.* a small 16th C. church that sits in the shadow of ➟Westminster Abbey

Considered for almost 400 years to be the "parish church" of the ➟House of Commons.

St Martin-in-the-Fields *pr. name, hist.* an early 18th C. London church, close by ➟Trafalgar Square

The design of this church, with its classical portico, tall steeple and internal balconies along the side walls, was the prototype of many hundreds of others in the years to come, especially in New England.

St Mary-le-Bow *pr. name, hist.* a church at ➟Cheapside, location of London's ➟Bow Bells

St Michael's Mount *pr. name, hist.* a part-time island, transformed into a peninsula connected to the southern ➟Cornish coast twice a day at low tide

This has been a holy place to Christians since the 5th C., and throughout the Middle Ages was both a military stronghold and a religious retreat. The present-day structure at the top of the island started out in life as a 14th C. priory and fort, but is now a private residence.

St Mungo *pr. name, hist.* founder of Glasgow Cathedral in the 6th C. and patron saint of ➟Glasgow

Also called St Kentigern, he lived in the 6th C.

St Pancras Station *pr. name* a principal railroad terminus in central London

For trains to and from north-central England, it was built in 1867 for the Great Northern Railway. St Pancras has been selected as the main terminus for trains using the high-speed track being built to connect the ➟Channel Tunnel and London.

St Partridge's Day *pr. name, coll.* September 1

Facetious name for first day of the partridge shooting season.

St Patrick *pr. name, hist.* the patron saint of Ireland

St Patrick's Cross *pr. name* the Irish national flag until the founding of the ➟Republic of Ireland

It consists of two diagonal red stripes on a white background and is a component of the ➟Union Flag. Today it is the flag of ➟Northern Ireland.

St Patrick's Day *pr. name* March 17, Ireland's national day

St Paul's Cathedral *pr. name, hist.* the cathedral church of the ➟City of London

The first church on this site date from 604. The present cathedral, the fifth, was built between 1675 and 1710 to a design by Sir Christopher Wren following the destruction of the previous St Paul's in the ➟Great Fire of London of 1666. It is considered to be one of the architectural gems of the world, although the one lost in that fire was in fact larger and taller.

Wren is buried within his wonderful baroque cathedral, with the Latin epitaph *Si monumentum requiris, circumspice* = "If you seek a monument to him, look around you."

Many other distinguished Britons, including Nelson and Wellington, are also buried there. The American War Memorial Chapel is located within St Paul's.

St Paul's School *pr. name* one of the leading English ➟public schools

Founded in 1509, it is located in central London.

St Peter's College *pr. name* a college of ➟Oxford University founded in 1929

St Peter's School *pr. name* one of the leading English ➟public schools

Founded in 627, it is located in ➟York, ➟North Yorkshire.

sair *adj., Sc.* (1) very; (2) severely painful; (3) dangerous; (4) oppressive or hard to bear; (5) severe or stormy; (6) difficult or serious; (7) grief-stricken or heartbroken; (8) harmful or damaging (5) refers to weather; (6) to a predicament or situation.

it's a **sair fecht** *idiom, Sc.* life is a hard struggle

salad cream *comp. noun* creamy salad dressing

saleable *spell.* salable

sale of work *comp. noun* a handicraft bazaar, typically for a charity or the local church

saleroom *noun* salesroom

sales assistant *comp. noun, pref.* sales clerk

Salford *pr. name* a city in ➟Greater Manchester

Incorporated as a city in 1835, its current population (also included within the Manchester urban area total) is 220,000 (1988 estimate)

salient *adj.* in heraldry, standing upon hind legs.

Usually it is a lion that is represented in this way, which is considered emblematic of valor.

St. Pauls Cathedral

Salisbury

Salisbury *pr. name* a city in ➡Wiltshire

The original site of the city, just to the north of the modern city, known as ➡Old Sarum and now abandoned, is where there was an Iron Age fortress that was successively occupied and adapted in turn by the Romans, ➡Anglo-Saxons and ➡Normans. Old Sarum is now remembered chiefly as the most rotten of all ➡rotten boroughs.

The Normans built a cathedral and castle alongside each other in the 11th C., but the commander of the castle and bishop could not agree, so the bishop built a new church a little way to the south, which is now the present-day cathedral in the center of the modern town. This cathedral was completed in 1258. The spire, at 404 ft the tallest in Britain, was added about 50 years later.

Salisbury was incorporated as a city in 1227. The current population is 105,000 (1988 estimate).

Salisbury Plain *pr. name* about 200 square miles of chalky upland in ➡Wiltshire largely reserved for military use by the army

This area also contains ➡Stonehenge.

the {**Sally » Sally Army**} *pr. name, abbr., coll.* nicknames for the Salvation Army

Sally Lunn *comp. noun* a slightly sweet tea cake

From the name of a woman who sold them in ➡Bath during the late 18th C. They are best served hot.

salmon and trout *idiom, rh. sl.* ➡stout beer

saloon *noun* a railroad parlor car

saloon bar *comp. noun* the better-furnished and better-served bar in a ➡public house

Also called a ➡lounge bar, this is where the drinks are pricier and ladies are encouraged to sit. SEE ALSO: ➡public bar.

saloon car *comp. noun* a sedan car

Salop *pr. name, hist.* ➡Shropshire

A former name for the county, derived from its Norman French name of *Salopesberis*, which is itself derived from the even earlier Anglo-Saxon name for ➡Shrewsbury, the county seat, which was: *Scrobbesbyig*.

Salopian *noun* (1) a native of ➡Shrewsbury; (2) a native of ➡Shropshire; (3) a student or former student of ➡Shrewsbury School

Derived from the alternate name for the county, ➡Salop.

Saltash luck *idiom, out., sl.* a grim or very depressing task that involves becoming thoroughly wet

From Saltash, a port in ➡Cornwall that is said to be home to some very unlucky sailors.

salt beef *comp. noun* corned beef

salt cellar *comp. noun* (1) a salt shaker; (2) a deep depression above the collarbone, which is mostly found in women

saltern *noun* a salt works

salt horse *comp. noun, coll.* (1) ➡salt beef; (2) a naval officer who performs general duties only

salting *noun* salt marsh, which is land regularly flooded by tides

saltpetre *spell.* saltpeter

From the Latin for "salt of the rock." It is usually considered to be potassium nitrate—KNO_3—but not sodium nitrate—$NaNO_3$—also, as is the case in the U.S.

the **Samaritans** *pr. name* a charitable organization, founded in 1953, that is devoted to helping the suicidally inclined and despairing

Its particular feature is to provide a telephone hot line that desperate people can call anonymously to have their troubles listened to and help offered.

Sam Browne belt *comp. noun, hist.* a leather belt supported by a light strap over the right shoulder

Named after its inventor, Sir Samuel Brown, a 19th C. army officer, it was formerly worn by army officers.

Samhain *pr. name, hist., Ir.* an ancient ➡Celtic festival celebrating the arrival of winter every November

This is the original ritual that has evolved into the modern ➡Hallowe'en observed in Scotland and the United States.

Sammy *noun, hist., sl.* nickname for a World War II G.I.

Derived from "Uncle Sam."

sanatorium *noun* a sickbay or small hospital attached to a school, college or similar institution

sandalled *spell.* sandaled

Sandhurst *pr. name, abbr.* the ➡Royal Military Academy

Sandinist *pr. name* Sandinista

Sandown Park *pr. name* a racecourse about 15 miles to the south west of London

sandpit *noun* a sandbox for children to play in

Sandringham *pr. name* a private royal residence in northern ➡Norfolk

This is where the ➡Royal Family traditionally spends Christmas. The estate was purchased by the future ➡Edward VII in 1861, who then spent the 1870s replacing the former house with the one standing there today.

sandshoe *noun* a tennis shoe

sand sugar *comp. noun, arch.* powdered brown cane sugar

sandwich cake *comp. noun* a layer cake

san fairy ann *idiom, Fr., sl.* nothing to it

From the French *ça ne fait rien*, meaning much the same thing.

sanitary towel *comp. noun* a sanitary napkin

Sankey's Horse *pr. name* a nickname for the 39th Regiment of ➡Foot

A unit of the British Army whose name reminds us of the habit of their commander, Colonel Sankey, of mounting his men on mules to reach the scene of battle faster while they were serving in Spain in the early years of the 18th C.

sapper *noun* an enlisted man in the ➡Royal Engineers

sapphire *noun* in heraldry, (1) azure; (2) a representation of the planet Jupiter

{**sapraemia » sapraemic**} *spell.* {sapremia » sapremic}

Blood poisoning.

302

Saracen corn *comp. noun, arch.* buckwheat

sarbut *noun, Mid., sl.* a police informer

sark *noun, arch, North, Sc.* (1) a man's shirt; (2) a woman's chemise or undershirt; (3) a priest's chemise

sarking *noun* a wooden lining between the roof and rafters of a building

sarky *adj., abbr., sl.* sarcastic

sarnie *noun, abbr., North, sl.* a sandwich

Sarum use *comp. noun, Lat.* divine service as ordered in ➡Salisbury diocese before the Reformation
From the Medieval Latin name *Sarum* = "Salisbury."

SAS *pr. name, abbr.* the ➡Special Air Service

sasine *noun, Sc.* (1) the possession of property on a ➡feudal basis; (2) the act of granting or registering possession of feudal property

Sassenach *noun, derog., Gae., Sc.* (1) a ➡Gaelic-speaking ➡Highlander's name for a ➡Lowland Scot; (2) a name incorrectly employed by many ➡Lowland Scots to delineate the English and all other foreigners from all Scots
From the Gaelic *Sassenach* = "Saxon." The reason that (2) is in error is that, of course, most Scots are themselves Saxon; or at least Angles, which is practically the same thing.

satellite town *comp. noun* a satellite community

satin paper *comp. noun* glossy, high-grade paper

saucepan lid *idiom, rh. sl.* a one ➡pound note
Derivation: pound > ➡quid > lid > saucepan lid.

sauce tartare *comp. noun, Fr.* tartar sauce
This is the French form.

sauch *noun, Sc.* (1) a willow tree; (2) a rod of willow

sauchen *adj., Sc.* (1) made of willow; (2) as tough as willow

Sauchiehall Street *pr. name* one of the principal shopping streets in ➡Glasgow

the **Saucy Seventh** *pr. name* a nickname for the 7th Queen's Own Hussars
A unit of the British Army, named for their smart appearance as portrayed upon a recruiting poster of 1809.

the **Saucy Sixth** *pr. name* a nickname for the 6th Regiment of ➡Foot
A unit of the British Army. While recruiting in 1795, the regiment set such high standards that few acceptable recruits were found but they did find they had acquired this name.

sausage *noun, arch., sl.* a nickname for a German

sausage dog *comp. noun, coll.* a nickname for a dachshund

sausage roll *comp. noun* a sausage wrapped in pastry and then baked

Save-As-You-Earn *pr. name* a payroll savings plan involving automatic deductions from pay by employers at the time of salary payments

saveloy *noun* a highly seasoned, ready-cooked sausage

Save the Children *pr. name, hist.* a charity founded in 1919 in the aftermath of World War I
It seeks to improve the health and welfare of children worldwide.

Savings Bond *comp. noun, abbr.* a ➡Premium Savings Bond

savings certificate *comp. noun* a government issued, interest-bearing certificate sold in small denominations suitable for small savers

saviour *spell.* savior

{**savour » savouriness » savoury**} *spell.* {savor » savoriness » savory}

savoury *noun* (1) a savory dish served at the start of a meal, as an appetizer; (2) a savory dish served at the end of a meal, as a dessert

the **Savoy** *pr. name* an area to the south of the ➡Strand, in London
Once a notorious theives' rookery but now occupied by one of the most luxurious hotels in London.

the **Savoy Operas** *pr. name, hist.* the collective name for the operettas of Gilbert and Sullivan, which were originally performed at the ➡Savoy Theatre, London, by the ➡D'Oyly Carte Opera Company

Savoy Theatre *pr. name, hist.* a theater in London, built by Richard D'Oyly Carte in 1881 specifically to perform the operettas of Gilbert and Sullivan.
When it opened, this was the first public building in the world to be illuminated by electricity.

sawn-off *adj.* sawed-off

sawn-off shotgun *comp. noun* a sawed-off shotgun

sawn timber *comp. noun* lumber

sax *noun, Sc.* six

Saxe-Coburg und Gotha *pr. name, abbr., hist.* the ➡Royal House of Great Britain from 1901 to 1917
The following English monarchs belonged to this house: ➡Edward VII and ➡George V. Saxe-Coburg und Gotha was the family name of Prince ➡Albert, consort of Queen ➡Victoria and thus the family name of his son, the future ➡Edward VII. The name was changed to ➡Windsor in 1917 because of anti-German feeling during World War I.

Saxon *pr. name, hist.* the earliest distinctive form of native English architecture
Of the period from the 7th to 11th centuries, and characterized by simplicity, small windows and round arches.

the **Saxon Shore** *pr. name, hist.* the coast of southeast England from the ➡Wash to the ➡Isle of ➡Wight
Fortified by the Romans in the 4th C. to protect against raids across the English Channel and North Sea from the Saxons and other Germanic tribes.

SAYE *pr. name, abbr.* ➡Save-As-You-Earn

SBS *pr. name, abbr.* (1) the ➡Special Boat Service; (2) the ➡Special Boat Squadron

SC

SC *noun, abbr.* a ➡special constable

scaafe *noun, East* a mischievous person

Scafell Pike *pr. name* the highest mountain in England
Located in the ➡Lake District, its height is 3,210 ft.

scaffie *noun, Sc.* a garbage collector
Perhaps a diminutive form of the word ➡scavenger.

scaffie cairt *comp. noun, Sc.* a garbage truck

scally *noun, abbr., sl.* a reprobate
Derived from ➡scallywag.

scallywag *spell.* scalawag

Scapa Flow [A] *pr. name, hist.* a large natural harbor
located among the islands of the ➡Orkneys
Before, during, and after the two World Wars, this was the
principal home base of the ➡Royal Navy.
[B] *idiom, rh. sl.* to go

Scarborough *pr. name, hist.* a coastal resort and spa
town in➡ North Yorkshire that has been a
destination for vacationers since the 17th C.
The current population is 46,000 (1991 estimate).

Scarborough warning *comp. noun, coll.* no
warning whatsoever
The approximate judicial equivalent of shooting first and
asking questions afterwards, from the summary justice
reputedly handed out by ➡Scarborough magistrates.

scarf-ring *comp. noun* an ornamental scarf fastener,
which is somewhat similar to a scarf-pin

scarper *verb, sl.* to escape, flee or run away

scart *verb, Sc.* (1) to scrape at the ground in search of
food; (2) to take the last scrap of food from a dish; (3)
to make a grating or rasping sound; (4) to mark or
scratch a surface; (5) to write or scribble carelessly
(1) as is done by animals.

scatty *adj., abbr., coll.* scatterbrained

scaup *noun, Sc.* (1) the scalp; (2) bare or stony ground;
(3) shellfish found on rocky seashores at low tide

scavenger *noun, out.* a street cleaner or garbage collector

the **scavenger's daughter** *comp. noun, hist.* an
instrument of torture
Devised by the ➡Lieutenant of the Tower of London in the
reign of ➡Henry VIII, it pushed the head forward towards
the knees until blood was forced out from nose and ears.

SCE *pr. name, abbr.* ➡Scottish Certificate of Education

scepsis *spell.* skepsis
Philosophical questioning.

{**sceptic** » **sceptical** » **sceptically**} *spell.* {skeptic »
skeptical » skeptically}

{**scepticalness** » **scepticism**} *spell.* {skepticalness »
skepticism}

{**sceptre** » **sceptred**} *spell.* {scepter » sceptered}

schedule *verb* to add a building to the official
schedule of ➡listed buildings

scheme *noun, abbr., Sc.* a ➡housing scheme

school *noun* (1) a group of people drinking or
gambling together; (2) a hall where a university
holds its examinations

school captain *comp. noun* a school's leading student
SEE ALSO: ➡head {boy = girl}.

School Certificate *pr. name, hist.* a certificate
formerly awarded to school students performing
to a satisfactory standard in an examination that
replaced ➡O-Level examinations in 1951

school dinner *comp. noun* lunch provided at school

school-keeper *comp. noun* a school janitor
The American word and meaning is usual in Scotland.

school-leaver *comp. noun* someone who is just
about to cease, or has just ceased, attending school

school year *comp. noun* an academic year, which
usually begins in late August or early September

schooner *noun, out.* a measure or glass of sherry

schottische *noun, Ger.* a variety of slow polka or
the music for this
From the German *der schottische Tanz* = "the Scottish dance"

sciamachy *spell.* skiamachy
Fighting with shadows.

the **Science and Engineering Research
Council** *pr. name* a government-funded research
council established by ➡Royal Charter
Responsible for establishing and maintaining fundamental
research into the natural sciences and engineering.

the office of **Science and Technology** *pr. name* a
government agency directly managed by the
➡Cabinet Office

the **Science Museum** *pr. name* a museum dedicated
to the history of science, medicine and technology
Originally part of the ➡Great Exhibition of 1851.
Afterwards, it was moved to ➡Kensington as part of the
➡Victoria and Albert Museum until it gained
"independence" in 1909.

Scillonian *pr. name* a native, citizen or inhabitant of
the ➡Scilly Isles

the **Scilly Isles** *pr. name* a group of some 140 small
islands lying about 30 miles west of ➡Land's End

SCM *pr. name, abbr.* (1) a State Certified Midwife;
(2) the Student Christian Movement

scoff *verb, coll.* to eat voraciously

scone [A] *noun* a small sweet quickbread or cake
containing oatmeal or barley flour, which is baked
in an oven, or more traditionally, upon a griddle
[B] *noun, sl.* the head

Scone *pr. name, hist.* the ancient ➡Pictish capital, and later the first ➡Scottish capital

Kings of Scotland were crowned at the abbey here from 1157 to 1488, and then finally ➡Charles II in 1651. Today, Scone is a suburb of the city of ➡Perth, in ➡Tayside.

scoobs *noun, rh. sl.* beer

Military slang derived from "Scooby-doo, where are you?" during the 1991 Gulf War in Saudi Arabia, land of no alcohol.

scorch *verb, arch.* to cut or slash

score *noun, sl.* £20 (twenty pounds)

SEE ALSO: ➡gorilla, ➡monkey, ➡pony.

scorpion *noun, sl.* a native or citizen of Gibraltar

Military slang.

Scot *noun* (1) a Scottish native, inhabitant or citizen; (2) a person of Scottish decent

scot *noun, hist.* a medieval tax similar to a modern local property tax

Scotch [A] *adj., abbr.* ➡Scottish

A word that is in general disliked in Scotland, this adjective should not be used except for the special cases listed in this dictionary. It is not now considered a correct name for the inhabitants of Scotland or their language although it certainly was in the past.

[B] *noun, abbr.* ➡Scotch whisky

Scotch broth *comp. noun* a thick soup made from barley, with beef or mutton

Scotch cap *comp. noun, out.* a man's rimless bonnet

Scotch egg *comp. noun* a hard-boiled egg wrapped in sausage meat and fried

Commoner in England than Scotland, as it happens.

{**Scotchman » Scotchwoman**} *pr. name* a {Scotsman » Scotswoman}

Not popular words to use in Scotland.

Scotch mist *comp. noun* a sort of fine drizzle that hangs in the air like an aerosol

Scotch Terrier *pr. name* a ➡Scottish Terrier

Scotch whisky *comp. noun* whiskey made in Scotland

Spelling the word with an "e" is considered rather insulting in Scotland, as it implies that Scotch whisky is no different from the vastly inferior (and misspelled) Irish concoction.

scot-free *adj., coll.* without harm or cost

Scoticise *verb* to imbue or overlay or model upon Scottish idioms or habits

Scotland *pr. name* the second-largest, second-most populous kingdom making up the ➡United Kingdom

The current population of Scotland is 5,108,000 (1990 estimate). ➡Edinburgh is the capital city of Scotland, but ➡Glasgow is by far the largest city.

Scotland has its own legal, educational and banking systems. It has its own Presbyterian ➡established church—the ➡Church of Scotland—and it is often represented separately from England in international sporting competitions.

Scotland Yard *pr. name, hist.* the former headquarters of the ➡Metropolitan Police

The reason for this name is that the headquarters building, located between ➡Whitehall and the ➡Embankment, was erected on ground that had once been where the Scottish embassy in London stood. The correct name of the present-day police headquarters in London is ➡New Scotland Yard.

ScotRail *pr. name (TM)* a railroad company operating services in Scotland

It is part of ➡British Rail.

Scots *pr. name, Sc.* the Scottish dialect or language

Emphatically *not* ➡Gaelic, which is the Celtic tongue of the ➡Highland Scots, a very small minority of the Scottish population as a whole.

(See box on following page.)

the Scots *pr. name, hist.* (1) today, the inhabitants of Scotland, who are a mixture of Angle, Celt, Jute and Viking; (2) historically, ➡Celts who migrated from ➡Ireland to ➡Scotland around about the year 500

the Scots Guards *pr. name* one of five regiments forming the ➡Guards Division of the British Army

Formed under this name for the first time in 1660.

Scotsman *pr. name* a male native, citizen or inhabitant of ➡Scotland

Scots Mile *pr. name, hist., Sc.* 1,976 yards or 5,928 feet

This unit is no longer in use. SEE ALSO: ➡Irish Mile.

scots pancake *comp. noun* a pancake

Of course, in Scotland it is just a pancake.

Scots pine *comp. noun* a Scotch pine

Scots pint *comp. noun, hist.* a former unit of liquid capacity in Scotland, equivalent to about three English or 3.6 U.S. pints, but no longer of any practical significance

Scots, wha hae! *pr. name, Sc.* one of Scotland's unofficial national anthems, more properly entitled *Robert Bruce's March to Bannockburn*, with words by Robert Burns

Scotswoman *pr. name* a female native, citizen or inhabitant of ➡Scotland

{**Scotticise » Scottishise**} *verb* to imbue with Scottishness; to emulate the Scottish way

{**Scotticism » Scottishism**} *noun* a Scottish expression, word, or idiom

Scottie [A] *adj., coll.* a diminutive version of ➡Scottish

[B] *noun* a ➡Scottish Terrier

Scottis *pr. name, hist., Sc.* a former name for the language that is now called ➡Scots or ➡Scottish

It was called ➡Inglis alone until 1494, when it was first called this new name by Adam Loutful. SEE ALSO: ➡Lallans.

Scottish *pr. name, Sc.* ➡Scots

305

The Guid Scots Tongue

Of all the different forms of English found in the British Isles, none is more different or more interesting than that found in Scotland. It is the only variety of British English that has ever had any grounds to claim linguistic independence. Scots is certainly more than just another dialect. It is distinct from standard English, with its own ancient history, literature, grammar, orthographic and other conventions; in other words, many of the trappings of a separate and distinct language, yet for all that it is not truly another language.

Unlike the history of English in Ireland or Wales, the English of Scotland is as home-grown in that land as the English of England is there. Old English, or Anglo-Saxon, was first brought to Scotland early in the seventh century by northern cousins of the same Germanic tribes that brought it to England at about same time. It shared the territory with Gaelic until late in the eleventh century when the arrival of Anglo-Norman kings marked a linguist turning point for Scotland. From that time there was to be a steady advance of English through all of the country excepting the inaccessible ➡Highlands and islands where the king's authority was weak anyway.

Of course, the royal court spoke ➡Norman French, not English. But the language of the king's representatives, their underlings and the common soldiery encouraged to settle the new ➡royal burghs established to secure the kingdom, was English, although it was a form heavily influenced by the Scandinavian tongue of the Vikings who had earlier settled much of the ➡Western Isles and the eastern parts of Scotland, and northern England too. This hybrid speech, a sort of Anglo-Danish Creole, was to evolve by the fourteenth century into the dominant language of Scotland south of the Highlands. The original ➡Celtic inhabitants, now heavily outnumbered, gradually abandoned their Gaelic, and Scotland's nobility discarded their Norman French.

So it came about that through the fifteenth and sixteenth centuries, there were effectively two "official" national languages in Britain There was what became the formal English of ➡Tudor England, originally the dialect of ➡Kent and London, but eventually exemplified by the ➡Authorized Version of the Bible and the works of William Shakespeare; and then there was the formal Scots of the ➡Stewart court and the lawyers and literati of ➡Edinburgh. The two languages were closely related; they were different from each other to about the same extent that Swedish and Danish, or Spanish and Portuguese for example, differ from each other today, which is to say not all that much. Southern English and Scots English have always had a large measure of mutual comprehensibility, although even today some none-Scots English speakers might just possibly have some difficulty with this proposition when listening to a drunken ➡Glaswegian holding forth on a topic close to his heart: soccer, for example.

However, the Anglicization of Scots—or rather, its convergence with English—is usually considered to have begun with the Reformation, especially when Scots Calvinists adopted the Geneva Bible after 1560. Then the process became greatly accelerated after the ➡Union of the Crowns in 1603.

This linguistic merging proceeded apace until by the middle of the eighteenth century virtually all Scots prose literature was written in the English of London. However, the same was not true of poetry; Robert Burns, Scotland's national poet, who lived from 1759 from 1796, almost always wrote in Scots. And the day-to-day spoken language of most Scots of that time remained resolutely embedded in the older tongue. Although even here there was compromise with the language of the south, there is also no doubt that there remained a major distinction between spoken Scots and "standard" English.

Since then the unifying process has continued. Nevertheless a very large measure of the older language can still be heard in Scotland, especially among the less well educated and older, more rustic folks living in rural Scotland. Most educated Scots speak what is best described as Standard English with a Scots accent, intermingled with words and phrases that reveal the speaker's Scottish background and can sometimes leave a listener from elsewhere in the English-speaking world at a loss.

Scots is also called ➡Scottish and ➡Lallans. In Medieval times, it was called ➡Inglis and ➡Scottis.

the **Scottish Ballet** *pr. name, hist.* the only professional ballet company in Scotland

Founded as the Western Theatre Ballet in ➡Bristol in 1957, it moved to ➡Glasgow in 1969 and took its present name.

Scottish Baronial style

Scottish baronial *pr. name, Sc.* an architectural style characterized by turrets, crow-step gables, and so on

It was especially popular in revival during the 19th C.
➡Balmoral Castle is an especially well-known example.

Scottish Certificate of Education *pr. name, Sc.* a certificate issued to every student who has performed satisfactorily in either ➡Standard or ➡Higher Grade examinations

Scottish Enterprise *pr. name* a government executive agency established to encourage and assist in the economic development of Scotland

Scottish Gaelic *pr. name, Gae., Sc.* the Scottish version of the ➡Celtic language

Today, it is spoken by some 65,000 people living in the western ➡Highlands and islands of Scotland. *SEE ALSO:* ➡Gaeilge, its very close relative spoken in Ireland.

the **Scottish Law Commission** *pr. name, Sc.* a commission set up by ➡Parliament to examine the laws of Scotland and to make proposals for modernization and improvement

the **Scottish National Gallery of Modern Art** *pr. name, hist.* a collection begun in ➡Edinburgh in 1950

the **Scottish National Orchestra** *pr. name, hist.* the name of the ➡Royal Scottish Orchestra until 1991

the **Scottish National Party** *pr. name* a political party advocating the independence of Scotland from the rest of the ➡United Kingdom

Founded in 1928, it won its first ➡Westminster seat in 1945, since when its fortunes have risen and fallen several times, but has never yet come close to its goal of independence.

the **Scottish National Portrait Gallery** *pr. name, hist.* a large and significant collection of portraits by famous artists or of famous people or both

Founded in 1882 in emulation of the recently-opened ➡National Portrait Gallery in London, it is located beside the ➡Royal Museum of Scotland in ➡Edinburgh.

the **Scottish National War Memorial** *pr. name, hist.* a marble Stone of Remembrance set upon a bare outcrop within ➡Edinburgh Castle

It was placed there in 1927 in remembrance of the many Scots who had fallen in World War I.

Scottish Natural Heritage *pr. name* a permanent independent agency set up by the government to promote the conservation and improvement of Scottish landscape and wildlife

the **Scottish Office** *pr. name* the office of state responsible for the internal government of Scotland

The Scottish Office is responsible for those functions which, in England, are looked after by the ➡Home Office, the ➡Departments of ➡Health, ➡Education, ➡Environment, ➡Agriculture and many others.

Scottish Opera *pr. name, hist.* Scotland's only professional opera company, which was founded in Glasgow in 1962 and is based there

the **Scottish Record Office** *pr. name, hist.* the office in ➡Edinburgh where the official government documents of Scotland are stored

Scottish Terrier *pr. name* a small rough-haired terrier with short legs and a large head

Scottish TV *pr. name* a local commercial TV company headquartered in Glasgow, and which is part of the ➡ITV network

the **Scottish verdict** *comp. noun, coll.* ➡not proven

the **Scott Monument** *pr. name, hist.* a 200-ft tall Gothic tower on the southern side of ➡Princes Street, ➡Edinburgh, built in remembrance of Sir Walter Scott

It was completed in 1844 and can be climbed to the top using an internal spiral staircase.

Scouse *noun, coll.* the dialect spoken in ➡Liverpool

Said to be derived from ➡lobscouse.

Scouser *noun, coll.* a native or inhabitant of ➡Liverpool

scout *noun* a college servant

Particularly at ➡Oxford University.

SCPS *pr. name, abbr.* the Society of Civil and Public Servants, a labor union for civil service clerks

SCR *noun, abbr.* a ➡senior common Room

scrag-end *comp. noun* low-grade mutton

scraggy *adj.* scrawny

scramble *verb* a motorbike race over rough terrain

scran *noun, sl.* military rations

scrape *noun* thinly applied butter on bread or toast

scraperboard *noun* black-surfaced board used to make white-line drawings by scraping at the surface

307

scrap merchant *comp. noun* a dealer in discarded materials and components

screenwasher *noun* an automobile windshield washer

screw *noun, sl.* (1) a miserable or mean person; (2) the value of salary or wages; (3) the curved motion of a billiard ball which has been hit eccentrically; (4) a small ⟶twist of paper

the **screws** *noun, Mid.* arthritis

screwtop *noun, out.* a bottle with a cap which can be screwed off and back on again
Once the kind normally used to contain beer, but now rare.

scribbling pad *comp. noun* a scratch pad

scrimshank *verb, sl.* to malinger or otherwise avoid military duty or responsibility

scrubber *noun, derog., sl.* a slut or prostitute

scrubbing brush *comp. noun* a scrub brush

scrum *noun, abbr.* (1) a situation in the game of ⟶Rugby where forwards from both teams come together in a tight group and attempt to gain possession of the ball with their feet; (2) a scrambling and muddled rush or crowd of people
Originally, this was an abbreviation of ⟶scrummage.

scrum-half *noun* the rugby half-back responsible for throwing the ball into a ⟶scrum

scrummage *noun, coll.* (1) a frenetic crowd; (2) a place of confusion
Derived from "scimmage."

scrump [A] *noun, West* a small apple
[B] *verb, coll.* to steal fruit from an orchard

scrumpy *noun* rough cider made with ⟶scrump apples

scruple *noun, arch.* a unit of weight, equal to 20 grains, formerly used by apothecaries

scrutineer *noun* a person who supervises the conduct of an election and counts the votes

scud *verb, Sc.* to slap with the open hand

scuddie *adj., Sc.* (1) naked; (2) possessing no clothes; (3) not large enough

scuffer *noun, North, sl.* a policeman

scunner *noun, Sc.* (1) a feeling of disgust, sickness or loathing; (2) a sudden shock or shudder of repugnance; (3) a loathsome or disgusting person or thing

scupper [A] *noun, sl.* a prostitute
[B] *verb* to sink a ship
[C] *verb, sl.* (1) to kill; (2) to stop or wreck a project

scutter *verb, Sc.* (1) to splash or spill; (2) to indulge in pointless or time-wasting activity; (3) to delay or prevent with pointless or irritating interruptions

scuttle *noun* that part of an automobile body between the windshield and the hood

scwad *noun, East* mud

SDLP *pr. name, abbr., hist.* the ⟶Social Democratic and Labour Party

SDP *pr. name, abbr., hist.* ⟶Social Democratic Party

the **Sea-girt isle** *pr. name, coll.* England, described in this manner because as Shakespeare put it, it is:

This precious stone set in the silver sea,
Which serves it in the office of a wall.

Of course this is not strictly true; England is but part of the isle.

the **Sealed Knot Society** *pr. name, hist.* a society whose members come together for the purpose of re-enacting historical military events (in particular, battles) of the ⟶English Civil War
The ⟶Civil War Society has a similar interest.

sea loch *comp. noun, Gae., Sc.* a narrow arm of the sea
SEE ALSO: ⟶sea lough.

Sea Lord *pr. name, arch.* a naval officer who is a member of the Board of ⟶Admiralty

sea lough *comp. noun, Gae., Ir.* a narrow arm of the sea
SEE ALSO: ⟶sea loch.

seals of office *comp. noun* the seals held by the ⟶Lord Chancellor and the various ⟶Secretaries of State during their tenure of office

Sealyham Terrier *pr. name* a short, wiry coat terrier
Named after Sealyham in Wales.

seam bowler *comp. noun* a bowler who deviates a ⟶cricket ball by causing it to bounce off its seam

Seanad *pr. name, abbr., Gae.* ⟶Seanad Éireann

Seanad Éireann *pr. name, Gae.* the upper house of the Parliament of the ⟶Irish Republic

SEAQ *pr. name, abbr.* the Stock Exchange Automatic Quotations, a computerized quotations system used by the London Stock Exchange

season *noun, abbr., coll.* a ⟶season ticket

season ticket *comp. noun, coll.* a ticket permitting the holder to make an unlimited number of visits, journeys, or similar over a set period such as a week, month, year, etc., as the case may be

seat *noun* an ⟶MP's parliamentary ⟶constituency

{**seborrhoea » seborrhoeal**} *spell.* {seborrhea » seborrheal}
The discharge of excessive sebum.

secateurs *noun* pruning shears

second *verb* to temporarily transfer a civil servant or military officer from their usual position to another

secondary modern school *comp. noun* a high school providing a more technical and less academic education than a ⟶grammar school

secondary school *comp. noun, pref.* a high school

the **Second Chamber** *pr. name* the ⟶House of Lords

second-class degree *noun, abbr., coll.* a university ➡first degree awarded with the second-highest of three possible classes of honor

Each class is further divided into upper and lower grades. The class and grade of a degree is often abbreviated in the form of, for example, 2-1, which is a second-class degree of the upper grade, or 2-2, which is one of the lower grade. See also: ➡first-class degree, ➡third-class degree.

second floor *comp. noun* the third floor
... and so forth.

the **Second Lord of the Treasury** *pr. name* the full official title of the ➡Chancellor of the Exchequer

second post *comp. noun* (1) the second mail collection of the day; (2) the second mail delivery of the day

Second Reading *comp. noun* the presentation of a ➡bill to ➡Parliament for approval of the general principle or broad idea behind it

the **Second Scottish Interregnum** *pr. name, hist.* the period between 1296 and 1306, from the overthrowing and abdication of ➡John Baliot until ➡Robert the Bruce was crowned king.

After Edward I of England's choice as king to end the ➡First Scottish Interregnum, ➡John Baliot, had abdicated, there was no clear successor. However this time the Scots did not seek the advice of the English king but determined to make their own choice, which unsurprisingly led to a chaotic situation similar to civil war.

secretary *noun* a government minister's principal assistant civil servant

secretary of state *comp. noun* a senior Cabinet minister who is responsible for a major government department

Secretary of State for Agriculture *pr. name* the senior Cabinet minister who is responsible for the Department of ➡Agriculture

the **Secretary of State for Defence** *pr. name* the senior Cabinet minister responsible for the ➡Ministry of Defense

the **Secretary of State for Education** *pr. name* the senior Cabinet minister who is responsible for the ➡Department for Education

the **Secretary of State for Employment** *pr. name* the senior Cabinet minister responsible for the Department of ➡Employment

the **Secretary of State for Environment** *pr. name* the senior Cabinet minister responsible for the Department of ➡Environment

the **Secretary of State for National Heritage** *pr. name* the senior Cabinet minister responsible for the Department of ➡National Heritage

the **Secretary of State for Northern Ireland** *pr. name* the senior Cabinet minister responsible for the ➡Northern Ireland Office

the **Secretary of State for Scotland** *pr. name* the senior Cabinet minister responsible for the ➡Scottish Office

the **Secretary of State for Social Security** *pr. name* the senior Cabinet minister responsible for the Department of ➡Social Security

the **Secretary of State for Transport** *pr. name* the senior Cabinet minister responsible for the Department of ➡Transport

the **Secretary of State for Wales** *pr. name* the senior Cabinet minister responsible for the ➡Welsh Office

the **Secret Intelligence Service** *pr. name* the proper current name for ➡MI6

section *verb* (1) to cut a sample, such as a portion of tissue, into very thin slices for the purpose of examining it under a microscope; (2) to commit a person to a psychiatric institution

(2) may only be done in accordance with the terms of the relevant section or sections of the mental health laws.

the **Security Service** *pr. name* the proper modern name for ➡MI5

sederunt *noun, Fr., Sc.* (1) a sitting of a court; (2) a sitting of a legislative body such as a parliament; (3) an informal or social gathering; (4) a list of those present at a meeting, recorded in the minutes
From the French *sedère* = "sit"

seed-corn *comp. noun* (1) seed stock kept for replanting; (2) a euphemism for seed money

seeder *noun* a spawning fish

seedlip *noun, arch.* a basket use in hand-seeding

seedplot *noun* an area set aside for development

seed potato *comp. noun* a potato used for the planting of a new crop

see off *verb, coll.* to remove or evict

see over *verb, coll.* to inspect
A house, for example.

see right *verb, coll.* to make sure things are all right

sees {a » us a} *imper., Sc., sl.* give me

Seidlitz powder *pr. name* Seidlitz powders
A laxative effervescent salt named after the mineral spring at Seidlitz, Bohemia, in what is now the Czech Republic.

seigniorage *noun, arch.* the right of the ➡Crown to keep for itself a portion of all bullion which is processed in the ➡Royal Mint

Seisyllwg *pr. name, hist.* an ancient kingdom in west-central Wales
Created out of the 9th C. union of ➡Ceredigion and ➡Ystrad Towy.

sejant *adj.* in heraldry, seated upright
Emblematic of counsel.

sel *noun, Sc.* self

Select Committee *pr. name* a committee of the ➧House of Commons formed for the specific purpose of looking at a specific issue and reporting back

self-cater *verb* to provide and prepare one's own food

self-catering accommodation *comp. noun* accommodations where tenants are responsible for providing and preparing their own food

{**self-centred** » **self-centredness**} *spell.* {self-centered » self-centeredness}

self-coloured *spell.* self-colored

self-denying ordinance *comp. noun, hist.* (1) originally, a measure of the ➧Long Parliament of 1645, requiring members of both ➧Houses to give up all military commands and civil offices within 40 days; (2) now an ironical description of the behavior of anyone declining a benefit for themselves

Naturally, (1) was more honored by its breach than observance. Perhaps (2) is also, but who can tell?

self-drive car *comp. noun* a rental car

self-feeder *comp. noun* a machine or other device that seeks out and replenishes its own fuel supply

self-fulfilment *spell.* self-fulfillment

self-raising flour *comp. noun* self-rising flour

Selfridges *pr. name (TM)* a large departmental store in central London

Selkirk *pr. name, hist.* a former Scottish county, now part of ➧Borders region

Selkirk bannock *comp. noun, Sc.* a kind of rich fruit loaf from ➧Selkirk

Sellafield *pr. name* a major nuclear energy complex on the coast of ➧Cumbria

sell a pup *idiom. phr. verb, sl.* to swindle by selling that which is worthless

Sellotape [A] *pr. name (TM)* a transparent adhesive plastic tape similar to Scotch Tape (TM)
[B] *verb* to use ➧Sellotape (TM)

sell under guise *phr. verb, sl.* to attempt to sell while pretending to carry out market research

sell up *verb* (1) to dispose of a business or house; (2) to sell goods belonging to a debtor as a way of paying off their debt

Selwyn College *pr. name* a college of ➧Cambridge University founded in 1882

semé *adj.* in heraldry, being covered all over with small devices such as stars

semibreve *noun, pref.* a whole note
A musical term.

semi-detached *adj., coll.* not paying proper attention

semi-detached house *comp. noun* a side-by-side duplex house

seminary *noun* a college for candidate priests to the Roman Catholic Church

semiquaver *noun, pref.* a sixteenth note
A musical term.

semmit *noun, Sc.* a man's undershirt

SEN *noun, abbr.* a ➧State Enrolled Nurse

sen *noun, East* self

senator *noun, Sc.* a judge of the ➧Court of Session

send *verb* to bowl a ➧cricket ball

send down *verb* to expel or rusticate from university

send to Coventry *verb, coll.* to ostracize

senior {**aircraftsman** » **aircraftswoman**} *comp. noun* the third-lowest rank in the ➧RAF

senior common room *comp. noun* the common living room used by the ➧fellows and other senior members of a college

senior lecturer *comp. noun* a university teacher approximately equivalent in grade to an associate professor in the United States
SEE ALSO: ➧lecturer, ➧professor and ➧reader.

senior nursing officer *comp. noun* a person responsible for the proper operation of nursing services in a hospital

senior private *comp. noun* a British enlisted soldier
Equivalent in rank to a private 1st class in the U.S. Army.

the **Senior Service** *comp. noun* the ➧Royal Navy
There had been a permanent naval fleet since the 9th C. By comparison, the army is a young upstart.

senior tutor *comp. noun* a tutor responsible for the teaching arrangements at a college

{**sentinelled** » **sentinelling**} *spell.* {sentineled » sentineling}

sentry-go *comp. noun* the process of marching up and down along a fixed path in the manner expected of a military sentry

sepoy *noun, arch.* a native Indian recruited as a soldier by the British Army in India

septendecillion *noun, num.* 10^{102}
The American septendecillion is 10^{54}.

{**septicaemia** » **septicaemic**} *spell.* {septicemia » septicemic}
Blood poisoning.

septic tank *idiom, rh. sl.* an American
Derivation: American > ➧Yank > tank > septic tank.

septillion *noun, num.* a tredecillion, or 10^{42}
The American septillion is 10^{24}.

septre *spell.* septer

sepulchre *spell.* sepulcher

SERC *pr. name, abbr.* the ➡Science and Engineering Research Council

sergeant-major [A] *comp. noun* a non-commissioned officer in the British Army
Equivalent in rank to a master-sergeant in the U.S. Army. [B] *comp. noun, sl.* military slang for (1) tea laced with rum; (2) a very strong, well-sugared tea

the **Serious Fraud Office** *pr. name* an autonomous department of the ➡Attorney General's Office
It was established in 1987 with responsibility for investigating and prosecuting serious and complex frauds.

serjeant *noun* a sergeant .
The official way of spelling this rank in British Army lists.

serjeant-at-arms *spell.* sergeant-at-arms
An official of a court of law, or of ➡Parliament.

serjeant-at-law *comp. noun, hist.* the highest rank of ➡barrister

the **Serpentine** *pr. name* a lake in ➡Hyde Park, where it is used for fishing, boating and swimming

SERPS *pr. name, abbr.* the ➡State Earnings Related Pension Scheme

serve out *phr. verb* to wreak vengeance upon

servery *noun* a small room adjacent to a dining room
Where cutlery, etc. is stored and from where meals are served.

service dress *comp. noun* a military uniform

service flat *comp. noun* an apartment with maid service included in the rent

services *noun* utilities such as electricity, water, etc.

serviette *noun* a table napkin

servit *noun, Sc.* a table napkin

set about *verb, coll.* to set upon or to attack

set fair *adj. phr.* likely to remain fine
Particularly of the weather.

set meal *comp. noun* a *table d'hôte* or fixed menu offered in a hotel or restaurant

set phrase *comp. noun* a standard arrangement of words

set piece *comp. noun* a formal or regular arrangement

set scrum *comp. noun* a Rugby scrum ordered by the referee

set the Thames on fire *idiom. phr. verb, coll.* to set the world on fire; make a great success in life, etc.

sett *noun, Sc.* a pattern of ➡tartan, many of which are now considered the specific "property" of a particular ➡Highland ➡clan

settling day *comp. noun, hist.* the biweekly payment day formerly used at the London Stock Exchange

set (something) to one side *phr. verb, coll.* to set (something) aside

the **Seven Years War** *pr. name, hist.* the European war from 1756 to 1763, whose central cause was the struggle for hegemony in central Europe between Austria and Prussia
As usual, Britain's goal was to prevent the European continent from being dominated by one power, so it fought on Prussia's side against the strongest power of the day, France, whose client Austria was.
Although not greatly involved in the European land battles, Britain had a very useful war elsewhere. In North America, the fall of Quebec to Wolfe secured Canada and the French gave up all of the continent east of the Mississippi except for New Orleans. In India, the French colony of Pondicherry fell to the ➡East India Company, effectively leaving all of the sub-continent open to British influence and eventual control.
At sea, victory over the French fleet at Quiberon Bay left Britain as master of the seas. At the end of this war, Britain had for the first time clearly moved well ahead of its great rival superpower, France.

the **Severn** *pr. name* ➡Great Britain's longest river
It rises in northeastern Wales and flows for about 220 miles until discharging into the Atlantic through the ➡Bristol Channel

the **Severn Bridge** *pr. name* a large suspension bridge over the estuary of the ➡Severn River to the north of ➡Bristol
This bridge carries the London to South Wales ➡motorway. It has a span of 3,240 ft and was completed in 1966.
Due to increased traffic, a second is under constructed, due to come into operation before 2000.

Severn capon *comp. noun, coll.* sole
The flatfish, that is

the **Severn Tunnel** *pr. name* the longest railroad tunnel entirely within Britain
Its 4¼ miles takes the principal railroad line between London and South Wales under the mouth of the ➡Severn River.

Seville orange *comp. noun* a bitter kind of orange used to make marmalade
From Seville in Spain, where they originate.

sewage {farm » works} *comp. noun* a sewage waste-treatment plant

sewer *noun, derog., out., sl.* a despicable individual

sewer rat *comp. noun* a common rat

sewin *noun* a Welsh salmon trout

sex bomb *comp. noun, arch., sl.* a very sexy woman

sexdecillion *noun, num.* 10^{96}
The American sexdecillion is 10^{51}.

sextillion *noun, num.* an undecillion, or 10^{36}
The American sextillion is 10^{21}.

Sezincote *pr. name, hist.* a very unusual house whose external appearance evokes Indian architecture but has a traditional neoclassical interior
It was built in the early years of the 19th C. some 20 miles to the north of ➡Cheltenham.

SFA *pr. name, abbr.* the Scottish Football Association
The body which regulates professional soccer in Scotland

SFO *pr. name, abbr.* the ➡Serious Fraud Office

SG *pr. name, abbr.* the ➡Solicitor General

SGM *noun, abbr.* the Sea Gallantry Medal

sh *noun, abbr., arch.* a shilling
This ia an abbreviation for the ➡shilling, which ceased to be legal tender in 1971. *SEE ALSO:* ➡s.

shackles *noun, sl.* a thick soup made from leftovers

the Shadow Cabinet *pr. name* the leading politicians of the largest non-government party in the ➡House of Commons
It is they who direct opposition to administration policies and constitute a potential alternate ➡Cabinet in the event of a change of administration.

shadow minister *comp. noun* a member of the ➡Shadow Cabinet

Shaftesbury Avenue *pr. name, hist.* a street that runs through the ➡West End of London
It opened for traffic in 1886, and is considered to be the heart of the London theater district. There are now just six theaters on Shaftesbury Avenue.

shagged out *adj., sl., taboo* exhausted

William Shakespeare

the **Shakespeare Memorial Theatre** *pr. name* a theater in ➡Stratford-upon-Avon
One home of the ➡Royal Shakespeare Company and location of an annual summer season of Shakespeare's plays.

Shakespearian *adj.* (1) in the style of William Shakespeare; (2) of or relating to William Shakespeare or his works, life and times

shaky do *idiom, arch., sl.* a difficult situation
This expression began life as ➡RAF World War II slang.

shamateur *noun, coll., derog.* a player or participant in any sport who claims amateur status but nevertheless makes money from the sport

shambolic *adj., coll.* chaotic, in a shambles

Shamrock *noun, Ir.* the vegetative emblem of Ireland

From the Irish *seamróg*, which is the diminutive of *seamar* + *og* = "clover" + "young."

shandy *noun, abbr.* a drink consisting of beer and either ➡lemonade or ginger beer in equal parts
An abbreviation of the 19th C. word "shandygaff."

shanks's pony *coll.* shanks's mare; one's own legs, used as a method of transportation
SEE ALSO: ➡Tamson's mear.

shanty *spell. pref.* chantey
A song sung by sailors, also spelled ➡chanty.

sharp end *comp. noun, coll.* (1) the bow of a ship; (2) where the action is

sharpish [A] *adj., coll.* quite rapidly
[B] *adv., coll.* quite sharp

shaw *noun* leaves and stalks of root crops like potatoes

sheading *noun* an ➡Isle of Man administrative unit
The island is divided into six sheadings.

shear *verb, Sc.* to reap wheat by means of a sickle

sheath *noun* a condom

shebeen *noun, Gae., Ir.* an illicit drinking establishment
From the Gaelic *séibe* = "mugful"

shed *noun, Sc.* a hair ➡parting

sheder *adj., East* female

sheepcote *noun* a sheepfold

sheep-dip *comp. noun* a bath-like structure where sheep are immersed in the chemical concoction also known as a sheep-dip

sheepshank *noun, Sc.* (1) the leg of a sheep; (2) a worthless person

sheepwalk *noun* a pasture for sheep

Sheffield *pr. name* ➡South Yorkshire's principal city
Sheffield has been at the heart of the British steel industry for a very long time indeed, and certainly known as a cutlery-making center since the 15th. C.
Incorporated as a city in 1843, the current population, including suburbs, is 650,000 (1988 estimate).

the **Sheldonian Theatre** *pr. name* the Senate House of ➡Oxford University
Designed by Sir Christopher Wren and opened in 1699.

Shell *pr. name (TM)* a large international oil company, headquartered in London.
Shell trades (as Royal Dutch-Shell) in partnership with the Royal Dutch Oil Company, of Amsterdam, Netherlands.

shell-suit *comp. noun* a kind of shiny track suit worn by people who want to look both energetic, fashionable and relaxed, all at the same time

Shelta *noun, arch., Ir.* a secret language of Irish gypsies

Shelter *pr. name* a charity founded in 1966 to campaign for homes for people with nowhere to live

sheltered housing *comp. noun* a housing development especially designed to be suitable for retired or disabled people

Normally with staff living there to help in an emergency.

Sheltie *noun, abbr.* (1) a ➠Shetland Pony; (2) a ➠Shetland sheepdog

shepherd's pie *comp. noun* a baked pie of minced meat with a top layer of mashed potatoes

For that authentic "shepherd" sensation, the meat should be mutton, but nowadays it's much more likely to be beef. *SEE ALSO:* ➠cottage pie.

sherardise *verb* to coat iron or steel with zinc by exposure to zinc dust at high temperature

A word devised from the merging of "galvanize" with the name of the inventor of this technique, Sherard Cowper-Coles.

Sheraton *noun, hist.* a style of English furniture that originated around 1800

A graceful and delicate style devised by Thomas Sheraton.

sherbet [A] *noun* a powdered candy, sometimes eaten like this; also a sweet drink when dissolved in water

[B] *noun, North, sl.* liquor or beer

Sherborne School *pr. name* one of the leading English ➠public schools

Founded in 1550, it is located in ➠Dorset.

sheriff *noun, abbr.* a ➠High Sheriff

Sheriff *noun, Sc.* the chief Crown officer responsible for the administration of justice in a Scottish ➠district

That is, the legal official responsible for the operation of the legal system and, in particular, the courts within a district.

sheriff clerk *comp. noun, Sc.* clerk of a ➠Sheriff Court

Sheriff Court *comp. noun, Sc.* a court presided over by a ➠Sheriff or ➠Sheriff Principal

Where most civil cases and all criminal cases too serious to be heard in a magistrate's court are heard in the first instance.

sheriff-depute *comp. noun, arch., Sc.* a lawyer appointed to be the principal judge of a ➠sheriffdom

sheriffdom *noun, Sc.* the ➠region or ➠district that a ➠Sheriff Principle or ➠sheriff is responsible for

the **Sheriff of Chancery** *pr. name, Sc.* the ➠Sheriff Principal of ➠Lothian and ➠Borders when acting on matters concerning the transference of heritable property to heirs throughout Scotland

sheriff officer *comp. noun, Sc.* an official who carries out the instructions of a ➠Sheriff

the **Sheriff of Nottingham** *pr. name, hist.* ➠Robin Hood's traditional enemy

Sheriff Principal *pr. name, Sc.* the chief officer of the Crown responsible for the administration of justice in a Scottish ➠region

In other words, the legal official responsible for the operation of the legal system and in particular the courts within a region.

sheriff substitute *comp. noun, arch., Sc.* deputy ➠Sheriff

Sherlock Holmes *pr. name, hist.* a fictitious detective

To much of the world, the personification of the private detective. The first Holmes story, *A Study in Scarlet,* appeared in *Beeton's Chritsmas Annual* in 1887.

He was the invention of Sir Arthur Conan Doyle, but probably based on the character and techniques developed by Dr. Joseph Bell of ➠Edinburgh University whom Doyle had met and been much influenced by when he was a medical student there.

Sherwood Forest *pr. name, hist.* a large forest in western ➠Nottinghamshire

This is said to have been where ➠Robin Hood and his colleagues lived during the 14th C. It is known that six or seven centuries ago when he was supposed to be around, the forest was very much larger than it is now.

Shetland *pr. name* a Scottish ➠Island Council

The current population is 25,000 (1991 Census).

Shetlander *noun* a native, inhabitant or citizen of the ➠Shetland Islands

Shetland lace *comp. noun* a kind of very fine lace that features open woolen trimming

Shetland pony *comp. noun* a small, rough-coated and hardy breed of pony from the ➠Shetland Islands

the **Shetlands** *pr. name* an archipelago of some 100 islands lying about 120 miles off the northern Scottish mainland, beyond the ➠Orkneys

The most remote inhabited part of the ➠United Kingdom. Until transferred, with the ➠Orkneys, to the Scottish ➠Crown in 1468 to compensate for the non-payment of the dowry of the bride of ➠James III, the Shetlands were Norwegian. More recently, the Shetlands have become a major center of the oil business, with Europe's largest oil terminal, ➠Sullom Voe on the northern coast of the largest island, serving the major oil fields of the ➠North Sea.

Shetland sheepdog *comp. noun* a heavily coated breed from the ➠Shetland Islands

They are said to somewhat resemble a small ➠collie.

Shetland wool *comp. noun* a fine soft kind of wool found on ➠Shetland sheep

sheugh *noun, Sc.* a trench, ditch or open drain

shice *noun, Ger., sl.* counterfeit money

From the German *Scheiss* = "shit."

shicer *noun, derog., Ger., sl.* a despicable parson

From the German *Scheisser* = "shiter."

shield *noun* the main component of a ➠coat of arms

Permitted colors are known as metals, other shadings or patterns are called furs, and items placed in the ground of the shield are called charges.

shieling

shieling *noun, Sc.* (1) a mountainous summer pasture; (2) a primitive mountain hut upon a (1)

shift *verb, sl.* to rapidly gulp large quantities of food

shillelagh *noun, Gae., Ir.* a cudgel of blackthorn oak
From Shillelagh, in County ➠Wicklow, Ireland

shilling *noun, hist.* a former British monetary unit
It was worth 12 old pence or 1/20th of a pound, and was commonly written using the ➠shilling mark or solidus in the following manner...
"1/-" was one shilling
"10/-" was ten shillings
"1/6" was one shilling and six pence
"15/11" was fifteen shillings and eleven pence
... and so forth.

shilling mark *comp. noun, hist.* the ➠solidus, a oblique backstroke thus: '/', used to separate ➠old pence and ➠shillings when written numerically thus for example: 2/6, which represented two shillings and six pence.
The solidus is still very commonly used for many purposes, such as the writing of dates, fractions, ratios, etc.
SEE ALSO: ➠shilling.

shilling Scots *comp. noun, hist., Sc.* a Scots coin worth two ➠bawbees
By 1707 when it ceased to be legal tender, one Scots shilling was worth one English ➠penny. For more about Scots currency, *SEE ALSO:* ➠pound Scots.

shilling shocker *comp. noun, arch., sl.* an upscale and more expensive variety of the ➠penny dreadful

shilpit *adj., Sc.* (1) thin, starved or puny; (2) insipid
(1) is of a person, (2) is of a drink

shin *noun* a shank cut of beef

shiner *noun, sl.* a diamond or other gemstone

shinner *noun, Ir.* a supporter or member of ➠Sinn Fein

shinty *noun, Sc.* a game like field hockey or

hurling, now most commonly played in the ➠Scottish Highlands

ship a sea *idiom. phr. verb, coll.* to ship a lot of water

ship-fever *comp. noun, arch., out.* typhus

ship money *comp. noun, hist.* a tax misused by ➠Charles I to raise money for the purpose of building up the ➠Royal Navy during the 1630s
It was an ancient right of the king to levy such a tax upon the coastal cities and ports of England in order to finance the navy, but when Charles I extended the tax to the whole country in 1635 and then again in 1636, this was seen as an attempt to get around ➠Parliament's long-accepted right to set taxes. This provoked Parliamentary ire, and led to their declaring in 1640 that the tax was illegal, so helping set the country moving toward civil war.

ship of the desert *idiom, coll.* a camel

ship-of-the-line *comp. noun, hist.* an 18th C. ➠line-of-battle ship
In the Royal Navy of that time, this would be a warship of the 1st to 4th rate, able to take its place in the line of battle.

shipping articles *comp. noun* ship's articles

shipping bill *comp. noun* a manifest of shipped goods

the shipping forecast *pr. name* a broadcast report on the current and forecast weather conditions in the sea areas around the ➠British Isles
Provided by the ➠Meteorological Office and broadcast by ➠BBC radio stations several times each day.

shipping master *comp. noun* an official who supervises the signing of ➠ships' articles, paying the crew, and so forth

ship-rigged *adj.* square-rigged

ship's biscuit *comp. noun* sea biscuit or hard tack

ship's corporal *comp. noun, out.* a non-commissioned ship's officer responsible for discipline under the

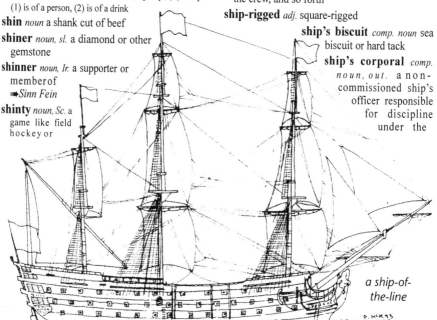

a ship-of-the-line

D. MCK 93

authority of the master of arms.

shipshape and Bristol fashion *idiom* everything in perfect order
Originally of a ship, now applicable to anything.

ship's husband *comp. noun, coll.* a port agent responsible for the provisioning of a ship

shire *noun, out.* (1) an English, Irish or Welsh county; (2) a former Scottish county

the **Shire Counties** *pr. name* (1) the English counties particularly prone to foxhunting; (2) all English counties that have or had names ending with "-shire"; (3) the English midland counties

shire horse *comp. noun* a breed of heavy draft horse originating from the English midland counties

the **Shires** *noun, abbr.* the ➡Shire Counties

shirt-lifter *comp. noun, coll., derog.* a male homosexual

shirty *adj.* irritated or annoyed

shitehawk *noun, derog., sl., taboo* a despicable person
This expression began life as ➡RAF World War II slang.

shoebox *noun, coll.* a very small or tight space

shoey *noun, arch., sl.* a military blacksmith working with a cavalry unit

shoogle *verb, Sc.* to shake, wobble or shuffle

shoot [A] *noun* (1) a ➡shooting expedition or party; (2) land over which ➡shooting takes place
[B] *verb* to bowl a ➡cricket ball so that it travels in a very low trajectory

shoot a line *idiom. phr. verb, coll.* (1) to lie; (2) to talk in a pretentious manner

shooter *noun* a ➡cricket ball that ➡shoots [B]

shooting *noun* hunting, specifically with guns
SEE ALSO: ➡hunting

shooting {box » lodge} *comp. noun* a small house occupied by sportsmen while ➡shooting

shooting-{brake » break} *comp. noun, out.* a station wagon
Originally, "break" was a 17th C. word meaning "framework"; later it came to mean a carriage-frame that was used to break in horses. Eventually, from this, the somewhat similar wheeled and horse-drawn framework that smaller game (such as birds and rabbits) were hung upon in the field for transportation away after the hunt became known as a "shooting-break." When automobiles replaced horse-drawn transport, these newfangled vehicles emulated their predecessors with an external wooden frame enclosing the large storage space at their rear; "-brake" is a 20th C. spelling innovation.

shop [A] *noun, pref.* a retail store
[B] *verb, sl.* to inform against someone
Especially to the police.

the **Shop** *pr. name, sl.* the ➡Royal Military Academy

shop assistant *comp. noun* a sales clerk

shopfitter *noun* a person who supplies and installs furniture and equipment into a store

shopfloor *noun, coll.* workers as a group, as distinct from management

shopkeeper *comp. noun* a storekeeper

shopman *noun, arch.* a storekeeper or assistant

shopping {centre » precinct} *comp. noun, pref.* shopping mall

shopping parade *comp. noun* a ➡parade of shops

shop-soiled *adj.* shopworn

shopwalker *noun* a floorwalker

shop-window *comp. noun, coll.* an opportunity to exhibit products, talents, etc.
Not necessarily in a window. It might be anywhere that the opportunity arises, such as an exhibition, a trade conference, at a place of work, and so forth.

short *noun* a small shot of liquor

short-armed *adj.* not fully extended

short back and sides *idiom, coll.* a man's hair, cut short at both the back and the sides of the head

short ball *comp. noun.* a short pitched ➡cricket ball

shortbread *noun, pref.* shortcake
SEE ALSO: ➡fruit shortcake

short commons *idiom, coll.* insufficient food

shortcrust *noun, abbr.* ➡shortcrust pastry

shortcrust pastry *comp. noun* a crumbly pastry made from flour and fat

short-dated *adj.* earlier or less time than usual
Of the period available in which to pay a bill, for example.

short {extra cover » fine leg » third man} *comp. noun* ➡fielding positions on the ➡cricket field

shorthand typist *comp. noun* someone who is both a stenographer and typist

short head *comp. noun* in horse racing, a length which is less than a horse's head

short hundredweight *comp. noun* a U.S. hundredweight of 100 lbs as opposed to the heavier imperial or British long ➡hundredweight of 112 lbs

short leet *comp. noun, Sc.* a short list

short pitched ball *comp. noun* a ➡cricket ball pitched close to the ➡bowler

shorts *noun* short pants, but not underwear

short ton *comp. noun* a US ton of 2,000 lbs as opposed to an ➡imperial or long ton of 2,240 lbs

shot *noun, sl.* a check in a restaurant or ➡pub

shot-blast *verb* to clean metal with a stream of shot

shot-tower *comp. noun, hist.* a tower where lead shot was manufactured

Molten lead was poured through a sieve at the top, so that by the time it had fallen the height of the tower into water at the base, it had hardened into a large number of small spheres.

shout *noun, sl.* the purchase of a round of drinks

shove-halfpenny *comp. noun* a kind of miniature shuffleboard game played in pubs

shovelboard *spell.* shuffleboard

{**shovelled » shovelling**} *spell.* {shoveled » shoveling}

show a leg *imper., coll.* an informal order or request to get out of bed

This expression originated in the 18th C. Royal Navy when sailors would be ordered to show a leg over the side of their hammock or bunk, to indicate that they were awake and ready to come on duty.

shower *noun, sl.* an objectionable or unacceptable person or group of people

showerproof *adj.* able to resist a shower of rain

Descriptive of, for example, a raincoat.

showjumping *noun* the competitive riding of horses around a course containing a number of fences and other obstacles that must be jumped over

Won by the rider and horse that complete the course with fewest penalty points for errors or failures.

show one's cards *idiom. phr. verb, coll.* to show one's hand, to declare one's intentions

show willing *verb, coll.* to demonstrate willingness

Shrewsbury *pr. name, hist.* a town, apparently established as early as the 5th C., which is the administrative center of ➡Shropshire

The current population is 65,000 (1991 estimate).

Shrewsbury School *pr. name* one of the leading English ➡public schools

Founded in 1552, it is located in ➡Shropshire.

the **Shrieking Sisterhood** *pr. name, derog., hist., sl.* suffragettes as a group

shrievalty *noun* a sheriff's jurisdiction or tenure

shrink *verb* to recoil, flinch or evade

{**shrivelled » shrivelling**} *spell.* {shriveling » shriveled}

Shropshire *pr. name* a county in west-central England, adjacent to the Welsh border

The county seat is ➡Shrewsbury and the current population is 400,000 (1991 Census).

shufti *noun, Arab., sl.* a glimpse or quick glance

Military slang derived from the Arabic *saffa* = "attempt to see"

shuit the craw *idiom. phr. verb, Sc.* to depart without ceremony

shut your gab *imper., sl.* be silent

shy [A] *adj., coll.* without, lacking or lost

[B] *verb, out.* to throw or fling an object

Sianel Pedwar Cymru *pr. name, Wal.* a special version of ➡Channel 4 Television transmitted in ➡Wales only, which contains a high proportion of ➡Welsh-language programs

From the Welsh, "Channel Four Wales." Although a commercial channel, significant portions of its Welsh-language programming are originated by the ➡BBC.

SIB *pr. name, abbr.* Securities and Investment Board

An investment regulatory agency.

sic *pronoun, Sc.* such

sick *noun, coll.* vomit

sick as a parrot *idiom, sl.* (1) spectacularly nauseous; (2) exceptionally dissatisfied

sick-call *comp. noun* a house call made by a physician

sicker *adj., Sc.* (1) secure; (2) dependable; (3) loyal

sick-flag *comp. noun* a yellow flag flown from a ship or building quarantined because of an infectious disease

The flag is a warning to others to stay away.

sick-making *adj.* sickening

{**sick » sickness**} **benefit** *comp. noun* a government allowance paid to those unable to work due to illness

sick up *verb, coll.* to vomit

side *noun, sl.* (1) a sideways spin placed on a ➡cricket ball; (2) a television channel; (3) pomposity or boastfulness

side-bet *comp. noun, coll.* a bet on a subsidiary matter

sideboards *noun, coll.* side-whiskers or sideburns

side-chapel *comp. noun* a subsidiary chapel at the side of a church

sidelight *noun* a vehicle's running or parking light

side note *comp. noun* a marginal note

side-on *adj.* facing to the side

side-plate *comp. noun* a bread plate

side-road *comp. noun* a minor road

side-salad *comp. noun* a salad served in a side-dish

sideseat *noun* a side-facing seat in a vehicle

sidesman *noun* an assistant churchwarden

side-trip *comp. noun* a detour

side-turning *comp. noun* a side street

sideview *noun* a view from the side

Sidney Sussex College *pr. name* a college of ➡Cambridge University founded in 1596

sidy *adj., sl.* affected with ➡side (3)

sightscreen *noun* a large white moveable screen located behind the bowler and near the boundary of a ➡cricket pitch to help the batsman see the ball

sightworthy *adj.* worth viewing

signal-book *comp. noun* a list of pre-arranged signals that might be required
A naval expression.

signal-box *comp. noun* a railroad signal tower

{signalled » signalling} *spell.* {signaled » signaling}

signalman *noun* a railroad switchman

signature tune *comp. noun, pref.* a theme tune

the **Signet** *pr. name, hist.* (1) the royal seal of England once used on certain formal state occasions; (2) the royal seal of Scotland once used on certain formal state occasions but now used as the seal of the ➡Court of Session

signing *noun, sl.* a sportsman who has signed a contract to play for a particular team

sign off *verb, coll.* to cease to ➡sign on

sign on *verb, coll.* to register as unemployed
A process which is necessary every two weeks, to qualify for unemployment payments from the state.

Silbury Hill *pr. name, hist.* Europe's largest prehistoric artificial hill
Possibly a burial mound, although there is no evidence of this. It was built at ➡Avebury in what is now ➡Wiltshire some 4,000 years ago. The structure is about 130 ft high and must have been an enormous project for those times.

silencer *noun* an automobile muffler

silk *noun, coll.* (1) a ➡{King's » Queen's} Counsel; (2) the silk gown worn by (1)

siller *noun, Sc.* (1) silver; (2) money

silly billy *comp. noun, coll.* a foolish or clown-like person, a figure of fun
Originally, a nickname for ➡William IV.

silly {mid off » mid on » point} *comp. noun* fielding players' positions on the ➡cricket field which are close to the ➡batsman
Called "silly" because being so close to the batsman is dangerous.

silly moo *comp. noun, derog., sl.* a stupid woman

silver band *comp. noun* a band that plays upon silver-plated instruments

silver jubilee *comp. noun* (1) any 25th anniversary; (2) in particular, the 25th anniversary of a ➡monarch's ascent to the throne

silver paper *comp. noun* fine tissue paper used for wrapping silver objects

silver sand *comp. noun* a very pure kind of sand used by gardeners

silverside *noun* an upper side of beef taken from the outer side of a leg

Silverstone *pr. name* a car racing circuit in ➡Northamptonshire, about 14 miles to the southwest of ➡Northampton
Where the British Grand Prix is held every other year and the British Grand Prix of Motorcycle racing is held every year.

silver wedding *comp. noun* the celebration of the ➡silver jubilee of a marriage

simnel cake *comp. noun* a richly spiced fruitcake coated with almond paste, which is usually eaten at Easter and before Lent

sin bin *comp. noun, sl.* where offenders are put

sin bosun *comp. noun, sl.* a naval ship's chaplain

since {Adam was a boy » the year dot} *idiom, coll.* since a very long time ago

singing hinny *comp. noun, North, Sc.* a currant cake that has been baked on a griddle
From the squeaking noise made as it fries there; "hinny" is Scots for "honey," an ingredient in an earlier form of this food.

single [A] *noun* a batter's hit in ➡cricket which is good for one run only
[B] *noun, coll., abbr.* a ➡single ticket

single cream *comp. noun* half-and-half cream

single-decker *comp. noun, coll.* a bus with one deck only, as opposed to a ➡double-decker

single malt *comp. noun* an unblended ➡malt whisky

the **Single Market** *pr. name, abbr., hist.* the single European market or economy that came into existence on January 1, 1993 throughout the ➡European Community, now the ➡European Union
On that day the United States formally or technically ceased to be the largest economy in the world, as the economy of the European Union is significantly larger.

singlet *noun* (1) an undershirt; (2) a kind of jersey used by an athlete

single ticket *comp. noun* a one-way ticket to ride

singsong *noun* an informal singing session

Sinn Fein *pr. name, Gae., Ir.* an Irish political party that seeks a united republican Ireland
The party was founded in 1902 and began by being in favor of non-violent protest, such as refusal to pay taxes, but by the time of the ➡Easter Rising had grown much more militant. It is now closely linked to the ➡IRA. The name is ➡Gaelic, meaning "We Ourselves."

Sinn Feiner

Sinn Feiner *pr. name, Gae., Ir.* a member or supporter of ➡*Sinn Fein*

sin-shifter *comp. noun, arch., sl.* a priest

sippers *noun, sl.* an additional sip of rum offered to a ➡RN ship's crew as a reward or in celebration

sippet *noun* (1) a small portion of bread toasted or fried and used as a garnish; (2) a small portion of bread soaked in a liquid

Sir *noun* a title used when addressing a man with the rank of ➡knight

The correct forms are "Sir John Smith" or "Sir John", but never "Sir Smith". *SEE ALSO:* ➡knight.

siren suit

siren suit *comp. noun, arch.* a one-piece whole-body garment, originally designed to be worn by women, who sought something that was easy to put on rapidly when the siren sounded to warn of an impending air raid during World War II

It was made popular with both genders when it began to be worn regularly by Winston Churchill, especially during the ➡Battle of Britain in 1940.

Sir Galahad [A] *pr. name, hist.* the noblest and bravest knight who sat at ➡Arthur's ➡Round Table

A late embellishment to the King ➡Arthur legends, who was invented by Walter Map.

[B] *comp. noun, coll.* a noble, pure and unselfish man

Sir Roger de Coverley *pr. name* a country dance similar to the Virginia Reel

Named after a fictitious country squire devised by the writers Addison and Steele in the columns of the *Spectator*, a London journal published in the 18th C.

SIS *pr. name, abbr.* the ➡Secret Intelligence Service

sister *noun, abbr.* a senior female nurse

sit *verb* to be a candidate in an examination

sit-down *comp. noun, coll.* a rest period

site of special scientific interest *comp. noun* an area protected because of its unique, rare, or interesting biological, zoological or geological examples

There are about 5,000 such locations throughout Britain The protecting agencies are the ➡English Nature, ➡Scottish Natural Heritage, and the ➡Countryside Council for Wales.

site rivet *comp. noun* a field rivet

sitting member *comp. noun, coll.* an incumbent ➡MP

sitting tenant *comp. noun, coll.* an incumbent tenant

situation vacant *comp. noun* a job vacancy

sit-upon *comp. noun, coll.* the buttocks

the **Six Articles** *pr. name, hist.* a statute passed in 1539 to ensure uniformity of form of worship and belief in matters of religion throughout England and Wales

It followed ➡Henry VIII's renunciation of Papal authority over the English Church in 1532, and was also known as the "Bloody Bill," as refusal to conform could lead to getting yourself burned at the stake.

the **Six Counties** *pr. name* the six counties constituting ➡Northern Ireland, commonly but inaccurately described as ➡Ulster

(See box on opposite page.)

sixer [A] *noun* a six-run hit in ➡cricket

[B] *noun, arch., sl.* ➡six of the best

six of the best *idiom, hist., sl.* the application of six strokes to the posterior with a cane

A punishment applied to miscreant schoolboys in those days when corporal punishment was still employed in schools.

sixpence *noun, arch.* a ➡sixpenny bit

sixpenny *adj., abbr.* ➡sixpence-worth

sixpenny bit *comp. noun, arch.* a former coin worth 6 old ➡pence or 2¹/₂ new pence

sixpenny-worth *adj.* worth or costing six ➡pence

sixth form *comp. noun* a high school class for students older than 16

sixth form college *comp. noun* a college for students older than 16

sizar *noun* a student at ➡Cambridge University or ➡Trinity College, ➡Dublin, who pays reduced fees

Originally in return for performing the duties of a servant.

Sizewell *pr. name, hist.* a site on the coast of ➡Suffolk that has become a major location for nuclear power production

The first two reactors (Sizewell A) came on-line in 1966, Sizewell B came on-line in 1995, and another two reactors, Sizewell C, are planned beyond that.

sizings *noun, arch.* a food allowance formerly provided to undergraduates by certain colleges at ➡Cambridge University

SJAA *pr. name, abbr.* the St John Ambulance Association

SJAB *pr. name, abbr.* the St John Ambulance Brigade

Skara Brae *pr. name, hist.* the best-preserved Neolithic village in Europe

It was built some 5,000 years ago upon the ➡Orkney ➡Mainland, and has been preserved almost intact, as it was buried by an inundation of blown sand about 4,500 years ago. Another storm in 1850 uncovered part of it again.

skate [A] *noun* a large, cartilaginous flat rhomboidal fish used as food, a member of the ray family

[B] *verb, sl.* to leave rapidly

Military slang.

skean dhu *comp. noun, Gae., Sc.* a black-handled, short-bladed sheath-knife worn in the sock as part of traditional Highland dress

From the Gaelic *sgian* + *dubh* = "knife" + "black"

skeely *adj., Sc.* skillful or experienced

skeleton in the cupboard *comp. noun, coll.* a skeleton in the closet

skelf *noun, Sc.* (1) a thin sliver of wood; (2) a thin person

(1) is especially one embedded under the skin.

skellie *adj., Sc.* lopsided

skellie-eyed *adj., Sc.* cross-eyed

skellum *noun, Sc.* a scoundrel or rogue

skelp *verb, Sc.* (1) to slap or smack with a flat object; (2) to hammer; (3) to kick; (4) to strike with misfortune; (5) to work energetically; (6) to move alone rapidly; (7) to gallop; (8) to splash a liquid

sketch *noun, coll.* (1) an amusing sight; (2) a comical or humerous person

sketching pad *comp. noun* a sketch book

sketch-map *comp. noun* a rough or tentative map that does not show many details

skew-eyed *adj.* squinting

skew-whiff *adj., coll.* out of alignment

skid-pan *comp. noun* a surface deliberately made slippery so that drivers can practice controlling their vehicles under difficult conditions

skier *noun* a ➡cricket ball hit high into the air

{**skilful » skilfullness » skilfully**} *spell.* {skillful » skillfulness » skillfully}

skillet *noun* a small metallic cooking pot with a long handle

skilly *noun* (1) a thin oatmeal gruel flavored with meat; (2) a beverage such as tea or coffee

(2) is sailor's slang.

skin *noun, abbr., sl.* a ➡skinhead

skin and blister *idiom, rh. sl.* sister

skinhead *noun, sl.* a teenage working-class hoodlum with very close-cropped hair

skink *noun* a drink or a thin guel

skinnymalink *noun, Sc.* a thin person or animal

skint *adj., sl.* completely without money

skip *noun* (1) a bucket or cage attached to a crane or hoist; (2) a large container

(1) is used to raise or lower men or materials into or out of mines, quarries, etc. (2) is used for the storage and transportation of trash, rubble and so forth, typically on construction sites.

skipper *noun, sl.* (1) an officer commanding an army unit; (2) the captain of a sporting team

skipping-rope *comp. noun* skip-rope

skirl *noun, Sc.* (1) a scream or cry of pain; (2) a shriek of laughter; (3) the cry of a bird; (4) a flurry of snow; (5) the shrill sound made by bagpipes

Six Counties in Ireland

The reason why six counties in the north of Ireland were not part of the ➡Irish Free State established in 1921 is that the majority there refused to have anything to do with it, and it could not be forced upon them without provoking a bloodbath. That's almost certainly still true.

While the majority of the Irish people are Roman Catholic ➡Celts, the area around Belfast in the northeastern corner of the island has a majority of Protestant (largely Presbyterian) ➡Anglo-Saxons, whose ancestors were sent there almost 400 years ago — most from the ➡Scottish lowlands, but also some from England — as colonists by ➡James I of England and VI of Scotland.

As Roman Catholics would be in a clear majority in a united Irish state and as at the time of the treaty in 1921 that majority were determined to establish a state which gave a special position to their church, effectively making it the state religion (which indeed remains the situation in the ➡Irish Republic today) the Protestant in the north, who had traditionally looked to the British ➡Crown as their protector against the Roman Catholic majority that surrounded them, flatly refused to become part of such a state.

They made it very clear indeed, especially through the activities and the words of Sir Edward Carson, who was the leading force behind the formation of the ➡Ulster Covenant and the ➡Ulster Volunteers, that if they were forced into an independent Irish state, they would fight. Carson, an ➡MP, both encapsulated and motivated Protestant opinion with effective, memorable slogans like "Ulster will fight, and Ulster will be right!" and "No Surrender!" and this position gained a great deal of support on the British mainland at that time.

The result was the partition of Ireland, and the present situation is the direct result of that.

skirl-in-the-pan

skirl-in-the-pan *comp. noun, Sc.* a food consisting of fried oatmeal and onions
From the noise they make while frying.

skirt *noun* meat cut from the lower flank

skirting *noun, abbr.* a ➠skirting board

skirting board *comp. noun* a baseboard

skit *noun, coll.* a large crowd

skite *verb, Sc.* (1) to slip or slither; (2) to throw a stone so that is skips over water; (3) to splash or squirt liquid; (4) to behave in a boisterous or belligerent manner; (5) to suddenly and forcefully throw or hit

skitterie *adj., Sc.* small, insignificant or unimportant

skittle *verb* to remove ➠batsmen rapidly one after the other in a game of ➠cricket

skive *verb* to goldbrick or goof off

skiver *noun* a goldbricker

skivvy *noun, derog., sl.* a female drudge or servant

skoosh *noun, Sc.* soda pop

skoosher *noun, Sc.* a sprinkler

skulk *verb* to avoid responsibility

sky *verb* to throw or hit a ➠cricket ball up into the air

the Isle of **Skye** *pr. name* the largest and one of the most beautiful islands of the ➠Inner Hebrides

Skye Terrier *pr. name* a variety of ➠Scottish Terrier

skyman *noun, sl., out.* a paratrooper

Sky Movies Gold *pr. name* a pay-TV movie channel
Part of the ➠BSkyB satellite broadcasting network.

Sky Movies Plus *pr. name* a pay-TV movie channel
Part of the ➠BSkyB satellite broadcasting network.

Sky News *pr. name* a 24-hour TV news channel
Part of the ➠BSkyB satellite broadcasting network.

Sky One *pr. name* a popular TV entertainment channel
Part of the ➠BSkyB satellite broadcasting network.

Sky Sports *pr. name* a pay-TV sports channel
Part of the ➠BSkyB satellite broadcasting network.

Sky Sports 2 *pr. name* a pay-TV sports channel
Part of the ➠BSkyB satellite broadcasting network.

Sky TV *pr. name (TM), abbr.* ➠British Sky Broadcasting plc

skywards *spell.* skyward

slab *noun* a mortuary table

slack *noun, out.* a pass between mountains

the **Slade School of Fine Art** *pr. name* a college of ➠London University founded in 1871

slag *noun, derog., sl.* (1) a prostitute or slut; (2) an unimportant or worthless person; (3) a tramp; (4) a petty criminal

slag off *verb, sl.* to slander or criticize pejoratively

sláinte *exclam., Gae., Ir.* a drinking toast

slán *exclam., Gae., Ir.* a form of friendly greeting

slang *exclam., Gae., Sc.* a drinking toast

slanging match *comp. noun, sl.* an extended and loud exchange of insults

slap and tickle *comp. noun, coll.* good-humored sexual teasing

slap-up *adj., coll.* first-rate or lavish
Usually descriptive of a meal.

slash *noun, sl., taboo* the act of urinating

the **Slashers** *pr. name* the 28th Regiment of ➠Foot
A unit of the British Army. While stationed in Canada in 1764, they were harassed by a local magistrate. Heavily disguised soldiers broke into the man's house at night and in a scuffle his ear was slashed off. They are also known as the ➠Braggs and as the ➠Old Braggs.

slate *verb* to strongly reprimand

slating *noun, coll.* a strong reprimand

SLD *pr. name, hist.* the ➠Social and Liberal Democratic Party

sledge [A] *noun* a sleigh or sled
[B] *verb* to ride or transport on a sleigh or sled

sleekit *adj., Sc.* (1) smooth in the sense of even and glossy; (2) smooth in the sense of sly and slippery

sleeper [A] *noun* (1) a railroad cross-tie; (2) a ring left in a pierced ear to prevent the hole from closing
[B] *noun, abbr.* a ➠sleeping carriage

sleeping carriage *comp. noun* a railroad sleeping car

sleeping partner *comp. noun* a secret or silent business partner

sleep rough *verb* to sleep outside upon the ground

sleepy sickness *comp. noun* the disease encephalitis letharigica, a brain infection causing sleepiness and possibly leading to a coma, which is called sleeping sickness in the U.S.
It should not be confused with any one of a number of tropical diseases caused by trypanosomes, also known as sleeping sickness in both Britain and America.

sleeve-link *comp. noun* a cuff link

slevers *noun, Sc.* nonsensical talk

sliding roof *comp. noun* an automobile sunroof

Sligo *pr. name* a county in the ➠Irish Republic
County Sligo in the ancient province of ➠Connaught.

slimming *noun* the deliberate losing of weight by dieting or other means

sling yer hook *imper, sl.* go away, get lost

slip-carriage *comp. noun, arch., hist.* a railroad passenger car detached from the rear of a non-stopping train in order to stop at a station while the rest of the train continued down the track without stopping or slowing

slip in the gutter *idiom, rh. sl.* bread and butter
Derivation: bread and butter> butter> gutter> slip in the gutter.

slipper bath *comp. noun* a bathtub that looks like a slipper and often has a covered end

slip-road *comp. noun* a ➠motorway access ramp

the **slips** *noun* a ➠fielding position suitable for intercepting balls glancing off the bat to the off-side

slipware *pr. name, hist.* a kind of earthenware pottery made in ➠Staffordshire in the 17th C.
Usually dishes decorated with figures in relief.

slitter *noun, Sc.* (1) a sloppy mess; (2) an untidy person

slive *verb, East* to slink

Sloane Ranger *comp. noun, sl.* an upper-class, non-intellectual, conventional, fashion-obsessed, wealthy, ➠green welly-wearing young person, especially in and around London
From amalgamation of "Sloane" Square, a fashionable area in London, with the Lone "Ranger" of Western TV series fame. Leading members of the group have included the Duchess of York and the ➠Princess of Wales.

Sloanie *noun, abbr., sl.* a ➠Sloane Ranger

slob *noun, Ir.* muddy ground

slog *noun, coll.* an extended spell of hard work

slogan *noun, Gae., hist., Sc.* originally, the war cry of a ➠Highland ➠clan
Their traditional war cry was the name of their chief. The literal meaning in Gaelic is *sluagh + ghairm* = "army" + "shout."

slop *noun, sl.* the police
An example of ➠backslang.

slop {basin » bowl} *comp. noun, arch.* a basin kept at table during a meal to hold the dregs from cups, etc.

slop out *verb* to dispose of food waste, typically in jail

slopperati *noun, sl.* a class of prosperous young people who flaunt a sloppy appearance

slosh *verb, sl.* to hit hard

slowcoach *noun* slowpoke

slow handclap *comp. noun* slow clapping in unison
Indicating impatience, displeasure, boredom, or all three.

slow off the mark *idiom, coll.* (1) slow to get started; (2) slow-witted

slow pitch *comp. noun* a ➠cricket pitch upon which the ball runs slowly or bounces little

slow puncture *comp. noun* a tire that has a very small puncture and thus deflates slowly

slow wicket *comp. noun* a slow game of ➠cricket

slubber *verb, coll.* to stain or spoil

slunge *verb, Sc.* to place or plunge into water

sma *adj., Sc.* small, thin or narrow

smacker *noun, sl.* one ➠Pound Sterling

small ad *comp. noun, abbr., coll.* a classified advertisement

small bundle *comp. noun, coll.* a newborn baby

smallholder *noun* the cultivator of a ➠smallholding

smallholding *noun* a portion of agricultural land that is smaller than a farm
Cultivated by an individual and his family to supplement a primary income usually earned in some non-agricultural way.

smalls *noun, coll.* small items of underclothing

the **Smalls** *pr. name* the mid-course examination for the Bachelor of Arts degree in classics and philosophy at ➠Oxford University

small wonder *comp. noun* no surprise

smart-arse *comp. noun, derog., sl.* a smart-ass

smartish *adj., adv., coll.* rapidly

smash-and-grab raid *comp. noun, coll.* a robbery where the thief smashes a store window and grabs what is displayed there

smasher *noun, coll.* a very beautiful or attractive girl

smashing *adj., coll.* (1) beautiful; (2) excellent; (3) exactly suitable

smelt *past tense* smelled
Of the verb "to smell."

smiddy *noun, Sc.* a blacksmith's workshop

Smithfield *pr. name, hist.* the popular name of London's main meat market since the 12th C.
Reputedly the world's largest, it has been located in the Smithfield area of the ➠City of London since the 9th C.

Smith Square *pr. name, coll.* a nickname for the headquarters of the ➠Conservative Party
Because it is located in this ➠London square.

the **Smoke** *noun, coll.* London

smokeless zone *comp. noun* an area where the creation of smoke is illegal, so only smokeless forms of coal and other fuels may be burned

smoke-room *comp. noun, arch.* a smoking room set aside for people of smoke

smoke-stone *comp. noun* smoky quartz, smoky topaz or ➠cairngorm

smoking-concert *comp. noun, arch.* a concert where smoking was permitted

smooth-faced *adj., coll.* falsely friendly

smoothing-iron *comp. noun, arch.* a flat iron

smore *verb, Sc.* to suffocate, choke or stifle

smoulder

smoulder *spell.* smolder

Snakes and Ladders *comp. noun* a board game similar to Chutes and Ladders

Snap *noun* a children's card game

Because players call out the word "snap" when two similar cards appear in sequence.

snap check *comp. noun* a spot check

the Snappers *pr. name* a nickname for the 15th Regiment of ➡Foot

A unit of the British Army. During the Revolutionary War, they participated in the defeat of the Continental Army at Brandywine in 1777. When ammunition was exhausted, they snapped their muskets, which caused the Americans to retreat because they believed they were being fired upon, it is said.

snark *noun* an imaginary creature, invented by Lewis Carroll in his *Alice in Wonderland*

sneak [A] *noun, sl.* a tattletale

[B] *verb, East* to steal surreptitiously

sneck [A] *noun, Sc.* (1) a small cut, mark or notch; (2) the latch of a door

SEE ALSO: ➡snib.

[B] *verb, North, Sc.* (1) to latch, shut or lock; (2) to switch or cut off; (3) to jam between two objects

SEE ALSO: ➡snib.

sneech *noun, arch.* snuff

snell *adj., Sc.* (1) piercing, cold, severe or bitter; (2) severe or sarcastic

(1) is of weather, especially wind; (2) is of speech.

snib *noun, Ir., Sc.* the catch or bolt of a door

SEE ALSO: ➡sneck (2).

snick *noun* an edge hit by a ➡cricket ball on the bat

snifter *noun, sl.* a small measure of liquor

snip *noun, coll.* a bargain

{**snivelled » snivelling**} *spell.* {sniveled » sniveling}

snochter-dichter *comp. noun, Sc.* a handkerchief

snog *verb, sl.* to kiss and caress in an amorous way

snooker [A] *noun* (1) a game superficially similar to pool but played on a billiard table; (2) a situation in (1) where a direct legal shot is impossible

There are 15 red and 6 other balls, which must all be pocketed in order. Originally known as "snooker's pool," it evolved among British officers serving in India during the 19th C, when "snooker" was a slang name for a new recruit.

[B] *verb, coll.* to prevent a continuation; to thwart

{**snorkelled » snorkelling**} *spell.* {snorkeled » snorkeling}

snotty *noun, sl.* a midshipman

snout *noun, sl.* (1) a cigarette or tobacco; (2) a police informer

Prisoners' or criminals' slang.

Snowdon *pr. name, hist.* the highest mountain in Wales

Located in ➡Snowdonia, its height is 3,560 ft A narrow-gauge rack and pinion steam-powered railroad giving access to the summit was opened in 1896.

Snowdonia *pr. name* a mountainous area in northwestern Wales, which was designated a ➡national park in 1951

It is named after its highest peak.

snowplough *spell.* snowplow

snowslip *noun, out.* a snowslide or avalanche

SNP *pr. name, abbr., Sc.* the ➡Scottish National Party

snuft *verb, East* to sniff

snug *noun, abbr.* a ➡snuggery

snuggery *noun* a small private area or room in a pub

snuid *noun, hist., Sc.* a ribbon once worn by young women to indicate their unmarried status

soakaway *noun* a rubble-filled pit where waste water percolates into the ground

soaking *noun, coll.* a very heavy fall of rain

sob *noun, sl.* one ➡Pound Sterling

socage *noun, hist.* a form of feudal tenure that did not entail military service

the Social and Liberal Democratic Party *pr. name, hist.* a short-lived former name for the ➡Liberal Democratic Party

Coined in 1989 when the ➡Liberal and the ➡Social Democratic Parties merged.

the Social Democratic and Labour Party *pr. name* a political party based in ➡Northern Ireland

The ➡SDLP is in favor of ➡Northern Ireland leaving the UK and becoming part of the ➡Irish Republic, but is totally opposed to the terrorist tactics adopted by the ➡IRA.

the Social Democratic Party *pr. name, hist.* a political party formed in 1981 and wound up in 1990

The party was founded mostly by breakaway members of the ➡Labour Party, including a number of ➡MPs, who disagreed with the extreme left-wing policies that were being adopted by the Labour Party of that time.

Within a year, the new party had formed an electoral pact with the ➡Liberal Party, which together became known as the ➡Alliance under which banner they fought the two general elections of the 1980s.

After the 1987 election the majority voted to merge with the Liberal Party, while the minority continued as a separate party for another two years before calling it a day.

social war *comp. noun, hist.* a war between allies

sod *noun, abbr., derog., sl.* (1) a male homosexual; (2) a worthless or despised person, usually male; (3) an average or typical man

Originally, an abbreviation of "sodomite".

soda bread *comp. noun* bread leavened with sodium bicarbonate

sod all *noun, sl.* absolutely nothing

soda water *comp. noun, pref.* club soda

sodding *exclam., sl.* a euphemism for "damned"

sodger *noun, Sc.* a soldier

sodger-clad but major-minded *idiom, Sc.* a strong sense of duty despite a lowly rank

sod it *exclam., sl.* a euphemism for "damn it"

sod off *imper., sl.* go away, get lost

Sod's Law *pr. name, coll.* similar to Murphy's Law
If something can go wrong, it will go wrong.

sod them *exclam., sl.* a euphemism for "damn them"

sod this for a game of soldiers *idiom, sl.* an expression of disgust at a frustrating situation

SOE *pr. name, abbr., hist.* ➡Special Operations Executive

soft *adj.* moist or rainy (of the weather)

soft drink *comp. noun* soda pop

soft fruit *comp. noun* small fruit, such as strawberries, that do not have stones

soft furnishings *comp. noun* rugs, drapes and so forth

soft goods *comp. noun* dry goods; textiles

soft option *comp. noun* the less difficult alternative

{**soft-pedalled » soft-pedalling**} *spell.* {soft-pedaled » soft-pedaling}

soft sugar *comp. noun* powdered sugar

soft tack *comp. noun* (1) bread; (2) the opposite of ➡hard tack

soft tyre *comp. noun, coll.* a partially deflated tire

soft wicket *comp. noun* a wet ➡cricket pitch

SOGAT *pr. name, abbr.* the Society of Graphical and Allied Trades, a labor union for printers absorbed into ➡SOGAT 82 in 1981

SOGAT 82 *pr. name, abbr.* the Society of Graphical and Allied Trades 1982
A labor union for printers, formed in 1981 by the merging of ➡SOGAT and ➡NATSOPA. Now merged into ➡GPMU.

Soho *pr. name* an area close to ➡Piccadilly Circus
London's red-light district, but also an area full of many excellent restaurants.

soke *noun, hist.* (1) a franchise issued to an individual under ➡Anglo-Saxon law empowering him to hold court and receive taxes within a specified territory; (2) the territory covered by such a franchise

Sol *noun* an heraldic representation of the sun

soldiers *noun, coll.* toast cut into thin strips, coated in yolk by dipping in a soft-boiled egg, and eaten

the Solemn League and Covenant *pr. name, hist., Sc.* a declaration of 1638 signed by almost the entire Scottish population

It asserted that the sole right to make and change law rest with a freely chosen Parliament and not with a king.

the Solent *pr. name* the channel between the Isle of ➡Wight and the English mainland

solicit *verb* to make an offer of sexual services that is conditional upon payment

solicitor *noun* a lawyer who advises clients, appears in lower courts, and instructs ➡barristers when cases go to higher courts
Most British lawyers are solicitors. *See also:* ➡barrister.

the Solicitor General *pr. name* a Law Officer of the ➡Crown
There are two. One is under the authority of the ➡Attorney-General in England, the other under that of the ➡Lord Advocate in Scotland.

solo *noun* a card game resembling whist but in which one player may play against all others

the Solway Firth *pr. name, hist.* a large estuary separating southwestern Scotland from ➡Cumbria, in England

Som. *pr. name, abbr.* ➡Somerset

{**sombre » sombrely » sombreness**} *spell.* {somber » somberly » somberness}

Somerset *pr. name* a county in western England, bordering on the ➡Bristol Channel
The county seat is ➡Taunton and the current population of the county is 460,000 (1991 Census).

Somerset House *pr. name* a large 18th C. building in the ➡Strand, London
Built upon the former location of the 16th C. palace of the Dukes of Somerset, it once contained all the records of births, marriages and deaths in England and Wales, but is now the home of the ➡Courtauld Institute.

Somerville College *pr. name* a college of ➡Oxford University founded in 1879
The college admits female students only.

something in it *idiom, coll.* something to it

something to be going on with *idiom, coll.* sufficient for the time being

the First Battle of the Somme *pr. name, hist.* one of the bloodiest battles of World War I
It lasted from June 1 until November 13, 1916. On the first day alone, there were 60,000 British casualties of whom 20,000 died, which is the greatest number ever to die in one day in the history of the British Army. Five and a half months later, at the end of the battle, there were 418,000 British soldiers killed or wounded, 195,000 French and 650,000 German.

After this carnage, the front line was advanced a mere eight miles; it was all quite futile. It was also noteworthy as the first occasion when tanks were used in battle, although due to inexperience and unsuitable terrain, their impact was minimal. The Somme is a river in northern France.

the Second Battle of the **Somme**

the Second Battle of the **Somme** *pr. name, hist.* the first battle of the final German offensive of World War I

It lasted from March 21 until April 5, 1918. By the end of the battle, there were 163,000 British soldiers killed or wounded, 77,000 French and approximately 250,000 German.

The Germans achieved a 40-mile deep salient before they were stopped by British reserves.

{**son » daughter**} **of the manse** *comp. noun, Sc.* the {son » daughter} of a ➡Church of Scotland minister

song of the thrush *idiom, rh. sl.* brush

sonsie *adj., Sc.* (1) hearty, friendly, cheerful or jolly (2) buxom or attractive; (3) sturdy or healthy

(2) descriptive of a woman, (3) descriptive of a child.

soor *noun, Hindi, sl.* an unpleasant person

From the Hindi *suar* = "pig."

soothing noises *idiom* calming or comforting words

soph *noun, abbr., out.* a sophomore or junior at ➡Cambridge University

From "sophist," not "sophomore" as might be supposed.

soppy *adj., coll.* (1) foolishly sentimental; (2) puerilely infatuated

sorbet *noun* sherbet

Sorbo rubber *pr. name (TM)* a hard yet spongy rubber

sorel *noun* a two-year-old fallow deer

sort *verb, Sc.* (1) to repair, mend or restore; (2) to punish or rebuke

sort out *verb, coll.* (1) to disentangle, separate or resolve; (2) to reprimand or punish

Sotheby's *pr. name* a firm of fine art auctioneers founded in London in 1744

soul-destroying *adj.* terminally tedious

souter *noun, North, Sc.* a shoemaker

Southampton *pr. name* a coastal city and port in ➡Hampshire in southern England

Established as a port in Roman times, it had became a significant center by the time the ➡Normans arrived. Traditionally, English armies leave for abroad from here. Southhampton was incorporated as a city in 1447, the current city population, including suburbs, is 270,000 (1988 estimate).

the **South Bank** *pr. name* a large arts complex on an impressive site upon the south bank of the ➡Thames River in central London

An area close to ➡Waterloo railroad station, largely devastated by German bombing during World War II. It was redeveloped as the main site of the ➡Festival of Britain exhibition of 1951 before being turned to its present use.

Southdown *noun* a breed of English sheep

Named for the South Downs area of ➡Hampshire and ➡Sussex, where the breed first appeared.

the **South-East** *pr. name* that part of England which surrounds London

Very roughly, everywhere east and south of an imaginary line which runs from ➡Bournemouth on the southern coast to Swindon to ➡Northampton to ➡Cambridge and then to ➡Ipswich on the eastern coast.

Southend-on-Sea *pr. name* a coastal town and resort center in ➡Essex

On the northern bank of the ➡Thames Estuary, about 35 miles downstream from London. Southend has the world's longest seaside pier at 1¹/₃ miles, with a railroad along its length. The current city population, including suburbs, is 275,000 (1988 estimate).

the **Southern Railway** *pr. name, hist.* a former railroad company, absorbed into ➡British Rail in 1947

It had a network stretching south from London to the south coast of England and the ➡Channel ports.

South Eastern *pr. name (TM)* a railroad company operating commuter services between London and its southeastern suburbs

It is part of ➡British Rail.

South Glamorgan *pr. name* a Welsh County

The current population is 385,000 (1991 Census).

---

the **South Sea Bubble** *pr. name, hist.* an 18th C. speculative mania centered around stock in the South Sea Company

The South Sea Company was founded in 1711 to trade with South America. Speculation in its share became hysterical in 1720 when it was rumored that the company was to take over the National debt in return for its own stock, but ended in a spectacular crash after shares in the company had risen over eight-fold in value in a few months.

The South Sea Bubble was an early precursor of the Wall Street Crash and other similar disasters brought about by the temporary triumph of greed over common sense and the economic laws of gravity.

Southwark *pr. name* a ➡Greater London borough

Its current population, which is also included within the ➡London urban area total, is 195,000 (1991 Census).

Southwell Minster *pr. name, hist.* a 12th C. cathedral in ➡Nottinghamshire

South West Trains *pr. name (TM)* a railroad company operating commuter services between London and its southwestern suburbs

It is part of ➡British Rail.

South Yorkshire *pr. name* an English ➡Metropolitan County

The principal city is ➡Sheffield and the current population is 1,250,000 (1991 Census).

sov *noun, arch., out.* a ➡sovereign

sovereign *noun* (1) a monarch, either king or queen; (2) a head of state; (3) a supreme ruler; (4) formerly, a coin

(4) consisted of 113 grains of gold, and had a face value of one ➡Pound.

---

the **Sovereign's Official Birthday** *pr. name* the day when the ➡{king » queen}'s birthday is celebrated, whenever {his » her} real birthday may be

Originally celebrated on May 24, which was Victoria's biological birthday, but by a mysterious and unexplained process of slippage it has transferred itself to the second Saturday in June. As well as not being the monarch's true birthday, it is also not a public holiday, so it is something of a non-event for most people. However, it is celebrated with the ceremony of the ➡Trooping of the Colour and the ➡Birthday Honours announcement.

---

soya bean *comp. noun* a soybean

spade guinea *comp. noun, hist.* a ➡guinea coin from the reign of ➡George III characterized by a spade-like shield upon its tail

spae *verb, Sc.* to foretell the future

spaewife *noun, Sc.* a woman fortune-teller

spaggers *noun, abbr., sl.* spaghetti

spaghetti junction *comp. noun* any complex road intersection between expressways

Spaghetti Junction *pr. name* Gravelly Hill ➡motorway intersection in ➡Birmingham

A particularly complex interchange of two ➡motorways and several other roads.

spalpeen *noun, Gae., Ir.* a rascal

Spam can *comp. noun, arch., sl.* a rather ugly type of steam locomotive once found on British railroads

Spam medal *comp. noun, hist., sl.* the nickname for a medal awarded to all members of the British Army who served during World War II

span *noun, arch.* a leg-shackle or hobbler for a horse

the **Spanish Armada** *pr. name, hist., Span.* the Spanish invasion fleet sent against England in 1588

The word means "armed" in Spanish, and the invasion fleet's full name was *La Flota Armada Invencible* = "the Armed Invincible Fleet" and the mission it was sent on had the grandiose title of "the Enterprise of England". It was defeated by the English Fleet under the command of Sir Francis Drake, helped rather extensively by the weather.

the War of the **Spanish Succession** *pr. name, hist.* a European war between 1701 and 1714, caused by Austrian objections to the Spanish monarchy falling into the hands of the French king following the death without issue of Charles II of Spain in 1700

As usual, Britain's goal was to prevent the European continent from becoming dominated by one power, so it fought on Austria's side against France. This was because the absorption of Spain—plus the Netherlands and much of Italy, both Spanish possessions in these days—by France would have created far too strong a continental power to suit British interests.

Eventually, under the Treaty of Utrecht of 1713, France ceded all of its claims in Canada except Quebec—Nova Scotia, Newfoundland, and the Hudson's Bay Territory—to Britian and recognized ➡Anne rather than ➡James Stuart to be the legitimate British monarch, while Spain ceded Gibraltar to Britain.

Again, here is a war that Britain ran at a profit.

Spanish tummy *comp. noun, coll.* another picturesque name for diarrhea, or Montezuma's revenge

Named in honor of the country which has played host to more British tourists than any other in recent years and thus the inevitable scene of many an outbreak of this misfortune.

Spanish windlass *comp. noun* a stick used as a winding-lever on a ship

spanner *noun* (1) a wrench; (2) a bridge cross-brace

spanner in the works *idiom, coll.* a problem or delay

spare *adj.* surplus to requirements

sparking plug *comp. noun* a spark plug

sparrashanks *noun, Sc.* thin legs

Literally, "sparrow legs."

spatchcock [A] *noun, Ir.* a game bird slit open and then grilled in this manner

[B] *verb, Ir.* to insert an irrelevant remark or statement into the midst of a speech or discussion

spatula *noun* a tongue depressor used by a doctor

the **Speaker** *pr. name* the presiding officer of the ➡House of Commons

Always an ➡MP elected by the citizens of a particular constituency in the same manner as all other MPs, and then elected to be speaker by fellow MPs from among their numbers. The first Speaker was elected in 1377; the name originates in the former role of this officer, which was to speak on behalf of the Commons to the monarch.

Speaker's Corner *pr. name* the northeastern corner of ➡Hyde Park, London

This area is traditionally set aside at weekends as a place where individuals or organizations make public speeches on any matter they wish.

It is not that free speech is denied elsewhere in Britain, but rather that this is a place where an audience can be assured. There are other Speaker's Corners in other British cities.

the **Speaking Clock** *pr. name* the former name for ➡Timeline (TM)

spean *verb, Sc.* to wean

spec *noun, abbr.* speculation

special

special *noun, Sc.* a kind of ➡heavy beer

the **Special Air Service** *pr. name* a special forces unit of the British Army

Founded in 1941, their motto is "Who dares wins."

Special Area *pr. name* an area designated by the government as economically depressed, thus qualifying for special financial assistance

the **Special Boat Service** *pr. name* the amphibious arm of the ➡Special Air Service

Not to be confused with the ➡Special Boat Squadron.

the **Special Boat Squadron** *pr. name* a commando unit of the ➡Royal Marines

It specializes in undercover amphibious operations. Not to be confused with the ➡Special Boat Service.

the **Special Branch** *pr. name* the police department responsible for political security and protection of important individuals within the ➡United Kingdom

special constable *comp. noun* a temporarily sworn police officer

special hospital *comp. noun* a hospital that more than somewhat resembles a prison, and where the criminally insane may be incarcerated upon the direction of a court

speciality *spell.* specialty

special licence *comp. noun* a license permitting immediate marriage without the delays normally required by law

Special Operations Executive *pr. name, hist.* a secret agency set up during World War II to recruit, train and infiltrate agents into occupied Europe

spectre *spell.* specter

speech day *comp. noun* an annual event at school when prizes are distributed and speeches made

the **Speech from the Throne** *pr. name* the ➡{King's » Queen's} Speech

speedo *noun, abbr., coll.* a speedometer

speir *verb, Sc.* to ask questions or make inquiries

speirin *noun, Sc.* an inquisition or questioning

Speke Hall *pr. name, hist.* a large 16th C. half-timber Tudor house seven miles south of ➡Liverpool

spelt *past tense* spelled

Of the verb "to spell."

spend a penny *verb, coll.* a euphemism for going to the bathroom

From the former necessity to put a ➡penny into the lock in order to gain access to a toilet stall in a public rest room.

speug *noun, Sc.* a sparrow

Spitfire

Spey *pr. name, hist.* a 110-mile long river in northeastern Scotland

It is best known for its quality salmon fishing. Also, many distilleries along its length use the river's water to help produce the finest ➡Scotch.

SPG *pr. name, abbr.* a ➡Special Patrol Group

A police unit somewhat similar to a SWAT team.

spicket *noun, Sc.* an outdoor water faucet

spider *noun* a devise consisting of a number of radiating elastic arms terminating in hooks

It is used to hold down anything that needs tying down when placed upon or in vehicles for transportation purposes.

spiderman *noun, coll.* a construction worker who works on tall buildings

spiffing *adj., out., sl.* spiffy

spike *noun, sl.* (1) a flophouse or cheap rooming house; (2) a ➡High Church ➡Anglican promoting or practicing Anglo-Catholic forms of worship

spike up *verb, derog., sl.* to make ➡Anglican worship more ➡High Church

spiky *adj., derog., sl.* very ritualistic or ➡High Church in form; ➡spiked up

spilt *past tense* spilled

Of the verb "to spill."

spin *verb, sl.* to search a suspect

A police expression.

spindle-shanked *adj.* spindle-legged or long-legged

spindle side *comp. noun, arch.* the distaff side

spinner *noun, abbr.* in ➡cricket, (1) a bowler who imparts spin to a ball; (2) a ball pitched by (1)

spinney *noun* an area of thicket

spin out *verb* in ➡cricket, to remove the ➡batsman by means of ➡spinners

spiraea *spell.* spirea
A shrub related to the rose family.

spiral balance *comp. noun* a device where the compression of a spiral spring under the object being weighed is used to measure its weight

{**spiralled** » **spiralling**} *spell.* {spiraled » spiraling}

spirit lamp *comp. noun* an alcohol-burning lamp

spirochaete *spell.* spirochete
Bacteria which have a spiral shape.

spit *noun* a depth of ground equal to one spade-length

the **Spitfire** *pr. name, hist.* one of the two front-line fighters with which the ➡RAF won the ➡Battle of Britain in 1940
Although the Spitfire is better known, there were actually more ➡Hurricanes flying in the battle.

Spithead *pr. name, hist.* the eastern part of the ➡Solent channel, lying between ➡Portsmouth and the Isle of ➡Wight
During the 17th and 18th Cs. this was the major anchorage of the British naval fleet, and it remains the usual location for reviews of the fleet.

Spithead pheasant *comp. noun, sl.* a bloater

spitting distance *comp. noun, coll.* a short distance

spiv *noun, arch., coll.* a flashy dresser who made his living by means of shady dealing
A term which originated during World War II, when many products were rationed and a black market flourished.

spiv up *verb, arch., sl.* to improve one's appearance

splash *noun, coll.* a small quantity of soda or some other dilutant added to liquor

splash out *verb, coll.* to spend money extravagantly

splendour *spell.* splendor

splice the mainbrace *imper, idiom, hist.* a naval order to issue an extra ration of ➡grog

splinter-bar *comp. noun* a whiffletree

split new *adj., coll.* brand-new

split pea *idiom, rh. sl.* tea

splitpin *comp. noun* a cotter pin

split ring *comp. noun* a spiral key-ring

the **splits** *noun* the feat of either leaping into the air or sitting down with legs positioned level on the ground but facing in opposite directions

split the vote *idiom. phr. verb* to attract voters from one choice to vote for a second in the secret hope or intention that a third may then win the election

splodge *noun* a splotch, spot or smear

splore *noun, Sc.* a celebration or party

Spode *pr. name, hist.* a kind of fine pottery
It was first manufactured by Josiah Spode of ➡Stoke in ➡Staffordshire, in 1770.

spoilt *past tense* spoiled
Of the verb "to spoil."

sponge bag *comp. noun* a waterproof bag containing personal toilet articles

sponge pudding *comp. noun* a baked or steamed dessert containing eggs, fat, flour and sugar

sponger *noun* one living at the expense of another

spool *noun, abbr., coll.* a roll of film or tape

sporran *noun, Gae., Sc.* a pouch worn on a belt at the front of a ➡highlander's ➡kilt
Usually made of leather and used to hold money and other valuables, which might otherwise lack a home as the kilt does not possess any pockets.
From the Gaelic *sporan* = "purse."

sporting cap *comp. noun* a cap worn or awarded as the visible badge of membership of a team

sports [A] *noun* sport
[B] *noun, coll.* a gathering for the purpose of participating in or observing a sporting activity

the **Sports Council** *pr. name* an organization set up in 1972 to promote and support sporting activities, especially at national and international levels
There are separate bodies for each of England, Scotland, Wales and Northern Ireland. The Sports Council owns and operates a number of national sporting facilities.

sports {**master** » **mistress**} *comp. noun* a {male » female} coach or teacher of physical education

sports saloon *comp. noun* sport coupe

spot *noun, coll.* a small quantity

spot of bother *idiom, coll.* some slight trouble

spot on *adj., coll.* exact or perfect

spotted {**dick** » **dog**} *comp. noun* a steamed or sponge pudding containing animal fat, dried currants, flour and sugar

spotted fever *comp. noun.* cerebrospinal meningitis
Not to be confused with *dermacentor andersoni*, better known as Rocky Mountain spotted fever.

Spr. *noun, abbr.* a ➡sapper

sprachle *noun, Sc.* (1) a struggle or scramble; (2) a weakling

sprang *past tense* sprung
Of the verb "to spring."

sprat *noun* a small, herring-like fish used as food
Its formal name is *sprattus sprattus*.

a **sprat to catch a mackeral** *idiom* a small risk but a large prize

sprauncy *adj., sl.* well-presented, flashy or showy

sprazer *noun, arch., sl.* a ➡sixpenny bit

the **Spring Bank Holiday** *pr. name* a public holiday held in late May

the **Spring Double** *pr. name* two horse races that occur around the same time every spring
They are the Lincoln Handicap and the ➡Grand National.

the **Springers** *pr. name* a nickname for the 62nd Regiment of ➡Foot
A unit of the British Army. During the Revolutionary War, they were used as light infantry, and the nickname is said to commemorate their speed and effectiveness in this role.

Springer Spaniel *pr. name* a kind of spaniel specially bred to "spring" partridges from their hiding places
There are two varieties of Springer, the English and the Welsh.

spring greens *comp. noun* leaves of young cabbages

spring onion *comp. noun, pref.* a green onion

sprog *noun, sl.* (1) a new military recruit; (2) a baby or young child

spruce *verb, sl.* (1) to evade work or responsibility; (2) to lie or deceive

spud bash *idiom, rh. sl.* to peel large numbers of potatoes as a military duty or punishment
Derived from ➡square bash.

spurrier *noun* a spur maker

spur royal *comp. noun, hist.* a coin issued in the reign of ➡James I of England and VI of Scotland
It had a face value of 15 shillings and bore an image of a sun emitting rays, which resembled a spur in appearance.

spurtle *noun, Sc.* a stick used to stir soup or porridge

spyhole *noun* a peephole

Spy Wednesday *pr. name, Ir.* the Wednesday before Good Friday
Because it was on that day that Judas made his bargain with the Sanhedrin.

sqireen *noun, Ir.* a petty Irish ➡squire (1)

Sqn. Ldr. *comp. noun, abbr.* a ➡squadron leader

squab pie *comp. noun* (1) a pigeon pie; (2) a mutton, apple and onion pie

squaddie *noun, sl.* (1) a private soldier; (2) a new recruit to the army

squadron leader *comp. noun* a commissioned officer in the ➡RAF
Equivalent in rank to a major in the USAF.

square *noun* in ➡cricket, (1) an area of close-cut grass where the ➡pitch is placed in the center of a field; (2) a line through the ➡stumps that is at right angles to the ➡wicket

square bash *verb, sl.* to drill upon a parade ground

square cap *comp. noun* a mortar board

square {leg » short leg} *comp. noun* fielding players' positions on the ➡cricket field

the **Square Mile** *pr. name* the ➡City of London
Which is indeed about one square mile in area.

square perch *comp. noun, arch.* a unit of area equal to $30\frac{1}{4}$ square yards, $272\frac{1}{4}$ square feet, or one ➡rod (2)

square-push *verb, arch., sl.* to go courting

square-rig *comp. noun, sl.* a ➡naval rating's uniform

squash *noun* a drink of crushed fruit or fruit juice

squew-whiff *adj., sl.* ➡squiffy

squidgy *adj., coll.* (1) soggy or damp; (2) squeezable

squiffy *adj., sl.* (1) somewhat drunk; (2) out of alignment or disordered

squillion *noun, sl.* an unimaginably vast number

squillionaire *noun, sl.* someone who is unimaginably rich

squire *noun, hist.* (1) the principal landowner in a district; (2) a male member of the traditional social hierarchy of England whose standing was higher than that of a gentleman but below that of a ➡knight; (3) a ➡knight's assistant; (4) jocular greetings from one man to another

squirearchy *noun* landowners as a political group

squireen *noun, Ir.* the owner of a small parcel of land

{squirrelled » squirrelling} *spell.* {squirreled » squirreling}

squit [A] *noun, coll.* a small or unimportant person
[B] *noun, East* foolish talk

the **squits** *noun, sl.* diarrhea

SR *pr. name, abbr., hist.* the ➡Southern Railway

SRC *pr. name, abbr.* the Science Research Council

SRN *noun, abbr.* a ➡State Registered Nurse

SSAE *noun, abbr.* stamped and self-addressed envelope

SSAFA *pr. name, abbr.* the Soldiers', Sailors', and Airmans' Families Association
A charity which looks after the families of service personnel.

SSC *pr. name, abbr., Sc.* the Solicitor to the ➡Supreme Court

SSP *noun, abbr.* ➡Statutory Sick Pay

SSRC *pr. name, abbr.* Social Science Research Council

SSSI *pr. name, abbr.* ➡Site of Special Scientific Interest

stable-lad *comp. noun* a man, of any age, who works in a horse stable

stable-mate *comp. noun* a person who is in the same unit, club, college, company and so forth, as another

stack *noun* (1) a tall, thin rock outcrop standing on its own in the form of a chimney; (2) a volumetric unit of wood, equal to 108 cubic feet

staff *noun, hist.* (1) the faculty of a college or university; (2) formerly, a token carried by the engineer of a train operating over a single-track railroad as his authority to proceed

(2) was a safety measure. As each sector of track had only one staff, it was impossible for there to be more than one train on a sector at any one time provided everyone followed the rules.

Staffa *pr. name, hist.* an uninhabited island west of ➡Mull in the ➡Inner Hebrides

Best known as the location of ➡Fingal's Cave.

staff college *comp. noun* a college where military officers are trained in the duties of ➡staff officers

staff nurse *comp. noun* a senior nurse ranking just below a ➡sister

staff officer *comp. noun* one of the ➡general staff

Staffordshire *pr. name* a county in central England

The county seat is ➡Stafford and the current population is 1,025,000 (1991 Census).

Staffordshire Bull Terrier *pr. name* a breed similar to the ➡English Terrier but smaller

Staffs. *pr. name, abbr.* ➡Staffordshire

staff sergeant *comp. noun* the senior sergeant of a military company, except in the infantry

staff wallah *comp. noun, arch., sl.* a ➡staff officer

stag *noun, sl.* (1) a purchaser of newly issued stock, for immediate resale for profit; (2) ➡sentry-go

(2) is military slang.

stage *noun, abbr.* a ➡fare stage

staging *noun* plant shelves in a greenhouse

staig *noun, Sc.* (1) a gelding; (2) a young horse which is not yet broken

stain *noun, Sc.* a stone

stairhead *noun* the landing at the top of a staircase

stair-rod *comp. noun* a carpet rod used to secure a carpet to a step of a stair

staithe *noun* a wharf used especially for the loading or unloading of coal

stale *noun, East* a long handle

Of the kind used for a rake, broom or pitchfork.

stall *noun* (1) a booth or stand in a market or exhibition where articles are offered for display or sale; (2) a seat in the ➡stalls of a theater

stallage *noun* (1) a rent paid to obtain the right to set up a booth at a market or exhibition; (2) the space set aside for a booth at a market or exhibition

stallholder *noun* someone who owns or operates a booth at a market or exhibition

the **stalls** *noun* the orchestra floor of a theater

This is usually the first floor.

stamp duty *comp. noun* a stamp tax

stance *noun, Sc.* (1) a building site or foundation; (2) a location for an open-air market or sideshow; (3) a place where taxis wait for passengers; (4) a place where buses halt for passengers

stand [A] *noun* (1) a booth at an exhibition, etc.; (2) an extended period of ➡cricket play when no ➡batsman has being removed from the field

[B] *verb* (1) to run for office; (2) to umpire ➡cricket

standard *noun, arch.* a former classification system for elementary schools

standard class *comp. noun* second-class rail travel

standard lamp *comp. noun* a standing or floor lamp

standard-rated *adj.* of that upon which VAT is charged at the standard rate

standard size *comp. noun* regular size

stand at ease *imper.* a military order to a squad of troops to relax with their feet apart

stand down *verb* (1) to cease running for office; (2) to relinquish an office that is already held; (3) to go off military duty

stand easy *imper.* permission to a squad of troops to relax further allowed by an order to ➡stand at ease

standing order *comp. noun* (1) a direction from a customer to a vendor to supply a product or service on a regular basis; (2) a formal written direction from a customer to his or her bank, to conduct the same transaction on the customer's account at regular intervals such as once every month

An example of (1): ask a ➡newsagent to deliver the same newspaper every morning. An example of (2): ask a bank to make regular payments of a mortgage every month

standing stone *comp. noun* a vertically-mounted megalith, characteristic of the Stone and Bronze Age inhabitants of Britain

stand of arms *comp. noun* a complete weapon-set suitable for one soldier

stand of colours *comp. noun* the ➡{King's » Queen's} Colours

stand off *verb, coll.* to lay off an employee

stand-off half *comp. noun* a rugby half-back serving as link between ➡three-quarters and ➡scrum-half

stand to *verb, coll.* abide to

The terms or conditions of an agreement or proposal, that is.

stand {to » to arms} *imper.* a military order to a squad of troops to assume defensive positions with their weapons at the ready

Stane Street

Stane Street *pr. name, hist.* a Roman road proceeding from ➡Colchester to link with ➡Ermine Street at Puckeridge, and also from London to ➡Chichester
A name not given it by the Roman but later, by the Saxons.

stang *noun, arch., Sc.* (1) a pole or wooden shaft; (2) formerly, a pole used to carry a man accused of ill-treating his wife around his village to the jeers and insults of neighbors; (3) a sting, ache or sharp pain

stanhope *noun, arch.* a 2- or 4-wheeled open carriage
Name for its inventor, a 19th C. English clergyman.

stank *noun, Sc.* (1) a pond or pool; (2) an area of stagnant water; (3) an open drain or watercourse; (4) a gutter

the **Stannaries** *pr. name* a district in ➡Cornwall where tin has been mined since Roman times

stannary *noun* a tin mine

the **Stannary Court** *pr. name* a court that regulates the tin mines of ➡Cornwall

Stanstead *pr. name* London's third airport, located about 35 miles north of central London
Operated by ➡BAA plc. During World War II, Stanstead was a USAAF bomber base.

star *noun, sl.* a ➡star prisoner

the **Star Chamber** *pr. name, hist.* a medieval criminal court consisting of the King's Council and judges
It had this name because it sat in a hall within the old ➡Palace of Westminster which had a ceiling decorated with stars. It acquired a largely undeserved reputation for unjust, irresponsible and arbitrary procedures, and was closed down in 1641.
The name is sometimes still employed as a sobriquet for a particularly harsh or penetrating inquiry, especially those held from time to time by the ➡Treasury into the allocation of funds between the various departments of state.

starkers *adj., sl.* (1) entirely naked; (2) entirely crazy

starn *noun, Sc.* (1) a star; (2) a speck or grain

the **Star of India** *pr. name, hist.* an order of knighthood instituted by Queen ➡Victoria in 1861
No new members have been appointed since Indian independence in 1947; the order is now considered defunct.

star prisoner *comp. noun, sl.* a first-time prisoner

starter *noun, sl.* the first course of a meal

starting handle *comp. noun, out.* the starting crank for an automobile

star turn *comp. noun* the principal feature or performer of a vaudeville theater show

stash it *imper., coll.* a request to stop some activity

statant *adj.* in heraldry, stationary

the **State Earnings Related Pension Scheme** *pr. name* a government-run ➡graduated retirement pension plan

State Enrolled Nurse *comp. noun, arch.* the former name for an ➡Enrolled Nurse

stately home *comp. noun* a large country house that is now or was formerly constructed for or owned by the aristocracy

state of nature *idiom* (1) completely naked; (2) the condition of an uncivilized or uneducated person; (3) the condition of a wild animal or plant

the **State Opening of Parliament** *pr. name* the formal opening by the ➡monarch of a new ➡Parliamentary session
Normally each fall, or shortly after a general election, the sovereign travels in procession to the ➡Houses of Parliament for the ceremony. The centerpiece is the ➡Speech from the Throne, delivered in the ➡House of Lords with the members of the ➡House of Commons present.

State Registered Nurse *comp. noun* a registered nurse

the **States** *pr. name* the regional or local governments of the ➡Channel Islands

state school *comp. noun* a public school

Stationers' Hall *pr. name, hist.* the Stationers' Company hall in the ➡City of London
Where the earliest copyright register was kept. The Stationers' Company is a ➡City Company.

the **Stationery Office** *pr. name, abbr.* ➡{His » Her} Majesty's Stationery Office

station sergeant *comp. noun* a police sergeant in charge of a police station

the **Statute of Westminster** *pr. name, hist.* the legal enactment that transformed the ➡British Empire into the ➡British Commonwealth in 1931

statute roll *comp. noun* a list all the statutes passed into law by ➡Parliament
It is kept in the ➡Public Records Office in London.

statutory sick pay *comp. noun* the minimum payment the law requires must be made to a sick employee for a maximum period of 28 weeks
Depending upon earnings and length of employment, this may be paid either by the employee's employer or by the government.

stave *verb, Sc.* to sprain or bruise a bodily extremity

stay *verb, Sc.* to dwell or reside on a permanent basis

stay-in strike *comp. noun, out.* a sit-down strike

STD *noun, abbr.* ➡subscriber trunk dialling

steading *noun, North, Sc.* the buildings of a farm, apart from the farmer's own dwelling house

steak and kidney pie *comp. noun* a hot savory pie made from beef and kidney in gravy, baked in pastry

steak and kidney pudding *comp. noun* a hot entrée made from beef and kidney in gravy, cooked in suet

steam *verb, sl.* to rush through a public place or vehicle such as a train, robbing all there

steamboats *adj., sl.* very drunk

steamer *noun, sl.* one who robs by ➡steaming

steamie *noun, hist., Sc.* a public building set aside for the washing of clothes, etc.

steamin *adj., Sc., sl.* very drunk

steam in *verb, sl.* to join an existing or start a new fight

steam organ *comp. noun* a calliope

{steam » steamed} pudding *comp. noun* a boiled dessert containing flour, fat, eggs and sugar

steatorrhaea *spell.* steatorrhea
An excess of fat in the stools.

steekit nieve *idiom, Sc.* a clenched fist

steer *verb, Sc.* to stir or disturb

{stencilled » stencilling} *spell.* {stenciled » stenciling}

Sten gun *comp. noun, hist.* a British-designed and made light sub-machine gun
A modified version of the Czechoslovakian-designed ➡Bren gun; the first two letters of the name "Sten" represent the initial letters of the names of the designers, Shepherd and Turpin Over two million were made and used during World War II.

Stephen *pr. name, hist.* King of England
Stephen, a member of the ➡Royal House of ➡Blois, styled himself *Dei Gratis Rex Anglorum* = "By the Grace of God King of England" and reigned for 18 years between 1135 and 1154 when he was usurped by ➡Henry, invading from Normandy.

steps *noun, abbr.* a ➡pair of steps

stereogram *noun, out.* a ➡radiogram with a stereophonic sound system

sterling *adj.* concerning British money

Sterling *pr. name, abbr.* the ➡Pound Sterling

Sterling Area *pr. name, hist.* the group of countries with currencies tied to the ➡Pound Sterling
At its maximum extent during the 1930s, it comprised all of the ➡British Commonwealth except Canada, together with ➡Eire, Jordan, Iraq, Libya, Burma and Iceland.
After 1945 its importance declined until today it is limited to Britain and a few minor members or former members of the ➡Commonwealth.

stevens *noun, rh. sl.* a bet with even odds
Derivation: even odds > even stevens > stevens.

stew *noun* (1) an artificial oysterbed; (2) a pond or large tank that edible fish are kept in

steward *noun* the title of several state officials and officials of the ➡Royal Household

Stewart *pr. name, hist.* the ➡Royal House of Scotland from 1371 until 1603
The following Scottish monarchs belonged to this house: ➡Robert II, ➡James I, ➡James II, ➡James III, ➡James IV, ➡James V, ➡Mary (Queen of Scots) and ➡James I of England and VI of Scotland.

Then, as ➡Stuart, the Royal House of Great Britain from 1603 to 1714. "Stewart" is the Scottish spelling of this name and ➡Stuart is the English, derived from the French; there is no letter "w" in French.

stewing streak *comp. noun* stew meat

stg *noun, abbr.* ➡sterling

stick [A] *noun, sl.* severe criticism or censorious advice
[B] *verb, coll.* to persevere, endure or tolerate

stick at trifles *idiom. phr. verb* to let small details get in the way of a larger issue

Stickie *noun, Ir., sl.* a member of the ➡Official IRA or ➡*Sinn Fein*

stickie-willie *comp. noun, Sc.* yard grass or cleavers

stick in {at » wi'} (something) *idiom. phr. verb, Sc.* persevere, work hard and doggedly (something)

sticky bun *comp. noun, coll.* a sweet bun with frosting

sticky wicket *comp. noun, coll.* (1) a ➡cricket pitch that has not yet dried after rain and thus is difficult for a ➡batsman to play; (2) a difficult situation

stiff-arsed *adj., derog., sl., taboo* (1) constipated; (2) stiff-necked or unbending

stiffener *noun, coll.* a shot of liquor

stiff upper lip *idiom* firmness and steadiness in the face of troubles
Although usually thought to be a very English expression for a very English attitude, the truth is it originated in America. It's only here because everyone expects it to be.

stiffy *noun, sl.* a formal invitation card

stilboestrol *spell.* stilbestrol
A synthetic estrogen.

stiletto heel *comp. noun* a spike heel

still-room *comp. noun* (1) a room where distilling occurs; (2) a storeroom in a large house where cakes, preserves and so forth, are kept

Stilton cheese *comp. noun* a strong, rich blue-veined cheese with a wrinkled rind
Originated in the village of Stilton, ➡Cambridgeshire.

stingo *noun, arch., sl.* a strong beer

stinks *noun, out., sl.* chemistry as a school subject

stirk *noun* a young bull or heifer

Stirling *pr. name, hist.* a town that is the administrative center of the Scottish ➡Central Region
Stirling has grown up around the great fortress of Stirling Castle, which sits upon the vast volcanic plug, dominating the country for miles around.
Strategically located at the first fording point over the Forth River and on the main route from Edinburgh to the Highlands, this has been the scene of many significant events in Scottish history, particularly the Battle of ➡Stirling Bridge and the Battle of ➡Bannockburn. The Princess ➡Mary, aged 9 months, was crowned ➡Queen of Scots in Stirling in 1543. The current population is 40,000 (1991 estimate).

Stonehenge

the Battle of **Stirling Bridge** *pr. name, hist.* a battle between an English army commanded by the Earl of Surrey and the Scots under the command of William Wallace in 1297, which ended in a decisive victory for the Scots that destroyed half the English army and caused the remainder to beat a hasty retreat back south from whence they came

Stirlingshire *pr. name, hist.* a former Scottish county, now part of ➡Central Region

Stir-up Sunday *pr. name, out.* the last Sunday in November when, traditionally, the ➡Christmas pudding is stirred up together by the whole family

stitherum *noun, East* (1) a long explanation; (2) a yarn

stob *noun, Sc.* (1) a fence post; (2) a short thick nail

stockbroker belt *comp. noun, coll.* those prosperous suburbs where stockbrokers live

the **Stock Exchange** *pr. name, abbr.* usually taken to mean the London Stock Exchange

stocking-filler *comp. noun, coll.* a stocking-stuffer

stockist *noun* a retailer who stocks goods

stockjobber *noun, arch.* a wholesale dealer on the stock exchange who could deal only with brokers
The job and name became redundant in the ➡Big Bang.

stocklist *noun* a price list published by a dealer

stocks *noun* bonds

the **Stockton and Darlington Railway** *pr. name, hist.* the world's first public railroad to use steam-powered locomotives
It opened in 1825 when a train with 450 passengers was hauled the 10 miles between these two towns in the northeast England, not far from Newcastle-upon-Tyne, at the breakneck speed of 15 mph.

stodge *noun, coll.* thick, heavy, unappetizing food

Stoke-on-Trent *pr. name* the city at the center of the ➡Potteries in Staffordshire
Formed by merging into a single borough the ➡Five Towns in 1810, later incorporated as a city in 1925; the current population, including suburbs, is 380,000 (1988 estimate).

stone *noun* (1) a unit of weight equal to 14 lbs; (2) the pit or kernel of a fruit

stone frigate *comp. noun, sl.* a shore establishment of the Royal Navy

Stonehenge *pr. name, hist.* the best-known and most significant megalithic site in Britain
Stonehenge consists of concentric circles of vast megaliths, several with horizontal stones lintels crossing from the top of one to the next. The exact purpose or reason for erecting Stonehenge is now unknown, but what is known is that it was erected some 5,000 years ago and was in continuous use for at least 2,000 years thereafter.

However, it seems quite likely that it was used as a sort of astronomical "computer" for the purpose of calculating such things as the timing of the seasons, and was also a mystical or religious site, possibly associated with a sun-worshipping cult of some sort. Certainly it was nothing to do with the ➡Druids as many suppose; it had already fallen into disuse by the time the ➡Celts arrived on the ➡British Isles.

Stonehenge is situated on ➡Salisbury Plain, about 10 miles north of the town of ➡Salisbury. This points to another mystery —how the stones that it is constructed from were transported there with the technology available 5,000 years ago. Some are known to have come from a location just 20 miles or so to the north of the site, but others, weighing some tons each, are known to have come from southwestern Wales, well over 100 miles and with one major river estuary (the Severn) lying in the way.

stone {me » the crows} *exclam., sl.* an exclamation of surprise

the **Stone of {Destiny » Scone}** *pr. name, hist.* the great ➡coronation stone of Scotland upon which the Scottish kings were once crowned at ➡Scone
Also known as ➡Jacob's Stone and the ➡Stone of Scone. It was removed to ➡Westminster Abbey in London by ➡Edward I of England in 1296, and remained there until it was stolen on Christmas Eve 1950 by a group of students from ➡Glasgow University favoring Scottish independence.
A stone, purporting to be the original, was returned to the abbey in February 1952, but there are many who believe that what was returned is not the original and the true Stone of Destiny remains hidden somewhere in Scotland ever since, waiting for an independent Scotland.

stonewall *verb* (1) to obstruct or delay a Parliamentary debate or decision; (2) in ➡cricket, to bat in a very cautious manner

stonk *noun, sl.* a large artillery bombardment

stonker *verb, Aus., sl.* to defeat, kill or outwit

stonkered *adj., Aus., sl.* (1) very drunk; (2) very exhausted or tired

stonking *adj., Aus., sl.* wonderful or fantastic

stony *adj., abbr., sl.* ➡stony-broke

stony-broke *adj., sl.* completely broke

stook *noun* sheaves of corn, etc., collected together and stood on end to dry in a field

stookie *noun, Sc.* stucco or plaster of Paris

stoolball *noun* a team game incorporating features similar to both ➡cricket and baseball

Stool of Repentance *comp. noun, hist., Sc.* where sinners sat in the ➡kirk on Sunday while subjected to public vilification by the minister during the service

stooshie *noun, Sc.* a loud brawl or argument

stop [A] *noun, abbr.* a ➡full stop
Especially when spelled out as in a telegram.
[B] *verb* (1) to punctuate text; (2) to fill a tooth
[C] *verb, coll.* to remain or wait

stop a packet *verb, sl.* to be killed or wounded, especially by a bullet

stop at home *verb, sl.* stay home

stop by *verb* to visit briefly

Stopes clinic *pr. name, coll., hist.* a birth-control clinic
From Marie Stopes, who opened the first one in 1922.

stop-go *adj., coll.* stop-and-go

stop-go economics *comp. noun, coll.* the use—or rather, the misuse—of government economic regulations and controls in such a way that there are alternate periods of fast and slow growth of business, employment, prices, etc.

stop lamp *comp. noun* a vehicle stop-light or brakelight

stopping *noun* a tooth filling

stopping train *comp. noun* a train that stops at every station along its route

stop press *comp. noun, coll., out.* late-breaking news
Called this because of the need to stop the press while late news is inserted in a newspaper.

storage heater *comp. noun* a room heater using cheaper overnight electricity to raise the temperature of bricks which then slowly release the heat accumulated through the following day

store *noun, out.* a computer memory device

store cupboard *comp. noun* a storage closet

{**storey » storeys**} *spell.* {story » stories}
The floor or floors of a building.

storm cone *comp. noun* a canvas cone raised to the top of a flagpole-like pole to warn of high winds

stormer *noun, sl.* a large or impressive entity

storm finch *comp. noun* a stormy petrel

storm in a teacup *idiom, coll.* much excitement over very little; tempest in a teapot

storm lantern *comp. noun* a hurricane lamp

Stormont *pr. name* the parliament building of ➡Northern Ireland
It is a large house situated in ➡Belfast.

Stornoway *pr. name* a port on the island of ➡Lewis
It is the largest town and administrative center of the ➡Western Isles; the current population is 8,000 (1991 estimate).

stoshious *adj., Ir.* very drunk

stot *verb, Sc.* to bounce

stotter [A] *noun, Sc., sl.* an attractive woman
[B] *verb, Sc.* to stagger or stumble

stottin fou *adj., Sc., sl.* spectacularly drunk

stour *noun, Sc.* (1) commotion or fuss; (2) flying or swirling dust; (3) a storm; (4) a blizzard

Stourhead *pr. name, hist.* one of the earliest Palladian mansions in England, built in the 1720s, some 27 miles from ➡Salisbury
Apart from the house itself, the grounds have been landscaped in a most spectacular fashion, resplendent with artificial lakes and classical structures such as a temple of Apollo, a pantheon and a grotto.

stout *noun* a dark, full-bodied beer made with roasted malt

stove *noun* an artificially heated greenhouse that is used especially for the forced growth of tropical plants

stovies *noun, Sc.* potatoes and onions cooked in beef drippings "on the stove"

Stowe School *pr. name* one of the leading ➡public schools in England
Founded in 1923 and located in ➡Buckinghamshire.

Strabane *pr. name* a district in ➡Northern Ireland, in what used to be County ➡Tyrone
The current population is 35,000 (1990 estimate).

strachle *verb, Sc.* (1) to struggle; (2) to move or walk with difficulty

strafe *verb, Ger., hist.* to rake with machine-gun fire, especially from an aircraft
From the German *strafen* = "to punish." *Gott strafe England* = "God punish England," was a German slogan in the early years of World War I, which became well known in Britain.

straight fight *comp. noun* an election contest with only two candidates

the Straits of Dover *pr. name* the narrowest part of the ➡English Channel, at the point where it meets with the ➡North Sea
Between ➡Dover in ➡Kent and Calais in northern France, where the strait is about 21 miles wide.

stramash *noun, Sc.* (1) a commotion or loud noise; (2) great excitement; (3) a loud argument

the **Strand**

the **Strand** *pr. name* a boulevard that links together the originally quite separate and distinct cities of ⟶London and ⟶Westminster

It traverses the northern bank of the ⟶Thames, hence its name.

stranger *noun* any person who is within the ⟶Chamber of the ⟶House of Commons, but is not a ⟶Member of Parliament or an official of the House

SEE ALSO: ⟶I spy strangers.

the **Strangers' Gallery** *pr. name* the public galleries in the ⟶Houses of Commons and Lords

SEE ALSO: ⟶stranger.

strap [A] *noun, Ir.* a loose woman or slut

[B] *noun, hist., out., Sc.* a ⟶tawse

Strata Florida Abbey *pr. name, hist., Lat.* a 12th C. Cistercian ⟶abbey, now a ruin, some 15 miles to the south of ⟶Aberystwyth

The name is Latin *Strata Florida* = "Carpet of Flowers."

Stratfield Saye *pr. name, hist.* an early 17th C. house about 10 miles south of ⟶Reading built and then rebuilt in the 18th C.

Purchased by the Duke of Wellington in 1817 who, abandoning his original plan to build a palace in its grounds, settled for the rebuilding of this house instead.

Stratford-upon-Avon *pr. name, hist.* the town in ⟶Warwickshire which is Shakespeare's birthplace

Stratford-upon-Avon is also the childhood home of the mother of John Harvard, founder of the university in Cambridge, MA which is named after him.

strath *noun, Gae., Sc.* a broad river valley

Strathclyde *pr. name, hist.* (1) an ancient Scottish kingdom; (2) a region in west-central Scotland

Strathclyde was a separate British kingdom until annexed by Alba in 1016 to create the kingdom of Scotland; earlier, it had been under the protection of the ⟶Anglo-Saxon kingdom of ⟶Northumbria.

The usual seat of the kings of ⟶Strathclyde was Alclyde, near the modern city of ⟶Glasgow on the ⟶Clyde River.

Present-day Strathclyde is the most populous Scottish region, with almost half the inhabitants of Scotland living within it, mostly in and around Glasgow.

The current population of (2) is 2,275,000 (1991 Census).

strathspey *noun, Sc.* a dance like a ⟶reel, but slower

Named for the Strathspey area of Scotland.

straun *noun, Sc.* a small stream or water channel at the side of a road

stravaig *verb, Sc.* to wander about in an aimless way

strawberries and cream *comp. noun* a traditional summer dessert

Strawberry Hill *pr. name, hist.* an 18th C. house some 13 miles to the south east of London

It is considered to be a particularly fine early example of the Gothic revival style of architecture.

straw potatoes *comp. noun* potatoes julienne

That is, potatoes cut into long thin strips.

stream *verb* to track school students by ability

streaming *noun* a student tracking system

streek *verb, Sc.* (1) to lay out a corpse; (2) to stretch

street cries *comp. noun, out.* the calls and cries made by ⟶street vendors seeking to attract customers

streets ahead *idiom* much superior

street vendor *comp. noun* a peddler

strewth *exclam., sl.* a variation of "God's truth"

strike a light *exclam., sl.* an exclamation of surprise

Strike Command *pr. name* the ⟶command of the ⟶RAF responsible for air strikes or attacks, air defense and military operations in general, including in-flight refueling and transportation

Formed in 1968 when ⟶Bomber and ⟶Fighter Commands were merged into one.

strike off the rolls *phr. verb* to bar a ⟶solicitor from working because of malpractice, dishonesty, etc.

striker *noun* the firing pin of a gun

Strine *pr. name, Aus., coll.* Australian English

From the way "Australian" is pronounced by many Australians.

string of beads *idiom, rh. sl.* the city of ⟶Leeds

string vest *comp. noun* a large-mesh undershirt

strip *noun* the playing dress or uniform worn by members of a sporting team

strip cartoon *comp. noun* a comic strip

stripey *noun, sl.* a long-serving Royal Naval seaman

From the good-conduct stripes on nautical uniforms.

strip lighting *comp. noun, coll.* fluorescent lighting

stroke *noun, sl.* a trick or deception

stroppy *adj., abbr., sl.* obstreperous

strunt *verb, Sc.* (1) to huff or sulk; (2) to strut; (3) to walk in an affected manner

Stuart *pr. name, hist.* the ⟶Royal House of Great Britain from 1603 to 1714.

The following British monarchs belonged to this house: ⟶James I of England and VI of Scotland, ⟶Charles I, ⟶Charles II, ⟶James II of England and VII of Scotland, ⟶William and Mary, and ⟶Anne. From 1649 to 1660, England had no monarch; it was a republic, known as the ⟶Commonwealth. Also, there was an interregnum of about two months in late 1688 and early 1689, after the departure of James II of England and VII of Scotland. It lasted until the arrival of William and Mary.

⟶Stewart is the Scottish spelling of this name and "Stuart" is the English, derived from the French; there is no letter

334

"w" in French. Previously, as ➡Steward, this had been the Royal House of Scotland from 1371 until 1603.

student *noun* a graduate paid a stipend by his or her college foundation

In particular a fellow of ➡Christ Church, Oxford.

student grant *comp. noun* a payment made from government funds to undergraduate students at a university or at certain other colleges, to enable them to finance their courses of study

student union *comp. noun* an organization run by and on behalf of the students of a university which provides them with the facilities of a social club and, in some cases, a debating society

The approximate equivalent of a students' fraternity house.

studio flat *comp. noun* a studio apartment

stuff *verb, sl., taboo* to copulate

stuff gown *comp. noun* a gown worn by a ➡barrister who is not yet a ➡silk

stumer [A] *noun, arch., sl.* a dud shell

A World War I expression.

[B] *noun, sl.* (1) a failure or bad bargain; (2) a counterfeit coin, forged ➡banknote or bad check; (3) an imaginary horse race; (4) a swindle; (5) a swindler

(3) is devised to alter the public perception of a horse's chances of winning in a real race so that its odds are run up and a killing can be made by those operating the scam.

stump [A] *noun* one of the three uprights of a ➡cricket ➡wicket

[B] *verb* (1) to baffle or puzzle; (2) to put out a ➡cricket ➡batsman by breaking the ➡wicket with the ball

stumped for an answer *idiom* unable to reply

stumper *noun, coll.* a ➡cricket ➡wicket keeper

stump up *phr. verb, coll.* to pay up

stumpy *noun* any member of a litter of ➡Manx kittens that is born with a short tail

SEE ALSO: ➡rumpy.

stushie *noun, Sc.* commotion, fuss or trouble

sub *noun, abbr., coll.* a subvention

A loan made in anticipation of future income.

subahdar *noun, arch.* a senior native officer of a native company in the former British Indian Army

subaltern *noun* a commissioned army officer below the rank of Captain

subcheese *noun, arch., Hindi, sl.* everything

Military slang, from the Hindi *sab* + *chiz* = "all + thing." An example of ➡hobson-jobson.

sub-edit *verb* copyread

sub-editor *comp. noun* a copy editor

subject *noun* anyone living within the territory or enjoying the protection of a monarch

sub-lieutenant *comp. noun* a commissioned officer in the ➡Royal Navy ranking below a lieutenant

Equivalent to a lieutenant junior grade in the U.S. Navy.

Sub-Lt. *noun, abbr.* a ➡sub-lieutenant

subscriber trunk dialling *comp. noun* direct distance dialing

SEE ALSO: ➡STD.

subscription *noun* the fee paid to become a member of a club, society, etc.

subsidy *noun, arch.* money granted by ➡Parliament to the ➡monarch for purposes of state

subsistence allowance *comp. noun* a traveling and living allowance

substitute *noun, Sc.* a deputy to the holder of a legal office, such as, for example, a ➡sheriff

subtopia *noun, coll.* ugly and unplanned urban or suburban sprawl

{**subtotalled » subtotalling**} *spell.* {subtotaled » subtotaling}

the **Subway** *noun, coll., hist., Sc.* the popular name for ➡Glasgow's underground rapid transit system

This is the second-oldest subway in the world, which came into service in 1886. Built in a circle, trains were originally hauled by cables powered from a central power station.

This entirely underground system was to a large extent excavated as true deep-level tunnels with small bores, which requires smaller cross-sectioned cars than is normal on most railroads. It is also the only subway in Britain (or, come to that, Europe) which is commonly *called* a subway.

{**succour » succourer**} *spell.* {succor » succorer}

Sudbury Hall *pr. name, hist.* a mid-17th C. house about 12 miles west of ➡Derby

It combines various styles and periods in a strange mixture of pretentiousness with simplicity and modesty.

suet pudding *comp. noun* a heavy pudding made from boiled or steamed suet

Suffolk [A] *pr. name* (1) a county on the eastern coast of England, between ➡Norfolk and ➡Essex; (2) a breed of black-faced hornless sheep

Formerly (1) was divided into the two counties of East Suffolk and West Suffolk. The county seat is ➡Ipswich and the current population is 630,000 (1991 Census).

[B] *pr. name, abbr.* a ➡Suffolk punch

Suffolk punch *pr. name* a breed of thickset draft horse

sug *verb, abbr., sl.* ➡selling under guise

sugar soap *comp. noun* an alkaline compound used to remove paint

suited *adj.* appropriate or suitable

Sulgrave Manor

Sulgrave Manor *pr. name, hist.* a 16th C. manor house about 18 miles southwest of ➡Northampton
This is the ancestral home of the Washington family; it has been maintained as a George Washington museum since 1921. *SEE ALSO:* ➡Washington Old Hall.

Sullom Voe *pr. name, hist.* an inlet on the northern coast of the main island of the ➡Shetlands group
It has been transformed since the discovery of oil in the ➡North Sea in the 1960s and is now the location of Europe's largest oil terminal.

sulphur *spell.* sulfur

sulph- *spell., prefix* sulf-
Containing sulfur.

sultana *noun* raisin

summat *noun, North* something

summer pudding *comp. noun* a dessert that consists of fruit in a ➡sponge pudding
The fruit, usually berries of various sorts, are pressed until their juice soakes right through the sponge pudding and darkened it.

summer time *comp. noun, abbr.* daylight saving time

sump *noun* (1) a vehicle crankcase; (2) an oil pan

Sun Alliance *pr. name (TM), abbr.* an insurance company

sun blind *comp. noun* a sunshade or window awning

sun cream *comp. noun* a sunscreen lotion

Sunday name *comp. noun, Sc.* one's formal first name

Sunderland *pr. name* a city and seaport upon the ➡Wear River in ➡Tyne and Wear
The port grew greatly in importance in the 17th C. as a shipping point for the coal being mined nearby, and then in the 18th C. it developed as a major shipbuilding center. Sunderland was incorporated as a city in 1992, the newest in Britain Current city population, including suburbs, is 200,000 (1988 estimate).

sundowner *noun, coll., out.* a drink taken at sunset

sun lounge *comp. noun* a sun parlor

Sunningdale *pr. name, hist.* a golf club in ➡Berkshire, not far from ➡Ascot
The original course opened in 1901 and a second in 1922.

sunny south *idiom, rh. sl.* mouth

sunshine *noun, sl.* a jocular form of address
Particularly to someone of unknown name.

sunwards *spell.* sunward

sup *verb, North* to drink, especially liquor

super *verb, arch., sl.* to remove a student from a school or a school grade because of {his » her} age was not thought suitable for that school or grade

superannuation *noun* a retirement pension

superannuation contribution *noun* a payment made into a retirement pension fund

supergrass *noun, sl.* a police informer supplying information or evidence that is especially incriminating or concerns a large number of people

superintendent *noun* a police officer below the rank of ➡chief superintendent but above ➡chief inspector

Supermac *pr. name, coll.* a nickname for ➡Prime Minister Harold Macmillan
From a political cartoon showing him in the form of Superman, after a successful period in office during which it appeared that he could do no wrong.

supertax *noun, hist.* an income tax formerly imposed, in addition to regular income tax, on those with an income above a certain level

supplementary benefit *comp. noun, arch.* a payment made from government funds to those not in full-time work and whose income had fallen below a certain level
Now replaced by ➡income support.

supply teacher *comp. noun* a substitute teacher

Support Command *pr. name* a ➡command of the ➡RAF responsible for training (including flight-crew training), engineering, logistics, medical services, and administration in general

the **Supreme Court of Judicature** *pr. name* the highest court of law in England and Wales other than the ➡House of Lords
There are three principal division of the Supreme Court. These are the ➡High Court of Justice, the ➡Crown Court and the ➡Court of Appeal.

supremo *noun, coll., Span.* the overall commander
The Spanish word for "supreme".

surf *verb, sl.* to joyride by clinging to the side or roof of a train, car, etc.

surgery *noun* (1) a physician's or dentist's office; (2) an office where an ➡MP or other politician meets with constituents and offers advice or help; (3) time devoted to advising or helping patients, clients or constituents; (4) formerly, an office where a lawyer met with clients to offer advice or help

surgical spirit *comp. noun* denatured alcohol used for cleansing during surgical operations

Surrey *pr. name* a county in southern England, immediately to the south of London
The county seat is ➡Kingston-upon-Thames (which is itself located within Greater London, not Surrey) and the current population is 1,000,000 (1991 Census).

surrogate *noun* a deputy bishop

surround *noun* (1) the edge or border of the floor of a room; (2) a covering for such an edge or border
(1) is especially the space between carpet and walls.

336

surtitles *noun, coll.* words projected onto a screen above the stage in a theater where an opera is being sung in a foreign language

suspender *noun* a woman's stocking-garter

suspender belt *comp. noun* a woman's garter belt

suss [A] *noun, abbr., sl.* (1) a suspect; (2) suspicion; (3) suspicious behavior

[B] *verb, abbr., sl.* to suspect

Sussex *pr. name, hist.* (1) an ancient kingdom in southeastern England; (2) a former English county; (3) a breed of red fowl

(1) was established by about 475, and remained independent until about 775 when it was annexed by ➡Wessex. The usual seat of the kings of Sussex was ➡Chichester.

(2) was abolished in 1974 when it was divided into two and replaced with ➡East Sussex and ➡West Sussex. This did little more than reflect reality because these two parts of the county had already been administered separately for about 400 years before this.

Sussex Spaniel *pr. name* a rare breed of short-legged, long-bodied spaniel with a golden coat

suss law *comp. noun, abbr., arch., sl.* a law that permitted the police to arrest someone on suspicion of his pr her intent to commit a crime

It was repealed in 1981.

suss out *verb, abbr., sl.* (1) to investigate; (2) to work out or understand

sussy *adj., abbr., sl.* suspicious

Sutherland *pr. name, hist.* a former Scottish county, now part of ➡Highland region

Sutton *pr. name* a ➡Greater London borough

Its current population, which is also included within the ➡London urban area total, is 165,000 (1991 Census).

Sutton Hoo *pr. name, hist.* an ➡Anglo-Saxon ship burial believed to date from about 625

Discovered in 1939 in Suffolk, this was one of the richest and most significant archeological discoveries ever made. Many of the most valuable artifacts, including armor and weapons, bowls and other items made from precious metals, are now on view in the ➡British Museum.

It is thought to be the burial place of an Anglo-Saxon king.

swallow and sigh *idiom, rh. sl.* collar and tie

swallow dive *comp. noun* a swan dive

swallow-hole *comp. noun* a sink hole

A cavity in rock which water drains into or through.

swan around *verb, coll.* to move around in a casual way while presenting a superior attitude to others

swankpot *noun, coll.* someone who behaves in a ostentatious manner

the **Swan of Avon** *pr. name* a poetic nickname for William Shakespeare

Devised by Shakespeare's contemporary and fellow playwright, Ben Jonson.

Swansea *pr. name* a coastal city and port located in ➡West Glamorgan, Wales

It was probably founded by the ➡Vikings, but certainly the ➡Normans built a castle here during the 12th C. It had become the largest Welsh port by the 17th C., and a center of heavy industry during the 19th C. Swansea was incorporated as a city in 1169 and the current city population, including suburbs, is 280,000 (1988 estimate).

Swansea porcelain *pr. name, hist.* a kind of earthenware pottery first made in south Wales during the 18th C.

swan-upping *comp. noun* the annual collecting and marking of swans on the ➡Thames River

Since the Middle Ages almost all swans living upon open lakes and rivers in England have belonged to the monarch. The exceptions are those living on certain stretches of the Thames, which are the property of two of the City Livery Companies, and are the ones marked every year.

Swan Vesta *pr. name (TM)* a brand of wooden matches

swath *noun, East* a rind or thick outer layer

swear blind *verb, coll.* to affirm in a very forceful and convincing manner

sweat [A] *noun, sl.* a long-distance run

A schoolboy's expression.

[B] *verb* to sauté gently

swede *noun* rutabaga

the **Sweeney** *noun, rh. sl.* a police flying squad, especially in London

Derived from Sweeney Todd, an early 19th C. London barber convicted of murdering his clients.

sweet *noun* a dessert

sweet biscuit *comp. noun* a cookie

sweet {fanny adams » FA} *idiom, sl.* (1) that which is worthless; (2) absolutely nothing at all

In 1867 an eight-year-old girl called Fanny Adams was brutally murdered, and there was much publicity over the case. At about the same time, sailors in the ➡Royal Navy were issued with tinned mutton for the first time, which with gallows humor they dubbed "Sweet Fanny Adams", so turning the phrase into a name for something worthless and eventually for nothing at all.

Sweetheart Abbey *pr. name, hist.* a Cistercian ➡abbey, now a beautiful ruin, dating from 1273 and located about six miles south of ➡Dumfries

It was founded by Devorgilla de Baliol, the mother of ➡John Baliol and founder of ➡Balliol College in Oxford. Originally known as New Abbey—as the village beside it still is—it became known by its present name because after her husband died, Devorgilla carried his heart with her until she too died in 1290, when she was buried with it in the abbey.

sweetie *noun, coll.* a candy

Sweet Nell of Old Drury

*Nell
Gwyn*

Sweet Nell of Old Drury *pr. name, hist.* a nickname for Eleanor—better known as Nell—Gwyn

She was, in turn, orange-seller, actress at the ➧Theatre Royal in ➧Drury Lane, and mistress of ➧Charles II.

sweets *noun* hard candy

sweet shop *comp. noun* a candy store

sweet trolley *comp. noun* a pastry cart or trolley

Swegn Forkbeard *pr. name, hist.* King of England

The son of ➧Edmond, and so a member of the Royal House of ➧Cedric, he ruled from 955 until his death in 959.

swill bin *comp. noun* a trashcan, especially one used for food waste

swill out *verb, coll.* to rinse or flush with water in order to clean or clear

swimming costume *comp. noun* a swimsuit

swing *verb* to cause a ➧cricket ball to diverge from a straight trajectory

swingeing *adj.* vast, extensive or excessive

Swinging London *pr. name, coll., hist.* London's nickname during the 1960s

Said to represent an uninhibited spirit of liberation in the area of ideas, fashion and sexual mores which supposedly characterized the city of that time.

swing {it » the lead} *idiom. phr. verb, coll.* to goldbrick or goof off

swingometer *noun* a device used to show voting swings when reporting election results on TV

swish *adj., coll.* elegant or fashionable

Swiss cheese plant *comp. noun* a houseplant so named because of the holes in its leaves, similar to those found in cheeses from Switzerland

Its formal name is *monstera deliciosa*, and it is similar to but distinct from the philodendron.

Swiss roll *comp. noun* a jelly roll

switch *noun* a tress of false hair worn at the rear so that the wearer's hair appears longer than it actually is

switchback railway *comp. noun* a roller-coaster

swither *verb, Sc.* to hesitate or doubt

{**swivelled » swivelling**} *spell.* {swiveled » swiveling}

{**swizz » swizzle**} *noun, coll.* (1) something that is unfair; (2) a swindle

sword dance *comp. noun, North, Sc.* (1) in northeastern England, a dance where participants hold the tip of the sword belonging to the dancer opposite them; (2) in Scotland, a solo dance over two swords laid crosswise on the ground

sword dollar *comp. noun, hist., Sc.* a silver coin worth 30 ➧shillings Scots

By 1707 when it ceased to be legal tender, this coin was equal to 2 ➧shillings and 6 ➧pence English, or ^{1}/sth of an English ➧pound. It was issued during the reign of ➧James I of England and VI of Scotland and it acquired this name because of the mark of a sword on its reverse side.

the **Sword of State** *pr. name* a ceremonial sword carried before the monarch on formal state occasions

swot *noun* (1) study that requires hard grind; (2) someone who indulges in such study

Typically, for an examination.

{**swot » swot up**} *verb, coll.* to study hard or quickly

{**symbolled » symbolling**} *spell.* {symboled » symboling}

synaeresis *spell.* syneresis

The merging of two vowels into one.

{**synaesthesia » synaesthetic**} *spell.* {synesthesia » synesthetic}

A subjective sensation other than the one being stimulated.

synd *noun, Sc.* a hasty wash or rinse

syndic *noun* the business agent of a university

In particular, of ➧Cambridge University.

syne *adv., Sc.* (1) since a pervious time; (2) previously; (3) therefore

the **Synod of Whitby** *pr. name, hist.* a church council held at Whitby in 664 to decide whether the kingdom of ➧Northumbria should follow the Irish or Roman form of Christianity

The Roman was chosen, which eventually led to its adoption throughout all Britain, including Ireland too in due course.

Syon House *pr. name, hist.* a castellated 16th C. house on the northern bank of the ➧Thames River some 10 miles west of London

The name, which is a variation of "Zion," reminds us that before the present-day house, there was a convent on this site.

syringe *noun* a spray gun used in kitchen or garden

t' *adj., adv., North* the definite article

T&G *pr. name, abbr., coll.* the ➡TGWU

ta *noun, coll.* thank you
An infantile form, but also used informally by adults.

TA *pr. name, abbr.* the ➡Territorial Army

tab [A] *noun* a red marker on an army uniform collar indicating that the wearer is a ➡staff officer
[B] *noun, North, sl.* (1) an ear; (2) a cigarette; (3) an old woman
[C] *noun, sl.* (1) a member of ➡Cambridge University; (2) a ➡yomp

tabard *noun* a coat, worn by a ➡herald, which is emblazoned with the ➡monarch's ➡coat of arms

tabby *noun, sl.* an attractive girl

table *verb* to place a matter upon an agenda
Particularly of the ➡House of Commons.

tablet *noun, Sc.* a kind of hard fudge candy

tabouret *spell.* taboret

tack *noun* an irrelevant additional clause attached to a ➡parliamentary bill

tacket *noun, Sc.* a small nail, especially a hobnail

tackety boots *comp. noun, Sc.* heavy-duty boots with ➡tacket-studded or hobnailed soles

tae *prep., Sc.* to

{**taenia » taeniacide**} *spell.* {tenia » teniacide}

{**taeniafuge » taeniasis**} *spell.* {teniafuge » teniasis}

the **Taffia** *pr. name, coll.* a supposed Welsh Mafia
Derived from ➡Taffy.

Taffy *pr. name, coll.* a nickname for a Welshman
Said to be derived from the Welsh pronunciation of the name "David," which is *Dafydd* in Welsh.

tag *noun* an aglet, the plastic or metal tip at the end of a shoestring

Taig *pr. name, derog., Ir., sl.* a Northern Irish Protestant nickname for a Roman Catholic

tail *noun* in ➡cricket, (1) the last in a team's batting order; (2) a team's weakest ➡batsman
(1) and (2) are usually the same person.

tailback *noun* a line of traffic stopped on the highway

tailboard *noun* a tailgate

tail-end Charlie *comp. noun, sl.* (1) a person bringing up the rear; (2) the rear gunner in a bomber; (3) the rear aircraft of a group
(2) and (3) began life as ➡RAF World War II slang.

tailored blouse *comp. noun* a shirtwaist blouse

Taiwan *noun, rh. sl.* an upper ➡second-class degree
Derivation: upper second > 2-1 > two-one > Taiwan

take against *verb, coll.* to start to dislike

take an early bath *phr. verb, sl.* to leave the field before the end of the game, for any reason

take a note *phr. verb, coll.* to write down

take a pew *phr. verb, coll.* to take a seat, sit down

take a purler *phr. verb sl.* to be hit in such a way as to fall lengthwise

take a shufti *phr. verb, coll.* to take a look
SEE ALSO: ➡shufti.

take as read *idiom. phr. verb, coll.* to accept as true or already known

take-away *comp. noun, abbr., coll.* (1) ➡take-away food; (2) a ➡take-away restaurant

take-away food *comp. noun, coll.* carry-out food

take-away restaurant *comp. noun, coll.* a restaurant specializing in carry-out food

take a wicket *verb* to remove a ➡cricketing ➡batsman from play

take ill *verb, coll.* to take sick

take in *verb, coll.* to buy or have delivered at regular intervals
For example, a daily newspaper.

take it in turns *phr. verb, coll.* to take turns

take it out of (someone) *phr. verb, coll.* to take it out on (someone)

take legal advice *phr. verb, coll.* to consult a lawyer

take no harm *phr. verb, coll.* to survive or endure without being damaged or hurt

take oneself out of oneself *idiom. phr. verb, sl.* to shrug off or brush aside excessive introspection

take service

take service *verb, arch.* to begin work as a servant

take ship *verb, arch.* to embark upon a ship for the purpose of going on a voyage

take {silk » the silk} *phr. verb, coll.* to become a ➡{King's » Queen's} Counsel

take stick *comp. noun* to be subjected to ➡stick [A]

take tea *phr. verb, coll.* (1) to drink a cup of tea; (2) to indulge in a meal such as ➡afternoon tea, ➡high tea, etc., either alone or, more usually, in the company of others.

take the biscuit *phr. verb, coll.* to take the cake

take the dick *phr. verb, abbr., sl.* to swear or affirm
"Dick" is a corrupted abbreviation of "declaration."

take the {King's » Queen's} shilling *phr. verb, arch., sl.* to join the army

take the {mickey » michael} *phr. verb, sl.* to tease or make a fool of someone

take the piss *idiom. phr. verb, taboo* to disparage or mock

take to the road *idiom. phr. verb, hist.* to take up a career as a highway robber

take under advisement *phr. verb, out.* to consult with others, especially one's superiors

take up *verb, coll.* to interrupt or question a speaker, especially at a public meeting

talk around *verb, coll.* to persuade by talking

talk Billingsgate *verb, sl.* to speak in a foul or abusive manner
SEE ALSO: ➡Billingsgate.

talking-shop *noun, coll., derog.* somewhere, such as a legislature, considered to be a place where talk is substituted for action

talk nineteen to the dozen *idiom. phr. verb, coll.* to talk in a rapid and continuous stream

talk out *verb* to successfully filibuster in ➡Parliament

talk round *verb, coll.* to avoid the issue; to talk of everything except what matters

tallage *noun, hist.* a medieval tax imposed upon towns
Abolished in the 14th C.

tallboy *noun* (1) a highboy; (2) clothespress

Tally *pr. name, derog., Sc., sl.* an Italian

tally clerk *comp. noun* one who keeps a tally of goods loaded and unloaded onto and off ships in dock

tallyman *noun, out.* someone who goes from door to door offering goods for sale on the installment plan

tally stick *comp. noun, hist.* a notched piece of wood, used in great numbers by the ➡Exchequer to record the financial transactions of the British government since early medieval times

These valuable historical records were stored in the crypt of the old ➡Palace of Westminster and, believe it or not, were used to fuel the stoves heating the building. The vast majority were destroyed in the great fire that engulfed the palace in 1834.

tam-o'-shanter *comp. noun, Sc.* a wide woolen cap with tight headband and central pompon
Named after the hero of Robert Burns's poem of this name.

Tam-o'-Shanter's mare *idiom, Sc.* a reminder of the dangers of buying pleasure at too high a price
From the fate of Meg, Tam-o'-Shanter's mare, who lost her tail to a winsome young witch wearing a ➡cutty sark:
When e're to Drink you are inclined'
Or Cutty-sarks rin in your mind,
Think, ye may buy the joys o'er dear—
Remember Tam-o'-Shanter's mare.
—Robert Burns, *Tam-o'-Shanter*

Tamson's mare *idiom, coll., Sc.* shanks's mare; one's own legs, when used for transportation
SEE ALSO: ➡Jock Tamson's bairns; ➡shanks's pony.

the Tangerines *pr. name* a nickname for the 2nd Regiment of ➡Foot
A unit of the British Army raised in 1661 for service in Tangiers, which was a British possession at that time.

tanist *noun, Gae.* a ➡Celtic chief's heir apparent, who is traditionally selected by election

tank *noun, sl.* a drink of beer, usually a pint

tank engine *comp. noun* a steam-powered railroad locomotive which carries water and fuel supplies on board rather than pulled behind on a tender

tanker *noun, sl.* a heavy drinker

tank up *verb, coll.* to fill up a vehicle with gasoline

Tanky *pr. name, sl.* a member of the ➡Communist Party of Great Britain who supports the "traditional" Stalinist worldview hook, line and sinker

tanner *noun, arch., sl.* a ➡sixpenny bit

Tannoy *pr. name (TM)* a public address system

Taoiseach *pr. name, Gae., Ir.* the ➡Prime Minister of the ➡Irish Republic
The Irish Gaelic word for "chief".

tap [A] *noun* a spigot or faucet
[B] *noun, abbr.* a ➡taproom
[C] *noun, Sc.* (1) the surface of water; (2) a tuft of hair or feathers; (3) a child's spinning top

tape *noun, sl.* the sleeve chevrons worn on military and other uniforms to indicate rank

tapper *noun, sl.* a beggar or scrounger

tappit hen *comp. noun, out., Sc.* (1) a crested or tufted hen; (2) a pewter tankard or decanter with a lid knob that resembles a hen's tuft

taproom *noun* a room in a pub or hotel where draft beer is sold and drunk

tapsie-teerie *adj., adv., Sc.* topsy-turvy, upside-down

{**ta-ra » ta-ta**} *exclam., coll.* good-bye
An infantile form, sometimes used informally by adults.

tart [A] *noun* a fruit-filled sweet pie
[B] *noun, rh. sl.* a prostitute or slut
Derivation: prostitute > sweetheart > raspberry tart > tart. The word "sweetheart" formerly meant "prostitute."

tartan *noun, Sc.* (1) a textile design comprising stripes of differing colors and widths crossing at right angles to form a ➡sett; (2) a heavy woolen fabric incorporating (1)
(See box below.)

tart around *verb, sl.* to behave in a promiscuous or ostentatious or tasteless manner or style

tart up *verb, coll.* to smarten up in an ostentatious or tasteless manner or style

{**tasselled » tasselling**} *spell.* {tasseled » tasseling}

tasty *adj., sl.* having a criminal record

tat *noun, coll.* (1) a grubby individual; (2) garbage or junk; (3) clothes that lack taste

Tate Gallery *pr. name* a leading art gallery with important collections of both 16th C. and 20th C. paintings and sculpture
The Tate Gallery, which was founded in 1897, has its main home in London, but there are also branch galleries at ➡Liverpool and St Ives in ➡Cornwall.

taters *idiom, rh. sl.* cold weather
Derivation: cold weather > cold > mold > potatoes in the mold > potatoes > taters. This is a somewhat tenuous trail, but we're stuck with it.

tattie *noun, Sc.* a potato

tattie-bogle *comp. noun, Sc.* (1) a scarecrow; (2) an unkempt or raggedly dressed person; (3) a child's toy consisting of a large raw potato with matchsticks stuck into it

tattie-howker *comp. noun, Sc.* a potato-harvester

Taunton *pr. name, hist.* a town that is the administrative center of ➡Somerset
There was a fortified ➡Anglo-Saxon settlement here in the 8th C. The current population is 36,000 (1991 estimate).

TAVR *noun, abbr., hist.* the Territorial and Army Volunteer Reserve
A division of the ➡Territorial Army, founded in 1922 and disbanded in 1967.

tawse *noun, hist., out., Sc.* a leather strip about 2 in wide and 2 ft long, with two or three tails at one end
Once used to administer corporal punishment in Scottish schools by striking upon the hands. *SEE ALSO:* ➡belt, ➡strap.

tax disc *comp. noun, coll.* a small paper disk that is a certificate of payment of the ➡Road Fund Licence
It is a legal requirement to display a current one of these upon an automobile's windshield.

taximan *noun, arch.* one who drives a taxi

taxi rank *comp. noun* a taxi stand

taxi stance *comp. noun, Sc.* a taxi stand

The Truth About Tartan

Tartan is arranged in various distinctive styles and patterns called ➡setts which are supposed to denote particular ➡Highland clans. However this modern notion of tartans being "owned" by particular clans is a fiction which was invented by Sir Walter Scott who came up with the idea when he was organizing the festivities surrounding a visit of ➡George IV to ➡Edinburgh in 1822. Until that time ordinary ➡kilt, ➡philabeg or ➡plaid wearers would normally use material that was devoid of any colored patterns that we would think of as tartan today, although clan chiefs and others of high rank would wear recognizably tartan-patterned and colored plaid. However, there was no thought of using particular setts to differentiate the membership of different clans, and those who could afford to, would wear whatever seemed a fashionable pattern at the time, but even this was rare and when Johnson made his famous highland journey with Boswell in 1773, he did not see tartan worn even once.

The use of a specific tartan as a badge or mark of belonging first developed among the Highland regiments of the British Army raised both before and after the ➡Forty-five, as all the men of a regiment would be required to wear the same sett, differentiating themselves from members of other regiments wearing other setts. Without doubt it was this example which put the notion of clan-specific tartans into the mind of Sir Walter Scott, and this rather spurious idea has survived and thrived down to the present day.

the **Tay** *pr. name* a river which at about 120 miles in length is the longest in Scotland

It rises in the ➡Grampians and flows eastwards into the ➡North Sea at the Firth of ➡Tay.

the Firth of **Tay** *pr. name* the estuary of the ➡Tay River, on Scotland's eastern coast

Bounded on the north by ➡Tayside and ➡Dundee and on the south by ➡Fife, this wide river mouth has been bridged by the lengthy ➡Tay Rail Bridge in the 19th C. and an even longer ➡Tay Road Bridge in the 20th C.

tayberry *noun* a soft fruit that is the product of crossing blackberry with raspberry

Named after the ➡Tay River, which flows through the area where they were first grown.

the **Tay Rail Bridge** *pr. name* 1¼ miles long bridge carrying a railroad across the Firth of ➡Tay near ➡Dundee in Scotland

There have been two railroad bridges over the Tay. The first, erected between 1871 and 1878, collapsed in December 1879 while a train was crossing it during a gale, killing 75. This is still remembered as the Tay Bridge Disaster.

A new bridge, still in use, was erected between 1883 to 1888. Some of the piers of the original bridge can still be seen from trains using the new bridge.

the **Tay Road Bridge** *pr. name* a bridge carrying a highway across the Firth of ➡Tay about two miles to the east of the older railroad bridge

About 1½ miles long and of box-girder construction, it rests on 42 piers and was built between 1963 and 1966.

Tayside *pr. name* a region in eastern Scotland

The current population is 395,000 (1991 Census).

TCD *pr. name, abbr.* ➡Trinity College, Dublin

TD [A] *noun, abbr.* (1) the Territorial Officer's Decoration; (2) the Efficiency Decoration of the Home Auxiliary Military Forces and ➡TAVR

(1) was issued between 1908 to 1930 only. (2) has been issued since 1930, when it replaced (1).

[B] *pr. name, abbr., Gae., Ir.* a *Teachta Dáil*, which is ➡Irish Gaelic for ➡Member of Parliament

tea *noun, abbr., coll.* ➡high tea

tea break *comp. noun* a short pause while tea is drunk, usually mid-morning

tea caddy *comp. noun* a small air-tight metal container used to store tea leaves or tea bags

tea cake *comp. noun* a light sweet cake, often toasted before being eaten

tea chest *comp. noun, out.* a light-weight wooden box about 2 ft high with thin internal metal foil lining, used to transport tea from India, etc.

After they arrived in Britain, they became widely used for the storage and transportation of household effects, once their tea-transporting duties were over.

tea cloth *comp. noun* a tea towel

tea cosy *comp. noun* a thickly padded cover used to keep teapots warm

tea lady *comp. noun, coll.* a woman who makes tea or coffee, taken around an office on a ➡tea trolley

tea leaf *idiom, rh. sl.* a thief

team *noun, sl.* a criminal gang

tearaway *noun, coll.* (1) a juvenile delinquent; (2) an unthinking or careless youth

tear off a strip *idiom. phr. verb, coll.* to rebuke in an angry manner

{**teaselled » teaselling**} *spell.* {teaseled » teaseling}

teashop *noun* a tearoom or small restaurant

Teasmade *pr. name (TM)* a machine which makes tea automatically at pre-determined times

teat *noun* the nipple on a baby's bottle

tea trolley *comp. noun* a tea {cart » wagon}

A small wheeled table that tea is served from.

tea up *idiom* here is tea ready to drink

TEC *pr. name, abbr.* a Training and Enterprise Council

One of a number of local agencies set up in England and Wales by the government to enhance job training and encourage job-creating employment.

In Scotland, similar agencies are known as ➡LECs

technical college *comp. noun* a junior college

technical school *comp. noun* a high school that specializes in technical education

technicolor yawn *idiom, sl.* projectile vomiting

ted *noun, abbr., coll.* a ➡tearaway

Derived from ➡teddy boy.

teddy boy *comp. noun, coll., hist.* a 1950s ➡tearaway who wore what was supposed to be ➡Edwardian dress

teedle *verb, Sc.* to hum a tune without the words

Tees *pr. name* a river some 80 miles in length

It flows from the Pennines into the ➡North Sea at ➡Teeside.

teg *noun* a sheep between one and two years old

{**telaesthesia » telaesthesic**} *spell.* {telesthesia » telesthesic}

The telepathic perception of distant events or objects.

telemessage *noun* the official name since 1981 of a British domestic telegram or cable

International ones are still called telegrams.

telephone box *comp. noun* a telephone booth

telephonist *noun* a telephone switchboard operator

teleprinter *noun* teletypewriter

telesales *noun* telemarketing

Teletex *pr. name (TM)* a teletext system for the transmission of information by electronic means

televisual *adj.* suitable for, related to, or concerned with television

telly *noun, abbr., coll.* a television set

Templar *noun* a barrister whose chambers at situated within the ➡Temple

---

the **Temple** *pr. name, hist.* a building in central London which houses two of the ➡Inns of Court, the ➡Inner and ➡Outer Temples
Originally this was the first house in England of the Knights Templar, hence this name.
(The Knights Templar were an order of knights, founded in 1119. They took monastic vows and dedicated themselves to protecting pilgrims coming to the Holy Land. They were name thus because their headquarters were on the site of the former Temple of Solomon in Jerusalem.)

the **Temple Bar** *pr. name, hist.* an old entrance to the ➡City of London, at ➡Fleet Street near to the ➡Temple
Once the western gate through the walls of the City, a prison was built above the gateway in the 14th C. and it became the place where the heads of executed traitors and rebels were displayed upon iron spikes until 1746. The gateway remained there until 1878, when it was dismantled and rebuilt at Waltham Cross, Hertfordshire, where it remains today.

Temple Meads Station *pr. name* the principal railroad terminus in central ➡Bristol

tenant right *comp. noun* a tenant's legal right to continue his or her tenancy even when the lease terminates, under certain special circumstances

{**ten a penny » two a penny**} *idiom, coll.* dime a dozen

ten bob note *comp. noun, arch., sl.* a ➡ten shilling note
SEE ALSO: ➡bob.

tenderloin *noun* the middle portion of pork loin

tenement *noun* a room or rooms that is a separate residence within a single building that contains other residences

the **ten minute rule** *comp. noun* a parliamentary procedure whereby an ➡MP, by means of a speech lasting no more than ten minutes, may request the ➡House to permit the introduction of a bill
After one opposing speech also lasting no longer than ten minutes, the ➡House votes for or against introduction.

tenné *adj.* the heraldic name for brown-orange

tenner *noun, abbr, coll.* a ten ➡pound note

tenour *spell.* tenor

ten shilling note *comp. noun, hist.* a ➡banknote worth ten ➡shillings
Ten shillings equalled half of one ➡pound. These banknotes were removed from circulation during the 1960s.

tent *noun, Sc.* attention or care

tenter *noun* (1) an unskilled assistant; (2) someone in charge of machinery or equipment

term *noun* the days when a court is in session

term-day *noun, Sc.* a Scottish ➡quarter-day
These days are:
{Candlemas » Canlemas}, February 28 *(formerly February 2)*
Whitsunday, May 28 *(formerly May 15)*
Lammas, August 28 *(formerly August 1)*
Martinmas, November 28 *(formerly November 11)*
English quarter-days fall upon different dates.

terminological inexactitude *comp. noun* a lie
An expression invented by Winston Churchill so that he could get around the ban on using the word "lie" in the ➡House of Commons where it is considered to be ➡unparliamentary language when used to describe the utterances of another ➡MP.
Of couse, politicians never lie; we all know that.

terms of reference *comp. noun* (1) points requiring to be discussed, settled or agreed; (2) constituent parts or scope of a project, case or inquiry

terms of trade *comp. noun* the ratio of the value of a nation's imports to the value of its exports

terrace *noun* a row of ➡terraced houses

terraced house *comp. noun* a row house

the **terraces** *noun, coll.* banked spectator areas surrounding an arena such as a soccer field
Traditionally there were no seats; spectators stood through the whole spectacle. But this is now changing rapidly and unseated terraces will soon be a thing of the past.

Terrier *noun, abbr.* a ➡Territorial

Territorial *noun* a member of the ➡Territorial Army

Territorial Army *pr. name* a force of part-time volunteer reserve soldiers, organized locally
Somewhat similar to the U.S. National Guard.

tertiary education *comp. noun* education at university or college level

Terylene *pr. name (TM)* a synthetic polyester fabric similar to Dracon (TM)

Tesco *pr. name (TM)* a national supermarket chain

TESSA *noun, abbr.* Tax Exempt Special Savings Account
A special savings account exempt from income tax.

test

the Thames
at London Bridge

test [A] *noun* a portable hearth that is used with a cupel to separate noble metals such as gold or silver from base metals such as lead

[B] *noun, abbr., coll.* a ⟿cricket ⟿test match

[C] *verb* to assay a metal

the Test Acts *pr. name, hist.* a collective name for various ⟿Acts of Parliament of 1661 to 1681 specifically intented to exclude Roman Catholics, ⟿Nonconformists and others from public office

They included the Acts of Abjuration, Allegiance, Supremacy, Corporation and Uniformity as well as the specifically so-named Test Act. All were repealed in 1828.

tester *noun, arch.* a ⟿sixpenny bit

test match *noun* (1) in ⟿cricket, a series of championship matches between national teams; (2) in emulation of cricket, a series of championship matches between national rugby teams

The name originated in a series of cricket matches played as "tests" throughout Australia by a visiting English team in 1862.

The dates of first Test Matches:

England v. Australia: 1876.
England v. South Africa : 1888.
England v. West Indies: 1928.
England v. New Zealand: 1929.
England v. India: 1932.
England v. Pakistan: 1952.

tetchy *adj.* irritable or touchy

teuchter *noun, derog., Sc.* a rustic individual, especially a ⟿Gaelic-speaker from the ⟿Highlands

tew *verb, East* to work very hard

TGWU *pr. name, abbr.* the Transport and General Workers' Union

A labor union for blue-collar workers

tha *pronoun., North.* you

the Thames *pr. name* the second-longest river in Great Britain and the longest entirely within England

It flows eastward 215 miles from Thameshead in the ⟿Cotswolds near ⟿Cirencester, to the North Sea. Its Roman name was *Tamesis*, and from its source to ⟿Oxford it is often called the ⟿Isis, which is a play on the river's Latin name. The two principal cities to sit astride the river are ⟿Oxford and, of course, ⟿London.

the Thames Conservancy *pr. name, abbr., hist.* an agency that was formerly responsible for managing the ⟿Thames

Now supplanted by the ⟿NRA

the Thames Flood Barrier *pr. name* a barrier, some 1,700 ft wide, which crosses the ⟿Thames at ⟿Woolwich Reach

This structure removes the risk of serious flooding in central London, possible because the Thames is tidal there.

These hydraulically operated gates normally lie flat on the riverbed to allow shipping to sail upon the river as normal, but they can be turned through 90 degrees to a height of about 50 ft above the riverbed when floods threaten.

Thameslink *pr. name (TM)* a railroad company operating services through central London from north of the city to south of it

It is part of ⟿British Rail.

Thames Trains *pr. name (TM)* a railroad company operating commuter services to and from the Thames valley and London

It is part of ⟿British Rail.

Thames TV *pr. name* a TV program production company headquartered in London, which was formerly part of the ⟿ITV network

thane *noun, hist., Sc.* (1) a ⟿Highland ⟿clan ⟿chieftain; (2) a baron who holds land directly from the king and has the rank of an earl's son

the Isle of **Thanet** *pr. name, hist.* the northeastern corner of ➠Kent
It was an island in Roman times but is not one today.

{thane » thegn} *noun, hist.* a rather lowly rank of landowner in ➠Anglo-Saxon England
A sort of proto-knight, later replaced by that rank.

that [A] *adv., coll.* so very
Example: "not that bad"
[B] *pronoun, coll.* the person being spoken to, especially by telephone
Used instead of "this." For example, on the telephone, "Is that Mary?" = "Is this Mary?"

thatch *noun* reeds, straw or similar, when used as a roof-covering

thatched roof *comp. noun* a roof made of ➠thatch
The normal way to cover a roof in Britain until slates and tiles became generally available about 250 years ago. Many thatched roofs can still be seen, especially in southern England.

thatcher *noun* a maker of ➠thatched roofs

Thatcherism *pr. name* the political philosophy of ➠Prime Minister Margaret Thatcher and her followers

that's torn it *exclam., coll.* that's wrecked things

the [A] *pronoun, Ir., Sc.* a function word sometimes found before the surname of a Scots or Irish ➠clan chief
For example, the Chief of ➠Clan MacDonald might be called "the Macdonald."
[B] *pronoun, Wal.* a function word placed between a family name and a description of someone's occupation or other principal characteristic, creating a Welsh dialectal nickname for the person which is descriptive of [his » her} occupation or role in life
For example: "Jones the Post" for Mr. Jones, a ➠postman.

{theatre » theatre-goer} *spell.* {theater » theatergoer}

theatre porter *comp. noun* a hospital orderly working at an operating room

Theatre Royal *pr. name, hist.* the oldest theater in London still in use today, founded in 1663

theatre sister *comp. noun* a principal surgical nurse

theatrical *noun* a professional actor

the noo *adj., Sc.* (1) presently; (2) momentarily

there it is *idiom, coll.* (1) that's what's been decided; (2) this is the problem

there's a good chap? *inter., coll.* you *do* agree with {me » us » this}, don't you?
A condescending expression.

there you are *idiom, rh. sl.* pub
Derivation: pub > bar > are > there you are.

thermaesthesia *spell.* thermesthesia
Temperature sensitive.

thermionic valve *comp. noun* an electron tube or thermionic tube

Thermos flask *pr. name (TM)* a Thermos or vacuum bottle

THF *pr. name (TM), abbr.* Trusthouse Forte
A major hotel and catering chain

thick ear *comp. noun, coll.* an ear swollen because of a blow upon it

thick on the ground *idiom, coll.* (1) in large numbers; (2) present everywhere

thick 'un *comp. noun, arch., sl.* a ➠sovereign coin, especially one made of gold

the **Thin Red Line** *comp. noun, hist.* the 93rd Highland Regiment of foot, called this when at the Battle of Balaclava during the ➠Crimea War, they had no time to form into squares yet were able to stop an enemy advance

thiopentone *noun* thiopental

{thiosulphate » thiosulphuric acid} *spell.* {thiosulfate » thiosulfuric acid}

thir *pronoun, North* these

third-class degree *noun, abbr., coll.* a university ➠first degree awarded with the lowest of three possible classes of honor
See also: ➠first-class degree, ➠second-class degree.

third man *comp. noun* a fielding player's position on the ➠cricket field
Positioned behind the slips and near to the field boundary

the **Third Programme** *pr. name, hist.* a BBC radio station that specialized in intellectual material such as classical and avant-garde music, drama, and literature, plus lectures and discussions on academic topics
In 1967 it was renamed ➠Radio 3.

third reading *comp. noun* the presentation of a ➠bill to ➠Parliament for final acceptance in detail as amended in committee
Also called the ➠Final Reading.

third wicket partnership *idiom* a pair of ➠cricketing ➠batsman working together to make runs

thirl *verb, Sc.* (1) to pierce or perforate; (2) to bore or drill a hole

the **Thirty-nine Articles** *pr. name* the central points of doctrine and belief that must be publicly accepted by those wishing to become priests in the ➠Church of England
They are based upon an earlier list of 42 articles prepared by Archbishop Cranmer in 1553 and finalized in 1571.

the **thirty-year rule** *comp. noun* a restriction on the release of confidential government papers that prevents most of them from being made available to the public until they are 30 years old

this day week *idiom, coll.* a week from today

This might be in either future or past sense; which one is to be determined from the context.

Thistle *noun* the national vegetative emblem of Scotland

It appears to have been adopted by ➡James III in the 15th. C. to symbolize defiance.

the Order of the **Thistle** *pr. name, abbr., hist.* the highest order of Scottish Knighthood

In full, "The Most Ancient and Most Noble Order of the Thistle," it is second in ranking only to the Order of the ➡Garter, and was reputedly founded in 787 by Achaius, a possibly mythical King of Scots. After being allowed to lapse, it was "re-founded" by ➡James II of England and VII of Scotland in 1687. The number of members of the order is restricted to 16 at any one time, plus the monarch.

It is also known as the Order of ➡St Andrew.

this weather *idiom, coll., Sc.* (1) today; (2) at this time

thole *verb, Sc.* to suffer, tolerate or endure with bravery or patience

tholeable *adj., Sc.* endurable or tolerable

thorp *noun, out.* a village

Now only used as part of a place name.

THORP *pr. name, abbr.* the THermal Oxide Reprocessing Plant

Located at ➡Sellafield in ➡Cumbria, THORP has been built to reprocess spent uranium oxide fuel rods used in both advanced gas-cooled and pressure water nuclear reactors. *SEE ALSO:* ➡Calder Hall.

thoucht *noun, Sc.* a thought

thowless *adj., Sc.* (1) listless; (2) ineffectual

thrash *noun, coll.* a lavish party

thrawn *adj., Sc.* (1) crooked or distorted; (2) twisted with pain or rage; (3) perverse or obstinate; (4) inclement or unpleasant

(2) refers to the face; (3) refers to people or to events; (4) refers to the weather.

Threadneedle Street *pr. name* the street at the heart of the ➡City of London financial district where the ➡Bank of England is headquartered

threap *noun, Sc.* (1) a dispute or quarrel; (2) a strongly held belief or strongly expressed opinion

three-cornered fight *idiom, coll.* an election contest with three candidates

three-day event *comp. noun* an equestrian contest lasting three days

three-decker *comp. noun, coll.* a novel or other literary work that is published in three volumes

the **Three Estates** *pr. name, hist.* a medieval term for the ➡Lords Spiritual, ➡Lords Temporal, and the ➡House of Commons

These were, respectively, the leaders of the church, of the nobility and of the common people. It is now an entirely outdated term, although the press, newspapers in particular, have been called the fourth estate since the early 19th C., and sometimes still is now.

3i *pr. name (TM)* Investors In Industry

A large venture-capitalist group.

three-line whip *comp. noun* the most urgent kind of ➡whip that can be issued by their party to ➡MPs

Called this because words are underlined three times to indicate particular urgency and importance.

Three Lions Passant Gardant *pr. name* the lions in the ➡coat of arms of England

threepence *comp. noun, arch.* (1) a ➡threepenny bit; (2) the sum of three pennies

threepenny *adj.* worth three pennies

threepenny bit *comp. noun, arch.* a former small 12-sided copper coin worth three old pennies

three-point turn *comp. noun* an automobile Y-turn

three-quarters *comp. noun* a rugby player standing just to the rear of the half-backs

thrift *noun, Sc.* gainful employment

Throgmorton Street *pr. name* a nickname for the London Stock Exchange

Because it is the street that the Stock Exchange is situated upon. Thus this should be the exact British equivalent of "Wall Street," but in fact is rarely if ever used in this sense; the more usual equivalent term is "the ➡City."

the **Throne** *pr. name, coll.* the office of ➡sovereign

throng *adj., East* busy

throughway *spell.* thruway

throw *verb* in ➡cricket, (1) to put out a batter by throwing a ball directly at the ➡wicket; (2) to return a ball from outfield

(1) is an illegal pitch.

thrustful *adj.* aggressive

thump *verb* to hit forcibly

thunderbox *noun, coll.* a chamber pot

the **Thunderer** *pr. name, hist.* a popular 19th C. nickname for London's *Times* newspaper

An allusion to the powerful effect its editorials had on public opinion and thus the government of the day.

thunderflash *noun* an explosive used in war games, yielding much smoke and noise but little blast

thundering *adj., coll.* vast or considerable

thunner *noun, Sc.* thunder

thuskin *adj., East* very large

thwaite *noun, arch.* former wild land now cultivated
Today only used as part of place names.

tice *noun* a ➡yorker

the **Tichborne Dole** *pr. name, hist.* an annual disbursement of bread to the people of the parish of Tichborne in ➡Hampshire
A ceremony carried out every ➡Lady Day since the 12th C.

{**tich » titch**} *noun, sl.* a tiny or insignificant person

tick *noun, coll.* (1) credit; (2) a brief interval of time
Originally, (2) was the time between two ticks of a clock.

ticket *noun, sl.* a military certificate of discharge

ticket barrier *comp. noun* a gate at the entrance to that area of a railroad depot or terminus where the tracks are and where trains are boarded
The point beyond which one may not proceed without a valid ticket to ride or a ➡platform ticket.

ticket day *comp. noun* a stock exchange ➡name day

ticket inspector *comp. noun* a railroad conductor

ticket-of-leave *comp. noun, hist.* a certificate granting a convict permission to leave prison before the formal end of {his » her} period of sentence
Superficially similar to a modern parole.

ticket-of-leave man *comp. noun, arch.* a convict who has been granted a ➡ticket-of-leave

tickety-boo *adj., coll., out.* all right, OK

tick over *verb, coll.* to operate at a minimal level
Of a person, business, machine, etc.

{**tic-tac » tick-tack**} *noun, coll.* a manual semaphore-like signaling system
It is used by race-course bookmakers to communicate odds and other information between each other.

tiddler *noun, coll.* (1) a small fish such as a stickleback; (2) an especially small person or thing

tiddly [A] *adj., coll.* very small

[B] *adj., rh. sl.* slightly drunk
Derivation: drunk > drink > wink > tiddly-wink > tiddly.

tiddly wink *idiom, rh. sl.* a drink

tidemark *noun, coll.* (1) a mark, often in the form of a ring, upon someone's body indicating the extent of the washed area; (2) a mark left around the inside of a bathtub by the water that had been in it

tidy sum *noun, coll.* a large sum of money

tie *noun* a match between two players or teams participating in a competition

tied {**cottage » house**} *comp. noun* (1) a dwelling that one lives in as a condition of employment; (2) a dwelling that is provided to an employee as part of a compensation package
SEE ALSO: ➡tied house.

tied house *comp. noun* a hotel or pub obliged by contract to sell beer manufactured by one particular brewer only
SEE ALSO: ➡tied {cottage » house}.

tierced *adj.* being heraldically divided into three different-colored parts

tiffin *noun* a light lunch

tig *noun* tag
The child's game.

tight-arsed *adj., sl., taboo* tight-assed

tights *noun, pref.* pantyhose

till [A] *noun* (1) a bank teller's counter; (2) a supermarket checkout counter
[B] *prep., Sc.* unto

tilliepan *noun, Sc.* a saucepan

till receipt *comp. noun* a tape printed out by a cash register as a record of transactions

Tim *noun, derog., Sc., sl.* a Roman Catholic

timber framing *comp. noun, hist.* ➡half-timbering

timbers *noun, sl.* ➡cricket ➡stumps or ➡wickets

time *noun* the moment when a ➡public house closes, as required by the licensing laws

time gentlemen, please *imper.* a ➡publican's warning call to customers to drink up as it is nearly ➡time

Time-honoured Lancaster *pr. name, hist.* ➡John of Gaunt, Duke of ➡Lancaster
A name coined for him by Shakespeare.

Timeline *pr. name (TM)* a telephone service that informs the user of the correct time by means of a recorded voice
Previously called the ➡Speaking Clock.

The **Times** *pr. name* the correct and complete name for the *Times* newspaper published daily in London
All other newspapers called the *Times*, such as, for example, the *New York Times* or the *Los Angeles Times*, can be said to be mere followers or imitators of this, the original *The Times*.

tin [A] *noun, abbr.* a ➡tin can
[B] *noun, sl.* money
[C] *verb, rh. sl.* to can
Derivation: can > ➡tin can > tin

Tina *pr. name, abbr., coll.* a nickname for ➡Prime Minister Margaret Thatcher
From her habit of saying, "There Is No Alternative."

tin can *noun* an airtight can made of tinplate or similar

tincture *noun* (1) the components of a ➡coat of arms; (2) a euphemism for a shot of liquor

tine

tine *verb, coll.* to become lost

tinker *noun, Ir., Sc.* a gypsy

tinkle *noun, coll.* a telephone call

the **tin lid** *comp. noun, coll.* the last straw

tin opener *comp. noun* a can opener

{**tinselled » tinselling**} *spell.* {tinseled » tinseling}

Tintagel *pr. name, hist.* a ruined castle on the coast of northern ➟Cornwall

Although the castle now there was built in the 13th C., nonetheless it is reputed to be the birthplace of ➟Arthur despite the fact that if he really did exist, he was around many hundreds of years before Tintagel arrived on the scene. That would be some neat trick.

tin tank *idiom, rh. sl.* bank

tip *noun* a place where garbage is dumped

tipper *noun* a dump truck

Tipperary *pr. name* a county in the ➟Irish Republic

County Tipperary in the ancient province of ➟Munster.

Tipperary rifle *comp. noun, Ir.* a ➟shillelagh

tippling house *comp. noun, arch.* a ➟public house

tipstaff *noun* a court official who carries out the directions of a ➟sheriff

tipsy cake *comp. noun* a sponge cake soaked in wine or liquor, usually served with custard

tip-up seat *comp. noun* a folding seat

For example, in a movie theater

TIR *pr. name, abbr., Fr.* ➟Transports International Routier

tired and emotional *idiom* a euphemism for drunk

tirl *verb, Sc.* to twirl, turn or spin

tiro *spell.* tyro

tit *noun, derog., sl.* a foolish or insignificant person

titbit *spell.* tidbit

titchy *adj., sl.* tiny

titfer *noun, rh. sl.* hat

Derivation: hat > tat > tit-for-tat > titfer.

tithe barn *comp. noun, arch.* a kind of barn originally built to hold the tithes once paid to the local church in the form of farm produce

tithing *noun, arch.* (1) a unit of ten households, grouped together and responsible for the behavior of each other; (2) land occupied by such a group.

titre *spell.* titer

The result of a titration.

tittlebat *noun* a stickleback

Its formal name is *gasterosteus aculeatus*.

tit willow *idiom, rh. sl.* pillow

tizzy *noun, arch., sl.* a ➟sixpenny bit

TLS *pr. name, abbr.* the *Times Literary Supplement*

A weekly publication, originally a free supplement that first appeared in 1902 with Friday's issue of *The* ➟*Times* newspaper. In 1914 it became a separate publication in its own right.

TML *pr. name, abbr., Fr.* Transmanche Link

From the French, meaning "Cross-channel Link." This is the consortium that constructed the ➟Channel Tunnel.

to *prep., pref.* of

Descriptive of time. For example, "ten to two" = "ten of two."

toad-in-the-hole *comp. noun* sausage-meat baked in batter

toby jug *comp. noun* a pottery ale-jug that resembles a stout man wearing a three-cornered hat

First made in ➟Staffordshire in the 18th C.

toerag *noun, derog., hist., sl.* (1) a vagrant; (2) a contemptible person

Supposedly, from a habit vagrants have of keeping their feet warm by wrapping them in rags rather than wearing socks.

toff *noun, sl.* (1) a dandy; (2) a well-dressed or upper-class person

toffee *noun* taffy or toffee, whether soft or hard

toffee-nosed *adj., sl.* stuck-up or pretentious

toft *noun* (1) a homestead; (2) the land (1) is upon

tog *noun* a unit of thermal resistance or insulating properties applied to quilts and clothes in general

togs *noun, coll., Lat.* clothes

From the Latin *toga* = "robe"

tog up *verb, coll.* to dress up

toilet *noun* a rest room

tolbooth *noun, hist., Sc.* (1) originally, an office or booth where taxes, tolls, etc. were collected; (2) a town hall; (3) a town jail

to let *idiom* available for rent

Typically, written on a notice outside the property in question.

the **Tolpuddle Martyrs** *pr. name, hist.* six 19th C. farm workers from Tolpuddle in Devon who formed a trade union for the purpose of resisting a wage cut

They were found guilty of administering illegal oaths and sentenced to be transported to Australia in 1834. After protests they were pardoned two years later.

tom [A] *noun, rh. sl.* jewelry

Derivation: jewelry > tomfoolery > tom.

[B] *noun, sl.* a prostitute

Tom and Jerry *pr. name, abbr., hist.* two fashionable but fictitious young men who were considered characteristic of early 19th C. London

From the two leading characters (Corithian Tom and Jerry Hawthorne) of Pierce Egan's *Life in London*, published in 1821. So far as we know, no felines or rodents were ever mentioned in this publication.

tombola *noun, It.* a lottery, typically found at fairs and other places of public entertainment, where winners are chosen by taking tickets from a revolving drum "tumble".

Tommy *noun, abbr., arch., sl.* a generic name for the typical enlisted man in the British Army

Abbreviated from "Thomas Atkins," a name chosen at random to use in a public-ation issued to troops in the 1890s to demonstrate how to fill out various official army forms. It was most commonly used as a generic name for a British soldier in World War I.

Tommy Rabbit *idiom, rh. sl.* a pomegranate

tomorrow week *idiom* one week from tomorrow

Tom Tit *idiom. phr. verb, rh. sl.* to defecate

ton [A] *noun, abbr.* a long or imperial ton

a Tommy

[B] *noun, sl.* (1) a speed of 100 miles per hour; (2) a score of 100 in a game such as darts; (3) £100 (one hundred pounds)

tonn *verb, East* to turn

tonne *noun* a metric ton

A unit of weight equal to 1,000 kg, 2,204.6 lbs or 1.1025 U.S. tons.

ton-up *comp. noun, sl.* a speed of 100 miles per hour

ton-up boy *comp. noun, sl.* a motorcyclist who makes a habit of traveling at 100 miles per hour

too Irish *idiom, rh. sl.* too true

Derivation: too true > too Irish stew > too Irish.

toom *verb, Sc.* (1) empty or vacant; (2) hungry; (3) hollow; (4) echoing; (5) empty-headed; (6) vain

toom-heidit *adj., Sc.* empty-headed or foolish

Toom Tabard *pr. name, hist., Sc.* the nickname of John Baliot, placed on the Scottish throne by Edward I of England

It means "empty cloak," a sobriquet earned by his perceived powerlessness as a puppet of the English king.

too much by half *idiom, coll.* far too much

toot *verb, Sc.* to drink to excess

tooth-glass *comp. noun* a drinking glass used to keep false teeth in overnight

top (A, B, C, etc. ...) *noun* high (A, B, C, etc. ...) Musical notes.

topaz *noun* heraldic representation of or or Sol

top drawer *comp. noun, coll.* (1) high social status; (2) the best quality available

top fruit *comp. noun* fruit grown on trees, not bushes

top gear *comp. noun* a vehicle's high gear

top-hole *adj., coll.* excellent

TOPIC *pr. name, abbr.* Teletext Output of Price Information by Computer

A viewdata-based London Stock Exchange information service.

topping *adj., arch.* excellent

topside *noun* the external portion of a round of beef

tor *noun, Gae., North, West* a rocky or steep hill

From the Welsh or Gaelic word *torr* = "bulging hill"

torch *noun* a flashlight

Torquay *pr. name, hist.* a popular coastal resort town in Devon

The current population is 125,000 (1991 estimate).

torse *noun* an heraldic representation of a wreath

Tory *pr. name, hist.* (1) together with the Whigs, one of the two alternating governing parties of Great Britain until they renamed themselves Conservative in 1830; (2) a member or supporter of the Conservative Party

Originally the name of bands of 17th C. Irish Roman Catholic bandits and rebels who attacked the English in Ireland. During the short reign of the Catholic James II of England and VII of Scotland, it evolved into a term of abuse directed at supporters of royal powers in general and Roman Catholics in particular.

In another sense, it could be said that the name was applied to those who during the then-recent English Civil War would have been called Cavaliers, or the "King's Party." "Tory" was first used as the name of what we might now recognize as a political party following the Glorious Revolution which swept away James and ushered in William and Mary in 1688.

Unlike the word Whig which has now fallen entirely out of contemporary usage, "Tory" is still in daily use as an alternate to "Conservative."

Toryism

Toryism *pr. name* the philosophies and policies of the ➡Conservative Party

the **Tory Party** *pr. name, coll.* an alternate name for the ➡Conservative Party

tosh [A] *adj., Sc.* neat or smart

[B] *noun, sl.* (1) money; (2) nonsense

Tosh *noun, sl.* a familiar form of general address made to any man whose correct name is unknown
SEE ALSO: ➡Jimmy, ➡John, ➡Kiddo, ➡Moosh and ➡Wack.

tosheroon *noun, arch., sl.* a ➡half-a-crown

toss *noun* a fall from a horse

tosser *noun, derog., sl., taboo* an undesirable or unpleasant person, especially a man
SEE ALSO: ➡to

tossing the caber

D. MCK. 93

tossing the caber *idiom, Sc.* a ➡highland sport
Very popular at ➡highland gatherings, it requires a heavy wooden pole (originally a tree trunk) to be thrown as far as possible. Typically, the ➡caber is about 20 ft long and weighs about 110 or 120 lbs.

toss off *verb, sl., taboo* to masturbate
SEE ALSO: ➡tosser

tot [A] *noun, out.* numbers requiring to be added up

[B] *noun, sl.* (1) a shot of liquor; (2) discarded items rescued by a trash collector for his own delectation

[C] *verb, sl.* to work as a ➡totter

{**totalled » totalling**} *spell.* {totaled » totaling}

the **tote** *noun, abbr.* a system of accumulating horse-racing bets similar to pari-mutuel

Tottenham Court Road *pr. name* a central London street with many electronic and computer stores

totter *noun, sl.* a ➡rag and bone man

tottie *adj., Sc.* young, tiny or both

totty *noun, sl.* (1) a small child or infant; (2) a promiscuous young woman

tot-up *verb* to add driving convictions together
Which will lead to automatic disqualification from driving if there are enough of them.

touch judge *comp. noun* a rugby linesman

touch-line *comp. noun* a sideline

touch up *verb, sl.* to touch in a sexually exciting or provocative way

touch wood *idiom. phr. verb, sl.* to knock on wood, as a talisman of good luck

tounbody *noun, Sc.* a city dweller

tounend *noun, Sc.* where a built-up area ends and open land begins; the urban-rural boundary

tourist class *comp. noun, pref.* coach class

tousie *adj., Sc.* (1) untidy or disordered; (2) tangled or disheveled (of hair)

tout [A] *noun* one who ➡touts

[B] *verb* to spy on racehorses in training to gain information that is useful when placing bets

tow *noun, Sc.* (1) rope, cord or string; (2) a jump rope; (3) a hangman's noose; (4) a winding rope; (5) a whip

towards *prep.* toward

towel *verb, sl.* to thrash

{**towelled » towelling**} *spell.* toweled

towel rail *comp. noun* a towel {bar » rack}

the **Tower** *pr. name, abbr.* the ➡Tower of London

tower block *comp. noun, coll.* a skyscraper

Tower Bridge *pr. name* a bridge over the ➡Thames River in London, whose twin Gothic towers are its most memorable features
It is a drawbridge, able to open up so that ships may pass though it on their way from the ➡North Sea to the ➡Pool of London. Its Gothic style is deceptive, as the bridge dates only from 1894 and was designed this way in order, supposedly, to fit in with the genuinely medieval ➡Tower of London, which is close by.

Tower Hamlets *pr. name* a borough within ➡Greater London
Its current population, which is also included within the ➡London urban area total, is 155,000 (1991 Census).

Tower Hill *pr. name* an open space beside the ➡Tower of London, where upper-class traitors once had the privilige of being executed

tower house *comp. noun, hist.* a medieval tower that was both fortress and residence
They were most common on the long-disputed border between England and Scotland.

the **Tower of London** *pr. name, hist.* a royal fortress on the northern bank of the ➡Thames River at the eastern extremity of the ➡City of London

The oldest part, the ➡White Tower, was built by ➡William the Conqueror in the years immediately following his victory at the Battle of ➡Hastings in 1066. It is said to have been erected upon the site of an earlier fortress put there by Julius Caesar when he visited Britain in 55 B.C., but there is no convincing evidence for this.

In addition to being a fortress, the Tower was also a residence of the monarch for many years, a role it continued to play until the early years of the 17th C.

But ever since it was new it has been a state prison (and sometimes place of execution) for prisoners of a broadly political hue, from the ➡Princes in the Tower through Sir Walter Raleigh, ➡Anne Boleyn, Lady ➡Jane Grey, various aristocratic supporters of ➡Bonnie Prince Charlie and Sir Roger Casement, to Rudolf Hess during World War II.

town *noun* (1) any hamlet or village that holds a regular market or fair; (2) the principal town or city of an area; (3) an urban settlement that is too large to be considered a hamlet or village but has not been endowed with the status of a city

Town *pr. name, coll.* a nickname for London

town clerk *comp. noun, arch.* the senior legal officer and secretary of a city's administration
Abolished in the local government reorganizations of 1974.

town council *comp. noun* a town's local government

town crier *comp. noun, out.* an official who declares public announcements in the streets
Before newspapers, radio or TV, this was one of the very few ways to make sure that a large number of people received accurate information about events in a timely manner. Well all right: *supposedly* accurate information.

townee *spell.* townie

town gas *comp. noun, out.* fuel gas manufactured from coal for commercial and domestic use
Now entirely superseded by natural gas supplied from gas fields under the North Sea.

town house *comp. noun* a town hall

town mayor *comp. noun* the chairperson of a ➡town council

township *noun, arch.* (1) a manor; (2) a parish; (3) a hamlet or village that was part of a larger parish; (4) the people who lived in (1), (2) or (3)

the **Townswoman's Guild** *pr. name* an organization for women who meet around the country for social activities and who act as local pressure groups on various topics

townee *noun, coll., derog.* (1) a town or city dweller; (2) a non-academic citizen or resident of a city or town that has a university associated with it.

{**toxaemia » toxaemic**} *spell.* {toxemia » toxemic}
Concerning blood poisoning.

toy *noun, arch., Sc.* a linen or woolen headdress once worn down over the shoulders of older married women as a badge of their status

toyboy *noun, sl.* a young man who is the kept lover of an older woman

Toy Manchester Terrier *pr. name* a small ➡Manchester terrier with erect ears.

TR1335 *pr. name, hist.* ➡Gee

tracklement *noun* a food item such as a sauce or jelly served with meat

tract *noun, arch.* a length of time

trad *adj., abbr.* traditional, especially of jazz

trade [A] *noun, abbr.* the ➡licensed trade

[B] *noun, arch., sl.* (1) aerial combat; (2) enemy aircraft available to be attacked
(1) and (2) began life as ➡RAF World War II slang.

the **trade** *noun, sl.* (1) the submarine service of the ➡Royal Navy; (2) espionage

the **Trade Board** *pr. name, hist.* an official body set up for the purpose of settling industrial disputes
Now replaced by ➡ACAS.

trade cycle *comp. noun* the business cycle

the **Trades Union Congress** *pr. name* (1) an annual meeting of all labor unions together in congress; (2) a body representing labor unions as a group

trade union *comp. noun* a labor union

trade unionism *comp. noun* the system and philosophy of ➡trade unions

trade unionist *comp. noun* a member of a labor union

trading estate *comp. noun* an area zoned for commercial and industrial use

the Battle of **Trafalgar** *pr. name, hist.* the great naval victory in 1805 when the British fleet under the command of Admiral Lord Nelson defeated the combined French and Spanish fleets off Cape Trafalgar on the southwestern coast of Spain
This victory led to Britain's hegemony on the oceans and, following the land victory at ➡Waterloo ten years later, the ➡Pax Britannica which was to endure until the rise of Imperial Germany and the outbreak of World War I in 1914.
Although he was victorious, Nelson was shot by a French sharpshooter during the battle and died later that same day.

Trafalgar Square

Trafalgar Square *pr. name* the principal square in west-central London

Opened in 1841, its name commemorates the great sea battle of this name. The centerpiece is, of course, ➡Nelson's Column.

trafficator *noun, arch.* a mechanical arm that was raised as a signal on the outside of a vehicle to indicate an imminent change of direction

traffic circus *comp. noun, arch.* a traffic circle

SEE ALSO: ➡gyratory circus, ➡roundabout.

traffic filter *comp. noun* a traffic management system allowing vehicles to proceed in one direction but not another

Typically to the right or left at a junction, while straight-ahead traffic remains halted.

traffic warden *comp. noun* a uniformed official employed by the police to control traffic

With especial emphasis on parking.

trail arms *imper* a military order to a squad of troops to hold their rifles parallel to the ground

trail one's coat *idiom. phr. verb, coll.* to go around looking for a quarrel or fight

trainband *noun, hist.* a militia

In particular, ones formed in London during the ➡Stuart monarchies of the 17th C.

trainers *noun* sneakers (the footwear)

training college *comp. noun* a teachers' college

Traitor's Gate *pr. name, hist.* the water gate of the ➡Tower of London leading to or from the ➡Thames, where in times past state prisoners were brought to the Tower for imprisonment or death

[tram » tramcar} *noun* a ➡streetcar

tram line *comp. noun* a streetcar route

tram {lines » way} *comp. noun* streetcar running tracks laid into a highway

{trammelled » trammelling} *spell.* trammeled

tranche *noun, Fr.* a share or portion, usually of money

In French, *tranche* = "slice."

trannie *noun, abbr., coll., out.* (1) a photographic transparency; (2) a transsexual; (3) a transistor radio

{tranquillisation » tranquillise} *spell.* {tranquilization » tranquilize}

transatlantic *adj., coll.* American

transfer charge call *comp. noun* a collect phone call

transfer charges *verb* to call collect

transire *noun* a permit issued by ➡HM Customs and Excise authorizing the passage of goods

transom window *comp. noun* a transom or fanlight

transportation *noun, hist., leg.* banishment as a penalty for a crime

The banished were sent first to North America, and then later, when this became impractical for reasons that became apparent during 1776, to Australia.

transport café *comp. noun* a trucker's diner

transporter *noun* a large vehicle used to transport other vehicles or particularly heavy loads

Transport House *pr. name, hist.* the London headquarters of the ➡TGWU

Until 1980, this was also the headquarters of the ➡Labour Party.

Transports International Routier *pr. name, Fr.* the regulations governing truck transportation within the ➡EU

Meaning, in French, "international road transport."

trapezium *noun* trapezoid

Being a quadrilateral with just one pair of sides in parallel.

trapezoid *noun* trapezium

Being a quadrilateral without any pair of sides in parallel.

Traquair House *pr. name, hist.* the oldest continually inhabited house in Scotland, some parts dating from the 10th C.

The house is located some 30 miles to the south of ➡Edinburgh. It is said that 27 monarchs have visited this house. The Bear Gates, in the grounds, have been closed since 1745 and reputedly will not open again until a ➡Stuart is once more monarch of Scotland.

trauchle *noun, Sc.* (1) a long exhausting walk; (2) tiring or dull work; (3) a state of complete confusion and muddle brought on by having too many things to do; (4) a burden or worry; (5) an incompetent or slovenly worker

{travelled » traveller » traveller's cheque} *spell.* {traveled » traveler » traveler's check}

traveller *noun, abbr.* a ➡commercial traveller

Travellers Club *pr. name, hist.* a club in ➡Pall Mall

Established in 1819, this club is traditionally the preserve of those who have traveled extensively abroad

{travelling » travelogue} *spell.* {traveling » travelog}

travelling rug *comp. noun* a lap robe, worn by a passenger to keep warm

Traverse Theatre *pr. name, hist.* a theater founded in ➡Edinburgh in 1963

Located in the ➡Grassmarket, it was a theater club until 1988, and has a tradition of performing new plays.

treacle *noun* molasses

treacle scone *comp. noun, Sc.* a biscuit made with molasses

treadwheel *noun* a treadmill

the **Treasury** *pr. name* the department of state responsible for management of the national economy and other governmental financial matters

This is without doubt the single most important and influential of the major departments of state. The nominal head of the ➡Treasury is the ➡Prime Minister, whose official or formal title is in fact ➡First Lord of the Treasury. However, in practice the Treasury is the responsibility of the ➡Chancellor of the Exchequer, whose official title is ➡Second Lord of the Treasury.

the **Treasury Bench** *pr. name* the ➡front bench in the ➡Commons where members of the government sit

treasury bill *comp. noun* a government bill of exchange issued to raise temporary funds

Treasury Solicitor *pr. name, abbr.* a department of the ➡Treasury that provides legal services for most government departments

treat *noun, coll.* what is enjoyable, well done or good

the **Treaty of Rome** *pr. name* the treaty that created the ➡European Economic Community

It was signed by the six original members (Belgium, France, Italy, Luxembourg, the Netherlands and West Germany) in 1957. The UK acceded to the treaty in 1973 after two previous attempts (in 1963 and 1967) had been vetoed by President de Gaulle of France. Ireland acceded in 1973 also.

treble chance *comp. noun* a method of betting on ➡football pools

Under this scheme, winning requires the participant to predict the number of drawn games and also the number of home wins and the number of away wins.

tredecillion *noun, num.* 10^{78}

The American tredecillion is 10^{42}.

tree sparrow *comp. noun* a breed of sparrow found in wooded districts

Its formal name is *passer montanus*, not *spizella arborea*, which is also known as the North American finch and often called a tree sparrow in North America.

trencher cap *comp. noun* a mortarboard

the **Trent** *pr. name, hist.* a 185-mile long English river

It rises in the Biddulph Moor in ➡Staffordshire and flows eastwards into the ➡North Sea through the ➡Humber Estuary.

tressure *noun* in heraldry, a narrow ➡orle

trews *noun, Gae., hist., Sc* (1) originally, ➡trousers worn by more prosperous highlanders in addition to the ubiquitous ➡plaid; (2) now, trousers made of ➡tartan-patterned material

(2) are worn as part of the uniform of some Scottish regiments of the British Army. The word derives from the ➡Gaelic *triubhas*, also the root-word of ➡trousers.

TRH *pr. name, abbr.* Their Royal Highnesses

trial at bar *comp. noun* a trial by the full court of judges of the ➡{King's » Queen's} Bench Division

tricar *noun* an automobile with three wheels

trick cyclist *idiom, rh. sl.* a psychiatrist

{**tricolour » tricoloured**} *spell.* {tricolor » tricolored}

trifle *noun* a dessert containing custard, gelatin, fruit, sponge cake and other ingredients, including perhaps sherry or other alcoholic liquor

trilby *noun* a soft felt hat with indented crown

From a hat illustrated in a line drawing in the novel *Trilby* by the French author George du Maurier, published in 1894.

trillion *noun, num.* a quintillion, or 10^{18}

The American trillion is 10^{12}.

the **Trinity Brethern** *pr. name, abbr.* the members of the ➡Corporation of Trinity House

Trinity College *pr. name* (1) a college of ➡Cambridge University founded in 1546; (2) a college of ➡Oxford University founded in 1554; (3) the first Irish university, founded in ➡Dublin in 1592

Trinity House *pr. name, abbr.* the ➡Corporation of Trinity House

SEE ALSO: the ➡Commissioners of Northern Lighthouses.

Trinity term *pr. name* the law and university term that follows Easter

tripe *noun, coll.* something nonsensical or useless

the **Triple Crown** *pr. name* (1) the national hockey team title; (2) the national rugby football team title; (3) the title awarded to a horse winning the ➡Triple Event

(1) and (2) are awarded to any team from England, Ireland, Scotland or Wales that defeats all the others in a single season.

the **Triple Event** *pr. name* the three horse races—the 2,000 Guineas, the ➡Derby and the ➡St Leger— winning all of which leads to the ➡Triple Crown

Triplex *pr. name (TM)* a brand of laminated or otherwise strengthened safety glass of the kind found in car windows and similar places

tripos *noun* the final examination for the honors BA degree at ➡Cambridge University

trippant *adj.* running, in heraldic representations of animals, etc.

tripper *noun* a tourist

Triumph *pr. name (TM), hist.* a motorcycle manufacturer, originally based in ➡Coventry

Triumph opened for business in 1902 and very soon had become one of the leading manufacturers of motorcycles in the world. It started to lose place ir the 1960s and went bankrupt in 1983. In 1991 the name was revived and a new Triumph motorcycle went into production in ➡Leicestershire.

troch *noun, Sc.* a trough or channel

trochie *noun, Sc.* a narrow passageway, such as there might be between buildings

trog [A] *noun, abbr., derog., sl.* a lout

Abbreviated from ➡troglodyte.

[B] *verb, sl.* (1) to stroll casually; (2) to trudge or plod

troglodyte

troglodyte *noun, derog., sl.* an intellectually disadvantaged person

troke *verb, Sc.* to truck, bargain, deal or trade

troll *noun, arch.* a casual walk or stroll

trolley *noun* (1) a shopping cart; (2) a luggage cart; (3) a hospital gurney; (4) a small open truck that runs on tracks similar to those of a railroad; (5) a wagon that can be pushed by hand

trolleys *noun, arch., sl.* a woman's panties

trolley wheel *comp. noun* a wheel at the end of a pole used to collect power from an overhead wire in order to operate a vehicle such as a trolley bus or streetcar

tron *noun, hist., Sc.* a public weighbridge
Which was usually found near a market place.

trooper *noun, abbr, sl.* a troopship

trooping the colour *idiom* the ceremonial display of a regiment's colors to members of that regiment
Originally this was done so that troops would be able to recognize their own colors in the heat of battle.

Trooping the Colour *pr. name* an annual ➡trooping the colour ceremony conducted in front of the ➡monarch in person on the second Saturday of June when his or her official birthday is celebrated
It takes place on ➡Horse Guard's Parade, off ➡Whitehall in London, and has been performed annually since 1748.

the Trossachs *pr. name, Gae.* the popular but inaccurate name for a large scenic region of mountains and lochs in the southwestern ➡Highlands, some 50 miles north of ➡Glasgow
In reality, "the Trossachs" is the name of a small wooded valley, between Loch ➡Katrine and Loch Achray. In Gaelic it means "the bristly country."

trotter *noun, sl.* a foot

trouble and strife *idiom, rh. sl.* a wife

trouble at t'mill *idiom, North* trouble at work

the Troubles *pr. name, hist., Ir.* (1) the sectarian divisions and terrorism in ➡Northern Ireland; (2) the period of the ➡Irish War of Independence and the ensuing ➡Irish Civil War, taken together
The modern Irish Troubles began in 1968, while the earlier ones lasted from 1919, throught the period of the the Anglo-Irish Treaty, and did not subside until 1923.

trouper *noun, coll.* a reliable friend or fellow-worker

trouser clip *comp. noun* a ➡bicycle clip

trousers *noun, pref.* pants, usually worn by men
The word is Scottish in origin, being derived from the Gaelic word *triubhas*. SEE ALSO: ➡trews.

trousersuit *noun* a pantsuit

{**trowelled** » **trowelling**} *spell.* {troweled » troweling}

truck *noun* an open railroad freight car

the Truck Act *pr. name, hist.* a 1831 law making it illegal to pay wages in anything but legal tender
More recently the law had to be modified to permit payment by check or directly into a bank account.

true blue *comp. noun* a loyal ➡Conservative
Blue is the ➡Conservative Party color.

trug *noun, out.* (1) a shallow gardening basket made of wooden strips; (2) a wooden milk pail

truncheon *noun* (1) a police officer's short billy club; (2) the ➡Earl Marshal's staff of authority

trunk call *comp. noun* a long distance telephone call

trunk road *comp. noun* a long distance highway
Designated by the prefix ➡A-

trunks *noun* undershorts

Truro *pr. name* a city, the administrative center of ➡Cornwall, that sits upon a river of the same name
In Medieval times, Truro was a significant port exporting tin from the ➡Cornish mines. Although incorporated as a city in 1589, the present cathedral was built between 1890 and 1910. The current population is 15,000 (1988 estimate).

truss *noun* a bundle of hay or straw

the Trustee Savings Bank *pr. name* a large national retail bank
It was founded in 1986 by the merging of a large number of local savings banks. The first savings bank was founded by a ➡Church of Scotland minister for the benefit of the members of his parish of Ruthwell, near ➡Dumfries, in 1810.

try *noun* in rugby, a touchdown
It scores four points and entitles the side making it to play for a ➡conversion.

try it on *idiom, coll.* to ➡try-on

try-on *phr. verb, sl.* (1) to attempt to deceive or delude; (2) to attempt to avoid responsibility

TSA *pr. name, abbr.* The Securities Association
An organization set up under the 1986 Financial Services Act to enforce codes of conduct in the London ➡Stock Exchange.

{**tsar** » **tsarevich** » **tsarina**} *spell.* {czar » czarevich » czarina}
The former Russian emperor, etc.

TT *adj., abbr.* teetotal

TT Races *pr. name, abbr.* the ➡Isle of Man Auto-Cycle Union Touring Trophy
The oldest motorcycle race in the world, first held in 1907. It is raced on the road that encircles the Isle of Man.

the Tube *noun, coll.* the popular nickname for London's subway system

Tube Alloys *pr. name, hist.* the code name of the secret British nuclear weapon development program during World War II
In 1943 it was decided that Tube Alloys, which had been under way for several years by then, should be merged with the new American Manhattan Project, with the explicit

agreement that the results should be shared equally between the British and American governments.

After the atomic bomb had been successfully developed in 1945, the U.S. government defaulted on this understanding, delaying development of the British bomb by about six years.

tube of peppermints *comp. noun* a roll of peppermint-flavored candies

tub-thump *verb, coll.* to orate in a ranting manner

TUC *pr. name, abbr.* the ➡Trades Union Congress

tuck *noun, coll.* food, especially candy and cakes eaten by children

Probably an abbreviation of the former British (now Australian) slang word "tucker" = "food."

tuck box *comp. noun* a box used to contain ➡tuck

tuck-in *comp. noun, coll.* an extensive meal

tuck in *verb, coll.* to eat up eagerly

tuck shop *comp. noun* a small store usually in or near a school, specializing in selling food to children

Tudor *pr. name, hist.* (1) the ➡Royal House of England from 1485 until 1603; (2) the architectural style of this period

Those English monarchs who belonged to this house were: ➡Henry VII, ➡Henry VIII, ➡Edward VI, ➡Jane Grey, ➡Mary I and ➡Elizabeth.

Tudor Rose *pr. name, hist.* a decorative emblem, symbolic of the House of ➡Tudor

A conventionalized five-lobed red rose enclosing a white one.

tug *noun, sl.* (1) an academic student; (2) that which is normal or common

(1) at ➡Eton College; (2) at ➡Winchester School.

{tularaemia » tularaemic} *spell.* {tularemia » tularemic}

A serious infectious disease in both animals and humans.

tum *noun, abbr., coll.* the tummy or stomach

tumble *verb* to realize a truth not comprehended earlier

SEE ALSO: ➡twig.

tumble-twist rug *comp. noun* a thickly twisted, long-piled cotton rug or carpet

tummle *verb, Sc.* (1) to tumble or fall; (2) to turn

tummle ower the wullcat *phr. verb, Sc.* to perform a somersault, or tumble head over heels

Literally, "fall over the wild cat."

tummock *noun, Sc.* (a) a knoll or hillock; (2) a molehill

tumour *spell.* tumor

tump *noun, out.* a mound or hillock

tumshie *noun, Sc.* a turnip

tumshie-heid *comp. noun, derog., Sc.* a stupid person

Literally, a "turnip-head."

{tunnelled » tunnelling} *spell.* {tunneled » tunneling}

tup *noun* a ram, a male sheep

{tuppence » tuppenny} *noun* ➡twopenny

tuppenny-halfpenny *adj., coll.* two cents worth, practically worthless, almost without value

turbary *noun* (1) the right to dig turf from land belonging to another, or from common land; (2) land where such rights apply

turf *noun, sl.* a police precinct

turf accountant *comp. noun* a bookmaker

the **Turf Club** *pr. name* a club for racehorse owners, founded in 1868

turf out *verb, coll.* to expel forcibly or kick out

turn *noun* (1) the difference between buying and selling price; (2) profit made by trading; (3) a short performance in a vaudeville theater

turn an honest penny *verb, coll.* (1) to work honestly; (2) to make an honest profit

Turnberry *pr. name* a ➡golf club in ➡Strathclyde, some 15 miles south of ➡Ayr on the Firth of ➡Clyde

The original golf course opened in 1905. During both World Wars it was converted into an airfield; after World War II, two courses were constructed.

turning *noun* a subsidiary road that branches away from a more important one

turn off *verb* (1) to discharge or fire from employment; (2) to go bad or spoil (of food)

turn on a sixpence *phr. verb, coll.* to turn on a dime

turnover *noun* a company's volume of business

Usually over a year, and expressed in monetary terms.

turn queer *verb, coll.* to become somewhat unwell

turn round *verb* to turn around

turn-up *comp. noun* a cuff at the bottom of a pant leg

turn up [A] *idiom, abbr., coll.* a ➡turn up for the books

[B] *verb* to look up in a book

For example, a reference in a textbook or a word in a dictionary.

turn up for the books *idiom, coll.* an unexpected but welcome event or discovery

turn up trumps *idiom. phr. verb, coll.* (1) to be very helpful; (2) to unexpectedly resolve difficulties; (3) to perform better than expected

turtle-dove *idiom, rh. sl.* a glove

tusser *noun* a tussah

Its formal name is *anthereae mylitta*, and it is a kind of silkworm native to India or China.

tutor *noun* (1) a university teacher providing individual tuition to students; (2) an instruction book, especially one upon an academic topic

tuts *noun, East* possessions

TV licence *comp. noun* an annual license required to operate a television receiver legally

One license covers all receivers in a single household; this revenue finances the ➡BBC.

twa

twa *noun, Sc.* two

{twat » twit} *noun, derog., sl.* a foolish or insignificant person

twee *adj.* affected, overly dainty, delicate or cute

tweed *noun, Sc.* a rough, twilled woolen fabric used to make suits and coats

The name is probably derived from the Scots "tweel" = "twill," and a mistaken association with the ➡Tweed River.

Tweed *pr. name, hist.* a river, some 100 miles long, which over much of its length forms the eastern portion of the border between Scotland and England

It rises in the Scottish ➡Borders and flows into the ➡North Sea at ➡Berwick-upon-Tweed.

tweeness *noun* the condition of being ➡twee

the Twelfth *pr. name, abbr., coll.* the ➡Glorious Twelfth

twelfth man *comp. noun* a cricket team's reserve man

Twickenham *pr. name* the large stadium in southwestern London where international rugby matches are played

twig [A] *noun, arch., coll.* a style or custom
[B] *verb* to realize a truth not comprehended earlier
See also: ➡tumble.

twilt *verb, East* to beat or punish

twin *verb* to link a town or city with a supposedly similar one in another country

This includes exchange visits and joint cultural events, all to encourage mutual understanding. At least, that's the theory.

twine *verb, Sc.* (1) to deprive a person of something; (2) to divide or separate; (3) to part company

twin set *comp. noun* a woman's knitted woolen jacket plus a matching knitted pullover sweater

twin town *comp. noun* a town or city which has been ➡twinned

twist [A] *noun, coll.* (1) a fraud or swindle; (2) a drink made by mixing two or more ingredients; (3) a paper packet with screwed up ends, used as a container
(3) is typically used to hold small quantities of tobacco, sugar, salt, etc. *See also:* ➡screw.
[B] *verb, coll.* to commit a fraud or swindle

twister *noun, coll.* (1) a cheat or swindler; (2) a ➡cricket ball that is pitched with a spin

twist the Lion's tail *idiom. phr. verb, arch., hist.* to insult Britain

twitcher *noun, coll.* an ornithologist who attempts to view rare birds

two and eight *idiom, rh. sl.* a condition of excitement or distress

Derivation: condition > state > eight > two and eight.

"Two and eight," meaning "two ➡shillings and eight ➡pence" is a typical example of the way money was described, particularly in speech, prior to decimalization in 1971.

two cities *idiom, rh. sl.* a woman's breasts

Derivation: breasts > titties > cities > *A Tale of Two Cities* (the novel by Charles Dickens) > two cities.
See also: ➡Bristols.

2IC *noun, abbr., coll., derog.* the second in command

{twopence » twopenny} *noun* two pennies
Especially ones prior to 1971.

twopenny *idiom, rh. sl.* head

Derivation: head > bread > loaf of bread > twopenny loaf > twopenny. It's a long time since a loaf cost two pennies; this idiom is showing its age.

twopenny damn *idiom, sl.* that which is worthless

two-stroke engine *comp. noun* a two-cycle internal combustion engine

two-up, two-down *idiom, coll.* a house with two rooms on both of its two floors

Tyburn *pr. name, hist.* a former name for the major street junction in London's ➡West End, which is now known as ➡Marble Arch

This was London's principal place of public execution until 1783. In that year the venue for this popular outdoor entertainment was moved to just outside ➡Newgate Jail.

the Tyburn Tree *pr. name, hist.* the gallows
For the reason why, refer to ➡Tyburn.

tyke *noun, derog., sl.* (1) a churlish or offensive man; (2) a ➡Yorkshireman; (3) a small child

Tyne *pr. name, hist.* a river, some 75 miles in length, in the northeast of England

Rising in the ➡Cheviot hills, it flows through ➡Northumbria and into the ➡North Sea at ➡Tyneside

Tyne and Wear *pr. name* a ➡Metropolitan County

The principal city is ➡Newcastle-upon-Tyne and the current population is 1,130,000 (1991 Census).

Tyne Metro *pr. name, abbr.* ➡Tyne and Wear Metro
A rapid-transit system in the ➡Newcastle-upon-Tyne area.

Tyneside *pr. name, hist.* the area around the mouth of the ➡Tyne in ➡Northumberland

Theis was the first industrial district in Britain, with coal mining already well established by the early years of the 17th C. The principal city of the district is ➡Newcastle-upon-Tyne.

Tynwald *pr. name, abbr.* the ➡Court of Tynwald

typewriter *idiom, rh. sl.* a fighter

tyre *spell.* tire

tyre lever *comp. noun* a tire iron

Tyrone *pr. name, hist.* a former Northern Irish County
County Tyrone in the ancient province of ➡Ulster.

U

U [A] *adj., arch., coll.* characteristic of the upper class
SEE ALSO: "non-U."

[B] *noun, abbr.* Universal
A movie classified as suitable viewing for all.

UB40 *pr. name* a certificate or registration card issued by the Department of ➡Employment to everyone registered with them as unemployed

UC *pr. name, abbr.* ➡University College

UCAS *pr. name, abbr.* the ➡Universities and Colleges Admissions Service

UCATT *pr. name, abbr.* the Union of Construction, Allied Trades, and Technicians
A labor union for construction workers.

UCCA *pr. name, abbr.* the Universities Central Council on Admissions
Absorbed, in 1992, into the ➡UCAS.

UCW *pr. name, abbr.* Union of Communication Workers
A labor union for TV and radio workers.

UDA *pr. name, abbr.* the Ulster Defense Association
A ➡loyalist terrorist organization in ➡Northern Ireland.

udaller *noun* someone holding ➡udal tenure

udal tenure *comp. noun, hist.* a system of land tenure based upon evidence of long-term possession
Predating the feudal system, it was once common throughout northern Europe and is still used in ➡Orkney and ➡Shetland.

UDC *pr. name, abbr., hist.* an ➡Urban District Council

UDI *pr. name, abbr., hist.* the unilateral declaration of independence made by the white government of what was then the British colony of Southern Rhodesia on November 11, 1965
Southern Rhodesia is now the independent nation of Zimbabwe.

UDM *pr. name, abbr.* Union of Democratic Mineworkers
A labor union for miners, formed in the 1980s as a breakaway from the ➡NUM during a national strike that was unconstitutional in terms of the NUM's own constitution and also illegal according to law.

udometer *noun* a rain gauge

UDR *pr. name, abbr.* the ➡Ulster Defense Regiment

UEFA *pr. name, abbr.* the Union of European Football Associations

UFF *pr. name, abbr.* the Ulster Freedom Fighters
A ➡Loyalist terrorist organization in ➡Northern Ireland.

the Uffington White Horse *pr. name, hist.* a large figure of a horse, stretching about 375 ft from head to tail, that has been cut into a chalk hillside some 20 miles southwest of ➡Oxford
There are a number of such figures in England, but this one is known to be more ancient than most. It is believed to have been formed as long ago as the 1st C. B.C.

Ugandan {affairs » discussions} *comp. noun, sl.* a euphemism for sexual intercourse
From the reputed discovery, *in flagrante delicto*, of the (female) Ugandan Foreign Minister in a public restroom at ➡Heathrow Airport in the early 1970s. However, it is now thought this story may have been invented in the columns of the satirical magazine *Private Eye*.
Whatever the truth, the euphemism remains.

UHT *noun, abbr.* ultra heat treated
Which is to say, long-life milk.

the UK *pr. name, abbr.* the ➡United Kingdom

UKAEA *pr. name, abbr.* the United Kingdom Atomic Energy Authority

UK Gold *pr. name* a satellite TV entertainment channel
It is jointly operated by the ➡BBC and ➡Thames TV.

Ullswater *pr. name* the second-largest lake in the ➡Lake District, it is about eight miles long

ulster *noun* man's long overcoat made from heavy and coarse cloth
Originally these were made in ➡Ulster.

Ulster *pr. name* one of Ireland's four ancient provinces
It consists of the counties of ➡Antrim, ➡Armagh, ➡Down, ➡Fermanagh, ➡Londonderry and ➡Tyrone, which are in ➡Northern Ireland, plus ➡Cavan, ➡Donegal and ➡Monaghan, which are in the ➡Irish Republic.

the Ulster Covenant *pr. name, hist.* a pledge, signed by the Protestants of ➡Northern Ireland, to resist the imposition of all-Irish independence upon them
The 1912 campaign to sign this pledge was led by Sir Edward Carson, an ➡MP who conducted a long parliamentary campaign against Irish independence under the slogan, "No Surrender!"
SEE ALSO: ➡Northern Ireland.

the **Ulster Defence Regiment** *pr. name, hist.* a former specialist regiment of the British Army
A reserve unit established in 1970 for the express purpose of assisting the police and other units of the army to maintain order and fight terrorism in ➡Northern Ireland. Because it turned out to have a 95 percent Protestant membership it tended to exacerbate the situation rather than help, and in the late 1980s it was merged with the ➡Royal Irish Rangers to form the ➡Royal Irish Regiment.

the **Ulster Democratic Unionist Party** *pr. name* a political party in ➡Northern Ireland with a strongly Protestant and pro-British stand

{**Ulsterman » Ulsterwoman**} *pr. name* a native of ➡Ulster

the **Ulster Museum** *pr. name, hist.* the leading museum in Northern Ireland, located in ➡Belfast

Ulster Orchestra *pr. name, hist.* founded in ➡Belfast in 1966, this is the only full-time professional orchestra in ➡Northern Ireland

Ulster Scots *pr. name, hist.* the Scotch-Irish

Ulster TV *pr. name* a local commercial TV company headquartered in ➡Belfast, part of the ➡ITV network

Ulster Unionist Party *pr. name* a strongly Protestant, pro-British political party in ➡Northern Ireland

Ulster Volunteer Force *pr. name, Ir.* a Loyalist Protestant terrorist group in ➡Northern Ireland
It modeled itself—at least so far as its name was concerned —on Sir Edward Carson's ➡Ulster Volunteers of 1913. The UVF was declared illegal in 1966.

the **Ulster Volunteers** *pr. name, hist.* a private army of northern Irish Protestants, established specifically to resist the imposition of all-Irish independence
It was set up in 1913 by Sir Edward Carson. Within a few months the organization claimed over 100,000 members and regularly marched and drilled in public.

Together with the ➡Ulster Covenant pledge, the activities of the Ulster Volunteers and the threats of the ➡Northern Irish Protestants convinced the British government that it would not be possible to establish a single independent state for the entire island of Ireland.

umpire *noun* the referee of a ➡cricket match
There are two umpires at each match.

unadopted road *comp. noun* a private road not maintained by public funds
And therefore not requiring publicly financed maintenance. *SEE ALSO:* ➡adopted road.

unalike *adj.* unlike

unbiddable *adj.* uncontrollable, disobedient

un-British *adj.* insufficiently British or British-like

uncannie *adj., Sc.* (1) dangerous or threatening; (2) unlucky or inauspicious

unchancie *adj., Sc.* (1) inauspicious; (2) not to be meddled or interfered with

uncle *noun, arch., sl.* a pawnbroker

Uncle Fred *idiom, rh. sl.* bread

Uncle George *pr. name, hist.* ➡George III

Uncle Joe *pr. name, coll., hist.* a World War II nickname for Joseph Stalin, Soviet dictator

Uncle Ned *idiom, rh. sl.* (1) a bed; (2) a head

Uncle Willy *idiom, rh. sl.* silly

unco [A] *adj., Sc.* (1) unknown, strange or alien; (2) changed beyond recognition; (3) foreign; (4) unusual, remarkable or peculiar; (5) shy or reserved
[B] *adv., Sc.* very or extremely

unco guid *idiom, derog, Sc.* (1) self-righteous; (2) ostentatiously religious
Literally, "unusually, remarkably or peculiarly good."

uncoloured *spell.* uncolored

uncome-at-able *adj. phr.* out of reach or unachievable

uncos *noun, Sc.* (1) news; (2) rare or strange things, events or people

uncrossed *adj.* not ➡crossed

uncrushable *adj.* wrinkle-free (of clothes)

undecillion *noun, num.* 10^{66}
The American undecillion is 10^{36}.

underarm *adj.* a ➡cricketing term for bowling with the arm held below shoulder level

underbodice *noun* a woman's undergarment, similar to a vest that covers the upper torso

undercart *noun, coll.* an aircraft's undercarriage

undercut *noun* a beef tenderloin

underdress *verb* (1) to dress plainly; (2) to wear insufficient clothes

underfug *noun, sl.* underclothes
Schoolboy slang.

the **Underground** *pr. name, abbr., coll.* the ➡London Underground subway system
In fact, the majority of the network, especially in the suburbs, is not actually under ground.

underground railway *comp. noun* a subway
Four British cities have subway systems. They are ➡London, ➡Glasgow, ➡Liverpool and ➡Newcastle-upon-Tyne.

underground station *comp. noun* a subway station

underhand *adj.* ➡underarm

undermanager *noun* an assistant manager

the **undermentioned** *adj.* that which is mentioned below or later in a document

underpants *noun* (1) men's undershorts; (2) women's panties

under-secretary *comp. noun* a junior ➡minister who is not a member of the ➡Cabinet

Unite

under starter's orders *idiom* (1) specifically, about to start a horse race; (2) in general, ready to begin

undertaker *noun, hist.* a ➡parliamentary lobbyist in the 17th C.

under the doctor *idiom, coll.* under the professional care of a physician

underthings *noun, coll.* underwear

undervest *noun* a vest

under weigh *spell., arch.* under way

uneppen *adj., East* clumsy or inept

unequalled *spell.* unequaled

{**unfavourable » unfavourableness**} *spell.* {unfavorable » unfavorableness}

{**unfavourably » unfavourite**} *spell.* {unfavorably » unfavorite}

unfunny *adj., coll.* not funny, although that may have been the intent

unhappy chappie *idiom, sl.* someone, usually male, who is extremely displeased

unharbour *verb* to dislodge a deer from its cover

unhonest *adj., Sc.* dishonest

unhonoured *spell.* unhonored

{**unicolour » unicoloured**} *spell.* {unicolor » unicolored}

union *noun, hist.* the consolidation of two parishes for the purpose of administering the ➡poor laws

the **Union** *pr. name, hist.* (1) the union of Scottish and English crowns in 1603; (2) the union of Scottish and English parliaments in 1707; (3) the union of Irish and British parliaments in 1801; (4) the present-day union of England, Scotland, Wales and Northern Ireland within the ➡United Kingdom

union-bash *verb, coll.* to attack or criticize labor unions, their members and their rights

the **Union Chain Bridge** *pr. name, hist.* Britain's first suspension bridge able to take vehicular traffic
It has a span of 437 ft and was built to link Scotland and England across the ➡Tweed River, near to ➡Berwick-upon-Tweed in 1820. It is still in use today.

Unionist *noun, hist.* (1) formerly, someone who was opposed to the dissolution of the union between ➡Great Britain and ➡Ireland; (2) now, someone opposed to the dissolution of the union between ➡Great Britain and ➡Northern Ireland
The word first took on political significance with the split in the ➡Liberal Party over ➡Irish Home Rule in 1886. Liberals who were opposed to this measure formed an alliance with the ➡Conservatives, later merging with them entirely. (2) is the revised meaning which has applied since the formation of the ➡Irish Free State in 1923.

the **Unionist Party** *pr. name, hist.* (1) a collective name for the ➡Ulster Unionist and the ➡Ulster Democratic Unionist Parties, taken together; (2) a former name for the ➡Conservative Party in Scotland

the **Union Jack** *pr. name* a common but inaccurate name for the national flag of the United Kingdom
Its more proper name is the ➡Union Flag.

the **Union of the Crowns** *pr. name, hist.* the constitutional event following the death of ➡Elizabeth I of England in 1603
When her nephew King ➡James IV of Scotland became King of England too, thus uniting both kingdoms under a single ➡crown for the first time.

union workhouse *comp. noun, hist.* a ➡workhouse built and operated by a ➡trade union

Unison *pr. name* a large labor union for civil servants and others working in public services
Formed by the merging of ➡NALGO, ➡NUPE and ➡COHSE in 1993.

unit *noun* (1) a single share in a ➡unit trust; (2) an item of furniture that fits together with other matching items to make a comprehensive system
(2) are typically found in kitchens and bathrooms.

Unite *pr. name, hist.* a gold coin, worth 20 ➡shillings, which was issued in 1604 during the reign of ➡James I of England and VI of Scotland
It was given this name to honor the ➡Union of the Crowns of Scotland and England the previous year. Although this was the coin's official name, it was also known as the ➡Jacobus and the ➡Broad. It bore the Latin motto *Faciam eos in gentem unam* = "I will make them one people" (Ezek. 37: 22). It was withdrawn in favor of the ➡Guinea in 1663.

---

the **Union Flag** *pr. name* the formal, correct name for the British national flag, although it is better known as the ➡Union Jack
The official description of the flag since the union with Ireland in 1801 is as follows:

The union flag shall be azure, the Crosses saltire of ➡St Andrew and ➡St Patrick quarterly per saltire, counter-charged, argent and gules, the latter fimbriated of the second, surmounted by the Cross of ➡St George of the third, fimbriated as the saltire.

the Union Flag,
or Union Jack

359

the **United Kingdom** *pr. name, hist.* (1) from 1603 until 1801, ➡Great Britain; (2) from 1801 until 1922, ➡Great Britain and ➡Ireland; (3) since 1922, ➡Great Britain and ➡Northern Ireland

the **United Reformed Church** *pr. name* a ➡Nonconformist church formed in 1972 out of the union of the Presbyterian and Congregational Churches of England

unit holder *comp. noun* a person with money invested in a ➡unit trust

unit trust *comp. noun* a mutual fund

the **Universities and Colleges Admissions Service** *pr. name* a clearinghouse through which students apply to join ➡first degree courses at British universities
This replaced both ➡UCCA and ➡PCAS in 1992.

University College *pr. name* a college of ➡Oxford University founded in 1249

University College, London *pr. name* a school of ➡London University
Founded in 1826, this was the first university college in England that was not in either ➡Oxford or ➡Cambridge. The reason it was established was that at that time only ➡Anglicans were admitted to these two traditional universities, and this new college was intended for the education of ➡Nonconformists. Anglicans responded two years later with ➡King's College, also in London. University College became linked to University College Hospital during the 1830s, and in 1836 the two colleges were brought together to form the ➡University of London.

{**unkennelled » unkennelling**} *spell.* {unkenneled » unkenneling}

the **Unknown Warrior** *pr. name* the Unknown Soldier

{**unlabelled » unlabelling**} *spell.* {unlabeled » unlabeling}

unlaboured *spell.* unlabored

unlicenced restaurant *comp. noun* a restaurant that is not permitted to sell alcoholic drinks

the **Unlisted Securities Market** *pr. name* a market trading in stocks not listed on the London Stock Exchange

unmade road *comp. noun* a dirt road

unmetalled road *comp. noun* a road made without road metal

unnameable *spell.* unnamable

unneighbourly *spell.* unneighborly

unobtainable number *comp. noun* a disconnected, out-of-order, or non-existent telephone number

unofficial strike *comp. noun* a strike called without the authority or formal approval of the labor union that the strikers belong to

unparliamentary language *comp. noun* (1) specifically, words and expressions prohibited from use in the ➡House of Commons; (2) generally, a euphemism for foul language or personal abuse

unpractised *spell.* unpracticed

unputdownable *adj., coll.* too exciting to stop reading
Descriptive of a book.

unquoted company *comp. noun* a company whose shares are not quoted on the London Stock Exchange

{**unravelled » unravelling**} *spell.* {unraveled » unraveling}

unrecognisable *spell.* unrecognizable

unrivalled *spell.* unrivaled

unsafe *adj.* not fully sound in law
Of a court verdict, for example.

{**unsavourily » unsavouriness » unsavoury**} *spell.* {unsavorily » unsavoriness » unsavory}

unseen *noun, abbr.* a translation from a foreign language text not previously seen into English, or from an English text not previously seen into that language, as part of a school or college examination

unsewn binding *comp. noun* perfect binding
A form of book binding where adhesive holds pages and covers together..

unshakeable *spell.* unshakable

unskilful *spell.* unskillful

unsocial hours *comp. noun* hours that are outside normal work hours

Unst *pr. name* an island in the ➡Shetland group that is the most northerly inhabited island of the British Isles

untrammelled *spell.* untrammeled

untravelled *spell.* untraveled

unwaged *adj., coll.* (1) unemployed; (2) unpaid

unwhipped *adj.* not answerable to a party ➡whip

unwiselike *adj., Sc.* indiscreet or foolish

unwritten constitution *comp. noun* one not based on a written document or formal basic law, but rather on custom and precedent as determined by the general body of laws and legal precedents

up [A] *adj.* (1) in a winning position; (2) attending or studying at university

[B] *noun* (1) a direction of travel towards the north; (2) a direction of travel towards a capital or major city, particularly London

up a gum tree *idiom* in serious trouble or difficulty

upcome *noun, Sc.* an outcome or result

updraught *spell.* updraft

uplift *verb, Sc.* to collect, take possession of, or gather

up line *comp. noun* a railroad track used by trains headed to London

upmak *noun, Sc.* an invention, composition, poem, plan of action, or work of fiction

upper *noun, sl.* (1) an upper-class person; (2) a student in the ➡upper school of an English ➡public school

the **Upper Chamber** *pr. name* the House of Lords

upper circle *comp. noun* the second gallery or curved balcony level of a theater
Equivalent to the third floor in a conventional building.

the **Upper House** *pr. name* the ➡House of Lords

upper school *comp. noun, sl.* that part of an English ➡public school where the oldest students are taught

Uppingham School *pr. name* one of the leading English ➡public schools
Founded in 1584, it is located in ➡Leicester.

upright chair *comp. noun* a straight-backed chair

upsides with *adv. phr., coll.* equivalent or equal to

upstanding *adj.* healthy and strong

up sticks *idiom. phr. verb* to move away or move on

up the spout *idiom, sl.* (1) hopeless; (2) useless; (3) pawned; (4) pregnant; (5) destroyed

up to and including *prep.* through
In the sense of being inclusive.

up to the {knocker » mark} *idiom, sl.* (1) of an acceptable standard; (2) in good condition or unspoiled

up train *comp. noun* a train heading toward London

up West *idiom, coll.* in London's ➡West End
As described by an ➡Eastender.

{uraemia » uraemic} *spell.* {uremia » uremic}
The presence of urinary matter in the blood.

urban clearway *comp. noun* a city street where parking is forbidden in order to speed traffic flow, especially at busy times

Urban Development Corporation *pr. name, hist.* a government agency set up to redevelop areas of inner-city dereliction
Operated in conjunction with enterprise zones sited in derelict areas, the first two were established in 1979, in London's ➡Dockland, and in ➡Merseyside. Since then eight others have been created in various urban areas of England. In Scotland, there is a similar agency in eastern ➡Glasgow.

urban district *comp. noun, hist.* an urban community or group of contiguous urban communities governed by an ➡Urban District Council
Replaced by the ➡District in the 1970s.

Urban District Council *pr. name, hist.* the elected body governing an ➡urban district

the **Urban Program** *pr. name* a major government spending program aimed at revitalizing inner cities

the **Urban Regeneration Agency** *pr. name* a government body charged with bringing back into productive use the large expanses of derelict land found in blighted inner city areas

Urdd Gobaith Cymru *pr. name, Wal.* a Welsh youth group who serve ➡Wales in particular and humanity in general, together with preserving Christian standards and the Welsh language
It is Welsh, meaning "Order of the Hope of Wales."

US *noun, abbr.* unserviceable or useless

USDAW *pr. name, abbr.* the Union of Shop, Distributive and Allied Workers
A labor union for sales clerks.

use your loaf *imper., idiom., sl.* think
SEE ALSO: ➡loaf.

usher *noun* a uniformed official who walks ahead of certain persons of high rank on ceremonial occasions

the **Usher Hall** *pr. name, hist.* the principal concert hall in ➡Edinburgh
It opened for the first time on August 4, 1914, the very day Britain declared war on Germany at the start of World War I.

USM *pr. name, abbr.* the ➡Unlisted Securities Market

{usquebaugh » usquebach} *noun, Gae., {Ir. » Sc.}* whiskey
From the {Irish » Scots} Gaelic {*uisce beathadh* » *uisge beatha*} = "water of life."

the **usual channels** *idiom* a euphemism for informal discussions between leaders of the various parties in the ➡House of Commons, which take place away from the floor of the House
These discussions are necessary so that the business of the House can be conducted in an orderly manner.

the **usual offices** *idiom* those things like kitchens, toilets, storage space and so forth, which turn a building into a suitable dwelling for human beings

usucaption *noun, Sc.* the acquisition of legal title to property by undisputed possession for an uninterrupted period of sufficient duration

usufruct *noun, Sc.* a right to enjoy the use of and the profit from another's property so long as it is not damaged or wasted

utility {clothing » furniture} *comp. noun, hist.* {clothing » furniture} made during World War II to specifications and prices set by the government
These products were made as economically as possible, with practicality rather than aesthetics the prime consideration, in order that as few resources as possible were diverted from the war effort.

UVF *pr. name, abbr.* the ➡Ulster Volunteer Force

.

V & A *pr. name, abbr.* the ➡Victoria and Albert Museum

the **V-1** *pr. name, abbr., Ger., hist.* a small pilotless aircraft carrying an explosive warhead of about one ton

> During World War II about 2,000 *V-1*s were launched by Germany against Britain, most targeted upon London. They were launched from specially built, steam-powered catapults in occupied France between June 1944 and March 1945. The *V-1* was propelled by a pulsed ram-jet, which had a characteristic sound that gave rise to the *V-1*s being known as ➡buzz-bombs.
>
> *V-1* is an abbreviation of the German *Vergeltungswaffe Eins* = "Revenge Weapon One."
>
> *SEE ALSO:* ➡V-2.

the **V-2** *pr. name, abbr., Ger., hist.* the first successful liquid fueled ballistic rocket, which carried an explosive warhead of about one ton

> In fact more damage was caused by the kinetic impact of the projectile than the high explosive it contained.
>
> During World War II about 1,200 *V-2*s were launched by Germany against Britain, most targeted upon London, from occupied France and Belgium between September 1944 and March 1945. *V-2* is an abbreviation of the German, *Vergeltungswaffe Zwei* = "Revenge Weapon Two."
>
> The *V-2* was the direct linear ancestor of the *Saturn* rocket that launched *Apollo 11* to the moon in 1969.
>
> *SEE ALSO:* ➡V-1.

VA *noun, abbr.* the Order of ➡Victoria and ➡Albert

vac *noun, abbr., coll.* a university vacation

vacant possession *comp. noun* the condition of owning a house that does not have any tenants or other occupants in residence

vacuum flask *comp. noun* a vacuum bottle

VAD *noun, abbr.* (1) a ➡Voluntary Aid Detachment; (2) someone who is a member of (1)

vair *noun, hist.* (1) the representation in heraldry of squirrel fur by small bell-shaped figures; (2) blue-gray or white squirrel fur that was used in ornamental linings in medieval times

valency *noun* valence

> The combining power of a chemical element expressed in terms of the number of hydrogen atoms that one atom of the element can combine with or replace.

valour *spell.* valor

value added tax *comp. noun* an incremental excise tax imposed on very many but not all transactions

> A system of ➡VAT operates in all countries that are members of the ➡European Union; a proportion of this tax is automatically transferred to the central treasury, where it forms the principal source of revenue for the ➡EU.
>
> VAT is levied on the cumulative value of a commodity at each stage of its production or distribution. Because the seller can offset against this the tax paid to his supplier, the net VAT paid by the seller is that levied on the value which has been added by himself only.
>
> For example, if a storekeeper buys goods for £100 (excluding tax) from his supplier and the rate of VAT is 17.5%, he pays altogether £117.50 to his supplier. However, if he sells these goods to his customers for £176.25 (£150 plus £26.25, which is the quantity of VAT payable on £150 at a rate of 17.5%), then the net amount of VAT which he has to pay to ➡HM Customs and Excise—the VAT collection agency in the ➡United Kingdom—is (£26.25 - £17.50), or £8.75. At the time of writing, VAT is not charged on food, books, newspapers and certain other categories.

value for money *comp. noun* something worth the money spent on it

valuer *noun* an appraiser

valve *noun, abbr.* an electron tube or thermionic tube

van [A] *noun* (1) an enclosed railroad baggage car; (2) formerly, a gypsy wagon

[B] *noun, abbr.* advantage in tennis

{vapour » vapourish » vapourishness} *spell.* {vapor » vaporish » vaporishness}

varicoloured *spell.* varicolored

varnish *noun, coll.* liquid nail polish

varsity *noun, abbr.* a university

VAT *noun, abbr.* ➡value added tax

VAT exempt *adj. phr.* upon which no VAT is charged

> *SEE ALSO:* ➡zero-rated. The two conditions are not the same, although the difference is not immediately apparent, except to an accountant perhaps.

Vatman *noun, coll.* an official responsible for assessing and collecting ➡value added tax

vauntie *adj., Sc.* vain, self-satisfied or proud

Vauxhall *pr. name (TM), hist.* a mass-production automobile manufacturer founded in 1903 at Vauxhall in south London, and now mostly at ➡Luton in ➡Bedfordshire

In 1925 it was bought outright by General Motors and remains one of the most important automobile manufacturers in Britain.

VC *noun, abbr.* the ➡Victoria Cross

VD *noun, abbr.* (1) the Colonial Auxiliary Forces Officers' Decoration; (2) the Volunteer Officers' Decoration; (3) the Volunteer Officers' Decoration for India and the Colonies

(1) was awarded from 1899 to 1930; (2) was awarded from 1892 to 1908; (3) was awarded from 1894 to 1930.

VDU *noun, abbr.* a ➡{visual » video} display unit

veg *noun, abbr.* vegetable

vegetable marrow *comp. noun* a variety of squash

Its formal name is *cucurbita*.

vehicle excise tax *comp. noun* the tax that must be paid in order to receive a ➡vehicle license

vehicle licence *comp. noun, coll.* a certificate of payment of ➡vehicle excise tax

The law requires that a current certificate be displayed upon an automobile windshield.

vehicle registration document *comp. noun* an official record of automobile registration details

the **Vein-Openers** *pr. name* a nickname for the 29th Regiment of ➡Foot

A unit of the British Army given this name by Americans following the accidental shooting, inaccurately known as the "Boston Massacre," of five members of a large crowd taunting, jeering and throwing stones at a small group of soldiers from this regiment in the vicinity of Boston Customs House late one dark night in 1770.

vennel *noun, Sc.* a narrow alley between buildings

venture scout *comp. noun* a Boy Scout who is more than 16 years of age

venue *noun* where a meeting, theatrical event or sports meet is appointed to happen

verbal *verb, sl.* to attribute to a suspect or witness a damaging statement that he or she did not make

verderer *noun, arch.* a judicial official responsible for guarding royal forests

verge *noun* the grassy edge or shoulder of a road or path

verger *noun* (1) a janitor of a ➡Church of England parish church; (2) an official who carries a verge or staff before a bishop or judge on ceremonial occasions

vernalisation *spell.* vernalization

versemonger *noun, derog., sl.* a poet

versicolour *spell.* versicolor

vert *noun* the heraldic name for the color green

vest *noun, abbr.* a man's sleeveless undershirt

vet *verb, coll.* to check over carefully and thoroughly

veteran *noun* (1) a soldier with many years service; (2) a soldier who has grown old while in the service

veteran car *comp. noun* (1) an automobile built before 1905; (2) an automobile built before 1916

(1) is the more strictly correct definition.

veterinary surgeon *comp. noun* a veterinarian

Vic *pr. name, abbr.* Victoria

vicar *noun* a ➡Church of England clergyman who receives the stipend but not the tithes of a parish

vicarage *noun* the benefice or residence provided for a ➡vicar of the ➡Church of England

{vice » vice-like} *spell.* {vise » viselike}

vice-chamberlain *comp. noun* the ➡Lord Chamberlain's deputy

vice-chancellor *comp. noun* the chief administrative officer of a university

viceregal *adj.* pertaining to a ➡viceroy

viceroy *noun* one who governs a province or colony on behalf of and with the authority of a ➡monarch

the **Viceroy** *noun, hist.* the person who governed India on behalf of and with the authority of the British ➡monarch before independence in 1947

Victoria *pr. name, hist.* (1) Queen of the ➡United Kingdom; (2) one of the principal railroad terminuses in central London; (3) one of the principal railroad terminuses in central Manchester

(1) styled herself "Queen of the United Kingdom of Great Britain and Ireland, Duchess of Braunschweig-Lüneburg, Defender of the Faith, etc., etc." until 1876, when she assumed the title of ➡Empress of India and so became, "Queen of the United Kingdom of Great Britain and Ireland, Duchess of Braunschweig-Lüneburg, ➡Defender of the Faith, Empress of India, etc., etc."

In all she reigned for 64 years, from 1837 until 1901. This is the longest reign of any British monarch.

Because she was a woman, Victoria was not eligible to become ➡Elector of Hanover, which office could only be held by a man, and thus this formal constitutional link that tied Britain so closely to Germany for a hundred years was broken. However, she remained a member of the Royal House of ➡Hanover, her first language was German, and she married a German, Prince ➡Albert of Saxe-Coburg und Gotha. Indeed, Kaiser Wilhelm II, who reigned in Germany during World War I, was her grandson.

The ethos of hard work and the certainty of moral righteousness that we now think of as one of the defining characteristics of her reign were in truth impressed upon the nation and empire rather more by Albert than by the Queen herself, although certainly her first words on hearing that she had inherited the throne were, "I will be good."

(2) is for trains to and from southeast England and ferry ports to the continent. The present terminus was created by merging two adjacent terminuses built in the 1860s.

(3) is for trains to and from the north.

Queen
Victoria

the **Victoria and Albert Museum** *pr. name* a large museum in central London

Named in honor of Queen ➡Victoria and her ➡Prince Consort, ➡Albert, it houses a vast collection of items of both fine and applied art from all areas of the world and all periods of history. Known originally as the South Kensington Museum, it was founded in 1852 to provide a permanent home for the many exhibits collected from around the world for the ➡Great Exhibition of the preceding year, moving to its present location in 1857. The present-day building was dedicated by Victoria in 1899 when she gave it its present name. In 1909 the science section was separated off as the ➡Science Museum.

the **Victoria Cross** *pr. name* the most distinguished British military medal

The award was created by ➡Victoria in 1856 and the medals are made from a cannon captured from the Russian army during the ➡Crimean War. It is in the shape of a Maltese cross with the words "For Valour" impressed upon it, and with one exception—a member of the Bengal Civil Service, Ross Lowis Mangles, who received his Victoria Cross for bravery during the ➡Indian Mutiny in 1857—has only ever been awarded to members of the armed forces, for feats of exceptional valor.

the **Victoria Line** *pr. name* one part of London's rapid-transit subway system

It extends from Walthemstow Central in the northeast to Brixton in the south.

the **Victoria Memorial** *pr. name, hist.* a large sculpture at the southern end of the ➡Mall, erected in 1911 as a memorial to ➡Victoria

Weighing over 2,000 tons, it sits at the center of the traffic circle in front of ➡Buckingham Palace.

Victorian *adj., hist.* relating to the time of or habits or attitudes pertaining during the reign of ➡Victoria

Victoriana *noun* objects from or relating to the ➡Victorian period

In particular, items of interest to collectors.

Victoria plum *comp. noun* a kind of large red plum

First identified as a species in 1840, it was named in honor of the then-very-new Queen.

Victoria {**sandwich** » **sponge**} *comp. noun* a cake of two sponge layers separated by a jam layer

HMS **Victory** *pr. name, hist.* the flagship of Admiral Lord Nelson at the Battle of ➡Trafalgar

Now preserved in ➡Portsmouth, ➡Hampshire as a museum open to the public, she entered service with the ➡Royal Navy in 1765 and still is a commissioned ship-of-the-line, although she has been placed in a dry dock since the 1920s. The *USS Constitution*, commissioned in 1797 and preserved in Boston, MA, is a relative youngster by comparison.

{**victualled** » **victualling**} *spell.* {victualed » victualing}

video nasty *comp. noun, coll.* a particularly violent or pornographic movie on videotape

video recorder *comp. noun* a videocassette recorder

{**video** » **visual**} **display unit** *comp. noun* a cathode-ray tube or other technology used to display information processed and presented by a computer

vigintillion *noun, num.* 10^{120}

The American vigintillion is 10^{63}.

vigour *spell.* vigor

vill *noun, hist.* a feudal village

villa *noun* a large private house that stands on its own grounds within an urban residential district

village *noun* a district or area within a city considered to resemble, in some way or another, a rural village

village fête *comp. noun* a village summer fair, outdoor celebration or festival

villain *noun, coll.* a professional criminal

villein *noun, hist.* a feudal serf

vintage car *comp. noun* a car that was built between 1917 and 1930

virgate *noun, arch.* a unit of measurement of land area

The size of this unit varied over the years and also varied between different parts of the country. Although usually equal to 30 acres, it was at other times considered to be equal to about one quarter of an acre. This must have somewhat limited its usefulness.

Virgin *pr. name* a national commercial radio station dedicated to pop/rock

the **virginals** *noun, hist.* a 16th C. keyboard instrument similar to the spinet or harpsichord

The name probably originated from the fact that the instrument was often played by young girls.

Virgin Atlantic *pr. name (TM)* Britain's largest intercontinental airline after ➡British Airways

Virgin Mary's Bodyguard *pr. name* a nickname for the 7th Dragoon Guards

A unit of the British Army, whose name refers back to the time it spent assisting Archduchess Maria Theresa of Austria during the reign of George II.

the **Virgin Queen** *pr. name, hist.* ➡Elizabeth I of England, called this because she never married

viscount *noun* a peer ranking above a ➡baron but below an ➡earl

viscountess *noun* (1) a woman who is a ➡viscount in her own right; (2) the wife or widow of a ➡viscount

visitor *noun* an educational official who visits colleges in order to inspect and report upon the academic and other standards of the establishment

vis major *comp. noun, Lat., Sc.* a legal term for a natural event or circumstance

Similar in legal standing to an act of God, its meaning in Latin is "superior force."

{**Vis » Visc**} *noun, abbr.* a ➡Viscount

vivers *noun, Sc.* food or provisions

Viyella *pr. name (TM)* the trade name for a fabric consisting of 55 percent merino wool and 45 percent cotton

VO *pr. name, abbr.* the Royal Victorian Order

Vodafone *pr. name (TM)* a cellular telephone network operated by ➡British Telecom plc

SEE ALSO: ➡Cellnet.

vogie *adj., Sc.* (1) arrogant, vain or proud (of people); (2) imposing or pretentious (of things)

voided *adj.* with the central part removed to show what is behind, in heraldry

volant *noun* the heraldic representation of flight or of birds

volley *noun* a ➡cricket ball pitched so as not to bounce

Voluntary Aid Detachment *pr. name, hist.* a voluntary group of first-aid workers and nurses formed during World War II

voluntary school *comp. noun* a school built by voluntary contributions, tbut thereafter maintained by taxation

Voluntary Service Overseas *pr. name* an organization, established in 1968, which sends volunteers to work in under developed countries

the **Volunteer Reserve Forces** *pr. name* a collective name for the various voluntary reserves of the different armed forces

vote *noun* (1) a proposal to spend money, which must be voted upon in the ➡House of Commons; (2) expenditure agreed upon by a vote in the ➡House of Commons; (3) money appropriated for a specific purpose

vote of {censure » no confidence} *comp. noun* a vote in the ➡House of Commons which if carried demonstrates that the majority of those present do not support the government

SEE ALSO: ➡vote of confidence.

vote of confidence *comp. noun* a vote in the ➡House of Commons which if carried demonstrates that the majority of those present do support the government

SEE ALSO: ➡vote of {censure » no confidence}.

voting paper *comp. noun* a ballot paper

vox pop *comp. noun, abbr., coll., Lat.* comments made by individual members of the public, purporting to represent public opinion on a radio or TV show

From the Latin *vox populi* = "voice of the people."

VR *pr. name, abbr., Lat. Victoria Regina*

The Latin form of "Queen ➡Victoria."

VRD *noun, abbr.* the Decoration for Officers of the ➡Royal Naval Volunteer Reserve

V-sign *noun, coll.* (1) a gesture of abuse or insult; (2) a gesture of victory made famous during World War II by Winston Churchill

(1) is made with the first two fingers extended and held apart in the form of the letter "V", with hand turned so that the back of the hand faces outwards. (2) is made with the first two fingers extended and held apart in the form of the letter "V," with hand turned so that the palm faces outwards. It is a good idea not to get one confused with the other.

VSO *pr. name, abbr.* ➡Voluntary Service Overseas

vulcanology *spell.* volcanology

The study of volcanoes.

W/Cdr. *noun, abbr.* ➡wing commander

WAAC *pr. name, abbr.* Woman's Army Auxiliary Corps
A non-combatant unit of women who served in World War I from 1917 to 1919. They should not be confused with the American WAAC of 1942 to 1948.

Waac *pr. name, coll., hist.* a member of the ➡WAAC

WAAF *pr. name, abbr.* Woman's Auxiliary Air Force
Formed in 1939 and renamed the ➡WRAF in 1948.

Waaf *pr. name, coll., hist.* a member of the ➡WAAF

wabbit *adj., Sc.* exhausted or worn-out

wabster *noun, Sc.* a spider

Wack *noun, North* a familiar form of general address especially in ➡Liverpool, made to any person whose correct name is unknown
See also: ➡Jimmy, ➡John, ➡Kiddo, ➡Moosh and ➡Tosh.

wad *noun, sl.* a sandwich
Military slang.

Waddeston Manor *pr. name, hist.* a late 19th C. country house near ➡Aylesbury, built for the Rothschild family in the style of a French Renaissance Revival château

waddin *noun, Sc.* a wedding

Wadham College *pr. name* a college of ➡Oxford University, founded in 1612

waesome *adj., Sc.* sorrowful

wage round *comp. noun, coll.* a general increase in wages or salaries

wages clerk *comp. noun* a payroll clerk

wages snatch *comp. noun, sl.* a payroll heist

wagger *noun, sl.* a trashcan

waggity-wa *comp. noun, Sc.* a wall clock with an exposed pendulum

{**waggon » waggoner » waggonette**} *spell.* {wagon » wagoner » wagonette}
Archaic; this use of "gg" is now very rare.

wagon *noun, abbr.* a railroad freight wagon

wainscot *noun, arch.* high-quality imported oak

waistcoat *noun* a man's vest

wait *verb* to park a vehicle for a short period

wait a mo *imper., abbr., sl.* wait a moment

wait at table *verb* to wait on a table as a waiter

waits *noun, out.* singers who perform in the street at Christmas time

wake *noun, hist.* an annual festival for the patron saint of a parish church

Wakefield *pr. name* a city in West Yorkshire that was a significant center of the woolen trade during the Middle Ages
Incorporated as a city in 1848. The current population is 305,000 (1988 estimate).

wake-robin *comp. noun* the European arum
Its formal name is *arum maculatum,* and it is also known as the ➡cuckoo-pint or ➡lords and ladies.

the **Wakes** *noun, abbr.* ➡Wakes week

Wakes week *pr. name* the annual summer vacation period in some industrial areas of northern England
Factories and other large employers in the area stop work at this time and all workers take vacations simultaneously.

wakey-wakey *imper., coll.* wake up

wale *verb, North, Sc.* to choose or select

Wales *pr. name* a principality that is a major component of the United Kingdom
Wales remains the most ➡Celtic of any major part of the British Isles and is the only area whose ancient Celtic language is still used in daily life by a large portion of the population. Cardiff is the capital city of Wales and the current population of Wales is 2,881,000 (1990 estimate).

walk [A] *noun* (1) a ceremonial procession; (2) the part of a forest looked after by one gamekeeper or forest ranger
[B] *verb* to depart from the ➡cricket field upon being ➡bowled out but without waiting for the ➡umpire to confirms this

walkabout *noun, Aus.* an informal mingling with the public by an important personage
Originally, time spent wandering in the Australian outback.

walking {**gentleman » lady**} *comp. noun, coll., out.* a theatrical term for a non-speaking extra

walking-on part *comp. noun* a walk-on part in a play

walk out with *phr. verb, arch., coll.* to be courting with

walk the streets *idiom. phr. verb* (1) to engage in prostitution; (2) to travel around looking for work

wallet *noun* (1) a billfold; (2) formerly, a bag used to carry food and personal items in while traveling

wall game *comp. noun* a sport, unique to ➡Eton College, which is similar to rugby

wallie *adj., Sc.* (1) attractive or beautiful; (2) glazed; (3) made of porcelain

wallie close *comp. noun, Sc.* a ➡tenement ➡close which has tiled walls

wallie dug *comp. noun, Sc.* an ornamental dog made of porcelain

wallies *noun, Sc.* false teeth

wallop *noun, coll.* beer or other drink containing alcohol

wally *noun, sl.* an incompetent or silly person

Walsingham *pr. name, hist.* a ➡Norfolk village about 30 miles northwest of ➡Norwich which possesses an 11th C. shrine to the Virgin Mary, following her appearance there in a vision

Walsingham was a major center of pilgrimage in medieval England. The shrine was largely destroyed during the Reformation but more recently has been restored and the village is again a popular pilgrimage destination. Indeed, it is now the most popular in England.

Waltham Forests *pr. name* a borough within ➡Greater London

Its current population, which is also included within the ➡London urban area total, is 205,000 (1991 Census).

Walworth Road *pr. name, coll.* the Labour Party

Its headquarters are located on this London street.

wame *noun, Sc.* (1) the belly; (2) the womb

Wandsworth *pr. name* a Greater London borough

Its current population, which is also included within the ➡London urban area total, is 240,000 (1991 Census).

wank *verb, sl., taboo* to masturbate

SEE ALSO: ➡wanker.

wanker *noun, sl., taboo* a foolish or trivial person

SEE ALSO: ➡wank.

wapentake *noun, hist.* a subdivision of a county, similar to a ➡hundred, in parts of England that were once part of the ➡Danelaw

wappenschaw *noun, hist., Sc.* (1) an inspection or muster of a local militia; (2) a shooting competition

Wapping *pr. name, hist.* the westernmost part of London's ➡Docklands area

War. *pr. name, abbr.* Warwickshire

the **War Box** *pr. name, hist., sl.* the ➡War Office

ward *noun* an electoral district that is a subdivision of a parliamentary constituency

County or city ➡Councillors each represent a ward.

warden *noun, out.* the senior official in charge of a school, hospital, etc.

warder *noun* (1) a male prison guard; (2) a warden

SEE ALSO: ➡wardress.

Wardour Street *pr. name, coll.* a nickname for the British movie industry

Called this because of the large number of movie companies that have their front offices in this central London street.

Wardour Street English *idiom, arch.* an affected use of archaic words and expressions such as "Wardour Street English."

wardress *noun* a female prison guard

SEE ALSO: warder.

wareday *noun, Sc.* the first day of spring

warehouse *noun* (1) a department store; (2) a wholesale repository

the **War Graves Commission** *pr. name, abbr.* the ➡Commonwealth War Graves Commission

the **War House** *pr. name, hist., sl.* the ➡War Office

war loan *comp. noun, hist.* British government stock issued during World War II

warm *noun, arch.* a heavy, warm overcoat

warmed-up *adj.* warmed-over

the **War Office** *pr. name, hist.* a former government department responsible for the British Army

It is now incorporated into the ➡Ministry of Defence.

warrant card *comp. noun* a police officer's ID and authorization card

warrant officer *comp. noun* a non-commissioned officer in the ➡RAF

Equivalent in rank to a master sergeant in the USAF.

the **Wars of the Roses** *pr. name, hist.* a dynastic civil war fought for 30 years from 1455 to 1485 over who should be King of England

It became known by this name because the central dispute was between the House of ➡Lancaster, whose emblem was a white rose, and the House of ➡York, whose emblem was a red rose. Eventually the wars ended with the defeat by the Lancastrian Henry ➡Tudor, of the ➡Yorkist ➡Richard III at the Battle of ➡Bosworth Field and the marriage of the new king, ➡Henry VII, to Elizabeth of York, thus uniting the two warring houses. Richard III has had a public image problem ever since, probably without any special justification.

Warwick *pr. name, hist.* a town with a ➠Norman castle; it is the administrative center of ➠Warwickshire
It was supposedly built as a fortress to repel the Danes in 915. The current population is 25,000 (1991 estimate).

Warwick School *pr. name* one of the leading English ➠public schools
Founded in 914, it is located in ➠Warwickshire.

Warwickshire *pr. name* a central English county
The county seat is ➠Warwick and the current population is 475,000 (1991 Census).

the Wash *pr. name* a large, very shallow inlet upon the eastern coast of England
Located between ➠Norfolk and ➠Lincolnshire, it is about 15 miles by 12 miles in extent.
Here, in 1216, ➠John lost his baggage while crossing it. Or, if you like, he lost his clothes in the Wash…

washer-upper *comp. noun, sl.* someone who washes cutlery and crockery

washeteria *noun* a Laundromat

washhand basin *comp. noun* a washbowl

washhand stand *comp. noun* a washstand

washing day *comp. noun* washday

washing line *comp. noun* a clothesline

washing powder *comp. noun* powdered detergent

Washington Old Hall *pr. name, hist.* a 17th C. house some five miles south of Newcastle-upon-Tyne
It is built upon the site of the 13th C. home of the ancestors of George Washington before they moved to ➠Sulgrave Manor.

washing up *comp. noun* (1) the washing of dishes, cutlery, etc.; (2) cutlery and crockery awaiting (1)

washing-up bowl *comp. noun* a dishpan

washing-up powder *comp. noun* dish-washing powder

wash up *verb* to wash cutlery and crockery
But *not* to wash *oneself*.

{wastebin » wastebasket} *noun* a trashcan

waste ground *comp. noun* (1) an empty lot; (2) wasteland

waste paper {basket » bin » can} *noun* a trashcan

watch *noun, hist.* an informal detachment of 18th C. Scottish ➠Highland troops
SEE ALSO: ➠Black Watch.

Watch Committee *pr. name, hist.* the committee formerly responsible for supervising the policing of a county, city or large town

watcher *imper., sl.* look out

watch-glass *comp. noun* a glass over the face of a watch

watch-strap *comp. noun* a watchband

watchword *noun, arch.* a password

water [A] *noun, out.* a body of water like a lake or pond [B] *noun, Sc.* a small river or stream

water bailiff *comp. noun* an official enforcing local fishing laws pertaining to a particular river or lake

water closet *comp. noun* (1) a compartment containing a toilet bowl; (2) a toilet bowl together with the associated equipment and furnishings

{watercolour » watercolourist} *spell.* {watercolor » watercolorist}

water-diviner *comp. noun* a dowser or diviner

Waterford *pr. name* a ➠Irish Republic county
County Waterford is in the ancient province of ➠Munster.

Waterford glass *comp. noun* a flint glass, distinguished for its clearness and colorlessness
It is made in Waterford, Ireland.

water ice *comp. noun* sherbet

watering *noun, Sc.* a drinking trough for animals

Waterloo *pr. name* one of the principal railroad terminuses in central London
This name commemorates the great victory over the French at the Battle of ➠Waterloo in 1815 and was thus considered to be an especially suitable, sensitive and appropriate name for the main terminal for trains arriving from France.
SEE ALSO: ➠Waterloo International.

the Battle of Waterloo *pr. name, hist.* a great battle in 1815, which was fought some 12 miles to the south of Brussels in Belgium, when the British and Prussian armies finally defeated Napoleon after his escape from Elba, ending the ➠Napoleonic Wars for good.
This was the decisive battle of the 19th C. It determined that France would not be able to counterbalance on land Britain's naval supremacy, established ten years earlier at ➠Trafalgar. The British army was led by the Duke of Wellington, the Prussian army by Blücher, who upon visiting London some time later looked around at what was then by far the greatest and richest city in the world and exclaimed, "*Was für plündern!*" = "What a place to plunder!"

the Waterloo and City Line *pr. name, coll.* an underground railroad that shuttles between Bank Station in the heart of London's ➠City, and ➠Waterloo railroad terminus
This is the oldest deep-tunneled line in London, and has earned its nickname of the ➠Drain from its dinginess and relative darkness in comparison with some of the more modern parts of the network. To be strictly accurate, it is not part of the ➠London Underground system as such, as it is owned and operated by ➠British Rail.

Waterloo International *pr. name* a major new railroad terminus built alongside the older ➠Waterloo terminus in central London
Built expressly to be the London terminus for trains arriving from France and Belgium via the Channel Tunnel, ensuring that the fine and longstanding British tradition of reminding French visitors of their nation's defeat at the Battle of ➠Waterloo in 1815 continues far into the future.

water meadow *comp. noun* a meadow on the flood plain of a river and so subject to occasional flooding.

waterproof *noun* a raincoat

the **waterworks** *noun, sl.* a euphemism for the human urinary system
A term sometimes used by doctors patronizing their patients.

Watling Street *pr. name, hist.* a Roman road that proceeds from ➟Dover through ➟London, ➟St Albans and ➟Dunstable, past ➟Birmingham, to Wroxeter on the ➟Severn river
Not its Roman name, but much later one, given by the Saxons.

wauchle *verb, Sc.* (1) to stumble; (2) to walk in a clumsy way or with difficulty

waukrife *adj, Sc.* (1) unable to sleep; (2) to be alert and on guard; (3) easily awakened

waur *adj., adv., Sc.* worse

the *Waverley* **Novels** *pr. name, hist.* the long series of historical novels written by Sir Walter Scott
Originally published anonymously by "the Author of *Waverley*", which was the title of his first novel. It is thought that Scott took the name from Waverley abbey in ➟Surrey.

Waverley Station *pr. name* the principal railroad terminus in central ➟Edinburgh
Opened in 1846 as the General Station, but renamed in memory of Sir Walter Scott in 1854.

the **Wavy Navy** *pr. name, sl.* the ➟RN(V)R
Because of the undulating stripes on officer's sleeves.

waxy *adj., sl.* bad-tempered

waybread *noun, arch.* a broad-leaved plantain shrub

Way In *comp. noun* entrance
A road sign.

Way Out *comp. noun* exit
A road sign.

wayzgoose *noun, arch.* an annual outing for the employees of a printing house

wazzoch *noun, sl.* a stupid or incapable person

WC [A] *noun, abbr.* a ➟water closet

[B] *pr. name, abbr.* West Central
A district in central London, originally devised by the Post Office as a sort of 19th. C. precursor of zip codes, to help it in the delivery of letters.

WD *noun, abbr.* a ➟Works Department

We *pronoun* I
This is the "Royal We," the way in which a ➟monarch refers to himself or herself, first used by ➟Richard I, it is said.
Certainly, it is traditional for the British monarch to refer to himself or herself in the plural, at least when speaking formally. This characteristic is most often associated with ➟Victoria and, in particular, her remark that "We are not amused," erroneously taken to mean that she lacked a sense of humor.

WEA *pr. name, abbr.* the ➟Workers Educational Association

the **Weald** *pr. name* a region in southern England incorporating parts of ➟Kent, ➟Surrey and ➟Sussex
Formerly wooded, which is the derivation of the name. It supplied charcoal for the 16th and 17th C. iron industries.

wealden *adj.* of an area with geology resembling that of the ➟Weald

wean *noun, Sc.* a baby or young child

wear *verb, coll.* to tolerate or put up with

{**weaselled » weaselling**} *spell.* {weaseled » weaseling}

weatherboard *noun* clapboard

wedding breakfast *comp. noun* the meal served after a wedding ceremony to celebrate that event

Wedgewood *pr. name* a style of pottery incorporating classical decorations in white on a pale blue base
Originated by Josiah Wedgewood, an 18th C. potter of ➟Stoke-on-Trent, Staffordshire.

wee bittie *comp. noun, Sc.* a very small piece or portion

the **Wee Frees** *pr. name, coll., hist.* the residual membership of the ➟Free Church of Scotland
An influential force in some parts of northern Scotland, where they insist upon strict observance of the Sabbath.

wee {**goldie » hauf » tottie**} *idiom, coll., Sc.* a small measure of ➟Scotch

wee hairy *comp. noun, derog., Sc.* a term of contempt for a young, low-class woman

wee heavy *idiom, coll., Sc.* a small bottle containing about half a pint of ➟heavy beer

wee hoose *idiom, Sc.* a euphemism for a rest room

weelfaured *adj. phr., Sc., sl.* (1) handsome, attractive; (2) respectable

weel-kent *adj., Sc.* well-known or easy to recognize

the **wee man** *idiom, coll., Sc.* the male sexual organ

the **Wee Man** *pr. name, coll., Sc.* the Devil

wee mannie *comp. noun, Sc.* an affectionate term for a small boy

weeping willow *idiom, rh. sl.* a pillow

weir *noun* (1) a small dam built across a river to regulate the flow of water; (2) an enclosure or fence across a river installed to trap fish

weird *noun, Sc.* fate, fortune or destiny
Usually not a good one.

weirdless *adj., Sc.* (1) unfortunate; (2) inept

well *noun* an closed-off area within a court of law, which is set aside for use by lawyers

well and truly *idiom* thoroughly or completely

wellie *noun, abbr.* a ➟wellington boot

wellie-wanging *comp. noun, coll.* the competitive throwing of ➡wellington boots as far as possible

the **Wellington** *pr. name, hist.* a bomber used by RAF ➡Bomber Command during World War II

wellington boot *comp. noun* a rubber or plastic waterproof boot that usually covers the shin
Named after its inventor, Arthur Wellesley, First Duke of Wellington, victor of the Battle of ➡Waterloo and later ➡Prime Minister of Great Britain.

Wellington College *pr. name* one of the leading English ➡public schools
Founded in 1853, the year after the death of the Duke of Wellington whom it is named after, it is located in ➡Berkshire.

wellingtons *noun, abbr.* a ➡wellington boot

well lined *adj. phr., coll.* well heeled, rich

Wells *pr. name* a city in Somerset, England
A city since 1201, current population is 10,000 (1988 estimate).

welly [A] *noun, abbr., sl.* (1) a ➡wellington boot; (2) a condom
[B] *verb, sl.* to kick forcefully

Welsh *noun* the language of Wales
The healthiest of the surviving ➡Celtic languages; about half a million Welsh people speak it as their first language.

the **Welsh** *noun* the people of Wales

Welsh cake *comp. noun* a small, flat biscuit cooked on a baking stone

Welsh Corgi *pr. name, Wal.* a breed of small, short-legged cattle-herding dogs with long bodies
The name is derived from the Welsh *cor + ci* = "dwarf + dog."

Welsh dresser *comp. noun* a sideboard with open shelves above cupboards

the **Welsh Folk Museum** *pr. name* one of the individual museums that constitute the ➡National Museum of Wales, situated in ➡Cardiff

the **Welsh Guards** *pr. name* the youngest of the five regiments that together form the ➡Guards Division of the British army
It was formed under this name for the first time in 1915 from Welsh members of the ➡Grenadier Guards.

Welsh harp *comp. noun* a large harp with three rows of strings

the **Welsh Industrial and Maritime Museum** *pr. name* one of the individual museums that constitute the ➡National Museum of Wales, it is situated in ➡Cardiff

{**Welshman » Welshwoman**} *pr. name* a {man » woman} who is ➡Welsh by birth or descent

the **Welsh National Opera** *pr. name, hist.* the only professional opera company in Wales
It was founded in ➡Cardiff in 1946 as an amateur society and is based at the New Theatre there.

the **Welsh Office** *pr. name* an office of state responsible for most aspects of the internal government of Wales
Created in 1964 in emulation of the ➡Scottish Office, it is responsible for those functions which, in England, are looked after by the Departments of ➡Health, ➡Education, ➡Environment, ➡Social Services, ➡Agriculture and others. It has special responsibility for ➡Welsh language and culture.

Welsh pony *comp. noun* a small and tough breed of pony originated from Wales
Popular for ➡pony-trekking.

Welsh {rabbit » rarebit} *comp. noun* grated and melted cheese on toast

Welsh Springer Spaniel *pr. name* a breed of small-eared spaniel with a red or orange and white coat

Welsh Terrier *pr. name* a small black-and-tan terrier

{**Welsh » Welch**} *adj.* that which relates to Wales
"Welch" is now archaic and very rare.

the **Welsh Wizard** *pr. name, coll., hist.* David Lloyd George, ➡Prime Minister during World War I
He acquired this name because, first, he was Welsh, and second, he had a particularly effective way of speaking and persuading people to do as he asked.

Welshy *pr. name, derog., sl.* a Welsh person

Wembley Stadium *pr. name* a large stadium in northwest London, where many important national and international sporting and other events are held, in particular the annual English soccer ➡Cup Final
Although not built especially for the purpose, this was the main stadium of the 1948 Olympic Games.

wen *noun* a big or busy city
SEE ALSO: the ➡Great Wen.

wendy *noun, derog., sl.* a particularly weak or small boy
A children's expression.

Wendy house *comp. noun* a small child's playhouse
From Wendy's house in J. M. Barrie's play *Peter Pan*.

Wensleydale *noun* (1) a breed of long-wooled sheep; (2) a kind of white or blue cheese
From Wensleydale in ➡Yorkshire.

Wessex *pr. name, hist.* the ancient kingdom of the West ➡Saxons, originally in southwestern England
It was founded by ➡Cedric about 520 and the usual seat of its kings was ➡Winchester. Eventually, it grew until it comprised all of England south of the ➡Thames River, and the Wessex King, ➡Alfred the Great, had become recognized as king of all the English outside the ➡Danelaw. Wessex had unified virtually all of what is now England under one ruler by 954, by which time other English rulers had accepted the king of Wessex as their overlord and king of all England.

West Anglia and Great Northern

West Anglia and Great Northern *pr. name (TM)* a railroad company operating commuter services between London, Cambridge, and other locations to the north of London

It is part of ➡British Rail.

West Coast *pr. name (TM)* a railroad company operating ➡InterCity services between London, ➡Birmingham, ➡Liverpool, ➡Manchester, ➡Glasgow, and other centers northwest of London

It is part of ➡British Rail.

the **West Country** *pr. name* the southwestern counties of England

Westcountry TV *pr. name* a local commercial TV company headquartered in ➡Bristol

It is part of the ➡ITV network.

the **West End** *pr. name* the main shopping and entertainment area of London

It was being called this in the 18th C. as it then formed the western boundary of the London urban area.

Western Isles *pr. name* a Scottish ➡Island Council

The current population is 30,000 (1991 Census).

West Glamorgan *pr. name* a Welsh County

The current population is 360,000 (1991 Census).

West Highland {Terrier» White Terrier} *pr. name* a small terrier dog with a white coat

Westie *pr. name, abbr.* a ➡West Highland {Terrier » White Terrier}

West Indian *pr. name* someone who originates from the Caribbean

the **West Indies** *pr. name* the Caribbean

West Lothian *pr. name, hist.* a former Scottish county, now part of ➡Lothian region

Westmeath *pr. name* a county in the ➡Irish Republic

County Westmeath in the ancient province of ➡Leinster.

West Midlands *pr. name* a Metropolitan County

The principal city is ➡Birmingham and the current population is 2,500,000 (1991 Census).

the **West Midlands** *pr. name* the western portion of the ➡Midlands area of England, especially the region around ➡Birmingham

Usually considered to be the counties of ➡Hereford and Worcester, ➡Shropshire, ➡Stafford, ➡Warwick and ➡West Midlands Metroplitain County.

Westminster *pr. name* (1) a district in central London, west of the ➡City; (2) a euphemism for ➡Parliament

(1) is where Parliament meets, hence (2).

the City of **Westminster** *pr. name* a city in ➡Greater London which, together with the ➡City, forms one of the two historic central areas of London

The name derives from a monastery established to the west of the original walled City of London during the 7th C. However,

it was ➡Edward the Confessor that built the Palace of ➡Westminster and ➡Westminster Abbey during the 11th C. In this way, it had already become joint seat—with ➡Winchester—of the English government before the ➡Conquest, and was incorporated as a city in 1201. Current population (also included in the London area total) is 180,000 (1991 Census).

Westminster Abbey

D. MK. 93

Westminster Abbey *pr. name* the cathedral church of the ➡Westminster and the location of English, later British, ➡coronations since that of ➡William the Conqueror on Christmas Day 1066

the present structure dates from the 13th C., although the two towers that flank the main entrance were erected in the 18th C., based on an earlier design by Christopher Wren. Within the abbey is ➡Poet's Corner.

Westminster Bridge *pr. name, hist.* a bridge over the ➡Thames River beside the ➡Houses of Parliament

The present bridge opened in 1862, replacing one of 1750.

Westminster Cathedral *pr. name* the principal Roman Catholic church in England, in ➡Westminster

Westminster Hall *pr. name* the only surviving part of the original medieval Palace of ➡Westminster, destroyed by fire in 1834

It was built by ➡William II in the 11th C.

Westminster School *pr. name* one of the leading English ➡public schools

The present school was founded in 1560, although there has been a school associated with ➡Westminster Abbey since the 12th C. at least. It is located beside the Abbey.

Westmorland *pr. name, hist.* a former county situated in the northwest of England, lying between Lancashire and Cumberland

It is now part of ➡Cumbria.

the **West Riding** *pr. name, hist.* a major administrative division of the former county of ➡Yorkshire

West Suffolk *pr. name, hist.* a former English County, now part of ➡Suffolk.

West Sussex *pr. name* a county on the southern coast of England, between ➡Hampshire and ➡East Sussex

It was formed out of the western part of ➡Sussex in 1974. The county seat is ➡Chichester and the current population is 690,000 (1991 Census). *SEE ALSO:* ➡Sussex.

West Yorkshire *pr. name* a ➡Metropolitan County

The principal city is ➡Leeds and the current population is 1,985,000 (1991 Census).

wet [A] *adj., coll.* feeble or spineless

[B] *noun, coll.* a Conservative politician who has a liberal stance

The term was particularly common during the ➡Prime Ministership of Margaret Thatcher, who is reputed to have invented the usage. *SEE ALSO:* ➡dry.

wet the baby's head *idiom. phr. verb, coll.* to celebrate the birth of a baby with an alcoholic drink

Wexford *pr. name* a county in the ➡Irish Republic

County Wexford in the ancient province of ➡Leinster.

Wg Cdr *comp. noun, abbr.* a ➡wing commander

whack *verb, sl.* to defeat or better an adversary

whacked *adj., coll.* exhausted or worn-out

whacking [A] *adj., coll.* whopping, huge

[B] *adv., coll.* very

whacko *exclam., out., sl.* an expression of pleasure

what *exclam., out., sl.* a terminating emphasizer

what-d'you-call-it *idiom, sl.* a doodad, thingamajig, or thingamabob

what the {deuce » dickens} *exclam., coll.* a euphemism for or variation of "what the devil"

whaup *noun, Sc.* a curlew

{wha » wham} *pronoun, Sc.* {who » whom}

wheech *verb, Sc.* (1) to whiz or rush through the air; (2) to make a whizzing sound

wheelie bin *comp. noun, coll.* a large, wheeled trashcan, sometimes issued by trash-collection agencies to simplify their work

SEE ALSO: ➡eurobin.

wheen *noun, Sc.* (1) a few; (2) several

wheesht *imper., Ir., Sc.* be silent

wheeze *noun* a cunning ploy

whelk *noun* an edible marine gastropod mollusk that can be consumed as a food

whelk-stall *comp. noun* a booth selling ➡whelks for immediate consumption

The proverbial smallest possible business venture.

when Dover and Calais meet *idiom, coll.* never

whennie *noun, sl.* someone who bores listeners with tales of their past exploits

From his or her regular use of the expression, "When I ..."

when one's ship comes in *idiom* when one becomes rich and successful

when the balloon goes up *idiom* when trouble starts

where the shoe pinches *idiom* where there are problems or difficulties

wherry *noun* (1) a fishing boat; (2) a large light barge

wherryman *noun* a crewmember of a ➡wherry

whiff *noun, coll.* a smell, especially an unpleasant one

whiffy *adj., coll.* possessing an unpleasant smell

Whig *pr. name, hist., Sc.* together with the ➡Tories, one of the two alternating governing parties of Britain until they started to be known as ➡Liberals, which name was apparently began as a jibe by their opponents, suggesting a lack of principles

"Whiggamore" was an old Scots word for cattle drover. Certainly "whig" was the nickname of the Scots ➡Covenanters who took part in the Whiggamore Raid of 1648. During the reign of ➡James II of England and VII of Scotland, the word was picked up and used as a term of abuse against groups of Scots and English Presbyterians opposed to the Roman Catholic ➡Stuarts remaining on the British ➡throne.

Then, it could be said that the name was attached to those whom during the earlier ➡English Civil War would have been called ➡Roundheads. "Whig" was first used as the name of what we would now call a political party after the ➡Glorious Revolution that swept away the ➡Stuart dynasty in 1688.

Unlike the name ➡Tory, which is still in common use as an alternative to ➡Conservative, the word "Whig" has now fallen entirely out of contemporary usage.

whigmaleerie *noun, Sc.* (1) a gimcrack; (2) a fantastic device or idea

Whig Party *pr. name, hist.* the former name of the political party renamed the ➡Liberal Party in 1877

SEE ALSO: ➡Whig.

whiles *adv., Sc.* occasionally

whilst *adv., conj.* while

whin *noun* (1) a hard basaltic rock, dark blue in color; (2) a spiny, yellow-flowered shrub, common upon open wasteland such as the Scottish ➡Highlands

(1) is often used as the base stone for roads. (2)'s formal name is *ulex europaeus*.

whinge *verb, coll.* to grumble, whine or complain

whip [A] *noun* (1) an ➡MP responsible for controlling the discipline and voting patterns of MPs of his party; (2) a written notice sent to MPs by (1) requesting or requiring their vote in a ➡division

The word is derived from "whipper-in," the person who controls hounds during a fox hunt. The number of times that the whipping notice is underlined signifies the urgency of the request. The most urgent are called ➡three-line whips.

[B] *verb, sl.* to steal

Whippet *pr. name* a dog similar to but smaller than a greyhound, used for racing in the north of England

whipping *noun* the business of a ➡whip [A](1)

whip-round *comp. noun, coll.* an informal collection of money for a charitable cause of some sort

whisky *spell.* whiskey

Irrefutable proof that it's not always American spelling that is the most simplified and rational.

whisky cocktail *comp. noun* a whiskey-based highball

whisky-mac *comp. noun* a drink consisting of a mixture of ➡Scotch and ginger wine

the **Whispering Gallery** *pr. name* a gallery around the inside of the dome in St ➡Paul's Cathedral

Due to an accident of the building's acoustics, someone whispering near to the wall on one side can be heard quite clearly near the wall on the opposite side, 107 ft away.

whist drive *comp. noun* a ➡drive where the participants play whist

whistle *noun, rh. sl.* a suit of clothes

Derivation: suit > flute > whistle and flute > whistle.

whistled *adj., sl.* drunk

Whitby *pr. name, hist.* a small fishing port on the coast of ➡North Yorkshire

The site of an abbey founded in 656, now in ruins. The current population is 15,000 (1991 estimate).

white-arsed *adj., derog., sl., taboo* (1) despicable; (2) scared

Whitechapel *pr. name, hist.* an area of London's ➡East End, once the haunt of ➡Jack the Ripper

the **White Cockade** *pr. name, hist.* a badge worn by supporters of ➡Charles Edward Stuart

white coffee *comp. noun* coffee with cream

white ducks *comp. noun* a pair of men's pants made from white, untwilled cotton

White Ensign *pr. name* the ensign flag of (1) the ➡Royal Navy; (2) the ➡Royal Yacht Squadron

white fish *comp. noun* various non-oily market fishes that have white flesh

Whitehall *pr. name* (1) a street in ➡Westminster, London; (2) a euphemism for the British government

(1) is where the principal government offices are, hence (2).

Whitehall warrior *comp. noun, sl.* (1) a civil servant; (2) a military officer engaged in clerical duties rather than on active service

Whitehall Palace *pr. name, hist.* a royal palace built as his personal residence just to the south of ➡Westminster Palace by ➡Henry VIII

It was almost entirely destroyed by fire in 1698; only the ➡Banqueting House, a 17th C. addition, survives.

white horse *comp. noun, hist.* a huge figure carved out of the chalk bedrock of southern England

There are many, but the best known are at ➡Uffington, south of Oxford, and the Vale of the White Horse in ➡Berkshire.

white horses *comp. noun* white foam upon the crests of sea waves

white meat *comp. noun* meat such as veal, poultry or rabbit, which is light in color when raw

white night *comp. noun, coll.* a night when sleep does not come

White Paper *pr. name* a government report, situation paper or proposal on a topic of public interest

white pudding *comp. noun, Sc.* a large sausage containing oatmeal, suet and onions

White Rose *comp. noun, hist.* (1) the emblem of the ➡House of York; (2) the emblem of ➡Yorkshire

White's *pr. name, hist.* the oldest London club

It evolved from a chocolate house opened by a Mr. Francis White in St ➡James's in 1693. During the 18th C. it was primarily a non-political gaming club, but then in the 19th C. it developed a ➡Tory political hue.

white spirit *comp. noun* a light and clear petroleum-based liquid solvent

the **White Tower** *pr. name, hist.* the square keep or stronghold which is at the center of the ➡Tower of London and is the oldest part of the fortress

whit for why? *inter., Sc.* what is the reason?

the Isle of **Whithorn** *pr. name, hist.* not an island at all but a peninsula on the southwest coast of Scotland where St Ninian founded his church in the late 4th or early 5th C. and began the process of Christianizing post-Roman Britain a good century before St Columbus arrived on ➡Iona
St Ninian's church, known as *Candida Casa* or the "White House" because it was built of light-colored stone, is believed to have been the origin of the name "Whithorn."

whitrat *noun, Sc.* a stoat or weasel

Whitsunday *pr. name* a Scottish term-day or ➡quarter-day,
Now May 28, but formerly May 15.

wholemeal *noun* whole wheat

the **whole shoot** *idiom, coll.* the whole shooting match; everything
Here "shoot" is a corruption of ➡shot.

whole time *idiom* full time

WH Smith *pr. name (TM)* the largest nationwide chain of stationers and bookstores

why for no? *inter., Sc.* why not?

the **WI** *pr. name, abbr.* (1) the ➡Woman's Institutes; (2) the ➡West Indies

wick *noun, arch.* (1) a dairy farm; (2) a hamlet or village
Now found only in place-names.

the White Tower

wicket *noun* in ➡cricket, (1) a batsman's inning; (2) one of two sets of three ➡stumps set 22 yards apart at either end of the ➡pitch

wicket keeper *comp. noun* the ➡cricket ➡fielder who is stationed close behind the active ➡wicket
In order to catch any missed balls; also to expedite a rapid return of the ball into play after it has been hit by the batter.

Wicklow *pr. name* a county in the ➡Irish Republic
County Wicklow in the ancient province of ➡Leinster.

widdie *noun, Sc.* (1) willow; (2) a rope made from twigs or willow or other flexible but tough material; (3) a hangman's noose

wide *adj., sl.* (1) shrewd; (2) dishonest

wide ball *comp. noun* in ➡cricket, a ball bowled to pass so far from the ➡wicket that it is out of the ➡batsman's reach

wide boy *comp. noun, sl.* a small-time crook

wide-weave *comp. noun* loose-weave fabric

the **Widow of Windsor** *pr. name, hist.* a nickname acquired by ➡Victoria after the death of ➡Albert
He died in 1861, leaving the Queen a widow for 40 years.

wife *noun, Sc.* a middle-aged or older woman

Wigan *pr. name, hist.* a town within ➡Greater Manchester that can trace its origins back to a Roman military camp
It also featured in the title of George Orwell's book *The Road to Wigan Pier* of 1937. The current population is 82,000 (1991 estimate).

wigging *noun, coll.* a scolding

the Isle of **Wight** *pr. name* the largest island situated off the southern coast of England
It has an area of about 147 square miles and is a county in its own right. The county seat is ➡Newport and the current population is 125,000 (1991 Census).

Wigmore Hall *pr. name* a concert hall in London which is a regular venue for chamber music recitals
Opened in 1901 as the Bechstein Hall, anti-German sentiment during World War I caused it to be renamed for the street it is on.

Wigtownshire *pr. name, hist.* a former Scottish county, now part of ➡Dumfries & Galloway region

the **wilderness** *noun* where politicians are said to go after ceasing to be in office
Especially if they fail to get themselves re-elected.

{**wilful » wilfullness**} *spell.* {willful » willfulness}

{**wilfully » willful**} *spell.* {willfully » willful}

William *pr. name, hist.* ➡King of Scots
The brother of ➡Malcolm IV, he reigned for 49 years from 1165 until 1214. He was known as "the Lion" but for all that, he accepted the overlordship of the king of England from 1174 until 1189.

William and Mary

William and Mary *pr. name, hist.* (1) the reign of William III and his wife Mary as the joint King and Queen of Great Britain; (2) an elegant 17th C. furniture style that made much use of walnut

A member of the Dutch ➡Royal House of Orange, William was associated with the British ➡Royal House of ➡Stuart by virtue of his marriage alone and thus was an acceptable candidate for the British throne vacated in 1688 by James, but only if in association with his wife Mary.

Accordingly they ruled together. William and Mary styled themselves "King and Queen of England, Scotland, France and Ireland, Defenders of the Faith, etc., etc." and reigned jointly for five years from 1689 after the short ➡Interregnum that followed the flight to France of ➡James II of England and VII of Scotland in 1688, until Mary died in 1694 without heir at the age of 32. Thereafter William reigned alone for another eight years, dying in 1702.

William I *pr. name, hist.* King of England

The illegitimate son of Robert, Duke of Normandy, he succeeded his father in 1035 but it took many years to establish his rule fully. His invasion of England in 1066 was based upon a reasonably strong claim to succeed ➡Edward the Confessor; indeed his claim was supported by the Pope.

He was crowned at ➡Westminster on Christmas Day 1066, just 10 weeks after the Battle of ➡Hastings and very soon had established his rule over the whole of England. He styled himself *Willielmus Rex Anglorum* = "William King of England" and reigned for 20 years after winning the Battle of Hastings, until 1087. The founding member of the ➡Royal House of ➡Normandy, he is better known as ➡William the Conqueror.

William II *pr. name, hist.* King of England

A member of the ➡Royal House of ➡Normandy and nicknamed ➡William Rufus, this third son of ➡William the Conqueror ruled aggressively, making enemies of his barons and the church whose coffers he raided.

He was unmarried, possibly homosexual, and died in a hunting accident in the ➡New Forest, although in truth that accident may have been murder by or on behalf of his brother, who was his successor and became ➡Henry I.

William styled himself *Dei Gratis Rex Anglorum* = "By the Grace of God King of England" and reigned a dozen years from 1087 until 1100.

William III *pr. name, hist.* King of Great Britain

SEE: ➡William and Mary.

William IV *pr. name, hist.* King of the United Kingdom

The third son of ➡George III, he served in the Royal Navy for many years. He had a long relationship with an actress, Dorothea Jordan, by whom he had 10 illegitimate children.

When the death of his cousin made him heir-apparent to ➡George IV, he eventually got married to a German princess, Adelaide of Saxe-Meiningen, who was considered a suitable choice for future queen, but there were no surviving offspring.

He styled himself "King of the United Kingdom of Great Britain and Ireland, Duke of Braunschweig-Lüneburg, Defender of the Faith, etc., etc." and reigned for seven years from 1830 until 1837. William was ➡Elector of Hanover and a member of the Royal House of ➡Hanover. He was succeeded by ➡Victoria, his niece.

William of Orange *pr. name, hist.* ➡William III

He ewas a member of the Dutch ➡Royal House of Orange, although in Britain he ruled jointly with his wife Mary as a member of the ➡Royal House of ➡Stuart. *SEE ALSO:* ➡William and Mary.

William Rufus *pr. name, hist.* ➡William II

William the Conqueror *pr. name, hist.* ➡William I

The victor of the Battle of ➡Hastings in 1066.

willie *noun, sl., taboo* the penis

will-o'-the-wisp *idiom* (1) an illusory hope or hopeless dream; (2) someone hard to find

willow *noun, coll.* a cricket bat

Because that's the wood it's made of.

Wilton *pr. name, hist.* a thick-piled woven carpet

From ➡Wilton, a small town three miles west of ➡Salisbury in ➡Wiltshire, a center of carpet making since 1655.

Wilton House *pr. name, hist.* originally a Tudor mansion four miles west of ➡Salisbury in ➡Wiltshire

It was rebuilt in Palladian style in the 17th C. and is now most celebrated for its Palladian style.

Wilts. *pr. name, abbr.* ➡Wiltshire

Wiltshire *pr. name* a county in western England

The county seat is Trowbridge and the current population is 555,000 (1991 Census).

Wimbledon *pr. name, abbr., coll.* (1) the All-England Lawn Tennis and Croquet Club; (2) the annual tennis championships they organize every summer

Wimbledon is the area of southwestern London the club is located in. Until 1968, the tennis championships were limited to amateur players only.

wimple *verb, Sc.* (1) to enfold or tangle; (2) to complicate; (3) to tell a story that confuses or deceives

The ***Wimpy*** *pr. name, abbr., hist.* a nickname for the World War II ➡*Wellington* bomber

wince *noun* a roller that pulls textile through a dye-vat

winceyette *pr. name (TM)* a lightweight cotton material, similar to flannelette

winch *verb, Sc.* to court or to go out with a person of the opposite sex

Winchester *pr. name* a city on the Itchen River; it is the administrative center of ➡Hampshire

Apparently this was already a place of significance before the Romans turned up and decided to call it *Venta Belgarum*. Later, it was the capital of ➡Wessex and thus eventually became the first capital of England during ➡Anglo-Saxon times. Indeed, Winchester remained joint capital with London until the 14th C. Incorporated as a city in 1155, its current population is 95,000 (1988 estimate).

Winchester College *pr. name* one of the leading English ➡public schools

Founded in 1382, it is located in ➡Winchester, ➡Hampshire.

windcheater *noun* a windbreaker

winder *noun* (1) a handle used to roll up or down the window of a car; (2) the stem of a watch

Windermere *pr. name* the largest lake in the ➡Lake District and in England

It is about 11 miles long.

windhover *noun* a kestrel

windmill *noun* a pinwheel

A child's toy.

the **Windmill Theatre** *pr. name, hist.* a small burlesque theater in London's ➡Soho district

Originally a movie theater, it became famous by remaining open throughout the worst days of the ➡Blitz in World War II with the slogan, "We never close".

window blind *comp. noun* a window shade

window-shop *phr. verb* to look at goods in store windows without buying anything

window tax *comp. noun, hist.* a tax on windows

Yes, really. Introduced in 1695, abolished in 1851.

windscreen *noun* an automobile windshield

windscreen wiper *comp. noun* a windshield wiper

Windsor [A] *pr. name, abbr., hist.* the ➡Royal House of Great Britain since 1917

The following English monarchs belonged or currently belong to this house: ➡George V, ➡Edward VII, ➡George VI and Elizabeth II of England and I of Scotland. The name is derived from the royal family's principal residence, ➡Windsor Castle. This has been the family name since 1917, when it was changed from ➡Saxe-Coburg und Gotha due to anti-German feeling during World War I. On hearing this news, the Kaiser suggested that a certain well-known light opera should henceforth be called *The Merry Wives of Saxe-Coburg und Gotha.*

[B] *pr. name, hist.* a town on the ➡Thames River in ➡Berkshire to the west of London, which has grown up around ➡Windsor Castle

The current population is 30,000 (1991 estimate).

The Duke of **Windsor** *pr. name* the title adopted by ➡Edward VIII following his ➡Abdication

Windsor Castle *pr. name* the principal official residence of the British monarch

It is located to the west of London, in ➡Berkshire, a few miles from ➡Heathrow Airport. Construction was begun by ➡William the Conqueror in the 11th C. and there have been frequent extentions and rebuilding projects since.

A large part of the castle, including the principal state banqueting room, St ➡George's Hall, and the ➡Round Tower, were gutted by a major fire in 1992.

Windsor chair *comp. noun* a dining chair with upright rods supporting a semicircular back

wind-up *comp. noun, sl.* a practical joke

wind up [A] *verb* to wind, typically, a clockwork mechanism

[B] *verb, sl.* to irritate or provoke

wine bar *comp. noun* a hostelry where wine is the principal liquid refreshment

wine-gum *comp. noun* a small wine-flavored candy with a gelatin base

They are available in a multitude of colors.

wing *noun* an automobile wheel fender

wing commander *comp. noun* a commissioned officer in the ➡RAF

Equivalent in rank to a lieutenant-colonel in the USAF.

winger *noun, sl.* (1) a friend; (2) a steward or passenger attendant on board ship; (3) a team player in a wing position

(1) is military slang. (2) is nautical slang. (3) is sports slang.

winkle *noun, abbr.* periwinkle

winkle out *verb, coll.* to displace, extract or evict

winkle-picker *idiom, out., sl.* a shoe that has a long pointed toe

Winnie *pr. name, coll.* a nickname for Winston Churchill, ➡Prime Minister during World War II

winter garden *comp. noun, out.* a large conservatory or greenhouse where summer conditions are maintained through winter so that flowers and other vegetation can thrive all year round

Usually open to the public, these establishments had their heyday in the ➡Victorian period, when they were particularly popular at coastal resorts.

wintle *verb, Sc.* to stagger or roll about

wipe over *verb* to mop a surface

Such as a table or counter, for example.

wipe the slate clean *idiom. phr. verb, coll.* (1) to cancel a debt; (2) to forget an earlier misdemeanor

wipe up *verb* to dry dishes, etc.

wireless [A] *noun, abbr., arch.* a ➡wireless set

[B] *verb, arch.* to make a radio transmission

wireless set *comp. noun, arch.* a radio receiver

wire netting *comp. noun* chicken wire

wire-walker *noun, arch.* a tightrope walker

Wisden *noun, abbr.* the standard reference book on ➡cricket, published annually

First published by John Wisden in 1864, and entitled in full, *Wisden Cricketers' Almanack.*

wiselike *adj., adv., Sc.* (1) reasonable or prudent; (2) respectable or decent; (3) handsome or pretty

the Wisest Fool in Christendom

the **Wisest Fool in Christendom** *pr. name, hist.* a nickname for ➟James I of England and VI of Scotland
SEE ALSO: the ➟English Solomon.

wisha *exclam., Ir.* an expression of surprise

witenagemot *noun, hist.* a kind of ➟Anglo-Saxon ruling council or parliament

withershins *adv., Sc.* (1) counterclockwise; (2) in the opposite direction to that of the sun; (3) in a direction or way of behaving that brings bad luck; (4) in the opposite direction to the normal

with it *adv., sl.* also

with knobs on *idiom, sl.* emphatically

witness box *comp. noun* a witness stand

witter on *verb, coll.* to speak at great length to no purpose or without coming to any sort of point

wivver *adv., East* however

wizard *adj., sl.* remarkable or outstanding

wizard prang *idiom, arch., sl.* an exceptionally accurate or successful ➟prang
This expression began life as ➟RAF World War II slang.

WO *noun, abbr.* a ➟warrant officer

Woburn Abbey *pr. name* a vast stately home some 15 miles to the southwest of ➟Bedford
Originally the site of a Cistercian abbey, it was gifted to the Russell family by ➟Henry VIII during the ➟Dissolution of the Monasteries. The house now there was built in stages between 1697 and 1769.

wock *noun, East* work

wodd *noun, East* a word

wodge *noun, coll.* a lump or clump

Wog *noun, derog., out., sl.* (1) a non-white foreign person; (2) the Arabic language
(1) is especially one from the Middle or Far East; reputedly the word is an abbreviation of "Worthy Oriental Gentlemen" but this is apocryphal.

Wolf Cub *comp. noun, arch.* a Cub Scout

Wolfe's Own *pr. name* the 47th Regiment of Foot
A unit of the British Army whose name honors their distinguished service at Quebec in 1759 under the command of General Wolfe.

Wolfson College *pr. name* (1) a college of ➟Cambridge University founded in 1965; (2) a college of ➟Oxford University founded in 1966

Wollaton Hall *pr. name, hist.* an ➟Elizabethan country house built in the late 16th C. about three miles to the west of Nottingham
It is considered to be the most ornate and spectacular of Elizabethen houses, and the inspiration for ➟Mentmore Towers.

wolly *noun, sl.* a policeman in uniform

Wolverhampton *pr. name, hist.* an industrial town about 13 miles northwest of ➟Birmingham
The current population is 250,000 (1991 estimate).

the **Woman's Institutes** *pr. name* an organization providing self-help cultural and educational activities for women, particularly in rural areas
Founded in 19th C. Canada, the movement established its first British branch in ➟Llanfair PG during World War I. Currently there are almost 10,000 branches in the United Kingdom.

the **Woman's Royal Air Force** *pr. name, hist.* a section of the ➟RAF which was reserved for women
First formed in 1918 and then dissolved in 1920, it was reformed in 1939 as the ➟WAAF but renamed the WRAF in 1949. It has now been absorbed into the rest of the ➟RAF.

the **Woman's Royal Army Corps** *pr. name, hist.* a section of the British Army reserved for women
Formed in 1949 from the ➟ATS, it was dissolved into the main body of the army in 1992.

the **Woman's Royal Naval Service** *pr. name, hist.* a section of the ➟Royal Navy reserved for women
First formed in 1917 and disbanded at the end of World War I, it was reformed again in 1939. Until 1990, members were restricted to shore duties.

the **Woman's Royal Voluntary Service** *pr. name* a voluntary organization that performs general social work and helps out in emergencies
Originally founded as the ➟Woman's Voluntary Service in 1938, the "Royal" appellation was added in 1966.

womble *noun, sl.* anyone who is considered unfashionably dressed or uninteresting
A children's expression, from the name of a family of TV puppets popular with young children in the 1970s.

woncer *noun, arch., sl.* a one ➟pound note

wonk *noun, derog., sl.* (1) a cadet or new recruit; (2) an ineffective person; (3) a male homosexual
(1) and (2) are nautical slang.

wonky *adj., sl.* (1) shaky or unsteady; (2) unreliable; (3) incorrect or wrong

wooden promenade *comp. noun* a boardwalk

the **wooden spoon** *comp. noun, coll.* a booby prize

woodentop *noun, sl.* (1) a policeman in uniform; (2) a slow-witted person
For (1), *SEE ALSO:* ➟woolly.

the **Wooden Walls** *pr. name, hist.* a popular nickname for the ➟Royal Navy in the days when it had a fleet of sail-powered wooden warships

wood-straw *comp. noun* excelsior used for packing

woodwork *noun, sl.* soccer goalpost frames

wool-fell *comp. noun* the skin of a sheep which is still carrying wool

{**woolled » woollen**} *spell.* {wooled » woolen}

woolly *noun, sl.* (1) a woolen garment such as a sweater; (2) a policeman in uniform

For (2), *SEE ALSO:* ➠woodentop.

the **Woolsack** *pr. name* (1) the official seat of the ➠Lord Chancellor in the ➠House of Lords; (2) a nickname for the office of ➠Lord Chancellor

(1) is a large seat, lacking back or sides, which is derived from the symbolic four sacks of wool that the king's Chancellor sat upon in medieval times, symbolizing the source of England's wealth in these days, which was wool.

Woolwich *pr. name, hist.* (1) an ancient town now incorporated within ➠Greater London, to the southeast of the center of the city; (2) a large national ➠building society

Woolwich first became significant when ➠Henry VIII established a royal dockyard there in 1512.

Although the dockyard closed in the 19th C., it was also a military garrison town until recently and it is still a center of the defense industry.

wop *noun, arch., sl.* an army radio operator

From the common abbreviation of the full former name: "Wireless Operator."

SEE ALSO: ➠wireless.

Worcester *pr. name, abbr., hist.* (1) a former English ➠County; (2) a city, on the ➠Severn River, which is the administrative center of ➠Hereford and Worcester; (3) ➠Royal Worcester

(1) is now part of ➠Hereford and Worcester. (2) is situated at the lowest fording point on the river and had become a significant center as early as the 7th C. The cathedral was began in the 11th C. Incorporated as a city in 1189, the current population is 80,000 (1988 estimate).

Worcester College *pr. name* a college of ➠Oxford University founded in 1714

Worcester sauce *pr. name* a thin pungent sauce containing soy, vinegar and garlic among other things

Its name reflects the fact that it was first made in ➠Worcester. Originally it was called "Worcestershire Sauce."

Worcestershire *pr. name, hist.* a former English county, now part of ➠Hereford and Worcester

word blindness *comp. noun* a form of dyslexia

the **Workers' Educational Association** *pr. name* a voluntary organization set up to educate people after they have completed their formal studies and commenced working

Currently this organization claims to have about 900 branches and some 180,000 students.

workhouse *noun, arch.* a poorhouse

working day *comp. noun* a workday

working men's club *comp. noun* a private club for working people, offering a place to go for a drink, socializing and entertainment

These have long been an important social institution, especially but not exclusively in the northern part of England. The first were established in the middle years of the 19th C. when they typically seem to have had a more serious and higher moral purpose than it would be realistic to expect from them today.

working party *comp. noun* a group established to study or resolve a particular problem

workmate *noun* a fellow worker

workpeople *noun* workers

works *noun* a factory or plant

works council *comp. noun* a group consisting of management and elected workers' representatives who meet together at regular intervals to discuss matters of mutual concern

works department *pr. name* the department of a local council responsible for carrying out construction work on behalf of the council

works outing *comp. noun, coll.* a company picnic

work the oracle *idiom. phr. verb, coll.* to influence events in secret or without being noticed

work to rule *comp. noun* a form of job action where employees follow rules with pedantic exactitude causing a work slowdown tantamount in effect to a strike, but without actually striking

the **world and his wife** *idiom, coll.* everybody

the **World Service** *pr. name* a worldwide multi-lingual radio service broadcast by the ➠BBC

World Service Television *pr. name* a worldwide television news service broadcast by the ➠BBC

worry *verb, Sc.* strangle or choke

the **worse for wear** *idiom, coll.* (1) quite drunk; (2) damaged through use; (3) injured

Worshipful *adj.* a title granted to certain people or organizations of distinction, particulary justices of the peace

{**worshipped » worshipper » worshipping**} *spell.* {worshiped » worshiper » worshiping}

wot *verb, out.* to know

wotcher *noun, sl.* a friendly greeting between men

Derived from "what cheer".

wpb *noun, abbr.* a ➠waste paper basket

WPC *noun, abbr.* a woman police ➠constable

WRAC *pr. name, abbr.* ➠Woman's Royal Army Corps

WRAF *pr. name, abbr.* ➠Woman's Royal Air Force

wrangler *noun* a person in the first class of the mathematical ➠tripos at ➠Cambridge University

wrap up *imper., sl.* a euphemism for "shut up"

Wren *noun, hist.* a member of the ➠WRNS

wrennery *noun, hist., sl.* where ➠Wrens lived

Wrexham

Wrexham *pr. name, hist.* an industrial town in northern Wales, which has a 14th. C. church tower containing the tomb of Elihu Yale, founder of Yale University

wrinkly *noun, sl.* an old person

writ *noun, Sc.* (1) handwriting; (2) a formal document, but not necessarily issued by a court

write off *phr. verb* to totally wreck a car

writer *noun, Sc.* a lawyer

Writer to the Signet *promp. noun, Sc.* a lawyer qualified to prepare ➡Crown writs
This refers to ➡Signet (2).

write to (someone) *phr. verb* write (someone)

writing block *comp. noun* a writing pad

writ of extent *comp. noun, arch.* a form of writ used to recover debts due to the ➡Crown

WRNS *pr. name, abbr.* ➡Woman's Royal Naval Service

wrong-foot *verb* to put an opponent on the defensive

wrongous *adj., Sc.* illegal

wrong'un *noun, coll., out.* a dishonest person

WRVS *pr. name, abbr.* ➡Woman's Royal Voluntary Service

WS *noun, abbr., Sc.* a ➡Writer to the Signet

WTN *pr. name, abbr.* Worldwide Television News
A subsidiary of ➡ITN, whose reports are seen on CNN.

wuid *adj., Sc.* (1) livid; (2) violent; (3) insane

wunna *verb aux., Sc.* will not

wur *pos. pronoun., Sc.* our

WVS *pr. name, abbr.* ➡Woman's Voluntary Service

wych-hazel *spell.* witch hazel

Wye College *pr. name* a school of ➡London University
It is located outside London at Ashford in ➡Kent.

Wykehamist *noun* a member of ➡Winchester College
From William of Wykeham, bishop of Winchester and founder of the college in the 13th C.

wyliecoat *noun, Sc.* warm underclothes

wynd *noun, Sc.* a narrow alley or street

Wypers *pr. name, coll., hist.* the British soldier's ➡hobson-jobson nickname for ➡Ypres, a scene of regular carnage throughout World War I

wyte *noun, Sc.* responsibility or blame

wyvern *noun* an heraldic representation of a two-legged dragon with wings and a tail that terminates in a barb

XYZ

yabber *noun, Sc.* to chatter or gossip loudly or excitedly

{Yank » Yankee} *pr. name, coll.* any American citizen from any part of the United States

yapp *noun* a form of leather bookbinding
The 19th C. London bookseller who invented the style.

the **Yard** *pr. name, abbr., coll.* (1) ➡New Scotland Yard; (2) the ➡Metropolitan Police

Yarmouth capon *comp. noun, coll.* a red herring

yarn *noun* embroidery thread

yauld *adj., Sc.* active, healthy or alert

ye *def. art., arch., hist.* the
An old-fashioned spelling of "the." There is a considerable confusion about this, as the word was never intended to be pronounced with its modern "y" sound.

In ➡Anglo-Saxon there was a letter, now lost, called *thorn*, pronounced like today's "th" yet looking somewhat like the modern "y," which had not yet been invented.

Indeed, the modern letter "y" evolved, quite separately, from the habit of merging the two letters "i" and "j" which when written together were pronounced as "y" is now. The "ij" combination is still found in present-day Dutch. When printing came along, *thorn* and "y" were confused, hence "ye."

the **year dot** *idiom, coll.* a very great time ago

yellow card *comp. noun* a card shown by a referee to a soccer player who is being warned for a breach in the rules

yellow {duster » flag » jack} *comp. noun, coll.* a ➡sick-flag flown from a ship

yellow line *comp. noun, coll.* a marking painted along the side of a road to indicted parking restrictions
Either a single line or two parallel lines may be there. Two lines indicates that parking is even more severely restricted than when there is one line only.

yeoman *noun, hist.* (1) a self-supporting small farmer; (2) a man who owned his own land and thus was qualified to serve on a jury; (3) a member of the ➡yeomanry

yeomanry *noun, hist.* a volunteer cavalry force, first raised in 1794 and disbanded in 1908

Yeoman Usher *pr. name* ➡Black Rod's deputy

Yeoman Warder *pr. name* a ➡Tower of London ➡guard

the **Yeomen of the Guard** *pr. name* the bodyguards of the ➡monarch
They should not be confused with the ➡Yeoman Warders of the ➡Tower of London who wear similar uniforms.

yersel *pronoun, Sc.* yourself

yestreen *noun, Sc.* yesterday or last night

yett [A] *noun, Sc.* (1) a gate; (2) a pass through hills
[B] *verb, East* to eat

yeuk *verb, Sc.* to scratch or itch

YHA *pr. name, abbr.* the Youth Hostel Association

yin *pronoun, Sc.* (1) one; (2) oneself

{yob » yobbo} *noun, sl.* a lout or hooligan
"Yob" is ➡backslang evolved from "boy."

yobbery *noun, sl.* hooliganism

yobbish *adj., sl.* in the manner of a ➡yob

{yodelled » yodelling} *spell.* {yodeled » yodeling}

yoghurt *spell.* yogurt

yomp *noun, sl.* a forced military march in full kit

yonks *noun, sl.* a very long time

yon time *idiom, coll., Sc.* very late at night

yoof *noun, sl.* youth

York *pr. name, hist., Lat.* (1) a city on the Ouse River in ➡North Yorkshire; (2) a subsidiary name used for the ➡Royal House of England from 1461 to 1485
(1) was established as a military garrison town called *Edoracum* by the Romans in the 1st C. It became the Roman military headquarters of their province of Britain and by the 7th C. it had become capital of the ➡Anglo-Saxon kingdom of ➡Northumbria. In 867 it became Danish, who called it *Jorvik*. There has been a cathedral at York since Anglo-Saxon times, and it was then that the city's bishop was made up to the rank of archbishop. Incorporated as a city in 1396, the current population is 100,000 (1988 estimate).

(2) was subsidiary because the Royal House before, during and after the years referred to was ➡Anjou, with "York" a subsidiary name without independent existence.

Both ➡Lancaster and "York" derive from the two sides of the ➡Wars of the Roses, who were the parties of the Duke of Lancaster and the Duke of York—both princes of ➡Anjou. The following English monarchs belonged to this subsidiary house: ➡Edward IV, ➡Edward V and ➡Richard III.

381

yorker *noun* a ➡cricket ball pitched so as to bounce immediately before the bat

Yorkist *noun, hist.* a supporter or member of the ➡House of York during the ➡Wars of the Roses

York Minster *pr. name, hist.* the largest medieval cathedral in the British Isles

Located in ➡York, the present structure dates from the 13th C.

Yorkshire *pr. name, hist.* a former English County

Now divided between ➡North Yorkshire, ➡West Yorkshire and ➡South Yorkshire, with other parts distributed between ➡Humberside, ➡Cleveland, ➡Durham, ➡Cumbria and ➡Lancashire. Yorkshire was the largest of the old English counties and was itself divided into three ➡Ridings, which were in effect counties in their own right.

the **Yorkshire Dales** *pr. name* part of the ➡Pennine mountain chain, made a ➡national park in 1954

Although mostly in ➡Yorkshire, part is in ➡Cumbria.

{**Yorkshireman » Yorkshirewoman**} *pr. name.* a native, citizen or inhabitant of ➡Yorkshire

Yorkshire pudding *comp. noun* a baked batter made from egg, flour and milk, baked with fat and traditionally eaten with roast beef

SEE ALSO: ➡roast beef and Yorkshire pudding.

the **Yorkshire Ripper** *pr. name, hist.* the nickname devised by the press for Peter Sutcliffe, a trucker from ➡Bradford in Yorkshire, who murdered 13 women and attempted the murder of 7 more, in the north of England between 1975 and 1980

Like ➡Jack the Ripper, he appeared to have a particular urge to murder and mutilate prostitutes. For a long time it seemed that like his 19th C. namesake, his identity would never be revealed but he was arrested in 1981.

Yorkshire Terrier *pr. name* a small long-haired terrier

Yorkshire TV *pr. name* a local commercial TV company headquartered in Leeds

It is part of the ➡ITV network.

you and me *idiom, rh. sl.* cup of tea

you lot *idiom, coll.* you-all, all of you

Young *noun, arch., Sc.* a ➡Highland chief's oldest son

As in "Young Lochinvar" or "Young Pretender"

the **Young Chevalier** *pr. name, hist.* the ➡Young Pretender, ➡Charles Edward Stuart

the **younger** *noun, out., Sc.* junior

A postscript name indicative that the bearer is the younger of two persons with the same name, especially if the two are father and son. Thus, "Douglas McPherson the younger" = "Douglas McPherson Junior."

young fogey *comp. noun, coll.* a young person with old-fashioned ideas, particularly those tending toward the right wing in politics

young offenders institution *comp. noun* a special prison for offenders under 21 years of age

Charles Edward Stuart, Bonny Prince Charlie, or the Young Pretender

the **Young Pretender** *pr. name, hist.* ➡Charles Edward Stuart, son of the ➡Old Pretender and grandson of ➡James II of England and VII of Scotland

He was popularly known as ➡Bonny Prince Charlie, and also as the ➡Young Cavalier or ➡Young Chevalier.

He was born in Rome and proclaimed ➡Prince of Wales that same day. He was brought up to speak French as his first language and had a very tenuous grasp of English, let alone its Scottish variety. In 1745 he arrived in Scotland and proclaimed his father King ➡James VIII of Scotland and III of England, so beginning the last ➡Jacobite attempt at the British Throne, the ➡Forty-Five Rebellion.

After considerable initial success, his army was routed by the Duke of Cumberland's army at ➡Culloden, near Inverness. Charles fled with a price of £30,000 (a very considerable fortune at that time, equivalent to perhaps $3 or $4 million in today's money) on his head, but was never betrayed and after five months escaped to France. The rest of his life was an anti-climactic decline into boorish drunkenness until he died, almost entirely forgotten, in Rome in 1788.

SEE ALSO: ➡pretender; ➡Old Pretender; ➡Young, ➡Jacobite.

your Grace *pr. name, hist.* (1) an honorific title used as a form of address to the monarch; (2) an honorific title used as a form of address to a ➡duke, ➡duchess or ➡archbishop

your {humble » obedient » humble and obedient} servant *idiom, out.* archaic ways to terminate a formal correspondence

your Ladyship *idiom* an honorific title used when addressing a ➡Lady

your Lordship *pr. name* an honorific title used when addressing a man with the rank of ➡lord

your worship *idiom* an honorific title used as a form of address to certain judges, mayors, etc.

youth court *comp. noun* a special magistrates court for young people aged between 10 and 17

yowe *noun, Sc.* ewe, a female sheep

the First Battle of Ypres *pr. name, hist.* a World War I battle fought in October and November 1914

This is where the newly-arrived ➡BEF prevented the advancing German Army from reaching the ➡Channel coast but were themselves almost exterminated in the process. Ypres is in Belgium, some 25 miles east of ➡Dunkirk.

the Second Battle of Ypres *pr. name, hist.* a World War I battle fought in April and May 1915

This is when the Germans became the first to use poison gas (chlorine) in warfare, against British troops.

the Third Battle of Ypres *pr. name, hist.* a World War I battle fought from June to November 1917

This time, mostly Canadian ➡British Empire troops advanced a few miles at a cost of almost 300,000 lives on each side.

Ystrad Towy *pr. name, hist.* an ancient kingdom that was in southwestern Wales

It is known to have been in existence by 700. During the 9th C., Ystrad Towy was united with ➡Ceredigion to form ➡Seisyllwg.

YTS *pr. name, abbr.* the Youth Training Scheme

A government program set up to train young people in the skills that will help them find employment.

zaffre *spell.* zaffer

A blue pigment.

zebra crossing *comp. noun* a pedestrian road crossing

Named from the way in which the alternate black and white stripes painted upon the highway surface to indicate where such a crossing is, resembles the coat of a zebra.

zed *noun* the letter "zee"

How the last letter of the alphabet is pronounced in Britain.

zed-axis *comp. noun* the zee-axis

The third coordinate of a geometric system.

zero-rate *adj. phr.* a VAT rate of zero percent

SEE ALSO: ➡VAT exempt. The two conditions are not the same, although the difference is not immediately apparent, except to an accountant perhaps.

Zetland *pr. name, hist.* a former Scottish county, now ➡Shetland Island Council

zibet *spell.* zibeth

A kind of skunk-like creature native to India, its formal name is *viverra zibetha*.

zimmer frame *comp. noun* a disabled or elderly person's tubular metal frame with rubberized feet, which helps them walk

zip *noun, abbr.* a zipper

zip fastener *comp. noun* a slide fastener or zipper

zizz *noun, coll.* a snooze or nap

{zoogloea » zoogloeal} *spell.* {zooglea » zoogleal}

A mass of bacterial matter.

Appendix 1: About Spelling

Although most people know that there are differences between American and British spelling, learning just how many words are in this category surprises many. Indeed, although considerably more than one thousand examples are listed in this dictionary, there are many times that number in the English language. Admittedly most of the unlisted ones are obscure or highly specialist or both, and so do not belong in a general dictionary like this, although a cross-section have been recorded to exemplify the way spelling differences permeate every corner of activity.

The reason for so many differences is usually put down to the efforts of Noah Webster, citizen of Hartford, Connecticut, a failed lawyer, itinerant schoolteacher and obsessive lexicographer. He lived from 1758 to 1843 and is now best-known for his *American Dictionary of the English Language*, published in 1828.

Webster believed that American English was just as good and proper and acceptable as the British version. On every possible occasion he preached his gospel to all who would listen and many who would rather not.

His campaign began forty years before he published his dictionary, when his *American Spelling Book* appeared in 1788. This rapidly became and then remained for many decades the standard spelling primer used in public schools throughout the United States. It is said that by the end of the 19th century it had sold as many as eighty million copies, making it the best-selling book in the history of the United States after the Bible. Considering that each copy had been used by at least one and sometimes by several school students, clearly this little volume must have had a huge influence upon the way generations of Americans were going to spell English.

From *Spelling Book* to *American Dictionary*, Webster worked tirelessly at his theme, writing polemics, revising his speller, writing to Congress and presidents, lecturing audiences throughout the land, visiting every printing shop he could find to cajole them into using his spelling list when typesetting.

However the truth is that although many of the spelling differences between America and Britain we have today can be laid a Webster's door, they are not all his, and not all his were adopted. Who now spells, except by accident, *groop* for *group*, *fantom* for *phantom*, or *hed* for *head*, as he proposed? And even within his own dictionary, Webster was not consistent; for example, he left *acre* and *glamour* alone.

After a visit to England, Webster was moved to write in his dictionary's preface that it was "desirable to perpetuate the sameness" of British and American spelling.

Well, we have and have not done that. There are differences, clearly, and they are many. But few are truly radical, and there are some rules that can provide at least some sort of hint about how they differ, although no rule is without its exceptions.

HOW BRITISH AND AMERICAN SPELLING DIFFER

(1)   Where Americans use the suffix *-er*, Britons tend to use *-re*.

For example, *center* becomes *centre*, and *meager* becomes *meagre*. However, both groups use *-er* in words that describe persons, for example *foreigner* or *adviser*; nouns denoting verbal action, such as *supper* or *catheter* and in many verbs, like *cater* or *plunder*.

By the way, this is a change from British spelling that Webster liked to take credit for, but the truth is it was already well established by the time he came along.

(2)   Where Americans use the suffix *-ize*, Britons will tend to use *-ise.*

However some authorities (especially the *Oxford English Dictionary*, which is too significant a source to be dismissed out of hand) contend that "-ize" is correct usage for Britons too. It must be said that very little justification for this assertion can be found in most British writings, but because of this divergence of view there are a large number of questionable spellings in this category which are not included in the main body of the dictionary and listed in Appendix Two instead. However, Britons undoubtedly do use *-ize* in the case of a number of synthetic verbs such as *transistorize* or—appropriately—*Americanize*, and there are also a number of examples of joint American and British use of the *-ise* form, as with *advertise* or *comprise*.

(3) Where Americans use *-e-* in many words of Latin origin, the British will tend to use *-ae-* or *-oe-*, which happens to be a more accurate rendition of the original Latin spelling of the root-word but plays no phonetic part in modern words derived from that source. For example in the case of *-ae-*, *encyclopedia* becomes *encyclopaedia* and *septicemia* becomes *septicaemia* in Britain; in the case of *-oe-*, *diarrhea* becomes *diarrhoea* and *maneuver* becomes *manoeuvre*. However there has been a discernible British tendency towards the American practice in this matter in recent years.

(4) Where Americans use the suffix *-or*, the British will tend to use *-our*.

For example, *clamor* becomes *clamour*, *rumor* becomes *rumour* and most famously, *color* becomes *colour*. Yet *governor* remains *governor*, *censor* is still *censor* and both groups use *glamour*.

Here is another change from British spelling that Webster liked to take credit for, but in fact was already well under way by the time he came along.

(5) Where Americans use *-l-*, the British tend to use *-ll-* in certain verbs inflected with suffixes such as *-ing*, *-ed* or *-or*.

For example, *leveled* becomes *levelled* although the root-verb *level* is unchanged, *jeweler* becomes *jeweller* but *jewel* does not change, and *traveling* becomes *travelling* yet *travel* is the same. However *sailor* and *sailing* are spelled identically in America and Britain, as are *mailed* and *mailing*.

(6) On the other hand (and confusingly) occasionally this rule seems to go into reverse, and words or morphones terminating with *-ll* in America will terminate with *-l* in Britain, as for example when the adjectival derivative of the commonly spelled *skill*, *skillful*, becomes *skilful*, the verb *distill* becomes *distil* in Britain, or the American *install* and its derivative *installment* become *instal* and *instalment*.

(7) There is an American tendency to use the suffix *-ense*, while *-ence* is more common among Britons, as with *license* and *licence*, or *defense* and *defence*. Yet *license* is how the word is spelled when it is employed as a verb in Britain, and *intense* and *immense* are the common spellings of these words among both groups.

(8) The American prefix *in-* is commonly rendered as *en-* by Britons, such as when *insure* becomes *ensure* or *inclose* becomes *enclose*.

(9) As a rule, the American suffix *-og* is transmuted into *-ogue* in Britain, as when for example *catalog* turns into *catalogue* or *prolog* into *prologue*. However, in computing, *catalog* is universal.

(10) The American word (and sometimes suffix) *(-)gram* normally becomes *(-)gramme* in Britain.

Thus *kilogram* becomes *kilogramme* and the word *program* is spelled *programme*. However in computing the American form is ubiquitous.

(11) The American habit of adding a period at the end of certain abbreviations such as *Mr.* or *Dr.* is much rarer in British usage.

(12) Hyphenation of compound words is commoner in British than American usage. For example, *cooperation* is rendered as *co-operation* and *passerby* turns into *passer-by*.

(13) There are a number of individual words where Americans and Britons employ different spellings, but are not part of a more general rule.

By the way, it is not always the American spelling that is more rational that the British, as most suppose. Sometimes the boot is on the other foot, as when *whiskey* becomes *whisky* in Britain, *spelled* becomes *spelt* or *curb* becomes *kerb*.

Appendix 2: Words Ending in *-ise*

Many words ending with "-ize" are regularly spelled with an "-ise" ending by users of British English. However, this is not a uniform practice and indeed, the Oxford English Dictionary insists that "-ize" endings are the correct ones. Because this is an area of some uncertainty or doubt, these words have been removed from the main dictionary and instead are listed here.

In practice, there should be little difficulty or confusion understanding or using either spelling in Britain.

acclimatise:acclimatize
Americanise:Americanize
anaesthetise:anesthetize
anatomise:anatomize
Anglicise:Anglicize
animalise:animalize
antagonise:antagonize
apologise:apologize
apotheasise:apotheasize
appetise:appetize
archaise:archaize
arterialise:arterialize
atomise:atomize
automatise:automatize
baptise:baptize
bowdlerise:bowdlerize
cannibalise:cannibalize
capitalise:capitalize
catechise:catechize
categorise:categorize
cauterise:cauterize
centralise:centralize
characterise:characterize
Christianise:Christianize
circularise:circularize
civilianise:civilianize
civilise:civilize
classicise:classicize
collectivise:collectivize
colonise:colonize
colourise:colorize
commercialise:commercialize
communalise:communalize
communise:communize
compartmentalise:compartmentalize
computerise:computerize
conceptualise:conceptualize
concretise:concretize
containerise:containerize
contextualise:contextualize
conventionalise:conventionalize
cosmopolitanise:cosmopolitanize
creolise:creolize
cretinise:cretinize
criticise:criticize
cross-fertilise:cross-fertilize

crystallise:crystallize
customise:customize
de-emphasise:de-emphasize
decarbonise:decarbonize
decentralise:decentralize
decimalise:decimalize
decolonise:decolonize
decolourise:decolorize
decriminalise:decriminalize
dehumanise:dehumanize
deinstitutionalise:deinstitutionalize
deionise:deionize
delocalise:delocalize
demagnetise:demagnetize
dematerialise:dematerialize
demilitarise:demilitarize
demineralise:demineralize
demobilise:demobilize
democratise:democratize
demonetise:demonetize
demonise:demonize
demoralise:demoralize
demythologise:demythologize
denationalise:denationalize
denaturalise:denaturalize
denuclearise:denuclearize
deodorise:deodorize
departmentalise:departmentalize
depersonalise:depersonalize
depolarise:depolarize
depoliticise:depoliticize
depolymerise:depolymerize
depressurise:depressurize
deputise:deputize
desensitise:desensitize
desexualise:desexualize
destabilise:destabilize
detribalise:detribalize
devitalise:devitalize
diabilise:diabilize
dialise:dialize
diarise:diarize
dieselise:dieselize
digitalise:digitalize
digitise:digitize
diphthongise:diphthongize

disharmonise:disharmonize
disillusionise:disillusionize
disorganise:disorganize
divinise:divinize
dogmatise:dogmatize
dramatise:dramatize
dualise:dualize
economise:economize
ecstasise:ecstasize
editorialise:editorialize
egotise:egotize
Egyptianise:Egyptianize
elasticise:elasticize
elegise:elegize
emblematise:emblematize
emotionalise:emotionalize
emphasise:emphasize
emulsionise:emulsionize
energise:energize
enigmatise:enigmatize
epimerise:epimerize
epitomise:epitomize
eternalise:eternalize
eternise:eternize
etherise:etherize
etymologise:etymologize
eulogise:eulogize
euphemise:euphemize
euphomise:euphomize
Europeanise:Europeanize
evangelise:evangelize
experimentalise:experimentalize
expertise:expertize
extemporise:extemporize
exteriorise:exteriorize
externalise:externalize
factionalise:factionalize
factorise:factorize
familiarise:familiarize
fanaticise:fanaticize
fantasise:fantasize
federalise:federalize
feminise:feminize
fertilise:fertilize
feudalise:feudalize
fictionalise:fictionalize

387

finalise:finalize
fluidise:fluidize
focalise:focalize
formalise:formalize
formularise:formularize
fossilise:fossilize
fractionise:fractionize
fragmentise:fragmentize
fraternise:fraternize
galvanise:galvanize
genealogise:genealogize
generalise:generalize
geologise:geologize
Germanise:Germanize
glamourise:glamourize
gluttonise:gluttonize
gorgonise:gorgonize
gormandise:gormandize
Gothicise:Gothicize
Græcise:Grecize
graphitise:graphitize
harmonise:harmonize
Hebraise:Hebraize
Hellenise:Hellenize
heparinise:heparinize
heroise:heroize
hierarchise:hierarchize
Hispanicise:Hispanicize
homogenise:homogenize
homologise:homologize
hospitalise:hospitalize
humanise:humanize
hybridise:hybridize
hypnotise:hypnotize
hypostasise:hypostasize
hypothesise:hypothesize
hysterectomise:hysterectomize
idealise:idealize
idolise:idolize
idyllise:idyllize
immobilise:immobilize
immortalise:immortalize
immunise:immunize
imperialise:imperialize
indigenise:indigenize
individualise:individualize
industrialise:industrialize
initialise:initialize
insolubilise:insolubilize
institutionalise:institutionalize
intellectualise:intellectualize
interiorise:interiorize
internalise:internalize
internationalise:internationalize
iodise:iodize
ionise:ionize
ironise:ironize
irrationalise:irrationalize
Islamise:Islamize
isomerise:isomerize
italicise:italicize

itemise:itemize
jargonise:jargonize
jeopardise:jeopardize
journalise:journalize
Judaise:Judaize
kaolinise:kaolinize
keratinise:keratinize
kyanise:kyanize
labialise:labialize
laicise:laicize
Latinise:Latinize
legalise:legalize
legitimatise:legitimatize
legitimise:legitimize
liberalise:liberalize
lingualise:lingualize
lionise:lionize
liquidise:liquidize
literalise:literalize
lithotomise:lithotomize
localise:localize
Lutheranise:Lutheranize
lyophilise:lyophilize
macadamise:macadamize
magnetise:magnetize
marginalise:marginalize
martyrise:martyrize
materialise:materialize
maximise:maximize
mechanise:mechanize
medievalise:medievalize
melodise:melodize
melodramatise : melodramatize
memorialise:memorialize
memorise:memorize
mercerise:mercerize
mesmerise:mesmerize
metabolise:metabolize
metastasise:metastasize
methodise:methodize
metricise:metricize
militarise:militarize
mineralise:mineralize
miniaturise:miniaturize
minimise:minimize
misanthropise:misanthropize
mithridatise:mithridatize
mobilise:mobilize
modernise:modernize
moisturise:moisturize
monasticise:monasticize
monetise:monetize
mongrelise:mongrelize
monologise:monologize
monopolise:monopolize
monotonise:monotonize
monumentalise : monumentalize
moralise:moralize
motorise:motorize
municipalise:municipalize
musicalise:musicalize

mythicise:mythicize
mythologise:mythologize
narcotise:narcotize
nasalise:nasalize
nationalise:nationalize
naturalise:naturalize
necrotise:necrotize
neologise:neologize
neutralise:neutralize
nicotinise:nicotinize
nomadise:nomadize
nominalise:nominalize
normalise:normalize
Normanise:Normanize
notarise:notarize
novelise:novelize
nuclearise:nuclearize
obelise:obelize
objectivise:objectivize
occidentalise:occidentalize
odorise:odorize
optimise:optimize
organise:organize
orientalise:orientalize
orphanise:orphanize
ostracise:ostracize
overcapitalise:overcapitalize
overemphasise:overemphasize
overgeneralise:overgeneralize
overspecialise:overspecialize
oxidise:oxidize
oxygenise:oxygenize
ozonise:ozonize
paganise:paganize
palatalise:palatalize
palletise:palletize
panegyrise:panegyrize
paralogise:paralogize
parametrise:parametrize
parasitise:parasitize
parenthesise:parenthesize
particularise:particularize
pasteurise:pasteurize
patronise:patronize
pauperise:pauperize
pedantise:pedantize
pedestrianise:pedestrianize
pelletise:pelletize
penalise:penalize
peptonise:peptonize
permanentise:permanentize
personalise:personalize
phagocytise:phagocytize
phantasise:phantasize
phenomenalise:phenomenalize
philanthropise:philanthropize
philologise:philologize
philosophise:philosophize
phlebotomise:phlebotomize
phoneticise:phoneticize
photosynthesise:photosynthesize

pilgrimise:pilgrimize
plagiarise:plagiarize
plasticise:plasticize
platinise:platinize
platitudinise:platitudinize
pluralise:pluralize
podzolise:podzolize
poeticise:poeticize
poetise:poetize
polarise:polarize
polemicise:polemicize
polemise:polemize
politicise:politicize
polymerise:polymerize
popularise:popularize
potentialise:potentialize
pragmatise:pragmatize
preconise:preconize
pressurise:pressurize
prioritise:prioritize
prise:prize *(As in "force open or apart".)*
privatise:privatize
professionalise:professionalize
proletarianise:proletarianize
prologise:prologize
pronominalise:pronominalize
propagandise:propagandize
proselytise:proselytize
Protestantise:Protestantize
provincialise:provincialize
psalmodise:psalmodize
psychologise:psychologize
publicise:publicize
pulverise:pulverize
pyritise:pyritize
quantise:quantize
racemise:racemize
radicalise:radicalize
randomise:randomize
rationalise:rationalize
realise:realize
recapitalise:recapitalize
recognise:recognize
recolonise:recolonize
recrystallise:recrystallize
regionalise:regionalize
regularise:regularize
remonetise:remonetize
reorganise:reorganize
reutilise:reutilize
revitalise:revitalize
revolutionise:revolutionize
rhapsodise:rhapsodize
ritualise:ritualize
robotise:robotize
romanise:romanize

romanticise:romanticize
routinise:routinize
rubberise:rubberize
ruralise:ruralize
Russianise:Russianize
sanitise:sanitize
Satanise:Satanize
satirise:satirize
Saxonise:Saxonize
scandalise:scandalize
schematise:schematize
scrutinise:scrutinize
sectarianise:sectarianize
sectionalise:sectionalize
secularise:secularize
segmentalise:segmentalize
Semitise:Semitize
sensitise:sensitize
serialise:serialize
sermonise:sermonize
sexualise:sexualize
signalise:signalize
singularise:singularize
skeletonise:skeletonize
slenderise:slenderize
socialise:socialize
sodomise:sodomize
solarise:solarize
solemnise:solemnize
soliloquise:soliloquize
solubilise:solubilize
Sovietise:Sovietize
spatialise:spatialize
specialise:specialize
spiritualise:spiritualize
stabilise:stabilize
standardise:standardize
sterilise:sterilize
stigmatise:stigmatize
stylise:stylize
subcategorise:subcategorize
subsidise:subsidize
substantialise:substantialize
subtilise:subtilize
suburbanise:suburbanize
sulphurise:sulphurize
summarise:summarize
supernaturalise:supernaturalize
syllabise:syllabize
syllogise:syllogize
symbolise:symbolize
symmetrise:symmetrize
sympathise:sympathize
synchronise:synchronize
syncretise:syncretize
synopsise:synopsize

synthesise:synthesize
syphilise:syphilize
systematise:systematize
tantalise:tantalize
tartarise:tartarize
tautologise:tautologize
telepathise:telepathize
temporise:temporize
tenderise:tenderize
territorialise:territorialize
terrorise:terrorize
tetanise:tetanize
texturise:texturize
theatricalise:theatricalize
theologise:theologize
theorise:theorize
thermalise:thermalize
totalise:totalize
tranquillise:tranquilize
transcendentalise:transcendentalize
transistorise:transistorize
traumatise:traumatize
tribalise:tribalize
trivialise:trivialize
tyrannise:tyrannize
undercapitalise:undercapitalize
underemphasise:underemphasize
unequalise:unequalize
unionise:unionize
universalise:universalize
urbanise:urbanize
utilise:utilize
valourise:valorize
vandalise:vandalize
vaporise:vaporize
vascularise:vascularize
vasectomise:vasectomize
vectorise:vectorize
ventriloquise:ventriloquize
verbalise:verbalize
vernacularise:vernacularize
vernalise:vernalize
verticalise:verticalize
victimise:victimize
visualise:visualize
vitalise:vitalize
vitaminise:vitaminize
vocalise:vocalize
vocationalise:vocationalize
volatilise:volatilize
vowelise:vowelize
vulcanise:vulcanize
vulgarise:vulgarize
westernise:westernize
winterise:winterize
womanise:womanize

Appendix 3: Bibliography

Allen, R.E., ed. *The Concise Oxford Dictionary of Current English.* 8th ed., Oxford and New York: Oxford University Press, 1990.

Augarde, Tony, ed. *The Oxford Dictionary of Modern Quotations.* Oxford and New York: Oxford University Press, 1991.

Ayto, John and John Simpson. *The Oxford Dictionary of Modern Slang.* Oxford and New York: Oxford University Press, 1992.

Bailey, Richard W. *Images of English: A Cultural History of the Language.* Ann Arbor: University of Michigan Press, 1991.

Barraclough, Geoffrey, ed. *The Times Concise Atlas of World History.* London: Times Books, 1986.

Baugh, A. C. and T. Cable. *A History of the English Language.* London: Routledge and Kegan Paul, 1978.

Borowski, E. J. and J. M. Borwein. *Dictionary of Mathematics.* Glasgow: Collins, 1989.

Brewer, E. Cobham. *Brewer's Dictionary of Phrase and Fable.* 8th ed., Ivor H. Evans, ed. London; Cassell, 1977 (first published 1870).

Brough, Stephen, ed. *The Economist Atlas.* London: Century Hutchinson, 1989.

Bryson, Bill. *Made in America.* London: Seeker and Warburg, 1994.

—— *Mother Tongue: The English Language.* London and New York: Penguin, 1990.

—— *The Penguin Dictionary for Writers and Editors.* London and New York: Penguin, 1991.

—— *The Penguin Dictionary of Troublesome Words.* London and New York: Penguin, 1984.

Burchfield, Robert. *Unlocking the English Language.* London: Faber and Faber, 1989.

Carpenter, Clive, ed. *The Guinness Book of Answers.* 8th ed., London: Guiness Publishing, 1991.

Chapman, Robert L., ed. *The Dictionary of American Slang.* London: Macmillan, 1988.

Clairborne, Robert. *The Life and Times of the English Language.* New York: Random House, 1983.

Clark, James ed. *The Encyclopedia of Modern History.* London: Hamlyn, 1978.

Clark, John O. E. *English Punctuation and Hyphenation.* London and Paris: Harrup 1990.

—— *Word Perfect: A Dictionary of Current English Usage.* London and Paris: Harrup, 1987.

Craigie, Sir William A. *The Growth of American English.* Oxford: Oxford University Press, 1940.

Crystal, David, *The Cambridge Encyclopedia of Language.* Cambridge and New York: Cambridge University Press, 1987.

—— *Who Cares About English Usage?* London and New York: Penguin, 1984.

Dear, I. C. B., comp. *Oxford English: A Guide to the Language.* Oxford and New York: Oxford University Press, 1989.

Eastway, Robert. *What is a Googly?* London: Robson Books, 1992.

Fowler, F. G. and H. W. Fowler. *The King's English.* 3rd. ed., Oxford and New York: Oxford University Press, 1985.

Fowler, H. W. *A Dictionary of Modern English Usage.* 2nd. ed., Sir Ernest Gowers, ed. Oxford and New York: Oxford University Press, 1974, (first published 1926).

Franklyn, Julian, *A Dictionary of Rhyming Slang.* 2nd ed., London and New York: Routledge 1961.

Fraser, Antonia, ed. *The Lives of the Kings and Queens of England.* London: Weidenfold and Nicolson, 1975.

390

Freeman-Grenville, G. S. P. *Atlas of British History.* London: Rex Collings, 1979.

Gascoigne, Bamber. *The Encyclopedia of Britain.* Basingstoke: Macmillan Press, 1993.

Gilbert, Martin. *American History Atlas.* London: Weidenfeld and Nicolson, 1968.

Gottfried, Robert S. *The Black Death.* London: Robert Hale, 1986.

Gowers, Sir Ernest. *The Complete Plain Words.* London: H.M. Stationary Office, 1954.

Green, Jonathon. *Slang Down the Ages:* London: Kyle Cathie, 1993.

Grimond, John. *The Economist Pocket Style Book.* London: The Economist Publications, 1986.

Harrison, J. F. C. *The Common People.* London: Fontana, 1984.

Hendrickson, Robert. *The Facts on File Encyclopedia of Word and Phrase Origins.* New York: Facts on File Publications, 1980.

Hobsbawm, Eric and Terence Ranger, eds. *The Invention of Tradition.* Cambridge and New York: Cambridge University Press, 1983.

Holt, Alfred. H. *Phrase and Word Origins.* New York: Dover Publications, 1961.

Hornby, A. S. *The Oxford Paperback American Dictionary.* Oxford and New York: Oxford University Press, 1986.

Kay, Billy. *Scots. The Mither Tongue.* Edinburgh: Mainstream, 1986.

McCrum, R., W. Cran, and R. MacNeil. *The Story of English.* New York: Viking, 1986.

Marsden, Hilary, ed. *Whitaker's Almanack.* 126th annual vol., London: Whitaker, 1994 (first published in 1868).

Mencken, H. L. and Raven I. McDavid. *The American Language: An Enquiry into the Development of English in the United States.* abbrev. 4th ed., New York: Alfred A. Knopf, 1989.

Mish, Frederick C., ed. *Webster's Ninth New Collegiate Dictionary.* Springfield, MA: Merriam-Webster, 1991.

Moore, W. G. *The Penguin Encyclopedia of Places.* London and New York: Penguin, 1971.

Morris, James. *Heaven's Command: An Imperial Progress.* London: Faber and Faber, 1973.

—— *Pax Britannica: The Climax of an Empire.* London: Faber and Faber, 1968.

—— *Farewell The Trumpets: An Imperial Retreat.* London: Faber and Faber, 1978.

Munro, Michael. *The Patter: A Guide to Current Glasgow Usage.* Glasgow: Glasgow District Libraries, 1985.

—— *The Patter: Another Blast.* Edinburgh: Cannongate, 1988.

Murison, David. *The Guid Scots Tongue.* Edinburgh: Blackwood, 1977.

O'Leary, John and Tom Cannon, eds. *Good Universities Guide.* London: Times Books, 1993.

Picard, Gilbert Charles, ed. *The Larousse Encyclopedia of Archaeology.* London and New York: Hamlyn, 1972.

Pickering, D., A. Isaacs, and E. Martin, eds. *Brewer's Dictionary of Twentieth Century Phrase and Fable.* London: Cassell, 1991.

Partridge, Eric, and J. W. Clark. *British and American English Since 1900.* London: Andrew Dakers, 1951.

Partridge, Eric. *The Dictionary of Historical Slang.* London and New York: Penguin, 1972.

—— *Slang Today and Yesterday.* London: Routledge and Kegan Paul,1970.

—— *Usage and Abusage.* London and New York: Penguin, 1971.

Robinson, Mairi, ed. *The Concise Scots Dictionary.* Aberdeen: Aberdeen University Press 1985.

Roget, Peter M. *Roget's Thesaurus.* new ed., Susan M. Lloyd, ed. London and New York: Longman, 1982.

Room, Adrian. *A Concise Dictionary of Modern Place-Names in Great Britain and Ireland.* Oxford and New York: Oxford University Press, 1983.

—— *An A to Z of British Life.* Oxford and New York: Oxford University Press, 1990.

Safire, William. *On Language.* New York: Avon Books, 1980.

Thorne, Tony. *Dictionary of Modern Slang.* London: Bloomsbury, 1990.

Tinniswood, Adrian, ed. *The National Trust Historic Houses Handbook.* London: The National Trust, 1993.

Todd, Loretto and Ian Hancock, eds. *International English Usage.* London: Routledge, 1990.

Tullock, Sara. *The Oxford Dictionary of New Words.* Oxford and New York: Oxford University Press, 1991.

Urdang, Laurence. *A Dictionary of Differences.* London: Bloomsbury, 1988.

Uvarov, E. B. and A. Issacs. *The Penguin Dictionary of Science.* London and New York: Penguin, 1987.

Walmsley, Jane. *Brit-Think. Ameri-Think.* London: Harrup, 1986.

Wedgewood. C.V. *The King's Peace.* Glasgow: Collins, 1955.

—— *The King's War.* Glasgow: Collins, 1958.

Wills, Garry. *Lincoln at Gettysburg: The Words that Remade America.* New York: Simon and Schuster, 1992.

Wood, Frederick T. *Current English Usage,* L. M. and R. H. Flavell, eds., London: Macmillan Press, 1981.

Appendix 4: Maps

The British Isles
Political

International frontier between the UK and the Irish Republic.

National borders within the UK; provincial borders within Ireland

Note (i): Northern Ireland is the only part of Ireland which is part of the UK. It lies entirely within the province of Ulster, but not all of Ulster is within Northern Ireland.

Note (2) The Isle of Man is British, but it is not part of the United Kingdom.

The Four Ancient Provinces of Ireland

(C) Connaught
(L) Leinster
(M) Munster
(U) Ulster

Northern Ireland

THE UNITED KINGDOM OF GREAT BRITAIN AND NORTHERN IRELAND

Scotland

Isle of Man

England

Wales

THE IRISH REPUBLIC

London

50 40 30 20 10 0   25   50   100
Scale   in miles

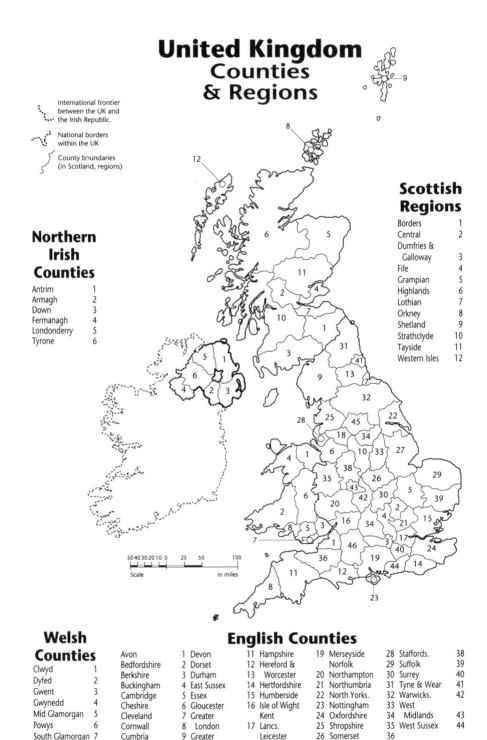

United Kingdom
Counties
& Regions

Scottish Regions

Borders	1
Central	2
Dumfries & Galloway	3
Fife	4
Grampian	5
Highlands	6
Lothian	7
Orkney	8
Shetland	9
Strathclyde	10
Tayside	11
Western Isles	12

Northern Irish Counties

Antrim	1
Armagh	2
Down	3
Fermanagh	4
Londonderry	5
Tyrone	6

Scale 50 40 30 20 10 0 25 50 100 in miles

Welsh Counties

Clwyd	1
Dyfed	2
Gwent	3
Gwynedd	4
Mid Glamorgan	5
Powys	6
South Glamorgan	7
West Glamorgan	8

English Counties

Avon		Devon	1	Hampshire	11
Bedfordshire		Dorset	2	Hereford & Worcester	12
Berkshire		Durham	3	Hertfordshire	14
Buckingham		East Sussex	4	Humberside	15
Cambridge		Essex	5	Isle of Wight	16
Cheshire		Gloucester	6	Kent	17
Cleveland		Greater London	7	Lancs.	18
Cornwall		Greater Manchester	8 / 10	Lincoln	18
Derbyshire					

Merseyside	19	Staffords.	28
Norfolk		Suffolk	29
Northampton	20	Surrey	30
Northumbria	21	Tyne & Wear	31
North Yorks.	22	Warwicks.	32
Nottingham	23	West Midlands	33
Oxfordshire	24	West Sussex	35
Shropshire	25		38
Somerset	26		39
South Yorks.	27		40
			41
			42
			43
			44

394

United Kingdom
Physical Features

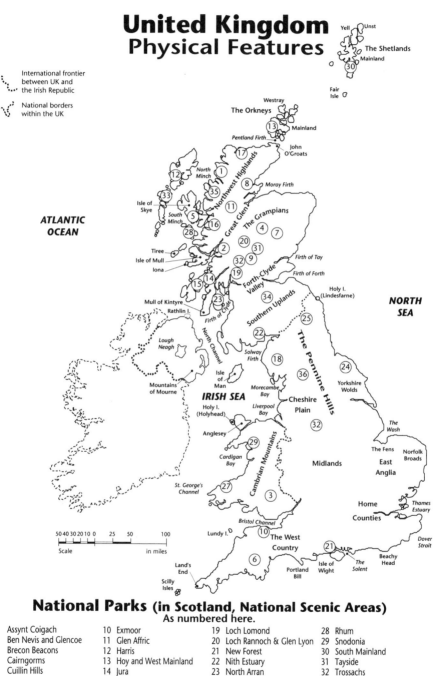

International frontier between UK and the Irish Republic

National borders within the UK

Yell · Unst
The Shetlands
Mainland

Fair Isle

Westray
The Orkneys
Mainland

Pentland Firth
John O'Groats

North Minch

Northwest Highlands

Moray Firth

Isle of Skye
South Minch

Great Glen

The Grampians

Tiree
Isle of Mull
Iona

Firth of Tay

Firth of Forth

Forth-Clyde Valley

Mull of Kintyre
Rathlin I.
Firth of Clyde

Holy I. (Lindesfarne)

Southern Uplands

ATLANTIC OCEAN

NORTH SEA

Lough Neagh

North Channel

Solway Firth

The Pennine Hills

Mountains of Mourne

Isle of Man

Morecambe Bay

Yorkshire Wolds

IRISH SEA

Holy I. (Holyhead)
Liverpool Bay

Cheshire Plain

Anglesey

The Wash

Cardigan Bay

Cambrian Mountains

The Fens · Norfolk Broads

Midlands

East Anglia

St. George's Channel

Home Counties

Thames Estuary

Bristol Channel

Lundy I.
The West Country

Dover Strait

Land's End

Scilly Isles

Portland Bill

Isle of Wight
The Solent

Beachy Head

National Parks (in Scotland, National Scenic Areas)
As numbered here.

1	Assynt Coigach	10	Exmoor	19	Loch Lomond
2	Ben Nevis and Glencoe	11	Glen Affric	20	Loch Rannoch & Glen Lyon
3	Brecon Beacons	12	Harris	21	New Forest
4	Cairngorms	13	Hoy and West Mainland	22	Nith Estuary
5	Cuillin Hills	14	Jura	23	North Arran
6	Dartmoor	15	Knapdale	24	North York Moors
7	Deeside and Lochnagar	16	Knoydart	25	Northumberland
8	Dornoch Firth	17	Kyle of Tongue	26	Peak District
9	Earnside	18	Lake District	27	Pembrokeshire Coast

28	Rhum
29	Snodonia
30	South Mainland
31	Tayside
32	Trossachs
33	Uist
34	Upper Tweeddale
35	Wester Ross
36	Yorkshire Dales

Scale 50 40 30 20 10 0 25 50 100 in miles

United Kingdom
Roads, Cities
& Airports

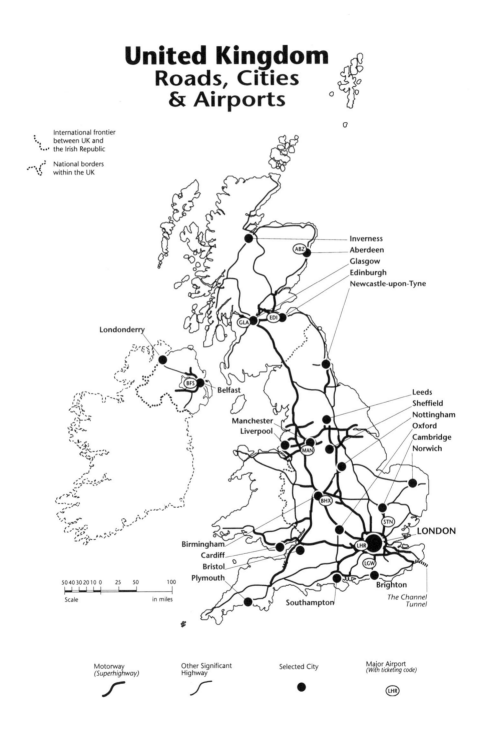

International frontier
between UK and
the Irish Republic

National borders
within the UK

Inverness
Aberdeen
Glasgow
Edinburgh
Newcastle-upon-Tyne

Londonderry

Belfast

Leeds
Sheffield
Nottingham
Oxford
Cambridge
Norwich

Manchester
Liverpool

LONDON

Birmingham
Cardiff
Bristol
Plymouth

Southampton

Brighton

The Channel
Tunnel

50 40 30 20 10 0   25   50   100

Scale   in miles

Motorway (Superhighway)	Other Significant Highway	Selected City	Major Airport (With ticketing code)

The European Union
Status on January 1st., 1995

At this time the European Union (EU) consists of 15 nations, as indicated above. The Union's total population, at 370 million, is over 100 million greater than that of the United States. Indeed, it is more than the combined population of the North American Free Trade Association (NAFTA) and the combined economy of the EU at current exchange rates is greater than that of NAFTA too.

The 15 member nations are: Austria, Belgium, Denmark, Finland, France, Germany, Greece, Ireland, Italy, Luxembourg, the Netherlands, Portugal, Spain, Sweden and the United Kingdom. The United Kingdom has been a member of the Union and its predecessor organizations, the European Economic Community and the European Community, since January 1973.

397

Arctic Ocean

Alaska
(to USA)

Dominion
of Canada

United
Kingdom

Irish
Free
State

Newfoundland

United States
of America

North
Atlantic
Ocean

Gibraltar

Bermuda

Hawaii
(to USA)

Bahamas

Puerto Rico
(to USA)

Leeward Islands

Jamaica

Barbados

Pacific
Ocean

British
Honduras

Trinidad & Tobago

British
Guiana

The Gambia

Sierra Leone

Gold Coast

Togoland

Nigeria

British Cameroons

Ascension
Island

St Helena

The British Empire
and dependent territories in 1922,
named as they were at that time.

*The Empire reached its maximum territorial extent—a quarter
of the land surface of the globe—at this time, and its population,
some 500 million people, comprised about one quarter of the
entire human race. For reference, the population of the United
States at that time was about one hundred million.*

South
Atlantic
Ocean

Tristan da Cunha .

☖ British Empire territories

☖ U.S. territories *(shown for reference)*

☖ All other countries & territories

Falkland
Islands

South
Georgia

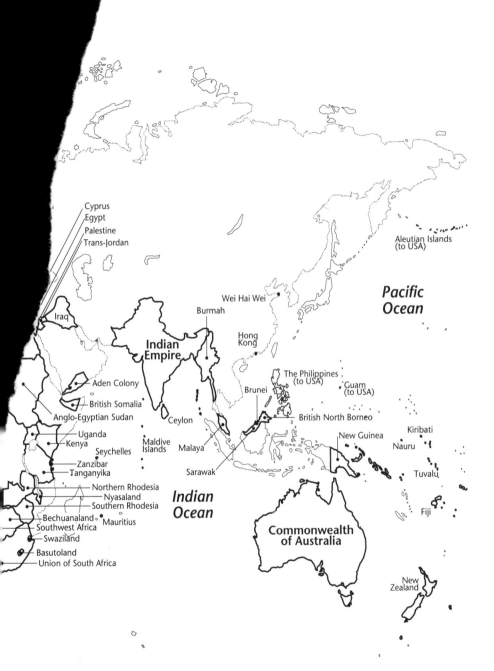

Cyprus
Egypt
Palestine
Trans-Jordan

Aleutian Islands
(to USA)

Pacific
Ocean

Wei Hai Wei
Burmah

Iraq

Indian
Empire

Hong
Kong

Aden Colony

British Somalia
Anglo-Egyptian Sudan

Ceylon

Brunei

The Philippines
(to USA)

Guam
(to USA)

British North Borneo

Kiribati

Uganda
Kenya

Maldive
Islands

Malaya

New Guinea

Nauru

Seychelles

Zanzibar
Tanganyika

Sarawak

Tuvalu

Northern Rhodesia
Nyasaland
Southern Rhodesia

Indian
Ocean

Fiji

Bechuanaland
Southwest Africa

Mauritius

Swaziland

Basutoland
Union of South Africa

Commonwealth
of Australia

New
Zealand

Antarctic Ocean

Ewart James was born in Scotland in 1942 and grew up there, but has spent most of his a[...] life working in England, Europe, the Middle East, and the United States. The differe[...] between the various strains of the English language have fascinated him for twenty years; t[...] dictionary is the result. He now lives in East Anglia, England.

Duncan J. McKinnon was born in Scotland in 1969 and grew up there. He lives in Lond[...] England, where he works as an architect.